District Gazetteers of India Series 153

MADRAS DISTRICT GAZETTEERS

TINNEVELLY

District Gazetteers of India Series 153

MADRAS DISTRICT GAZETTEERS

TINNEVELLY

H. R. PATE

23 VOLUMES (IN 25 BINDINGS)

(VOL. 20th)

GYAN

Published by

Gyan Publishing House
5, Ansari Road
Daryaganj, New Delhi-110002
Phone: 011-47034999, 9811692060
E-mail: books@gyanbooks.com

Distribution Network
gyanbooks.com
India, USA, Canada, UK, Australia, France

ISBN: 978-93-6208-562-7 (Set) 23 Volumes (In 25 Bindings)
978-81-212-5839-5 (PB)

First Published, 1917

2nd Impression 2024

Printed at: Gyan Press, Delhi.

MADRAS DISTRICT GAZETTEERS (Vol. 20th)
Author: H. R. PATE

LIST OF VOLUMES

S. NO.	ISBN NO.	VOLUME	TITLE	AUTHOR	PRICE	PAGES
			ASSAM DISTRICT GAZETTEERS			
1	9788121285926	1st	Cachar	B. C. Allen	600	300
2	9788121285919	2nd	Sylhet	B. C. Allen	750	378
3	9788121285902	3rd	Goalpara	B. C. Allen	400	203
4	9788121285896	4th	Kamrup	B. C. Allen	675	344
5	9788121285889	5th	Darrang	B. C. Allen	725	364
6	9788121285872	6th	Nowgong	B. C. Allen	560	280
7	9788121285865	7th	Sibsagar	B. C. Allen	675	343
8	9788121285858	8th	Lakhimpur	B. C. Allen	690	347
9	9788121285841	9th	Naga Hills and Manipur	B. C. Allen	580	294
10	9788121285834	10th	The Khasi And Jaintia Hills, The Garo Hills And The Lushai Hills	B. C. Allen	675	363
11	9788121285827	11th	The Sadiya and Balipara Frontier Tract	B. C. Allen	375	190
			BENGAL DISTRICT GAZETTEERS			
12	9788121218672	1st	Angul	L. S. S. O'Malley	340	168
13	9788121259637	2nd	Bakarganj	J. C. JACK	970	194
14	9788121218696	3rd	Balasore	L. S. S. O'Malley	450	228
15	9788121259590	4th	Bankura	L. S. S. O'Malley	1000	199
16	9788121218375	5th	Bhagalpur	J. Byrne	390	194
17	9788121218290	6th	Birbhum	L. S. S. O'Malley	300	150
18	9788121259651	7th	Eastern Bengal and Assam - Bogra	J. N. Gupta	940	188
19	9788121218351	8th	Burdwan	J. C. K. Peterson	450	227
20	9788121259538	9th	Calcutta District Gazetteer - Statistics, 1901 - 02		340	68
21	9788121218313	10th	Champaran	L. S. S. O'Malley	410	205
22	9788121259613	11th	Eastern Bengal District Gazetters - Chittagong	L. S. S. O'Malley	1080	216
23	9788121259552	12th	Chota Nagpur Tributary		130	26
24	9788121259415	13th	The Cooch Behar Gazette: Statistics		1460	292
25	9788121218412	14th	Cuttack	L. S. S. O'Malley	490	248
26	9788121261357	15th	Eastern Bengal District Gazetteers Dacca	B. C. Allen	400	207
27	9788121218436	16th	Darbhanga	L. S. S. O'Malley	360	180
28	9789362089335	17th	Darjeeling	L. S. S. O'Malley	500	248
29	9788121259453	18th	Eastern Bengal District Gazetteers - Dinajpur	F. W. Strong	890	178
30	9788121259392	19th	Faridpur	L. S. S. O'Malley	700	140
31	9788121218474	20th	Gaya	L. S. S. O'Malley	540	270
32	9788121214032	21st	Bihar and Orissa District Gazetteer: Hazaribagh	E. Lister	715	234
33	9788121218337	22nd	Hooghly	L. S. S. O'Malley	680	340
34	9788121218191	23rd	Bengal District Gazetteer Howrah	L. S. S. O'Malley	390	199
35	9788121259293	24th	Eastern Bengal and Assam - Jalpaiguri	John F. Gruning	890	178
36	9788121259279	25th	Jessore	L. S. S. O'Malley	960	192
37	9788121259231	26th	Khulna	L. S. S. O'Malley	1100	220
38	9788121259217	27th	Malda	G. E. Lambourn	670	134
39	9788121267854	28th	Manbhum	H. Coupland	600	313
40	9788121218498	29th	Midnapore	L. S. S. O'Malley	500	252
41	9788121218597	30th	Monghyr	L. S. S. O'Malley	560	280
42	9788121259156	31st	Murshidabad	L. S. S. O'Malley	1250	250
43	9788121259576	32nd	Bengal District Gazetteers - Muzaffarpur	L. S. S. O'Malley	940	188
44	9788121259132	33rd	Mymensingh	F. A. Sachse	960	192
45	9788121259118	34th	Nadia	J. H. E. Garrett	1070	214
46	9788121259095	35th	Eastern Bengal and Assam - Noakhali	J. E. Webster	580	115
47	9788121218450	36th	Feudatory States of Orissa	L. E. B. Cobdenramsay	790	395
48	9788121259071	37th	Pabna	L. S. S. O'Malley	710	142
49	9788121218511	38th	Palamau	L. S. S. O'Malley	380	190
50	9788121218634	39th	Patna	L. S. S. O'Malley	500	250
51	9788121218535	40th	Puri	L. S. S. O'Malley	650	328
52	9788121218757	41st	Purnea	L. S. S. O'Malley	440	220
53	9788121258937	42nd	Rajshahi	L. S. S. O'Malley	1080	216
54	9788121256681	43rd	Bihar and Orissa District Gazetteers: Ranchi	M. G. Hallett	1350	278
55	9788121258913	44th	Eastern Bengal and assam - Rangpur	J. A. Vas	890	178
56	9788121218559	45th	Sambalpur	L. S. S. O'Malley	480	242
57	9788121214056	46th	Santal Parganas	L. S. S. O'Malley	940	308
58	9788121218610	47th	Saran	L. S. S. O'Malley	380	190
59	9788121218658	48th	Shahabad	L. S. S. O'Malley	380	190
60	9788121256704	49th	The Gazetteer of Sikhim	H. H. Risley	960	481
61	9788121218573	50th	Singhbhum, Saraikela And Kharsawan	L. S. S. O'Malley	560	280
62	9788121259439	51st	Eastern Bengal District Gazetteers - Tippera	J. E. Webster	730	146
63	9788121259033	52nd	24 Parganas	L. S. S. O'Malley	1420	284

S. NO.	ISBN NO.	VOLUME	TITLE	AUTHOR	PRICE	PAGES
			CENTRAL PROVINCES DISTRICT GAZETTEERS			
64	9789362081728	1st, Vol. A	Akola (Descriptive)	A. E. Nelson, C. Brown	870	436
65	9789362085481	2nd, Vol. A	Amraoti (Descriptive)	S. V. Fitzgerald, A. E. Nelson	1050	524
66	9789362089267	3rd,Vol. A	Balaghat (Descriptive)	R. V. RUSSELL	430	216
67	9789362083494	4th, Vol. A	Betul (Descriptive)	R. V. RUSSELL	610	306
68	9789362085146	5th, Vol. A	Bhandara (Descriptive)	R. V. RUSSELL	580	292
69	9789362088390	6th, Vol. A	Bilaspur (Descriptive)	R. V. RUSSELL	870	434
70	9789362086044	7th, Vol. A	Buldana (Descriptive)	A. E. Nelson	1090	543
71	9789362089014	8th, Vol. B	Chanda (Descriptive)	R. V. RUSSELL	470	234
72	9789362086938	9th	Chhattisgarch Feudatory State	E. A. De Brett	880	440
73	9789362082961	10th	Chhindwara (Descriptive)	R. V. RUSSELL	550	274
74	9789362089342	11th, Vol. A & B	Damoh (Descriptive and Statistical Tables 1891-1901)	R. V. RUSSELL	830	414
75	9789362081230	12th, Vol. A	Durg (Descriptive)	A. E. Nelson	460	232
76	9789362086037	13th, Vol. A	Hoshangabad (Descriptive)	R. V. RUSSELL	860	430
77	9789362086792	14th, Vol. A	Jubbulpore (Descriptive)	A. E. Nelson	950	474
78	9789362089663	15th, Vol. A & B	Mandla (Descriptive and Statistical Tables 1891-1901)	R. V. RUSSELL	370	186
79	9789362086419	16th, Vol. A	Nagpur (Descriptive)	R. V. RUSSELL	790	394
80	9789362080646	17th, Vol. A	Narsinghpur (Descriptive)	R. V. RUSSELL	510	257
81	9789362084835	18th, Vol. A	Nimar (Descriptive)	R. V. RUSSELL	600	299
82	9789362087737	19th, Vol. A	Raipur (Descriptive)	A. E. Nelson	790	396
83	9789362080264	20th, Vol. A	Saugor (Descriptive)	R. V. RUSSELL	570	285
84	9789362081117	21st, Vol. A	Seoni (Descriptive)	R. V. RUSSELL	460	232
85	9789362084965	22nd, Vol. A	Wardha (Descriptive)	R. V. RUSSELL	600	302
86	9789362083401	23rd, Vol. A	Yeotmal (Descriptive)	R. V. RUSSELL	550	277
87	9789362080325	24th, Vol. I, Pt. I	Gwalior (Text and Tables)	R. V. RUSSELL	980	489
88	9789362087133	24th, Vol. I, Pt. II	Gwalior (Maps)	R. V. RUSSELL	400	198
89	9789362086341	24th, Vol. I, Pt. III	Gwalior (Village List)	R. V. RUSSELL	810	406
90	9789362085467	24th, Vol. I, Pt. IV	Gwalior (Photos)	R. V. RUSSELL	1400	698
91	9789362087393	25th, Vol. II	Indore (Text and Tables)	C. E. Luard	1050	524
92	9789362084422	26th, Vol. III	Bhopal (Text and Tables)	C. E. Luard	540	272
93	9789362086815	27th, Vol. IV	Rewah (Text and Tables)	C. E. Luard	500	250
94	9789362087584	28th, Vol. V, Pt. A	Western States - Malwa (Text)	C. E. Luard	1520	762
95	9789362087300	29th, Vol. VI, Pt. A	Eastern States - Bundelkhand (Text)	C. E. Luard	930	463
96	9789362082169	30th, Vol. VI, Pt. B	Eastern States - Bundelkhand (Tables)	C. E. Luard	830	417
			GAZETTEER OF THE BOMBAY PRESIDENCY:			
97	9788121283441	1st, Part I	History of Gujarat	Ed.: James M. Campbell	3220	644
98	9788121285582	1st, Part II	History of the Konkan Dakhan and Southern Maratha Country	Ed.: James M. Campbell	4200	840
99	9788121285568	2nd	Gujarat, Surat and Broach	Ed.: James M. Campbell	2990	598
100	9788121285544	3rd	Kaira and Panch Mahals	Ed.: James M. Campbell	1690	339
101	9788121285520	4th	Ahmedabad	Ed.: James M. Campbell	1860	372
102	9788121285506	5th	Cutch, Palanpur, and Mahi Kantha	Ed.: James M. Campbell	2390	478
103	9788121285483	6th	Rewa Kantha, Narukot, Cambay, and Surat States	Ed.: James M. Campbell	1450	290
104	9788121285469	7th	Baroda	Ed.: James M. Campbell	3260	652
105	9788121285445	8th	Kathiawar	Ed.: James M. Campbell	3790	758
106	9788121285421	9th, Part I	Gujarat Population - Hindus	Ed.: James M. Campbell	3170	636
107	9788121285407	9th, Part II	Gujarat Population - Musalmans and Parsis	Ed.: James M. Campbell	1520	304
108	9788121285384	10th	Ratnagiri and Savantvadi	Ed.: James M. Campbell	2500	501
109	9788121285360	11th	Kolaba and Janjira	Ed.: James M. Campbell	2550	513
110	9788121285346	12th	Khandesh	Ed.: James M. Campbell	3190	638
111	9788121285322	13th Part I	Thana	Ed.: James M. Campbell	2050	413
112	9788121285308	13th Part II	Thana	Ed.: James M. Campbell	1770	357
113	9788121285285	14th	Thana - Places of Interest	Ed.: James M. Campbell	3290	659
114	9788121285261	15th Part I	Kanara	Ed.: James M. Campbell	2340	348
115	9788121285247	15th Part II	Kanara	Ed.: James M. Campbell	1740	348
116	9788121285223	16th	Nasik	Ed.: James M. Campbell	3490	698
117	9788121285209	17th	Ahmadnagar	Ed.: James M. Campbell	3860	772
118	9788121285186	18th Part I	Poona	Ed.: James M. Campbell	2930	586
119	9788121285162	18th Part II	Poona	Ed.: James M. Campbell	2680	537
120	9788121285148	18th Part III	Poona	Ed.: James M. Campbell	2500	503
121	9788121285124	19th	Satara	Ed.: James M. Campbell	3450	692
122	9788121285100	20th	Sholapur	Ed.: James M. Campbell	2730	547
123	9788121285087	21st	Gazetteer of the Bomaby Presidency: Belgaum	Ed.: James M. Campbell	2570	514
124	9788121285063	22nd	Dharwar	Ed.: James M. Campbell	4200	841
125	9788121285049	23rd	Gazetteer of the Bombay Presidency:Bijapur	Ed.: James M. Campbell	3550	712
126	9788121285025	24th	Kolhapur	Ed.: James M. Campbell	2250	450

S. NO.	ISBN NO.	VOLUME	TITLE	AUTHOR	PRICE	PAGES
127	9788121285001	25th	Botany	Ed.: James M. Campbell	2040	408
128	9788121284981	26th, Part I	Materials Towards a Statistical Account of the Town and Island of Bombay - History	Ed.: James M. Campbell	2500	504
129	9788121284967	26th, Part II	Materials Towards a Statistical Account of the Town and Island of Bombay - Trade and Fortifications	Ed.: James M. Campbell	2690	538
130	9788121284943	26th, Part III	Materials Towards a Statistical Account of the Town And Island of Bombay - Administration	Ed.: James M. Campbell	2450	702
131	9788121284929	27th	General Index	Ed.:R. E. Enthoven	2190	428

MADRAS DISTRICT GAZETTEERS

S. NO.	ISBN NO.	VOLUME	TITLE	AUTHOR	PRICE	PAGES
132	9788121258814	1st	Anantapur	W. Francis	1140	227
133	9788121258555	2nd	Malabar	C. A Innes & F. B Evans	3010	602
134	9788121258791	3rd	Bellary	W. Francis	1890	377
135	9788121258777	4th	Statistical Appendix For Chingleput		280	56
136	9788121258753	5th	Coimbatore	K. N. Krishnaswami Ayyar	3420	628
137	9788121232814	6th	Madras District Gazetteers District Gazetteer Cuddapah	C. F. Brackenbury	1120	285
138	9788121258715	7th	Statistical Appendix For Ganjam		370	73
139	9788121256766	8th, Vol. 1st	Godavari District Gazetteer	F. R. Hemingway	650	320
140	9788121256803	8th, Vol. 2nd	Godavari District Gazetteer	F. R. Hemingway	160	83
141	9788121258678	9th	Statistical Appendix For Kistna		640	127
142	9788121258654	10th	Statistical Appendix For Kurnool		270	54
143	9788121258616	11th	Madura	W. Francis	1900	379
144	9788121258579	12th	Statistical Appendix For Madura		740	148
145	9788121258630	13th	The Nilgiris	W. Francis	2190	437
146	9788121234276	14th	Madras District Gazetteers Gazetteer Of The Nellore District Brought Upto 1938		1150	386
147	9788121258517	15th	North Arcot		590	118
148	9788121258494	16th, Vol. 1, Part I	Salem	F. J. Richards	1710	343
149	9788121258593	16th, Vol. 1, Part II	Salem	F. J. Richards	1800	360
150	9788121258456	17th	South Arcot	W. Francis	2400	480
151	9788121258470	18th	Statistical Appendix For South Canara		400	80
152	9788121258432	19th, Vol. 1st & 2nd	Tanjore: Main Volume and Statistical Appendix		2070	401
153	9788121258395	20th	Tinnevelly	H. R. Pate	2740	547
154	9788121258418	21st	Statistical Appendix For Tinnevelly		320	64
155	9788121258371	22nd, 1st & 2nd	Trichinopoly: Main Volume and Statistical Appendix	F. R. Hemingway	2440	487
156	9788121241953	23rd	Vizagapatam District Gazetteer	W. Francis	760	385

PUNJAB DISTRICT GAZETTEERS

S. NO.	ISBN NO.	VOLUME	TITLE	AUTHOR	PRICE	PAGES
157	9788121255943	1st	Ambala District 1883-84		620	124
158	9788121255967	2nd	Amritsar		1180	236
159	9788121255981	3rd	Delhi		1300	260
160	9788121256001	4th	Ferozepore		950	188
161	9788121256025	5th	Faridkot		350	70
162	9788121256049	6th	Gujranwala 1893-94		1270	254
163	9788121256063	7th	Gujrat	C. E. Luard	1140	228
164	9788121256087	8th	Gurdaspur 1891-92		1260	252
165	9788121256100	9th	Gurgaon 1883-4		1020	203
166	9788121256124	10th	Hazara	H. D. Watson	2290	458
167	9788121256148	11th	Hissar district and Lohar State		1840	367
168	9788121256162	12th	Hoshiarpur		1420	283
169	9788121256186	13th	Jhang		1070	213
170	9788121256209	14th	Jhelam		1010	202
171	9788121256223	15th	Jalandhar District 1883-84		540	108
172	9788121256247	16th, Vol. XIV-A	Jullundur District, with maps and Kapurthala		1990	398
173	9788121256261	17th, Pt. I	Kangra (Proper)		1450	290
174	9788121256285	17th, Pt. II	Kangra (Kulu, Lahual, Spiti)		1800	357
175	9788121256308	18th	Karnal		1930	386
176	9788121256322	19th	Kohat		1540	307
177	9788121256346	20th	The Lahore District 1883-84		1220	244
178	9788121256384	21st	Ludhiana and Maler Kotla		1680	335
179	9788121256407	22nd	Lyallpur		735	147
180	9788121256421	23rd	Mianwali		1170	234
181	9788121256445	24th	Montgomery	P. J. Fagan	1590	318
182	9788121258364	25th	Multan (1901-02)	E. D. Maclagan	2400	480
183	9788121258708	26th	The Rohtak District 1883-84		980	196
184	9788121258746	27th, Vol. III A	Dujana State 1904		500	16
185	9788121256483	28th	Shahpur District		1780	356
186	9788121256506	29th	Simla District		800	159

S. NO.	ISBN NO.	VOLUME	TITLE	AUTHOR	PRICE	PAGES
187	9788121256520	30th	The Chamba State		2040	408
188	9788121256544	31st	The Chenab Colony 1904		1550	310
189	9788121256568	32nd	Kalsia State		270	53
190	9788121256582	33rd	Suket and Mandi		770	154
191	9788121256605	34th	Phulkian States, Patiala Jind And Nabha 1904		2070	414
192	9788121256643	35th	Simla Hill States		2220	443
193	9788121256667	36th	Sirmur		920	183
			RAJPUTANA DISTRICT GAZETTEERS			
194	9789362088994	1st, Vol. I-A & B	Ajmer-merwara (Text and Statistics Tables)	C. C. Watson	1230	246
195	9789362080882	2nd. Vol. II-A & B	Mewar Residency (Text and Statistics Tables)	K.D. Erskine	1700	339
196	9789362088444	3rd, Vol. III-A & B	The Western Rajputana States Residency And The Bikaner Agency	K.D. Erskine	3590	718
			UNITED PROVINCES OF AGRA AND OUDH DISTRICT GAZETTEERS			
197	9789362087560	Vol. I	Agra	H. R. Nevill	2260	452
198	9789362082466	Vol. II	Aligarh	H. R. Nevill	1300	260
199	9789362089779	Vol. III	Allahabad	H. R. Nevill	2050	409
200	9789362081346	Vol. IV	Almora	H. G. Walton	1670	333
201	9789362085658	Vol. V	Azamgarh	D. L. Drake Brockman	1750	349
202	9789362080547	Vol. VI	Bahraich	H. R. Nevill	1410	281
203	9789362085214	Vol. VII	Ballia	H. R. Nevill	1750	350
204	9789362084668	Vol. VIII	Banda	D. L. Drake Brockman	1750	349
205	9789362086518	Vol. IX	Bara Banki	H. R. Nevill	1720	344
206	9789362084101	Vol. X	Bareilly	H. R. Nevill	1640	327
207	9789362086631	Vol. XI	Basti	H. R. Nevill	1610	321
208	9789362083814	Vol. XII	Benares	H. R. Nevill	2290	458
209	9789362086105	Vol. XIII	Bijnor	H. R. Nevill	1820	363
210	9789362081674	Vol. XIV	Budaun	H. R. Nevill	1890	378
211	9789362086891	Vol. XV	Bulandshahr	H. R. Nevill	2100	419
212	9789362081520	Vol. XVI	Cawnpore	H. R. Nevill	2210	442
213	9789362088031	Vol. XVII	Dehra Dun	H. G. Walton	1710	342
214	9789362088710	Vol. XVIII	Etah	E. R. Neave	1600	320
215	9789362082992	Vol. XIX	Etawah	D. L. Drake Brockman	1390	277
216	9789362082220	Vol. XX	Farrukhabad	E. R. Neave	1620	324
217	9789362083869	Vol. XXI	Fatehpur	H. R. Nevill	1890	377
218	9789362085962	Vol. XXII	Fyzabad	H. R. Nevill	1700	339
219	9789362087997	Vol. XXIII	Garhwal	H. G. Walton	1270	254
220	9789362089892	Vol. XXIV	Ghazipur	H. R. Nevill	1600	320
221	9789362085436	Vol. XXV	Gonda	H. R. Nevill	1650	330
222	9789362080271	Vol. XXVI	Gorakhpur	H. R. Nevill	1890	378
223	9789362086129	Vol. XXVII	Hamirpur	D. L. Drake Brockman	1390	277
224	9789362087638	Vol. XXVIII	Hardoi	H. R. Nevill	1680	336
225	9789362081636	Vol. XXIX	Jalaun	D. L. Drake Brockman	1180	236
226	9789362084309	Vol. XXX	Jaunpur	H. R. Nevill	1750	350
227	9789362084187	Vol. XXXI	Jhansi	D. L. Drake Brockman	1960	391
228	9789362089168	Vol. XXXII	Kheri	H. R. Nevill	1650	330
229	9789362086778	Vol. XXXIII	Lucknow	H. R. Nevill	1760	352
230	9789362088635	Vol. XXXIV	Mainpuri	H. R. Nevill	1740	348
231	9789362080424	Vol. XXXV	Meerut	H. R. Nevill	2170	434
232	9789362081087	Vol. XXXVI	Mirzapur	D. L. Drake Brockman	2430	486
233	9789362085443	Vol. XXXVII	Moradabad	H. R. Nevill	1900	380
234	9789362082763	Vol. XXXVIII	Muttra	D. L. Drake Brockman	2140	428
235	9789362089915	Vol. XXXIX	Muzaffarnagar	H. R. Nevill	2260	451
236	9789362086143	Vol. XL	Naini Tal	H. R. Nevill	1890	377
237	9789362086761	Vol. XLI	Partabgarh	H. R. Nevill	1560	312
238	9789362081124	Vol. XLII	Pilibhit	H. R. Nevill	1570	314
239	9789362084453	Vol. XLIII	Rai Bareli	H. R. Nevill	1610	322
240	9789362088284	Vol. XLIV	Rampur	H. R. Nevill	1170	234
241	9789362083654	Vol. XLV	Saharanpur	H. R. Nevill	2190	438
242	9789362083142	Vol. XLVI	Shahjahanpur	H. R. Nevill	1510	302
243	9789362083623	Vol. XLVII	Sitapur	H. R. Nevill	1590	317
244	9789362089939	Vol. XLVIII	Sultanpur	H. R. Nevill	1330	266
245	9789362080851	Vol. XLIX	Unnao	H. R. Nevill	1530	305

MADRAS DISTRICT GAZETTEERS

TINNEVELLY

VOLUME I

MADRAS DISTRICT GAZETTEERS

TINNEVELLY

BY

H. R. PATE, I.C.S.

VOLUME I

MADRAS:
PRINTED BY THE SUPERINTENDENT, GOVERNMENT PRESS.

1917

PREFACE.

THE old District Manual, the chief value of which lay in its statistics, was published so long ago as 1879. The present Gazetteer is entirely new. The greater part of the book was written before the outbreak of the present war; consequently, a few statements, those, for instance, which relate to foreign trade and to shipping, will be found now to be out of date. In the hope that normal conditions will soon return, I have thought it unnecessary to alter these passages. My thanks are due to the numerous gentlemen, official and non-official, who have assisted me in the preparation of the book; where possible, I have acknowledged such help in the foot-notes. Among the authorities consulted by me there is none to which I am so deeply indebted as Bishop Caldwell's *History of Tinnevelly*.

TUTICORIN,
12th March 1916.

H.R.P.

PLAN OF CONTENTS.

TABLE OF CONTENTS.

CHAPTER I.

PHYSICAL DESCRIPTION.

CHAPTER II.

POLITICAL HISTORY.

PAGE

CHAPTER III.

THE PEOPLE.

PAGE

CHAPTER IV.

AGRICULTURE AND IRRIGATION.

CHAPTER V.

FORESTS.

CHAPTER VI.

OCCUPATIONS AND TRADE.

CHAPTER VII.

MEANS OF COMMUNICATION.

CHAPTER VIII.

RAINFALL AND SEASONS.

CHAPTER IX.

PUBLIC HEALTH.

CHAPTER X.

EDUCATION.

CHAPTER XI.

LAND REVENUE ADMINISTRATION.

PAGE

PAGE

CHAPTER XII.

SALT, ABKARI AND MISCELLANEOUS REVENUE.

CHAPTER XIII.

ADMINISTRATION OF JUSTICE.

CHAPTER XIV.

LOCAL SELF-GOVERNMENT.

CHAPTER XV.

GAZETTEER.

GAZETTEER

OF THE

TINNEVELLY DISTRICT.

CHAPTER I.

PHYSICAL DESCRIPTION.

GENERAL DESCRIPTION—Position and boundaries—Taluks and chief towns —The headquarters. HILLS—Chief peaks—Agastyamalai—Forests—Coffee estates—Hill-tribes; the Paliyans—The Kānis. RIVERS—The Tāmbraparni: its course—Its flood banks—Its name—Its fame—Its tributaries: in the hills —In the plains; the Manimuttār—The Varāhanadhi—The Gatanānadhi—The Pachaiyār—The Chittār—The Uppōdai—Basin of the Tāmbraparni—The Nānguneri rivers—The Sankaranainārkōil rivers; the Vaippār basin—The Kōilpatti rivers. THE PLAIN COUNTRY—Its natural divisions—The river-valleys—The dry red lands—The "palmyra forest" or *tēri* country—The black-cotton country. THE SEA-COAST—Harbours: Tuticorin—Kulasēkhara-patnam—Kāyalpatnam—Vaippār and Vēmbār—The weather of the coast —Pearl and chank fisheries. SOILS—Their distribution—The black soils—The red soils. GEOLOGY. MINERALS. CLIMATE—Rainfall—Temperature and winds. FLORA. FAUNA—Domestic animals—Semi-wild cattle—Buffaloes —Goats and Sheep—Wild animals—Birds—Reptiles and fishes—Insects.

CHAP. I. GENERAL DESCRIPTION.

Position and boundaries.

THE Tinnevelly district, 4,326 square miles in extent, forms the southernmost Collectorate of British India. It is bounded on the east and south by the Gulf of Manaar; on its northern boundary, the line of which is dictated by administrative convenience only, lies the district of Rāmnād; on the west is Travancore, the frontier following, with a few important exceptions, the watershed of the Western Ghats. To the west of the Tenkāsi taluk, where the mountains drop to form the Ariyankāvu pass, the frontier turns eastward to include with Travancore not only the slopes of the hills but also the taluk of Shencotta in the low country. Again, above Panagudi the boundary descends from the crest of Mahēndragiri down the eastern slope of the hills and continues southward along the level country till it meets the sea at a point four miles east of Cape Comorin. The official literature dealing with the Tinnevelly-Travancore boundary

CHAP. I. GENERAL DESCRIPTION.

(many details remain still unsettled) would fill a volume of respectable size; some reference to the subject will be found in Chapter XV in the notice relating to the taluk of Tenkāsi.

Taluks and chief towns.

The district is made up of the eight taluks of Tenkāsi, Tinnevelly, Ambāsamudram, Nānguneri, Tiruchendūr, Srīvaikuntam, Kōilpatti and Sankaranainārkōil, and dates its present constitution from the year 1910, when the newly-formed Collectorate of Rāmnād absorbed two northern taluks, Sāttūr and Srīvilliputtūr, which till then had belonged to Tinnevelly. To secure a convenient boundary for the re-formed district of Tinnevelly a few villages were interchanged between these two taluks and the country to the south of them; the old Ottapidāram, extended on the north, and diminished on the south by the transfer of twenty villages (including Tuticorin) to the Srīvaikuntam taluk, became the present Kōilpatti taluk, with its headquarters at Kōilpatti; enlarged on the north, the old Srīvaikuntam taluk was greatly reduced in area by the constitution of its southern half into the new taluk of Tiruchendūr.

There are few really large towns in the district, the principal, in the order of their population, being Palamcotta, the district headquarters, Tinnevelly and Tuticorin. Large villages, however, known for administrative purposes as "towns," are more numerous than in any other district, and occur, as might be expected, chiefly in the fertile valley of the Tāmbraparni. Ambāsamudram, Kallidaikurichi, Vīravanallūr, Sērmādēvi, Srīvaikuntam and Alvārtirunagari are the chief of these; the high figure returned for Tiruchendūr (25,531) is chiefly due to the fact that at the time of census a largely-attended festival was going on in the place.[1]

The head-quarters.

The district gets its name from the town[2] which, from the times at least of the Nāyakkan rulers, formed the headquarters of the "Province." During the poligar wars Palamcotta with its fort, three miles from the town of Tinnevelly on the opposite side of the Tāmbraparni, assumed importance as a strategical position and from the earliest days of the Company's interference in the district became the military headquarters. The civil offices of the Company were not established in the district till 1801, when Mr. Lushington moved from Rāmnād, the old headquarters of the successive Collectors of Poligar Peshkash. The offices of the new Collector of Tinnevelly were at first located in Kokkarakulam on the Palamcotta side of the river, then in a building near the temple in the town of Tinnevelly; thereafter they changed

[1] See p. 86. [2] See also p. 494.

CHAP. I.
GENERAL DESCRIPTION.

their situation more than once, until finally, in 1831, the Cutcherry was established in Kokkarakulam, a mile from the fort, in the buildings vacated by the old Commercial department on its abolition. At that time Palamcotta comprised only the fort and its immediate surroundings, Kokkarakulam belonging neither to Tinnevelly nor to Palamcotta. In 1902 the village was definitely incorporated with the municipal town of Palamcotta; and from that date it may strictly be said that Palamcotta has been the headquarters of the district.[1]

HILLS.

The hills which form the western boundary of the district are a continuation of the great irregular chain of the Western Ghats, which here attain comparative regularity. Save for a recess enclosing a bay of the Tenkāsi taluk, they march in a straight line from the northern limit of the district as far as Pāpanāsam and the valley of the Tāmbraparni; thence, sweeping for twelve miles in a bold curve towards the south-east, they once more resume their southward trend towards the sea.

Chief peaks.

This immense and rugged barrier of hills, towering along the western side of the district and visible from almost any point of the level country, presents for the denizen of the plains the most fascinating object of the landscape. Above Sivagiri, where the Tinnevelly district is entered, and southward as far as the northern boundary of the Tenkāsi taluk, they rise (as in Rāmnād) with great suddenness from the plains to the water-shed, which, measured by a horizontal line, is only some three or four miles from their base. Along the sky-line the range averages 5,000 feet, at least twenty peaks running up to over that height. Conspicuous amongst them are the Kallakadai Mottai (5,721 feet) above Sivagiri, the great dark mass of Kottaimalai (6,335 feet) over Puliyangudi, and Kulirātti (5,876 feet) towering up behind Krishnāpuram. Southward from this point the hills lose in height; at Kadaiyanallūr they throw out low arms into the plain, and the main range drops rapidly to the Ariyankāvu pass. Recovering again, they climb gradually upwards until above the valley of the "Five-falls river" they reach 5,000 feet, culminating in the splendid peak of Panjantangi (5,135 feet) above Kuttālam and the still more striking, though somewhat lower, Kulirātti, or "General's hill", above Mattalampārai on the border of the Tenkāsi and Ambāsamudram taluks. Here the ghats begin to widen out, and above Pāpanāsam the range attains its greatest thickness. Low hills skirt their base, and behind these extend higher

[1] See also p. 477.

CHAP. I. HILLS.

undulating hills and broad valleys, with here and there extensive plateaus, leading gradually up to the great range of high rugged mountains which mark the watershed.

Agastyamalai.

The glory of this mass of mountains is the famous Agastyamalai (6,125 feet), known to the natives as the Eka Pothigai, the place to which the *rishi* Agastya, after the achievement of his great life's work (which included treatises on medicine, theology and Tamil grammar), retired to rest; there, mindful of the human race, he created the Tāmbraparni, over whose fortunes he still presides from his mountain hermitage. A perfect cone in shape, standing on a low base in a wide gap on the sky line, Agastyamalai, whether viewed from Travancore or Tinnevelly—but especially when seen from Tinnevelly in the glory of a March sunset—is the most striking peak in the whole range of hills. Often for weeks together it is wreathed in clouds, enjoying as it does the full benefit of both monsoons. Next to it on the south, but at a respectful distance, stands the great Ainthalai Pothigai, five-headed, as its name implies; and, seen from the plain country to the east, its line of peaks silhouetted against the sky seem, with the rugged Nāgamalai, their neighbour, to stand sentinel six deep over the enthroned majesty of Agastyamalai.

With the Ainthalai Pothigai the watershed turns south-east as far as the Nānguneri frontier, which marks the point from which the ghats again march southwards. Here they lose in thickness and become steeper, retaining an average height of 5,000 feet. Above Tirukkurungudi they tower up to close on 6,000, dropping slightly to the Mahēndragiri range, which dips to rise again and ends abruptly in a magnificent scarp of bare precipitous rock. This is the last of the Tinnevelly ghats; for north of Panagudi, where a low pass occurs, the boundary leaves the watershed and turns south-east towards the plain. After Panagudi the mountains rise once more to half their height, dropping after a few miles to the Arāmboli pass in the level country. Their final effort is a comparatively low detached hill, whose southern base is two or three miles from the sea and slightly west of Cape Comorin.

Forests.

Some account of the forests which these hills contain will be found in Chapter V. They partake generally of the character of the ghat forests further north and, though possessing a special botanical interest of their own, contain but little timber of commercial importance. Kōngu *(Hopea parviflora)*, which is found in the evergreen region, is perhaps the most valuable among the trees, but its distribution is limited and confined to the southern part of the district. Holding as they do, however, the sources of innumerable streams which go to irrigate and refresh the level country, the forests possess a protective value of the highest importance.

Coffee estates.

In the earliest days of the Company's interference in the district the possibility suggested itself of turning to the uses of exotic cultivation the peculiar climate of these hills. Kuttālam[1], with its exceptional advantages, was selected, and a number of valuable plants were imported at considerable expense from the Moluccas and laid out in the valleys of that neighbourhood. The experiments, however, were not a commercial success and were abandoned finally in 1853. Mr. Hughes (p. 487) conceived a scheme of planting coffee on a large scale in the same region, but apparently gave up the idea; his natural son, Ramsingh, obtained extensive grants of hill-land in 1844 for the same purpose and opened up the plantations now known as the Terkumalai and Hope estates above Kuttālam.

It was from about this time forward that a number of small coffee estates were laid out on the Nānguneri hills. Tradition says that the earliest of these clearances (afterwards known as the Mahēndragiri estate) was actually made and planted up with spices by Mr. E. P. Thompson so far back as 1840; he subsequently presented it to the head of a well-known Muhammadan family in Panagudi, who planted the estate with coffee and managed it successfully for many years. The idea quickly became popular; and from about 1850 onwards a large number of similar plantations were opened up on these hills by Indian enterprise. The competition of Travancore coffee, however, leaf disease and the depreciation of the product combined to ruin these experiments, and from about 1880 most of the estates went by degrees out of cultivation. At the time of the forest settlement of 1902 the Nānguneri hills contained not less than twenty-seven such estates, some of which had been definitely abandoned, whilst others possessed a name but no local habitation. At the present day there are thirteen plantations still in the hands of private owners. Most of them are left to nature; some still produce a few fruits, pomeloes loquats, and pomegranates, and such coffee as will grow without any serious attempt at cultivation. In the little Mambōdai estate,

[1] The details regarding the Kuttālam enterprises will be found on pp. 462 foll.

CHAP. I. HILLS.

near the Kumāraswāmi Pillai anicut, a few acres have been laid out with tea.

Hill-tribes: the Paliyans.

The only inhabitants of the ghats are a few Paliyans and Kānis. The Paliyans confine themselves to the hills overlooking the Sankaranainārkōil taluk, and number all told only about 40 or 50 persons. People of the same tribe inhabit in larger numbers the hills bounding (on the west and north) the Srīvilliputtūr taluk of the Rāmnād district and the Varshanād valley of the Madura district. These hill-men are a malodorous and unsightly race, with short bodies, square faces, thick lips and unkempt hair. Men and women wear a small dirty cloth about their thighs; they scarcely ever bathe, and, when they do so, it is only (as they explain) to make themselves cool, not clean. Their language is a corrupt form of Tamil, spoken with a curious sing-song intonation. They live in groups of one or two families in holes and caves—*pudais*, as they are called—in the lower slopes of the hills and occasionally rig up a rough shelter of teak-leaves to lend a little comfort to the home. They live on roots of various kinds, tamarind fruit mixed with wood-ash, unripe dates, wild mangoes, all of which they search for on the hill sides. Some of them collect the minor produce of the forest, such as roots, cardamoms, honey and wax, for the renters under Government and receive grain in payment from their employers. This they cook, and eat with avidity; otherwise their foods are generally taken raw. To get honey from the face of precipitous rocks they let themselves down, pot and torch in hand, by twisted creepers to the level of the hive, their bodies being entirely unprotected. To produce fire they take a piece of steel and cotton-wool and strike a flint on the metal. Taken as a class, the Paliyans of this district are a little in advance of their brethren further north. By their dealings with the contractors they come more into contact with the people of the plains; occasionally they get money from the villagers who employ them to watch their crops. Some, owing to the exertions of missionaries, have become Christians and have somewhat smartened their dress. After exhausting the resources of a tract the family moves on to a new *pudai*, a stay usually lasting a month or two. They are not by nature hunters of game and, so far as is known, are of no use as trackers; they have some primitive devices for catching birds, and a few of them are known to possess old muzzle-loading guns, with which they now and then bring down a sambhur. They keep no cattle and never cultivate. Marriage ties are made without ceremony and are easily dissolved; promiscuous relationships are common, and polygamy is general. Women work as hard as the men, and those who have babies carry them slung in a cloth over the left shoulder. Child-birth is a simple matter and is considered to require not more than two days' holiday. Old and useless people are neglected and left to die. No man is greater than another; they have no headman, and every one must settle his own quarrels.

The Kānis.

The habitations of the Kānis (or Kānikkārs), of whom there are only about two hundred in this district—they are numerous in Travancore—are in the regions of Kannikatti and the Singampatti forests. They are a simple straightforward folk and are in all respects greatly in advance of the Paliyans. Their settlements, which they call *vādis*, consist of huts made of bamboo and grass and are situated, as a rule, away from the tracks of men and animals. Around their dwellings are the patches of land they are cultivating for the time being. The ground is first cleared and roughly chopped up with a bill-hook and, after it has been set on fire, is ready, without further tillage, to be sown. Cholam, tapioca, sweet potatoes, plantains and chillies are the usual crops and form their staple food. They also collect and eat a few wild roots. In addition each settlement has, with the special permission of the Abkāri authorities and subject to their control, its little plot of ganja, which men, women and children smoke. They generally manage to find a few palmyras to supply themselves with liquor. When their land shows signs of loss of vigour, that is after a year or two, they move on to another spot and repeat the process of clearing, burning and planting. In these days their ravages are controlled by the Forest department, who allot them sites from time to time and greatly restrict the area of their operations. Some of them have on this account moved across the Tāmbraparni to the Singampatti zamindari, where they are not subject to such severe restraint. In the Kattalamalai estate, the property of the Jesuit mission, a number of Kānis have become Christians and have settled down as agriculturists with a fixed abode. Though their physique is poor and fever seems to be almost general amongst them, they make excellent forest guides and show wonderful powers of endurance. They have been tried as watchers by the Forest department; but they do not like the job and do it badly. There are a few old muzzle-loading guns amongst them, and most of them have bows and arrows. They appear to be very poor archers; and it is difficult to believe their statement that they bring down birds

CHAP. I. HILLS.

with these weapons. Each settlement has its hereditary headman, who exacts implicit obedience and is much feared; the use of abusive language when in his cups is considered an excess of authority, and on one occasion the Forest Range Officer was appealed to in the hope that he would intervene to prevent a recurrence of such unpleasantness. They have a number of gods ranking in the class of Mādaswāmi and his fellows, to whom they make offerings; at the time of festivals they go to the famous temple of Sorimuthayyan (in the Singampatti forest), where the worship of the numerous attendant devil-gods evokes perhaps more enthusiasm than that of the Sāstā himself. The lonely parts of the jungle are inhabited by vaguely conceived but powerful spirits, and for sixteen days after a relative's death a man who wishes to avoid them should either stop at home or keep to the frequented paths. The marriage tie is respected; but divorce is permitted on the initiation of either party. Their language is a mixture of Tamil and Malayālam.

RIVERS. The Tāmbraparni: its course.

It is in the Western Ghats that all the rivers of the district take their rise. The Tāmbraparni, the chief river of the district, drains an area of about 1,750 miles and from its source in the Periya Pothigai to its mouth in the Gulf of Manaar is 75 miles long. Possessing in the ghats alone a catchment area of 200 miles, it enjoys the full benefit of both the monsoons [1], and its bed is never dry. For some miles the stream flows with a rapid current through a densely-wooded valley, till it precipitates itself over a ledge of rock about 100 feet high; thence, by a succession of rapid falls, amounting in the aggregate to 100 feet, it reaches, after receiving the Pēy-ār and Ullār on its left, the Bānatīrtam precipice, over which the water falls in a magnificent cascade. At the foot of this fall the river is joined on the right by the Pāmbār, which rises in the Singampatti zamindari, and a mile-and-a-half further down, at the lowest end of the Kattalaimalai estate, the Kāriyār flows in on the left. From the Pāmbār junction to the famous Sorimuthayyankōil, a distance of about three miles, the river falls about twenty feet in a mile; but the slope varies, and near the temple, where the river flows between precipitous rocks, its current resembles a rapid. Thence for five miles the river traverses a table-land, receiving on its left, near Mundanthurai, the Sērvaiyār, a most important tributary. Dividing into two arms which enclose two rocky

[1] Between 1855 and 1860 the rainfall on the top of Periya Pothigai was recorded by the Travancore Government. The annual fall averaged nearly 200 inches but varied greatly from year to year.

islands in succession, the river reaches the Pāpanāsam barrier of rocks, over which it plunges in a fine cataract of 300 feet known as the Kalyānatīrtam fall. Striking high rocky ground in the plain, the river almost immediately divides into three streams, which finally reunite in less than half a mile. From Pāpanāsam eastwards to its mouth at Punnaikāyal on the Gulf of Manaar, a course of about 60 miles, the fall of the river gradually decreases from an average of about six feet a mile, in the Ambāsamudram taluk, to less than half that figure after the Srīvaikuntam taluk is reached. Its general depth, in times of normal flood, diminishes from 15 feet, in Ambāsamudram, to 6 feet, below the Srīvaikuntam anicut, as the breadth of its bed increases from about 300 feet, in the Ambāsamudram taluk, to more than a quarter of a mile, below Alvārtirunagari, some 12 miles from the sea. As will be seen from Chapter VIII, floods, sometimes serious, have been not infrequent; the highest for which authentic records exist occurred in 1914, when the water rose to 20½ feet at the Srīvaikuntam anicut.[1]

Its flood-banks.

Above and below most of the anicuts flood-banks of varying length have been thrown up; from a point some two and a half miles above the Srīvaikuntam anicut such banks are continuous for sixteen miles, to within two miles of the river's mouth. The process by which the river delta has within historical times advanced at the expense of the sea is referred to in the notices relating to Korkai and Kāyal.[2] As the coast is reached, the water meanders through winding back-waters to the sea; of the two main mouths, in Punnaikāyal, one is always open, the other being closed for a few months of the year.

Its name.

The origin of the name Tāmbraparni has been much discussed. The Sanskrit *tāmra* means either "copper" or "red," and the second half of the word is identified variously with *parna*, "a leaf" or "a tree," and *varna*, "colour." Hence we have either "the copper-coloured river" or "the river of the red leaves." The first derivation seems reasonable enough; but the second one, which was evidently in the mind of the writer of Tāmbraparni Mahātmyam, an ancient account of the river from its rise to its mouth, is undoubtedly the more popular. Agastya, the story runs, was sent to the south to right the balance of the world at the time when all the gods and goddesses were assembled in Kailāsam for the marriage

[1] The corresponding figure for the highest flood recorded before 1914, that of 1895, was 20 feet.

[2] See p. 256 below.

CHAP. I. RIVERS.

of Paramasivan and Pārvathi and he took with him a string of lotus-flowers. The chaplet soon transformed itself to a damsel, pink and fresh like the lotuses themselves, who, on the appearance of the newly-wedded god and goddess before Agastya on Pothigai, was bidden to turn into a river. The command was obeyed; and the sage Agastya, following the course of the river's progress in a *vimānam*, or aeroplane, established along its course many holy shrines and also bathing-ghats, thirty-two above Pāpanāsam, intended for the Dēvas, and eighty-six below, for mortal men. Other stories told in explanation of the name need not be related here.

Its fame.

The river is one of ancient fame. In the geographical section of the Purānas we read: "The principal town of the Pāndya country is Madura. The chief mountain is the great Pothi, the chief rivers the Tāmbraparni and Vēghavathi (Vaigai)." The Tāmbraparni is referred to in the Mahābhāratha; and again, in the Rāmāyana, Sugriva addressing his monkey corps says:—"By the leave of the high-souled Agastya ye will cross the great river, Tāmbraparni, abounding in alligators.[1] Like a maid with her lover, she with her waters and islets concealed beneath beautiful sandal trees,[2] bathes in the sea. Proceeding thence ye shall see the grand golden gates in the walls of the capital of the Pāndyas.[3]" The great Buddhist emperor, Asōka, relates in his inscription at Girnar that he planted the pillar of victory in (the) Tambapanini.[4]

Its tributaries: in the hills.

The chief tributaries of the river in the ghats, the Pēy-ār, Ullār, Pāmbār, Kāriyār and Sērvaiyār, have already been referred to. The Pāmbār rises in the ghats immediately to the south of the Periya Pothigai in what is known as the Nāga Pothigai; and after breaking through an intervening range of hills, in doing which it forms the splendid double cascade of Pāmbanarivi, it flows for six miles in a

[1] Alligators are still to be seen above the Kannadiyan anicut.

[2] Suggesting another derivation: "the river flowing among red (sandal) trees."

[3] Presumably Korkai. See below, p. 429.

[4] Dr. Caldwell identifies Tambapanini here referred to, and consequently the word Tambraparni, with Taprobane, the name by which Ceylon was known, to the Greeks at least, before the Christian era. Megasthenes (302 B.C.) so refers to Ceylon; and the author of the Periplus (A.D. 80) states that the former name of the island (Ceylon) was Taprobane. Incidentally it may be remarked, this was the name adopted by Milton: "And utmost Indian isle Taprobane." Dr. Caldwell, after discussing whether the island owed its name to the river or the river to the island, inclines to the opinion that the name was brought over to the mainland by immigrants from Ceylon to the Tinnevelly country. *History of Tinnevelly*, p. 10.

north-easterly direction to its junction with the main river. Both the Pāmbār and the Sērvaiyār come more completely than any other affluent under the influence of both monsoons.

In the plains; the Manimuttār.

The first tributary to join the river in the plains is the Manimuttār. Rising in deep shola above Sengaltēri, it is reinforced by the united waters of the Varattār and Kusankuliyār, the latter of which takes up the surplus of the Kīla Manimuttār escaping over the Karumandi-amman dam.[1] By means of the channel—Perunkāl—which takes off at an anicut at the foot of the hills the stream becomes the principal source of irrigation to the Singampatti zamindari; it joins the Tāmbraparni two miles west of Kallidaikurichi, immediately above the Kannadiyan anicut. A short distance before it reaches the plains it forms a fine cascade.

The Varāhanadhi.

The Jambunadhi, rising in the eastern slopes of General's Hill to the west of Kadaiyam Perumpattu, joins at Ravanasamudram the Rāmanadhi, which has its sources further south in the steep hills above Mēla Kadaiyam, and their united stream is known thereafter as the Varāhanadhi. The Jambunadhi is crossed by three anicuts, the Rāmanadhi by one, and the Varāhanadhi by two.

The Gatanānadhi.

The Gatanānadhi, rising far back in the hills above Sivasailam, is joined by the Varāhanadhi in Pāppānkulam, and flows into the Tāmbraparni on its left bank at Tiruppudaimarudūr. There are six anicuts on this tributary. Next is the Kōraiyār, a stream which carries the drainage of low hills in the south of the Ambāsamudram taluk and enters the Kannadiyan channel at Vellankuli.

The Pachaiyār.

The Pachaiyār, rising in the north-eastern slopes of Vellimalai and supplemented by the Karumandi-amman channel, which is diverted from the Kīla Manimuttār, flows through the Nāngunēri and Tinnevelly taluks and, after doing its own work of irrigation, enters the Pālaiyan channel at Taruvai.

The Chittār.

The last affluent is the Chittār, "the little river," or, in its Sanskrit form, Chithrānadhi, "the beautiful river," second in importance to the Tāmbraparni itself. It is 40 miles long, is crossed by 18 anicuts, and, after irrigating together with its tributaries a total area of over 27,000 acres in the taluks of Tenkāsi and Tinnevelly, joins the Tāmbraparni at Sīvalappēri. Its main flood-season is the period of the north-east monsoon. The source of the river is in the hills above Kuttālam, into which village it precipitates itself over a succession of beautiful falls, the principal being, in order of

[1] See p. 186.

CHAP. I. RIVERS.

descent, the Tēnarivi, or "Honey Fall," the Shenbagādēvi fall and the well-known Kuttālam fall itself. Unlike the country in which the Tāmbraparni rises, the ghats here are steep, and the watershed is but a short distance back from the plain. Consequently the catchment basin in the hills is small, floods descend swiftly, and for its supply the river is largely dependent on the vast area it drains within the plains. Though rains both light and heavy are blown through the Ariyankāvu or Shencotta gap during the south-west monsoon and drive along the eastern face of the hills around Kuttālam, the slopes which hold the sources of the Chittār do not enjoy to the full the benefit of the south-west monsoon. When this monsoon is heavy, rain is beaten over the hill-tops, and the river then descends in force; but the flood in this season is quickly absorbed in tanks and seldom extends beyond 10 or 15 miles of the river's course. Its chief tributary is the Hanumānadhi, which rises in the hills above Panpuli and, receiving the Karuppānadhi from the Chokkampatti hills on its left, joins the Chittār at Vīrakēralampudūr after a course of 12 miles. From the amphitheatre of hills which enclose Kuttālam a number of streams descend to mix with the main river; amongst these may be mentioned the Aludakannīr, descending from the hills above Mattalampārai; and the Ainthalarivi, or "Five-falls" river, so called from the beautiful five-fold cascade in which it tumbles just before leaving the forest.

The Uppōdai.

Another affluent of the Chittār, scarcely deserving the title of a river, is the stream somewhat vaguely described as the Uppōdai, "the salt stream," which first assumes definite shape as a water-course in the region of Kalugumalai (Kōilpatti taluk). It drains a nominal area of 272 square miles, the greater part of which consists of the broad tract of country extending eastwards from the hills overlooking Chintāmani (Sankaranainārkōil taluk). From this side the supply is slight, most of the rain being trapped in the innumerable tanks—there are nearly two hundred included in the Uppōdai basin—lying between the hills and the eastern borders of the Tinnevelly and Sankaranainārkōil taluks. The defined course of the stream lies roughly along the common boundary of the Sankaranainārkōil and Kōilpatti taluks, its chief feeders coming from the sharper slopes lying immediately to the east and west of its bed. It joins the Chittār in Gangaikondān (Tinnevelly taluk) a few miles above the confluence of the latter with the Tāmbraparni.

Basin of the Tāmbraparni.

With its numerous tributaries the Tāmbraparni comprises in its basin the Tenkāsi, Ambāsamudram and Tinnevelly taluks, most of the Srīvaikuntam taluk, much of Tiruchendūr and parts of Nānguněri, Sankaranainārkōil and Kōilpatti. A number of outlets, extending from Tuticorin on the north to Kulasēkharapatnam on the south, discharge the drainage of its irrigation system; as the coast is reached the country becomes an almost dead flat, and much of it is water-logged for many months of the year. Most remarkable is the great depression extending for six miles from Tiruchendūr to Kulasēkharapatnam behind the sand-dunes of the coast; in the rainy season water overflows into the low land from the Ellappanāyakkan tank, the last on the Srīvaikuntam south-main system, and stagnates, often for months, until it can find its way by a process of slow drainage to the Karumanaiyār and thence to the sea. Proposals for turning to the advantage of the cultivator the bed of this great swamp are at present under consideration.

The Nānguněri rivers. Southward from the Pachaiyār basin, the Nānguněri taluk is drained by the Karumanaiyār, the Nambiyār and the Hanumānadhi.

The origin of the Karumanaiyār, which only by courtesy can be called a river, is explained in Chapter IV. The Nambiyār, rising in the Māyamparambu shola on the Mahēndragiri slopes, augmented by the channel diverted from the Kīla Manimuttār at Vengayya Nāyakkan's anicut and by the Tamaraiyār, the Kōmbiyār and the Kōdamadiyār, reaches the plains at Tirukkurungudi and flows thence in a southerly direction to the sea, which it reaches a mile or two east of Kūttanguli.

The Hanumānadhi, a swift and fitful river, rises within the limits of Travancore and, after a course of twenty miles, reaches the sea some five miles east of the boundary of the district.

Generally speaking, these rivers are in flood only during the north-east monsoon; the occasional "freshes" which occur during the south-west monsoon extend only to villages at the very foot of the hills.

The Sankaranainārkōil rivers; the Vaippār basin. Northwards from Chintāmani the Sankaranainārkōil taluk drains itself into what is known as the Vaippār basin. The rivers of the taluk are, from south to north (they are all quite small), the Vālamalaiyār, Kōttaimalaiyār, Nikshēbanadhi, Kākānadhi and Pālaiyār; they derive practically no benefit from the south-west monsoon, and the water they bring down between October and January is almost entirely absorbed in a net-work of tanks. The slope of the country is towards the north-east, and it is in this direction that the surplus water

CHAP. I. RIVERS.

collects (together with the drainage of a large part of the Srīvilliputtūr and Sāttūr taluks of the Rāmnād district) to form the Vaippār. Draining an enormous area in the districts of Rāmnād and Tinnevelly, this river is subject to occasional tumultuous floods, which rise and subside with amazing rapidity; during the greater part of the year its bed is completely dry. Its course lies chiefly in the Rāmnād district; about fourteen miles east of the town of Sāttūr the river enters the Kōilpatti taluk, through which it flows south-east, reaching the sea at the little village to which it gives its name.

The Kōilpatti rivers.

A few water-courses, chief of which is the Malattār, carry the surface drainage of the Kōilpatti black-cotton country to the sea. A stream liable to heavy flood during the north-east monsoon, known (like so many of the kind) as the Uppōdai, carries the drainage of the high lands to the north-west of Ottapidāram southward through Pudukkōttai in the Srīvaikuntam taluk and thence through the Kōrampallam tank to the sea a mile south of Tuticorin.

THE PLAIN COUNTRY.

Eastwards from the foot of the ghats the district as a whole is one great plain, sloping almost imperceptibly towards the sea. Kuttālam and its neighbourhood stand 500 feet or more above sea level, and the country of that part is somewhat undulating. Occasional low hills—locally called pothais—some capped with gneissic rocks of the most fantastic formation (many may be seen in the Ambāsamudram taluk), others with rounded quartzite tops, emerge here and there from the plain and form important landmarks. Their eastern faces often show patches of brilliant red, the effect of the sand blown over and deposited by the high winds which rage from July to September. The most sustained of these formations is, perhaps, the quartzite ridge extending almost unbroken from the neighbourhood of Uttumalai (Tenkāsi taluk) as far as Tālaiyūttu and forming the watershed between the Tāmbraparni and the Chittār. More striking are the isolated hills referred to below, where the geology of the district is discussed.

Its natural divisions

Still, the plain country possesses wide diversity of scenery and, as has been said,[1] forms an epitome, a facsimile on a miniature scale, of the whole Madras Presidency. Broadly speaking, four types of country may be distinguished, owing their special characteristics to differences of soil and climate and to the presence or absence of river-irrigation.

[1] By Mr. A. J. Stuart, in the old *District Manual*.

CHAP. I. THE PLAIN COUNTRY.

First, there are the river valleys of the Tāmbraparni and Chittār and the country around the upper reaches of the smaller rivers; next, the dry lands, mostly red, which comprise the centre of the district (the river valleys excepted); third is the region of sand-hills; and last, the plains of black-cotton soil.

The river valleys.

In the first class chief in interest and importance is the well-watered valley of the Tāmbraparni, varying in width from two to five miles and extending from the middle of the line of ghats to the sea. Many large villages and towns, set in a sea of green fields and marked by tiled houses and temple-towers, occur at intervals along the banks of the river and display the real riches of the district. The land irrigated by the Chittār is less compact; starting in terraces from around Kuttālam, the wet lands form for a few miles one continuous expanse but soon break up into scattered patches, each watered by a tank connected by a long leading-channel with the river. From north to south along the foot of the Sankaranainārkōil and Nānguneri hills occur at intervals the blocks of rice-fields irrigated by the smaller rivers.

These irrigated tracts are the best favoured parts of the district. Here at intervals along the banks of rivers and channels and clustering often in thick masses near the base of the hills, groves of fruit-bearing trees, cocoanut, mango, illuppai and tamarind, spread their deep shade; most of the rice-fields yield two good crops every year, and the best of them are green for ten months out of twelve.

The dry red lands.

Rising from these river valleys and embracing much of Sankaranainārkōil and western Kōilpatti, the uplands of Ambāsamudram and Tinnevelly, the greater part of the Nānguneri taluk and much of north Srīvaikuntam, there extend wide areas of dry red sandy lands, spotted with numberless tanks and small patches of paddy land and broken by the steep water-courses which the rains scour out from year to year. Palmyras (there are nearly nine millions of them in the district) grow everywhere throughout the tract, here scattered and there in dense masses; for shade there are the road-side avenues and the thick clusters of banyan, peepul and tamarind which shelter the villages. Except where wells have been sunk, the lands are largely waste and, when cultivated, yield comparatively poor crops of pulse and gram. The rich red loamy lands lying around and above the rice-fields beside the ghats, especially those about Kuttālam, are quite exceptional; they enjoy a bounteous rainfall and yield heavy crops, often two in a year.

CHAP. I.
THE PLAIN COUNTRY.

The "palmyra forest" or *tēri* country.

The most peculiar division of the district is the great undulating expanse of red sand—the *tēri* country, as it is called—which dominates the southern part of the Nānguneri taluk and a great part of the taluk of Tiruchendūr. Starting as an insignificant strip within a few miles of Cape Comorin, the formation continues, almost unbroken, but varying greatly in width, depth and elevation, to within six miles of the eastern sea-board of the Tiruchendūr taluk. The level country of the tract and indeed the slopes of many of the dunes are studded with thousands of palmyras; "the palmyra forest" is a phrase by which this region of 150 square miles is often comprehensively described. Idaiyangudi, Naduvakkurichi or Arasūr, and Kuthiraimoli are the villages which give their names to the chief sand-hills of the tract; and it is to these uplands rather than to the level sandy country that the term *tēri* is in correct speech more particularly applied. The surface formation of these masses of sand is constantly changing under the action of the south-west winds, a phenomenon which has given rise to the widespread belief that many of the sand-hills are the tombs of buried cities. The highest and best defined of these is that lying in the two villages of Arasūr and Naduvakkurichi, which at its centre rises to an elevation of 219 feet; the Kuthiraimoli *tēri*, which covers an area of approximately twenty-one square miles, is the largest. *Tēri* country, on a much less extensive scale, reappears to the north of the Tāmbraparni in the neighbourhood of Sawyerpuram (Srīvaikuntam taluk), and the dunes of white sand to the north of Tuticorin appear to be similar in formation.

The danger of these drifting sands has long been recognized. In 1848, Mr. E. B. Thomas, the Collector, initiated the policy of encouraging ryots to plant them up with trees on favourable terms; more recently the Kuthiraimoli was formed into a "forest reserve," and the efforts of the Forest department to arrest the progress of the drifts by the plantation of palmyras and coarse grasses continue to the present time.[1] An extensive area at the highest point of the Arasūr-Naduvakkurichi *tēri* has recently been assigned, subject to the condition that plantation shall be carried out in accordance with a defined programme; so far, however, the results have been unsatisfactory.

In curious contrast to these barren masses of sand are the fertile patches of land found at intervals along their bases. Practically all the rain which falls on these dunes is at once

[1] See p. 205.

CHAP. I
THE PLAIN COUNTRY.

absorbed and flows out continuously into the surrounding level country within a few feet of the surface. Channels are dug and water is led off by gravitation into the surrounding flats. In a large number of villages adjoining these sand-dunes—Kāyāmoli, Pallippattu, Nālumāvadi, Kachināvilai, Tenmāvadi, Pannai and Arasūr—paddy is regularly cultivated by this means, and the plantain cultivation of Vīramānikkam, similarly raised, is famous. In other places, such as Padugai, Udangudi, Kommattikkōttai, Sāstāvinallūr, Naduvakkurichi (Tiruchendūr taluk) and Kuttam (Nānguneri), wells are sunk to a slight depth, water is baled, usually by means of baskets *(iraipottis)* attached to hand-picottas, and excellent crops of the more valuable kinds of garden produce, betel, plantains, chillies, and vegetables of all kinds, and even paddy, are obtained. Under the action of water and manure the red sand quickly converts itself to a black mealy soil of great richness.

In the occasional deep depressions which occur amongst these sand-dunes the local rain, augmented by the subsoil water of the dunes and by the drainage carried in innumerable water-courses from the south-eastern quarter of the Nānguneri taluk, creates the great inland lakes, or *taruvais*—the most striking features of this remarkable landscape. The largest of these, the Puttantaruvai, some three square miles in extent, lies in a deep basin within a mile of the sea, from which it is separated by a high barrier of red sand. Other such lakes are the Vairavantaruvai in Sāstāvinallūr, the smaller Sundan-kōttai and Kannu *taruvais* near the village of Padugaipattu, and the Mēla-Tangai in Kadākshapuram, all to the south of the Karumanaiyār, and, north of that river at the foot of the Kuthiraimoli *tēri*, the large *taruvai* of Semmarikulam. During the north-east monsoon their beds are filled and, as the water subsides, their slopes are quickly ploughed and planted up with garden crops and paddy. Pits are dug, and water is baled as the contents of the lake recede and the surface becomes drier. Exceptionally heavy rain precludes this cultivation and occasionally produces widespread floods, which, in a country with no natural fall and with great sand-hills barring any possibility of an outlet to the sea, necessarily take months to subside. Until 1914 one of the most serious inundations on record had been that of the years 1810–11, when the waters of the three largest *taruvais* in the south overflowed and, by means of channels, united in one common flood. The phenomenon recurred on a smaller scale from time to time; and many years later, in 1856, a cut was made to drain the water of the Puttantaruvai to the Karumanaiyār. The fall to

CHAP. I. THE PLAIN COUNTRY.

this river, however, was so slight, that the cutting has never proved really effective. During the recent floods of 1914, which appear to have exceeded even those of 1810, the channel was found to be quite unequal to its task; when the Karumanaiyār itself came down in flood, its water actually surged up the channel to swell the volume of water that was already pouring from all sides into the deep basin of the lake. Investigations have shown that, even if the channel is further excavated and a device provided by which the Karumanaiyār water may be locked out from entrance to the *taruvai*, it will scarcely be possible to drain off sufficient water to render possible in the near future the resumption of cultivation on a normal scale.

The black-cotton country.

The "black-cotton" country occupies the greater part of the Kōilpatti taluk and a large tract in the north of Srīvaikuntam. It is perhaps unfortunate for the reputation of the district that the main line of the railway takes travellers from Tuticorin to Madras wholly through this stretch of country; for of all parts of the district it is, for nine months of the year, the most uninviting. During the remaining three months tall waving crops of cumbu and cholam lend some cheerfulness to the scene; the cotton plants, which remain much longer in the ground, make at their best but a poor show. Umbrella trees and dancing heat are the main features of the landscape; occasional clumps of shade-giving trees, marking the sites of villages, occur at wide intervals to break the hard monotony.

THE SEA-COAST.[1]

The sea-coast, about 85 miles in length, extends along the Gulf of Manaar from Vēmbār, an insignificant port, on the north to a point about four miles east of Cape Comorin. Southwards as far as Tiruchendūr the coast, like that of Rāmnād, is low and presents generally the appearance of a continuous forest of palmyras and scrub jungle fringed with sand. The first prominent point is the low sand-stone cliff of Tiruchendūr, on the extremity of which is situated the temple of Subramanyaswāmi, its *gōpuram* visible at sea for twelve miles and looking, as has been said, like a brig under full sail. The coast-line then drops to a lower level for seven miles, until the high sandy promontory of Manappād is reached. Jutting boldly into the sea, it forms the southern arm of the Kulasēkharapatnam harbour; at this point the coast turns somewhat sharply to the south-west, rising in undulating sandy hills, which in places run up to a height of a hundred feet or more. Towards the south, at Kūttanguli, Idintakarai and

[1] For assistance with this section I am indebted to Mr. G. Leverett of the Port department.

CHAP. I. THE SEA-COAST.

elsewhere, the gneissic rocks of the Nānguneri taluk jut out a little distance into the sea.

Between the southern limit and Manappād the only projection of the coast affording shelter is a cape, near Kūttanguli, northwards of which a bay is formed sufficient to protect small craft from westerly winds. From Manappād Point northwards a series of rocky shoals extends as far as Vaippār. A reef fronts Kulasēkharapatnam, and small vessels bound to that port anchor inside it; during the south-west monsoon the anchorage is subject to heavy breaking seas, and except for very small craft, which can anchor close in shore, the harbourage is then somewhat unsafe. Off the point a dangerous rocky shoal, known as the Manappād outer shoal, extends ten miles from north to south with an average breadth of one mile, and between this shoal and the point is a navigable channel. It was to guide vessels clear of this reef that the Manappād light-house (rebuilt in 1901) was erected in 1888. North of Manappād off the village of Alantalai lie a series of shoals, inside of which small vessels can find good anchorage. From the Tiruchendūr cliff a dangerous reef, which projects three miles to the north-east, gives shelter to small vessels anchored off Vīrapāndyanpatnam. Another reef, about three miles from shore, fronts the town of Kāyalpatnam; between the rocks composing it are small channels, of which native craft can take advantage, anchoring in the water which lies between this reef and a smaller reef near the coast. Off Punnaikāyal, a small fishing village at the mouth of the Tāmbraparni, there is, rather more than a mile from the shore, good anchorage, which, protected during the period of the south and south-west winds by the Kāyalpatnam reef, provides a safe passage for small vessels bound to Kāyalpatnam. About three miles from the coast is a remarkable natural basin in the rocks extending eastwards about four miles, its depth ranging from ten fathoms on the west to twenty on the east, with a bottom of fine sand and mud. The formation is said to be similar to the deep swatches which, on a very much larger scale, exist off the mouths of the Hugli and Indus. Two miles south of "Devil's Point" begins a reef, on the northern continuation of which stand the islands of Punnaiyadi Tīvu, Cronjee Tīvu and Pāndyan Tīvu [1], facing Tuticorin. The islands extend at intervals northwards to Vaippār,

[1] At the present day the "Devil's Pass" is closed and the Punnaiyadi Tīvu is united with the mainland; and, except on the occasion of high tides, the three "islands" themselves form one continuous stretch of land. Punnaiyadi and Cronjee islands have long been permanently united. Proposals to reopen the Devil's Pass are made from time to time. The chart of 1879 showed a passage of 16 feet depth at this point.

CHAP. I. THE SEA-COAST.

ending with the Sali Tīvu group, the last of which is three-and-a-half miles south of Vaippār. The water off this part of the coast is very shallow and generally smooth; only small craft can pass inside the islands.

Harbours: Tuticorin.

The Tuticorin harbour is formed by a low sandy cape—the "Devil's Point" referred to—projecting eastward from the mainland on the south, whence in a northerly direction extend the Punnaiyadi, Cronjee and Pāndyan islands; a mile north of Pāndyan island is a rocky shoal, partly exposed at low water, extending in a north-westerly direction towards the mainland. Within this circular chain of islands and reefs lies the harbour. For fairly large coasting craft perfect shelter is found within the reef in eight or nine feet of water. Ocean-going vessels anchor in the road-stead outside Pāndyan Island[1] five or six miles from the town; and even coasting craft of large size have to proceed to this road-stead to complete their loading. The entrance to the harbour is a channel about half-a-mile wide, lying between two sets of submerged rocks. There is no distinct bar, the twelve feet line of soundings running parallel with the coast and shoaling gradually towards the land. An entrance from the south existed until quite recently between Devil's Point and Punnaiyadi Tīvu, but is now completely closed.[2] It is in this direction and also in the southern part of the harbour generally that the silting, of which so much complaint is heard, has chiefly taken place. The local currents, which set with the wind and vary accordingly in direction and strength, are operating constantly to bring about changes in the coast line.

As a port, Tuticorin stands second in the Madras Presidency and fifth in British India. Regular lines of steamers trading with Europe call there, and the British India Steam Navigation Company maintains a daily service with Colombo and a weekly service of coasters. The Asiatic Company's steamers call fortnightly.[3]

Kulasēkharapatnam.

Kulasēkharapatnam is a small port, with which small country craft trade all the year round. Larger vessels going to and from Ceylon and the more distant ports of India generally avoid the period of the south-west monsoon; it is difficult then both to negotiate the reef and to land goods.

Kāyalpatnam.

Kāyalpatnam, a little port protected by a reef, is visited by country craft all the year round. As at Kulasēkharapatnam, the south-west monsoon does not interfere with this class of trade.

[1] Popularly known as Hare island.

[2] See footnote on page 19.

[3] This was written, as will be evident, before the outbreak of the present war.

CHAP. I. THE SEA-COAST.

Vaippār and Vēmbār.

Vaippār and Vēmbār, 15 and 20 miles north of Tuticorin, are two unimportant ports, visited on an average by two or three small country vessels a month.

The weather of the coast.

The weather on the coast is governed by the north-east and south-west monsoons. Northwards of Manappād the south-west winds blowing off the land are not felt by coasting vessels; at ten to twenty miles off the coast, as the protection of the Manappād Point is lost, bad weather is often experienced. The unsettled period begins with the middle of October and lasts till the end of January. During these months cyclonic storms form in the south of the Bay of Bengal and usually pass westward across the southern coast of India. A serious storm of this kind occurred in 1906 (on the 13th November), in which a schooner of 60 tons foundered off the Manappād Point and several cargo boats were driven ashore along the coast.

Pearl and chank fisheries.

It is through its pearl-fisheries[1] that the Gulf of Manaar is best known. The so-called "pearl-banks" are rocky outcrops on the sandy submarine plateau which fringes the whole length of the coast. The rocks appear to be of recent origin, composed of more or less pure limestone, the irregularities of which are as a rule covered with fine sand. As compared with the Ceylon banks, the Indian reefs labour under several disadvantages. Exposed to the force of both monsoons, they enjoy rest only for four brief months in the year. The Ceylon banks, on the other hand, are sheltered from the north-east monsoon by the land and from the south-west by the shoal known as Karaitīvu. A special enemy of the oyster, peculiar to the Tinnevelly banks, is the mud, which, with the gradual encroachment of the land on the sea, comes down in increasing quantities and mixes itself with the sand.

Every rocky outcrop from Rāmēsvaram to Cape Comorin is charted as a pearl-bank, though many have not yet proved that they deserve the name. In fact, the limits within which successful fisheries are known to have been conducted are Vaippār on the north and Manappād on the south, a region which corresponds exactly in latitude with the profitable banks on the Ceylon side.[2] This stretch, forming what is generally known as the "central division," comprises

[1] See also pp. 229 foll. My authority for this section is mainly Mr. J. Hornell's *Report on the Indian Pearl-Fisheries*, Madras Government Press, 1905.

[2] Quite recently (1914) a fishery was held off Tondi on the Rāmnād coast. So far as can be ascertained from records, no fishery had till then been held in those waters. The fishery was scarcely a success.

CHAP. I. THE SEA-COAST.

fifty-four distinct banks, or *pārais*, varying in size from a few hundred square feet to eight or ten square miles. Geographically they have been divided into seventeen groups and their characteristics have been scientifically examined and recorded. The "Tulāyiram Pār," ten miles off Tuticorin, consisting, as its name ("nine-hundred rocks") correctly suggests, of a number of rocky patches, and the "Kudumutti Pār," lying some six miles east of Punnaikāyal, have hitherto proved the most productive.

The undoubted decadence of the pearl-fisheries in modern times has given rise to a great deal of speculation and discussion. The mollusc known locally as killikāy *(avicula)*, the ray *(trygon)* and the trigger-fish *(balistes)* have all been blamed; and it is known that to a greater or less extent all these fish do prey on the oyster. But most baneful of all is the mollusc, known locally as *suran*, which clusters in dense masses on the sea-bottom, spreading over the surface of the coral blocks, smothering and crowding out the delicate young of the oyster; and the records of inspection made by the Superintendents of Pearl-banks amply prove the case against this mischievous little creature. The old theory that the chank was an enemy of the oyster received its quietus from Mr. H. S. Thomas in 1884. There are two species of the chank, the spined horse chank and the spined elephant chank, which at times attack oysters; but they are rarely found off the Tinnevelly coast. The habitat of the local chank—*turbinella pyrum*—is a mixture of sand and mud, a combination which would smother the oyster, whilst on the oyster's rock the chank would starve. The natural result of the conditions of the Gulf is that, when compared with Ceylon, Tinnevelly produces poor oysters but good chanks.

SOILS. Their distribution.

The soils of the district are, broadly speaking, divided between the black and red series, the usual gradations occurring in the two classes, according as clay or sand predominates in their composition. The table in the margin shows (so far as ryotwari areas are concerned) the distribution in the various taluks of these two main classes of soil. The regions covered by each of the two kinds are as a rule well defined.

Taluk.	Percentage of soil classified (at the last settlement) as Black.	Red.
Ambāsamudram ...	11	89
Kōilpatti	69	31
Nānguneri ...	3	97
Sankaranainārkōil	33	67
Srīvaikuntam ...	57	43
Tenkāsi	8	92
Tinnevelly	27	73
Tiruchendūr ...	11	89
Percentage for the district	25	75

Soils.

Along the foot of the hills lies a stretch of red sandy loam (the more loamy called *semman* and the less loamy *sevval*), extending in the north half-way across the Sankaranainārkōil taluk, embracing towards the south the whole of the Tenkāsi and Ambāsamudram taluks, the south and middle of Tinnevelly, west Srīvaikuntam, north-west Tiruchendūr, and the northern and central parts of Nānguneri. The greater part of the Kōilpatti taluk forms, with the north-western region of Srīvaikuntam, an almost unbroken stretch of black soil; the western side of the Kōilpatti taluk is mostly red, a wedge of black earth intervening on the west to separate it from the red soils of western Sankaranainārkōil. Smaller pockets of black soil are found here and there throughout the district. Red sand covers a great part of the Tiruchendūr taluk and the southern regions of Nānguneri. Outside the two main series is the belt of grey sand, varying greatly in width, that extends throughout the length of the sea-coast.

The black soils.

The black soil of the northern plain, a lighter earth than the prevailing type found in the Ceded Districts, is very dark in colour and comparatively easy to plough, opening out in the hot weather into wide cracks. Towards the south it becomes greyer, and kankar is often found near the surface. The belt of paddy land on either side of the Tāmbraparni, though classed as regar, or "black-cotton," is a very different soil; it is much stiffer, well suited to irrigation, and is in reality a good red loam, blackened by constant flooding and manuring. The tract is not of uniform quality, the subsoil varying in its degree of fineness. Where the subsoil is less stiff and drainage is consequently more difficult, the earth is generally known as *veppal*; a worse type of soil, impregnated with soda, is that known generally as *pottal*.

The red soils.

The red soil near the hills, the finest example of which is found in the bay enclosing Tenkāsi, is a stiff and rich loam, believed by geologists to be a fluvial deposit direct from the hill sides. Water as a rule is obtainable at a slight depth, and irrigation from wells is common in this strip. Further east the red soil is lighter in colour, more sandy and often very stony. Large heaps of termite earth of a brilliant red colour form a striking feature of the landscape near the hills in south Nānguneri. The real red sand is found in the "palmyra forest" already referred to.

Geology.[1]

Owing to the general flatness of the district the rivers have, as a rule, cut out but shallow valleys, which afford poor

[1] This section is based on a memorandum furnished by the late W. R. Bruce Foote.

CHAP. I.
GEOLOGY.

geological sections; and on this account the correlation of some of the more recent sedimentary formations has been found difficult and doubtful. Another obstacle to geological study is the fact that a great part of the country, notably the Kōilpatti taluk, is heavily overlaid with black soil. It is as a rule only where the hills stand up from the plain that outcrops of the rocks are to be seen; and, as these hills are few and widely scattered, a geological map of the district becomes little more than patchwork.

The rocks met with during geological survey, arranged in descending order, are the following:—

1. Archæan rocks, gneisses and granites.
2. Gritty sandstones (Cuddalore sandstones), Rajahmundry beds, Conjeeveram gravels.
3. Lateritic conglomerates, gravels and sands.
4. Sub-recent marine beds, limestones and grits (upraised coral reefs).
5. Fluviatile and marine alluvia, kankar deposits.
6. Blown sands, red *(tēris)*; white (coast-dunes).
7. Soils and sub-aerial deposits.

Most conspicuous among the outcrops are the numerous masses of granular quartz occurring in the eastern central part of the district. Amongst these may be enumerated the Kurumalai ridge near Kumārapuram (Kōilpatti taluk), the ridges to the south and north-east of Kōilpatti, to the west of Ottapidāram and again near Pudukkōttai, and—most striking of this class—the Vallanād hill, nine miles east of Palamcotta, which rises to a height of over a thousand feet. Other conspicuous outcrops forming considerable ridges occur north-east, east and south of Palamcotta, and west of the town of Tinnevelly. The western arm of the Mēlapāttam horse-shoe out-crop, north-east of Palamcotta, re-appears under the alluvium of the Tāmbraparni northward and in all probability joins on to the great granular quartz band forming the Tālaiyūttu ridge. Inter-bedded with all these granular quartz bands are bands of granitic gneiss. Economically the rock is valueless, the only mineral found as a rule in the minute spaces between the quartz granules being an earthy, apparently decomposing, hæmatite.

The crystalline rock series, occurring to the south and west of the region of the granular quartz bands just enumerated, is pre-eminently granitoid, the prevalent variety being a pale-grey quartzo-felspathic banded rock, with very little black mica but very numerous pale red or pink garnets.

From its large development near Cape Comorin, it has been called the Cape Comorin type, and is regarded by Mr. Holland as an acidic form of his Charnockite series. To this class belongs the low ridge of rock at Singikulam (Nānguneri taluk), ten miles south-west of Palamcotta, and connected with it on the west are some considerable rocky hills, which culminate in the beautiful Kolundumāmalai (at Sērmadēvi), perhaps the finest isolated mass in the district. A few miles to the south of Singikulam rise several sharp-peaked hills, just to the north of the road from Nānguneri to Kalakkād; and, further south again, the perfect cone of naked rock overlooking Tirukkurungudi affords a magnificent specimen of the gneissic type. The outcrops to the west and north-west of Sērmadēvi, occurring at intervals throughout the Ambāsamudram taluk and again lying close into the ghats in the Tenkāsi and Sankaranainārkōil taluks, have not been geologically examined; but they appear to belong to this definitely granitoid class. Amongst them the great mass known as the Periyūr malai (1,378 feet), in the Sankaranainārkōil taluk, is perhaps the most striking.

Resting on the eastern extensions of the granitic bands are thin beds of sandstone, "whitish grits," which, on grounds of strong petrological resemblance and similarity of stratigraphical position, are held to be the equivalents of the Cuddalore sandstones, a formation met with at frequent intervals along the eastern coast of the peninsula from the neighbourhood of Cuddalore up to and beyond Rajahmundry. Nowhere has this formation been found to contain fossils by which to fix its age positively, but the several small exposures of it met with in the south of the district underly a set of marine beds in the shape of sandy clays, full of sub-fossil shells of recent species, *ostræa*, *arca*, *cythera*, etc., and in two sections seem to pass up into it. The better one of these sections is at Tōppuvilai, on the right bank of the Nambiyār, about two miles above its embouchure.

These marine beds are not always sandy or clayey; in some places they are calcareous, as in the small limestone plateaus at Kodunkulam, twelve miles from Cape Comorin, which stand some 150 feet above the sea level. Fossils are not numerous, though some beds are largely composed of comminuted marine shells; those recognizable belong to species now living. The limestone varies, as a rule, from 50 to 60 feet in thickness, and in colour from greyish white to brown. At the eastern end of the eastern plateau an impure tufa has been found above the limestone, enclosing very large

CHAP. I. GEOLOGY.

numbers of the living *helix vitata.* Other interesting outcrops of the marine beds, mostly limestones, occur at the mouth of the Nambiyār, in the banks of the Ellava Odai, and near Tisayanvilai; a valuable building-stone obtained at the last-named place was used by Bishop Caldwell in the construction of his church at Idaiyangudi. The rock is limestone, very largely composed of comminuted shells.

Other shelly limestones with recent shells occur at and near Christianagaram (Udangudi) and at Panampārai, seven miles away. North of the Tāmbraparni only one exposure of these marine beds worth noticing occurs, eighteen miles north of Tuticorin, at Vēdanattam. The gritty calcareous sandstone, both fine and coarse, is a good building-stone and is largely quarried and much used in Tuticorin. The fossils are all of living species.

The lateritic formations, so important and widespread in the Trichinopoly, Tanjore and Madura districts, demand but little attention; it is only in the south of the Nānguneri taluk, near Rādhāpuram, that notable patches of this ferruginous conglomerate are met with.

The alluvia of the rivers are, as a rule, of a pale reddish colour and very sandy, the Vaippār, with its accumulations of regar, being the only exception. Calcareous tufa appears in the banks of the Tāmbraparni in large quantities near the town of Tinnevelly; and at and above the Tinnevelly bridge is a considerable spread of coarse tufaceous conglomerate, on which substantial *mantapams* have been built. The advance of the Tāmbraparni delta is a matter as much of historical as of geological knowledge; and, were it not for the scouring action of the current which flows north-eastward up the coast during the south-west monsoon, the advance would have been faster. Of the marine alluvia it is impossible to say much, as they are almost entirely covered by the blown sands, so largely developed in this district.

The *tēris*, or dunes of red sand, already referred to, are composed of grains of quartz, with an admixture of fine red clay-dust in very variable quantity. Their origin is ascribed to the action of the fierce and continuous winds of the south-west monsoon, which sweep up vast clouds of dust from the dry surface of the red loam skirting the base of the hills and deposit their burden near the coast over the plains to the east. It is believed, however, that the red sands of all these *tēris* are piled up over small plateaus of the marine series described above and that, as a rule, the depth of pure sand does not exceed a hundred feet. The north-east monsoon, which not only brings rain but is more fitful in its action, has comparatively little effect on the formation of these sand-dunes.

Quite distinct from the *tēris* and forming a sharp contrast of colour are the dunes of white sea-sand thrown up at many points along the coast by the combined action of the surf and the prevailing south-west wind. They are of importance only near Manappād, where the ridge they form is fully a hundred feet high, and the sand, which consists very largely of comminuted shells, has on the sea-ward slope become sufficiently consolidated to serve as a building-stone. The results of this process are especially marked at Manappād Point, where the coast comes under the influence of both monsoons. At Tiruchendūr too, further north, the sand has so far hardened as to permit the sea to cut it into a cliff some fifty feet high, part of which has been excavated to form the temple of Subramanyaswāmi.

MINERALS.

The minerals of the district are not interesting. Iron was formerly worked on a fairly extensive scale in many places along the foot of the ghats, and large deposits of slag may still be seen at Vāsudevanallūr, Kadaiyanallūr, Vallam and elsewhere. Old men who still profess to remember the days of iron-smelting say that the ore used was the black metallic sand to be found in the local watercourses. They add regretfully that a European who came and saw the process went home and gave the secret to his own people; thus the import of cheap iron began, and the indigenous industry disappeared.

Graphite, or plumbago, of good quality is found in the Singampatti hills, but it has not, apparently, been found possible to work it profitably.

The gneissic rock which outcrops at many places in the centre and west of the district is used largely for building purposes; excellent fine-grained stone, which lends itself to sculpture, is obtained at Brahmadēsam. The cream-coloured Pannampārai stone, referred to above, is in great demand in the south of the district and was used, in modern times, in the construction of the handsome churches at Megnānapuram and Mudalūr.

Kankar, or limestone, is found in abundance in many parts of the black soil country.

The coral stone excavated from the bed of the sea close in to the islands lying off Tuticorin develops, after long exposure to rain and sun, into a serviceable building-stone of a rough kind and is extensively used.

CHAP. I. CLIMATE.

Rainfall.

The climate of the district is peculiar, its principal characteristics being light rainfall and an equable temperature. Lying immediately under the ghats, the plain country receives very little rainfall from the south-west monsoon, though large areas derive the benefit of irrigation during that season from the rivers which rise in the hills. The average rainfall of the district is 27·57, three-quarters of which is received between October and December. Further details will be found on page 251.

Temperature and winds.

Since 1911 the temperature has not been officially recorded at any station in the district. The appended table shows in degrees Fahrenheit the average maximum, minimum and mean temperature for each month, as recorded at Palamcotta during the nineteen years ending with 1911; the average velocity of the wind in miles per hour is also given.

Month.	Average maximum tempera-ture (1893–1911).	Average minimum tempera-ture (1893–1911).	Average mean tempera-ture (1893–1911).	Normal wind direction.	Average wind velocity in miles per hour (1902–11).
	°	°	°		
January	88·1	71·8	79·9	N 19° W	3·2
February	92·6	72·8	82·7	N 17° W	3·2
March	96·7	75·3	86·0	N 25° W	3·1
April	98·5	78·3	88·4	N 48° W	2·8
May	100·9	80·3	90·6	N 75° W	3·6
June	96·9	79·4	88·1	N 73° W	5·3
July	95·3	78·9	87·1	N 72° W	6·1
August	96·5	78·6	87·5	N 75° W	6·2
September	97·3	78·4	87·9	N 74° W	5·5
October	93·7	76·3	85·0	N 51° W	2·5
November	88·5	74·2	81·3	N 24° W	2·3
December	86·2	72·2	79·2	N 11° W	2·7
For the year ...	94·3	76·4	85·3	...	3·9

The highest temperature on record is 107·1 (May 17th, 1906), and the lowest, 64·9, registered on three occasions during January and February. As a rule, however, the temperature varies little from the averages given in the table.

The average mean temperature is the highest for any district in the Presidency, and is a degree and a half higher than that of Madura, the nearest district for which statistics over any considerable period are available. The hottest months of the year are April and May, and those who can do so escape to the sea-coast of the Tiruchendūr and Nānguneri taluks to enjoy the continual sea breezes which then prevail.

CLIMATE.

Early in June strong westerly and south-westerly winds set in, and about the 15th the first floods come down the Tāmbraparni. With the wind blowing through the monsoon rains which fall on the hills, the air throughout the district then becomes perceptibly cooler; the country along the foot of the ghats benefits most, and at places situated near gaps in the hills, as Kuttālam (Tenkāsi taluk) and Panagudi (Nānguneri), the climate is delightfully cool, and rain falls in plenty. In July and August the winds become more violent, and sand-storms, which obliterate the sky and often overlay the fields with masses of sand, occur frequently in the red soil tracts. With October or early November the north-east monsoon sets in; and for two months the mean temperature falls below 80. The lowest temperatures of the year are usually experienced in January.

FLORA.[1]

The flora of the district combines the characteristic features of Malabar and the Coromandel coast, on the one hand, and of Ceylon, on the other. At the same time we find some species peculiar to the district, and such endemic species are by no means few. Further, we have in this region many plants which very much resemble, but are yet different from, the species found in the Malay peninsula.

The eastern region supports a vegetation which is more or less the same from Ganjām to Cape Comorin, although there may be well-defined areas with different sets of plants, and hence distinguishable one from the other, while at the same time we meet with plants of very wide and even distribution. The sea, especially in the neighbourhood of Tuticorin, abounds in sea-weeds, and there are over a hundred species flourishing there. However, the following are the most common species:—*Caulerpa scalpelliformis, C. plumaris, C. peltata, C. sedoides, Sargassum Wightii, S. dentifolium, Udotea flabellata, Dictyurus purpurascens, Polysiphonia corymbosa, Valonia Forbesii, Halimeda Tuna, Turbinaria conoides, Gracillaria multipartita, G. lichenoides, G. tænioides, Ulva fasciata* and *Enteromorpha intestinalis.*

Besides these we find in the seashore in shallow water the following aquatic monocotyledonous plants:—*Cymodocea serrulata, C. australis, Halophila ovata* and *Halophila stipulacea*, a species not previously recorded from India.

In salt marshes plants such as *Salicornia brachiata, Arthrocnemum indicum, Suæda monoica, S. nudiflora, Sesuvium Portulacastrum, Avicennia officinalis* and *Sonneratia acida* (with their

[1] This section has been kindly contributed by M.R.Ry. Rai Bahadur K. Ranga Achariyar Avargal, M.A., L.T., Government Lecturing Botanist.

CHAP. I. FLORA.

breathing roots standing erect several inches above the soil) and *Atriplex repens* abound. In somewhat dry places in the sand we find *Salvadora persica, Lippia nodiflora, Solanum xanthocarpum, Ipomœa biloba,* the sedge *Cyperus arenarius* and the grasses *Zoysia pungens, Sporobolus virginicus* and *Spinifex squarrosus,* and some other sand-binding plants.

As we proceed inland, we pass gradually to the flora characteristic of the east Coromandel coast. But the herbaceous and shrubby vegetation of this region is very much stunted in growth and, compared with similar regions in other districts, is very meagre as regards number, except for a few months after the rains in the year. The very poor stunted state of the vegetation is due to the very dry condition of the soil and the extreme heat, the result of the shutting off of the monsoon from the district by the hills on the north and west and by the island of Ceylon on the east. Xerophilous plants, such as *Barleria cuspidata, Lepidagathis pungens* and the columnar leafless *Euphorbias,* occupy these tracts, and from amidst them rise the trees *Acacia arabica, A. latronum, Borassus flabellifer* and *A. planifrons* with its conspicuous flat-topped head. Other common trees, such as the tamarind, banyan, *Terminalia Arjuna, Bassia longifolia, Melia Azadirachta* and *Thespesia populnea* are found here, as elsewhere in the Presidency.

The black-cotton soil supports a vegetation consisting of some or other of the plants, *Chrozophora plicata, Triumfetta rhomboidea, Alysicarpus monilifer, Indigofera trita, Cassia auriculata, C. obovata, C. angustifolia,* and the grasses *Cynodon dactylon, Tragus racemosus, Andropogon pumilus* and *A. pertusus.*

There is not much change in the character of the vegetation until we come up to the vicinity of the base of the hills. As we approach the hills, scrubby jungle consisting of the usual thickets composed of the trees and shrubs, such as *Zizyphus œnoplia, Z. jujuba, Z. xylopyrus, Canthium parviflorum, Albizzia amara, Capparis horrida, Terminalia belerica* and *T. chebula* make their appearance. Though there is a great uniformity of vegetation with strong affinities to the flora of the plains elsewhere in the Presidency, yet here and there we meet with special features. The region at the foot of the hills and lower elevations of the hills near Pāpanāsam, for instance, is characterised by the predominance of *Coleus aromaticus, Asystasia coromandeliana, Sarcostemma intermedia* and *Mundulea suberosa.* At Kuttālam such places harbour the common plants of the plains, but *Indigofera uniflora, Andropogon Nardus,* and a few others are very prominent. The compositaceous plant, *Gynura lycopersicifolia,* so far collected only from here, is very abundant. Here the introduced lantana has established itself firmly and is spreading very rapidly on every side. Some of the neglected coffee estates are completely overrun by this plant. Another plant which is spreading aggressively is *Stachytarpheta indica*, the moist condition of the soil being very favourable for its growth. The sensitive plant, *Mimosa pudica*, was a rarity some fifteen years ago, but now it has become quite common, and, if it is not checked from spreading at an early date, it is certain to become a serious pest, as it has done in certain parts of Malabar and Coorg.

At the foot of the Kalakkād hills we find *Barleria cuspidata*, *Erythroxylon monogynum*, *Dalbergia spinosa* and *Indigofera aspalathoides* dominant, with a sprinkling of the common plants, *Vicoa auriculata*, *Sida humilis*, *S. carpinifolia*, *Tephrosia purpurea*, *Cassia auriculata*, *Hibiscus micranthus*, *Vitis quadrangularis* and *Rivea hypocrateriformis*. The nature of the vegetation does not change at the foot of the hills and even up to a certain height. For instance, from Pāpanāsam to Mundanthurai we find only plants characteristic of the plains forming the bulk, though plants such as *Cochlospermum Gossypium*, *Givotia rottleriformis*, *Stenosiphonium Russelianum*, usually flourishing at low elevations, are also found mixed with them. In the neighbourhood of Mundanthurai *Strobilanthes*, *Cadaba trifoliata*, *Strychnos colubrina*, *Murraya exotica*, *Abutilon crispum*, *Eugenias*, *Vitex leucoxylon*, *V. altissima*, several species of *Grewias* and *Zizyphus* abound. Here again we find a mixture of plants of the plains and the lower elevations, but plants such as *Aglaia Roxburghiana*, *Eugenia rubicunda* (a species recorded only from this district), *Croton Klotzschianus*, *Polyalthia cerasoides*, *Alphonsea sclerocarpa*, a species found only in Ceylon and Tinnevelly, predominate. The frequent denudation of the forest at the lower elevations by the clearing of coupes exerts a profound influence on the vegetation. The plants flourishing on the plains gradually creep up and occupy the area.

As we proceed higher up towards Kannikatti, *Anonaceous* species become very common, thus showing Malayan affinities. Other species that are also predominant are those of *Diospyros* and *Grewia*. One species of each of these genera, *Diospyros Barberi* and *Grewia pandaica*, were recently found to be new species confined to this region. A species *Aglaia* growing between Mundanthurai and Kannikatti was found to be a new species by Mr. Gamble, and he has named it *Aglaia Barberi*. Besides these, on the rocks in the Tāmbraparni river, especially

CHAP. I. FLORA.

near Mundanthurai, grow two species of plants *Lawia zeylanica, var. malabarica* and *Farmeria indica*, both belonging to the same interesting and peculiar family, *Podostemonaceæ*. All the plants of this order are liverwortlike aquatics. The latter, *Farmeria indica*, is an endemic species. Another herbaceous plant, *Ionidium travancoricum*, endemic to Tinnevelly and Travancore hills, is very abundant here as well as on the Kalakkād hills between Kaḷakkād and Sengaltēri. The creeper *Pyrenacantha volubilis*, a Ceylon plant occasionally met with in the Avadi forests near Madras and on the Sirumalai hills in Madura district, is abundant here and also in and around Netterikāl. Scandent shrubs, such as *Combretum*, *Calycopteris*, *Symphorema*, and the climbers, *Cissampelos Pareira*, *Thunbergia fragrans*, *Atylosias* and *Aristolochia Roxburghiana*, are fairly common. The undergrowth consists of a very rich herbaceous vegetation, composed of plants of the orders *Compositæ*, *Rubiaceæ*, *Leguminosæ*, *Acanthaceæ*, *Labiatæ*, *Scitamineæ* and *Gramineæ*. However, the most widely distributed and striking species are *Curculigo Finlaysoniana*, *Commelinas*, *Scutellaria violacea*, *Oxalis corniculata*, *Sporobolus diander* and *Panicum patens*.

On rocks where there is moisture *Aneilema paniculatum*, *Cyanotis arachnoidea*, *Pouzolzias*, *Hibiscus surattensis* and ferns such as *Hemionitis orifolia*, *Cheilanthes mysorensis*, *Pteris aurita*, *Drynaria quericifolia* and *Selaginellas* flourish.

The vegetation of the Kalakkād hills is more or less similar to that of the Papanāsam and Mundanthurai hills. In the lower elevations herbaceous plants are abundant, the most common being *Crotalaria prostrata* and other species of *Crotalaria*, *Polygala javana*, *P. elongata*, *Indigoferas*, *Euphorbia hirta* and *E. cristata*.

The higher elevations present the same characters as those of the Anamalai, Pulney and Nilgiri hills, in most places. But, as we proceed southward, we notice features peculiar to the district. The forests are evergreen and are always moist and, therefore, the trees grow very tall, and several species usually flourishing at higher altitudes (4,000 or above) on other hills grow on these hills even so low as 2,500 feet. Some plants which are usually shrubby in other places grow and become tall trees in the sholas of these forests. For instance, the verbenaceous plant, *Clerodendron infortunatum*, which grows only into a shrub at lower elevations on these hills and on the west coast and the Nilgiris, becomes a tall tree in these sholas. Exposed grassy downs, so characteristic of the higher regions of the Nilgiri and Anamalai Hills and the

Pulneys, do not occur here. Long stretches of the endemic bamboo, *Ochlandra travancorica*, eagerly sought by elephants, are met with in many places, especially close to the Travancore boundary. CHAP. I. FLORA.

Both near Kannikatti and Sengaltēri the endemic species *Hedyotis purpurascens* grows in abundance and is very conspicuous on account of its violet massive inflorescence. From about 2,000 feet upwards plants characteristic of higher elevations, such as *Cynoglossum furcatum*, *Hypericum mysorense*, *Clematis smilacifolia*, *Gordonia obtusa*, *Vaccinium Leschenaultii*, *Lonicera*, *Gouania microcarpa*, *Clerodendron serratum*, begin to appear. All around Sengaltēri, Netterikāl and Kannikatti we find a very large leaved Labiate, *Anisochilus robustus*, a species not recorded from any other part of the world. Another Labiate, also endemic to the Kalakkād hills, *Orthosiphon comosus*, is very common amidst grass and is most attractive when in flower, on account of its purple flowers and bracts forming terminal spikes. The ground gets covered in many a place by the pretty flowered *Acranthera grandiflora*, especially after the rains. A very pretty creeper with yellow flower heads, abundant in the valley a little below Sengaltēri bungalow, is another species endemic to Kalakkād, and this was recently named *Senecio Calcadensis*.

The undergrowth in the sholas of the forests consists mostly of ferns, *Selaginellas*, *Hydrocotyle javanica*, *Begonia malabarica*, *B. floccifera*, *B. fallax*, *Balanophora indica*, several species of *Phyllanthus*, two or three species of *Ophiorrhiza*, *Plectranthus menthoides*, *Peliosanthes courtallensis*, *Pancratium triflorum*, *Ophiopogon intermedius*, *Arisæma Leschenaultii*, and several species of sedges. By the sides of streams we find the Acanthaceous plant, *Asystasia travancorica*, the balsams, *Impatiens grandis*, *I. Henslowiana* and *I. subcordata*, *Pouzolzias*, two or three species of *Didymocarpus*, species of *Osbeckia*, *Elatostema*, *Polygonum chinense*, and grasses such as *Zenkeria elegans* and *Ischæmums*. Exposed moist places harbour *Utricularias*, one or two species of *Eriocaulons* and *Xyris* and the ground orchid *Spiranthes australis*.

As already remarked the sholas consist of very tall trees, and the main bulk of them are such as are met with elsewhere on the Western Ghats. However, there are also many species of trees quite peculiar to these hills. All along the streams and also within the sholas we find the trees *Mesua ferrea* and *Mesua coromandeliana*, *Eugenia rubicunda* and two other species of *Eugenia*. The trees *Hopea parviflora*, *Balanocarpus utilis*, *Pœciloneuron indicum*, *P. pauciflorum*, *Xylopia*

CHAP. I. FLORA.

parvifolia, Ormosia travancorica are very common, and are quite special to these hills. Another tree, *Filicium decipiens*, a Ceylon tree, is very abundant all over the hills.

The teak tree is abundant in several places at the base of the hills, but everywhere its growth is poor. The most valuable timber trees of these mountains are the following :—*Balanocarpus utilis, Heritiera Papilio, Pterospermum rubiginosum, Chloroxylon Swietenia, Schleichera trijuga, Gluta travancorica, Ougeinia dalbergioides, Pterocarpus marsupium, Hardwickia binata, Acrocarpus fraxinifolius, Xylia dolabriformis, Acacia sundra, Terminalia tomentosa* and *T. paniculata, Eugenias, Diospyros foliolosa, D. Ebenum, D. sylvatica* and other species, *Bischofia javanica, Myristica laurifolia, M. attenuata, Bridelia retusa. Artocarpus hirsuta* and *Artocarpus integrifolia.*

Orchids are very common about Kannikatti, Agastyamalai and Kuttālam, and the common ground orchids found are *Microstylis Rheedii, Pogonia carinata, Calanthe Musuca, Habenaria jantha* and *Disperis zeylanica.* Several species of *Dendrobium, Eria reticulata, Pholidota imbricata, Saccolabium nilagiricum, Oberonia zeylanica* are fairly common. The orchid *Ania latifolia* is confined to Tinnevelly and Travancore. Several species of *Loranathus* and two species of *Viscum* are met with in the district.

Many of the plants and trees figured as new by Beddome in *Flora Sylvatica* and *Icones Plantarum* are those found about Sivagiri, Kannikatti and Kalakkād hills. Of the several new species discovered subsequently, some were collected by Dr. Barber. Plants so far known to be endemic to the Tinnevelly hills (and Travancore also in some cases) are the following :—*Aglaia Barberi, Andrographis elongata, A. viscosula, Anisochilus robustus, A. scaber, Anaphyllum Beddomei, Balanocarpus utilis, Coleus parviflorus, Cinnamomum gracile, Diospyros Barberi, Diotacanthus albiflorus, D. grandis, Farmeria indica, Hedyotis purpurascens, H. albonervia, H. viscida, Homalium travancoricum, Leptonychia moacurroides, Mallotus Beddomei, Psychotria nudiflora, Ochlandra travancorica, Orthosiphon comosus, Eugenia rubicunda.*

FAUNA. Domestic animals.

The district is not noted for any special breed of cattle. The ordinary village herds, though little cared for, are distinctly superior to those of the neighbouring districts. The cattle owned by ryots of the black-cotton country are amongst some of the best in the Presidency. They are all imported from outside the district and are mostly of the Kāngayan breed. "Salem" and "Alambādi" cattle are occasionally seen in the plough, but they have not the stamina of the Kāngayan animals and are chiefly used for draught purposes. In the cotton country cattle are well looked after; except during the season which follows sowing, when pasture is plentiful and work is scarce, they are fed daily with cotton-seed and sometimes with horse-gram as well. Their fodder is *chōlanāttu* or a mixture of this and cumbu straw. The pack bullock *(pothi mādu)* of the south is generally a small creature with a light and springy gait, which constant journeying in the sandy country of the "palmyra forest" has no doubt developed.

CHAP. I. FAUNA.

Semi-wild cattle.

A peculiar breed of cattle, whose characteristics are due to the neglect of their owners, are the half-wild creatures found in the neighbourhood of the forest reserves of Vallanād, Mīlavittān and Vaippār. These animals are, it appears, deliberately turned out from their earliest years to graze in the adjoining forests; some return to their houses at intervals; others—apparently very few—take such a fancy to life in the scrub jungle that they cut themselves permanently adrift. Not only the forests (which in the places referred to are mostly poor) but also crops suffer an immense amount of damage from these vagabond animals; most of the cattle are perfectly well known, it is believed, to their individual owners, and, as they decline to keep them under control, it has been found necessary to declare that, if found in the forest, the animals are liable to be shot. They are extremely timid and fleet of foot, and it is impossible therefore to capture them in the open.

Buffaloes.

Buffaloes are of the ordinary type and are used as plough-animals in the wet fields. In the production of ghee, butter and curd the milk of the she-buffalo is generally preferred for its richness to that of cows.

The numerous fairs and markets at which cattle are bought and exchanged are referred to on page 237.

Goats and sheep.

Goats and sheep are plentiful everywhere, and do not differ from those of other districts.

Wild animals.[1]

Big game, which is confined to the ghats, is varied and on the whole plentiful; as a rule, however, the forests are so thick, thorny and extensive that both beating and tracking are extremely difficult. The elephant is not resident in the district; but small herds and solitary animals migrate occasionally from Travancore and stay for short periods on the Tinnevelly side, rarely descending from the upper slopes. Bison are to be found in a few favoured spots in the Sankaranainārkōil, Ambāsamudram and Nānguněri forests. Tigers

[1] For what follows, to the end of the chapter, I am indebted to the kind assistance of Mr. W. A. Hasted and Mr F. H. Hannyngton, I.C.S.

CHAP. I. FAUNA.

are distinctly common throughout the ghats; they prey mainly on game, but at certain seasons of the year pay some attention to village cattle grazing on the lower slopes. In the south of the Nānguneri taluk they occasionally make raids into the plain country. Panthers are, or seem to be, decidedly rare, an impression which may be due to the fact that, like the tigers, they confine themselves as a rule to thick forests, rarely, as in other districts, visiting the villages. The sloth bear is found throughout the ghats; and his tracks may be seen on almost every fire line in the forests.

Sambhur are numerous; but as compared with the animals on the Travancore side carry poor heads. Ibex are to be found on the hills above Kuttālam and Tirukkurungudi. The barking deer or jungle sheep *(Cervulus muntjac)* is distributed here and there throughout the forests, but, like the mouse deer *(Tragulus meminna)*, which is commoner, is seldom seen owing to its retiring habits. The wild boar is found in large numbers in the forests. It raids the paddy-crops at the foot of the hills, and just before harvest will be seen many little *machāns* in which the cultivator sits up at night to protect his fields. The Indian wolf is by no means abundant and is usually found in the neighbourhood of the antelope. The Indian antelope or black buck is fairly common, being most plentiful in the neighbourhood of Gangaikondān and Vallanād. Unlike its fellows in other districts, whose haunts are usually open grass plains or cultivated lands, the Tinnevelly black buck is invariably found in the neighbourhood of low hills covered with scrub jungle. Retiring to their shelter soon after day-break, they do not emerge again till sunset, a habit which would seem to indicate long years of merciless persecution. The jackal, though not so often seen here as in the neighbouring districts, can be found in almost any place that offers cover. Wild dogs are far too plentiful in the ghats; moving about, as a rule, in small parties up to about eight in number, they destroy a large number of sambhur and spotted deer. The forests on the Travancore border harbour some of the hill monkeys of South India, amongst them a race of Nilgiri langur *(Presbytis johnii)* being perhaps the most conspicuous.

Birds.

Among birds, the green imperial pigeon *(Carpophaga aenea)* and great hornbill *(Dichoceros bicornis)* are interesting denizens of the ghat forests. On the plains the bird life is similar to that of the rest of the Peninsula, except that it is reinforced in the cold weather by a few partial migrants from Ceylon. Grey pelicans *(Pelecanus philippensis)*, for instance, have been seen on the Vijayanārāyanam tank (Nānguneri taluk) in

CHAP. I.
FAUNA.

January and February, and these birds were almost certainly cold weather visitors from Ceylon, where they are known to breed. The district is poor in migrants from the north, especially in representatives of the duck tribe. The cotton teal *(Nettopus coromandelianus)* alone amongst this family is a permanent resident and breeds in the larger tanks during the south-west monsoon. Snipe are fairly common in all suitable localities, and the woodsnipe *(Gallinago nemoricola)* has been shot occasionally in the lower ghat forests.

Reptiles and fishes.

Among poisonous snakes, the cobra and Russel's viper are common enough, while two species of krait *(Bungarus coeruleus* and *Bungarus fasciatus)* are fairly plentiful in the ghat forests, whence also the hamadryad *(Naia bungarus)* has been recorded.

The Gulf of Manaar teems with fish and crustacea of great interest to the naturalist and of commercial importance. The pearl-oyster and the chank have been referred to.

Except in a few favoured localities the fresh-water fish carry on an unequal struggle for existence, each tank and pool being thoroughly fished out in the dry weather. They are also sacrificed in myriads in the interests of irrigation. The upper reaches of the Tāmbraparni contain a good supply of carp, and in the lower reaches the "fresh-water shark" *(Wallago attu)* attains a fair size.

Insects.

Insect life is most plentiful in the ghats, favouring the area of heaviest rainfall and merging into the extraordinarily rich insect fauna of Travancore. The local representatives of the genera *Mycalesis*, *Ypthima* and *Lethe* among butterflies are all to be found on the grassy slopes in the neighbourhood of the reed bamboos *(Ochlandra travancorica)*, where the trees give way to grass and scrub. In the dry south-east portion of the district the insects are closely related to those found in the vicinity of Jaffna on the opposite side of the Gulf of Manaar. Here predominate the genera *Colotis* and *Terias* among butterflies, whose headquarters are to be sought in Africa; and many species of fossorial wasps find the loose sand of the Tāmbraparni delta to their liking. Systematic collecting throughout the district has never been done; if undertaken, it would probably yield interesting results.

CHAPTER II.

POLITICAL HISTORY.

PREHISTORIC PEOPLES. EARLY HISTORY—Pāndyas, Chōlas and Chēras—Pāndya kingdom; its antiquity—The evidence of Tamil literature - Sixth century—Pressure of the Pallavas—Is relieved by the appearance of the Chālukyas—The Kalabhra interregnum—Seventh, eighth and ninth centuries—Pāndya ascendancy—Decline of the Pallavas—The Ganga-Pallavas—Tenth to twelfth centuries—Ascendancy of the Chōlas—The Pāndyas take the aggressive—Subjection of the Pāndyas—The Chōla empire—Pāndya rebellions—Revival of the Pāndya power, twelfth century—War of the Pāndya succession about A.D. 1175—Thirteenth century—Chōla decline and Pāndya ascendancy—Māravarman Sundara-Pāndya I (1216—1235)—Relations of the Pāndyas with the Hoysalas—Māravarman Sundara-Pāndya II (1238—1251)—Jatāvarman Sundara-Pāndya I (1251—1261)—Disappearance of the Chōlas and Hoysalas—Māravarman Kulasēkhara I (1268—1308)—Jatāvarman Sundara-Pāndya II (1275—1290)—Splendour of the Pāndya dominions. MUHAMMADAN INVASION—Fourteenth century—The later Pāndyas. VIJAYANAGAR DOMINION (1365—1532)—Aggression of Travancore—Fifteenth and sixteenth centuries—Invasion of Achyuta (about 1532) and suppression of Travancore—Period of transition (1532—1559)—The Portuguese and the Dutch. THE NAYAKKAN RULE (1559—1736)—Its foundation—Extent of their dominions—Visvanātha (1559—1563)—Kumāra Krishnappa (1563—1573)—Krishnappa Visvanātha II (1573—1595)—Lingayya (1595—1602)—Muttu Krishnappa (1602—1609)—Muttu Vīrappa (1609—1623)—Decline of Vijayanagar—Tirumalai (1623—1659)—Throws off allegiance to Vijayanagar—And calls in the Muhammadans whose feudatory he becomes—His wars with Mysore—His public works—His capital—Muttu Alakādiri (1659—1662)—Chokkanātha (1662—1682): His troubles with the Muhammadans and the Maravans—His conquest and loss of Tanjore—Invasions of his kingdom by Mysoreans and Marāthas—Who seize his territories—Ranga Krishna Muttu Vīrappa (1682—1689)—Mangammāl (1689—1704)—Vijaya Ranga Chokkanātha (1704—1731)—Mīnākshi (1731—1736)—Interference of Muhammadans—End of the Nāyakkan dynasty. MUHAMMĀDAN DOMINION—Chanda Sāhib (1736—1740)—Marāthas again intervene (1740—1749)—Intervention of the English and the French. ENGLISH PERIOD—Muhammad Ali sends an expedition to the south, 1751—Colonel Heron's expedition—The Poligars—Revolt of western poligars who are assisted by Travancore—Western poligars joined by those of Madura are defeated by Māhfuz Khān—Muhammad Yūsuf despatched to Tinnevelly, 1756—The Nawāb's renter unites with Māhfuz Khān and poligars against Muhammad Yūsuf and is defeated, 1756—Māhfuz Khān proclaims himself the Nawāb's renter, 1757—Muhammad Yūsuf returns and is again recalled, 1758—Muhammad Yūsuf returns to find eastern and western poligars united, 1759—Assisted by Travancore he attacks Vāsudēvanallūr without success—Appearance of the Dutch inland, 1760—Muhammad Yūsuf's position, 1761—Major Campbell sent to Tinnevelly; negotiations concluded with Travancore (1764—1766)—The poligars again in revolt, 1767—The

"Assignment," 1781—Colonel Fullarton's expedition, 1783—He attacks Pānjālankurichi and Sivagiri—Surrender of the "Assignment," 1785—The "Assumption," 1790—Treaty of 1792—Anarchy once more—Excesses of Pānjālankurichi—Murder of Lieutenant Clarke at Rāmnād, 1798—The western poligars hold aloof (1798—1799)—Major Bannerman's expedition against Pānjālankurichi, 1799—Pursuit and capture of the rebels—Their fate—The last insurrection, 1801—Major Macaulay marches to Pānjālankurichi—And is obliged to retire—Reinforcements arrive and Pānjālankurichi is again attacked—Lieutenant-Colonel Agnew is sent with a large force; the fort captured—Escape and final capture of the defenders—Cession of the country to the English—Mr. Lushington, Collector of Tinnevelly.

PRE-HISTORIC PEOPLES

OF palæolithic man in Tinnevelly no evidence has yet been discovered. Mr. Bruce Foote, while exploring the district in 1883, discovered a number of fragments of chert, silicified wood and limpid quartz imbedded in the red loam underlying the *tēri* sands in the neighbourhood of Sāwyerpuram, Srīvaikuntam taluk. These specimens he assigned to the neolithic age. The iron and bronze objects discovered at Adichanallūr (p. 424) and elsewhere belong to a later period. With them are associated the sepulchral urns which contained these objects and which have been unearthed in numbers in all parts of the district.[1] The problem of deciding who this race of people was that buried its dead, apparently unburnt, in urns and with them ornaments and implements of all kinds, remains yet for archæologists to solve. The earthen vessels found inside the urns show unmistakeable skill in pottery; they are well-baked, and some are ornamented and highly polished. The iron, bronze and gold objects indicate considerable artistic skill. The current traditions describe these people as a race of dwarfs who did not die but, as they became old, grew smaller and more mischievous every year, until their fellow creatures lost patience with them and buried them alive. It would be rash to infer from the wildness of this legend that the age of this buried race was necessarily very remote; indeed it has been seriously doubted whether the remains should properly be described as prehistoric. It seems difficult, however, on any other hypothesis to account, in a conservative country, for a mode of sepulture of which no trace remains to the present day. Buried town-sites are often found in the immediate vicinity of these places of burial, so frequently, indeed, that the fact can scarcely be explained as a mere coincidence;[2] and the further examination of these ancient sites may yet supply some evidence as to the age of the neighbouring remains.

[1] See the notices relating to the various taluks in Chapter XV.
[2] See pp. 409–10, 428.

CHAP. II.
EARLY HISTORY.[1]

Pāndyas, Chōlas and Chēras.

When history first faintly dawns, the Pāndyas are found in possession of the greater part of the district; and, with intervals, they remained either its rulers or intimately associated with its history till the seventeenth century A.D.

The Pāndyas were the rulers of one of the three great kingdoms into which Southern India was divided in the earliest times. Whether we look to native tradition or to the more reliable data provided by inscriptions and ancient writings, our information about the country commences with the story of the Chēras, Chōlas and Pāndyas. Mr. Kanakasabhai,[2] a recent Hindu writer, has, it is true, inferred from a study of some of the early Tamil poets that, before the advent of the Pāndyas, the country was occupied by a ferocious race of men called Nāgas (the supposed ancestors of the present Kallans, Maravans and Paravans), and that the Pāndyas, Chēras and Chōlas were a body of non-maritime invaders from Bengal, coming from a stock which crossed the sea to Burma, Cochin China, Ceylon and Southern India. His inferences, however, are not certain; and in any case nothing is known of the Nāga rule.

Native tradition[3] represents the eponymous ancestors of the Pāndyas, Chēras and Chōlas as three brothers living together at Korkai, a town which tradition and historical research alike have identified with the place of that name, now an obscure village, four miles from the mouth of the river Tāmbraparni, in the modern Srīvaikuntam taluk. Eventually a separation took place, Pāndyan remaining at home, while Chōlan and Chēran went forth to seek their fortunes. Chōlan founded a kingdom in the north, while Chēran founded one in the west. The Chōlas seem to have ruled in the Tanjore and Trichinopoly districts and, perhaps, at the highest point of their greatness, extended their influence as far as the Kurnool district.[4] The Chēras established themselves in Travancore, Malabar and Coimbatore, and the Pāndyas in Madura and Tinnevelly. This traditional account of the boundaries of their dominions is roughly borne out by all that we know of them from properly historical sources.

[1] The original draft of this section to the end of the Nāyakkan dynasty (intended both for this and for the Madura Gazetteer) was written by Mr. F. R. Hemingway, I.C.S. With the kind and valuable assistance of M.R.Ry. Rao Sahib H. Krishna Sastri Avargal, Assistant Archæological Superintendent for Epigraphy, Southern Circle, I have revised it and brought it up to date.

[2] *The Tamils Eighteen Hundred Years Ago*, by Mr. V. Kanakasabhai Pillai (Madras, 1904), page 47.

[3] Caldwell's *History of Tinnevelly* (Madras, 1881), page 12.

[4] *Govt. Epig. Ann. Report* for 1904-05, pp. 48 and 49.

CHAP. II. EARLY HISTORY.

Pāndya kingdom; its antiquity.

Veryl ittle can be said with certainty about the Pāndya kingdom in its earliest days; but of its antiquity there is clear evidence. According to some versions of the Mahābhārata[1], Arjuna visited the country, and the Sanskrit grammarian, Kātyāyana, who lived probably in the fourth century B.C., knew enough of the kingdom to venture a derivation of the name.[2] References are also found to the Pāndya kingdom in the works of Greek and Roman writers.[3] Megasthenes, who about 302 B.C. was sent as ambassador by Seleucus Nicator, one of the successors of Alexander the Great, to the Court of Chandra Gupta, king of Pātaliputra near Patna, speaks of a country called "Pandaia" after the name of the daughter of the "Indian Hercules"—Krishna. "To his only daughter, Pāndiya, he assigned that portion of India which lies to the southward and extends to the sea." "The Pāndae" and "King Pandion" as well as "his mediterranean emporium of Modoura" are mentioned by Pliny (A.D. 77); and that writer adds the curious statement that these were the only Indian people who were ruled by women.[4] That the Pāndyas at this time occupied no mean political and social position may be inferred from the fact that they sent an embassy to the Roman Emperor Augustus.

According to the Singhalese chronicle, Mahāwamsa, Vijaya, the first invader of Ceylon, arrived in the island on the very day of the *Nirvāna* of Buddha. It is related that he selected as his queen a princess of the house of Pāndu, king of Southern Madhura, to whom he sent annually large sums of money.[5]

Another interesting reference to the Pāndyas is found in an inscription of Asoka,[6] the emperor and militant evangelist of the great Buddhist Mauryan empire, who came to the throne

[1] The Mahābhārata is of great antiquity, though its date is obscure. A work of that name was in existence before the seventh century B.C.

[2] Both he and Dr. Caldwell derive the name from Pāndu, the father of the five Pāndava brothers; and Dr. Caldwell supposes that the title was adopted by the Pāndyas so as to claim adoptionship with that family. Whatever be the merits of this derivation, we have on more than one occasion references to "five Pāndyas" as ruling in the country. Thus the Chōla Kulōttunga (1070–1118) subdued the "five Pāndyas," and there is evidence of the rule of the five Pāndya kings in 1292.

[3] For the following references to classical writers, see Caldwell's *History of Tinnevelly*, pp. 15, 16.

[4] The reference is probably to the peculiar social customs of the West Coast, where, in Pliny's time at least, the Pāndyas of Madura had colonies.

[5] *Indian Antiquary*, XL, p. 209.

[6] *Epigraphia Indica*, ii, 471, and *Ind. Antiq.*, XX, p. 240.

CHAP. II. EARLY HISTORY.

in 269 B.C. and made extensive conquests in Southern India. One of the inscriptions contains the proud statement that the "conquest through the sacred law extended in the south where the Chōdas and the Pānidas (i.e., the Pāndyas) dwell as far as Tambapanini" (the Tāmbraparni), and indicates, if not a political conquest, at least the acceptance by the Chōlas and Pāndyas of the Buddhist religion, an event of which we have evidence from other sources. It is to the second and third centuries B.C. that the inscriptions found in the fairly numerous caverns and stone beds of the Madura and Tinnevelly districts have been assigned.[1] Indeed, till the seventh century A.D. the Chōlas, and, more certainly, the Chēras and Pāndyas, seem to have remained untouched by pressure from the great empires of the north which extended their power from time to time from northern into central India; wars with one another, family disputes and conflicts with jungle tribes and the Singhalese[2] appear to have been their main occupation.

The evidence of Tamil literature.

Mr. Kanakasabhai Pillai[3] has attempted, on the authority of some ancient Tamil poets, to give some account of the kingdoms of Southern India in the age corresponding to the early years of the Christian era. Though recent epigraphical research has completely upset his chronology, a few important facts remain uncontested.

The capital of the Pāndyas according to these poems is the modern Madura, a fact which Pliny, as has been seen, confirms. It was called Northern Madura to distinguish it from another city of the same name in the extreme south of the Peninsula, which had been formerly a Pāndya capital but had been submerged by the sea. Another important Pāndya town was Korkai[4], which was well-known to the writer of the *Periplus Maris Erythræi* (about A.D. 80) and to Ptolemy (A.D. 140). The Pāndyan king is often referred to in the poems as well as in inscriptions as *Korkaiāli*, "Lord of Korkai." The Pāndya royal emblem was the fish, that of the Chōlas a tiger, a fact borne out by the united testimony of ancient

[1] These were appropriated in later times by the Jains and we find in them images of Jaina teachers and inscriptions of about the seventh and eighth centuries A.D. (*Govt. Epig. Ann. Reports*, 1907 and later; see under *Early Lithic Monuments, Caverns and Brahmi Inscriptions* in Part II), cf. also p. 380 below.

[2] The Andhras who followed the Mauryans in central India seem not to have extended their empire further south than the north of Mysore. Rice's *Mysore* I, 292–293.

[3] *The Tamils Eighteen Hundred Years ago*, Madras, 1904.

[4] See below pp. 429 foll.

coins, inscriptions and literature; the Pāndya warriors wore garlands of margosa when they went to battle, the Chōlas garlands of "Ar", and the Chēras wore garlands of palmyra leaves. These few gleams of light excepted, the internal history of the Pāndya kingdom during the first five centuries of the Christian era is shrouded in obscurity.

Sixth century.

For the sixth century the recent discovery[1] of the so-called Vēlvikudi grant and Sinnamanūr plates has given us the name of Palyāga-Mudukudumi-Peruvaludi, a king already familiar from the Tamil poem *Madurai-Kānchi,* where he is referred to as an ancestor of the Pāndya king, Nedunjeliyan. From the *Puranānūru*, a poem found in the Tamil anthology, we gather that Palyāga was a great conqueror: "the extensive forts captured from his foes he destroyed by yoking herds of white-mouthed asses and ploughing the streets. In the countries of hostile kings he drove into rice-fields his chariot drawn by restive horses. Into the fresh-water tanks of his enemies he forced his angry elephants with broad feet and stout necks." Of the existence of this king there is thus no longer any doubt; but of his achievements and his date nothing is known beyond the fact that he reigned not later than the sixth century.

Pressure of the Pallavas.

The earliest rivals of the Pāndyas in the continent of India appear to have been the Pallavas. By the second century the Andhras, with their capital at Amarāvati in the Kistna district, had succeeded the Mauryas in their dominions in central and eastern India and by the end of the second century were in their turn giving way to the advancing Pallavas. Descending from central India, the Pallavas appear to have almost at once succeeded in establishing themselves at Conjeeveram on the border of the Chōla country[2]; but there is nothing to show what their relations were with the ancient kingdoms of the south till the end of the sixth century A.D. About this time claims are made in the inscriptions of three successive Pallava kings that they conquered the Chōlas, and their records are found so far south as Trichinopoly.[3] Two of these kings,

[1] *Govt. Epig. Ann. Reports* for 1907–08, pp. 62 foll.

[2] The Pallava name first occurs in an inscription at Gujarat (d. 150 (A.D.) in which a king Rudradaman speaks of a Pallava chief as his minister *(Bombay Gazetteer*, 1896, p. 317). The Andhra king Gautamiputra (A.D. 172–202) boasts of having defeated the Pallavas; but it is clear the Andhras were subverted by the Pallavas very shortly after his time. Their inscriptions came to an end in A.D. 236 (V. A. Smith's *Early History of India*, Andhra dynasty; table facing p. 202).

[3] *South Indian Inscriptions*, I, 29, 30, 152 and II, iii, 356.

CHAP. II. EARLY HISTORY.

Simhavishnu and his grandson Narasimhavarman I.,[1] also proclaim that they conquered the Pāndyas; and there is evidence to show that their power extended to the Cauvery.

Is relieved by the appearance of the Chālukyas.

Almost at once, however, pressure from this quarter was relieved by the arrival in central India of a new power which gave the Pallavas sufficient employment in the north to divert their attention from their southern neighbours. These were the Chālukyas of Bādāmi (in the Bombay Presidency), who suddenly appear about this time as the owners of a vast empire in western and central India. By A.D. 615 they had driven the Pallavas to the walls of Conjeeveram; they claim even to have conquered the Chōlas, crossed the Cauvery and invaded the country of the Pāndyas and Chēras.[2] Whatever may be the precise truth of this assertion, it seems that it was against the Pallavas that the main efforts of the Chālukyan king Pulakēsin II. (A.D. 610–634) were directed; for (we read) " he caused the prosperity of the Pāndyas, Chōlas and Chēras to grow while he destroyed the Pallavas." [3]

The Kalabhra interregnum.

But before they attained " prosperity " the Pāndyas appear to have suffered a complete check from a new enemy, the Kalabhras; [4] and it is probably to the deliverance of the Pāndyas from their yoke and to the aggressive Pāndya policy which followed that Pulakēsin's inscription particularly refers.

When the Pāndyas first came into conflict with the Kalabhras, or who, in fact, the Kalabhras were, are still matters of great uncertainty. They are mentioned frequently amongst the tribes overcome by the Chālukya and Pallava kings. The Chālukya, Vikramāditya I., is reported to have " subdued with the thunder-bolt, which was his prowess, the mighty tumult of mountains which were the Pāndya and the Chōla and Kērala and the Kalabhra and other kings." The Pallavas of Conjeeveram claim frequently to have defeated

1 The existence of friendly relation between the Pallavas and the Singhalese prince Manavamma referred to in the Mahāwamsa (Ch. XLVII) indicates the possible influence of the Pallavas in the intervening Chōla and Pāndya countries. The Kāsakudi plates also state that Narasimhavarman I. conquered Lanka (Ceylon) (*S. Ind. Inscr.*, II., p. 343). Saint Siruttonda of the Tanjore district served as a general under Narasimhavarman I. and helped him in the conquest of Vātāpi (Ep. Ind., III, p. 277).

2 Sewell's *Lists of Antiquities*, ii, 155. Vikramāditya I. (A.D. 655–680), son of Pulakēsin II., actually issued a grant while he was encamped at Uragapura on the southern bank of the Kāvēri river after invading the Cholika-Vishaya (*Ep. Ind.*, X, p. 101). *Bombay Gazetteer* (Bombay, 1896), I, ii, 183.

3 *Ep. Ind.*, VI, p. 11.

4 *Govt. Epig. Ann. Report* for 1907–08, p. 65.

the Kalabhras. From these details nothing can be inferred beyond the fact that the Kalabhras were a tribe of southern India; the conjecture that they came from the Kanarese country has yet to be confirmed. The evidence of epigraphy to the effect that they definitely occupied the Pāndya country and drove out its native rulers receives corroboration in a curious form from the Tamil *Periya Purānam.* Madura, it is there stated, was invaded and occupied by the king of Karnāta during the time of the Saiva devotee, Mūrti Nāyanār, whose date is about the seventh century A.D.; the Karnāta king became a Jaina and persecuted the Saivas at Madura. He died without issue, and the choice of succession was left to an elephant which was let loose for the purpose. The elephant picked up Mūrti Nāyanār, and he accordingly became king of Madura. The story is referred to in the *Kallādam,* an old Tamil work, and may be taken to relate to the temporary occupation of Madura by the Kalabhras. The Kalabhra interregnum, now an established fact of history, is believed to have ended at the beginning of the seventh century.

Seventh, eighth and ninth centuries.

Thereafter we have the names of thirteen Pāndya kings, extending over nearly three centuries, the seventh, eighth and ninth.

Pāndya ascendancy.

The succession is as follows :—

1. Kadungōn Pāndyādhirāja.

2. Adhirāja Māravarman.

3. Seliyan Sēndan.

4. Māravarman Arikēsarin Asamasaman.

5. Kōchchadaiyan Ranadhīra.

6. Arikēsarin Perānkusa Māravarman Tēr-Māran.

7. Jatila Nedunjadaiyan Parāntaka (donor of Vēlvikudi grant) A. D. 769–70.

8. Rājasimha II.

9. Varaguna Mahārāja.

10. Srīmāra Srīvallabha Ekavīra Parachakrakōlāhala Pallavabhanjana.

11. Varagunavarman (*alias* Māranjadaiyan), came to the throne in 862–863.

12. Parāntaka Vīranārāyana Sadaiyan.

13. Rājasimha (III) Mandaragaurava Abhimānamēru.

Kadungōn, No. 1 in the list, was the rescuer of his country. For a long time (so runs the Vēlvikudi grant), the Adhirāja

CHAP. II. EARLY HISTORY.

(the Pāndya king) was sent into exile and the country occupied by the Kalabhra. Afterwards, the Adhirāja appeared "like the sun springing out of the stormy ocean and quickly removed the right which other (kings) had spread over the goddess of the earth and established his exclusive right over her." Kadungōn's son (No. 2) "made the earth his exclusive possession and wedded Prosperity." Māravarman Arikēsarin (No. 4), son of No. 3, defeated the army of Vilvēli at the battle of Nelvēli [1] and conquered the king of Kērala, who was "the undisputed Lord of the earth." Arikēsarin's son and successor is credited with a victory at Marudūr; but the details of the battle are lost. His successor is said to have defeated the Pallavas twice; and we may infer from this that the ascendancy of the Pāndyas had by this time (the middle of the eighth century) been completely established in the south. More important still are the extensive conquests ascribed to Srīmāra (No. 10), who not only defeated the kings of the Pallavas and of Kērala but crossed to Ceylon and "defeated the king of that country at Kunnūr." Another enemy whom he subdued was Māya Pāndya, whom we can only suppose to have been one of the king's own family and possibly the author of the dissensions which brought the Pāndya ruler into conflict with Ceylon. The close of Srīmāra's reign is placed in 862-863; and of his two successors in the list given above the first at any rate continued the aggressive policy of his ancestors. Inscriptions show that he conducted an expedition into the heart of the Chola country.[2]

Decline of the Pallavas.

It is to this period, the later middle years of the ninth century, that we may safely assign the rapid decline and the extinction, as a political force, of the Pallavas. The Pallava king who suffered defeat at the hands of the Pāndya Arikēsari Māravarman must be identified with the Nandivarman Pallavamalla, whose general Udaiyachandra had gained a victory over the Pāndyas at Mannaikudi,[3] the last defeat the Pāndyas were to suffer at the hands of the Pallavas. The might of the Pallavas, assailed first by the Chālukyas and then by the Pāndyas, was thus quickly broken; and the next power that appears on the scene to contest the supremacy of the Pāndyas is that of the Ganga-Pallavas.

The Ganga-Pallavas.

Like the Pallavas, this dynasty seems to have ruled at Conjeeveram, and at the end of the ninth century extended its

[1] Vilvēli and Nelvēli are unfortunately unknown names.

[2] *Govt. Epig. Ann. Report* for 1907–08, inscription No. 43 of 1908.

[3] *S. Ind. Inscr.*; ii, 364. The site has not been identified.

power for a few years into the north of the Chōla country. Almost at the same time, they turned their arms against their southern neighbours, the Pāndyas. Among some inscriptions[1] found near Tanjore, which have been assigned to the end of the ninth century, is one in which the Gango-Bāna king, Prithivipathi I., claims to have defeated Varaguna-Pāndya[2] at Srīpurambiyam Tiruppurambiyam (near Kumbakōnam) and to have lost his life on behalf of Aparājita, whose ally he was. Aparājita was the last great king of the Ganga-Pallava line, and many stone inscriptions of his reign have been discovered.

Danger, however, was threatening the Pāndyas from another quarter. Whilst the Ganga-Pallavas were measuring their strength with the southern kingdom, the Chōlas once more raised their heads and began to lay the foundation of an empire, which, with a few slight breaks, was to continue supreme in Southern India for three centuries.

Tenth to twelfth centuries.

Ascendancy of the Chōlas and decline of the Pāndyas.

It was apparently in the reign of the Chōla King Parāntaka I. (about A.D. 906—946) that the Pāndyas for the first time fell definitely under the Chōla yoke.[3] He defeated the Pāndyas thrice in the field, Rājasimha-Pāndya being his opponent. He defeated also the king of Ceylon, who came to the assistance of the Pāndya, and assumed the title of *Madiraiyum Ilamum-konda*—"the captor of Madura and Ceylon." His inscription at Anaimalai, six miles from Madura, the capital of the Pāndyas, is significant of the effectiveness of his conquest. A record at Kumbakōnam speaks of a Pāndya army stationed at that place in the time of Parāntaka I.

The Pāndyas take the aggressive.

Seizing the opportunity for rebellion afforded by the crushing defeat in A.D. 949 of the Chōlas near Arkōnam at the hands of the Rāshtrakūtas of Mālkhēd, who now occupied the country formerly held by the Chālukyas of Bādāmi, the Pāndyas openly revolted; their ruler Vīra-Pāndya defeated the Chōlas under Aditya Karikāla and, according to more than one inscription, "took the head of the Chōla king."[4] But later the Pāndyas again succumbed, for the Chōla Rājarāja (A.D. 985–1013) claims in a contest with the Pāndya king, Amarabhujanga, to have "taken away the splendour of the

[1] Nos. 51 and 10 of the *Govt. Epig. Ann. Report* for 1903–04, para. 12.

[2] An earlier king, believed to be identical with No. 11 in the Pāndya list on page 45 above, appears to have carried his conquests into the Tondai-nādu (South Arcot district). His inscription at Ambāsamudram records a grant from his camp at Araisūr on the Pennār river.

[3] *Ep. Ind.*, V., 42 and *S. Ind. Inscr.*, ii, 379.

[4] See inscriptions in the Nellaiyappar temple, Tinnevelly, and in the Ericha-Udaiyar temple at Ambāsamudram. (*Govt. Epig. Ann. Report* for 1904–05.)

CHAP. II. EARLY HISTORY.

Pāndyas." All we know of this victory is that it formed one of a series which ended with the year A.D. 998–999.[1]

Subjection of the Pāndyas.

The completeness of the Pāndya subjection at this period is proved by the immense number of Chōla inscriptions of the succeeding years which are found in the Madura and Tinnevelly districts[2] and by the large number of copper coins of Rājarāja which to this day are to be obtained in the Madura bazaar.[3] Even the name of the old Pāndya capital of Korkai was changed into Chōlēndrasimha-Chaturvēdimangalam; and the Pāndya country in general became a province of the Chōla empire under the name Rājarāja-Pāndinādu, which it retained for at least the next hundred years.[4]

The Chōla empire.

Of the external history of the Chōla empire during the eleventh century[5] it is unnecessary to say much. Rājarāja extended his rule throughout the Madras Presidency and in some directions even beyond it. On the west it extended as far as Quilon and Coorg and in the north-east to the borders of Orissa; his conquests included Ceylon and "twelve thousand ancient islands of the sea."[6] Parts of Burma and the Malay Archipelago were added to these dominions by his immediate successors. Their conquests were least secure in the north-west, and their most formidable rival at this period were the western Chālukyas who had ousted the Rāshtrakūtas of Mālkhēd and returned to power with their capital at Kalyāni in the Hyderabad country. In spite of the numerous inscriptions in which Rājarāja and his successors claim to have defeated these Chālukyas, it is clear that the Chōlas never succeeded in incorporating more than a small part of the Chālukya dominions in their empire. The scene of conflict seems generally to have been confined to the Ceded Districts and the north of Mysore.

Pāndya rebellions.

Of the Pāndyas it may with certainty be said that they were not submissive subjects. Early in his reign Rājēndra Chōla I. (A.D. 1011—1044) had once more to reduce them[7];

[1] *S. Ind. Inscr.*, III, i, 29.

[2] See *Govt. Epig. Ann. Report* for 1894.

[3] Capt. Tufnell's *Hints to Coin Collectors in Southern India*, i, 11.

[4] *Govt. Epig. Ann. Report* for 1903–04, para. 20. Eleven inscriptions of Rājarāja exist in the Alagar temple at Sīvalappēri (Tinnevelly taluk); one of them mentions Mudikonda-Chōla-Vallanādu. The present village of Vallanādu is in the neighbourhood.

[5] This is more fully described in the Tanjore and Trichinopoly *Gazetteers*.

[6] See also, under Tiruppudaimarudūr, p. 370.

[7] It is during the reign of this king (about A.D. 1021) that we first hear of the Chōla-Pāndya rulers in this country. An inscription of a king of this line, who apparently came to the throne in A.D. 1021, is found at Mannārkoil near Ambāsamudram. (No. 112 of 1905.)

and in order to bring the country under effective control he appointed one of his sons, Jatāvarma-Sundara Chōla-Pāndya, as viceroy of the Pāndya territory.[1] Following his example, Rājādhirāja I and Vīrarājēndra I made similar appointments. Rebellion again broke out during the reign of Rājādhirāja I (1018—1053). The Pāndyas were apparently united with the Chēras and Singhalese with the common purpose of throwing off the Chōla yoke. The revolt was suppressed; the Singhalese king was killed in battle, the Chēra king captured and the Pāndyan put to flight. "Among the three allied kings of the south," to quote an inscription[2] of the victor, "he cut off on the battle-field the beautiful head of Mānābharanan, which was adorned with large jewels and was inseparable from the golden crown; he captured in battle Vīra-Kēralan of the wide ankle-rings and was pleased to have him trampled by his furious elephant, Attivārana; and he drove to Mullaiyūr[3] Sundara-Pāndya of endless great fame, who lost in a hot battle the royal white parasol, the wisps of the hair of the white yak and his throne, who ran away with his crown dropping from his head, his feet full weary and his hair dishevelled."

CHAP. II. EARLY HISTORY.

Another rebellion which occurred during the reign of Vīra-Rājēndra II (1062—1070) was sternly put down, the Pāndya King or "pretender" being captured and "trampled to death by a *mast* elephant."[4] The conqueror gave the Pāndya "province" to his son Gangai-konda-Chōla with the title Chōla-Pāndya. The death of Vīra-Rājēndra (1070) was followed by a fierce domestic contest for the Chōla crown[5]; and it was not apparently until about 1074 that the great Kulōttunga I[6] (who reigned till about A.D. 1118) succeeded in establishing himself firmly on the throne. His hands were too full during these years to look after the outlying portions of his empire and for a time, at least, a great part of them fell away; Ceylon, indeed, appears during his reign to have been lost to the Chōlas beyond recall. The Pāndyas and the Chēras once more united in a rebellion against the Chōla empire and were again suppressed. The operations of Kulōttunga in the Pāndya country seem to have been prolonged

[1] Several of these Chōla-Pāndya inscriptions are found in this district—see *Govt. Epig. Ann. Report* for 1910, p. 89, para. 20.

[2] *S. Ind. Inscr.*, iii, 56.

[3] Not identified. The inscriptions refer only to Mullaiyūr, which must be a village and not the river Mullaiyār.

[4] *S. Ind. Inscr.*, iii, 37.

[5] See either the Tanjore or Trichinopoly *District Gazetteer*, Chapter II.

[6] Inscriptions of this king are found at Sīvalappēri, Gangaikondān, Sērmādēvi and Tinnevelly.

CHAP. II. EARLY HISTORY.

and elaborate. An inscription of his fourteenth year records that he put the "five Pāndyas" to flight and subdued the Gulf of Manaar, "the Podiyil mountain" (i.e., Agastyamalai), Cape Comorin and Kōttāru, the last of which places he took by storm. He limited the boundary of the Pāndya country and posted garrisons at Kōttāru and other strategically important places in the recently conquered country. He also conquered the hilly country of Malabar (whose warriors perished to a man in defending their independence) and twice destroyed the ships of the Chēra king.[1]

Revival of the Pāndya power, twelfth century.

The position of affairs in the Pāndya kingdom at the beginning of the A.D. twelfth century is obscure. It appears that the line of Chōla-Pāndya viceroys[2] instituted by Rājēndra Chōla I had ceased. The Pāndya dynasty, at any rate, revived; for inscriptions have revealed to us the names of four Pāndya kings who reigned before A.D. 1190. Of three of them, however, we know nothing beyond their names:

(1) Māravarman Srīvallabha.
(2) Jatāvarma Srīvallabha.[3]
(3) Vīra-Pāndya (the hero of the war of succession described below).
(4) Parākrama.

War of the Pāndya succession about A.D. 1175.

About A.D. 1171 we find a civil war of succession for the throne going on between two Pāndya princes, the kings of the Chōlas and of Ceylon being ranged on opposite sides in the struggle. The two rival claimants were Parākrama-Pāndya and his son Vīra-Pāndya on the one side and Kulasēkhara-Pāndya and his son Vikrama-Pāndya on the other. The Singhalese took the side of Parākrama-Pāndya, whilst Kulasēkhara-Pāndya was assisted by the Chōlas. The war is described in great detail in the annals of Ceylon, and is referred to in the inscriptions of the Chōla kings Rājādhirāja II about (1171—1178) and Kulōttunga III (1178—1215). Briefly stated, the facts appear to have been as follows[4]:— Receiving an appeal for help from Parākrama-Pāndya, the great Singhalese king Parākrama Bahu (A.D. 1164—1190)[5]

[1] For Kulōttunga's conquests in the south, see *Govt. Epig. Ann. Report* for 1900-01, p. 9.

[2] A certain Vikrama Chōla-Pāndya, apparently a prince of the same family, was probably (to judge from his name) a contemporary of the Chōla king Vikrama-Chōla (A.D. 1118-1135).

[3] Many stone inscriptions of this king are found in the Madura and Tinnevelly districts.

[4] The materials available for a history of these events are given fully in the *Govt. Epig. Ann. Report* for 1898-99, paras. 23 foll.

[5] This date is that given by the Singhalese annals, whose chronology is not beyond question.

sent his general, Lankāpura-Dandanātha, to suppress Kulasēkhara and establish Parākrama-Pāndya on his kingdom. Before the Singhalese army had embarked, however, news arrived that Kulasēkhara had captured Madura and put his rival, with his wife and children, to death. Vīra-Pāndya, the youngest son of the murdered monarch, escaped to the Malabar country. Lankāpura, however, was ordered to proceed and, after subduing Kulasēkhara, to bestow the kingdom on some relative of the dead Parākrama-Pāndya. The Singhalese troops for some time carried all before them. After several battles they captured the island of Rāmēswaram and took away "the sacred door" and all the treasures of that holy place. Here they were for some time besieged by Kulasēkhara, who had collected a large force from Tinnevelly and the Kongu country (Salem and Coimbatore), "which belonged to his maternal uncles," and numerous conflicts took place between the two armies. The result was complete victory for the Singhalese; their troops marched inland, everywhere successful. Vīra-Pāndya was now invited to return and on arrival was received with honour by the Ceylon troops. Meanwhile, the Singhalese had gained some further desultory success in the Pāndya country. Kulasēkhara again managed to raise an army and once more set out against the invaders. The latter, reinforced at this juncture by more troops from Ceylon, succeeded in inflicting more than one crushing defeat upon Kulasēkhara, who fled in utter discomfiture to the forests of "Tondamana," i.e., the Pudukkōttai country. Madura was now occupied by the Singhalese.

It was at this stage that the Chōlas seem first to have given Kulasēkhara effective support. With their help a stand was made at Pon-Amarāvati (the site of which has not been identified), but the Singhalese were again victorious, and a space of three leagues was covered with the corpses of the vanquished. Lankāpura returned to Madura and placed Vīra-Pāndya on the throne. Supported by certain Chōla chiefs, Kulasēkhara again took the field and was again defeated, this time at Palamcotta, and fled for refuge to the Chōla country. Though the Chōla king assisted him with a large army, he was once more defeated, and the Ceylon troops advanced to the north and even burnt some villages in the Tanjore district. After one more victory over the Pāndya and Chōla troops the Singhalese returned to Ceylon, leaving Vīra-Pāndya in possession of his kingdom.

Here the Singhalese annals fail us; but an inscription of Kulōttunga III shews that that ruler subsequently took up the cause of Vīkrama-Pāndya, son of Kulasēkhara-Pāndya, against Vīra-Pāndya and the Singhalese, defeated the combined forces of the enemy, "cut off the noses" of the soldiers of Ceylon and drove them into the sea, captured Madura and made over the Pāndya crown to his protégé, Vikrama, and assumed the title of "conqueror of Madura and Ceylon." With these events the twelfth century closes.

Thirteenth century.

Chōla decline and Pāndya ascendancy.

It was during the reign of Rājarāja III (1216 to at least 1239) that the first fatal blows to the Chōla power were dealt. His feudatories revolted on all sides, and one of them, Kōpperunjinga, a prince of some power in the Tondaimandalam country, actually took Rājarāja captive (1230-1231). He was only released by the intervention of the Hoysala Ballālas, a newly-risen power which had recently subverted the western Chālukyas of Kalyāni and, with their capital at Halēbīd in Mysore, now began to interfere in the affairs of the south.

The Pāndyas were not slow to take advantage of the Chōla collapse, and the close of the twelfth century marks the beginning of the period of their greatest power. Epigraphical research has provided us with a long list of rulers from this time forward; some are kings of great power and well known to us, the great majority remain for the present no more than names. The initial year of each reign has been definitely ascertained, but the last year, when given, is merely the latest date, as yet discovered, which contains details admitting of verification:—

(1)	Jatāvarman Kulasēkhara	1190—1214
(2)	Māravarman Sundara-Pāndya I ...	1216—1235
(3)	Do. do. II ...	1238—1251
(4)	Jatāvarman Sundara-Pāndya I ...	1251—1261
(5)	Vīra-Pāndya	1252—1267
(6)	Māravarman Kulasēkhara I ...	1268—1308
(7)	Jatāvarman Sundara-Pāndya II ...	1275—1290
(8)	Māravarman Kulasēkhara II ...	1314—1321
(9)	Māravarman Parākrama-Pāndya ...	1334—1352
(10)	Jatāvarman Parākrama-Pāndya ...	1357—1372
(11)	Parākrama-Pāndyadēva	1365
(12)	Parākrama-Pāndya	1384
(13)	Jatilavarman Kulasēkhara ...	1395
(14)	Jatilavarman Parākrama-Pāndya Arikēsaridēva and	1422—1461
(15)	Māravarman Vīra-Pāndya ...	1422
(16)	Alagan Perumāl Kulasēkhara [1] ...	1430

[1] Younger brother of No. 14.

(17)	Vīra-Pāndya	1437
(18)	Vīra-Pāndya [1]	1475
(19)	Jatilavarman Parākrama-Pāndya Kulasēkhara	1479—1499
(20)	Parākrama-Pāndya	1516
(21)	Jatilavarman Srīvallabha or Abhi-rāma-Parākrama and	1534—1537
(22)	Māravarman Sundara-Pāndya III.	1531—1555
(23)	Kulasēkhara or Perumāl Parākrama and [2]	1543
(24)	Vikrama-Pāndya	
(25)	Konērimaikondān Kulasēkhara Dharmaperumāl [3]	1550
(26)	Jatilavarman Srīvallabha Ativīra-rāman [4]	1562—1567
(27)	Kulasēkhara Parākrama Alagan-Sokka	1572
(28)	Abhirāma Varatungarāma and	1586
(29)	Vīra-Pāndya	
(30)	Sivala Mārar	1615

Māravarman Sundara-Pāndya I (1216–1235).

The second on the list, Māravarman Sundara-Pāndya I, invaded the Chōla country and captured Tanjore and Uraiyūr, a suburb of Trichinopoly and a former capital of the Chōlas. According to his own version, he finally gave back his kingdom as a gift to the Chōla king; and the reality of his success is proved by his inscriptions in the Tanjore and Trichinopoly districts and by the fact that his coins bear the legend, "The conqueror of the Chōla country."

Relations of the Pāndyas with the Hoysalas.

But the decline of the Chōlas brought the Pāndyas into touch with the Hoysalas, who about this time established themselves near Srīrangam, in a town newly built by their king "in order to amuse his mind in the Chōla country, which he had conquered by the power of his arm." As early as 1222 the Hoysala king had "marched against Ranga" (i.e., Srīrangam) in the south, had "cleft open the rock that was the Pāndya", and assumed the title of the "establisher of the Chōla kingdom."

Māravarman Sundara-Pāndya II (1238–1251).

As to the political relationship between the Pāndyas and the Hoysalas, our information is slight; but of Māravarman Sundara-Pāndya II (A.D. 1238—1251) we know that he was a contemporary of the Hōysala Sōmēsvara and perhaps also, as his inscriptions suggest, his nephew. He actually founded

[1] Perhaps a joint ruler with No. 19.
[2] Sons of No. 21.
[3] Son of No. 21.
[4] Son of No. 25.

CHAP. II.
EARLY HISTORY.

a Brahman village in the name of Sōmēsvara and called it Sōmidēva-chaturvēdimangalam [1] (the modern Murappanādu, in the Srīvaikuntam taluk). The mention in some Mysore records of Sōmēsvara's army as being present on the banks of the Tāmbraparni and the grant recorded in a Tinnevelly inscription [2] as having been made by one of the officers of Vīra-Sōmēsvara show that the latter was actively helping his nephew Sundara-Pāndya in what may have been a local disturbance in Tinnevelly. During this period, therefore, we may at least infer that the Hoysala king was on distinctly friendly terms with, if not subordinate to, the Pāndya ruler.

Jatāvarman Sundara-Pāndya I (1251–1261).

Jatāvarman Sundara-Pāndya I (1251 to at least 1261), who succeeded, adopted a policy of bold aggression. He invaded the island of Ceylon, defeated and killed the Hoysala king Sōmēsvara, the friend of his predecessor, came into conflict with the rapidly growing power of the Kākatīya kings of Warangal, in Haidarabad, defeated the king of Karnāta, and extended his conquests as far as Nellore, where he was "anointed as a hero."

Vīra-Pāndya, his contemporary, was a still mightier conqueror. His victories extended as far as the Ganges and China; he encountered the kings of the Chōla, Chēra and Karnāta countries and defeated them; he killed "one of the two kings of Ceylon," captured his throne and all his royal treasures, and planted the Pāndya flag "with the double fish" on the Kandy hills.[3]

Disappearance of the Chōlas and Hoysalas.

The Chōlas, whose relations at this time with the Pāndyas are obscure, seem under Rājēndra Chōla III (A.D. 1246 to about 1267) to have succeeded, about 1252, in inflicting on the Hoysalas a defeat which enabled their king to assume the title of "the hostile rod of death" to Sōmēsvara. They reappear at Srīrangam as early as 1256, and from this until the end of the thirteenth century Chōla and Hoysala inscriptions alternate and overlap in a most puzzling manner. The inference is the Hoysalas were not permanently weakened by the blows dealt them by the Chōlas and the Pāndyas, but continued till the following century as the effective rivals of the latter in the Trichinopoly district.

The Chōlas still remained a power to be reckoned with. Though the Pāndyas had reached Nellore before 1261, there

[1] *Govt. Epig. Ann. Report* for 1906–07, Nos. 431–435 of 1906.

[2] In the Nellaiyappar temple. (*Govt. Epig. Ann. Report*; No 138 of 1894.)

[3] *Govt. Epig. Ann. Report* for 1911–12, para. 39.

are inscriptions to show that the Chōla Rājēndra-Chōla III retained his independence till as late as 1267.[1] Thereafter, however, the Chōlas seem to have dropped completely out of the race; and that part of their country which was not held by the Hoysalas was occupied by the Pāndyas.

Māravarman Kulasēkhara I (1268–1308). Jatāvarman Sundara-Pāndya II (1275–1290).

The succession of the Pāndya kings after Jatāvarman Sundara-Pāndya I, whose last known date is 1261, is not very clear. Māravarman Kulasēkhara I (1268 to at least 1308) and Jatāvarman Sundara-Pandya II (1275 to at least 1290) are kings of considerable power and are both well known to us, the former as the "Kalēs Dēvar" of Muhammadan historians, and the latter as the "Sender Bandi" of Marco Polo.[2] As the overlapping of the dates of these and other rulers in the list indicates, it was apparently the custom with the Pāndyas of this period to divide the sovereignty of the country amongst several members of the ruling house. Marco Polo, who visited the coast of Tinnevelly in 1292, tells us that the kingdom was divided between five brothers[3]—"own brothers," he calls them. That their relations were not always harmonious is perhaps to be inferred from the fact that the Muhammadan Rashid-ud-din speaks of the "opponents and adversaries" into whose hands the power and wealth of Sundara-Pāndya fell on his death in 1290. But that they occasionally acted in harmony is to be inferred from the description in the Singhalese annals of an invasion of Ceylon by "five brothers who governed the Pāndya kingdom" about 1288.[4] Even here, however, Kulasēkhara is described as the Pāndya king, and it is to him that the booty is given.

Splendour of the Pāndya dominions.

All our authorities agree in extolling the wealth and magnificence of "Ma'bar"[5] as they call the Pāndya kingdom of this period. It extended along the coast from Quilon to Nellore. Marco Polo says it was called "the greater India" and adds that "it is the best of all the Indies" and "the finest and noblest province in the world." The Chinese annals contain a description of an embassy which the Pāndyas sent to the Moghul emperor, Kublai Khān, in 1286. Muhammadan

[1] *Govt. Epig. Ann. Report* for 1912, p. 69, para. 32.

[2] See Caldwell's *History of Tinnevelly*, pp. 32 foll., and his *Grammar of the Dravidian Languages* (London 1875), pp. 535 foll.

[3] See page 433.

[4] The Mahāwamsa (Chapter XC) places this invasion in the reign of Bhuvanekha-Bahu I, who, according to Mr. Wijesinha, reigned from A.D. 1277 to 1288. Caldwell says the invasion took place at the end of this reign. (*Grammar of Dravidian Languages*, p. 537.)

[5] Apparently not the same word as "Malabar," though the two have been confused. See *Ind. Ant.*, xxxi, 347–350.

CHAP. II. EARLY HISTORY

ministers were employed by the Pāndya kings and attained great influence and wealth. The chief city of the Pāndya country is still Madura, but a town of great commercial importance, described with admiration by Marco Polo, is Cail—Palayakāyal or "Old Kāyal"—now an obscure village near the mouth of the Tāmbraparni, about a mile and a half inland. Cail was a thriving city and the centre of a large sea-borne trade. The Pāndya king, says Marco Polo, encouraged merchants of the country and foreigners, and all the ships from the west touched at the place. And the contemporary Persian historian, Wassaf, in a rhetorical passage says that all the products of India and China were constantly arriving there and that all the splendour of the west came from Ma'bar "which is so situated as to be the key of Hind."

MUHAMMADAN INVASION. Fourteenth century.

Jatāvarman Sundara-Pāndya II died in 1290, and Kulasēkhara was murdered by his son, Sundara-Pāndya, about the year 1308, because he had appointed Vīra-Pāndya, a half-brother of Sundara-Pāndya, as his successor. A conflict ensued between the brothers; Sundara-Pāndya was defeated, and thereupon fled to Delhi to implore the assistance of the emperor Alla-ud-din. Indeed some Muhammadan historians ascribe to his importunity at the Delhi Court the invasion of South India by Malik-Kāfur, the general of Alla-ud-din, which took place in 1310 and caused the most momentous changes in the political configuration of central and southern India. After capturing Halēbīd, the capital of the Hoysala Ballālas, Malik-Kāfur swept down into the Carnatic, and made his way, it is said, as far as Rāmēswaram, where he founded a mosque.[1] He returned almost at once; but both the Pāndyas and the Hoysalas seem to have endured a humiliation from which neither kingdom ever recovered itself completely. The Pāndya kings, it is true, continued to rule in a spasmodic fashion over dominions of varying size and with varying power for the next two-and-a-half centuries; but their feebleness may be judged from the fact that a king of the Chēras, a nation long sunk out of all importance in Indian politics, marched right across the peninsula, defeated Vīra-Pāndya and made his way in 1313 to Conjeeveram.[2]

The Chēra occupation was short-lived; but from the north repeated blows were dealt during the next half century to the Hindu kingdoms of central and southern India. The emperor Mubārak Khilji of Delhi is credited with a conquest of

[1] Elphinstone's *History of India* (London, 1857), p. 340.

[2] *Ep. Ind.* iv, 146.

CHAP. II.

MUHAMMADAN INVASION.

"Malabar"[1] in 1318, the Yādavas of Dēvagiri in the north were time after time reduced, and finally, in 1323, Pratāpa Rudra of Warangal was carried captive to Delhi. By 1327[2] some Muhammadan chieftains had advanced through Tondaimandalam and occupied Trichinopoly and Madura and founded a dynasty that for forty years ruled these districts, at first as feudatories of the Delhi emperor and later as independent kings.[3]

The later Pāndyas.

The list of the Pāndya kings already given shows that chiefs of this line were also ruling throughout this period and indeed continued to rule as late as the seventeenth century. They are contemporaries first of the Muhammadan kings referred to, then of various Vijayanagar princes and adventurers, and finally of the more or less independent Nāyakkans of Madura. It appears from the frequency of their inscriptions in this district that they confined themselves to the Tinnevelly country, and that the successive paramount governments did not interfere in the internal management of the diminished Pāndya province, but were content to receive tribute and, occasionally, military aid.[4]

VIJAYANAGAR DOMINION (1365–1532).

The Muhammadan kings of Madura ultimately fell before the new Hindu empire of Vijayanagar which was founded about 1335 at Hampi (in the Bellary district) upon the ruins of the Hoysala kingdom and succeeded for over two centuries in stemming the tide of Muhammadan invasion from the north. It was apparently about 1365[5] that Kampana Udaiyār, a prince of the Vijayanagar royal line, with his servant Gopana, overthrew the Muhammadans and brought Madura nominally under the rule of the Vijayanagar house. This dynasty, which does not seem to have lasted beyond the end of the century,[6] was followed by a succession of chieftains, apparently of

[1] Elphinstone's *History of India* (London, 1857), p. 345. This is a confusion for Ma'bar.

[2] For this date we are indebted to a Tamil work (the *Koyil-olugu*) which registers the donations, etc., made to the Renganātha temple at Srīrangam. Mr. Nelson in his *Madura District Manual* gives a dynasty of eight Muhammadan kings who ruled from 1310 to 1358, beginning with Malik-Kāfur (1310—1313).

[3] Ibn Batuta, a servant of the king of Delhi, who landed somewhere in the Rāmnād Country in 1348–1349, found the whole of 'Malabar,' including the Chōla and Pāndya countries, in the hands of a Muhammadan family who had shortly before acquired it in consequence of the revolt of one Jalal-ud-din Hasan, formerly a subject of Muhammad Tughlik of Delhi. (1325–1353). See Caldwell's *History of Tinnevelly*, p. 42 and Elphinstone's *History of India*, p. 341.

[4] Caldwell's *History of Tinnevelly*, p. 54.

[5] Kampana Udaiyār's victory is referred to in an inscription of that year. *Ep. Ind.*, vi. 324.

[6] Sewell's *Lists of Antiquities*, ii, 160 and 223.

CHAP. II. VIJAYANAGAR DOMINION (1365-1532).

Telugu extraction, who shared the sovereignty of the Madura and Tinnevelly country with the so-called Pāndya kings. Lists of these Telugu chieftains (of whom nothing is known beyond their names) compiled from ancient Tamil manuscripts and from inscriptions will be found in the old *Madura District Manual* and also in Sewell's *List of Antiquities.*[1]

Aggression of Travancore. Fifteenth and sixteenth centuries.

The middle years of the fifteenth century mark the beginning of a period during which the Chēra king of Travancore succeeded by a series of invasions in wresting, temporarily at least, from the paramount power considerable portions of the Tinnevelly district. Inscriptions of Travancore kings ranging from 1439 to 1532 are found in Tirukkurungudi, Sērmādēvi, Kalakkād, Mannārkōil, and Tirukkalūr. One of their local palaces seems to have been at Sērmādēvi,[2] and another at Kāyal, where, a Portuguese Captain states (in 1516), "the king of Quilon" used generally to reside.[3]

Invasion of Achyuta (about 1532) and suppression of Travancore.

About 1532, however, a change came over the scene. Not content with overrunning a great part of the Pāndya country, the Travancore ruler was rash enough to defy the suzerainty of Vijayanagar; and it was apparently in order to effect the reduction of Travancore as well as to defend the Pāndya king from the encroachments of two Nāyakkan invaders that Achyuta, the king of Vijayanagar, organised a great expedition into the extreme south of India about this time. He was, if we are to trust his own inscriptions,[4] conspicuously successful. He planted a pillar of victory in the Tāmbraparni, exacted tribute from the king of Travancore, suppressed two troublesome Telugu chieftains, and married the daughter of the Pāndya king. The Pāndya country was now held firmly in the grasp of Vijayanagar.

From this time onwards, until at least the early years of the eighteenth century, there is nothing to show that the Chēra ruler again obtained possession of any part of the Tinnevelly country. In fact (to anticipate the narrative which follows) we find from the Jesuit letters of the 17th century that the "Badages," (i.e., Vadugans, or northerners) the emissaries of the Madura rulers, were constantly extending their

[1] ii, 223.

[2] Caldwell's *History of Tinnevelly*, pp. 251 foll. The full name of the village is Chēran-mahā-dēvi (see also page 365 below).

[3] *Ibid*, p. 67.

[4] *Govt. Epig. Ann. Report* for 1899–1900, paras. 70 foll. There is at present no support for the theory advanced by Dr. Caldwell (*History of Tinnevelly*, p. 55) that Krishnarāja (of Vijayanagar) had already interfered in the affairs of Pāndya.

VIJAYANAGAR DOMINION (1365–1532).

"incursions," apparently in quest of tribute, into the very heart of the Travancore country. "The king of Travancore", wrote Father Jean De Britto, in 1683, "is one of the petty princes of India and is tributary to the kingdom of Madura."

Period of transition.[1] (1532–1559).

The period 1532 to 1557 is occupied in a confusing manner by Telugu princes and Pāndya kings, each of whom is treated in turn by the chronicles as though he were the supreme ruler. From among this mixed company there emerges the distinct and important figure of Vitthala Rāja, a prince of the Vijayanagar house, who invaded Travancore in 1543 and was recognized by that power as overlord in 1547–1548.[2] The death of Vitthala was followed by anarchy in the Madura kingdom; a quarrel between a Pāndya king named Chandrasēkhara and a so-called Chōla chieftain again drew down the intervention of the Vijayanagar king and thereby laid the foundation of the famous Nāyakkan dynasty, which was to hold the country for nearly two centuries.

The Portuguese and the Dutch.

It was during this period of confusion, in 1532, that the Portuguese first set foot on the Tinnevelly coast. Their doings (so far as our records go) centred entirely on the pearl-fishery of the gulf of Manaar and can scarcely be regarded as forming a chapter in the political history of the district. Some account of their occupation, which terminated with the capture of Tuticorin by the Dutch in 1658, will be found in Chapter VI (pp. 231 foll.).

The Dutch first entered the main current of Tinnevelly history at the time of the poligar rebellions; some further details regarding them will be found in their place and in the article dealing with Tuticorin (Chapter XV).

THE NAYAKKAN RULE (1559–1736).

Its foundation.

In response to an appeal from Chandrasēkhara an expedition was sent to restore the Pāndya king under a certain Nāgama Nāyakkan. He suppressed the disorder and then attempted to make himself king of Madura. Hearing that Nāgama Nāyakkan had failed to reinstate the Pāndya, the Vijayanagar ruler sent Visvanātha, Nāgama's own son, in command of an army, with orders to reduce his father to submission. This he succeeded in doing and was equally successful

[1] For the next two centuries neither inscriptions nor reliable histories give much assistance and we are driven to rely on ancient vernacular historical manuscripts of very doubtful value. Mr. Nelson has embodied the result in the old *Madura District Manual*, and it is from that book that the present account of the Nāyakkan period is mainly derived. Fortunately, light is often thrown on current events by the letters of the priests of the Madura Mission.

[2] A Kērala chief named Būtala-Vīra Rāmavarma made a grant to the temple a Suchīndram for the merit of Vitthala on his birthday.

CHAP. II. The Nayakkan Rule (1559–1736)

in procuring the pardon of his father, which was no doubt the object with which he so readily undertook the expedition. Visvanātha obeyed the orders of the Vijayanagar king so far as to place the Pāndya on the throne; but, as policy and self-interest were alike opposed to the course of handing over the actual government to the old and feeble dynasty, he took the supreme control into his own hands. The peculiar feature of the new régime was that, whether by the design of its founders or not, it became first a hereditary governorship and subsequently developed into what was, in effect, a hereditary monarchy. The Nāyakkans never assumed, it is true, the titles of royalty, but were content, even after they had ceased to pay tribute, to call themselves the *karthākkals* or "lieutenants" of Vijayanagar.[1] The Pāndyas as an effective political force now disappear from history, and Visvanātha, the chronicles say, was crowned by the emperor of Vijayanagar.

It will be convenient here to give in tabular form the names and dates of the Nāyakkan rulers.

Visvanātha	1559
Kumāra Krishnappa	1563
Krishnappa *alias* Periya Vīrappa ... / Visvanātha II	1573
Lingayya *alias* Kumāra Krishnappa Visvappa *alias* Visvanātha III.	1595
Muttu Krishnappa	1602
Muttu Vīrappa	1609
Tirumalai	1623
Muttu Alakādri *alias* Muttu Vīrappa	1659
Chokkanātha *alias* Chokkalinga	1662
Ranga Krishna Muttu Vīrappa	1682
Mangammāl (Queen-Regent)	1689
Vijaya Ranga Chokkanātha	1704
Mīnākshi (Queen-Regent)	1731–1736

Extent of their dominions.

The dominions to which Visvanātha succeeded, or rather, over which he and his successors gradually extended their power, included, apparently, the districts of Trichinopoly, Madura and Tinnevelly and the greater part of Coimbatore; Travancore also occasionally paid tribute. Tinnevelly and perhaps Coimbatore were governed by Deputies (*kārya-karthās*) subordinate to the Nāyakkan ruler. To the north-east of Visvanātha's dominions were those of the Nāyakkans of Tanjore and Gingee; beyond them, the dominions given

[1] Caldwell's *History of Tinnevelly*, p. 61.

towards the end of the century, to Jagadēva Rāya and, to the far north-west, the kingdom—as yet a small one—of Mysore. Like Madura, all were subordinate to Vijayanagar.

CHAP. II. THE NAYAKKAN RULE (1559–1736).

Visvanātha (1559–1563).

Early in his reign Visvanātha is credited with the acquisition of Trichinopoly, at that time (so the manuscripts tell us) in the possession of the Nāyakkan of Tanjore. Its rulers were too weak to police the town adequately, and the pilgrims from Madura to Srīrangam were constantly plundered by bandits. Visvanātha accordingly proposed, and the Tanjore chieftain accepted, an exchange of Trichinopoly for Vallam (in Tanjore), which was then in the possession of Madura. The new ruler improved the fortifications and town of Trichinopoly and the temple of Srīrangam and cleared the banks of the Cauvery of robbers. According to some copper-plate grants [1] he conquered in battle the Tiruvādi (i.e., the ruler of Travancore) and other kings and annexed their dominions. The fabulous stories of "the five Pāndyas", with whom Visvanātha had so successful an encounter, may be accepted as further evidence of the consolidation of Nāyakkan dominion in the south. Of his heroic general, Aryanātha Mudaliyār, many stories are told; the greatness of his achievements is established by the fact that an equestrian statue was erected to his honour in the *Pudu-mantapam* at Madura. The poligars used to pray to him as their patron saint, and he is credited with a "thousand-pillared *mantapam*" in the great Madura temple. The Palamcotta fort and many irrigation works [2] of the district are ascribed to him; and he is said to have rebuilt the town of Tinnevelly. Tradition represents him as the real master of all the Vijayanagar viceroys in the south, and adds that after the battle of Talikōta (1565) he confirmed the rulers of Madura, Tanjore and Mysore in their respective dominions.

An administrative measure which is attributed to Visvanātha was the establishment of poligars in the Pāndya country. The system was based on a principle which no previous rulers had adopted in the south; and it seems more reasonable to attribute its origin to the self-assertion of local leaders than to the deliberate action of a paramount authority.

Kumāra Krishnappa (1563–1573).

Visvanātha was succeeded after a short rule by his son, Kumāra Krishnappa [3] (1563–73), who is represented as an able

[1] See *Govt. Epig. Ann. Report* for 1906, p. 85; and same for 1912, p. 82.

[2] Perhaps the Ariyanāyakapuram anicut owes its origin to him.

[3] Called also Periya Krishnappa Nāyakkan. He built and endowed the temple at Krishnāpuram (Tinnevelly taluk) *Govt. Epig. Ann. Report* for 1912. See also p. 474 below.

CHAP. II. THE NAYAKKAN RULE (1559–1736).

and victorious monarch. He is said to have conquered Ceylon, but, in view of the silence of the candid annals of Ceylon on the point, the truth of the story may well be doubted.

Krishnappa Visvanātha II (1573–1595). Lingayya (1595–1602).

The next two reigns (1573–1602), first Krishnappa Nāyakkan and Visvanātha II jointly, and then Lingayya, son of Krishnappa, were uneventful.

Muttu Krishnappa (1602–1609).

Muttu Krishnappa (1602–1609), who followed, is said to have founded the dynasty of the Sētupatis of Rāmnād and to have given that house a considerable slice of land in the Marava country, on the condition that they should suppress crime and protect pilgrims in that wild and inhospitable region.

Muttu Vīrappa (1609–1623).

Muttu Vīrappa (1609–1623), who succeeded, is a scarcely more distinct figure. It was this ruler, apparently, who first made Trichinopoly definitely his capital.

Decline of Vijayanagar.

Meanwhile, at the battle of Talikōta, in 1565, the power of Vijayanagar had been dealt an irreparable blow by the combined Muhammadan kings of the Deccan. The rulers of this house were compelled to abandon a large part of the districts of Bellary and Anantapur to their victorious opponents, to retreat from Vijayanagar, and to establish their capital successively at Penukonda (in the Anantapur district) and at Chandragiri and Vellore (in North Arcot). The rulers of Trichinopoly and Tanjore still paid the usual tribute to their overlord; but, during the reigns which now follow, we find traces of the weakening of the suzerain and of contempt and, finally, rebellion on the part of his feudatories.

Tirumalai (1623–1659).

Muttu Vīrappa was succeeded by Tirumalai Sēvari Nāyakkan, the most powerful ruler and the best known to us of this dynasty. The peace imposed upon the south by the kings of Vijayanagar was dissolving owing to the weakness of that power, and the old Pāndya country was now torn by the quarrels of the once feudatory rulers of Madura, Tanjore and Mysore, by the unavailing attempts of the last rulers of the dying empire to re-assert their failing power, and, finally, by the incursions of the Muhammadans of the Deccan, who now begin to press southwards to reap the real fruits of their victory of Talikōta. An added trouble lay in the insubordination of the Sētupatis of Rāmnād, who took advantage of the embarrassments of the kings of Madura to disobey their commands and finally to make themselves independent.[1]

[1] A few copper-plate inscriptions of the Sētupatis of Rāmnād and of some later Nāyakkan rulers of Madura are noted on pp. 88–90 of the *Epig. Report* for 1911.

CHAP. II. THE NAYAKKAN RULE (1559–1736).

Throws off allegiance to Vijayanagar.

One of Tirumalai's first acts was to withhold the tribute due to the king of Vijayanagar. He still sent a complimentary message every year, and this sufficed for some time to appease the resentment of the incapable representative of that ancient line. But a change came, about 1638, when king Ranga succeeded to the throne of Chandragiri and declared war against Tirumalai and prepared to march south with a large and formidable force. The Madura ruler had long expected such an attack; and, besides strengthening the fortifications of Trichinopoly and strongly garrisoning the town, he had persuaded the Nāyakkans of Tanjore and Gingee to join in his rebellion. The Tanjore king recanted on Ranga's threatened invasion and sent in his submission as well as news of the plans of the confederates. Ranga thereupon advanced upon Gingee.

And calls in the Muhammadans whose feudatory he becomes.

He was frustrated by a desperate move of Tirumalai, who, regardless of the claims of a larger patriotism, implored the Muhammadan king of Golconda to invade the Vijayanagar kingdom from the north. The Muhammadan complied and Ranga had to retrace his steps. Defeated by the king of Golconda, he came south again, this time to invoke the help of the Nāyakkans against the Mussalmans; but the parties could come to no agreement, and Ranga fled without friends or power to take refuge with the king of Mysore. For some time the king of Golconda was content to consolidate his conquests in the north; but shortly afterwards (about 1644) he marched upon Gingee, and the Nāyakkan of Tanjore at once submitted. Tirumalai now had recourse to the rival Muhammadan of Bijāpur, who sent a force to his assistance. The allies marched to the relief of Gingee; but hardly had they arrived there when the Bijāpur troops went over to the enemy and joined in the siege. The Golconda king was soon recalled by trouble in other parts of his newly conquered territories, and Tirumalai threw himself into Gingee; but owing to dissensions among the garrison the gates were opened to the troops of Bijāpur. Thus the first of the old Nāyakkan dynasties fell before the Muhammadans; and Gingee remained in the possession of Bijāpur for nearly forty years.

Tirumalai retreated in dismay to Madura; the Muhammadans advanced to the south and, having exacted submission from Tanjore, proceeded to lay waste the Pāndya country. Tirumalai submitted, apparently without striking a blow; he paid a large sum to the invaders and agreed to furnish an annual tribute to the Sultan of Bijāpur. Thus,

CHAP. II. THE NAYAKKAN RULE (1559–1736).

after an interval of nearly 300 years, the Muhammadans were again recognized as supreme in the district.

His wars with Mysore.

Tirumalai's next conflict was with Mysore. In the early years of his reign and before his troubles with the king of Vijayanagar and the Muhammadans he had been involved in a short war with that kingdom. Madura had been invaded by the Mysore troops; the raiders had been driven out, and Mysore was successfully invaded by a general of Tirumalai's. Since then, as has been seen, the Vijayanagar king had taken refuge with the king of Mysore; and now these two monarchs invaded the territories recently conquered by Golconda and inflicted a defeat upon that power. Inspired by jealousy or fear, Tirumalai now invited a Muhammadan invasion of Mysore from the south and threw open the passes in his own country for the purpose. His proposal was accepted; Mysore was invaded, and a general war ensued, which resulted in the final extinction of the power of Vijayanagar and the humiliation of Mysore. The victorious Muhammadans came down to Madura, levied an enormous tribute from their submissive friend Tirumalai, moved on to Tanjore and treated its Nāyakkan in a similar manner.

These events appear to have constituted the last violent interference of the Muhammadans in the affairs of Tirumalai. His only other external wars were directed, towards the close of his reign, against Mysore. In these he is represented as eminently successful. They began with an invasion of Coimbatore by the Mysore king, apparently in revenge for Tirumalai's contribution to his recent humiliation by the Muhammadans. The district was occupied by the enemy with ease, and Madura itself was threatened. The Mysore troops, however, were beaten, chiefly owing to the loyal assistance of the Sētupati of Rāmnād, and after a second defeat, apparently near Dindigul, were driven in disorder up the ghats to Mysore. A counter-invasion of Mysore was now undertaken under the command of Kumāra Muttu, the younger brother of Tirumalai, and was so successful that the king of Mysore was captured and deprived of his nose. He had similarly maltreated his prisoners during his own irruption into the Madura country, and his war with Mysore was known in consequence as "the hunt for noses." In Rāmnād Tirumalai had trouble with the Sētupati and his Marava followers as the result of an unsuccessful attempt to impose his nominee on that principality. In Tinnevelly he came into conflict with the poligars, headed by Ettaiyāpuram, whose suppression was finally effected by the grateful Sētupati.

Tirumalai died before he could receive the news of his brother's victory in Mysore. He was about sixty-five years of age and had reigned for thirty-six eventful years. His character is summed up, probably with justice, in a letter written by a Jesuit Father just after the king's death and dated from Trichinopoly in 1659. "It is impossible to refuse him credit for great qualities, but he tarnished his glory at the end of his life by follies and vices which nothing could justify. He was called to render account to God for the evils which his political treachery had brought upon his people and the neighbouring kingdoms. His reign was rendered illustrious by works of truly royal magnificence. Among these are the pagoda of Madura, several public buildings, and above all the royal palace, whose colossal proportions and astonishing boldness recall the ancient monuments of Thebes. He loved and protected the Christian religion, the excellence of which he recognized; but he never had the courage to accept the consequences of his conviction.[1] The chief obstacle to his conversion came from his 200 wives, of whom the most distinguished were burnt on his pyre."

CHAP. II. THE NAYAKKAN RULE (1559–1736).

His public works.

Of Tirumalai's public works the largest and most magnificent was the great palace at Madura. He erected another palace on a much smaller scale, but in the same style of architecture, at Srīvilliputtūr (in the present Rāmnād district), where he occasionally resided.[2] The *Pudu-mantapam* at Madura, a number of fine *gōpurams* (called Rāya gōpurams) and additions to the temples of Srīrangam and Madura were among his other important works.

His capital.

Unlike his predecessor, Tirumalai made Madura his capital. But he resided a good deal at Trichinopoly; and his successors, though they went to Madura to be crowned, generally lived at Trichinopoly.

Muttu Alakādiri (1659-1662).

Tirumalai's son, Muttu Alakādiri (1659–1662), who succeeded, made an ineffectual attempt to repudiate his allegiance to the Muhammadans, who replied by marching into the Trichinopoly and Madura districts, devastating the country.

Chokkanātha (1662–1682): His troubles with the Muhammadans and the Maravans.

He was succeeded in 1662 by his son Chokkanātha (1662–1682), a boy of sixteen, who repeated his father's policy and was equally unsuccessful. He was threatened by a domestic conspiracy; and, though the plot was detected and quashed, the commander-in-chief, who had taken a leading part in the

[1] It has been supposed by some that his title Sēvari (Xavier ?) was taken from the Christians.

[2] The building now serves as the taluk office.

CHAP. II
THE NAYAKKAN RULE (1559-1736).

plot, now openly went over to the Muhammadans and joined them in an attack upon Trichinopoly. The Tanjore Nāyakkan, if he did not actively assist, at least encouraged the besiegers. Again unfaithfully served, Chokkanātha at length took command of the army himself and drove the invaders back to Tanjore. Soon after, he made a sudden attack upon that place, exacted the submission of the Nāyakkan and drove the Muhammadans back to Gingee. So far successful, Chokkanātha within a year or two (1663 or 1664) had to pay a heavy price for his good fortune. A Muhammadan army burst into the Trichinopoly and Madura districts and ravaged the country with incredible cruelty. Again the siege of Trichinopoly was unsuccessfully undertaken; but Chokkanātha had to buy off the invader with a large sum of money. He consoled himself by attacking and conquering the faithless Nāyakkan of Tanjore and by garrisoning Vallam; and he attempted without success similar reprisals on the Sētupati of Rāmnād, who had failed to assist him against his enemies.

His conquest and loss of Tanjore.

From 1666 to 1673 the Jesuit letters fail us; and it is unfortunate that about the end of that period there should have occurred so important an event as the capture of Tanjore by Chokkanātha and the final extinction of the Nāyakkan dynasty of that city. The details of this crisis, derived from a vernacular manuscript, are given at length in the old Manuals of Madura and Tanjore. Chokkanātha handed over Tanjore to his half-brother, Alagiri, who soon attempted to assert his independence. In 1674 a Marātha general, named Venkāji, appeared before Tanjore at the head of a Bijāpur force, with orders to turn out the Madura usurper and instal the petitioner. Alagiri was defeated, Venkāji occupied Tanjore, and Chokkanātha had exchanged a Nāyakkan neighbour for a Marātha. Meanwhile Gingee had been taken from Bijāpur by Sivāji, the nominal agent of Golconda, and remained in the possession of the Marāthas for the next twenty years.

Invasions of his kingdom by Mysoreans and Marāthas.

Chikka Dēva Rāya of Mysore (1672–1704), who for some time had been massing troops on his frontier, now burst upon Coimbatore. Chokkanātha was deposed; and his brother, who was put in his place, was soon turned out (in 1678) by a Muhammadan adventurer. Two years later the Muhammadan was assassinated, and Chokkanātha was for a time restored to his throne. His capital was being besieged by the Mysoreans, and at his request the Marāthas both of Tanjore and Gingee had come to help him against his assailants. A force of Maravans was also outside the walls of Trichinopoly, having come ostensibly to assist their lord but in reality to share the booty which the sack of the city was expected to yield.

Who seize his territories.

While Chokkanātha sat helpless behind his defences, matters were taken out of his hand by the more virile actors upon this curious scene. The Marāthas of Gingee inflicted a crushing defeat on the Mysore troops, and drove them out of the greater part of the Madura and Trichinopoly districts. They then turned against Chokkanātha, their pretended ally, and laid siege to Trichinopoly itself.

The actual siege was apparently unsuccessful; for in the following year we find the capital in the possession of Chokkanātha's son and successor. The Mysoreans, the Marāthas of Tanjore and the Marāthas of Gingee and the Maravans each divided up the greater part of the Nāyakkan's territories amongst themselves. Tinnevelly, apparently, was from its position immune from invasion and continued to acknowledge the Nāyakkan's authority.

Ranga Krishnamuttu Vīrappa (1682–1689).

Chokkanātha died in 1682 and was succeeded by his son, Ranga Krishnamuttu Vīrappa (1682–1689). Shortly after his succession a new disturbing factor in South Indian politics appeared on the scene in the person of the Moghul emperor Aurangazeb, who, in 1685–86, conquered the kingdoms of Golconda and Bijāpur and was for many years engaged in a war with the Marāthas. The young Nāyakkan succeeded during his short reign in recovering a great part of the territory of his ancestors.

Mangammāl (1689–1704).

He died in 1689 at the early age of 26 and was succeeded by his mother Mangammāl, who for the next fifteen years acted as regent on behalf of her infant grandson.

She was a popular administrator, and is widely known as a maker of roads and avenues, and as a builder of choultries. During her reign Zulfakar Khān was sent by Aurangazeb to attack the Marātha stronghold of Gingee, and, though he did not succeed until five years later in taking the place, he exacted tribute both from Trichinopoly and Tanjore in 1693. In 1704–05 Mangammāl's grandson, Vijaya Ranga Chokkanātha, came of age and succeeded to the throne.

Vijaya Ranga Chokkanātha (1704–1731).

It was during his reign, which lasted 26 years (1704–1731), that the Rāmnād territory was divided into two parts, the newly-formed province of Sivaganga being assigned to a successful rival of the Sētupati. At the same time Pudukkōttai finally severed its connection with Rāmnād and became independent under its Tondaman.

CHAP. II. THE NAYAKKAN RULE (1559–1736).

Mīnākshi (1731–1736).

Vijaya Ranga Chokkanātha died in 1731, and was succeeded by his widow Mīnākshi, who acted as regent on behalf of a young boy whom she adopted as the heir of her deceased husband. Within a year or two an insurrection was raised against her by Vangāru Tirumalai, who, as the father of Mīnākshi's adopted son, pretended to have some claims on his own account to the throne of Trichinopoly. But the appearance on the scene at this juncture of the Moghuls gave an unexpected turn to the history of the south.

Interference of Muhammadans.

Since 1693 the Trichinopoly ruler had been nominally the feudatory of the emperor of Delhi; and the Carnatic to the north of the Coleroon had been since 1698 under direct Muhammadan rule. The local representative of the Moghul was the Nawāb of Arcot, and an intermediate authority was held by the Nizam of Haidarabad, who was in theory the subordinate of the emperor and the superior of the Nawāb. In 1734, when Mīnākshi and Vangāru Tirumalai were fighting for the crown, an expedition was sent by Dost Ali, the Nawāb of Arcot, to exact tribute and submission from the kingdoms of the south. The leaders were the Nawāb's son, Safdar Ali Khān, and his nephew and confidential adviser, the well-known Chanda Sāhib. Tanjore was taken by storm, and, leaving the stronghold of Trichinopoly unattempted, the invaders swept across Madura and Tinnevelly into Travancore, carrying all before them. On their return Vangāru approached Safdar Ali Khān with an offer of three million rupees if he would oust the queen in favour of himself. Unwilling to attack Trichinopoly, the Mussalman prince contented himself with declaring Vangāru Tirumalai to be king and taking a bond for the three millions. He then marched away, leaving Chanda Sāhib to enforce his award as best he could. The queen approached Chanda Sāhib with substantial offers and had little difficulty in persuading that facile politician to accept her bond for a crore of rupees and to declare her duly entitled to the throne. Vangāru Tirumalai was allowed to go off to Madura with permission to rule over that country and Tinnevelly. Chanda Sāhib proceeded to Arcot and, returning two years later (1736), obtained admission to the fort and proceeded to make himself master of the kingdom.

End of the Nāyakkan dynasty.

He then turned against Vangāru Tirumalai, who was still ruling in the south, defeated him at Dindigul and Ammayanāyakkanūr, compelled him to take refuge in Sivaganga, and occupied the southern provinces of the Trichinopoly kingdom. He imprisoned the queen and proclaimed himself ruler.

The queen thereupon took poison; and with her the dynasty of the Nāyakkans of Madura came to an end.

CHAP. II.

MUHAMMADAN DOMINION.

Chanda Sāhib (1736–1740).

Chanda Sāhib's success was regarded with suspicion by the Nawāb of Arcot; but family reasons prevented a rupture, and Chanda Sāhib was left undisturbed while he strengthened the fortifications of Trichinopoly and placed his two brothers as governors in the strongholds of Dindigul and Madura.

Marāthas again intervene (1740–1749).

To defend themselves against Chanda Sāhib, Vangāru Tirumalai and the king of Tanjore determined to invite the help of the Marāthas of Satāra. The latter had their own grievances against the Muhammadans of Arcot, with whom Chanda Sāhib was still identified, and gladly answered the call. Early in 1740 a vast Marātha army appeared in the south and defeated and killed the Nawāb, Dost Ali, in the pass of Dāmalcheruvu in North Arcot. They allowed his son Safdar Ali to succeed as Nawāb, and then retired. At the end of the same year, on the secret invitation of Safdar Ali, the Marāthas suddenly appeared before Trichinopoly. They invested the town closely, defeated and killed the two brothers of Chanda Sāhib as they advanced to his help from Madura and Dindigul and, after a siege of three months, compelled the garrison to surrender. Chanda Sāhib was taken captive to Satāra, and Morāri Rao of Gooty was appointed governor of the conquered kingdom. In 1743 the Nizam marched south and established his authority in the Carnatic. He appointed Anwar-ud-din to be Nawāb, and the whole of the Madura kingdom now fell under the rule of that potentate. Morāri Rao retired from the scene, and Vangāru Tirumalai disappeared (poisoned, some say) shortly afterwards.

Intervention of the English and the French

The next scene opens, in 1748, with the release of Chanda Sāhib (partly by the influence of Dupleix) and the joint invasion of the Carnatic by Chanda Sāhib and the would-be Nizam, Muzaffar Jang. Anwar-ud-din, who derived his authority from the real Nizam, Nazir Jang, was defeated and killed in July 1749 at Ambūr, and Chanda Sāhib was appointed by Muzaffar Jang to be Nawāb of Arcot. Anwar-ud-din's son, Muhammad Ali, fled to Trichinopoly and proclaimed himself Nawāb; and soon most of the south of India was involved in the struggle between these rivals. The French and the English took sides in the conflict, the former supporting Chanda Sāhib and the latter Muhammad Ali, and from this time begins what was in effect a struggle between these two European nations for the mastery of the Carnatic.

CHAP. II. ENGLISH PERIOD [1].

Muhammad Ali sends an expedition to the south, 1751.

To make sure of the adhesion of the people of Tinnevelly, Muhammad Ali despatched to the district a force of a few thousand men, amongst whom was a small detachment of English under Lieutenant Innis. Abdul Rahim, however, who was appointed to the supreme command, encountered more difficulties in dealing with his own troops than in securing the allegiance of the inhabitants of the country. Meanwhile, an adventurer named Alum Khān, who had served first Chanda Sāhib and then the king of Tanjore, peacefully entered Madura, where his reputation as a soldier aided him, and held the city in the name of Chanda Sāhib, thus cutting off Muhammad Ali's communications between Trichinopoly, the stronghold of the north, and Tinnevelly in the south. Captain Cope, in command of a force of Europeans and sepoys, attempted to regain the place, but was repulsed.

Colonel Heron's expedition.

Finally, in 1755, a force consisting of 2,000 sepoys and 500 Europeans was equipped and placed under the command of Colonel Heron. Māhfuz Khān, the Nawāb's elder brother (of whom we hear more later), was put in charge of the native troops. Madura fell without a blow; and the poligar of Rāmnād signified his submission by surrendering to the Company two seaports on the coast opposite Ceylon. Heron then proceeded to capture Kōvilgudi, a temple-fortress, in which the fugitive governor of Madura had taken refuge. Proceeding south, he took Tinnevelly without opposition; and renters, both in the capital and the surrounding country, gave in their submission. Many of the poligars rejected the demands of tribute made in the name of the Nawāb, chief among the recalcitrants being Kattaboma Nāyakkan, of Pānjālankurichi. An attempt was made to reduce his stronghold but had to be abandoned, as the whole force was almost immediately recalled to Trichinopoly. A detachment of the force was sent to attack a fort called (by Orme) Nellikottah, the site of which Dr. Caldwell has identified with a place called Nattakōttai, six miles to the east of the Arāmboli lines. The capture of the place was attended with great savagery, almost the whole population, including women and children, being put to the sword. On his way back Colonel Heron made a diversion towards the fort of Nelkattanseval, the head-quarters of the Pūli Tēvan, the leading poligar of the

[1] The chief authorities for what follows are: Orme's *pistory of Indostan*; Cambridge's *Military History of the Madras Engineers; A View of the English Interests in India*, by William Fullarton, M.P.; Colonel James Welsh's *Military Reminiscences*; Caldwell's *History of Tinnevelly*. *Some Account of the Panjalamcourchy Poligar*, a compilation from official records, by the Rev. J. F. Kearns, has also been referred to.

Sankaranainārkōil country. The attempt proved a failure, and the force withdrew to Madura. The revenues collected by means of the expedition had not been sufficient to cover its expenses, and finally Colonel Heron was induced by a large present to allow Māhfuz Khān to rent the countries of Madura and Tinnevelly for the small sum of 15 lakhs of rupees. On his return to Madras Colonel Heron was tried by court-martial on a charge of bribery and dismissed the service.

The Poligars. The origin of the poligars, who for the next fifty years were to dispute with the English the sovereignty of the Tinnevelly district, has been already referred to (p. 61). Their Tamil name, *pālaiyakkāran,* "holder of an armed camp," sufficiently describes the basis on which the power of these chieftains rested. The services of the poligar were, in theory, at the disposal of the sovereign; and in return for his assistance he was allowed, subject to his rendering a tribute, to hold complete sway over a certain tract of country and to collect for his own use what revenues he could. At the time when the English first set foot in Tinnevelly (probably Lieutenant Innis was the first Englishman to do so) there were in the district (that is, in the district as it existed till 1910) no less than thirty-one such baronies. Of the modern district practically the whole of the Sankaranainārkōil taluk, a great part of the Tenkāsi and Ambāsamudram taluks and more than half the modern Kōilpatti taluk were under the control of these chieftains. The poligars of the Kōilpatti country were almost all of the Tottiyan caste, owing their establishment, doubtless, to the favour or at least the acquiescence of their fellow-Telugus, who constituted the Nāyakkan dynasty of Madura; prominent among them were the chieftains of Pānjālankurichi and Ettaiyāpuram. The western poligars, with the exception of Sivagiri and the unimportant Alagāpuri, who were Vanniyans, belonged to the Marava caste; their leaders were the poligar of Nelkattanseval (always known as the Pūli Tēvan) and the poligar of Chokkampatti. Each chieftain was surrounded by a horde of armed retainers, mostly Maravans. By Orme and other writers of the period they are referred to as "Colleries," a word invented for the Trichinopoly and Tanjore districts, where the corresponding race of freebooters belonged to the caste of Kallans, or "Cullers." Referring to the Marava "Colleries" of Tinnevelly, Orme says [1]:—

"The Colleries of this side [i.e., the west] of the Tinnevelly country possess nothing of the ugliness or deformity which

[1] *History*, Vol. ii, p. 568.

CHAP. II. ENGLISH PERIOD.

generally characterize the inhabitants of the hills and wilds of India. They are tall, well-made, and well-featured. Their arms are lances and pikes, bows and arrows, rockets and matchlocks, but whether with or without other weapons, every man constantly wears a sword and shield. In battle the different arms move in distinct bodies; but the lancemen are rated the most eminent, and lead all attacks. This weapon is eighteen feet long. They tie under the point a tuft of scarlet horse-hair and when they attack horse, add a small bell. Without previous exercise, they assemble in a deep column, pressing close together, and advance at a long steady step, in some degree of time, their lances inclining forward, but aloft, of which the elasticity and vibration, with the jingle and dazzle, scare the cavalry; and their approach is scarcely less formidable to infantry not disciplined with fire-arms."

Revolt of western poligars who are assisted by Travancore.

On Heron's departure the western poligars at once made up their minds to revolt. They were assisted by three Pathan soldiers of fortune who had been stationed in the southern countries as the representatives of Chanda Sāhib. The king of Travancore, whose army had been trained under the famous Flemish officer De Lanoy, sent a force of 2,000 Nāyars, who joined the united rebel forces at Kalakkād.[1] Though Māhfuz Khān was defeated, the Travancore force returned home in haste, apparently smitten with fear of the cavalry of Māhfuz Khān which was known to be approaching. The following year however (1766) they returned, and inflicted another defeat on Māhfuz Khān's troops.

Western poligars joined by those of Madura are defeated by Māhfuz Khān.

The Pūli Tēvan, the leader among the poligars of the west, now began to contemplate a union with his comrades of the east, the chief of whom was Kattaboma Nāyakkan. Both he however and his vassal at Ettaiyāpuram refused. The poligars of Madura, on the other hand, promised assistance, and a formidable league was now threatening. The confederates concentrated their efforts on Srīvilliputtūr, the main stronghold of the northern part of the district. Abdul Rahim, to whom Māhfuz Khān had deputed the charge of the country, was defeated; the fort was taken and reduced. The united forces of the poligars now amounted to 25,000 men, of whom 1,000 were cavalry. Māhfuz Khān had meanwhile won over Kattaboma Nāyakkan and the poligar of Ettaiyāpuram, but relied mainly on his 1,500 cavalry and the sepoys, 1,000 in number, who were under the command of Jamanul Sāhib. A

[1] It appears that since 1734 the Travancore ruler had (at intervals, perhaps) been in nominal possession of various portions of the Tinnevelly district, including Kalakkād. Shangoony Menon's *History of Travancore*, p. 129.

battle took place seven miles to the north of Tinnevelly, which resulted in the defeat of Pūli Tēvan and his confederates.

CHAP. II. ENGLISH PERIOD.

Muhammad Yūsuf despatched to Tinnevelly, 1756.

It was wellknown in Madras that the object of this confederacy was nothing less than to get possession of Madura. The Company had, out of deference to the Nawāb, so far treated Māhfuz Khān with indulgence, but were at the same time convinced of his untrustworthiness. Muhammad Yūsuf was a commander who had already proved his ability in the service of the Company, and it was decided to send him immediately to the south. He arrived in May 1756 and with a mixed force, which included a detachment of European artillery, joined Māhfuz Khān at Kayattār. Owing to the devastation caused by the previous campaigns both commanders found themselves unable to collect sufficient money to maintain their troops. In spite of difficulties, however, the combined forces proceeded to Srīvilliputtūr, re-captured the fort and received the submission of most of the poligars, including Pūli Tēvan himself.

The Nawāb's renter unites with Māhfuz Khān and poligars against Muhammad Yūsuf and is defeated, 1756.

Leaving a strong garrison in Srīvilliputtūr to overawe the poligars of the west, Muhammad Yūsuf started for Tinnevelly, where he found that the Nawāb had handed over to a Hindu, named Alagarappa Mudaliyār, the management of the Tinnevelly district, for a yearly rental of eleven lakhs; in return for this payment the renter was to possess the usual plenary powers, civil and criminal. Māhfuz Khān's agent, Mir Jaffar, was still on the spot, and friction inevitably arose. The Mudaliyār rashly turned to the Pūli Tēvan and his friends for help, and at the same time sought and obtained reconciliation with Māhfuz Khān. Muhammad Yūsuf Khān demanded from the Mudaliyār payment for the Nawāb's sepoys and, being refused, confined him to jail. The allies mustered in force and plundered the town of Tinnevelly; the Mudaliyār regained his liberty and, occupying the fort of Palamcotta (which even at that date was in a ruined condition), managed to defy the musketry attacks of the sepoys. Muhammad Yūsuf (who had meanwhile been recalled to Madura) hurried to the scene and, meeting a large force of the allies at Gangaikondān, inflicted a severe defeat.

Māhfuz Khān proclaims himself the Nawāb's renter, 1757.

Far from being disheartened, the confederates took the bold step of negotiating with the Mysoreans, who were then before Dindigul. The position of the English looked serious; and, as the vital necessity of securing Madura was realized, Muhammad Yūsuf was sent there with troops. No sooner had he left the district than Māhfuz Khān, who had been at Madura in negotiation with the rebels in the town, saw his opportunity, hurried back to Nelkattanseval, and took the field once more

CHAP. II. ENGLISH PERIOD.

with the Pūli Tēvan and his allies. A proclamation was issued announcing Māhfuz Khān as the Nawāb's renter; and negotiations were opened with the Travancore sovereign for the surrender to that ruler of Kalakkād and its neighbourhood. The town of Tinnevelly was taken and Palamcotta besieged; the defenders made a sally and, with the aid of the poligars of Ettaiyāpuram and Pānjālankurichi, obliged the enemy to retire.

Muhammad Yūsuf returns and is again recalled, 1758.

Muhammad Yūsuf returned once more to the district to find a strong conspiracy formed against him by Māhfuz Khān and the western poligars; the Travancore troops were in possession of Kalakkād; many towns in the Ambāsamudram and Srīvaikuntam taluks had become strongholds of the confederates, and Palamcotta itself was threatened. Muhammad Yūsuf was beginning to make some progress, when he was suddenly called away to Madras, then being closely besieged by the French.

The crisis appeared to Pūli Tēvan to be his opportunity. Relying on the expectation of French assistance, he succeeded in effecting a momentary alliance between the two leagues of poligars, the eastern and the western, a task rendered easier by the fact that Kattaboma Nāyakkan, the leader of the eastern section and a supporter of Muhammad Yūsuf, had just died. His successor declared himself from the outset an enemy of the English.

Muhammad Yūsuf returns to find eastern and western poligars united, 1759.

Such was the situation which Muhammad Yūsuf found on his next return in 1759. His first efforts were directed towards the disruption of this confederacy and the restoration of the old antagonism between the east and the west. Kollankondān, a fort near Srīvilliputtūr under the Pūli Tēvan's occupation, was captured; Kōlārpatti, the stronghold of an eastern poligar, was next attacked and after some resistance overpowered and razed to the ground. The Uttumalai poligar, controlling the country to the north-west of Tinnevelly, who had hitherto shown little activity, was reduced to submission and his fort of Surandai occupied. From Kalakkād to Cape Comorin the Travancore troops were plundering the country, and in his anxiety to reduce the poligars Muhammad Yūsuf took the invaders into alliance. Vadagarai, the original stronghold of the poligar of Chokkampatti, not far from Shencotta, was captured, and the poligar fled to his neighbour the Pūli Tēvan for refuge. The Pūli Tēvan, however, was equal to the situation. The news of a battle at Wandiwash had already reached Māhfuz Khān, and the current version obtained from French sources was that the English had been defeated. Travancore wanted the district of Kalakkād, and Māhfuz Khān promised to secure it for him, provided

Travancore would join the confederates. The situation was explained to Muhammad Yūsuf, who, disappointed in his expectation of guns and ammunition consigned for his use to Tuticorin and recognizing the overwhelming superiority of the newly threatened alliance, decided to secure the adherence of the ruler of Travancore by offering him Kalakkād and its neighbourhood. The bargain was accepted, and the Madras Government approved Muhammad Yūsuf's action.

CHAP. II. ENGLISH PERIOD.

Assisted by Travancore, he attacks Vāsudēvanallūr, without success.

Aided by the Travancore troops, Muhammad Yūsuf, who by now had received ammunition from Anjengo, proceeded to attack Vāsudēvanallūr, one of the outlying strongholds of the Pūli Tēvan. The fort, though of mud, was exceptionally strong and, situated as it was only three miles from the foot of the ghats, was closely protected on the west and south by low hills and jungle. The position was considered by the poligars to be of first importance, and an immense army of "colleries" rallied to its defence. Muhammad Yūsuf turned his 18-pounder against the defences; it did some damage but burst after a day's firing. A storm was attempted, when instantly the Pūli Tēvan, issuing from Nelkattanseval in the rear, fell upon Muhammad Yūsuf's camp. The garrison was exultant, but Muhammad Yūsuf continued the attack in the face of fire from the fort and the surrounding forest. The position became more and more hopeless, and before evening Yūsuf decided to retire. The Travancoreans returned to their homes through the passes, and Muhammad Yūsuf departed to Tinnevelly, where news of a new kind from an unexpected quarter reached him.

Appearance of the Dutch inland, 1760.

Since 1658 the Dutch had been in possession of Tuticorin, having taken it from the Portuguese. They had factories on the coast at Vēmbār, Vaippār, Punnaikāyal, Palayakāyal, Manappād and Cape Comorin, and at Alvārtirunagari in the interior. The Dutch in Ceylon had lately received reinforcements from Batavia, some of which were despatched to Tuticorin and the other Dutch stations on the Tinnevelly sea-coast. As will subsequently appear, their appearance was due probably to the invitation of the poligars and also to offers of assistance from the king of Travancore. Muhammad Yūsuf sent troops to Tuticorin to demand an explanation, but none was given. The Dutch troops marched to Alvārtirunagari, whilst Manappād was also occupied. Muhammad Yūsuf collected four thousand sepoys and some cavalry and marched to Alvārtirunagari. The Dutch immediately decamped to Tuticorin and sailed away; Manappād was also abandoned; and this curious alarm subsided as swiftly as it had arisen.

CHAP. II. ENGLISH PERIOD.

Muhammad Yūsuf's position, 1761.

Muhammad Yūsuf now claimed that he had reduced the Tinnevelly district to submission and offered to take the rental of the district for four years at an annual rental of seven lakhs of rupees a year. The Nawāb was reluctant to accept the offer, but the Presidency insisted. Māhfuz Khān, who had apparently effected a reconciliation with his brother, the Nawāb, left the district for good in 1760. In 1761 Pondicherry was taken by the English, and the poligars' long-cherished design of a French alliance was fading. Indeed, so strong was the position of Muhammad Yūsuf that by 1762 the gravest suspicions were felt at Madras regarding his loyalty to the Company. In December it was discovered that he was enlisting troops in Tanjore; his negotiations of 1759 with Travancore had by now awakened mistrust; he had provided the forts of Palamcotta and Madura with stores, and the forces at his command were estimated (irregular levies included) at 27,000 men. Though his immediate charge was the Tinnevelly district, he had made his headquarters at Madura, and was daily receiving reinforcements from the French and Haidar Ali. A strong force was equipped and despatched under the command of Colonel Monson to besiege him in Madura; and after a protracted siege the place was taken on the 14th October, 1764. Muhammad Yūsuf was captured and hanged.

Major Campbell sent to Tinnevelly; negotiations concluded with Travancore, 1764-1766.

Major Charles Campbell, who in January 1764 had succeeded to the command of the army before Madura, set out on the 18th October for Palamcotta, which surrendered immediately on his arrival. Major Call was deputed to make a settlement with the king of Travancore, and an arrangement was effected by which all the districts to the east of the mountains should be surrendered to the Nawāb. Campbell and Call returned to Madura. Further negotiations ensued; and finally, in 1766, the districts of Kalakkād and Panagudi were definitely ceded to the Nawāb, certain reservations in regard to the Shencotta tract being admitted in favour of the Rāja. The precise nature of the Travancore claims over these villages continued in dispute for many years.[1]

The poligars again in revolt, 1767.

Meanwhile the poligars were ransacking the country once more and refusing to pay their dues. Major Flint was at Srīvilliputtūr and attempted unsuccessfully to reduce the Sivagiri outpost of Kollankondān. In February 1767 he marched against Pānjālankurichi and attempted to storm the fort, but was repulsed with heavy loss; a blockade was then decided on, but the defenders escaped in the night. In the north of the district Colonel Campbell, who had again returned from

[1] See p. 452.

Madura, marched on Sēttūr and Sivagiri and dislodged their garrisons; the forts were levelled. Thence he marched to Vāsudēvanallūr, which he captured and garrisoned with troops. A cantonment was at the same time established at Sankaranainārkōil; a cessation of hostilities was announced, and, through the agency of the Nawāb's manager, Hakmid Ram, negotiations were opened with the poligars.

The situation, however, remained in reality unchanged. The poligar of Sivagiri was in open revolt and was soon joined by the other poligars. He was in treaty with the Dutch at Colombo and had collected ammunition sufficient to supply the force that was expected from that Government; he was negotiating with Haidar Ali, and the Nawāb's Muhammadan renter was suspected of similar treachery. The Dutch at Tuticorin, on the other hand, were posing as the common enemy with the English of Haidar Ali; and the Governor-General was, in 1781, actually trying to negotiate with them an agreement by which, in return for a force of 1,000 European infantry, 200 European artillery and 1,000 Malays, the district of Tinnevelly should be ceded to the Dutch, the nominal sovereignty of the Nawāb remaining undisturbed. The Madras Government, however, declined to forward the treaty and referred the matter to the Court of Directors. In the following year open hostilities with the Dutch broke out; Tuticorin was captured, and no more was heard of these proposals.[1]

The "Assignment," 1781.

The year 1781 marks an important epoch in the history of the Tinnevelly district and of the Carnatic provinces in general. Towards the close of the year the Nawāb assigned by treaty to the East India Company the management and control of the whole of the revenues of those districts, on the condition that he should be allowed one-sixth part of them for his personal uses.[2] Superintendents were appointed to the districts to administer them on behalf of the Company and to receive the revenues. Mr. George Proctor was posted in 1781 to Tinnevelly; his management gave general dissatisfaction, and in 1783 he was succeeded by Mr. Irwin.

Colonel Fullarton's expedition, 1783. He attacks Pānjālankurichi;

The country, however, was still in a state of utter disorder, and Mr. Irwin represented the case plainly to the Madras Government. Finally, Colonel Fullarton, who in 1783 had succeeded to the command of the southern army, marched southwards by way of Sivaganga, which he reached on August 8th; on the 12th he was before Pānjālankurichi, 100 miles distant. Capitulation was refused, and it was decided to storm the fort.

[1] Mill, Vol. IV, Book 50.

[2] Aitchison's *Treaties*, VIII, 26.

CHAP. II. ENGLISH PERIOD.

A battery was hastily constructed, and fire was opened on the north-east bastion. This proving ineffectual, it was decided to breach the adjoining curtain. The enemy, who manned the defences in thousands, kept up a constant fire, and it was dark before a practicable breach was effected. A strong hedge fronting the breach was removed, and about 10 P.M. the assault commenced. The defenders replied with pikes and musketry and obliged the storming party to retire to their battery after considerable slaughter on both sides. The poligars, however, lost heart and abandoned the place, sallying by the eastern gate. An enormous quantity of guns and ammunition was captured; a find of 40,000 star pagodas was distributed among the troops, and the original of a treaty between Kattaboma and the Dutch Government of Colombo was discovered in the fort.

And Sivagiri.

Leaving a garrison in the place, Colonel Fullarton proceeded by way of Palamcotta to Sivagiri. The poligar, as usual, took refuge in his *kōmbai*, or ravine, and Colonel Fullarton prepared to attack him. After a desperate contest the summit was reached, the Sivagiri troops in the *kōmbai* were taken in the flank, and the position was captured. Summoning the leading poligars to his camp, Colonel Fullarton informed them that he was leaving on the 21st September, "but that if they did not return to their allegiance, he would make a vow to Siva, the Gentoo God, whose attribute is vengeance, to march back and spread destruction through every possession of the defaulting poligars."

Surrender of the "Assignment," 1785.

The improvement in the situation promised by the concentration in the hands of the Company of all control, both civil and military, was short-lived; for in 1785 the "Assignment" was surrendered [1], and Mr. Irwin, under orders, handed over the management of the district to the Nawāb's Amildars.

The "Assumption," 1790.

Five years later, the Madras Government, finding it impossible to induce the Nawāb to pay his share of the Company's expenses, "assumed" by proclamation the management of the country and established a Board of Assigned Revenues (a department of the Board of Revenue, established in 1786) to administer the revenues. Mr. Benjamin Torin was sent down to Tinnevelly as "Collector of Tinnevelly and the dependent poligars."

Treaty of 1792.

In July 1792 a definite treaty was effected with the Nawāb, by which the Madras Government undertook at their own risk

[1] Aitchison's *Treaties* VIII, 35. This engagement was reiterated with some modifications in 1787. *Id.* VIII, 40.

and expense to collect the whole of the peshkash or dues of the poligars and to allow the Nawāb credit for this amount in the contribution due by him to the Company.[1] The management of the district was to rest with the Company until an amount equal to the arrears due had been collected. In virtue of this agreement Mr. Torin was in the same year appointed "Collector of the Zamindar and Poligar Peshkash in the Tinnevelly, Madura, Trichinopoly and Rāmanādhapuram and Sivaganga districts."

Anarchy once more.

Colonel Maxwell was also deputed to Tinnevelly, and with Mr. Torin proceeded to make a settlement with the poligars. The Sivagiri poligar had just put the Sēttūr chief to death; Sivagiri was again attacked, but the poligar seems to have escaped punishment. The Sēttūr pālaiyam was seized by a usurper, but Major Stevenson, who had gone to attack the place, was told by Government to confine himself to giving warnings. Kattaboma Nāyakkan was plundering Alvārtirunagari and Srīvaikuntam; and the records of the time are little more than a catalogue of acts of freebooting and violence. In 1797 the poligar of Singampatti shot his colleague of Urkād; the Sivagiri estate had been wrested from the poligar by his own son. In fact the anomalies of the situation created by the treaty of 1792 were becoming daily more apparent. Though the Company was responsible for the collection of the peshkash, the Nawab's ultimate sovereignty was recognized even over the poligars; the administration of the "Circar territory" and its inhabitants was actually in the hands of the Nawāb's officers. By means of their *kāval* system the poligars exercised as much control over the sirkar villages as any Government officer, and in these villages the Company had by the terms of the treaty no concern.[2] The system was clearly unworkable, and none recognized more clearly than the poligars the opportunities which such divided control offered.

Excesses of Pānjālankurichi.

The centre of disaffection was the poligar of Panjālankurichi. Almost the whole of the eastern country lay at his mercy, and, as soon as the great rebellion broke out, in 1797, in the Rāmnād district, he was the first of the Tinnevelly poligars to join the insurgents. His powerful leadership had secured a strong following, chief amongst whom were the poligars of Nāgalāpuram, Kādalgudi, Mēlmāndai, Kulattūr, and Elāyirampannai. Mr. Jackson, who succeeded to the

[1] Aitchison's *Treaties*, VIII, 47.

[2] For a full discussion of the situation, see letter from the Honourable Court of Directors Public Department, dated 10th June 1795.

CHAP. II. ENGLISH PERIOD.

Murder of Lieutenant Clarke at Rāmnād, 1798.

post of Collector of Poligar Peshkash in 1797, realized the importance of settling with Kattaboma Nāyakkan and summoned him to his headquarters at Rāmnād. The poligar evaded appearance, and it was not till four months later that the order was obeyed. The interview was proceeding, when the poligar asked permission to retire. Leave being given, "he ran" (to quote Mr. Jackson's report to the Board of Revenue) "precipitately to the gate of the Fort which was at the distance of 150 yards and with his attendants forced the gateway. Lieutenant and Adjutant Clarke, coming up at the moment, spoke to the poligar, and urged him to return to the Cutcherry, calling out at the same time to the sepoys not to injure the person of the poligar. But the latter, without uttering a word, drew his short sword or dagger, plunged it into the right breast of the Adjutant and killed him on the spot. He then effected his escape. Upon the death of the Adjutant, the sepoys fired and in the scuffle two sepoys were wounded mortally; and several of the poligar's people were killed and wounded; the latter were carried off."

A commission of three was appointed to investigate this somewhat curious affair; in the end, Mr. Jackson was condemned for want of tact and recalled, and Kattaboma Nāyakkan was acquitted of the murder of Lieutenant Clarke. Popular opinion, however, declared the poligar to be the actual assassin, and a fresh impetus was given to the depredating hordes of Pānjālankurichi peons who were terrorizing the country.

The western poligars hold aloof, 1798–1799.

A fortunate result of the excesses of Kattaboma Nāyakkan was the entire alienation from his side of all the Marava poligars in the western parts of the district. The Sivagiri chief, a Vanniyan, was appealing to the Collector for help. At the invitation of Subramania Pillai, the chief agent and evil genius of Pānjālankurichi, and Māppillai Vanniyan of Kōlārpatti, the son-in-law of the poligar of Sivagiri, two thousand armed men had encamped in the Sivagiri territory and were looting the country. From Uttumalai came complaints that a dangerous confederacy of the eastern poligars was concentrating on Elāyirampannai, with the intention of "having a battle at Sivagiri" and then descending on all the pālaiyams of the west. West was closely united against east, even the Pūli Tēvan having in the course of the year seceded from the ranks of the rebels. A conspicuous exception, however, amongst the eastern chieftains was the poligar of Ettaiyāpuram, who, although a Tottiyan like Pānjālankurichi, proved himself in the troubles that were to follow the staunchest adherent of the Company; he was in fact the only

CHAP. II. ENGLISH PERIOD.

poligar who rendered effective assistance. Mr. Stephen Rumbold Lushington,[1] who succeeded on the 12th June 1799 as Collector of Poligar Peshkash, realized that until a proper force could be obtained coercion was impracticable. His first act was to try persuasive measures with Kattaboma Nāyakkan, and he succeeded no better than had Mr. Jackson before him.

Major Bannerman's expedition against Pānjālankurichi, 1799.

In response to the Collector's representations to Government, Major Bannerman was despatched with a strong force, and arrived before Pānjālankurichi on the 5th September. Without waiting for a detachment of European troops which was due to arrive, he attempted to storm the fort. A gate was completely shattered and a partial breach effected, but panic seized the sepoys and they refused to enter. Four European officers were killed. Two days later the European detachment arrived late in the evening with two 12-pounders. That night the poligar and his followers evacuated the fort.

Pursuit and capture of the rebels.

Two troops of cavalry and four hundred grenadiers were sent off in pursuit, and in reply to a letter addressed to various poligars a message was received from Ettaiyāpuram promising to assist. True to his word, he sent out troops, which united with the Company's forces and traced Kattaboma Nāyakkan to the fort of Kōlārpatti. Kattaboma Nāyakkan was engaged; his troops were dispersed, but the poligar himself escaped. Subramania Pillai, his chief minister, was captured and afterwards publicly hanged at Nāgalāpuram. Meanwhile Bannerman himself advanced to Nāgalāpuram, where the poligar of the place surrendered, and his more dangerous brother, Sundarapāndia Nāyakkan, was captured and executed. Kattaboma Nāyakkan, who had fled to the Pudukkōttai country, was captured and brought back a month later to Major Bannerman's camp at Kayättār. In the presence of all the poligars, who had been summoned to attend, the full story of the indictment against him was read by Major Bannerman and sentence of death was passed. The poligar was then carried off to execution and hanged in a conspicuous spot near the old Kayattār fort.[2]

Their fate.

A proclamation was issued by Major Bannerman to all the poligars notifying the commands of Government. The pālaiyam of Pānjālankurichi was declared confiscated; likewise the estates of the five poligars, Elāyirampannai, Nāgalāpuram, Kōlārpatti, Kādalgudi and Kulattūr, who had joined in the recent rebellion. Orders were given that all forts should be

[1] Afterwards Governor of Fort St. George, 1827–32.

[2] See p. 383.

CHAP. II. ENGLISH PERIOD.

destroyed and that every "firelock, matchlock, pike or spear" should be surrendered on pain of death. In consultation with the poligars it was decided that the work of demolishing forts and of disarmament should be left to their owners, the conduct of the Ettaiyāpuram poligar being held up to them for emulation. The poligars of Nāgalāpuram and Elāyirampannai were sent as prisoners to Madras, where they died. The Kōlārpatti poligar, "a poor weak thin youth," and the Kulattūr poligar, "a weak infirm old man between 60 and 70 years of age," were considered sufficiently harmless to justify their detention at Rāmnād. The Kādalgudi poligar was at large. Several members of the Pānjālankurichi family, amongst whom the most important were the two brothers of the executed poligar, surrendered themselves at Tuticorin and were sent to Palamcotta and there imprisoned. Peace appeared to have been restored to the country, and Major Bannerman left the district, the main body of troops returning to Trichinopoly. The command devolved on Major Turing; he was shortly afterwards succeeded by Major Colin Macaulay, who held at the same time the post of Resident in Travancore. A regiment of native infantry was left at Sankaranainārkōil, one or two companies at Kayattār, and Palamcotta was garrisoned by a small force.

The last insurrection, 1801.

Peace had continued for little more than a year, when trouble broke out in a most unexpected quarter. "On the 2nd of February 1801 (to quote the graphic narrative of a contemporary writer)[1] while our force was cantoned at Sankaranainārkōil, about 30 miles to the northward, and the whole of the remaining community, about twenty ladies and gentlemen, were dining at Major Macaulay's garden-house at Palamcotta, a number of Poligar prisoners confined in the fort made their escape by overpowering their own guard and the one at the fort-gate, whom they disarmed. As men of consequence and State prisoners, they had been hitherto kept in irons and very strictly guarded; but the small-pox having recently broken out amongst them, their chains had been removed a few days before. This evening a number of their adherents in disguise and with concealed weapons had entered the fort and at a pre-concerted signal forced the prison gate, whilst the prisoners attacked the two sentries in front. A few of the guard were wounded, and the whole instantly disarmed; when the prisoners, seizing the musquets of their *ci-devant* jailers, headed their adherents, and rushing on the gate-guard

[1] This was Captain (afterwards General) Welsh, who served as Staff Officer throughout the ensuing campaign.

CHAP. II. ENGLISH PERIOD.

succeeded in overpowering them when passing through the gates. They made such good use of their heels that, before morning, they had arrived at Pānjālankurichi, a distance of 30 miles; having surprised nearly one hundred men at different stages on the road, and at one place an entire company under a native officer. In their haste to secure a safe retreat, they, however, let slip the fairest opportunity they ever could have enjoyed of crippling our force, for the party assembled at our commandant's included the civilians of the station, all the staff-officers, and several others of the force; the house was protected by a Naigue's guard only, and not above a mile out of their route; and there we must all have perished unprepared and unresisting since they were several hundred strong, even before they left the place. Unaware of the extent of the mischief, small parties were sent out, as soon as they could be collected to overtake the fugitives and lucky it was for them that they returned unsuccessful. Indeed, all the sepoys then in Palamcotta would have been inadequate for that purpose."

Major Macaulay marches to Pānjālankurichi.

Major Macaulay hastened immediately to Kayattār with what troops he could collect, and Major Sheppard was ordered to join him from Sankaranainārkōil. The whole force, amounting to nine hundred native infantry and a detachment of Bengal Artillery with four guns, assembled on the 8th February, 19 miles beyond Kayattār. No sooner had the camp been formed than a numerous force of poligar troops attacked but did little damage. After a wakeful night the force marched off to Pānjālankurichi, which was reached by 9 o' clock. To the surprise of all, the walls presented exactly the same appearance as when they had last been seen, and were manned by several hundreds of armed men. The attacking force had no battering-guns to breach the fort and no Europeans to lead a storming party. An assault by day was deemed hopeless, and a move was made to the east of the fort with a view to prepare for a night attack. News soon came in that the rebels, five thousand strong, were contemplating a descent on the camp.

And is obliged to retire.

The situation appeared hopeless, and finally it was decided to retire past the fort in the direction of Palamcotta, there to await the expected reinforcements from Trichinopoly. Palamcotta was reached on the 10th. One by one the outlying forts fell again into the hands of the poligars. Tuticorin, which was defended by a subaltern and a few sepoys, was captured by the rebels and the Master-Attendant taken prisoner.

CHAP. II. ENGLISH PERIOD.

Reinforcements arrive and Pānjālankurichi is again attacked.

On the 27th March the troops from Trichinopoly reached Kayattār, the combined forces now amounting to about three thousand men. After two days' marching, in the course of which a skirmish was fought with the enemy, the force appeared before Pānjālankurichi, "the Gibraltar of these insurgents." A determined attempt was made to breach the north-west bastion, the artillery fire continuing from half-past eight till three in the afternoon. Some signs of a breach appearing, the storm was ordered. "The party for assault was composed of the two companies of the 74th Regiment, all the native grenadiers, and a Battalion Company of the 3rd; the whole line being close to them, disposed to the right and left, to keep down the enemy's fire. They advanced with alacrity, under the heaviest fire imaginable from the curtains and five or six bastions, the defences of which we had not been able to demolish. Our men fell rapidly, but nothing impeded their approach; even the hedge was speedily passed, and repeated attempts were made to surmount the breach, but all in vain. Every man who succeeded in reaching the summit was instantly thrown back, pierced with wounds from both pikes and musquetry and no footing could be gained. At length a retreat was ordered, and a truly dismal scene of horror succeeded: all our killed, and many of the wounded being left at the foot of the breach, over which the enemy immediately sprung, and pursued the rear, while others pierced the bodies both of the dying and the dead."

Lieut.-Col. Agnew is sent with a large force; the fort captured.

It was evident that the guns were not equal to the task of reducing the fort, and reinforcements were demanded. A large force of native and European troops with powerful siege-guns was despatched under the command of Lieut.-Col. Agnew from Malabar and Trichinopoly. In two months the new force had arrived before Pānjālankurichi. Two batteries were opened on the south-west bastion, and the fire soon proved effective. The storming party advanced, and was received with a hot rain of fire. The summit was gained, and the defenders in the breach were soon levelled by hand grenades. At the same time entrance was gained on the flanks; the enemy were panic-stricken and fled, leaving about four hundred and fifty killed. Six hundred were cut off by the cavalry, the rest to the number of about 2,000 making good their escape. The losses on the English side were 47 killed and 187 wounded.

Escape and final capture of the defenders.

The fugitives made their way to Sivaganga in the Rāmnād district and there joined in the rebellion of the "Marudus," the suppression of which after a difficult campaign was effected with the capture of Kālaiyārkōvil, on the 1st October 1801. In a few days Kattaboma Nāyakkan and his younger brother were captured, sent to Pānjālankurichi and there hanged. Colonel Agnew who had commanded the force in Sivaganga returned to Palamcotta. The Pānjālankurichi fort was razed to the ground; the site was ploughed over and sown with castor seed, and the name of the place was expunged from all the registers of the district. During Colonel Agnew's absence Mr. Lushington had been busy hunting down gangs of rebels that were still at large; the "Dalavāy Pillai," one of the chief supporters of Pānjālankurichi, fled to the Maravans of Nānguneri for refuge, and a little rebellion which they got up together in October had to be suppressed by troops. Some of the rebels were sent to the fortress of Kamudi in the Rāmnād country, others to Madras.

Cession of the country to the English.

But before the insurgents in Sivaganga and in Nānguneri were reduced, the Tinnevelly district had become a possession of the East India Company. On the fall of Seringapatam and the death of Tippu Sultan in 1799 correspondence came to light which showed that the Nawāb had been engaged in a treasonable conspiracy with Tippu. Whilst the matter was under enquiry, the Nawāb died, and, as his heir declined to accept the conditions which the Madras Government thought it necessary to impose on him, the Nawābship was given to a junior member of the family. On the 31st July, 1801, an agreement was effected with the new Nawāb, by which the sole and exclusive administration of the civil and military Governments of all the territories and dependencies of the Carnatic was handed over to the Company in perpetuity.

Mr. Lushington, Collector of Tinnevelly.

On the same day Mr. Lushington was appointed the first Collector of the district under the new sovereign power, and moved from Rāmnād to Tinnevelly. A week afterwards he reported to Madras that the "Province of Tinnevelly has been brought without the smallest disturbance under the Company's authority." "By the energy and justice of Government," he added later, "the rebellions have been subdued; the oppressed have been upheld and exalted; the obedient have been liberally rewarded; and the extinction of a divided authority has restored the fairest province of the Carnatic from an acknowledged state of anarchy and confusion to a state of subordination and prosperity."

CHAPTER III.

THE PEOPLE.

GENERAL CHARACTERISTICS—Density of the population—Its growth—Parent tongue—Religions. THE CHRISTIANS—Roman Catholic Mission—Church of England and Protestant Missions—Earlier history—The S.P.C.K.—The C.M.S.—The S.P.G.—Later history: the C.M.S.—The S.P.G.—Missions of other denominations. THE MUHAMMADANS. THE JAINS. THE HINDUS—Villages—Houses—The village community—Food—Amusements—Religious life; Brahmanism—Dravidian forms of worship—Minor deities: Ayyanār—His festivals—Ammans—The Grāmadēvatas—Festivals—Other forms of worship: the "Etteluttu-mārgam"—The demon-gods—Names and characteristics of some—Others—The pisāchas—Festivals of the Mādan tribe—The animal sacrifice—The devil-dance—Origin of "Mādans"—Vows. PRINCIPAL CASTES. PARAVANS—Their Christianity—Their occupations—History of the caste—Their headman—Marriages—The "Vāsapadi Mariyal." SHĀNĀNS—Their aspirations—Attempts to realize them—The riot at Kalugumalai—The riots of 1899—A threatened disturbance, 1902—Characteristics of the caste—Origin of the caste; traditional account—Subdivisions—Caste customs—Their titles. MARAVANS—Subdivisions—Characteristics of the caste—Marriages—Funerals. VELLĀLANS—Their occupations and characteristics—Subdivisions—The Nangudi Vellālans—Marriage customs—Funerals. KAMMAVANS—Their characteristics—Caste customs—Marriages. ILUVANS—Their occupations—Social position—Subdivisions—Caste organization. KATASANS—Occupations—Social status—Caste organization—Subdivisions.

CHAP. III. GENERAL CHARACTERISTICS.

Density of the population.

TINNEVELLY stands eighth among the districts of the Presidency (Madras and Anjengo excepted) in regard to the density of its population, containing on an average 411 persons to the square mile.

According to the figures of the last census (1911) Tiruchendūr is the most thickly populated taluk and contains as many as 661 inhabitants to the square mile. By an unfortunate coincidence the important *Māsi* festival was at the time of enumeration in progress in the head-quarter town of the taluk, and the figures returned from that place are, in consequence, enormously inflated. If a deduction of 10,000 (which is perhaps rather under than above the mark) is allowed on that account, the density for the taluk drops to 630 persons to the square mile, and Tinnevelly with its two large municipal towns heads the taluks with 649. Tiruchendūr, on the whole a poor taluk, still takes precedence over the remaining taluks and appears to owe its high position chiefly to the fertility of its large Christian population. The density of population is lowest (287 to the square mile) in Nāngunēri and Sankaranainārkōil (319). The population in the river-valley taluks is in all cases, as might be expected, well above the district average.

Its growth.

Owing to the fact that the district was reconstituted in 1910, it is impossible to gauge correctly the increase of its population over any considerable period. During the last census (1911) the figures obtained in 1901 for the district as a whole and for each taluk were recast in such a way as to render possible a comparison of the population contained, in 1891, 1901 and 1911, in the areas now comprised in the newly-formed taluks and in the new district. The result is to show that in the present district as a whole the population advanced in the twenty years ending with 1911 by 17 per cent, a figure exceeding both the average for the east coast districts of the south (14·1 per cent) and for the Presidency (16·1 per cent). A reference to the census figures relating to the old district of Tinnevelly shows that, in spite of the great famine of 1876–1878, the population increased slightly (by 0·3 per cent) in the decade 1871–1881; in the next ten years the rebound usual after scarcity took place, the advance being as much as 12·7 per cent; in the period 1891–1901 the growth of the population, in the district as re-formed in 1910, was 8·3 per cent, or slightly greater than the Presidency average. In the decade 1901–11 the increase was 8 per cent, a figure slightly below the Presidency average (8·3 per cent).

In every one of the ten years the birth-rate of the district exceeded that of the Presidency; but in nine years of the ten a corresponding excess of deaths occurred. This fact, added to the emigration which took place, mostly to Ceylon, contributed to check an increase which otherwise would have been far greater. Statistics show that in these ten years the result of emigration to British colonies (excluding those persons that returned to the district) was a net loss of 112,000 to the population of the district. The increase in the decade 1901–1911 was highest (21·9 per cent) in the Srīvaikuntam taluk, a fact which is accounted for partly by the growing prosperity of the port of Tuticorin and partly by the extension of wet cultivation under the Srīvaikuntam system. Tenkāsi, with its rich irrigation at the foot of the hills, its exceptionally light assessments and its industrious Shānān population, who have taken largely in these parts to well-cultivation, comes next, with an increase of 11·8 per cent. Tiruchendūr, where the density of population is high, seems to have reached its limit; much of this taluk and of Nānguneri is at the mercy

CHAP. III. GENERAL CHARACTERISTICS.

of the seasons, and these areas contribute most largely to emigration.

Parent tongue.

Tamil, which is the language of nine-tenths of the population, is spoken with greater purity, but with a more pronounced drawl, than in the northern districts. In rustic speech consonants are often transposed—for instance, *kuthīrai* becomes *kurithai*, *abarātham* becomes *abathāram*—and with all classes the letter ழ degenerates to the equivalent of a simple "l". The Vadugans, Kammavans and Kambalattāns (all of whom bear the title Nāyakkan or Nāyudu) and the Reddis constitute the bulk of the Telugu-speaking section (which forms altogether 9 per cent of the population) and are found chiefly in the black-cotton country of the Kōilpatti taluk. Telugu Brahmans are found in small numbers in all parts of the district. Canarese is spoken by less than 1 per cent of the population. The language spoken by the Pattunūlkārans, known as Pattunūli, is a dialect of Gujarāti which the caste brought with it from the country of its origin. They number about four thousand and are found chiefly in Palamcotta and Vīravanallūr and a few other villages of the Ambāsamudram taluk.

Religions.

In every hundred of the population eighty-four are Hindus, ten are Christians and six are Muhammadans. The proportion of Christians to the total population is higher than in any other Madras district.

THE CHRISTIANS.

In the decade 1901–1911 the Christians (almost entirely Indians) increased by 17 per cent. They are most numerous (amounting to nearly one-fourth of the total population) in the Tiruchendūr taluk, which contains a number of villages wholly inhabited by Paravans (who are all Roman Catholics) and also many settlements, including the important village Nazareth, of adherents of the S.P.G. Nānguněri (17 per cent) and Srīvaikuntam (12 per cent) come next. The Christians belong in about equal proportions to the Roman Catholic and Anglican churches, an odd three thousand being adherents of minor Protestant denominations.

Roman Catholic Mission.

The Roman Catholic Mission [1] is older than any other by more than two centuries.

In 1532 the Paravans of the sea coast, with whom the Muhammadans had recently come into serious conflict over the question of the pearl-fishery, sent a deputation to Cochin asking for assistance from Michael Vaz, the Vicar-General

[1] For valuable assistance with this section I am indebted to the Rev. Fr. Causannel, S.J. I have also made use of the recently published *Mission du Maduré* by Fr. Léon Besse, S.J., Trichinopoly, 1914.

of the Bishop of Goa. Michael Vaz sailed back with the Paravans and, in consideration of their becoming Christians, undertook, with the aid of a number of Portuguese followers who accompanied him, the chastisement of the Muhammadans. The terms were accepted; the Moormen were repressed; the Paravans became Christians, and in 1532 was established "the Christianity of the Fishery Coast" under the supervision of the See of Goa. In 1542 the celebrated Francis Xavier, a member of the Society of Jesus, visited the new Christians, and during the two years that he laboured among them gave them their first practical lessons in the doctrines of their new faith. Having taught himself Tamil, he translated into the vernacular the Creed, the Lord's Prayer and the Ave Maria, and travelling, bell in hand, from village to village collected the inhabitants, instructed and baptized them. The numerous letters written by him to his Society in Rome from Tuticorin, Manappād, Vaippār, Vīrapāndyanpatnam, Alanthalai, Punnaikāyal, Tiruchendūr and other places give a most interesting account of his activities.

From the sea-coast Christianity spread into the interior, but little is known of its progress in the district during the next hundred years. According to an original authority quoted by Dr. Caldwell[1], there were in the year 1600 twenty-two congregations scattered over the district of Tinnevelly and Madura, no less than sixteen of which were on the coast. The work was in charge of seventeen fathers and three brothers, the chief residence of whom was the college already established at Tuticorin.

In 1606 the Mission of Madura was established by Father Robert de Nobili; and, though formally it continued to be under the jurisdiction of the "Malabar province," the new society had from the first its own methods and sphere of action and managed its own finances. It took under its nominal control the inland parishes of the Tinnevelly district, the missionary in charge being stationed far away, at Mullipādi, now in the Trichinopoly district. The Fishery Coast still remained an integral part of the "Malabar province," under the authority of Goa.

In its early years the Madura Mission was too much occupied with its work in Trichinopoly, Tanjore and Madura to pay much attention to Tinnevelly. In 1638 Father Emmanuel Martin, a member of the Madura Society, toured through the district. "The results of the mission," he writes from Kurukkalapatti (near Andipatti, Tenkāsi taluk), "are in

[1] *History of Tinnevelly*, p. 235.

CHAP. III. THE CHRISTIANS.

proportion to the excursions we make, after the manner of hunters. My time is spent in running all over the district." By 1666 the mission had got seriously to work and congregations are found existing all over the district, at places as far apart as Tenkāsi, Mārandai, Palamcotta, Pannikulam, Kayattār, Perunkulam, Punnavanam and Kāmanāyakkanpatti. It was a period however of great political commotions, and in 1676 were added the horrors of a famine. "How can religion," writes Father Britto in 1683, "become securely established in a land whose population is unstable as the waves of the sea, shifting like the sands of the desert, in a country where it wants only a war, an epidemic, a famine, a political change, a foreign invasion, to destroy one-half of its inhabitants and to change almost its whole population?"

In 1683 Father John de Britto succeeded to the charge of the Madura Mission and in the following year, after visiting almost every part of the Tinnevelly district, ordered the establishment of a permanent residence at Kāmanāyakkanpatti instead of Mullipādi. It was during this visit that the first steps were taken in that important movement by which Christianity ultimately spread so widely amongst the Shānāns. Father de Britto who had penetrated as far south as Vadakkānkulam (Nānguneri taluk) was called back unexpectedly to Kumbakōnam. A congregation, however, of Shānāns appears definitely to have been formed by 1685 at Vadakkānkulam; and, under Father Borghese, the first resident missionary of Kāmanāyakkanpatti, the work of conversion amongst that caste, whose members now constitute nearly one-half of the Roman Catholic population of the district, progressed rapidly in the south of the taluk of Nānguneri and in south Travancore. "By its numbers and its wealth," wrote Father Calini in 1716, stationed at Vadakkānkulam, which had two years previously become a residence, "the Shānān caste is in comparison with all other castes admirably adapted to Christianity. In fact the Shānāns could easily observe the Christian practices. The nature of their life, the necessity of climbing palmyras, preserves them from laziness, the fountain of all disorders. Besides, they are gifted with an excellent disposition, most inclined to religious matters."

Meanwhile the Fishery Coast remained under the control of the Bishop of Cochin. In a letter of 1604 we read of six principal residences occupied by Jesuit Priests, and of the seacoast villages the "Catalogus" reports: '*Omnes hi Vici instar magnarum urbium Sunt, Et omnes Christianis incoluntur.*' The chief place of the coast was still Tuticorin; but here, as elsewhere, constant troubles were experienced by the Paravans at the hands of their Hindu neighbours, and on several occasions the Jesuit Fathers of Tuticorin had to seek shelter in the islands opposite the town.

Finally, in 1612, under the orders of the Bishop of Cochin, who had quarrelled both with the Archbishop of Cranganore and the Viceroy of Goa, all the Jesuit Fathers withdrew from the Fishery Coast and retired to Ceylon, Travancore and Cochin. They returned again some eleven years later; but the mission of the Fishery Coast had fallen on evil days. In Tuticorin the college had disappeared; and even the Church which remained had "neither altar nor images nor doors" and was used as a stable and a store-house. The Portuguese officials, "who to increase, they say, the royal treasure take away our endowments," were in alliance with the Jāthitalavaimōre and his local representatives against the priests and people.

In 1658 the Dutch took Tuticorin, and the Portuguese establishments passed one by one into the invaders' hands. The final blow was the capture of Cochin in 1663. In 1683 Father de Britto, of the Madura Mission, reported that all that was of importance had been abandoned and destroyed, only a few miserable villages, amongst which he mentions Tālai, Manappād, Alantalai and Punnaikāyal, being left. Though the college had passed to Manappād, Tuticorin was still the headquarters of the mission, and with regard to this place Father de Britto incidentally makes the astonishing statement[1] that it contained 50,000 inhabitants. Most of the churches along the coast had been turned by the Dutch into warehouses, the missionaries often being turned out of their homes to accommodate merchants. Baldaeus writing in 1703 evidently judged by appearances: "all along the Coast," he writes, "inhabit the Paruas who being for the most part Christians, you see the Shore all along as far as Comoryn and even beyond it to Tutecoryn full of little churches some of wood, others of stone."

The Paravans clung to their Christianity, and in 1742 were fortunate enough to obtain the services of the famous divine, scholar and poet, Father Beschi of the Madura Mission. This remarkable man, remembered chiefly as the author of a number of Tamil poems (the best known of which is the epic styled Tēmbāvani) and of many books on history, religion and philosophy, arrived in Tinnevelly in 1711 and was placed

[1] It seems certain that the writer was mistaken in this. We can only conclude that it was already at that time an important place.

under the resident missionary of Kāmanāyakkanpatti. He was posted to Kurukkalpatti (Tenkāsi taluk), where shortly afterwards he narrowly escaped death at the hands of the inhabitants. In 1716 he was in Madura, and from 1720 onwards was put successively in charge of two stations near Trichinopoly, Vadugārpatti and Avūr, and afterwards of Tanjore. Hoping to be able to influence Chanda Sāhib, who since 1736 had been in possession of Trichinopoly, to give his support to the Christians, he went to see that potentate, having learnt Persian, it is said, expressly for this purpose. He was received with courtesy, but little benefit accrued to the mission. In 1741 Chanda Sāhib surrendered his capital to the Mahrattas, and, with the transfer of authority to these invaders, the missionaries had to take refuge at a distance from the seat of political power. Beschi went to the south and in 1742 reached the Fishery Coast, of which he took charge. In 1744 he was made Rector of the "Collegium Orae Piscariae" at Manappād. In the next year he was posted as teacher of theology and Sanskrit in the college of Ambalacat (in Travancore), where he died in 1747. With 1752 the series of "Catalogues of the Malabar Province" closes and with it the authentic story of the decline of the mission of the Fishery Coast.

In 1773 the Society of Jesus was formally abolished by Pope Clement XIV; and for sixty years the congregations of the interior, following the fate which had already slowly overtaken the Fishery Coast, came gradually, as the Jesuit missionaries died, under the control of the native priests of the diocese of Goa. The details of the history of the period which followed are obscure. The priests were few in number and seem to have had no fixed abodes. "They ran about the country, passing from congregation to congregation, partly, it is true, to administer the sacraments but also to realize the contributions which the Faithful were accustomed to pay for their marriages and other religious services." It is generally believed that many congregations relapsed during the period from Christianity or passed under the control of the Protestant missionaries, whose activities began with the close of the eighteenth century.

The Society was revived in 1814, but it was not till 1837 that the first detachment, of two missionaries, deputed to the district reached Palamcotta. Trouble not unnaturally arose with the priests of Goa, who had stepped into the places of the old Jesuits and now showed a reluctance to surrender their charges. Several attempts were made by Rome to induce Portugal to

CHAP. III. THE CHRISTIANS.

withdraw the priests sent by Goa, but they proved for many years ineffectual. Finally, in 1886, by the Bull *Humanae Salutis* Pope Leo XIII created the Catholic hierarchy in India, by which the Madura Mission was placed under the jurisdiction of the newly-established bishopric of Trichinopoly. In the settlement which followed the Christian congregations of the district were apportioned between the priests of Goa (now under the Bishop of Mylapore) and the Jesuit missionaries subordinate to the See of Trichinopoly. Roman Catholics in the district number, all told, 86,000, and to this figure the Goanese congregations, which are confined to five sea-coast villages, contribute less than six per cent.

Roman Catholic churches are to be found in every quarter of the district, the Jesuits alone owning more than 150 substantially built ones. Many date their foundation from the seventeenth and even the sixteenth century; but practically all have been rebuilt, many more than once. The diocese of Trichinopoly is divided into the three districts of Trichinopoly, Madura and Palamcotta, each comprising a varying number of *pangus*, or parishes. One of the four vicariates of the Mylapore diocese is the Tinnevelly district, generally known as the "Fishery Coast," which is administered by a "Vicar-vara" stationed at Tuticorin.

The Jesuit society maintains in the district two high schools, a number of convents and some hundreds of elementary schools.

Church of England and Protestant Missions.[1] Earlier history.

The history of Protestant missionary effort in Tinnevelly goes back to the era of the poligar wars. As early as 1771 the memorable Schwartz mentions in his diary that one of his Trichinopoly converts was in that year engaged in preaching to the people of Tinnevelly. Seven years later Schwartz himself visited Palamcotta and found a few Christians there. He baptized a Hindu woman of the place, who afterwards was chiefly instrumental in getting built the little church which exists to this day near the present English church. In 1786 Schwartz paid the congregation a second visit, and in 1790 ordained Sathyanāthan, one of his catechists, and put him in charge.

The S.P.C.K.

Very soon a beginning was made amongst the Shānāns of the south, the first convert from this class being a man of Kālankudiyiruppu, some ten miles east of Sāttānkulam. Receiving the name of David, he was put to work in his native

[1] Authorities: Caldwell's *Records of the Early History of the Tinnevelly Mission*, Madras, 1881; *History of the C.M.S.*, by Eugen Stock; and official publications of the S.P.G. and C.M.S.

CHAP. III. THE CHRISTIANS.

place and the conversion of Shānāns, who now form the bulk of the Protestant community, began on a large scale. Mudalūr, "First-town," was established as a definitely Christian settlement before 1800; and between 1800 and 1803 over five thousand Shānāns in the south of Tiruchendūr and Nāngunēri taluks were admitted to Christianity. Since 1791 German missionaries, sent out by the Society for the Promotion of Christian Knowledge, had been in charge of the district, Jaenicke from 1792 till his death in 1800 and after him Gericke, who died in 1804. In 1806 Ringeltaube, a member of the London Missionary Society, was sent down by the S.P.C.K. to take charge. He was an eccentric person and, although devoted to his work, was not a practical success. He lived in the humblest fashion; "scarcely an article of his dress was of European manufacture. He seldom had a coat to his back except when furnished with one by a friend (especially Captain Trotter) in his occasional visits to Palamcotta." In 1815 he suddenly left the district for Madras, where he appeared ready for a voyage, wearing a straw hat of native manufacture and without a coat. No one knew where he went, nor was he heard of again. Towards the end of his time Ringeltaube had settled in south Travancore and as early as 1808 had severed his connection with the S.P.C.K.

By 1816, when James Hough was appointed Chaplain at Palamcotta, half the converts had given up their Christianity. Hough, though it was no part of his duty, brought about a complete revival. He started schools, distributed bibles and prayer-books, and, other resources failing, appealed to the Church Missionary Society for help.

The C.M.S.

In 1820 that Society sent down C. E. Rhenius, perhaps the most notable missionary that the district has known. As a preacher he commanded audiences of Christians and non-Christians alike; he founded numerous societies, the most important of which was the "Dharma Sangam", or "Philanthropic Society", for the purchase of lands and houses for converts. It is to him that a large number of the existing Christian settlements of the district owe their origin, such as Suvisēshapuram, Kadākshapuram, Nallūr and Megnānapuram. He instituted a Poor Fund, a Widow's Fund and Bible Societies; he made numerous converts and at the same time supervised the congregations belonging to the old S.P.C.K. mission.

The S.P.G.

In 1824 the S.P.C.K. transferred the charge of their mission to the Society for the Propagation of the Gospel; but it was not till 1829 that the latter society sent a missionary (in the person of David Rosen) to the district. Rosen left the district in the following year, and the Tanjore missionaries once more resumed nominal charge of their Christians in Tinnevelly. Meanwhile the organization started by Hough and carried on and expanded by Rhenius continued to exist side by side with the Society of the "Tanjore Christians" (as they came to be called), managed by the S.P.C.K. Shortly after David Rosen's appointment in 1829 signs of friction between the two Societies appeared, the native pastors of either mission "appropriating" each other's congregations and property. In 1834 the C.M.S. suggested that the Tinnevelly missions should be handed over to their sole charge, the S.P.C.K. being compensated by receiving the Māyavaram (Tanjore) mission in exchange. The S.P.C.K. declined the offer, and the two Societies continued to work side by side in the district. In 1835 Rhenius, who was still in the district, quarrelled with the C.M.S. authorities on a subject of doctrine and quitted the mission. He was succeeded by George Pettitt, and peace was soon restored.

In 1836 the S.P.G. sent their first English missionary to the district, and from that date a regular succession of English workers, both for the S.P.G. and the C.M.S., has followed. In 1841 Robert Caldwell (afterwards Bishop) came out to the S.P.G., and it was shortly after this that the districts of the two societies were carefully marked out, each mission developing thereafter on its own distinctive lines.

As a consequence of the neglect of the earlier mission the C.M.S. obtained the greater part of the field, the work of the S.P.G. being confined to the south-east of the district.

Later history: the C.M.S.

By 1855 the C.M.S. had mapped out their territory into nine districts—Palamcotta, Megnānapuram, Kadākshapuram, Suviseshapuram, Dōnāvūr, Pannaivilai, Pannikulam, Nallūr and Surandai, all except one (Kadākshapuram) under European missionaries. North Tinnevelly formed a separate division, an itinerating mission having been started there about 1855.

By degrees the missionaries in charge of the nine stations (except Megnānapuram) retired or died, and in 1876 the Rev. E. (afterwards Bishop) Sargent at Palamcotta was the only European missionary left. In 1877 both he and the Rev. Robert Caldwell of the S.P.G. were appointed Assistant Bishops to the Bishop of Madras and were placed in episcopal charge of their respective missions. Bishop Sargent died in 1889 and Bishop Caldwell in 1891; and in 1896 a new bishopric was established for the general superintendence of all Church of England missions in the districts of Tinnevelly and Madura. The out-stations of the C.M.S., each of which had

CHAP. III. THE CHRISTIANS.

for many years past been managed by a local council, were brought under central control, a Superintending Missionary and Chairman being appointed at Palamcotta. Associated with him are one or two European missionaries, who, however, hold no pastoral charge.

The Society owns over one hundred and fifty churches in the district, amongst which may be specially mentioned Trinity Church, Palamcotta, built by Rhenius in 1826, and St. Paul's, Megnānapuram, completed in 1868, one of the finest churches in Southern India. From the earliest times education, mainly with a view to evangelization, has been a marked feature of the Society's work. Besides the Sarah Tucker College for women and the Church Missionary Society College, the mission maintains two high schools, five incomplete secondary schools, several hundreds of elementary schools and one training school. Some account of the more important of these institutions, and also of the schools for the blind and the deaf and dumb, will be found in Chapter X.

The native adherents of the mission, the bulk of whom are Shānāns, number about fifty thousand.

The S.P.G.

From the earliest times Mudalūr and Nazareth had been the two chief centres of the missionary work of the S.P.C.K. In 1836 J. L. Irion, the first English missionary sent out by the S.P.G. to take charge of the mission, settled at Nazareth, but remained only for two years. The appointment in 1839 of the Rev. A. E. Caemmerer (1839–58) marked the beginning of a period of revived energy. Considerable accessions to Christianity followed, and in 1844 the Rev. G. U. (afterwards Dr.) Pope, who had two years previously been placed in charge of the newly-formed "district" of Sawyerpuram, reported that "a more encouraging movement to Christianity had never taken place in India." A new church was opened in 1844 at Sawyerpuram (since replaced by the present church, which was dedicated in 1887), a "Church Building Society" was formed, and four of the largest churches belonging to the Society, those at Puthiyamputtūr, Kadayanōdai, Christianagaram and Mukkupēri, were erected within the five years following. From 1839 onwards the mission area was by degrees parcelled out into a number of districts. The Mudalūr district was definitely separated from Nazareth and placed under the charge of the Rev. G. Y. Heyne (1839–45). In 1841 the southern part of the Mudalūr area was formed into a new district, called Idaiyangudi, under the superintendence of the Rev. Robert Caldwell (1841–83); in 1842 the district of Sawyerpuram was carved out of

CHAP. III. THE CHRISTIANS.

the Nazareth area, the Rev. G. U. Pope taking charge. The Christianagaram district (formerly attached to Mudalūr) was formed in 1845, and in 1856 the Puthiyamputtūr district was separated from Sawyerpuram. There are now eleven S.P.G. districts in Tinnevelly, whose congregations aggregate about 30,000. The evangelistic movement of 1844 was followed by an extension of education, which received a special impetus in an entirely new direction by the foundation in that year of Mrs. Caldwell's school for girls at Idaiyangudi.

The mission possesses many fine churches, amongst which the most conspicuous are those at Mukkupēri, Sawyerpuram, Idaiyangudi, Mudalūr, Christianagaram and Nāgalāpuram. It maintains one hundred and sixty-five elementary schools, five secondary schools and three training schools, besides industrial schools and orphanages. Of the secondary schools one is a high school for girls, at Nazareth; it attained its present status in 1836 and was the first of its kind in the Presidency.

Missions of other denominations.

Indian Christians, other than the adherents of Anglican and Roman Catholic Societies, are mainly Baptists and number altogether about 3,000. Kōilpatti, Nāraikkinar (Tinnevelly taluk), and Prakāsapuram, near Nazareth, are the chief centres of these smaller missions.

THE MUHAMMADANS.

Muhammadans, who constitute only six per cent of the population of the district, are, proportionately to the adherents of other faiths, most numerous in the three taluks of Tinnevelly (over 10 per cent) and Tiruchendūr and Tenkāsi (10 per cent). They belong, with few exceptions, to that widespread class which speaks Tamil and it is generally designated by the comprehensive term "Lebbai." Of the four religious sects, deriving their origin from four disciples of the Prophet, only two, Shāfi and Hanafi, are represented in any considerable numbers in the district. As a rule, members of different divisions do not marry into one another's families though in regard to ordinary social intercourse with one another the two classes observe no restrictions. Amongst themselves the title Lebbai is as a rule reserved for priests or men of some learning; Sāhib (in theory only) is a title confined to men of still greater learning, such people as the Hindus might style Guru; ordinary persons who make no pretension either to learning or unusual piety are known as Rāvuttans or Taragans. From their speech, customs and dress it is evident that most of them belong to the same race as the bulk of the Hindus of the district; and, though scarcely any tradition survives as to the circumstances in which they adopted their present faith,

CHAP. III. THE MUHAMMADANS.

it is reasonable enough to suppose that most of them were forcibly converted to Islam during past periods of Muhammadan domination.

The Muhammadans of the coast towns of the Tiruchendūr taluk (Kāyalpatnam[1] is their most important centre) are perhaps an exception. There is every reason to accept in its general outlines the local tradition that the Muhammadan settlement of Kāyalpatnam owes its origin to immigrants who came by sea from Arabia "many centuries ago." They took wives from among the women of the country, and to the present day their descendants have maintained an exclusive attitude towards the other Muhammadans of the country. Even in Kāyalpatnam itself, though Tamil is the general speech of all, there is an "inner circle" some of whom are learned in Arabic, while most of them (unlike the majority of Tinnevelly Muhammadans) are taught a certain amount of Arabic, or at least learn to write Tamil in Arabic characters. The members of this upper class claim to be Saiyids, or descendants of the Prophet; as the champions of orthodoxy, they affect contempt for the Hindu elements which so many Tamil Muhammadans like to impart to their religious and social ceremonies; their women observe *gōshā*; and the men who trade by sea adopt the superior title of Marakkāyar. Kāyalpatnam seems to have been the earliest settlement of these Muhammadans; they are to be found also in Kulasēkharapatnam and here and there in the Srīvaikuntam and Tiruchendūr taluks.

In his dress the ordinary Muhammadan man may as a rule be distinguished from a Hindu by his coloured squat cap or variegated turban and by the tartan pattern of his *vēshti* or waistcloth. Unlike her Hindu neighbour, the Muhammadan woman brings the single cloth which forms her dress up over her head and wears a jacket covering the upper part of the body.

Numerous instances could be quoted in which Hindu customs are observed. On the occasion of births and marriages their women raise that peculiarly Hindu wail known as *kulavai*; the tying of the *tāli* at marriage and the payment by the bride's father of a substantial sum (crudely called *kaikūli*) to the bridegroom are customs derived from the Hindus; the celebrations connected with "taboots," wooden frames adorned with coloured paper and tinsel in which offerings of sandal dedicated to saints are carried in proces-

[1] See also pp. 499–500.

sion, is an almost exact imitation of the ordinary " chapram " ritual of the Hindus. Examples are to be found in the district of a curious kinship in religious feeling between Muhammadans and Hindus. The mosque at Pottalpudūr[1] attracts, it is said, more Hindu worshippers than Muhammadans; attached to the Attankarai mosque near the mouth of the Nambiyār (in the extreme south of the Nānguneri taluk) is the tomb of a Muhammadan saint to which Hindus make offerings in fulfilment of vows; at Mēlappālaiyam, a suburb of Palamcotta, there is a tomb similarly respected by Hindus; at a small mosque in Gangaikondān Hindus gladly receive consecrated offerings from the Muhammadan priest; and probably instances might be multiplied. Muhammadans in their turn take offerings, it is said, to the famous temple of Subramanyaswāmi at Tiruchendūr and often join with great enthusiasm in the processions of Hindu festivals. Quarrels, as at Tenkāsi, occasionally arise over religious matters between Muhammadans and their Hindu neighbours; as a rule, however, the two classes live together on terms of amity.

Following the precept given, according to tradition, by the Prophet to those who asked what a man should do in order to prosper in this world, the majority of the Muhammadans of the district are traders. The chief exchange-mart of the district, Pēttai, is almost entirely in their hands and has made the fortunes of many; in Kulasēkharapatnam, Udangudi, Kāyalpatnam and elsewhere many have grown rich through trade with Ceylon and the Straits; large numbers, believing in all senses that " maior in externas fit qui descendit harenas," go abroad to Ceylon, Burma and the Straits Settlements, set up as traders, and return after they have made enough money. An occupation next in importance is weaving. The richer Muhammadans of Mēlappālaiyam, which is the chief centre of this industry, supply the yarn and in many cases the warp, ready made, to their employees, Muhammadan men and women, there and in various parts of the district. The finished articles, tartan cloths, *muris*, and carpets (the last are made in Mēlappālaiyam only) are sent to the capitalists, who arrange for their export or local distribution. The important *kōrai* mat industry of Kayattār is similarly under the control of Pēttai merchants.

Muhammadan agriculturists are found in small numbers in all parts of the district, being most numerous, perhaps, in the Srīvaikuntam and Tiruchendūr taluks. The richer among them often buy land by way of a safe investment from the

[1] See p. 360.

CHAP. III. THE MUHAMMADANS.

proceeds of their trade; so general in fact is the practice among Pēttai and Mēlappālaiyam merchants that the best irrigated land in the neighbourhood of Tinnevelly and Palamcotta now fetches more than Rs. 4,000 an acre, though quoted, and very often sold, in units of a *kuruni* (8 cents). Poorer Muhammadans are labourers and retail shop-keepers; and in the sandy tracts of the south some make a living out of pack-bullocks.

THE JAINS.

The district contains no Jains or Buddhists. The revival of the Saiva religion and the consequent disappearance of the Jaina and Buddhist influence in southern India is known to have begun about the beginning of the seventh century A.D.; and the *Periya Purānam* contains a number of stories which relate how the cause of Saivism was advanced by the miraculous deeds of the famous saints of that era, Appar, Tirugnāna Sambandar, and Sirutonda Nāyanār.

The memory of the Jains, however—*Samanāl,* as they are popularly called—is kept green in many parts of the district by the ceremony known as *kaluvēttal* (lit., "impaling"), which is celebrated with enthusiasm on the sixth day of the great festivals held in connection with many Siva temples of the district. Tiruchendūr, Kalugumalai, Vilāttikulam and Tinnevelly afford the best known examples. In popular belief the ceremony is associated with the Jains of old. The model of a human head is stuck on a spike and carried in procession. To lend spirit to the performance, temple servants turn out with their bodies bedaubed with black and red paint; some suspend false tongues from their mouths and coil round their bodies the intestines of a sheep, or sit as if impaled on a stake; others appear to be hanging from gibbets, or have a leg bent double and tied up to suggest that it has been cut off; others again lie in pits in the ground, showing only what pretends to be a head cut from its body. The idea of the performance is to suggest mutilation; and there can be little doubt that it is intended to commemorate the savage treatment which the Jains of old received at the hands of their Saiva persecutors.

Evidence of the former widespread influence of Jainism and of the existence also of Buddhism in the district is seen in the stone remains which are to be found in places so far apart as Kalugumalai, Marugāltalai (a hamlet of Sīvalappēri, Tinnevelly taluk), Vīrasikhāmani, Kulattūr, Muramban, Mandikulam and Pudukkōttai.[1] It is not easy to say whether these monuments are to be traced to Buddhist or Jaina origins. The

[1] A note regarding most of these places will be found in Chapter XV.

so-called *Pancha Pāndava padukkai*, a set of stone beds carved out in a recess of a rock, at Marugāltalai, contains a Brāhmi inscription, and is believed on this account to be the work of Buddhists; the remaining monuments are generally attributed to Jains.

THE HINDUS.

The Hindus constitute the bulk of the population, and it remains to give some account of their manner of living, their religion and customs.

Villages.

The villages of the district conform as a rule to a more or less uniform type, consisting of blocks of houses, each inhabited by different castes and divided from one another by streets and lanes, which usually run from east to west or north to south. If the village possesses a tank or is situated near a river or channel, the houses cluster, as far as possible, near the waterside, with every facility at hand for bathing and drinking and for washing clothes. The houses of the Brahmans (if there are any) stand in one block, arranged as a rule in double rows facing one another across the street. Unlike the Vishnu temple which looks down the street, the temple of Siva should be a little distance away and is usually found in the north-east corner of the village. The Sūdra houses, grouped two or three together in separate compounds, form a compact block. If any particular caste is found in large numbers, it has its own distinct quarter; otherwise, Vellālans, Idaiyans, Maravans and so on inhabit the same region. The "half-polluting" castes, such as Iluvans and Shānāns, always have their separate habitations just outside the main villages; Pallans and Paraiyans live in a still remoter site, or *chēri*, consisting, in the river valley, of a mound of dry land surrounded by the wet fields in which they labour.

The Parava villages of the coast such as Manappād, Alantalai and Vīrapāndyanpatnam stand in a class by themselves and resemble rather small European towns than Indian villages.

Houses.

In the river valley tiled houses are almost the rule, only the houses of the poorer labourers being thatched. Even in *paracheris* tiled roofs are occasionally to be seen; and the thatched roofs of the proverbially poor weavers are rapidly disappearing. In the Tenkāsi taluk and in all villages lying along the foot of the hills in this and other taluks, in many of the richer villages in central and south-east Nānguneri, thatch has for many years past gradually been giving place to tiles. And this means, of course, that walls and ceiling must be substantial. All the better houses, most numerous in the rich villages of the river valley, are founded on a solid basement,

CHAP. III.
THE HINDUS.

the walls being made either of stone (especially when, as in the Ambāsamudram taluk, stone is plentiful and is quarried above the ground) or of bricks and mud. Kōngu *(Hopea parviflora)*, a timber which possesses a peculiar fascination for the people of this district, is largely used, even in preference to teak, for rafters, the latter wood serving for door-frames and windows. In the towns and in the smaller villages in which a good deal of wealth is concentrated (Brahmadēsam is a good example) houses run often to two or three storeys and are finished with great elaborateness. In the black soil country, where incendiarism is too common a pastime, substantial houses with Mangalore tiles are constantly replacing the old mud walls and thatch of cumbu stalks. In the ordinary unpretentious houses of the less well-to-do palmyras provide the rafters, mud the walls and an upper storey is rarer; the roof may be either thatched or tiled. The labouring classes everywhere and most of the poorer agriculturists live in small houses of mud and thatch.

When it is remembered that to a great extent every domestic act of a Hindu, especially of a Brahman, forms part of a prescribed ritual, it is not surprising to find that the houses of the Brahmans, on the one hand, and of the Sūdras, on the other, conform as a rule to a defined type. In a Brahman house the pial or raised verandah faces the street. This is often fenced in from the roof to the ground with a lattice of wood or iron, a row of houses presenting often the appearance of a series of menagerie cages. The front door opens from the street into a room *(ulluthinnai)*, along one side of which there is often a raised platform *(thinnai)*. Behind this comes a series of small rooms or compartments, a door on one side of the *ulluthinnai* leading into the first *rēli*, or hall, to the other side of which are a couple of store rooms; from the first *rēli* a door opens into the second *rēli*, which occupies the whole width of the house, and behind this is the kitchen on one side and on the other side the *nālām vāsal*, or lobby, leading to a small courtyard *(mittam)* open to the sky. Beyond this is a room *(pattāsālai)* which serves as the women's apartment, and next behind them live the cattle, which come in by the compound at the back. The pial is surrounded by a slanting roof, and over the *ulluthinnai* and the first *rēli* is usually an upper room; half of the second *rēli* is often terraced, the other half supporting a small attic. The upstair-rooms are used as grain stores.

The feature which at once distinguishes a Sūdra house is the absence of a regular verandah in front. A doorway in a front wall leads into an open courtyard *(mittam)* which is common to a number of houses, and within it, facing the house, is a raised platform *(kūdam)* with a pent-roof, which serves as the general lounge. The internal arrangements differ, but only slightly, from those of the houses of Brahmans.

The houses of the labouring and poorer classes are little more than square huts with one or two rooms.

The front door of almost every house, whatever caste may inhabit it, is daubed with numerous impressions of the open hand—palm, fingers and thumb. This decoration, which is laid on with flour paste, is said to commemorate Mahābali Rāja, "the Giant King." The god Vishnu, according to the familiar story, once appeared before Mahābali as a dwarf and craved three feet of the earth's space. The request was granted, and Vishnu, once more a god, proceeded to measure out his allotment. Two feet measured the whole length of the earth and, as the god sought to measure out the third, he thrust Mahābali down to the underworld, Pāthālam. Once a year, however, by the favour of Vishnu, this king is allowed to re-appear on earth, and in the month of Kārtigai, when his visit is expected, Hindus renew the impressions on their front-doors and light up their houses and streets. The impression of the hand—this seems to be the theory—is sure evidence that the Rāja has pushed open the door and entered.

The village community.

The small communities which inhabit these villages possess in themselves almost all the elements which should go to form a strong corporate spirit: a common temple and a choultry in which the villagers collect and gossip, a village watch and a company of artisans to whose support every one makes a rateable contribution, pasture-grounds, cattle-yards and threshing-floors common to all, often tanks and channels in the maintenance of which almost all alike have an interest. Sometimes there are village funds *(samudāyam)* derived from the proceeds of communal lands or from the annual sale in auction of the right to the fishery of the tank and from trees which are jointly owned by the whole community. In a few villages, particularly in the Srīvaikuntam and Tiruchendūr taluks, funds of comparatively recent origin, known as *oppadis*, are maintained by proportionate contributions from all land-owners. The money raised by these various methods is spent on the clearing of tanks and channels, the purchase and distribution of manure, the support of temple festivals, the feeding of travellers and sometimes, it is to be feared, in securing the favour of the lower ranks of the officials. Many of these funds, especially the *oppadis*, are well administered;

CHAP. III. THE HINDUS.

too frequently however their control passes into the hands of privileged classes, and complaints of misappropriation are not unknown.

And with all these inducements to co-operation it can scarcely be said that the average Tinnevelly village possesses the strength born of unity. General panchayats are practically unknown, disputes are too readily taken to the law-courts instead of being settled in the village, and the best efforts of the revenue and irrigation officers and of the police are often hampered by deep-seated faction. It is among the individual castes that the spirit of cohesion is most clearly seen. This often takes the practical form of a *mahimai*, or general fund, levied by each community for its own uses. In many villages, especially those in which Shānāns and Paravans preponderate, members of a caste collect small subscriptions from those who trade in the local markets; Kaikkilaiyans sometimes pay a fixed sum on every loom to a common purse, and Muhammadan weavers do the same; in Kallidaikurichi the Brahman capitalists have organized a regular fund of this kind. The objects of expenditure are usually the support of temples, mosques or churches owned by the contributors; occasionally the money is diverted to petitions or litigation in which the caste as a whole is interested.

Food.

Generally speaking, the staple food of the richer classes throughout the district is rice, the chief exception being the black soil country, where even the wealthier agriculturists usually prefer the "dry" grains, cumbu, cholam, *kādaikkanni* and ragi, which their fields produce. In those parts of the district which grow rice that grain forms the usual diet of all classes, even the poorest. Dry food-grains are seldom imported to any part of the district, and in those regions (such as south Nānguněri, south Tiruchendūr, north Srīvaikuntam and a great part of the Sankaranainārkōil taluk) which produce almost no paddy and very little dry grain, rice is obtained from the irrigated tracts for consumption by all classes. In western Tenkāsi cholam, which is there produced in such abundance, forms the staple diet of all but Brahmans and the wealthiest. Brahmans, as in other districts, invariably take rice, a local peculiarity being that the paddy is boiled before it is husked, instead of being pounded in its raw state. Rice so treated (known as *pulungal*) is believed to be more digestible and is more palatable as a cold food than rice treated in the ordinary way. Among his Tamil brethren in the north the rural Brahman of Tinnevelly, who cooks his food in earthen pots and prefers as a rule a cold supper at night to a hot one, has earned a reputation for frugal habits. While Brahmans go in for a hot dinner at noon, Sūdras and lower classes have their hot meal at night, preserving what is left over *(palaiyathu)* for consumption on the morrow at midday. The hot meals of Brahmans and the wealthier Sūdras consist of rice, dholl and ghee with a curry of vegetables (and, in the case of flesh-eaters, meat), pepper-water and butter-milk, the meals of the poorer classes being in proportion plainer. The old practice of taking *kanji*, or cold rice-water, in the early morning is rapidly giving way to coffee drinking, a degenerate innovation at which the older generation shake their heads. Even Pallans in some parts insist on having their cup of coffee before they go out to work; with the younger members of the richer classes the custom of drinking coffee is almost general. Palmyra juice *(pathanir)* in its season forms almost the staple food of the tapper, especially in those parts of the country which yield little else besides palmyras; and those who have had opportunities to observe declare that the climbers thrive better on this diet than on any other.

All Brahmans, most Vellālans and a number of other Sūdra castes are forbidden to take meat or liquor. Meat food seldom goes beyond fish, eggs and fowls, mutton being only an occasional luxury of the richer people. A drink of toddy often serves field labourers as their midday meal.

Amusements.

Grown up men and women seldom play games. *Pathinainthāmpulli*, which is something like "halma," is a quiet indoor game sometimes played by men; in one or two clubs a few play billiards, and of late years "bridge" has become distinctly popular. In the northern parts of the district, especially among the Kambalattāns, cock-fighting is a popular sport. Boys and girls have a number of pastimes, most of which have their rough equivalent in European countries. *Pachaikuthirai*, or "green horse," is the same as "leap-frog"; *kiliyanthattu*, a kind of "fox and geese," is an exciting game and very popular; *chadukudu* is similar. In *rājāmanthiri* each boy draws a ticket which shows the part he has to play—king, minister, thief, kāvalgār, and so on; the thief bolts, the kāvalgār gives chase, the minister makes enquiries and the king passes judgment. *Nilāpūchi* is a game rather like "prisoner's base," in which one party occupy the moonlight and one the shade; safety for one party is the shade, and as they run from one patch to another their adversaries try to catch them. Standing on one foot and kicking tamarind-pods in competition into squares, and a game like "dibs" played also with tamarind-pods, are instances of quieter games with which little boys and girls amuse themselves. Football and cricket are played in the secondary schools, and tennis is played by schoolboys and in a few men's clubs.

Religious life; Brahmanism.

The existence in the district of many important temples dedicated to Siva and Vishnu—at Tinnevelly, Tiruchendūr, Alvārtirunagari, Nānguneri, Tirukkurungudi, Pāpanāsam, Sankaranainārkōil, to name only a few—which attract annually thousands of worshippers, might suggest to the casual observer the omnipotence of Brahmanism and the gods to whose worship the Brahmans minister. In the social relations of life it is possible to point to the general rule which requires or prefers that Brahmans should officiate in all marriage ceremonies. In the villages in which Brahmans are found the traditional respect due to them both individually and as a class is still rendered, an attitude which the Brahmans are as a rule all the more able to command as the owners in many parts of the district of most of the better irrigated lands. Though the poor Brahman may in recent years have grown poorer, his richer brother, benefiting from the extraordinary rise of prices which the past generation has experienced, from the increase of foreign trade, the regulation of assessments which began forty years ago and their general moderateness, has raised his material resources to a position of security before unknown. These advantages, added to education, which has given him a preponderant position in the administration, assist the Brahmans indirectly in maintaining the social leadership and to some extent the religious authority which as a caste they claim to exercise.

In numberless small matters other castes pay them the flattery of imitation. A Vellālan who wants to command respect gives up meat; many Vellālans, like the Brahmans, perform daily worship in their own houses and study the writings of their Saints, as Brahmans read the Vēdas. The Pattunūlkārans pose as Brahmans and adopt many of their social customs; the Vāniyans adopt the peculiarly Brahmanical ceremony of *upanayanam;* the Kammālans go in for a *tāli* shaped like that of the Brahmans; the men wear threads and shave their faces clean to look like Brahmans, whilst the women adopt a Brahman fashion in their dress. Many of the humbler castes, Shānāns, Katasans, Savalaikkārans, affect disapproval of divorce and the remarriage of widows and seek to earn merit by a prolongation of their funeral ceremonies.

It must however be remembered that from another point of view these tendencies are only part of a process of beating the Brahman on his own ground. Vellālans havé now their own religious societies and in parts of the district have developed a strong sectarian spirit, whose aim is spiritual self-sufficiency, with a consequent disregard of the Brahman priesthood. They probably do not forget that, compared with themselves, the Brahmans generally are recent immigrants to the district. In Tinnevelly town itself, in many of the river-valley villages, in Tenkāsi and Nānguneri, distinct traditions survive which trace the origin of the Brahmans to settlements made by Pāndyan or even Nāyakkan rulers. And in spite of all the wealthy temples of Siva and Vishnu, the rich *matams*, the wealth and undoubted social influence of Brahmans, the religion of the great mass of the population remains essentially, in form and spirit, as purely Dravidian to-day as we may imagine it was before ever the Brahmans set foot in the country.

Dravidian forms of worship.

The accounts which will shortly be given of the hosts of lesser deities and of the enthusiasm with which they are worshipped may serve to show that the gods who for the mass of the people rule and direct their daily lives, who bring evil and can if willing remove it, who are intelligible beings—men on the grand scale—are not Siva and Vishnu, but Kāli in her various forms, and Sudalaimādan "and his horrid crew."

The Brahmans themselves have appreciated the situation. Their attitude is not one of opposition (that would indeed be futile and fatal) but of mild acquiescence and, to some extent, active approval. When a festival or *kodai* is to be performed in honour of a Kāli or of Sudalaimādan, a Brahman performs the initiatory ceremony of cleansing the idol; contributions to the rituals, which as a rule involve animal sacrifice, are received from the Brahmans as from others; in some cases the Brahman priest by his touch consecrates the sacrificial knife before the blood of the victim is spilled; and the dance in honour of Sāstā, which the Brahman himself performs, is certainly not of Vēdic origin. Many of the Dravidian gods have received the dignity of a pedigree which connects them with Siva or Vishnu; and in some cases spirits of the lower type have found their way into the circle of a Brahman's domestic gods. A pyramid of mud is found in his backyard, and to it, under the directions of the householder and at his expense, offerings of liquor and flesh are made. In regard to its spiritual masters aboriginal Tinnevelly has undoubtedly "led captivity captive"; respected and even venerated as Brahmans are, the religion they brought with them has not become the religion of the bulk of the people.

CHAP. III. THE HINDUS.

Minor deities: Ayyanār.

First in rank among the lesser deities comes Ayyanār, or Sāsta (as he is more usually called), who has a shrine in almost every village of the district. By his pedigree he is raised to the level of the great gods and called Hariharaputhra, his father being Siva and his mother Vishnu, who once took the form of a goddess. Represented in his image as a handsome youth with a wife on either side of him, he is known by a variety of local names differing from place to place. Sometimes a square block of stone does duty for an image or even, though rarely, a pyramid of earth. In his temple is placed an image of his son, Chella Pillai, and beside the son stands a retinue of servants, chief amongst whom is Sangili Būthattān—"pride in his port, defiance in his eye"—brandishing a club over his head. In the outer yard stands the gigantic and ferocious Ali, the Sāsta's watchman, and beside him, Karuppaswāmi, the hunter, the fore-runner of the god. His priests are Brahmans, where one can be found; otherwise Vēlāns or Othuvāns (Vellāla caste) do duty.

As elsewhere, Sāsta is here the god who brings rain in its season, and it is appropriate therefore to find his temple situated, as a rule, on the bund of a tank or beside a channel. He is also the general custodian of the village, and it is for the use of him and his followers in their task of riding round the fields at night to drive out disease, blight and evil spirits that the horses, dogs and elephants which face his shrine are provided by his grateful devotees. Master of the tribe of demons and hobgoblins, though not of them, he can reduce them to impotence. In Mānād and Kuthiraimoli (Tiruchendūr taluk) are two well-known Sāstās who frequently exchange visits. They are seen riding horses and elephants at night over the *tēri,* with a thousand torch-bearers in attendance and followed by packs of dogs, the whole train appearing and re-appearing like summer-lightning.

As a family deity, Sāsta occupies a peculiarly important position and in this capacity especially is worshipped by people of all castes. Families, either singly or in groups, look up to some particular Sāsta as their household god, styling themselves his servants *(adimaikārar)*. Those who have moved from one village to another continue, even after the memory of the migration has long passed away, to visit the Sāsta of their original home and to make offerings; such as cannot go or send a representative of their family ask friends to take their contributions. The district is singular in possessing some Sāstās who are far more than family gods and village guardians and on the occasions of their festivals attract crowds from all parts. Amongst these are the Sorimuthayyan, whose temple is on the right bank of the Tāmbraparni, three miles above the Pāpanāsam falls, Pūlā-udaiyār of Sīvalappēri (Tinnevelly taluk), and the Chittūr Sāstā of Kannanallūr (Nānguneri taluk).

His festivals.

The festival—the Sāstāprīthi, as it is called—of all Sāstās is performed at various seasons, the *Panguni Uttiram*, or failing that any Saturday, being preferred. In the morning the image is washed with water, milk and the juice of fruits, and decorated; offerings of rice, milk and sugar are made, and the afternoon is given over to feeding. In the evening the grand ceremony begins. The image is purified again and plastered with sandal-paste, the features of the god are picked out with colours, jewels and chaplets of flowers are hung about him and offerings of sugar-cane, in which Sāstā specially delights, fruit and rice are placed before him.

The lamps are swung and the dance begins. Four "kōmarattādis"[1] or prophets—they are all Brahmans as a rule—stand forth, impersonating Sāstā, Chella Pillai his son, and his two servants Sangili Bhūthattān and Yakshi. Pots of burning camphor are set beside them, and as they breathe its fumes the afflatus of the god or of his servants possesses them. A party of musicians recites the stories of the birth and exploits of Sāstā and his retinue; the kōmarattādis are moved; they shout and jump and bang their hands on the wall or floor—sure sign that the god has taken possession. The bystanders run forward and seize the very present deity by the arms to hold him steady; he shakes them off, declares his godhead and utters prophecies. The worshippers ply him with questions, stating their troubles and asking for remedies; the god replies and the questioner is satisfied. The servants of the god are still more frantic, but do not prophesy. When all have had enough, the kōmarattādis are taken in procession to the river where they bathe; returning to the temple, the kōmarattādi of the god continues for a while to prophesy and then distributes sacred ashes to the worshippers. All four fall prostrate before the god and are relieved of their possession (*kōmaram*). The offerings placed before the god are distributed and the Sāstā's festival is over. A shrine of Sudalaimādan and his fellows is often just beside the Sāstā temple; a festival (or *kodai*) in their honour is generally arranged for these occasions, and, as the Sāstā's rites are closing, the wild ceremonies of the *kodai* are well in progress.

[1] That is, "one who is inspired"; *kōmaram*, "possession" or "inspiration."

CHAP. III. THE HINDUS. Ammans.

Midway between the orthodox gods and the demons (described further on) come the female deities or Ammans, whose worship is an interesting blend of brahmanical and Dravidian ritual. These goddesses have their own proper pūjāris, either Ochans or Vellālans (who in this capacity assume the title of "Othuvamūrti"); and in the more important temples daily pūja is performed. On feast days a Brahman usually officiates as priest. Their non-brahmanical character is seen in the fact that on days of festival they are given offerings of rice, meat and liquor and are honoured by the sacrifice of sheep and even (at Palamcotta and Gangaikondān [1]) buffaloes.

In front of the Amman's temple an array of minor deities of the demon class will invariably be found; and often the more orthodox will seek to explain that it is for them, not for the Amman, that the meat-offerings and animal sacrifices are made. Popular belief, however, does not support this theory; and there can be no reasonable doubt that for all practical purposes it is the Amman who is the object of these unorthodox rituals. Ammans who receive no flesh offerings are to be found everywhere; but the vast majority, those who under various names are manifestations of Kāli, exact blood. Badrakāli is the prototype of these goddesses, a terrible creature, whose appearance is described in the invocation recited at the time of her festival by the pūjāri:

"Come, come in haste, O goddess, with thy locks bedraggled, thou who hast three eyes, whose skin is dark, whose clothes are stained with blood, who hast rings in thy ears, who hast a thousand hands, and ridest upon a monster and wieldest in thy hands tridents, clubs, lances and shields."

Uchinimākāli, Muttāra, Ulaga, Muppidāri—these are some of the commonest of the innumerable names by which the Kāli is known in the district. Epidemics are the speciality of Uchinimākāli-amman (as of Māri-amman in Tanjore); she can inflict small-pox and cholera but also, if appeased, she can remove them. Ulagamman has the power of making the human race fertile, and it is pathetic to see that the Kōttai Vellālans [2] have recently made a somewhat tardy attempt to stave off extinction by establishing just beside their fort a temple for this goddess.

The Grāmadēvatas.

It is however as "Grāmadēvatas," general guardians of the village, that these deities play their most important part. Standing on the limits of the village and facing (almost

[1] The goddess in both these temples is Ayirattamman.

[2] See pp. 438–439.

invariably) the north, whence alone all calamities come, they are the first objects of attention with all castes when any crisis occurs or is feared in the village or in the family. If disease breaks out, a *kodai*, or festival, is performed; individual sufferers promise to place models of their bodies or single limbs in the Amman's temple, provided they are cured; women with child promise to give bangles or cradles if they are safely delivered and to call the child by the goddess's own name. Others in distress vow to make offerings of rice, milk and cocoanut or a sheep at the next festival. In most villages there are many temples, sometimes one to each street, dedicated to Kāli Amman under her various names; but one Amman is usually regarded as pre-eminently the village guardian.

Many Ammans have more than a local reputation; and perhaps the most famous of all is Muttumālai of Korunganni, a hamlet of Māvadippannai (Tiruchendūr taluk), in whose temple beside the river thousands of sheep are sacrificed at the time of her festival in May.

Festivals.

An *ammankodai* is an elaborate business and often lasts for three days. The last day marks the climax, and at midday all turn out to see the procession of professional dancers who, balancing on their heads pots containing water or fire and decorated with flowers and tinsel, amuse the crowd and induce them to make contributions. At midnight meat-offerings and a decoction of toddy are carried round the village and brought back to the temple and there offered to the goddess. The sacrifice of sheep and fowls then begins; the heads are severed at one blow and placed on the *balipītam* in front of the shrine. Music, dancing and "prophesying" follow; the dancer, or kōmarattādi, receives the inspiration of the goddess and often performs marvellous feats. Hook-swinging was at one time common on these occasions; in the festivals of Draupadi Amman (as at Vīravanallūr) the dancer walks through fire; in Udaiyārpatti (near Tinnevelly) the villagers speak with regret of a kōmarattādi who, under the influence of the goddess, used to produce iron chains from his mouth and swallow them again. As a rule the performance is limited to acrobatic dancing.

Other forms of worship: the "Ettelut-tu-mārgam."

A curious sect of people whose chief place of worship is Chettiyārpattu in the centre of the *tēri* country of the Tiruchendūr taluk is that composed of the followers of the "Eight-letter" persuasion. There are six shrines within the temple precincts, the most important of which is that dedicated to Attiswāmi. This god delights in all kinds of flesh offerings,

CHAP. III. THE HINDUS.

but most acceptable of all is a pig. A devotee who wishes to offer such a sacrifice has only to whisper in the ear of his chosen victim a few mystic words, and of its own accord the animal will start and—accompanied by the votary—will find its way to the god's shrine. The priest who conducts the ceremonies of the temple is a *paradēsi*, or ascetic, but may be of any caste. The floor in front of the shrine is strewn with a layer of red powder and on it a diagram, as illustrated, is drawn.

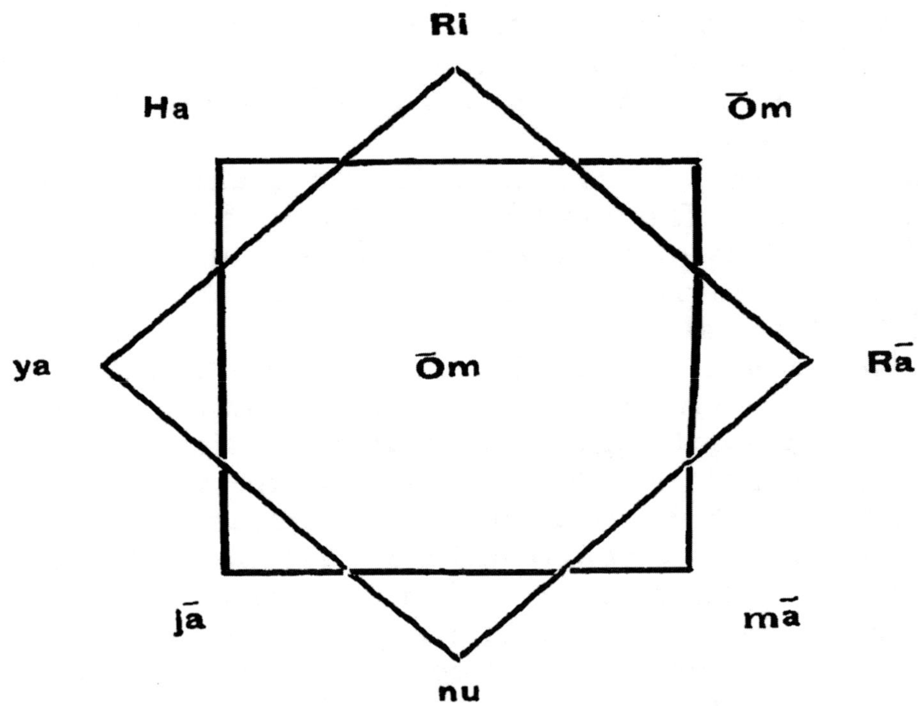

The eight letters (a consonant with a vowel following form in Tamil one letter) at the corners of the squares starting with *Ha* form an invocation to the great apostle of the Vaishnavite religion: *Hari Om Rāmānujāya.* Eight arecanuts and eight betel leaves are placed on the diagram and a decorated bottle of arrack is set in the middle. When the pūja is over, the bottle is opened and its contents distributed to all. Meats and other offerings are also distributed; and then all lie down together for the night in the temple-yard.

Followers of the faith are contributed by practically every caste (Shānāns are the most numerous), and the remarkable feature of their ritual is that all eat and drink together. No unpleasant social consequences follow. The temporary abrogation of caste rules is one of the principles of this queer sect. "Oh Goddess," runs their hymn, "there is no Holy Scripture higher than thou art, no place which thou dost not inhabit, no wisdom or knowledge besides thee. Thou art the leader of a faith that transcends all caste differences. I am thy devoted and unworthy slave."

The goddess is apparently Sakti, the basis of a wide-spread form of worship usually associated with extreme Saivism. The adherents of the sect, however, all claim to be Vaishnavites, and in some places converts to the faith are made to take Vaishnavite names. In keeping with the mysterious nature of the sect is their habit of referring to things connected with the rituals by cryptic names: arrack is "holy water"; pig is "master"; skin (of the animal) is "coat"; sheep is "the walker"; a spoon is "the accountant"; and there are many others. "Eight-letter" people are found in all parts of the district; thousands are said to attend the two festivals held each year in Chettiyārpattu, but it is impossible to estimate the numbers of the sect.

The demon-gods.

No visitor to the district can fail to notice the numberless truncated, often shapeless, obelisks of brick or plastered mud, which are to be seen almost everywhere—on the roadside, on waste grounds (which generally prove to be places of cremation), on mounds standing dry above the paddy fields, often in the half shade of a withered—looking thorn-tree, in the village lanes and even in the backyards of inhabited houses. Often these rude pyramids stand in groups or clusters of groups; they are placed as a rule on a pedestal cut into two or three steps, and they vary in height from two feet to ten from top to base. A ferocious human figure may be depicted in colours on one face of the pyramid; often one face bears at least a crescent and dot, much like the emblem of the Turkish empire; sometimes all the faces are perfectly plain. These are the symbols—*pūdams* they are called—of the innumerable gods or devils (according to the point of view) which, to judge by their ubiquity, the enthusiasm which their festivals excite and the close relations they are believed to have with mankind in almost all his doings, are the chief objects of worship among the masses of the people. They are in fact the old Dravidian deities whose power, despite the invasion of Brahmanism, remains undiminished to the present day. Again, in front of the temples of the Grāma dēvatas and of Sāsta, occasionally in their own rough structures of mud and thatch or within the enclosure of a mud wall, groups of stone images of all sizes will be seen, some standing on stone platforms, others on the ground in circles, squares or irregular lines. These figures represent the same gods; and with them may be *pūdams* and sometimes square or

CHAP. III. THE HINDUS.

rounded blocks of stone intermingled. It is only an expert—even the villagers cannot as a rule agree—who can decide what deity each *pūdam* in a group represents; some are pre-eminent by their size, a few have unmistakable marks and often a certain order or arrangement is observed; but, speaking generally, *pūdams* are all as much like one another as mud-pies.

The characteristics common to all these godlings—*pēy*, that is "demon" or "spirit", is their generic name—are that they delight in the sacrifice of animals, their festivals are invariably accompanied by a dance performed by one whom the demon possesses for the occasion, they go about the world giving trouble, and they have no priests and (with few exceptions) no temples. If not propitiated, they inflict disease on men and cattle; they attack lonely women, especially if they are with child; night and midday are the worst times and the blackest days are Tuesday and Friday. Margosa leaves in such cases carried in the hand do some good; but flowers are merely an invitation to the malign influences of these spirits.

In some parts of the district—roughly speaking the Kōilpatti taluk, where the bulk of the population consists of the Telugu Kammavans and Kambalattāns, and the northern part of the Sankaranainārkōil taluk—the worship of these deities is very rare indeed. Elsewhere all classes of Sūdras, Pallans and Paraiyans indulge in it.[1] Maravans and Idaiyans are perhaps the greatest enthusiasts, and it would be difficult to find a settlement of either of these castes without its group of demons. Every *pēykōil* (that is a cluster of *pēys*) is the property of some particular caste; and from that community will be provided the funds required for festivals, the controllers of the rituals and (as a rule) the "kōmarattādi", or dancer. The pūjāri whose duty is to perform sacrifice may be of any caste other than Brahman; daily service is extremely rare, the important act of worship being the *kodai* which occurs as a rule once or twice in a year.

Names and characteristics of some.

The names of these hobgoblin deities are countless, and it would be tedious to enumerate and describe many of them. There is no doubt they differ in status, as they do in character, form and (to some extent) functions; but an attempt to classify

[1] The Sudalaimādan of Sīvalappēri, the prototype, according to some, of all the Sudalaimādans of the district, is worshipped as a "household deity" by some Brahmans. The *pūdams* found in the backyards of some Brahman houses (referred to on page 107) appear to represent deities of the type referred to in this section.

even the better known amongst them might savour of presumptuousness. Standing in the first rank and king among a company of five[1] is Sudalaimādaswāmi, for whom a pedigree, tracing his descent from Siva, has been prepared. In all *pēykōils* he has the place of honour; whether he be in the form of a *pūdam* or an image, he is the biggest. He wears a high hat rather like that of an archbishop or a Parsee; he has a fierce moustache and gleaming eyes, in his right hand he brandishes a short sword and his left hand rests on a thick club. But in actual life he assumes many forms; he is seen as an elephant, as a man riding on a white horse in coat and breeches, as a great white bull trampling down the crops, as a pig, as a bear—"omnia transformans sese in miracula rerum"—he is Protean. He is heard screaming at night. His sharp cry calls Mundaswāmi, his brother and subordinate, to attention; something wrong has happened, it means, and a *kodai* must be performed. Sheep and pigs are the sacrifices in which he delights; the heart and the unborn young cut out and laid before him, and the *tiralai*[2], performed at the burning-ground, will alone appease his passion.

Mundaswāmi, on the other hand, is a low grovelling creature like a pig and is very ferocious. Karuppaswāmi (his pedigree goes back to Vishnu) in his images is armed like Sudalaimādaswāmi. His hair, beneath a turban shaped to fit it, is bunched up into a knot on the left side of his head; round his neck are strings of beads, which reach below his waist, and a dog often stands at his side. He is a great hunter and (as has been seen) is one of Sāstā's outriders. Irulappan (descended from Brahma) has little individuality. Sivananainjaperumāl was created by Siva for the express purpose of picking red flowers at dawn. Duped by Vishnu, he failed in this task one day and was consequently sent with a curse to earth by his creator. Bad policy though it may seem to recall so unpleasant an incident, all things connected with his rituals are red. The sheep slain in his honour are red, and the time of sacrifice must be dawn, when the sky is red; his image is adorned on feast days with red flowers and red cloths, and is smeared with red paint.

Associated with these five are two demonesses, Pēchi and Brahmarākshasi. They were on earth from the beginning of things, and were appointed by Siva to be the foster-mothers of Sudalamādaswāmi, when he was banished from Kailāsam. Pēchi is a horrible and dangerous creature. Corpses and

[1] The other four are Mundan, Karuppan, Irulappan, and Sivananainjaperumāl.

[2] See p. 118.

CHAP. III. THE HINDUS.

babies are her favourite food; and she is generally represented as eating one infant with others ready to follow. In one place at least (Ottapidāram) she has a skull in one hand and a string of skulls round her body. Brahmarākshasi, associated in song with Pēchi, has similar tastes. The two are usually placed on either side of Sudalaimādan, their foster-son, Brahmarākshasi on the right and Pēchi on the left.

Others.

This company of seven is found in almost every *pēykōil*; their personalities are familiar to everyone and the distinguishing details of the rituals due to each are everywhere understood and observed. Others, like Isàkki, have no distinguished ancestry, or are known and worshipped only here and there. Isakki is a powerful she-devil of exceptional wickedness and widespread fame. She was once the concubine of a Brahman, who in revenge for her treachery took her life. To this day she is seen going about in the guise of a beautiful dancing-girl of sixteen, and at midday may be heard weeping. She decoys young men and women that cross her path and, having got them into her snares, brings untold misery upon them. Her images represent her, like Pēchi, eating infants; by her side is usually a box in which many, to avert worse evils, drop their pice. Bangles, winnowing-fans and models of the demoness herself are given to her in fulfilment of vows; and, to judge by the continual increase in the number of her shrines, Isakki may claim to be the most dreaded of the demon-tribe. Padhalakandi-amman, a virgin, is found chiefly in the form of a *pūdam*; occasionally (as in Kayattār) she is represented as peeping out from the nether-world, which she inhabits, half her head alone appearing above the ground. Dalavāy Nallamādan *alias* Komba Mādan, "horned Mādan," represented in his images with a bull's head, Karadimādan, with a bear's face, and Pannimādan, with a pig's face, are particular manifestations of Sudalaimādan; in these capacities he often has a wife placed beside him, whose face is either similar or borrowed from another animal.

The Pisāchas.

Besides the demons who have names (only a few have been enumerated) there are the hosts of *bhūthams* or *pisāchas*, nameless spirits or hobgoblins, who wander about the earth giving trouble and seeking to be "laid." They are subordinate to Sudalaimādan, who can, and, if properly treated, will, control them. They are, it is said, the spirits of men who have met with violent deaths; they haunt the burning grounds and all desolate places, above all, the grim *tēris*. Trees, especially those that stand near *pēykōils*, are infested by them; and lest the spirits should be disturbed, the leaves of such trees are not cut. Smears of saffron are sometimes daubed on trees by way of honouring the "spirit of the grove."

Festivals of the Mādan tribe.

The propitiation which Sudalaimādan and his retinue demand is usually concentrated on the time of their occasional festivals. Offerings, mostly of the mild type, rice, ghee and cocoanuts, are made at any time by a devotee to suit a particular occasion; vows are taken and *ex voto* symbols are placed before the images. Most vows, however, are fulfilled at the time of the festivals, when each person, according to the promise made, brings an animal to be slaughtered.

A festival which lasts for three days is called a *kodai;* a one-day festival is a *padukkai*. Strictly speaking, a festival of some kind should occur twice a year; often only one is held, and sometimes even that falls through. A *kodai* conducted on a grand scale is a very expensive affair and may cost its promoters as much as two or three thousand rupees. Sometimes it is done at the expense of one or more worshippers by way of fulfilment of vows; more often the caste owning the temple meets the expense by the levy of contributions. After the idols or *pūdams*, as the case may be, have been purified by a Brahman priest, the festival is ready to begin. The villagers and visitors are welcomed by a song from the musicians, and then follows an orgy of animal sacrifice (with which often human blood is mingled) music and dancing, which continues at intervals till the morning of the third day; the climax of excitement is then reached and the *kodai* ends.

The animal sacrifice.

The right to slay the victim and, consequently, to appropriate its head rests with the village *kāvalgār*, who is usually a Maravan; the refusal of this right implies a denial of the *kāval* claim and has been known to lead to trouble. In the absence of a *kāvalgār*, the pūjāri or any willing substitute performs the act of sacrifice. The slaughter is attended by a ritual, which varies from place to place. Water is sometimes poured over the victim, a goat, a sheep or a pig, before it is slain; if the animal shivers, the omen is acclaimed. The animals are then strapped on to a wooden frame, and the bodies are split open lengthwise. The hearts are taken out and placed on leaves, one before each deity. The kōmarattādi [1] (or, if there are several, the chief among them) stoops down and drinks the blood flowing from the hearts of the animals. Sometimes the blood is let down into a pit and mixed with water; the kōmarattādi gets into the pit and drinks some of the mixture; a few of the bystanders run

[1] The office is hereditary and is held sometimes by boys and even women.

CHAP. III. THE HINDUS.

forward with plantains, soak them in the blood of the victims and give them to the kōmarattādi to eat. Human blood is contributed by the Kaniyāns [1], one or two of whom lend their services on the occasion of most *kodais*. They are not kōmarattādis, but, like them, they dance and sing under the inspiration of the deities. When his frenzy is at its height, the Kaniyān takes a knife and cuts his arm till the blood flows. Plantain leaves (fifty-one is the correct number) are laid out to receive the drops ; the kōmarattādis catch some of the stream in their hands and drink.

A remarkable item on the programme of many *kodais* is what is known as the *tiralai*. Towards midnight on the day of festival the kōmarattādis accompanied by the Kaniyāns with their drums march off to the burning-ground, bearing in a pot the *tiralai*, a dumpling of rice and meat. A sheep and a pig (which become the perquisites of the Kaniyān) are slain; their blood mixed with another contribution from the arms of the Kaniyāns is drunk by the kōmarattādis. One of the Kaniyāns then takes the *tiralai* and throws it over his shoulder in the air. It never falls to the ground; for Sudalaimādan, the haunter of burning-grounds, in whose honour the rite is done, invariably catches it.

It is on the return of this party to the place of revelry that the music and dancing which have gone on at intervals by day and night throughout the festival attain their highest pitch of fury.

The devil-dance.

The chief instrument of music (if the word may be used) is the *vil*, or bow. A number of bells of varying sizes is fastened to the frame of an enormous bow, the string of which is tightened so as to produce a twang when struck. One man has a plectrum and plays this instrument, whilst another beats with a flat blade of wood on the mouth of an earthen pot attached to the bow. A third man bangs a pair of cymbals, another blows a trumpet, others beat drums. Beside these sit the choir, who sing songs dealing with the exploits of the deities; the leader sings his solo and the rest take up the refrain. The resultant noise added to the taste of blood and liquor provide the dancer with his inspiration. The kōmarattādi is dressed to represent the deity whom he honours and whose personality he will presently assume. A highly decorated cap, with three conical peaks, tails of shaggy hair, a hatchet in his right hand, a spear with jingling bells in his

[1] The caste of Kaniyān is generally graded below the Sūdras and above the Pallans and Paraiyans.

left, a gaudy jacket and breeches worked with figures of demons, bells on his ankles—these, subject to variations, are the trappings of Sudalaimādan and his fellows. The female deities are represented by men or women, and women (though rarely) impersonate gods.

At first, when the devil-dance is beginning, the accompaniment is slow; the dancer starts with a few convulsive movements, which, as the music quickens and his inspiration grows, develop into more excited leaps and plunges. The music becomes louder and faster, and the dancer's antics grow more furious; the god is not far off. A flaming torch is handed to him, and to increase his frenzy he applies the fire to his breast and face. The pace rises to madness, the musicians bang and thump and scream; the Kaniyāns dressed as men and women come in beating their cylindrical drums and throw themselves madly about; the kōmarattādi is now possessed. His personality is in abeyance, his movements and speech are completely under the deity's control. He is regarded by all as a god and answers out of the fullness of his superhuman knowledge all the questions with which the bystanders ply him.

Origin of the "Mādans."

A "rationalistic" explanation commonly given of the origin of these demons is that, like the *bhūthams* and *pisāchas*, they are the troubled spirits of men and women who died by violence or were terrible in their lives. The theory, which is two-fold, is probable enough and possibly would fit most cases. The nameless *pisāchas* are almost certainly to be accounted for in this way; the *kuladeyvams*, or "household gods", are said to commemorate unnatural deaths; and occasionally other *pūdams* can be found for which a definite explanation of this kind is offered. In front of the temple of Sudalaimādan in Ittamoli (Nānguнēri taluk) is a flat unornamented slab of stone, placed there, the villagers say, in memory of a European who came from Travancore "in the days of Khān Sāhib" and lost his life fighting on the *tēri*. The details of the incident are completely lost; the known facts are that the person commemorated was a European and died a violent death. The *pūdam*—as it is called—does not cover his place of burial, but serves as a mark to which men may repair to "lay" the ghost of the deceased. For this purpose offerings are made, from time to time, suitable to the taste of the departed—bread, fowls, cheroots and brandy.[1] At Kayattār offerings are made to Kattaboma Nāyakkan

[1] See also the section on Mānūr, p. 476.

CHAP. III. THE HINDUS.

on the spot where he was hanged in 1799; a *pūdam* has not yet been formed, but is almost certain to arrive in time. Whether Sudalaimādan and his train are to be traced to similar origins, it is impossible to say.

Vows.

Vows are the means by which a worshipper seeks to interest the deity in his mundane affairs and to obtain divine blessing or guidance. A pinch of sacred ashes, some turmeric and money, and perhaps an ornament, are taken and tied up in a cloth, and a solemn promise is made that, if the particular object of the devotee's desire is accomplished, an offering, of which the coins and ornament are as it were the earnest-money, will be made to the deity. Vow-takers are people in sickness, women in child-birth, persons whose cattle are sick, and, when an epidemic is prevalent, those who fear its attack. Amongst the larger temples the most popular with vow-takers are those at Tiruchendūr and Pāpanāsam; and in all of them *ex voto* cradles, images of babies and models of limbs affected by disease may be seen hanging in fulfilment of promises made to the god; in the temples of Sankaranainārkōil and Tiruppudaimarudūr the goddess Gōmati Amman has a great reputation among women and receives in consequence innumerable presents from her thankful worshippers.

But it is to the village goddess, Kāliamman in her numerous manifestations, that vows are most commonly made. Whilst small-pox or cholera is prevailing and the goddess, as the belief is, is playing with the disease, vows are taken both by the sufferers and by those who as yet have escaped—perhaps a sheep to be sacrificed at the next festival or models of limbs in brass, silver or gold, or a figure in pottery of the Amman herself to be placed before her shrine. In gratitude for safe delivery a mother gives bangles to the goddess; if children or calves are sick, money is sent to the Amman's temple so that offerings of cocoanut and rice may be made. Vows too are made to Sudalaimādan and his brethren, not so much to avert special calamities as to secure general prosperity. Isakki, as has been seen, and Pēchi also, receive *ex voto* offerings in plenty.

THE PRINCIPAL CASTES.

At the census of 1901 as many as sixty-five distinct castes were enumerated in the district.[1] The social and religious characteristics of a large number of these communities have been investigated in all parts of the district; but space permits of a more or less detailed account of only a few of them. The Paravans, though belonging without exception to the Roman Catholic communion, form a society which has

[1] At the census of 1911 separate figures were not recorded for all castes.

CHAP. III. THE PRINCIPAL CASTES.

all the characteristics of a caste and have consequently been included in the descriptions which follow. They, as well as the Iluvans and Katasans, are found either solely or almost solely in this district and on that account specially deserve mention. The other castes dealt with have been selected as being numerically or in other respects important.

PARAVANS.

Paravans are found chiefly in Tuticorin (where they constitute about one-fourth of the population) and, to the practical exclusion of all other castes, in a number of sea-coast villages in the Nānguneri, Tiruchendūr, Srīvaikuntam and Kōilpatti taluks. Scattered colonies are found also in several villages in the interior of the district. They have never been officially enumerated; thirty thousand is an approximate figure. The only other districts in which members of the castes are found are Rāmnād and Madura; and with the exception of a very few in those districts who are Protestant Christians the entire community is Roman Catholic.

Their Christianity.

Their Christianity dates[1] from 1532, and the miracles wrought by St. Francis Xavier, who baptized their ancestors in thousands, are still related in the villages.[2] At the present time the Paravans of the district are distributed unequally between the episcopal jurisdictions of Trichinopoly and Mylapore, some few villages containing congregations of both sections.[3] Their numerous handsome churches, especially conspicuous at intervals along the sea-coast, are only the external signs of the devotion of the caste to their adopted religion. Congregations are almost everywhere self-supporting; and in the coast villages, where fishing is the chief occupation of the poorer members of the community, contributions levied rateably on the daily catch of fishes are paid to a common fund *(mahimai)* for the support of the church.

Their occupations.

The richer members of the community are traders, brokers, contractors and boat-owners. Their usual method of trade is to migrate to Ceylon, where they set up as importers of goods from the Indian mainland and as general dealers in all kinds of grocery and haberdashery. The merchant leaves his family behind and, after an absence of a year or less, is relieved by another member of his family. As may be judged from their many well-built and commodious houses which form so striking a feature of their sea-coast settlements, Tuticorin, Vīrapāndyanpatnam, Manappād and Periyatālai,

[1] See pp. 88–89.

[2] In one coast village (Kūttapulli) it is related that St. Francis Xavier hung up a light by a chain made of sea-water.

[3] See p. 93.

CHAP. III. PARAVANS.

they study comfort to a degree almost unknown among other communities of the district. As a class they are shrewd men of business, intelligent and public-spirited; comparatively few have gone in for English education and for the learned professions.

The poorer classes follow the traditional occupations of the caste: fishing and sailing, diving for chanks and pearls, and cutting coral-stone from the bed of the sea. Evidence of their general hardihood is seen in their ability to carry their catches of sea-fish day after day to enormous distances into the interior of the country. There are no cultivators among them. As a community they are far too fond of drink, a vice which some of their leaders deplore and are attempting, though with little success, to check. To this habit is ascribed their growing inferiority to Arabs as divers, a fact which recent fisheries have proved.

History of the caste.

According to their own account they are descendants of king Bharata (Parava is said to be a corruption of this name) of the lunar race who ruled in Oudh, and in support of their tradition they refer to their custom of displaying at their marriage-feasts banners and emblems peculiar to the distinguished race to which they belong. They make their first appearance in history as fishermen and divers for pearls; and some account of the fortunes of the caste under their successive masters, Pāndyan, Portuguese and Dutch, will be found in Chapter VI (pp. 230 follg.). To the present day the leaders of the community cherish pleasant traditions of the consideration with which they were treated by the Portuguese officials; the Portuguese surnames which were universally adopted are still preserved; and their headman, the Jāthitalavaimore, owes to the Viceroy of Goa the distinguished address "Don" which he still prefixes to his name and also, apparently, the honorific suffix of his title.[1] The Dutch, who took Tuticorin in 1658, did their utmost, but entirely failed, to suppress the Roman Catholicism which the Portuguese had imposed on their former subjects.

Their head-man.

The Jāthitalavaimore, whose office is hereditary, is the secular headman of the caste; he enjoys the dignity of a specially distinctive dress and commands considerable respect among the bulk of the Parava community. Under the Dutch succession to the post required the ratification of Government, a practice which in early days the English Government continued; at the present time the appointment is left entirely

[1] The Tamil form is, correctly, Jāthitalaivan.

to the community to settle, official recognition limiting itself to the understanding that the duly-constituted headman undertakes the privileges and responsibilities connected with the pearl-fishery.[1] In almost all the Parava settlements (Tuticorin is a partial exception) the authority of the Jāthitalavaimore is accepted without question. His deputies, known as Adappans (with their assistants, Sittāttis) or Pattangattis, are found in every village; they are the nominees of the Jāthitalavaimore and perform the duties of settling social disputes and collecting *kānikkai*, or contributions, for their master's support.

In Tuticorin, however, the upper circles of Parava society are divided between those who support the authority of the Jāthitalavaimore and those who do not. The adherents of this chief are generally known as *Mēsaikārar*, i.e., "those who eat at a table," a practice derived by the Paravans from their intercourse with the Portuguese. The Jāthitalavaimore upholds this custom; and the word has consequently come to imply in a general sense not only those who by their habits are in a position to dine with the Jāthitalavaimore but also, generally, his supporters. This class consists mostly of well-to-do merchants; and in opposition to them is the party, sometimes called *Kamārakkārar*, also consisting partly of merchants but including boat-owners and others, who impugn the authority of their professed caste-leader and resent his social interdictions. The poorer classes, composed of fishermen, sailors and divers, who constitute about one-half of the local Parava population, though they cannot aspire to be *Mēsaikārar*, are apparently as a whole supporters of the Jāthitalavaimore. The literal distinction between *Mēsaikārar*, "those who eat at tables," and others who do not, is found in other Parava villages but does not appear to imply any division of feeling with regard to the authority of the Jāthitalavaimore. Roughly speaking, merchants are *Mēsaikārar*, boatmen and fishermen are not.

Marriages.

The marriage of a member of the upper classes is conducted with much ceremony. The ritual is in many essential features similar to that observed by the Hindus, and dates, no doubt, from the time when the Paravans were a Hindu caste. A peculiar feature of the wedding is the procession from the church (where the rite of marriage is performed) to the bride's house with *virudhus* or banners, supposed to be the insignia of the kingly ancestors of the race. The emblems consist of

[1] See again p. 234.

CHAP. III. PARAVANS.

twenty-one flags embroidered with representations of various objects, animate and inanimate, such as a snake, a peacock, a palmyra, a chank, the sun, an elephant, a fish, and so on. In addition to these a large umbrella, a shield and other trappings are carried. The bridegroom wears a costume called *kapa*, resembling the state robes of the Jāthitalavaimore, and white cloths are spread before him in his path.

The 'Vāsapadi Mariyal."

Being no longer Hindus, they do not observe the *morai* system by which a man should always marry, where possible, a particular relation; but a picturesque ceremony which points to the former observance of this rule is still occasionally performed. It is known as the "Vāsapadi Mariyal"—"obstruction of the entrance"—and consists in a mock contest of words between the bridegroom and the bride's cousin, who, according to the *morai* rule, should have taken her in marriage. When the bridegroom reaches the bride's house, after the church ceremony is over, the "*morai* candidate" appears and asks:—

Tell me why you came here in procession through the town
With garlands of sweet-scented flowers—
Attired like a bridegroom in head-dress and new cloths
With a scarf over all to match.

Bridegroom—

Hear, you assembly of Catholics, the justness of my cause!
In the glorious church, dedicated to the Virgin, Our Lady of the Snows,
Our holy priest gave me a bride this morning in marriage;
To seek for that bride have I come.

Morai-bridegroom—

Meet and right is it that you should come:
But why comes not the bridegroom all this while since the marriage was made?
What means all this pompous procession with torches,
This spreading of carpets, these banners and this great gathering?

Bridegroom—

Hear the reason of my coming.
It is the will of Jesus our Saviour that I take the bride to be my wife.
A truce to your prating vainglorious chatter!
Bring out the bride to the marriage-tent.

Morai-bridegroom—

The bride in the tent is my rightful bride.
Give me a thousand pieces of gold,
Elephants, horses, and cows with calves,
And I give her to you to be your wife.

Bridegroom—

At sunrise tomorrow I give all that you ask;
In token of my promise I surrender this gold ring
You know well, as the old poetess Auvaiyar says;
In making gifts we are the foremost.

SHĀNĀNS.

The Shānāns, best known as the great palmyra-climbing and toddy-drawing caste of the district, number 15 per cent of the population.

"Not content to pollute without eating beef,"[1] writes Mr. Molony in the census report of 1911, "they claim to be Kshatriyas." In the decade 1891 to 1911 the "Kshatriyas" of the Madura, Rāmnād and Tinnevelly districts increased by as much as 63 per cent, and it is evident that the exceptional growth of this caste (of which there are, so far as is known, no true representatives in these districts) is to be explained by the growing habit among Shānāns of arrogating to themselves this pretentious description. In spite of these "defections" however and of the conversion of some to Christianity (how many is impossible to say) the caste as a whole increased between 1901 and 1911 by 8 per cent.

Their aspirations.

The endeavours of the caste to obtain a status in Hindu society higher than other Hindus are willing to allow them and in particular their efforts to attain recognition as Kshatriyas have a long history; and within the last fifteen years their pretensions have been elaborately set out in written statements. Pamphlets on the subject, originating from a member of the caste living near Nazareth, are now in circulation and are duly presented to any one who is suspected of the intention of publishing any account of the community. The arguments contained in these papers have been discussed and met in the census report of 1901.[2] Briefly stated, the contentions raised are that the proper form of the name Shānān is "Sānrōr," a word which means "the learned" or "the noble"; and that the community belongs to the Kshatriya caste. The active exertions of the caste towards enforcing the recognition of their independence claims date at least from the year 1858, when a riot occurred in Travancore owing to the opposition created by female converts giving up the caste custom of going about without an upper cloth.

1 The phrase alludes to the position assigned to the community in the classification of castes contained in the Madras Census Report of 1891. In popular estimation the Shānān caste comes below the Sūdras and somewhat above Pallans, etc.

2 Vide *Census of India*, 1901, *Madras, Part I*, p. 178. The arguments contained in these pamphlets are there fully discussed.

CHAP. III. SHĀNĀNS.

Attempts to realize them.

The most important test, however, of the social position of a caste is the extent of its privileges in regard to temples; and in 1874 the Shānāns of Madura attempted by means of a criminal complaint to assert their right to enter the great Saivite temple of Mīnākshi in that place. The case failed; but a similar attempt, which was also unsuccessful, was made two years later at Tirutangal in the Srīvilliputtūr taluk (transferred in 1910 to Rāmnād district). In 1885 trouble arose in a village in the Sāttūr taluk (now also part of the Rāmnād district) over an attempt made by the local Shānāns to take a procession through the streets of other castes in opposition to the wishes of the whole village.

The riot at Kalugumalai.

In 1895 a similar dispute, one which by that time existed in a smouldering condition in many villages of the district, led to a serious riot at Kalugumalai. The zamindar of Ettaiyāpuram, as trustee of the local temple, had obtained an injunction restraining the Shānāns from making processions in the car-streets, a move which the Shānāns countered by turning Roman Catholics in a body. To provide a place of worship for this band of converts the mission bought a shop in one of the car-streets, and, just before the day arrived on which the Hindus were in the course of their festival to drag their car through the street, a *pandal* was rigged up across the road in front of the new chapel. The car reached the site, and it became obvious that unless the *pandal* were removed the procession could not get past. Seventy Shānāns manned their premises and began throwing stones on the crowd; the Brahman manager of the Ettaiyāpuram estate came up to reason with the defiant Shānāns and was immediately stabbed to death by one of their number. A general riot ensued, in which seven Shānāns and two of the manager's followers were killed. The infuriated crowd set fire to the thatch roof of the chapel and burnt and looted the Shānān quarters. A force of additional police was thereupon stationed at Kalugumalai; it was withdrawn in March 1899 just a month before the most serious Shānān disturbance broke out.

The riots of 1899.

The incidents immediately preceding the memorable outbreak of 1899 belong rather to the history of Rāmnād than of this district. In 1895 the Shānāns of Sivakāsi (in the Sāttūr taluk of the district), the home of many wealthy representatives of the caste, applied by petition to the Tinnevelly Temple Committee for the appointment of a Shānān trustee on the managing body of the local Siva temple. Their request was rejected, and other disputes followed. Some Shānāns tried to force their way into the temple, and in the disturbance which followed some temple property was burnt. The Shānāns were tried, and acquitted, by a Deputy Magistrate and almost immediately repeated their attempt. Again they were acquitted and, in fact, justified by the same court; whereupon the temple was shut, and the Shānāns appeared to have scored a partial victory. Meanwhile a suit, in which the Rāmnād zamindar (a Maravan by caste) was seeking to obtain a decree prohibiting the Shānāns from entering his Saivite temple, was in progress in the sub-court of Kamudi, 40 miles from Sivakāsi. The case was conducted with great bitterness of feeling on both sides and excited much bad blood between the Shānāns and the rest of the Hindu community.

On the 26th April 1899 the Shānāns of Sivakāsi boldly took the aggressive and set upon the Maravans, burning fifty-five of their houses. The local Maravans, joined by their neighbours across the Madura border and a number of Pallans, retaliated with a systematic campaign of arson and pillage against several Shānān villages in the north of the old Tinnevelly district (now Rāmnād). On the 6th June a united attack was made by over five thousand Maravans on Sivakāsi, in the defence of which 16 Shānāns were killed. A general attack immediately followed on a number of villages in the Tenkāsi taluk inhabited by Shānān Christians, who by their jaggery trade are closely associated with the Shānāns of Sivakāsi. A military force requisitioned from Trichinopoly reached the district on the 7th June, and a large number of additional police was obtained from neighbouring districts. By the 16th June all the gangs were rounded up and order was restored. Nineteen hundred and fifty-eight persons were arrested; special magistrates and three additional Sessions Judges were appointed for the trial of the offenders at Tinnevelly; and forces of additional police, the cost of which was met by fines levied on the inhabitants of defined areas, were stationed at Sivakāsi (in the present Rāmnād district), Surandai and Kōilpatti.

As a fighting race by tradition it was but natural that Maravans should take the leading part in the campaign; and perhaps to some extent, not only as sympathisers with their fellow-casteman, the plaintiff in the Kamudi suit, but also as being nearer (though still far away) to the Shānāns in the social scale than many other more influential castes, the Maravans had special reasons for their hostility. The hostility, however, was shared by practically the whole Hindu community, the feeling of Vellālans being possibly as bitter as any.

CHAP. III. SHĀNĀNS.

The riots evidently cleared the air; for the decisions in the Kamudi suit and in the suit instituted by the Ettaiyāpuram zamindar regarding the site of the Roman Catholic chapel at Kalugumalai, both of which went against the Shānāns, were received quietly.

A threatened disturbance, 1902.

In 1902 a curious movement which seemed at the time to threaten trouble was started at Ovari, in the extreme south of the Nāngunēri taluk. The Shānāns decided in combination that their women should no longer carry headloads or wear beads or leaden bracelets and should not go to market. A rumour was started that the scheme had the sanction of Government, and an attempt was made to collect subscriptions in support of the cause. These audacious pretensions, added to a dispute regarding the contributions due by the Shānāns to the *mahimai* or village fund, soon brought them into collision with their neighbours, the Paravans of Periyatālai; some rioting ensued, but the disturbance was quickly suppressed.

Characteristics of the caste.

Though their social aspirations may be deemed ill-judged and though their methods of expressing them have from time to time been deplorable, it must in fairness to the caste be said that, as persevering and resourceful cultivators, as traders both at home and abroad, as unwearied tappers of the palmyra and as capable clerks and officials in the service of Government, the Shānān community by their own merits are steadily earning for themselves a position and reputation infinitely more valuable than any social pre-eminence attainable by violence or pamphleteering. One of the most noticeable features of the resettlement recently concluded was the enormous increase of Shānān pattas (both in wet and in dry lands) in almost every quarter of the district. Cultivation with the aid of wells is perhaps their speciality; if water exists under the ground a Shānān will find it, and will quickly convert into a luxuriant garden a patch of poor soil which, in the time of its previous owner, had been a dreary waste. Should pressure on the land some day reach a point of danger, the Shānān, who has already shewn signs of beating his fellows at intensive methods, will be the last to feel the strain. In some villages (Kāyāmoli, Arasūr, Arumuganēri, Kānam are good examples) Shānāns have long been well-to-do landowners; in the centres of trade rich Shānān merchants are numerous; in many villages the labourer is steadily converting himself into a peasant-owner, and the tapper (as in south-east Nānguneri and in the Tiruchendūr and Tenkāsi taluks) is often known to invest his savings in lands. If land cannot be had, he buys, transports and sells jaggery, or breeds sheep, goats and fowls, which he exports to Colombo. Some go abroad with a little capital and make a living in the towns of Ceylon as writers or shop-keepers or as maistris in the tea and rubber estates. Large numbers (mostly Christians) obtain a cheap and serviceable education in the mission schools and find employment in Government service, in the railways and in commercial houses. Among members of the caste are graduates in law, theology, medicine and the arts; and from the Christian community missionaries have been sent to Madagascar, Natal, Mauritius and the Straits.

And it must not be supposed that the "Sānrōr" theory has by any means spread a general infection over the whole community. In villages near the source of its origin it finds often vehement supporters; but one need not go far, for preference to a village where hard work is the order of things, to find the story either treated with mild derision or even not known. Possibly it may die of inanition.

Origin of the caste; traditional account.

The popular account (which forms no part of the "learned" version) of the origin of the caste is that its founders were the sons of seven maids—*kannis*—formed from the eye-sight of the god Nārāyana. The god brought up the seven boys on the milk of the cow of the god Indra and then left them under the protection of Badrakāli (to the present day the household deity of the community). One day, the story goes on, the river Vaigai (in the Madura district) breached, and flood after flood was threatened. The king of the country was told that, if the seven boys took mud in baskets on their heads and closed the breaches, the remedy would be permanent. The Shānān boys said their heads were made to carry crowns, not baskets, and refused to obey the king. The king was furious and ordered that one of the boys should be buried in the sand up to his neck. The order was obeyed, and an elephant came up and kicked off the boy's head, which was then thrown into the river. The other boys were still defiant, and a second victim was treated likewise. As his head floated down the stream, it cried out: "Shall this head prove false to the other?" The king heard, and was appeased; and the remaining five, from each of whom originated a subdivision of the caste, were spared.

Subdivisions

The subdivisions are:—(1) Mānattan, more generally known as Karukkumattaiyan, (2) Mēnattan, (3) Kodikkāl or Nattātti Shānān, (4) Kāvadipurathān or Kāvēripurathān, (5) Pulukka Shānān. In some places more classes are enumerated, but the additional ones are on examination found to be

CHAP. III. SHANANS.

identical with one or other of the five here given. Members of one section may, so far as the rules go, dine with those of any other, but intermarriages are not allowed. As a community all are flesh-eaters, but some seek merit by abstaining.

The divisions appear to be territorial in origin. The first class, by far the most numerous of all and by general repute the highest in the social scale, is said originally to have inhabited the country around Mānād (Mahānādu, "the great province"), four miles from Tiruchendūr. Their alternative title, Karukkumattaiyan (*karukku*—"sharp edge", *mattai*—"the leaf-stalk of the palmyra"), suggestive of their association with tree-climbing, is unpopular and by a simple change is generally given the form Karukkupattaiyan, *pattaiyam* meaning "a sword." The Mēnāttans, or "westerners" (*mēlnādu*, "western country"), are generally believed to have come from Nānjanād in south Travancore, still the home of Shānāns. Members of the third sect are now found chiefly in the Ambāsamudram taluk, where, as their description implies, they are largely employed in the cultivation of betel-nut gardens (*kodikāl*); their original home is said to be Nattātti (Srīvaikuntam taluk). The fourth division, Kāvēripurathān, those who immigrated from the banks of the Cauvery, is spoken of in many villages but appears not to be represented in this district.[1] The Pulukka Shānāns are, properly, the domestic servants of the other classes and are, in fact, often so employed. They are generally spoken of as an inferior class and are in many places not allowed to feed with members of the other sections. The prohibition is perhaps only one instance of a general system of class distinctions by which, apart from the "rules" of the caste, the relationship between members of one subdivision and another is governed. In villages where both agriculturists and tappers are found, the two classes tend to grow mutually exclusive in regard to social matters. Each section lives by itself; an agriculturist seldom marries a bride from a tapper's family unless she can bring with her a substantial dowry. On the other hand an ambitious Shānān who values his position may have to pay heavily for a son-in-law.

Caste. customs.

In regard to the re-marriage of widows, the custom appears to differ from place to place. Members of the first two subdivisions allow but as a rule deprecate it; Kodikkāl Shānāns allow it and in some places even encourage it; Pulukkans appear generally to allow it. Questions of divorce come occasionally for decision before a *Nāttāmai* or local headman,

[1] I have been unable to find any of this division.

if such a personage exists; otherwise one is appointed for the purpose. Generally speaking, divorce is unusual but is not forbidden. Girls are married either before or after puberty; the *tāli*-tying ceremony should take place just before sunrise. The dead (with the usual exception of first-born infant children) are generally buried, not burnt.

Converts from the caste to Christianity live on friendly terms with their Hindu brethren, and the fact that some members of a family may be Hindus and others Christians does not give rise to dissension. If a Hindu wishes to marry a Christian, one or the other must change his or her religion. Shānāns, as we have seen, constitute the bulk of the Protestant community and half the total number of Roman Catholics; as a class they are staunch supporters of the church of their choice and rally to its festivals with enthusiasm and open hands.

The corporate spirit which is such a marked characteristic of the community is due less to any caste organization (of which beyond the existence of a *Nāttāmai* here and there little trace is to be found) than to its freedom from outside control. Almost every settlement of Shānāns has its own Amman temple, which they themselves control; the important Amman shrine at Koranganni on the right bank of the Tāmbraparni in the Tiruchendūr taluk, to which thousands of all classes congregate on feast days, is the property of their caste. Here and there, as for instance at Nallūr (Tenkāsi taluk) and Ovari (Nānguneri taluk), are Siva temples which belong to Shānāns, and in which they control, if they do not perform, the services. With the aid of their barbers, who are the repositories of the ritual, they conduct their own marriages, Brahmans very rarely officiating.

Their titles.

Nādān is the usual caste title; two others, Mukkundan and Sērvai, are also found. Mukkundan, which seems originally to have implied a local headmanship, is now falling into disuse and conveys no particular meaning. Sērvai[1] is the title borne by the Shānāns of Kadaiyam and Kalakkād, in both of which places the hereditary *kudikāval* is in the hands of this caste; and it is possible that they owe the appellation to their position. In Kadaiyam the story is told that, when one of the old native renters, according to the custom of those potentates, ordered the Sivagiri zamindar to grovel before him in the mud specially prepared for the purpose, the zamindar refused to do so; the Shānāns were told to

[1] The title is also used by some Maravans.

CHAP. III. SHĀNĀNS.

cut his head off and did so. So they earned the honourable title of Sērvai, or Sērvaikāran. Elsewhere the title conveys no sort of distinction ; and curiously enough it is in some parts borne by the humble Pulukkans.

MARAVANS.

The Maravans, who form nearly one-tenth of the total population of the district, are members of the widespread race to which the Kallans and Agamudaiyāns of the other Tamil districts also belong.

The origin of their name has been much discussed. One fanciful derivation connects it with *maravēn*—"I will not forget"—the expression used by Rāma, speaking in appropriately high Tamil, when he thanked the members of the caste for the assistance they gave him in his pursuit of the demon Rāvana. Others associate the name with the story which traces the origin of the caste to the clandestine (*maravu*, "secret") intercourse of the god Indra with Gautama's wife, Ahalya. Another explanation—the least improbable—is one which connects the name with *maram*, a word denoting "ferocity," a striking characteristic, if not of the present race of Maravans, at least of their ancestors. Tēvan and Talaivan are their usual titles, the latter, which means "headman," implying either local leadership or descent from a chieftain.

It has been conjectured[1] that they are the descendants of the race of Nāgas, believed to have been the rulers of the southern districts before the Pāndyas came ; but it is not till many centuries later that we obtain any historical view of the caste. It was during the time of the Madura Kartākkals that the Maravans developed and consolidated their power as poligars. In the north-west of the district they had banded themselves into a formidable league, which did its utmost to resist the attempts of all invaders, the Nawāb and the English in turn ; elsewhere, by means of the *dēsakāval* and the *stalam-kāval*, they had become the self-constituted protectors (during generations of rapine and bloodshed) of most of the villages of the district. The story of the suppression of the confederacy will be found in Chapter II ; some details regarding the *kāval* system are given in Chapter XIII.

Subdivisions.

The two main subdivisions found in this district are the Sembināttu (otherwise called Kottāli) and the Kondaiyan-kōttai. Other sections found in small numbers are called Kārkurichi, Vannikutti[2] and Uppukatti. The servants of Marava zamindars forming another subdivision are known as Pulukka Maravans, or Parivārams, and usually bear the

[1] By Mr. V. Kanakasabhai Pillai in his *Tamils Eighteen Hundred Years Ago.*
[2] To be distinguished from Vanniyans, an entirely separate caste.

title Sērvaikāran. Though all these subdivisions are, strictly speaking, endogamous, intermarriages occasionally take place between members of the different sections; a Kottāli sometimes marries in a Kondaiyankōttai family and even the humble Pulukkan has been known to marry into other classes of the community. The Kārkurichi people never contract marriages outside their own sect. The Pulukkans and Kārkurichi Maravans dine together but not as a rule with members of other subdivisions; otherwise any Maravan may feed with any other.

The Kottāli section again divides itself into two main classes, which are generally regarded as endogamous, viz., the Periyatāli people, those whose women wear a big *tāli*, and the Siriyatāli sect, whose *tāli* is small. Even here the prohibition regarding intermarriages is sometimes disregarded, the zamindars of Singampatti (Siriyatāli) and of Urkād (Periyatāli) having by their marriage connections set a leading example.

The Kondaiyankōttai sect are elaborately subdivided into six endogamous *kothus*, or "trees" (they are named after trees), each kothu being again split up into three exogamous septs, or *kilais*. The names of the *kothus* are:—*Vettilai* (betel-vine), *Milagu* (pepper-vine), *Kamugu* (areca), *Icham* (date), *Thennai* (cocoanut), *Panai* (palmyra). The *kilais* are the names of persons, as is the case with the *gōtrams* among Brahmans. A point of difference, however, between the Marava *kilai* and the Brahman *gōtram* is that children inherit the *kilai* not of their father but of their mother. The rule forbidding members of the same *kilai* to marry one another is strictly followed; that prohibiting members of one *kothu* from marriage into another is frequently ignored. A visitor in search of hospitality in a strange village will always ask for a household belonging to his own *kilai*.

Like the Kondaiyankōttai sect, the Kārkurichi people divide themselves into *kilais*, or exogamous septs, but they have no subdivisions corresponding to the *kothus*. They are able to name six *kilais* and add that the members of a nameless seventh fled from their country during the wild days of the Pānjālankurichi rebellions. The country over which Kārkurichi Maravans are now distributed may be almost exactly defined as that lying east of a line drawn due south through Pudukkōttai and south of a line passing due west from Tuticorin. A clear tradition survives amongst these people that they were very roughly treated by Pānjālankurichi and his Kambalattān followers; some members of their section, with the curious title of Manikāran, now living in Sankarappēri (near Tuticorin), are said to be the descendants of families who were reduced to the position of *parivārams,* or servants, of that ruthless poligar. Whether the oppressive treatment of Pānjālankurichi is the cause or not, there is little doubt that the entire Kārkurichi section is regarded by other Maravans as possessing a status no better than that of Pulukkans or Parivārams.

Characteristics of the caste.

The social niche of the Maravans is next below that occupied by Vellālans. They are not, as a caste, in the least obsessed by theories of precedence, and their attitude in regard to the Shānān dispute (p. 126) was defensive rather than aggressive. They are meat-eaters and will exchange hospitality with Idaiyans. In the matter of religion some compromise by wearing the sacred ashes of Siva and professing to be adherents of Vishnu; most, however, are avowedly Saivites. Tirumanja Alvār, the Tirukkurungudi saint, is claimed by the Maravans as a member of their caste.[1] Their gurukkal is a Vellālan.

"A large section of the population of the district, the Maravans," says the Madras Police report of 1903, "are criminal by predilection and training." It is now some years since the caste received this severe condemnation, and police vigilance and, to some extent, education have in the interval produced a marked change for the better. The subject is dealt with in Chapter XIII and needs little discussion here. The training referred to in the quotation is that derived chiefly from the practical monopoly of the *kudikāval,* or "village watch", which the community has enjoyed for centuries. "Set a thief to catch a thief" is a principle which naturally appeals to a primitive society. The assumption that the licensed pursuer was necessarily a thief was perhaps unjustified; but the corollary to the proposition—"if he cannot catch the thief then let him loot some one else"—inevitably followed. To the present day the old *kāval* survives in almost every village of the district, and it is a factor with which magistrates and the police have constantly to reckon. As a rule, the institution is willingly supported by the villagers, who make annual contributions among themselves towards its maintenance. A landowner pays rateably according to the extent of his property, sometimes one-eighth of a *kōttai* of paddy for every superficial *kōttai* of his wet land; the landless man gives a few annas or a measure of grain. In return he secures the protection of sturdy fearless watchmen for his crops and cattle during night,

[1] See p. 403.

with a fair certainty that his losses, provided they are not too large, will be made good. The strength of the system is that it stimulates a corporate life and a feeling of self-reliance and to a great extent prevents crimes; its obvious weakness is that it encourages the people to hush up offences when they occur and provokes retaliation against invading thieves. Without the connivance of the *kāvalgārs* offences against property will not occur; but when they do occur, the policeman in search of a clue is often at the mercy of the Maravan informer. In the face of such a system, police work in Tinnevelly will always be a difficult and delicate task.

Incidental to the post of *kāvalgār* (as has been stated above) is the important duty of slaying, not only in their own *pēykōils* but in those of other Sūdra castes, the sacrificial animals offered on feast days to Sudalaimādan and his host of attendant deities; and, taken as a whole, there is no caste which bestows so much undisguised enthusiasm on these primitive forms of worship. Existing as it does in almost every settlement of Maravans, the demon-temple serves as a strong rallying-point for the community. Before a "hunting expedition," in other words a dacoity, is undertaken, offerings are made to Sudalaimādan, and omens are sought from him; his yearly festivals are celebrated by Maravans on a scale which no other caste can emulate. At the head of each community there is as a rule a *Nāttāmai*, whose office is hereditary; questions of divorce, of fines in cases of misconduct, and of the apportionment of the amount to be paid in restitution to the victims of thefts come before him for decision.

Marriages.

Marriage ceremonies, which are more or less the same with all sections, take two or three days and are generally performed in the bridegroom's house. Before the appointed day a formal agreement is made orally between the parties, and the bridegroom's people go to the bride's house and give the *parisam*, usually a present of jewels (to accommodate which Marava women dilate their ear-lobes enormously) and a silk cloth to the bride's parents. On an auspicious day just before the marriage the bride is taken to the bridegroom's village and lodged in a convenient house. When the day arrives, she is taken in procession accompanied by her female relatives, who unite in a chorus of shrill cries *(kulavai)*, to the bridegroom's house and is seated inside on a silk mat. The bridegroom enters the courtyard of the house accompanied by his maternal uncle, both of them are garlanded, and a pot of earth is set up before them, in which they sprinkle dry grains, horse-gram, black gram, cotton seeds, and so on. They retire

CHAP. III. MARAVANS.

into the house, and the bride with her maternal uncle comes out and sows seeds, as the bridegroom had done, but in another pot, and then goes inside. Bride and bridegroom then come out together and receive from the Brahman priest a silk cloth with his blessing. They put on new cloths, the present of the bridegroom, and while they are seated together the Brahman (or sometimes the maternal aunt) ties a string of saffron silk round the wrist of each and asks the bride's father whether he consents to the marriage. The bridegroom's sister then appears, dressed in new clothes, receives the *tāli* from the Brahman and, after the bridegroom has touched it, ties it round the neck of the bride. The bride's father makes a solemn declaration that he has made a gift of his daughter and ties together with a silk thread the little fingers of the pair. Two cups of milk are placed before the bride and bridegroom; and, invoking blessings on the pair, everyone in turn throws betel and margosa leaves or small coins into the vessels. The bride's brother then leads the pair thrice round the platform on which they were seated and the couple then retire into the house and have a light meal. The bride's brother unties the fingers of the pair and for his trouble receives a present *(kaippidisurul)*. The next day is given up to feasting at the expense of the bridegroom's parents, and on the third day the guests return the compliment by giving presents (known as *moy*) to their entertainers.

A man may marry as many wives as he can afford to support. Divorce is easy and is generally ratified by a deed which serves the woman as a passport for re-marriage. "As long as there is cotton to be spun," says the proverb, "the Marava woman will be able to find a *tāli* "; or, as one villager more naïvely put it, "when the husband goes to jail the wife may marry again." Widows are eligible for re-marriage; and the brother of the deceased husband is expected to take his place. Adult marriage is the rule.

Among the Kondaiyankōttai people, when marriages have to be arranged secretly or when it is inconvenient for the bridegroom to be present, the bridegroom may send a *tāli* to the bride's house; a stick is used to represent him, and his sister ties the *tāli* to it. The ceremony, which has usually been a prerogative of the richer classes, is now falling into disrepute. The Kondaiyankōttai women wear two *tālis*, one which is put on during girlhood before marriage, known as the *tumbamani*, the other, known as *mayirkodi*, which is given at the time of marriage. The latter, which is much the larger of the two, is, as a rule, worn only on festival occasions and even, for the purpose of marriage, is sometimes obtained on loan.

Funerals.

All classes of Maravans, rich and poor, practise either cremation or burial indifferently; if the deceased, as sometimes happens, has expressed such a wish, some of his posses sions, a stick, a knife or a vessel, are put in the grave with his body.

VELLALANS.

Vellālans, who by general consent come next to Brahmans in the social scale, number nine in every hundred of the population.

Their occupations and characteristics.

The variety of their occupations is infinite; in the ryotwari areas they form, probably, the largest land-owning class; they are employed in every grade of Government service; they are merchants, shop-keepers, lawyers and even priests; and they are to be found almost everywhere. In the service of Government, though far behind, they are the nearest competitors with the Brahmans; and it is amusing now to read, at a time when their rivals have so far out-stripped them, that Mr. Puckle, finding (in 1866) the Collector's establishment practically monopolized by Vellālans, applied for their transfer to other districts in favour of Brahmans. It was from the most distinguished section of the Vellāla caste that most of the old race of renters—the Dalavāys—were drawn; Vellālans were the chief advisers of those most rebellious of poligars, Pānjālankurichi and Sivagiri; and the Vellālans of the town of Tinnevelly are still inclined (with some justice) to regard their Brahman fellow-citizens as recent interlopers. Elections to local bodies in Tinnevelly, municipal councils, college committees and boards of temple management, bring out all the inherited love of authority that distinguishes the community, and on these occasions their rivalry with the Brahmans is seen at its keenest. In the villages too, where Brahman and Vellālan live side by side, the race for the best land is hotly contested; and, provided he is not handicapped too much at the start, thrift and perseverance will carry the Vellālan to victory in the end. Occasionally Vellālans work in their own fields and do everything but reap; mostly they employ hired labour or lease their land.

In matters of religion they compete closely with Brahmans. They have their own religious institutions, or mutts, at Tiruvāduthurai, Dharmapuram (in the Tanjore district) and at Perunkulam (Srīvaikuntam taluk), presided over by members of their own caste; subordinate to these presidents are not only the local gurukkals who officiate in the religious ceremonies of the Vellālans but also all the other nominees who serve as gurukkals to many of the lower castes. Like the Brahmans,

CHAP. III. VELLALANS.

all Vellālans perform *srāddhas* in memory of the dead and invoke the spirits of their ancestors on new moon days; many perform daily pūja in their own houses, wear strings of *rudrākshams*, the mark of piety, and study the Dēvāram, the work of the four Vellāla Alvārs. The Saiva Sabha, recently instituted by Vellālans at Palamcotta with the object of promoting the study of the sacred books, is only one symptom of a growing movement amongst the community towards self-help in matters of religion.

Subdivisions.

Three main endogamous divisions of the caste represented in the district are: (1) the Tondamandalam Vellālans most of whom bear the title of Mudali or (more honorific) Mudaliyār; (2) Kāraikattārs or Kārkāttārs; (3) "other Vellālans," possessing no distinctive class-name, but known generally (from their caste title "Pillai") as "Pillaimārs."

The Tondamandalam class divides itself into two endogamous sections: one (which has no particular name) consists of those who are said to come originally from the neighbourhood of Conjeeveram and is invariably distinguished by the title of Mudaliyār; the other section consists of Tuluvas, believed to have emigrated from the Tulu country.[1] The usual title of these latter people is Pillai; a few, bearing the title Nāyakkan, say they were given it by Tirumalai Nāyakkan of Madura in whose service they came to the southern districts. The Mudaliyārs (to use a convenient but inaccurate expression), who are found mostly in and near Tinnevelly itself, are Saivites and vegetarians, and claim to form the highest class among Vellālans; the section is now composed almost exclusively of the old families who in pre-British days wielded extensive powers as renters of the district. The Tuluva Vellālans, of whom there are very few representatives in the district, are followers of Vishnu and are not forbidden to eat meat.

The Kārkāttārs (whose title is Pillai) form a small community possessed of a strong corporate spirit and proud of their generally admitted superiority to the great mass of the Vellāla population which is comprised in the third division. They are found in small colonies in almost all parts of the district, but altogether number probably only a few thousands. They have a tradition that they migrated from the north and, as has been suggested,[2] their name may be derived from the country, perhaps called Kāraikādu, from which they

[1] The title Mudali or even Mudaliyār is used by the Kaikkilaiyans and some other castes. The classification of Tuluvas as a section of the Tondamandalam class is doubtful; the "Mudaliyārs" resent it.

[2] *Census Report* of 1901, Madras, Part I, p. 184.

came. A more fanciful explanation is found in their own story that once, when the god Indra was at war and famine oppressed his country, the ancestors of the caste called away the clouds from the enemy's country and brought rain to the stricken crops. They thus came to be called "those who waited *(kāttār)* for the clouds *(kār)*". They have ninety-six exogamous *gōtrams*, or septs; all are Saivites and abstain from flesh. The gurukkal of every family is a Brahman selected from one of two households in Mēlapāttam, near Tinnevelly.

Most of the Vellālans of the district belong to the third class—"Pillaimārs." Broadly speaking, they fall into two main sections: those who do not eat meat ("Saiva Pillai" or "Saivāl" is their usual description) and those who do. Between members of these two sections there can be neither intermarriage nor "interdining." The qualifying test for admission to the "Saivāl" class is rigorous in the extreme. It is not enough that a man should be a vegetarian; if his ancestors are suspected of having eaten meat, even (it is said) to the two-hundred-and-third generation, he can claim neither meals nor marriage in the house of a "Saivāl." Risks in regard to meals have sometimes to be faced in the case of strangers; "are you Saivāl?" however is invariably the first question put, and, if any doubt arises, a cross-examination follows. If the stranger breaks down, hospitality is refused, or, if begun, is stopped. In the villages, especially, minute and otherwise inexplicable distinctions between one batch of families and another find their origin in the suspicion that the ancestors of one batch once ate meat. As may be inferred, abstention from meat conveys marked social superiority; and amongst "Pillaimārs" more than any other caste strenuous efforts are everywhere being made towards such advancement, either by not eating meat or by seeming not to do so.

They have a few defined endogamous subdivisions, two of which are sufficiently important to deserve mention, viz., Nangudi Vellālans and Kōttai Vellālans. They are referred to below. Apart from these subdivisions distinguished by name, and subject always to the gulf separating vegetarians from flesh-eaters, there is no rule preventing any member of a "Pillaimār" family from marrying into the family of any other. In practice, however, things are very different. The *morai* system in regard to brides is the same in this caste as in most others, that is, a man should marry the daughter either of his paternal aunt or of his maternal uncle. The rule cannot always be observed, and in many parts, in towns especially, there is a tendency to disregard it altogether. It does not however follow that the choice of the bridegroom's parents then becomes a free one; in theory it is, but in practice the circle of families from which a choice may be made is always limited. It is a defined circle and continues from generation to generation. The origin of these exclusive societies is extremely hard to trace. The families of the two parties may live in the same place or far from one another; sometimes the bond is community of occupation, sometimes it can only be a common place of origin or perhaps even a common ancestor. Whether these distinctions are increasing in number it is difficult to say; all that can be said is that they represent in effect an infinity of endogamous subdivisions. One reason for the limitation of choice and for distrusting the formation of connections with strange families is to be found, no doubt, in the fact that members of many other castes, e.g., Iluvans ("Illattu Pillai"), Shānāns, the sons of dancing-girls, and even sometimes Paraiyans, assume the name of "Pillai" and, with a view to a good marriage, attempt (sometimes with success) to pass themselves off in society as Vellālans.

Pillai, as has been said, is the title of most Vellālans of the third main subdivision; a few have titles indicative of the occupation of themselves or of their ancestors. Chetti is the surname of some, but does not necessarily imply that its owner is a trader; if he is not, it may be assumed that his family were once traders. A Vellālan who officiates in the temple of a minor deity, Pillaiyār or an Amman, is styled Othuvān or Othuvāmūrti; Pandāram is the title assumed by an ascetic, often distinguishable by his orange-coloured cloth, his beads and smears of ashes. The wearers of these titles do not constitute themselves separate subdivisions; they may intermarry with one another and with any family of the main subdivision to which they belong.

The Nangudi Vellālans.

The Nangudi Vellālans, often called Sevalai Pillaimārs, after the name of the place (in the Srīvaikuntam taluk) in which they are found in considerable numbers, are scattered over several places, mostly in the Srīvaikuntam taluk, their largest settlement being in Mudittānēndal. According to their own story, they came "from the north" and took service under the ruler of Korkai. A quarrel arose over the conduct of one of their party and split them into two factions, one of which became the Kōttai Vellālans[1], the other the Nangudis. They have eight exogamous septs, or *kilais*, children inheriting the *kilai* of their mother. They are agriculturists (often cultivating their lands themselves), merchants and petty traders,

[1] See p. 438.

and on the whole are a remarkably prosperous and energetic community. They may eat meat and by religion are Saivites. They have a headman, whose name, "Irunkol Pillai," interpreted as meaning "Please-sit-down Pillai," is attributed to the fact that when he comes into the company of his fellow-castemen he is given a seat on a dais whilst the others stand up. A peculiar feature of their marriage system (observed also by the Kōttai Vellālans) is that the bride always brings as a dowry a furnished house for the married couple to live in and, if her parents can afford it, landed property in addition. The dowry remains the property of the bride and goes on her death either to her daughter or her mother.

Marriage customs.

Much might be written on the subject of the marriage ceremonies of the Vellālans; but it will be sufficient to refer only to one or two of their more peculiar customs and to those which especially distinguish one section from another. The rule amongst all Vellālans (the Tondamandalam subdivision excepted), unlike the Brahmans, is that their girls should marry after puberty. "Pillaimārs" and Tuluvas frequently do without Brahmans at their marriages, preferring to employ a gurukkal of their own caste; Mudaliyārs and Kārkattārs always employ Brahmans. The purely Brahmanical custom of paying a premium to secure a suitable bridegroom is, unfortunately, gaining ground amongst the wealthier members of all sections, that is, amongst those who can afford to disregard the custom regarding the *morai*-bride. The crudeness of the commercial transaction is often softened by the inclusion of additional jewellery in the bride's dowry; sometimes the bride's parents contract to pay the educational expenses of their prospective son-in-law.

A peculiar ceremony observed by the Kārkattārs preliminary to a girl's marriage is that known as the *vilakidu kaliyānam*, which is performed in every alternate year from the girl's fifth year until she is eleven. On the first of *Thai* (January-February) three lights are kindled and offerings are made; a *tāli*, known as *nāmatāli*, is tied round the girl's neck by an old married woman of the family, and at the expense of the girl's maternal uncle friends and relations are fed. Should the girl become widowed before she is eleven, the ceremony is not repeated. Three days after her marriage some of the beads are taken out of the *nāmatāli* and put in the *tāli* which is tied at the time of marriage.

Funerals.

Amongst all Vellālans funeral ceremonies last for sixteen days, on each of which (in imitation of Brahmans) the sons of the deceased after bathing bring water in a small pot and

CHAP. III. VELLALANS.

place it beside the spot on which their parent died. On certain days cakes are offered to the spirit of the deceased as represented by the pot of water; on the last day a stone is planted, and, by way of propitiation to the spirit, rice and vegetables are given to the Brahmans. The stone is then taken up and flung into the river. Widows (other than those of the Kārkāttār section) remain at home for a year and substitute cakes for a rice diet for any period up to three months.

The treatment accorded to the Kārkāttār widow is incredibly severe. For two days after the loss of her husband she is given absolutely nothing to eat. On the next day vegetables cooked without salt and then soaked in butter milk (fruit is sometimes substituted for vegetables) are put out for the crows to eat and, when they have finished with the food, the remains are given to the widow. This process continues till the tenth day with the exception of the seventh day, which is a strict fast. Until the end of three months fruit and vegetable constitute her diet; after that for another three months her food is rice gruel without salt. She is then free to eat what she likes, subject to abstinence on eighteen successive new moon days. This brings her to the end of two years; but her troubles are not yet over. After the expiry of another year she calls her near relatives together and joins them in a meal of rice, and for a year from that date she has to go without salt in her food. During this year she performs the penance of walking 1,008 times round the temple, but may credit towards this figure any rounds which her dāyādis may consent to make on her behalf. When the year is over restrictions in regard to food are removed, and she may appear in public; if she is widowed when young, her seclusion may last for ten years or even more.

KAMMAVANS.

The Kammavans, who numbered 41,829 at the census of 1901,[1] are a Telugu-speaking people, found chiefly in the Kōilpatti and Sankaranainārkōil taluks.

Their characteristics.

They are a fine, sturdy, hardworking race of agriculturists and in the cultivation of the black-cotton land which they inhabit have only one rival—the Reddi. When the season requires it, a Kammavan will work in his fields from morning to night, not even going home for his midday meal. Squatting down beside his plough, he makes short work of the food sent out to him and, plunging his fingers into the black

[1] It is probable that a large number of Kammavans were included in the 37,296 "Vadugans" returned in the census of 1901. The term Vadugan, "northerner," is a description often adopted by Kammavans, Balijas and Reddis. In 1911 the Kammava caste was not separately enumerated.

earth to clean them, resumes his labours. Of all castes the Kammavans (and their fellow-Telugus, the Reddis) have responded most readily to the efforts which for many years the Agricultural department through its farm at Kōilpatti and its scattered agencies has been making towards the improvement of cultivation. With the Kammavan agriculture is a profession, not merely a means of livelihood. "Turn a pound of earth to a pound of dust," says one of his proverbs, "and you will want no manure." "Make your cultivation in the proper season, and the golden age of Lakshmi will return." They live almost invariably in villages, often to the entire exclusion of other castes; they are either peasant-owners or paid cultivators.

Caste customs.

Though they have no defined endogamous subdivisions, there are a number of sections, apparently of local origin, the members of which contract marriages only amongst themselves. On the other hand, they say they have 100,000 exogamous septs, members of the same sept being, as usual, forbidden to marry one another. Children follow the sept of their father. The question of prohibited degrees of marriage, however, cannot often arise, as the *morai* system, by which a man must marry either his father's sister's daughter, his maternal uncle's daughter or his own sister's daughter, is invariably observed. So rigidly in fact is the principle enforced, that a boy may find himself married to a woman old enough to be his mother; and, when there are girls who cannot otherwise be provided for under the rule, a man may have to marry several wives. In the former case the boy's father performs the duty of begetting children for his son; the boy is however the "statutory" father, and the complication of relationships which follows can be easily imagined. The rules of morality are lax; but adultery outside the family circle is condemned and, as a rule, severely avenged.

Marriages.

Their marriages last for three days. On the first day the bride and bridegroom go to the *manthai*, or common cattle-yard, of the village, worship the family deity and then proceed to the bridegroom's house. The floor is strewn with grain, and on it five pots painted with various colours are set in a row with inverted pots placed over them. Eleven lamps are lighted and continue to burn for three days and nights. The *tāli* is taken from one of the pots, and when the important persons present have blessed it by their touch the bridegroom places it on the bride's neck, his sister tying the knot. The Panjānga Brahman ties the little fingers of the couple with silk. The second day is given up to a procession of the bridal pair

CHAP. III. KAMMAVANS. in palanquins. On the third day a little earth is spread on the floor, and husband and wife go through a ceremony of mock-ploughing, in which a stick serves the purpose of a plough. A painted pot containing water is then brought, and in it are thrown a nose ornament, a bangle and a writing-style. The husband and wife compete with one another to see what each can fish out with their fingers, and on the result depends the question whether their first-born will be a boy or a girl.

ILUVANS. The Iluvans of the Presidency numbered in the census of 1901 (in which they are classed as Panikkans) 30,406; more than half of them were found in this district as then constituted, and almost all the rest belonged to the Madura district.

Their occupations. Until the introduction (in 1881) of the modern Abkāri system one of their chief occupations was the distillation of arrack under the supervision of a renter, who took in auction the "farm" for the supply of the district; the spirit was obtained from the juice of the palmyra, the fermentation of which was aided by the use of the bark of *Acacia leucophlœa*, and between them the members of the caste owned thousands of small stills. At present their most characteristic calling is weaving; and in the Ambāsamudram taluk, in addition to those working on their own account, many are employed by Brahman capitalists in the important business of manufacturing rough cloths for export to Travancore. The use of the fly-shuttle is more general amongst them than with any other community of weavers. Others are renters of arrack shops, petty traders and agriculturists; and in Vikramasingapuram, where they are found in large numbers, they supply a great part of the labour employed in the local cotton-spinning mills.

Social position. They employ Brahmans for their marriages and funerals, and owe allegiance to a gurukkal of that caste who lives in the Madura district; but their social status is estimated differently by themselves and by their Hindu brethren. The view of the orthodox is that Iluvans may not go beyond the *kodimaram*, or flag-staff, of the temple and that they may not enter Brahman streets; their own contention is that they are subject to neither restriction. Their efforts towards social advancement may be seen in the fact that they prefer to drop their caste-title, Panikkan, or "teacher" (which however seems respectable enough), and style themselves in documents and so on as "Illattu Pillai," or simply "Pillai," and sometimes define their caste as "Siruvādi Vellālan." Adult marriage and the re-marriage of widows (provided they are not more than 21 years old) are two of their excellent caste customs; social aspirations are now leading them to substitute in both cases the more advanced practices of the castes above them. They still eat meat.

Subdivisions.

The caste is divided into three endogamous sections, or *vagais*: Pattanam, Midālam and Malayām. The third is not (so far as enquiries go) represented in the district; it is said that it is confined to the Malayālam country. Consequently, it is considered that members of this section cannot feed with members of the other two. Each endogamous division has five exogamous septs, called *illams*, or "households," viz., Mūttillam, Pallikkillam, Tōranattillam, Manjanāttillam and Sōlivillam. Children follow the *illam* of their mother. In addition to the usual prohibition that members of the same sept may not marry one another, there is the further restriction that a member of one of the first two septs may marry only into the other of those two septs, whilst members of the remaining three septs confine their marriages amongst themselves.

Caste organization.

The most remarkable feature of the caste is the existence among them of a regular constitution for the management of their common affairs. The country over which they are scattered is divided into eleven divisions, or *nādus*, each corresponding roughly in area and boundaries to a taluk. A *nādu* is again subdivided into a number of *gadistalams*, five, six or seven; the last unit is the village. Each village selects two representatives for the *gadistalam*, and the body so formed elects five members to the *nādu*, the vote usually being decided, they say, by the opinion of the leading man. The functions of the body representing the *nādu* are to settle the arrangements for their own festivals and the contributions to be made to the larger temples and to discuss social questions of all kinds. Some *nādu* assemblies meet occasionally, about once a year; others are more or less defunct; but the organization is recognized and well understood. In addition each village, sometimes each street in a village, has its own panchayat, presided over by a headman, known variously as Nāttāmaikāran, Kanakkupillai and Ambalam.

KATASANS.

The Katasans are a small caste (in 1901 they numbered 1,811) found (so far as is known) only in this district and are scattered in small colonies over the central and southern taluks.

Occupations.

Their usual caste title is Pattangatti.[1] Nīttarasan, "lime-king," a name which they sometimes use to describe themselves, indicates the business of lime-burning in which some of them are employed in Tuticorin, and is derived, they

[1] Means, properly, "headman," a title in use also amongst the Paravans.

say, from the days when, by extracting lime from the coral-rock, they provided material for the bridge constructed between Ceylon and the mainland for Rāma's expedition. In Ambāsamudram a few call themselves Pulavan or Maistri; some declare they are "Chōliya Vellālans" and use the title Pillai. The chief occupation of the community is the manufacture of mats, baskets, fish-traps and winnowing-fans from the leaf of the palmyra. In Ambāsamudram a few work in wood and horn and make neat little boxes to hold snuff or trinkets. Some have a reputation as medicine-men and effect their cures by the recitation of *mantrams.*

Social status.

Their guru is a Vaishnavite Brahman of Mannārkōil (Ambāsamudram taluk), but, in the villages at least, they are not supposed to enter Brahman streets. They have washermen of their own, sharing a barber with the Paravans. Curiously enough, as a caste they appear scarcely to be recognized in some places, and in Vīravanallūr it was stated that by their profession of basket-making they gave the impression that they were Shānāns and that their exclusion from the Brahman streets was due to this misapprehension. Their privileges in the matter of temples differ also from place to place; in the Saivite temples at Tinnevelly, Pāpanāsam and Attūr they may go as far as the *kodimaram;* in most other temples they are refused admittance even to this extent. At Tinnevelly and Pāpanāsam the members of this caste conduct the procession on one of the days of the great festivals, the necessary funds being raised by means of a *mahimai*, or general subscription, to which Hindu and Christian members of the caste alike contribute. The headman receives the offerings made to the god, and the Brahmans are then given a sumptuous meal.

Caste organization.

The various local settlements have as a rule their own leader—"Ur-Pattangatti"—and at the head of the caste is a general headman, who is known as the "Nāttu-Pattangatti." He and his family, who live at Kadaiyanōdai (Tiruchendūr taluk), are now Christians; but the post, which involves the important duty of managing the processions referred to, does not seem to have lost any of its authority on this account. Appeals from the decisions of the local headman are occasionally made to the chief of the locality; his attendance is secured, when possible, for marriages and funerals.

Subdivisions.

The caste is divided into seven exogamous sects or *kilais*, children following the *kilai* of their mother. Once upon a time, they say, the Katasans took part on the side of the Kammālans in a fight between the right and left hand castes, the Kavarai Chettis leading the opposite faction. The Katasans were all killed except seven men, and these took refuge with the Kondaiyankōttai Maravans at Kalangal, in the Uttumalai country. The Chettis pursued but, being informed by the Maravans that there were none except people of their own caste in the place, desisted. The seven Katasans then took wives, each from a different caste, and following the practice of their protectors divided themselves into *kilais*, seven in number. The names of the *kilais* and of the caste which furnished the female ancestors of each are as follows :—(1) Kuttini : Kosavan ; (2) Attukkutti : Idaiyan ; (3) Thomba Pulâvan : Thomban[1] ; (4) Nayinān Chakravarti : Pāṉan ; (5) Nēttali : Paravan ; (6) Kavadi : Shānāṉ ; (7) Tachīlai : Vannān. It cannot be said that there are any defined endogamous subdivisions in the caste.

As a matter of practice, intermarriage and common feeding are restricted to members either of the same locality or of one or two fixed places ; the Katasans of Sērmādēvi and Nallūr (Tenkāsi taluk), for instance, are considered inferior by those of Pēttai ; Pēttai people again have no social relations with Katasans of Tuticorin. All are flesh-eaters ; adult marriage is the rule ; divorce and the re-marriage of widows are permitted.

[1] This is identified (by the Katasans) with the Dāsi caste. The identification seems however doubtful.

CHAPTER IV.

AGRICULTURE AND IRRIGATION.

AGRICULTURAL STATISTICS—Chief crops. WET LANDS—Fully irrigated crops—Sunn-hemp—Its cultivation—Paddy; season of cultivation—Kinds of paddy—Methods of its cultivation—"Irrigated dry" crops. DRY LANDS—Their cultivation—Chief crops on the red soils—"Tinnevelly senna"—Well-irrigation—Extent of it—Cultivation on the black soils—Chief crops—Other crops—The agricultural year—The Kōilpatti Agricultural Station—Cotton: The indigenous varieties—The "dealer"—Work of the Agricultural Station; the fixing of types—Seed farms—Outturn of lint—The seed-drill—Exotic cultivation—Cambodia—Its introduction—Subsequent history—Its cultivation and outturn—Early attempts to improve cotton cultivation. IRRIGATION—Statistics—The Tāmbraparni system—Anicuts—Area irrigated under each—The Kōdaimēlalagiyan anicut—The Nadhiyunni anicut—The Kannadiyan anicut—The Ariyanāyakapuram anicut—The Palavūr anicut—The Suttamalli anicut—The Marudūr anicut—The Srīvaikuntam anicut—Earliest project—Subsequent history—Execution of the work—Description of the anicut and its system—Flood-banks—The system at work—Revision of the project—Later experience of the system—Remedies suggested—Extent of cultivation—Financial results of the scheme—The Pāpanāsam reservoir project—Captain Horsley's proposal—Its investigation—Mr. Puckle takes it up—The scheme is condemned—Again revived, 1894—The Chittār system—Quality of its irrigation—Area of irrigation—The rivers of the Vaippār basin, Sankaranainārkōil taluk—Area irrigated—The Kīriyār project—Another scheme—The rivers of the Nānguneri taluk—Area irrigated—Nature of the irrigation—The Kila Manimuttār—The Karumanaiyār—Area irrigated—A project relating to Puttantaruvai—Another project—Rain-fed irrigation—Wells. ECONOMIC CONDITION OF THE AGRICULTURISTS—Tenures—Position of the tenant—"The non-cultivating owner"—The "cultivating owner"—The agricultural labourer—Indebtedness of agriculturists.

CHAP IV. AGRICULTURAL STATISTICS.

THE appended table shows at a glance the distribution in the district of the different classes of land, ryotwari, inam, and zamindari, and the extent to which the ryotwari area is cultivated.

CHAP. IV.
AGRICULTURAL STATISTICS.

Taluk.	Percentage of total (i.e., atlas sheet area) which is				Percentage of area according to village accounts which is			
	Government forest.	Ryotwari including minor inam.	Whole inam.	Zamindari.	Not available for cultivation.	Culturable waste other than fallows.	Current fallows.	Net area cropped.
Ambāsamudram ...	28·1	50·1	0·8	21·0	26·7	0·5	31·0	41·8
Kōilpatti	0·4	30·4	4·4	64·8	17·6	0·8	10·6	71·0
Nāngunēri	12·5	82·5	5·0	...	5·3	2·5	49·8	42·4
Sankaranainārkōil ...	6·0	42·0	11·5	40·5	33·5	0·3	18·0	48·2
Srīvaikuntam... ...	2·5	77·0	8·0	12·5	17·5	...	30·3	52·2
Tenkāsi	10·0	42·0	...	48·0	16·2	1·5	24·6	57·7
Tinnevelly	2·0	86·0	12·0	...	18·5	1·8	36·5	43·2
Tiruchendūr	7·6	87·8	4·6	...	8·1	1·6	32·8	57·5
District total ...	8·0	56·0	6·0	30·0	17·4	1·2	30·4	51·0

Zamindaris, it will be seen, constitute thirty per cent of the total area of the district. In the Kōilpatti taluk, which in addition to smaller estates contains the large Ettaiyāpuram zamindari, the proportion of zamindari land is as much as two-thirds of the whole area; in Tenkāsi, which contains the estate of Uttumalai and twelve of the eighteen Chokkampatti mittas, the proportion is one-half; in Sankaranainārkōil it is two-fifths; the zamindari land of the Ambāsamudram taluk is almost entirely composed of ghat forests. In the remaining taluks the area of zamindari land is negligible, Tinnevelly, Nāngunēri and Tiruchendūr possessing none. In the Ambāsamudram taluk, which contains enormous tracts of both Government and zamindari forests, three-fifths of the total area is beyond the reach of cultivation.

Of the ryotwari and minor inam country only one in every hundred acres of cultivable land is waste. Even this figure may perhaps be higher than the facts warrant; for in the Tiruchendūr and Nāngunēri taluks (which together account for a great part of the cultivable waste) large areas of sandy soil recorded in the accounts as "available for cultivation" are really unfit to produce any crops at all. The high proportion of fallows in the Nāngunēri taluk is accounted for partly by the general poorness of the soil and the precariousness of the rainfall and also partly by the difficulty of determining, in the case of lands in which palmyras alone are grown, the extent to which a holding should be deemed cultivated or not. The principle followed in these cases is to consider that a certain minimum number of palmyras in a survey field renders that

CHAP. IV
AGRICULTURAL STATISTICS.

area "cultivated"; if this density is not attained, the field is returned as fallow. In Kōilpatti and Sankaranainārkōil, much of the "cultivable waste" is only theoretically cultivable; in the remaining four taluks, Ambāsamudram, Tinnevelly, Tenkāsi and Srīvaikuntam, cultivation has reached its utmost limit.

Chief crops.

The table following shows both the total cultivated area of the district and, of that area, the proportion of land on which each of the different crops was grown in the year 1913–14. Only the more important crops are specified by name :—

Crops.	District total.	Ambāsamudram.	Kōilpatti.	Nānguneri.	Sankaranainārkōil.	Srīvaikuntam.	Tenkāsi.	Tinnevelly.	Tiruchendūr.
Cereals and pulses—									
Rice	20·6	63·4	2·0	28·0	15·0	31·8	24·0	45·2	24·3
Chōlam	7·1	0·9	7·9	6·1	10·2	0·8	17·0	3·4	0·4
Cumbu	15·1	0·1	34·0	2·5	8·8	18·0	1·0	5·7	3·4
Ragi	2·6	1·2	2·1	1·0	6·1	0·5	5·0	1·9	0·4
Others	20·7	20·5	9·2	46·1	25·1	11·2	35·0	16·7	21·0
Oil-seeds—									
Gingelly	3·5	8·1	0·5	2·1	5·2	0·8	7·5	6·4	4·5
Others	0·2	0·1	0·1	0·1	0·3	0·3	0·2	0·3	0·3
Fibres—									
Cotton	19·2	0·3	36·4	7·6	22·1	20·8	4·0	8·5	1·8
Other sorts of fibres	0·1	0·2	...	...	...	...	0·1	0·3	...
Condiments and spices	1·8	0·6	3·0	0·7	1·5	0·9	2·8	0·9	0·5
Sugar	2·8	1·4	0·1	1·9	0·2	5·8	0·2	2·6	23·0
Dyes	0·1	0·4	...	0·1	...	...	...	0·2	...
Drugs and narcotics	0·7	0·3	0·1	0·6	0·3	0·7	0·5	5·4	0·4
Fodder crops	1·9	...	3·8	0·1	4·3	4·3	0·5	1·4	...
Orchards and gardens	1·2	1·8	0·4	1·5	0·9	1·4	2·2	0·9	2·0
Fuel trees and topes	2·4	0·7	0·4	1·6	...	2·7	...	0·2	18·0

WET LANDS.
Fully irrigated crops.

Among the regularly irrigated crops paddy easily comes first. Of the total cultivated area of the district this crop occupies one-fourth; the proportion in the Ambāsamudram taluk, which possesses the best of the lands irrigated by the Tāmbraparni, rises to nearly two-thirds. Other fully irrigated

WET LANDS.

crops grown on wet lands are plantains (included under "orchard and garden"), betel-vine ("drugs and narcotics"), turmeric ("dyes") and sugar-cane; the last-named crop accounts for only 150 acres of the area shown under "sugar," the rest consisting of palmyras. Sunn-hemp comes under "other fibres." The area under plantains is small, the crop being cultivated chiefly in Vēlūr Pudukkudi, Vēlūr Kasba, Attūr (Srīvaikuntam taluk), in villages at the foot of the *tēris*, from which spring-water is drawn off for the purpose, and here and there in several villages under the lower irrigation of the Tāmbraparni. The betel-vine is grown in various places throughout the Tāmbraparni valley (chiefly at Seydinganallūr, Mangalakurichi, Korkai, Mukkāni and Attūr) and occasionally under the minor river systems. The most noteworthy example of sugar-cane cultivation is at Gōvindappēri (Ambāsamudram taluk), where an enterprising landowner has introduced cane of the Mauritius variety, has installed a water-pump worked by an oil-engine, and devotes a great deal of care to the scientific treatment of the crop. Turmeric is very little cultivated, and is to be met with in one or two villages (Kīlaseval, Nayinārkulam, Gōpālasamudram) of the Ambāsamudram taluk.

Sunn-hemp.

Another crop deserving mention is sunn-hemp, which, though not irrigated to the extent required by the crops just referred to, is cultivated only on wet lands. As may be inferred from the figures relating to "other sorts of fibre" to which this crop is the chief contributor, its cultivation is confined, as a rule, to small areas in the three taluks of Ambāsamudram, Tinnevelly and Tenkāsi. Being an industrial crop, its cultivation and subsequent treatment are fettered by the well-known rule which prescribes that every industry shall be the monopoly of a caste. In this case it is the Saluppans; and, in villages where these people live and the conditions of the land are suitable, sunn-hemp is grown and made ready for use.

Its cultivation.

The season of its cultivation is the interval between the *pisānam* and *kār* crops, and it is grown on wet lands which retain a little moisture and can get one or two floodings during that period. The land is ploughed once while it is still moist early in March, and the seed is sown before the month is out. By the end of May or early in June the field is covered with a thick growth of tall golden flowering stalks, and the crop is then ready for harvest. The plants are cut off flush with the ground and left to dry in the sun for a few days. The seed is beaten out, and the stalks removed to a storehouse to dry thoroughly. They are then taken out in bundles, at leisure, and left in water for a few days until they become thoroughly soaked, a stage which is recognized by the fetid smell which they then emit. The stalks are taken in handfuls, first by one end and then the other, and slashed against the surface of the water until the fibre round the stalk is loosened and collects in bunches adhering to the stem. The fibre is removed and formed into bundles and is ready to be spun into yarn. This is woven into sacking of exceptional durability; and professional cartmen say that bags made of this material will stand hard wear for twenty years. It is used also for the trapping and harness of pack-bullocks, and serves the purpose of the leather generally used in other districts in the manufacture of the necks of mhote-buckets. The stalks are used as thatch. Much of the fibre is sent out of the district in an unworked state; and, in spite of the competition of the cheap jute sacking of Bengal, the Saluppans appear to drive a fairly prosperous trade.

A part of their earnings has to go in rental to the landowner, as the Saluppan never owns the lands he thus cultivates. The crop pays the landowner handsomely. He gets a rental varying from Rs. 12 to Rs. 25 an acre; and, though the lands on which the crop is grown are among the best wet lands in the district, this rental will often more than pay the whole assessment for the year. The seed not required by the Saluppan for his next year's sowing is often bought by the owners of wet lands, who sow it in their fields and, after 30 or 40 days' growth, cut the plants before they flower. The stalks and roots are left in the field and puddled in with the plough to form manure for the paddy crop.

Paddy; season of cultivation.

The cultivation of paddy is regulated by the north-east and the south-west monsoons, the period of the former being, approximately, October 15 to January 15, that of the latter, June 15 to September 15. All the rivers of the district are in flood during the north-east monsoon; but the Tāmbraparni alone receives ample supplies from June to September. The Chittār is affected more than any of the minor rivers by the south-west monsoon; but under this system, as also under those commanded by the rivers of the Nāngunēri taluk, it is only in the villages close up to the hills that water sufficient for a wet crop is received during the period. Paddy cultivation during this season under any of the Sankaranainārkōil rivers is extremely rare. In several villages of the Tiruchendūr taluk lands irrigated by the *tēri* springs regularly yield two crops of paddy.

The season of the south-west monsoon is known as *kār*, that of the north-east monsoon as *pisānam*. The single-crop lands, which include practically all lands under rain-fed tanks, all the wet lands below the uppermost reaches of the minor rivers in the Nānguneri, Tenkāsi and Sankaranainārkōil taluks and about 6 per cent of the total area under the Tāmbraparni system, produce only a *pisānam* crop. Under a few tanks, chiefly the better sources fed by the Chittār, some tanks supplied by the Nānguneri and Sankaranainārkōil rivers, and very rarely under rain-fed tanks, if the supplies of the north-east monsoon have been ample and the tanks are again replenished by the hot-weather rains, a second short-termed paddy crop—one of the *kuruvai* series—is taken. The supplies received in the tanks are, in such cases, usually supplemented by privately owned wells.

Kinds of paddy.

The varieties of paddy grown in the district are too many to enumerate. Some grains are thick, some thin, some long and some short. The rice obtained may be yellow, reddish, dull white or pure white. The most highly valued paddy is the *ānaikomban* with its long thin white grain, and next come the varieties known as *sambā* (with many sub-species), *kulavālai*, *vellai* and so on, which yield a short thick grain; least prized are the dark grained sorts, such as *maikuruvai* and *puluthiviratti*. The choice of a particular kind of paddy for a field is determined by a number of conditions: the length of time available for its growth, the level of the land, the nature of the soil and the prospects of irrigation. The *pisānam* season is considered to last for five months and where possible *ānaikomban* is grown during this period; on the best single-crop lands under the Chittār, where cultivation is begun in August and the closing months of *kār* are made to form one season with *pisānam*, *kulavālai*, a crop of heavy yield taking seven to eight months to mature, is preferred. The *kār* season is a month shorter and the favourite crop of that period is *sambā*; *puluthiviratti* and *maikuruvai* mature in 100 days and are sown when time is limited.

Methods of its cultivation.

Paddy is cultivated by two methods, either by direct sowing in the field or by transplantation from a seed-bed. Speaking generally, the sowing method is adopted in *kār* and transplantation in *pisānam*. The land is ploughed immediately after the *pisānam* harvest; sheep are sometimes penned in the field and cow-dung and ashes are applied just before the sowing season. As soon as the earliest rains are received (which should be in May), the field is ploughed again, the seed sown, and the land once more turned up so that the

CHAP. IV. WET LANDS.

seed may be covered. The surface is then smoothed over with a plank (*maram*) drawn by bullocks, and for two or three weeks no water is admitted. Regular irrigation is then begun, and in four months from the start the crop should be ready for harvest.

Under the system of transplantation seed-beds are prepared as soon as the earliest freshes of *pisānam* are received, or even, if the *kār* crop was started early, advantage will be taken of the later freshes of the *kār* season for the purpose. The seedlings remain in the nurseries for 20 to 50 days according to the nature of the paddy, the theory being that the young plants should be kept in the seed-bed for a period equal to one-fourth of the time that the crop takes to mature in the field. Meanwhile the fields have been flooded, leaf manure, *kolinji* or *āvāram* for choice, is churned up with a light plough and levelled up with a plank. The seedlings are brought from the nursery and planted out in clumps of four or five to ten plants at a time at short intervals. The field is partially drained to enable the young plants to root themselves firmly; water is then admitted once more and allowed to stand until the crop begins to shoot. From that stage onwards the soil is kept moist but should not be flooded. The process of harvesting or threshing is the same in *kār* as in *pisānam*. The stalks are cut by hand close to the ground and carried off in bundles to a suitable high and dry place, a mound or a rock; the bundles are beaten on the ground till most of the grain falls out; they are then spread out on the ground, and cattle yoked three or four abreast are made to perform endless circles over them until the last grain is trodden out.

The above account of paddy cultivation is necessarily sketchy; and all general statements are subject to exceptions. For instance, there are extensive areas in the lower reaches of the Tāmbraparni valley and elsewhere in which *ānaikomban* is not raised in *pisānam*, either because the freshes are received too late or the land is not sufficiently well drained to suit the crop. Towards the eastern side of the Tinnevelly taluk and in the Srīvaikuntam and Tiruchendūr taluks generally, the method of transplantation, not sowing, is the rule for the *kār* crop, the general reason being that the hot-weather rains cannot be relied on here to render early sowing possible. Even when broadcast sowing is adopted, the seed is sown after the field has been puddled (*tholi* is the word used to describe this state of the ground); further east, under the lower channels of the Srīvaikuntam anicut system, where supplies are often received late and the seasons for both crops are short, broadcast sowing in *tholi* is often adopted both for *kār* and *pisānam*.

The absence of uniformity in methods of paddy cultivation is the most striking feature of the wet lands under the Srīvaikuntam system.

A farmer's stock-in-trade of implements is small: a light wooden plough for use in puddled fields and perhaps also a slightly heavier one for use when the field is ploughed in a comparatively dry state (*podi* this state is called) with a view to broadcast sowing; a wooden plank attached to a yoke for use in levelling the surface and a *manvetti* or spade. Total value, including two ploughs, about six rupees.

"Irrigated dry" crops.

In addition to the regularly irrigated crops, a number of "dry" crops requiring only occasional irrigation are cultivated on wet lands—the species of cultivation described in the old accounts as *nanjai mēl punjai*, "dry crops on wet lands." These comprise cholam, ragi, gingelly, chillies and vegetables of various kinds. Gingelly is grown chiefly in the best lands of the Tāmbraparni valley between the *pisānam* and *kār* crops; the other crops are grown mainly during the *kār* season on lands whose supply of water is scanty during that period. Wells are generally used to supplement the supply. Senna (see below) and gingelly are also raised occasionally on single-crop paddy lands after the *pisānam* harvest is over.

Agricultural practice on the dry lands of the district divides itself according as the soil is black or red. The table on page 22 shows the distribution of these two kinds of soil over the various taluks, and, as the rates of assessment abundantly prove, the black soils as a class are infinitely more valuable than the red. The Tenkāsi taluk and, to some extent, Sankaranainārkōil form an exception to this rule; Kuttālam and a dozen villages adjacent to it in the Tenkāsi taluk contain much red loam of exceptional fertility, which, as a rule, produces two good crops in a year. During the south-west monsoon, when the rainfall in these parts (known as *sāral*) varies between a gentle drizzle and heavy showers, most of the fields are cultivated with cholam. Labour and manure are applied in plenty, and the result is usually a heavy crop. In October or November sāmai, varagu, horse-gram or gingelly forms a second crop. The red loamy lands at the foot of the Sankaranainārkōil hills also repay cultivation and are comparatively valuable.

Elsewhere in the district the red soils get little attention and, in the neighbourhood of good wet lands, especially those watered by the Tāmbraparni, are practically neglected. It does not, however, follow that the lands are valueless; for in many parts their owners derive a fair income by letting them

CHAP. IV.
DRY LANDS.

for pasture during a few months of the years. "Want of care ruins a wet field, care ruins a dry field" is the proverb which at least sums up the general practice in these parts. Over large tracts of the Nānguněri, Tiruchendūr and Srīvaikuntam taluks, much of which is assessed at three annas an acre, palmyras and acacias are the chief products of soil. Where palmyras are found alone, the soil is ploughed or roughly hacked up with a spade and planted with the usual inferior dry crops. Acacias, which form valuable firewood, are cut down every eight years, and the land is then turned to cultivation or re-stocked with acacia seed.

Chief crops on the red soils.

The crops usually raised on the red soil are inferior cereals and pulses such as sāmai *(Panicum miliare)*, varagu *(Paspalam scrobiculatum)* and pulses, horse-gram, black gram and gingelly. When the north-east monsoon has broken, the land is ploughed two or three times and the seed is sown; after sowing, the land is ploughed again, and the seed more or less covered. Planks are occasionally used to level the soil. Gingelly cannot stand much rain and is not sown until December or January. The period from seed-time to harvest in the case of all these crops is three to four months. Two crops are occasionally mixed in one field, the idea being apparently that a season which will not suit one of them may suit the other.

"Tinnevelly Senna."

A crop possessing a peculiar interest is that which is known as Tinnevelly senna (in Tamil *āvarai ilai* or *nilavāgai*). The plant was introduced into the district in the early years of the century by Mr. G. A. Hughes, who imported the seed from Arabia and sowed it (apparently on wet lands) in the neighbourhood of Tachanallūr. It is still grown on wet lands in several villages, chiefly in the Tinnevelly taluk, between the *pisānam* harvest and the *kār* sowing. Elsewhere, as in Gangaikondān, Chattram-pudukkulam and Mānūr (Tinnevelly taluk) and in Nānguněri, it is raised as a second or supplemental crop after the main crop on single-crop lands has been harvested. Fair crops of less valuable senna are obtained also on the better red dry lands in several villages of the Tinnevelly taluk and in the north of Nānguněri.

Sowing on the dry lands takes place in December, and the soil should be thoroughly moist at the time. Flowers begin to appear after forty days and are picked at once. Thereafter the plants are allowed to flower and to produce pods or beans, which, like the leaves, form an industrial product. Two-and-a-half months after sowing and again after another month and yet again after another three weeks, the leaves are picked and are put in a shed to dry gradually, in such a way that they do not become brittle. They are then screened through a sieve with a half-inch mesh, and what does not pass through forms the valuable portion of the crop. The good leaves and pods are tied up in sacks and sent to Tuticorin to be pressed and are thence exported to Europe, where they are largely used in medicinal preparations. In a good year the crop is a profitable one, the gross yield representing not less than Rs. 50 an acre. The return from a crop grown on wet land is proportionately higher.

Well-irrigation.

A saving feature of the dry red lands of the district is to be found in the complete transformation which well-irrigation can produce. Given an enterprising cultivator and a water-level within reasonable distance of the surface, a well is sunk; black soil, when obtainable, and tank-silt are carted to the field in large quantities, farm-yard refuse is saved up for the precious plot and in a few years the most barren, coarse and useless red soils will become rich and valuable gardens. Wells are, as a rule, built square and revetted with stone above the level of the rock; twenty to thirty feet is their ordinary depth, and in normal seasons their supply lasts throughout the year. The water lifts generally in use are the hand-picotta and the familiar double-bullock mhote *(kamalai)* in which the bullocks walk backwards and forwards up a ramp, lowering and raising the bucket over a pulley. The most notable well of the district is one at Palavūr (Nānguneri taluk) in which as many as eighteen pairs of bullocks are sometimes employed in lifting water. Oil-engines and pumps have been installed in eight places, the most successful examples being at Karunkulam (Nānguneri taluk) Gōvindappēri (Ambāsamudram) and Chintāmani (Sankaranainārkōil). The well-cultivation in the *tēri* regions of Tiruchendūr and Nānguneri is referred to in the notices relating to those taluks; Padugai, Udangudi, Kommattikōttai, Sāstāvinallūr, and Nālumāvadi in the Tiruchendūr taluk and, in the Nānguneri taluk, Kuttam and Ovari are the chief centres. In all parts of the district the Shānāns stand out as the most enterprising of garden cultivators; and nowhere is their success so conspicuous as in the *tēri* areas.

Extent of it.

Detailed figures of the area irrigated in each taluk ten years ago or more from private wells are difficult to obtain. The area so watered in the whole district in 1913–14 was 42,453 acres, which represent, so far as ascertainable, an advance on the figures of 1902–03 of 34·24 per cent. Nearly one-third of the total area occurs in the Sankaranainārkōil taluk.

CHAP. IV. DRY LANDS.

In addition to these wells, used for irrigation of dry lands, a number of wells, usually substantially built with masonry walls, are used in wet lands to supplement the precarious supplies of tanks and channels in the raising of a second crop of paddy or an "irrigated dry" crop, such as cholam, ragi or chillies. These are most numerous in the Nānguněri, Tenkāsi and Sankaranainārkōil taluks and in villages on the lower reaches of the Chittār.

Cultivation on the black soils.[1]

The finest farmers of the district are to be found on the black-cotton soil (mainly in the Kōilpatti taluk and in the north of Srīvaikuntam), and the best of these are the Telugu Kammavas and Reddis who now own the greater part of this class of land.

Here the ryot is by instinct a real farmer; he does his work himself and prefers the assistance of his family—men, women and boys—to that of hired labourers. His pride is in his cattle, his *cumbu adi* (see below) and the cleanness of his land, and he is ever on the look-out for the time when his less industrious neighbour may fail in the great competition. Hariali grass *(Arugam pullu)* is the enemy of the black soil, and the ryot who neglects it is the man to whom money should be advanced on the security of his field; soon the mortgage will be foreclosed upon, and the land will change hands. So the industrious farmer reaps his reward, and the fittest alone survive.

There are three main crops on the black soil, viz., cumbu, cholam and cotton.

Chief crops.

The cultivation of cumbu in the place of the more usual cholam as the main cereal of the black soil tract is peculiar to the district; and the reason for this local difference is probably that the temperature of the district is high throughout the year and cumbu is a better food for such a climate than cholam.

The cholam crop *(chōlanāthu)* of the black-cotton soil is also an unusual sub-species, known as *Sorghum saccharatum* (var. *irungu*), and is peculiar to the southern districts. It is not a grain crop in any sense of the word. It is grown solely for cattle fodder, and, though seed is collected, it is rarely that this provides more than what is required for the sowing of the following season.

Other crops.

Bengal gram is occasionally grown pure, usually a late-sown crop on land where the sowing season has been lost for cotton occasionally also coriander or horse-gram is sown for the same reason. Kuthiraivāli *(Pannicum frumentaceum* var. *crus galli)* occasionally takes the place of cumbu, especially on poor

[1] For valuable assistance with this section I am much indebted to Mr. H. C. Sampson, Deputy Director of Agriculture.

shallow soils inclined to be saline or in places where water is liable to stand. Red gram is also grown on the mixed or shallow soils which do not crack, but only if rain happens to fall in July or August, which is the sowing season. Other pulses are usually sown as mixtures with cotton or cumbu, but never with cholam, which on black-cotton soils is always a pure crop. Cow gram, green gram and mochai *(Dolichos lablab)* are sown in furrows eight feet or so apart in a cumbu crop, and horse-gram, green gram, black gram, cow gram, Bengal gram and, occasionally, cluster beans are similarly sown in the cotton crop. Castor and coriander are sometimes broadcasted in the cotton crop, especially in the south of the district. Pulichai *(Hibiscus cannabinus)*, which yields a fibre and serves also as a vegetable, is also occasionally sown in rows in the cotton. Owing to the high prices which coriander has commanded during the last few years, the admixture of this crop with cotton, though harmful to the latter, has very greatly increased.

The agricultural year.

The black soil is seldom more than six feet deep and often is not more than half this depth. To save these lands from exhaustion rotations are, therefore, essential and are, in fact, generally practised. Well-to-do ryots, however, reserve land near the village, on which they grow cumbu year after year; they take a special pride in such plots—cumbu *adi* as they call them—and manure them heavily. Fodder cholam is also grown year after year alongside paths and cart-tracks through the black soil. Cotton never follows cotton on well-farmed land. Ploughing commences immediately the cumbu is harvested in February; and there are several Tamil proverbs which emphasize the importance of thorough work at this stage—தை உழவோ நெய் உழவோ—"ploughing in *Thai* (January-February) is ploughing ghee." சித்திரை மாதம் புழுதி பத்தரைமாத்துத் தங்கம்—"*Chittirai* (April-May) tilth is like pure gold." After this follows the ploughing on the harvested fields of chōlanāthu, and the land receives anything from three to seven ploughings between this time and the next sowing season. The land under cotton, which is allowed to remain under this crop until July, naturally has much less cultivation given to it, and, unless cropped with a cereal the next year, soon becomes foul with weeds. In many places much time and labour is expended on improving the lands by repairing washes, carting soil, tank silt and manure, and digging out hariali grass. Each man has his own pit, into which all his cattle-manure, house refuse and threshing-floor sweepings are dumped. This mixture is periodically covered with black-cotton soil or silt, and the whole forms a more or less homogenous mass of

CHAP. IV. DRY LANDS.

wellrotted manure. Here "bratties" are seldom used for fuel. Manure is too precious to be thus wasted, and the fuel supply is met from the cotton stalks, which are pulled up and neatly stacked in the village stackyard. Practically all the manure goes to the cumbu crop. Chōlanāthu is seldom manured; and with cotton, if it is manured at all, the process is usually to pen sheep on the land. The sowing season commences in September in the north of the district and a month later in the south, and lasts for about six weeks. Sometimes rain is insufficient and at other times is too much for these heavy soils, with the result that often the fields have to be sown a second time.

Chōlanāthu is usually sown first, with a very heavy seed rate, often as much as 40 to 50 Madras measures per acre. Such a crop, if it is to grow to any height and produce a fine straw, naturally requires all the rain that it can get, and even in good seasons it seldom attains more than 3 or 4 feet. It gives a very fine leafy straw. After this, cumbu is sown, with a seed rate of one Madras measure per acre. Then follows the cotton sowing. Before the rains are over, the ryot ploughs through the cumbu crop to loosen the surface soil and to thin out the plants. As the Tamil proverb says: சோளம் நட்டாப் போல், கம்பு கெட்டாப்போல்—"cholam should look as though just planted: cumbu as if it had been spoiled." Weeding in the cotton fields then begins, and a good surface mulch is at the same time made and maintained. Next follows the harvest of cumbu and of the earlier mixed pulses, then the harvest of chōlanāthu, and by this time ploughing again commences. The cotton harvest, as will be shown below, extends over several months. Thus the black soil peasant makes work for himself throughout the year and, in spite of his shallow and easily exhausted soils, produces as good an outturn to the acre as any other ryot in the Presidency.

The Kōilpatti Agricultural Station.

It was in this country of good farmers that in 1901 the Madras Government opened, as an experimental farm, the Kōilpatti Agricultural Station. The farm comprises two blocks of land of average quality, one of red and one of black soil. The red soil block, 25 acres in extent, is situated less than a mile from the Kōilpatti railway station and contains the farm buildings and office and quarters for the staff. One-and-a-half miles away on the road to Sāttūr lies the black soil tract, its area, after a great extension made in 1906, amounting to 115 acres. On the black soil attention has been directed to the introduction of new cereals, the study of the different kinds of irungu cholam (*Andropogon sorghum* var.

irungu), the rotation of crops and the use of manures. On the red soil experiments have been made with new crops and new methods of well-irrigation; the value of concentrated manures has also been tested.

Most important of all, however, have been the efforts directed towards improving the cotton crop by means of seed selection and better methods of cultivation.

Cotton: The indigenous varieties.

The indigenous cotton of the district, though occasionally sown in red and mixed soils, is mainly a black soil crop and is therefore produced chiefly in the Kōilpatti taluk, in the north of the Srīvaikuntam taluk, in east Sankaranainārkōil and in the occasional pockets of black soil which are found here and there throughout the district. The two main species known as *karunganni (Gossypium obtusifolium)* and *uppam (G. herbaceum),* though often, and in fact generally, grown together in the same field, can be readily distinguished. Its rounded short sepals, spherical bolls and harsh, though snowy white, lint mark the *uppam* variety; whilst the *karunganni* can be known by its elongated deeply serrated sepals, by its conical bolls and the creamy tinge and comparative fineness of its lint. *Karunganni* likes the sea-breeze and, except when grown on red or mixed soils, is seldom found more than thirty miles from the coast; further inland the *uppam* predominates. Both species are included in the general term "Tinnies"—the name by which the cotton of Tinnevelly, Rāmnād and Madura is quoted in the London markets.

The bolls of the *karunganni* crop begin to burst by the middle of March; picking commences at once, and the "season picking" will continue till the middle of May. About this time, or sooner, the heavy hot-weather rains are expected; if the rainfall is good, the plants will produce a second flush and will go on yielding cotton till July and sometimes even longer. The harvest of *uppam* begins two or three weeks later than that of *karunganni*; its rate of production is far more rapid, and, though its net yield is about the same as that of *karunganni,* it exhausts itself in the early season and seldom gives a second flush.

A normal outturn on ordinary black cotton soil is one-and-a-half to two *pothis* [1] of raw cotton, or *kappās.* The daily pickings are dried in the sun and are then stored until the ryot makes his own arrangements to convey the cotton to a ginning factory or until the local dealer, or *taragan,* calls for it. The cotton is ginned at the factory on payment of a fee; and,

[1] A *pothi* = 248 lbs. Thus two *pothis* practically equal a candy (500 lbs.).

though the ginning merchant is also, as a rule, an exporter, the sale of the cleaned lint forms a separate transaction.

The "dealer."

With the introduction to this district, in 1894, of the steam ginning factory, the use of the old hand-gin *(manai)* has become comparatively rare; and its partial displacement has been by no means an unmixed blessing. To make up their bundles for the factory the dealers deliberately mix cotton of all kinds, using good samples to grade up bad and judiciously blending bad cotton with good, the result being that the seeds are handed back in a mixed state and a deterioration of type inevitably follows. A few of the more intelligent growers, it is true, keep back a part of their crop for seed and clean it themselves with the hand-gin. By this means they are able to select the best seed of a uniform type for sowing purposes. Taken as a whole, however, the ryot seldom selects his seed and, if left to himself, is unlikely to produce a pure strain of either type of cotton.

Work of the Agricultural Station; the fixing of types.

Recognizing the importance of teaching and diffusing the habit of seed selection, the Agricultural department, by means of the Kōilpatti Agricultural Station, have given their special attention to this aspect of cotton cultivation. From the beginning the two species were separated and grown as pure crops at the agricultural station; and the lint so obtained was submitted to experts, whose unanimous opinion it was that *karunganni* was the true "Tinny" of commerce, to be preferred for its longer staple and its consequent suitability for the relatively higher counts of cotton. After further improvement had been made by selection, it was found that the *karunganni* plant was a far more variable type than *uppam*; it was also noticed that natural crossing was of common occurrence, and the operations of 1908 showed *uppam* to be actually the better yielder of lint. In 1909, however, *karunganni* proved superior. The difficulty of fixing a type in the case of *karunganni* still continued; but by degrees the fertilization of one sort of *karunganni* with another resulted in the production of a fairly fixed strain. A similar process applied to the *uppam* species has produced a very vigorous strain of that variety. Samples of the two kinds of cotton were sent in 1910 to the Director of the Imperial Institute, London, and the opinion then obtained agreed substantially with that which had already been expressed by the local cotton merchants. The Director stated in the course of his report: "The *karunganni* cotton is thus seen to approximate in fineness to Egyptian cotton, whilst the *uppam* has the ordinary coarse character of most Indian cottons."

CHAP. IV. DRY LANDS.

Seed-farms.

To give practical effect to the scientific work accomplished at the farm, the Agricultural department have recently started a system by which selected ryots contract to grow cotton and supply seed to the department. The department buys the *kappās*, gins it by hand and sells the seed to cotton-growers. These seed-farms, distributed in various parts of the district, extend now (1914) to upwards of 1,300 acres, and the stock of seed produced in a year is sufficient to sow several thousands of acres. The success of the scheme may be gauged from the fact that, while the ryot can buy back his seed at the ginning factory at Rs. 6 a *pothi*, the whole of the stock obtained by the department was sold at the rate of Rs. 10 a *pothi*. *Karunganni*, it seems, is assuming a fixed type, and the European merchants assert that its improvement is being maintained.

Outturn of lint.

Efforts are also being made to improve the ginning outturn of the local cotton. Attempts so far have met with considerable success, and one unit strain of *karunganni* is already being distributed, which not only gives an outturn of 31·3 per cent of lint but is also a heavier cropping strain than the ordinary plant. Another strain suitable for the tract where *uppam* predominates and which gins at 33⅓ per cent of lint, is now being grown on seed-farms for distribution. Special importance is attached to this last experiment, as it is hoped that the strain will replace a short coarse cotton, known locally as *mailam* or *pulichi*, which has been recently imported from North India and, owing to its high outturn of lint, is obtaining a grim forthold in the district.

The seed-drill.

Another improvement which the Kōilpatti station is trying to effect is in the method of sowing. Under the present system of broadcast sowing, much seed is wasted, the plants grow up irregularly, and interculture is difficult. The "seed-drill" of the Ceded Districts obviates all these difficulties, and, since its foundation, the farm has, by precept and example, done its best to popularize the instrument. There were several difficulties in the way, one of the principal being that the use of the seed-drill rendered it difficult to sow mixtures with the cotton. Pulses, coriander and tennai (*Setaria italica*) are usually mixed in small quantities with cotton ; and, as these are the perquisites of the women of the household, there were naturally objections to sowing cotton pure. However, as greater experience has been obtained in drilling, this objection has largely been overcome bullock-hoeing, which follows as a corollary to the use of the seed-drill, has considerably lightened the woman's share in the cultivation, and, in villages where the people are still dependent on the department for the loan of implements, it is the

CHAP. IV. DRY LANDS.

women who lead the scramble for the bullock-hoes. It is estimated that about 12,000 acres in the district are now being treated with the seed-drill.

Exotic cultivation.

Besides these two indigenous kinds of cotton, a large number of extra-provincial and exotic (including American) varieties have been tested on the farm; most of the experiments, however, did not justify themselves, and, with one notable exception—"Cambodia"—, these cottons were abandoned.

Cambodia.

Cambodia cotton closely resembles American and is a variety of *hirsutum*; in a tropical climate, however, it is much harder and gives a stronger and fuller lint than either newly-introduced American or acclimatized Dharwar-American stock. Unlike the indigenous "Tinnevelly" which has a long tap-root and slender feeding-roots penetrating deep into the soil, both the Cambodia and the American possess a tapering tap-root with strong feeding-roots given off near the surface. Being thus unable to withstand prolonged drought, Cambodia thrives best, not on the black-cotton soils which depend on the rainfall, but under regular irrigation and heavy manure. Given these two conditions, the quality or colour of the soil is comparatively of little account. Cambodia cotton may be seen growing in garden lands which formerly produced valuable crops of vegetables, and new wells are being sunk in many places with the primary object of irrigating this plant. Even on well-drained wet lands, irrigated by tanks and channels, the certainty of a good crop of Cambodia is in some cases preferred to the risk which paddy cultivation may involve.

Its introduction.

Cambodia cotton was introduced into this Presidency in 1904 by Mr. C. Benson, then Deputy Director of Agriculture, who obtained a small quantity of seed from the President of the Pondicherry Chamber of Agriculture. It was sown in the Kōilpatti farm in 1904 and the three following years on the ordinary unirrigated black-cotton soil and soon showed that it could not resist drought. In 1905, Mr. A. Steel of Messrs. A. & F. Harvey & Co., Virudupatti (now in the Rāmnād district), happened to find in a bundle of cotton some Cambodia *kappās* and sowed some of the seed by way of experiment in a plot of black-cotton soil near his office. The rainfall was short that year, and, as in the Kōilpatti farm, the crop was a comparative failure. The next season (1906–07) proved more successful; but even then the ryots who had flocked to see the new "American" cotton—as it was then named and as it is generally called by the ryots to this day—thought the results were not quite satisfactory and themselves suggested that it should be irrigated. This idea having once got abroad, there was a regular scramble for Mr. Steel's stock of seed. The crop of 1907–08 amounted to 40 bales (of 500 lbs.), and the seed of this crop was eagerly sought for and bought at fabulous prices. In 1908–09 the number of bales pressed had risen to 1,650, the figure for the next year being 7,500. The demand for this cotton has by now thoroughly established itself, being greatly in excess of the supply. In 1911 the Council of the British Cotton Growing Association expressed their highest appreciation of the species and said Lancashire could take 500,000 bales of it annually. From the Kōilpatti farm seed has been distributed to several districts of the Presidency, Madura, Coimbatore, Trichinopoly, Salem and South and North Arcot, and has even found its way to Burma and the Punjab.

Subsequent history.

When the *kappās* of ordinary Tinnevelly cotton was selling a few years ago at Rs. 25 a *pothi*, Cambodia was fetching as much as Rs. 40. In 1912, however, the price of Cambodia fell to the level of, and even below the level of, Tinnevelly. The drop was partly due to the fact that long-staple American, the competitor of Cambodia, was cheap that year; but it was due also to causes within the control of ryots and the local dealers. To save himself trouble, the ryot sometimes leaves the cotton in the ground to yield a second crop in the second year; the additional crop is poor and encourages the development of insects. Often too the ryot sows his crop mixed with plants of the indigenous species, and, even if he does so accidentally, it goes to his heart to root up the other varieties before they have yielded. The more deliberate mischief-makers are the dealers who, in the hope of securing a Cambodia price, stuff their Cambodia bundles with Tinnevelly. Deceived at first by the dealers' stratagem, the merchant infers thereafter that the presence of Cambodia means a mixed bundle of no definite type and values it even less than a similar weight of pure Tinnevelly.

Its cultivation and outturn.

Cambodia is an exhausting crop, and heavy manuring is essential. The seed is sown in a thoroughly wet soil in October at the rate of about 10 lbs. an acre. It receives no further attention except occasional weeding until December, when, in the absence of rain, irrigation is necessary. According to the state of weather and the nature of the soil, irrigation will be repeated at intervals of a fortnight or more. The bolls begin to burst early in February; regular picking starts in the following month and continues till the end of April. A second flush will follow in June. The plants are sometimes left in the ground till the following March, with the

CHAP. IV. DRY LANDS.

consequence, however, that they deteriorate. The yield of an acre during the first year varies between three and six *pothis*. The *kappās* gives a high proportion of lint, varying between 33 and 35 per cent; with the ordinary Tinnevelly, the percentage is about 25. Hand-ginning in the case of Cambodia is especially difficult and is therefore practically unknown.

Early attempts to improve cotton cultivation.

In the light of these achievements of the modern Agricultural department it is of interest to recall the early efforts of the East India Company to improve the cotton of the Madras Presidency and of this district in particular. In 1790 Dr. Anderson was sent to Madras and was given the duty of distributing a variety of foreign cotton seeds. One important result followed, namely, the introduction of Bourbon cotton, which became naturalized subsequently in three districts—Tinnevelly, Salem and Coimbatore. The results in this district were due largely to Mr. G. A. Hughes, a private merchant, whose efforts towards developing the resources of the country are referred to elsewhere. His cultivation of Bourbon cotton was, however, at the time a still greater triumph than his Tinnevelly senna; and for more than 20 years "Hughes' Tinnevelly cotton" (Bourbon variety) continued to be quoted in the Liverpool market as the best in India. It was actually sold at a higher price than the American-stapled cotton, and 3*d*. a lb. above the best Surats.

Mr. Hughes sent in his views in 1819 regarding the method of growing this cotton. His main contentions were that the soil should be red or brown loam and that black-cotton soil was to be entirely avoided; the land should be near the sea; sowings should be in September; and the plant should be cultivated as a perennial. Mr. Hughes' successful cultivation, however, did not long survive him. He died in 1835; and in 1840, the Collector, Mr. Thompson, reported that Bourbon cotton was cultivated only by one man and on a small scale, namely a hundred chains. At the present day its cultivation has almost disappeared from the district.

In 1836 Dr. Wight was appointed by the Madras Government to enquire into the methods of cotton cultivation in South India; and on the report of Government the Court of Directors decided to start experimental farms under American planters. Ten planters were procured from America, and in 1840 three of them were sent to the Tinnevelly district. Their duties were to demonstrate the value of the "saw-gin" and to popularize American seed and American methods of cultivation. The gins did not arrive, and the ryots did not take kindly to the foreign methods and seed; and after frittering away a year in the neighbourhood of Sivakāsi, the planters were removed from the district.

A few years later, in 1845, Mr. Finnie, another of the original ten planters, was transferred from South Arcot to Tinnevelly. His instructions were similar to those which his predecessors had received, but Mr. Finnie had notions of his own and put them into practice. He had no faith in the saw-gin and recognized that the fatal obstacle to the success of the indigenous cotton was that it passed through too many hands. The local merchants used up all the best cotton on their domestic trade, and the rubbish, amounting to fifty thousand bales a year, was exported to Europe. Mr. Finnie asked permission to act as a private agent for the purchase of locally-grown hand-ginned cotton, and after some difficulty was permitted by Government to do so. In 1849 he bought 230 bales of indigenous cotton from the ryots, ginned it himself by hand and sent it home for sale on behalf of the East India Company. The Manchester Commercial Association found it to be fine, clean, bright cotton, so clean and of so good a colour that the entire quantity was disposed of at the satisfactory price of 5*d*. a lb.

Meanwhile Mr. Finnie had, according to his instructions, made experiments with the New Orleans seed; and though in one place, Kuttālam, his cultivation was successful, the ryots distrusted him and declined to try his seed. Gin-houses had been built at Aruppukōttai and Sivakāsi (Rāmnād district), but Mr. Finnie could not get good cotton at a reasonable price, and the expenses of ginning were prohibitive.

In 1849 the Madras Government decided to give up their cotton experiment and to dispense with the services of Mr. Finnie and Dr. Wight. "The continuance of this experiment," Government observed, "is calculated to do harm to the cause which it was originally intended to promote, inevitably leading the natives to imagine that Government alone have the means and facility of raising American cotton." And, after two years' employment in the Tinnevelly district, Mr. Finnie left for England. The gins and instruments were handed over to the East Indian lads then under Dr. Wight's tuition at Coimbatore. The gin-house of Sivakāsi was handed over to the Collector and was subsequently sold. Dr. Wight's services, however, were retained at Coimbatore until 1853, when he retired.

IRRIGATION. Statistics.

In the total (ryotwari) area of the district 15 acres in every hundred are under irrigation from Government tanks and channels; and of the irrigated area 82 acres in a hundred

CHAP. IV. IRRIGATION.

derive their supply from rivers and streams, the remainder being dependent on rain-fed tanks. The following table exhibits in one view the distribution over the eight taluks of the four classes of irrigation-sources and also, as judged by the rates of assessment, the relative values of wet lands in the different parts of the district. It may be explained that all fourth-class sources are rain-fed tanks and all first and second class sources and almost all third-class sources are tanks and channels supplied by rivers; a very few exceptionally good rain-fed tanks are included in the third class.[1]

Taluks.	Percentage of the occupied area which is wet.	Percentage of the total (ryotwari) irrigated area of the district which is registered under each class of source.				Average assessment per acre on wet lands.			
						River-fed.		Rain-fed.	
		First.	Second.	Third.	Fourth.	Single crop.	Double crop.	Single crop.	Double crop.
(1)	(2)	(3)	(4)	(5)	(6)	(7)	(8)	(9)	(10)
	ACS.	ACS.	ACS.	ACS.	ACS.	RS. A.	RS. A.	RS. A.	RS. A.
1. Ambāsamudram ..	28	10·5	2·5	2·5	2·5	6 6	14 2	4 3	4 13
2. Kōilpatti ...	2	..	...	...	2·0	...	...	4 12	4 10
3. Nānguneri ...	12	...	3·0	11·0	4·0	7 10	11 12	6 1	6 3
4. Sankaranainārkōil	10	...	0·5	5·0	2·5	5 15	6 11	5 1	5 6
5. Srīvaikuntam ...	19	8·5	2·5	0·5	2·5	6 10	14 1	4 12	5 15
6. Tenkāsi	24	1·0	6·5	4·0	0·5	5 11	7 13	4 11	5 3
7. Tinnevelly ...	22	8·0	2·0	5·0	1·0	5 10	13 2	4 15	5 9
8. Tiruchendūr ...	16	...	4·0	4·0	4·0	6 11	11 14	5 5	6 8
Total ...	15	28	21	32	19	6 14	12 5	5 4	5 10

Perhaps the most striking feature of the table—one which the facts entirely justify—is the wide difference between the rates paid by the compounded lands under river-fed irrigation on the one hand and under rain-fed irrigation on the other. In the Tinnevelly taluk one-half, and in Ambāsamudram and Srīvaikuntam more than one-half, the irrigated area falls under the highest class. In these taluks and in Tiruchendūr almost all the river-fed lands are compounded for two crops and, in

[1] The principles on which this classification was made are explained in the resettlement notifications relating to the various taluks. A uniform system was adopted throughout the district. Cf. p. 304 below.

CHAP. IV. IRRIGATION.

estimating with reference to the assessment the general value of the lands so irrigated in these tracts, it is necessary to take into account only the double-crop charge (in column 8). A conspicuous exception to the rule that the assessment is an index of land values is afforded by the extremely favourable rates in force in the Tenkāsi taluk. The Chittār and its affluents are the main source of irrigation in this tract, and, as will be seen, more than one-half of the area so watered (mostly compounded lands) has been placed in the second class. In general quality the wet lands of this taluk (at least of the river-irrigated portion) are considerably superior to those of Nānguněri, and indeed the best of them are scarcely inferior to those under the first-class irrigation of the Tāmbraparni. It will be noticed that the Tiruchendūr taluk, which comprises the whole of the south-main system under the Srīvaikuntam anicut, has been leniently treated, no sources having been placed in the first class.

The Tāmbraparni system.

The Tāmbraparni would be an important river in any district; and in Tinnevelly its importance is enhanced by the contrast presented by the lands it irrigates to those situated near it but beyond its influence. Of all the rivers south of Madras that have their source in the Western Ghats, the Tāmbraparni and the Cauvery alone obtain the full benefit of the south-west monsoon; and, though insignificant as regards its length and the area of its catchment basin, the Tāmbraparni is for its size probably the most valuable river in the Presidency. On 94 per cent of the area which it irrigates two crops are raised in all good years, and the richest lands, for instance, those lying on the upper reaches of the Kannadiyan, Kōdagan and Pālaiyan channels, produce annually over two tons of rice an acre. Many of them bear a double-crop assessment of Rs. 22–8–0 an acre, a rate unknown elsewhere in the Presidency. Under the seven upper anicuts remissions are very rare, and even during the famine of 1876-1877 the Tāmbraparni gave a bountiful supply. As paddy-growing land the valley derives much of its fertility from its subsoil of stiff yellow clay, which, effectually preventing all soakage, keeps the water, vegetable matter and manure in suspension near the surface. The surface soil is mostly a light black loam, the exceptions being chiefly in eastern parts of the Tiruchendūr and Srīvaikuntam taluks, where sand predominates.

Anicuts.

Eight anicuts span the river, all of which, except the lowest, at Srīvaikuntam, are ancient works; but as to when and by whom they were built, nothing unfortunately is known.

CHAP. IV. IRRIGATION.

Area irrigated under each.

The following table shows the area irrigated by means of each of the eight anicuts :—

Name of anicut.	Single crop.	Double crop.	Taluk.
	ACS.	ACS.	
Kōdaimēlalagiyan	14	1,976	Ambāsamudram.
Nadhiyunni	20	1,607	
Kannadiyan	245	11,005	Ambāsamudram and Tinnevelly.
Ariyanāyakapuram...	49	5,122	
Palavūr	246	8,039	Ambāsamudram, Tinnevelly and Srīvaikuntam.
Suttamalli	586	5,485	Tinnevelly.
Marudūr	1,074	16,235	Srīvaikuntam and Tiruchendūr.
Srīvaikuntam	2,568	*19,247	
	4,802	68,716	

* To these double-crop figures may be added almost the whole of an area of 1,198 acres permanently under wet cultivation on payment of water-rate, in the Kārkurichi mitta (357 acres) and in the ryotwari villages of Mīlavittān, Mullakād and Kōrampallam (north main channel) and Nālumāvadi and Pallipattu (south main channel). These lands, the figures relating to which are based on the average of four faslis, are mostly cultivated with two crops each year. On some lands a third crop is occasionally raised. The areas within the ryotwari villages were not converted to "wet" at the resettlement as it was thought that the extension of wet cultivation had been dangerously rapid.

In the phrase, the "Tāmbraparni system," is also as a rule included the irrigation supplied by a number of tributaries, chiefly the Rāmanadhi, Gatanānadhi, Kōraiyār, and Jambunadhi, which join the main river within the Ambāsamudram taluk. To the figures given in the foregoing table, for channels and tanks under these affluents, add: for single crop, 1,295 acres; for double crop, 13,619 acres.

From the eight anicuts named above water is conveyed to the fields, either direct by means of channels or through tanks. Under the first two anicuts almost all the irrigation is direct, and under the middle anicuts, the fourth to the sixth, small tanks, most of which require several fillings in a season, are used to irrigate about an equal extent with channels. In the Marudūr and Srīvaikuntam areas channels account for only one-third of the irrigation; tanks become more capacious, and a few of them, if once filled, can hold enough water to bring a crop to maturity.

The Kōdaimēlalagiyan anicut.

The Kōdaimēlalagiyan anicut or dam is a primitive affair. After descending the Pāpanāsam rocks the river passes through a level reach and thence through a narrow gorge, partly blocked up by huge boulders, which have fallen from the hill into a deep pool; a reef of rock at the lower end of this pool has been utilized for the dam. Holes have been cut in the rock in which posts are inserted; cross-bars with brushwood and stuffing are fastened to the uprights, and the channels on both sides are thus supplied with water. Though liable to be washed away by any heavy flood, it can be quickly reconstructed; the channels taking off to right and left secure the benefit of the very earliest freshes and, provided the dam survives, the very latest.

The Nadhiyunni anicut.

A few miles above Ambāsamudram is the next anicut, the Nadhiyunni, "that which raises the level of the river." Like most ancient works of its class, it stands, as do the next six anicuts below it, at an oblique angle to the course of the river. Built on rock, it gives off one channel only, on the left bank of the river, which irrigates the villages of Kīla Ambāsamudram, Mēla Ambāsamudram, Brahmadēsam, Urkād and Sāttapattu.

The Kannadiyan anicut.

The next barrier, about a mile-and-a-half away, is the Kannadiyan anicut, just below the junction of the Manimuttār with the Tāmbraparni. It was rebuilt by Captain Horsley in 1842 and has lately undergone extensive repair. It is a carefully built cut-stone work, nine feet high with a top width of six feet and is supported on a foundation of solid rock; the channel takes off from the right or southern bank of the river. The work is undoubtedly one of considerable antiquity, and an elaborate myth has grown up in explanation of its origin. The author is believed to have been a Brahman who acquired wealth by effecting a successful cure on a king of Vellore. Coming to the south with the intention of performing some charity, the Brahman decided first to consult Agastya in his mountain home on Pothigai. The *rishi* advised him to build an anicut across the Tāmbraparni and dig a channel and, to give him a line for the channel, sent forth a cow; where the cow walked the channel should be dug, and where it sat down a tank was to be made. The tank at Mēlasevval called Kādavarāyapēri is the last place at which the cow sat down, the name being merely a corruption (it is said) of *Kānāmalānapēri*, "the tank where (the cow) disappeared." The lower tanks fed by the Kannadiyan channel are believed to be later additions. Bishop Caldwell places the date of the anicut between the fourteenth and sixteenth century and thinks it may safely be inferred that it was the work of a Brahman of Kanara (Kannada).

The Ariyanāyakapuram anicut.

Next is the Ariyanāyakapuram anicut, six miles below, supplying the Kōdagan channel to the north of the river. Its

CHAP. IV. IRRIGATION.

name, which is also that of the village in which it is situated, suggests a Nayakkan origin.[1] Its head-sluice was built in 1877.

The Palavūr anicut.

The Palavūr anicut, the fifth, situated in the village of the same name (Tinnevelly taluk), gives off the Pālaiyan channel, 27 miles long, from the right bank of the river. At Taruvai (Tinnevelly taluk) the Pachaiyar enters the channel, a surplus weir being provided at this point to carry off the flood water of this river. Eleven Tamil inscriptions set in the anicut crest record the restoration piece by piece from fasli 1219 to 1230 (A.D. 1809 to 1820) of the left flank of the work. The names of two Collectors are inscribed: against 1808 Mr. Hepburn, and against 1820 Mr. Hudleston.[2]

The Suttamalli anicut.

The Suttamalli anicut, which comes next, gives off the Tinnevelly channel, 17 miles long, at the left bank of the river; so obliquely does it stand that its length is four times the width of the river at this point. The head-sluice was constructed in 1877.

The Marudūr anicut.

The Marudūr anicut, the last of the old anicuts and by far the largest of them, is of a curious irregular horse-shoe shape, about three-quarters of a mile in length, with its curve up the river. As an effective anicut, it may almost claim a British origin. "It is constructed," wrote the first Civil Engineer of the district, Captain Caldwell, "upon no definable principle, the whole consisting of a rude mass (the result of repeated ruin and repair) which at the same time it manifests a considerable degree of enterprise on the part of the ancient inhabitants of the country displays a very moderate share of corresponding skill or judgment." The blocks of stone composing it had been thrown together without any binding material, and generally the anicut was in a state of hopeless dilapidation. Its repair (in 1808) cost nearly Rs. 15,000, a work apparently commemorated by the simple inscription (in Tamil) on the crest of the dam near the left-hand end: "Mr. Hepburn." Two pillars engraved with inscriptions refer to repairs carried out by Mr. Torin in 1792 and seem to mark the limits of the reconstruction then carried out. Debris of the old work are still to be seen lying about below the present dam. It gives off channels both on the right (the Kīlakāl) and on the left side (the Mēlakāl) of the river and provides irrigation for a larger area than that commanded by any of the anicuts above it. Classed

[1] Quite possibly the work of Aryanātha Mudaliyār, who is often given the title Nāyakkan in the old chronicles. (See p. 61.)

[2] The vernacular forms of these names are Epran and Adalshan; the former was Collector from 1806 to 1812, the latter from 1820 to 1823.

as a "provincial" work, it is the only one of the seven pre-British anicuts for which capital accounts are kept.

CHAP. IV. IRRIGATION.

The Srīvaikuntam anicut.

The last anicut, that at Srīvaikuntam, is a work of comparatively modern origin.

Of the area now commanded by this work some 12,800 acres were formerly being irrigated, partly by the surplus water of the tanks fed by the Marudūr Kīlakāl and partly by two main channels which led off, one on either side of the river, at Srīvaikuntam itself. Six miles below this point channels cut direct from the river supplied on the north bank the Korkai tank and on the south the Attūr tank. In addition to the area which they irrigated direct, the north and south main channels supplied also a chain of tanks extending on the north side almost to Tuticorin and on the south as far as Tiruchendūr. The so-called system, however, was most defective; the head-sluice of the southern channel was so completely silted up that the lands on this side had come to be solely dependent on the Marudūr anicut.

Earliest project.

A project designed to enlarge and improve this decrepit and wasteful system was first brought forward in 1855 by Captain Horsley, the District Engineer. Briefly, the scheme provided for building an anicut at Srīvaikuntam with main channels, intended both for irrigation and navigation, as far as Tuticorin on the north and Kulasēkharapatnam on the south. Provision was made also for a bridge over the anicut and for a supply of drinking-water to Tuticorin. The estimate, amounting to Rs. 3·85 lakhs, was finally sanctioned in 1857 by the Court of Directors.

Subsequent history.

The Mutiny, however, intervened, and no further action was taken in the matter until May 1862, when the project was again taken into consideration; it was then found that, owing to the great rise in rates of labour that had occurred since 1855, the original estimates were wholly inadequate. The scheme remained in abeyance until Mr. Puckle appeared on the scene, in 1866, to throw his tremendous enthusiasm and energy into it. In a little over a year money to the extent of Rs. 20,000 was subscribed by the ryots interested, foremost among them being the people of Tentiruppērai, and more than half of this sum was spent in carrying to the site cut-stone from the ruins of the dismantled Palamcotta fort.

An estimate was prepared by Captain Prendergast and submitted to Government in 1867. In January 1868, owing to the partial failure of the monsoon and the consequent short supply received by the Kadambā tank and the other tanks

CHAP. IV. IRRIGATION.

south of the river, Mr. Puckle, who was engaged in the settlement of the district, urged the necessity of cutting immediately a channel at the point where the south flank of the proposed anicut would rest. The subscriptions now amounted to Rs. 32,450, and sanction was obtained to spend the unused balance of over eighteen thousand rupees on this work. Captain Prendergast's estimate had meanwhile been returned, and a revised one sent up in 1868 by Lieutenant Shepherd, R.E. With the exception that no provision was now made for navigation, the scheme was substantially the same as that prepared in 1855 by Captain Horsley. In spite of this important modification, however, the rise in prices had sent the estimate up to Rs. 8·31 lakhs. The area ultimately to be irrigated twice a year was calculated at 33,000 acres, and a return of 16 per cent on the project was estimated.

Execution of the work.

The work was put in hand at once; but, owing to the great trouble that was experienced with the contractor to whom the whole of the project had been committed, operations came practically to a standstill in 1870, and it was not till the following year that the anicut was completed. The works on the southern side were by this time well advanced, and irrigation under the anicut dates from this year. The original idea of carrying a channel round the foreshore of the Kadambā tank to feed the lower tanks was given up in favour of a regulating sluice, known thereafter as the Poraiyūr head-sluice, built in the bund of the Kadambā tank itself. From this sluice the supply to eleven tanks is now controlled. By January 1873 the whole system was on the point of completion, and in June of the next year Tuticorin received its first supply of drinking water from the Kōrampallam tank. In 1875 the sale of waste lands commanded by the new channels in Tiruchendūr and other villages realized over Rs. 60,000, a sum which was spent in the construction, of five tanks [1] on the south side of the river, of fifty-two masonry works, sluices and calingulas, sixteen miles of roadway and sixteen miles of drainage channel, all carried out under the direct supervision of Mr. Puckle and his subordinates.

Description of the anicut and its system.

The anicut, as it stands, is 1,380 feet long between the wing walls rising eight [2] feet above the general level of the river with a breadth, at the crown, of 7½ feet. The piers were at the time of the construction of the work brought up to

[1] Nallūr-kīlakulam, Nattaikulam, Nālaiyiramudaiyārkulam, Avudaiyārkulam, Ellappanāyakkankulam.

[2] Of these, two feet were added in 1894–95, as the bed of the river had silted badly in front of the anicut.

the level of the crest, in order to accommodate a bridge, should one be built, as was then intended. The existing bridge was built in 1890 by the District Board, the funds originally subscribed by the ryots towards the construction of the anicut being diverted from the credit of Imperial funds to this purpose.

The system dependent on the anicut is a simple one and needs no detailed description. The two channels taking off above the anicut are known as the "north main" and the "south main." The first subsidiary channel leading from the northern channel branches to Korkai. Immediately beyond the Korkai head-sluice, the main channel supplies Arumugamangalam, the first big tank on the system, through another head-sluice; thence running alongside the bund of the tank, it broadens out into the so-called Pēykulam tank, whence, by way of the calingula, water goes to Pottaikulam and Kōrampallam. The wet lands of Palayakāyal depend at present entirely upon the surplus over the Arumugamangalam calingula.

In the "south main" system the Kadambā tank corresponds generally in position with the Arumugamangalam tank in the north. Immediately above it a subsidiary channel leads to Attūr, feeding the Attūr and Kīranūr tanks. The south main channel, however, falls directly into Kadambā, and the lower systems derive their water through this tank. After the water rises to a certain height in this tank—below calingula level—the surplus is drawn off by means of a channel through the Poraiyūr head-sluice. From this a branch leads to the Nallūr Mēlakulam and Kīlakulam and Arumuganēri, whilst the main channel fills the Ammanpuram and Kānam tanks; through the sluices of the Ammanpuram tank water is taken to Sīnimāvadi, Nattaikulam, Tulukkānkulam and Nālaiyaramudaiyārkulam. The surplus from Kānam—when there is any—flows to Ellappanāyakkankulam and Avudaiyārkulam in Tiruchendūr. Sugantalai is a small tank, which is situated above the Nallūr tanks and is practically within the ayakat of Kadambā, from the drainage of whose lands it derives its supply.

Flood-banks.

The flood-banks above and below the anicut are of more recent origin. During the north-east monsoon of 1869 the works then in progress suffered serious damage. The embankments of the river breached; and Alvārtirunagari and Attūr on the south and Srīvaikuntam on the north were flooded. Heavy damages were again caused by the flood of 1874, the embankments of the river, of the Attūr channel and of the Korkai and Kōrampallam tanks being broken. In 1877

CHAP. IV. IRRIGATION.

the Kadamba tank gave way, and finally in 1881 the Kōrampallam tank breached again. The old flood-bank on the northern side of the river was abandoned, and between 1882 and 1883 the bank of the north main channel was strengthened and made to serve the purpose of a river flood-embankment for seven miles below the anicut. From Mangalakurichi eastwards the river was provided with a flood-bank of its own as far as Mukkāni; the bank for the southern side from Srīvaikuntam almost to the sea was put in hand at the same time. The banks above the anicut, each about two-and-a-half miles in length, were constructed between 1888 and 1890.

The system at work.

At the time when the project was first put in hand, the most sanguine ideas prevailed as to its ultimate success. It was assumed generally that the capabilities of the Tāmbraparni were extremely ample, if not inexhaustible; and in forwarding to the Government of India the estimate of 1868 the Madras Government said they were satisfied there need be no fear of any deficiency of water. From observations of the river made at Srīvaikuntam for five years it had been found that the minimum discharge during March, the driest month of the year, was 198 cubic feet per second. Observations, however, made between 1868 and 1874 resulted in the unpleasant discovery that the discharge was not 198 but 90. The effect of yet another year's tests was to reduce the figure to 46. That reliance should in the first instance have been placed on the result of observations during so short a period as five years is perhaps explained by the general confidence in the Tāmbraparni which the almost unfailing success of the upper system had engendered. It so happened, however, that at this very time the area of cultivation under the old anicuts was rapidly expanding, and it is only reasonable to suppose that at Srīvaikuntam the effects were beginning to be seen.

Revision of the project.

So serious was the diminution of the water-supply that by 1874 it was realized that some revision of the project was necessary. After a good deal of discussion this took the form of raising the bunds of several tanks both on the north and south sides and thus increasing their storage capacity. In 1878 it was found necessary to add two to the existing three vents in the southern head sluice and to widen the channel from 36 (as originally designed) to 45 feet.

Later experience of the system.

When, in 1882, the last revised estimate was submitted to Government, it was impossible to conceal the fact that the project would not be as successful as had been generally anticipated. The crucial period of the year was found to be, as subsequent experience has also shown, from June to the

CHAP. IV. IRRIGATION.

middle of October, the season of the *kār* crop. In some years, during the whole period of the south-west monsoon, the water fails to top the anicut; and the freshes, even when they come, are often too late to enable the ryots to start their *kār* cultivation in time to admit of their fields being ready by November for the *pisānam* crop. The *pisānam* crop is then delayed; and there may, in that case, be no water to mature it in March. On the other hand, there has seldom been any lack of water during the north-east monsoon; the difficulty has rather been to carry off the heavy freshes down the channels quickly enough to prevent the wastage of water over the anicut. Added to this is the fact that many of the tanks, being of slight capacity, are unable to retain all the water that may come and to store it against the coming weeks of low supplies. The system accounts in most years for more than two-thirds of the remission of assessment granted on the whole Tāmbraparni valley.

Remedies suggested.

The earliest remedy suggested was to deal with the regulation of the Tāmbraparni supply *as a whole*, provision being made that, during periods of low freshes, water should be passed on, whenever possible, to Srīvaikuntam, instead of being idly stored in the tanks dependent on the upper anicuts. The proposal, though plausible, was found to present not only practical, but possibly also legal, difficulties and was definitely abandoned in 1883. Since then efforts have been mainly directed to the improvement of the details of the Srīvaikuntam system itself; and proposals to secure this object are now under consideration.[1]

Extent of cultivation.

The area which, according to the estimate of 1868, was ultimately to come under irrigation was, it will be remembered, 33,000 acres. From the annexed statement it will be seen that, after the construction of the anicut, the irrigated area began slowly to increase until 1874–75, the year of the introduction of the settlement, when a very rapid expansion set in.

Year.	Area actually irrigated for one crop.	Area actually irrigated for two crops.
	ACS.	ACS.
Before construction of anicut, 1869–70 ...	13,409	6,988
After construction of anicut, 1870–71 ...	13,161	7,121
After settlement, 1874–75	17,605	16,128
Do. 1880–81	20,492	17,253

(These figures as well as those given in the table next following include a large area of mitta and inam lands raising wet cultivation on payment of water-rate—see note on page 170.)

[1] See G.O. No. 171 I., dated 8th May 1912.

CHAP. IV. IRRIGATION.

In 1883 the ultimate area of irrigation was fixed at 25,000 acres (all double-crop); and, after the recent resettlement of 1910, the actual figures were the following:—

Area irrigated (including permanent water-rate)—

					Acs.
For one crop	...	...	...	...	23,014
For two crops	...	...	...	...	20,445

Financial results of the scheme.

During the course of the work numerous unforeseen charges arose; rates of labour had to be revised from time to time, and a great deal of damage occurred now and then from floods. No less than five revised estimates of the cost were submitted, and it was not until 1882 that a final calculation was made. The total charges were found to be Rs. 14,96,809, very nearly double the figure estimated in 1868. On the 31st March 1882 there was a deficit on the undertaking of Rs. 4 lakhs. Allowance being made for an expected increase of cultivation, it was calculated in 1882 that, including the credit to be given on account of enhanced land revenue, a return of 7·51 per cent would be realized from the year 1886–87 on the total charges. The return actually realized up to date is, according to the recent calculations of the D.P.W., 8·25 per cent.[1]

The Pāpanāsam reservoir project.

The disappointment experienced over the Srīvaikuntam anicut brought once more under discussion a project which had its origin so long before as the thirties of the last century. Though the scheme had taken various forms, its general object was to provide a reservoir somewhere among the hills in the upper reaches of the Tāmbraparni by means of which it would be possible to hold up the flood waters of the river and to regulate their distribution. It was intended that, by such an arrangement, all parts of the irrigation system should be served alike and that remissions of assessment and the waste of water, which in times of flood flowed to the sea, should be saved. The original author of the suggestion appears to have been Colonel A. T. Cotton; but it was left for Captain Horsley (1854) to formulate a definite scheme.

Captain Horsley's proposal.

His proposal was to throw across the river, about a mile above the Sorimuthayyan temple and five miles from the Pāpanāsam fall, at a point where the river is not more than a hundred yards broad, a dam 50 feet high which would throw back the stream for a distance of three miles and flood the valley of the Tāmbraparni and its upper affluents. The reservoir was to extend up the valley of the main river as far as the foot of the famous cataract of Bānathīrtham. Below

[1] See G.O. No. 531, dated 22nd January 1913.

the fall the Tāmbraparni is reinforced on the left bank by the Kāriyār and on the right bank by the Pāmbār which descends from the Singampatti hills. The storage thus effected was to be supplemented, if necessary, by a second lake about a quarter of a mile above the first aṇicut on the Tāmbraparni river, at a point where the river narrows to a breadth of three or four hundred feet and flows between high rocky hills. An important feature of the project, as now conceived, was the construction of navigable canals which should link up the ports of Tuticorin, Punnaikāyal and Kulasēkharapatnam with the rich paddy lands of the Ambāsamudram taluk. The scheme came before the Government in 1855 and its investigation was ordered.

Its investigation.

In 1856 Lieutenant Roberts, Captain Horsley's successor, prepared an estimate amounting to one-and-a half lakhs for the formation of the Sorimuthayyankōil reservoir. It was calculated that the drainage of 25 square miles would be stored in the basin and that eight inches of rainfall would be sufficient to fill it. The contents of the reservoir, though estimated as capable of irrigating only 3,000 acres, would serve, it was thought, in the last stages of a failing season to save ten times that area. The scheme, however, had not been thoroughly investigated, and Lieutenant Roberts confessed as much. A further small sum was sanctioned by Government, and in 1858 and 1859 two more engineers investigated the project. No real progress, however, seems to have been made in the matter; and it was not till 1869, apparently, that any further action was taken in the matter.

Mr. Puckle takes it up.

In 1872 Mr. Puckle, in a comprehensive report to the Board on the irrigation of the district, brought forward the subject once more, adding another similar proposal of his own in regard to the Gatanānadhi. Mr. Norfor was sent to survey the site of the Sorimuthayyankōil reservoir, but it was found that a dam 80 feet high would impound only 22 million cubic yards of water. This finding disposed of the proposals for a reservoir at this place or higher up.

In 1875, when the difficulties at Srīvaikuntam had revived a serious interest in the scheme, Major Mullins, the Civil Engineer, came to the conclusion, after further investigation, that the most suitable site for a dam was a spot about a mile above Pāpanāsam, at a place where the river passes in two channels through low rocky hills, the valley above being wide and open and the ground of little or no value. Here he thought it would be possible to construct a reservoir of considerable

CHAP. IV. IRRIGATION.

capacity and at a moderate cost. No practical results followed. In 1881, the Collector, Mr. J. B. Pennington, brought the matter again to notice and urged the appointment of a special officer. "It is not the direct pecuniary gain to Government," he observed, "by such improved irrigation that is the measure of its value. Government gets revenue all the same from land, the assessment of which has been compounded for two crops, even though the second crop may have failed and the ryot have lost half his rent; so that such projects ought not to be made contingent on the direct benefits to Government alone. It should be considered that Government cannot fail to benefit also by the increased prosperity of the people though it may be impossible to estimate such direct returns in figures, . . . There is one satisfactory feature about all irrigation schemes in this district. . . . and that is the extraordinary enterprise of the people. Only provide water and the people will do the rest."

The scheme is condemned.

The Board supported the Collector, and Government directed the early consideration of the scheme. Engineering opinion had, however, veered round to the view that the place for a reservoir of the kind was the foot of the hills, and with this modification the Pāpanāsam project was put down in the list of protective works to be examined by one of the newly-formed project divisions of the Public Works Department. The Chief Engineer, however, who had meanwhile visited the district, practically condemned the scheme, and in 1884, under the orders of the Government of India, it was struck off the list.

Again revived, 1894.

In 1894 Mr. Macleod, the Collector, dissenting from the views expressed by the Chief Engineer, brought the matter once again to the notice of Government. Under their orders the scheme was again examined; surveys were made in 1902 of the site above the Pāpanāsam fall, but no final decision was reached, as in the opinion of the Chief Engineer the investigation had not been adequate. On a further reference the Executive Engineer reported that no better site than the one above Pāpanāsam could be found; but he considered that the area of drainage had been wrongly calculated and the rainfall statistics incompletely compiled. The Superintending Engineer thereupon issued orders that fresh rain-gauges should be erected in the catchment and that the river should be gauged at a short distance below the Pāpanāsam fall. At the same time he quietly condemned the scheme, pointing out that the existence of seven anicuts between the reservoir and the Srīvaikuntam anicut would largely discount any advantage to the latter system from the additional storage.

In 1911 Mr. Ashe once more revived the subject, but, beyond the steps taken to compile an accurate record of the rainfall and the discharge of the river, no progress has been made with the scheme.

The Chittār system.

The irrigation system of the Chittār with its numerous affluents, the chief of which are the Hanumānadhi and the Karuppānadhi, comes next in importance to that of the Tāmbraparni. The river is crossed by eighteen anicuts, the last of which (at Gangaikondān) is eight miles above the point where, in the village of Sīvalappēri, the river joins the Tāmbraparni. Three miles lower down there was once another dam which supplied a large tank in Sīvalappēri. It breached in 1796, and the tank-bed has now been under cultivation for a century. In 1856 a scheme for restoring the anicut and tank was examined, but nothing came of the investigation. In 1868 Mr. Puckle again brought the project to notice, but again nothing was attempted.

Quality of its irrigation.

It is only in the villages of the Tenkāsi taluk near the hills that two crops of paddy a year are regularly raised. The hills in which the Chittār rises are steep, and its catchment area above the plains is small; consequently the supplies received during the south-west monsoon, when the rainfall is confined to the ghats, are only enough to supply a few villages on the upper reaches of the river. But the lands within this favoured zone are scarcely inferior to the wet lands of the upper Tāmbraparni; their soil is a deep and rich red loam, and the crops have the further advantage of the *saral*, or light rains, from June to August. With the railway passing through them, these villages are now among the wealthiest in the district; and it was calculated at the recent resettlement that in no part of the district had land risen so much in value during the past thirty years as in western Tenkāsi.

The catchment area of the Chittār within the plains is enormous; and the local rains added to the floods descending from the hills assure in almost all years a plentiful irrigation supply between October and January. In addition to the *pisānam* crop of paddy which is raised during this season, a subsidiary crop of one of the more valuable cereals or millets, such as ragi or cholam, is cultivated in many of the ayakats during the *kār* season. Wells are largely used to supplement the uncertain supplies of the tanks and channels. Under some tanks, when water received during the north-east monsoon is ample and good rain falls during March and April, a crop of ragi, cholam, senna, or even paddy is taken after the *pisānam* harvest. So good are the chances of obtaining a crop of this

CHAP. IV. IRRIGATION.

kind that the owners of well-situated fields are always anxious to be given the privilege of paying compounded assessment for two crops.

The largest tanks under the system are the Mānūr tank (forming one with Ettankulam) with an ayakat of 1,843 acres; the Kīla Pāvūr tank (Periyakulam), ayakat 1,659 acres; the Gangaikondān tank (Sirukulam), ayakat 793 acres; and the Pālamadai tank of Pallikkōttai with an ayakat of 681 acres. With two exceptions, all the remaining tanks irrigate areas of less than 200 acres each.

Area of irrigation.

The following table shows the area irrigated by the Chittār and its affluents in the three taluks which they command:—

Taluk.	Area irrigated by channels and tanks.		
	Single crop.	Double crop.	Total.
	ACS.	ACS.	ACS.
Tenkāsi	1,284	19,178	20,462
Sankaranainārkōil	433	65	498
Tinnevelly	2,388	4,187	6,575
Total ...	4,105	23,430	27,535

* In the village of Virasikhāmani, irrigated by the affluent Karuppānadhi.

The rivers of the Vaippār basin, Sankaranainārkōil taluk.

The five rivers which form part of what is known as the Vaippār basin and supply the irrigation of the Sankaranainārkōil taluk are (they have been already detailed on page 13 above), from south to north, the Vālamalaiyār, the Kōttaimalaiyār, the Nikshēbanadhi,[1] the Kākānadhi and the Pālaiyār. Of these the first two furnish the best supply, and the narrow strip of country fed by them in the villages of Puliyangudi, Mēla Puliyangudi, Subramanyapuram, Nāranapuram and Vāsudēvanallūr contains the finest paddy lands of the taluk. The Kākānadhi is a poor feeder, its own supply being derived mainly from the surplus of a few tanks dependent on other streams. The Nikshēbanadhi is another precarious river and can scarcely be relied on for a supply except to the first two or three villages through which it flows. The supply received by ryotwari lands from the Pālaiyār, whose chief duty is to fill a large tank serving over 800 acres in Tirumalāpuram, has lately been much improved owing to the settlement in the law-courts of a dispute between Government ryots and the Sivagiri zamindar. A dam to regulate the distribution of water between the zamin and ayan areas was erected in 1910,

[1] The Sanskrit equivalent of the word "Vaippār."

and it is believed that the benefit to Tirumalāpuram will be permanent.

More than five-sixths of the area dependent on these five rivers consists of single-crop lands. When a second crop is obtained, it is usually one of the "irrigated dry" species, such as cholam or ragi; it is raised during the *kār* season, its cultivation being assisted by wells. Under a few of the very best tanks near the hills a second crop of paddy is obtained after the *pisānam* harvest.

Besides these rivers are two or three "jungle streams," dependent partly on springs and partly on local rains, which irrigate about 250 acres in the different villages of the taluk. Of these the so-called Sambōdai (in Chintāmani), maintained apparently by natural springs, is remarkable for the almost perennial supply which it affords.

The little water that remains after all the tanks and channels of the taluk have been supplied drains away to the north-east of the taluk and, uniting with the surplus water of a great part of the Srīvilliputtūr taluk of the Rāmnād district, helps to form the Vaippār river, a name which this basin first assumes about the point where the three taluks of Srīvilliputtūr, Sattūr (of the Rāmnād district) and Sankaranainārkōil meet.

Area irrigated.

The following table shows the area irrigated in the Sankaranainārkōil taluk by each of the rivers which drain into the Vaippār basin:—

River.	Area irrigated direct and through tanks.		
	Single crop.	Double crop.	Total.
	ACS.	ACS.	ACS.
Pālaiyār	925	...	925
Kōttaimalaiyār	2,481	666	3,147
Nikshēbanadhi	1,834	467	2,301
Vālamalaiyār	856	184	1,040
Kākānadhi	1,760	226	1,986
Total ...	7,856	1,543	9,399

The Kiriyār project.

An interesting suggestion, having for its object the improvement of irrigation in the northern part of the Tinnevelly district, proceeded some years ago from the ryots of the Sankaranainārkōil, Sāttūr and Srīvilliputtūr taluks (the two last named are included now in the Rāmnād district). The proposal, evidently inspired by the great Periyār project then in hand in Madura, was that a stream rising on the western side of the ghats should be diverted to the Sankaranainārkōil taluk. The scheme was examined; but, as the river (the name of which was found to be the Kiriyār) was believed to be a tributary of the Periyār, it was decided that any thought of its diversion to Tinnevelly must be abandoned. That the river was in fact an affluent of the Periyār had, however, not been determined with certainty; and in 1892 Mr. C. W. Wood, Assistant Engineer at Sērmadēvi, was sent up to verify this point. It was found that the river did not flow into the Periyār; on other grounds, however, the scheme was decided to be impracticable. At no point in its uppermost course did the river approach the dividing range, and its catchment area in the higher ranges was small; a tunnel 8,000 feet long would be required, and this alone would cost not less than Rs. 2 lakhs. Government agreed with the Superintending Engineer in condemning the scheme. The subject was again revived in 1902, and six years later Mr. Medlicott, the Superintending Engineer, after inspection, suggested a project, at an estimated cost of Rs. 6 lakhs, which provided a dam across the stream, a tunnel through the hill and a reservoir on the eastern slopes. The financial prospects of the scheme were not examined, and the matter was no further advanced than it had been in 1892. In 1909 the proposal was definitely abandoned.

Another scheme.

A less ambitious, but equally abortive, scheme, which was started in the time of Mr. Puckle, aimed at the utilization of the surplus water of the Malaiyadikurichi and Talaivankōttai tanks for the supply of the rain-fed tanks of the village of Mēla Sankaranainārkōil and its neighbourhood. Money was subscribed, and a channel was dug for the purpose. Objections were raised by the ryots of Ariyūr and other villages to the diversion of the Talaivankōttai surplus water, and the work was abandoned in 1878. The remains of the channel are still to be seen in the neighbourhood of Nagaram and alongside the Sankaranainārkōil-Puliyangudi road.

The rivers of the Nānguneri taluk.

The rivers supplying irrigation to the Nānguneri taluk are from north to south: the Pachaiyār, the Kīla Manimuttār (though the Karumāndi-amman, Nettēri, Nānguneri, and Sīvalappēri channels), the Nambiyār, the Hanumānadhi and (if it may be called a river) the Karumanaiyār.

The areas irrigated from these sources are detailed in the following table :—

Area irrigated.

River.	Area irrigated direct and through tanks.		Total.
	Single crop.	Double crop.	
	ACS.	ACS.	ACS.
Pachaiyār	3,907	639	* 4,636
Karumāndi-amman-kāl	469	752	1,221
Nettēri-kāl	552	338	890
Nānguneri-kāl	3,648	1,042	4,690
Sīvalappēri-kāl	550	527	1,077
Nambiyār	7,663	3,265	10,928
Hanumānadhi	1,944	465	2,409
Karumanaiyār (see below)	...	...	...
Total ...	18,823	7,028	25,851

* In addition, this river irrigates 2,550 acres in the Tinnevelly taluk and 138 acres in the Ambāsamudram taluk. Of this additional area 1,707 acres are registered as double-crop (compounded).

Nature of the irrigation.

Of the total area thus irrigated, nearly nine-tenths receives its supply through tanks. The main crop is that raised in *pisānam ;* and, though compounded assessment for two crops is levied on more than one-fourth of the river-fed lands of the taluk, the cultivation of paddy during the *kār* season is confined to a few villages situated immediately at the foot of the hills ; in other villages, less favourably placed, a second crop, either a short-termed variety of paddy or one of the " irrigated dry " series, such as cholam, vegetables, senna and so on, is raised immediately after the *pisānam* harvest with the aid of such water as is left in the tanks in March or April. Unless this supply is supplemented by heavy showers during these two months, paddy stands very little chance of success.

The Kīla Manimuttār.

Of the rivers which affect the irrigation of the Nānguneri taluk, the Kīla Manimuttār, supplying as it does the Karumāndi-amman, Nettēri, Nānguneri and Sīvalappēri channels and augmenting the rivers Pachaiyār and Nambiyār, is the most interesting. The river, descending from the watershed of the hills about Mahēndragiri (5,839 feet), is just about to take a sharp turn to the north, when its course is arrested at the head of the valley by a huge barrier of earth, some 150 feet in length, revetted with rough stones. This is the so-called Venkayya Nāyakkan's anicut, to which reference is made in a

CHAP. IV. IRRIGATION.

stone inscription in the Alagiyanambirāyar temple of Tirukkurungudi.[1] Thence dropping some 2,000 feet down its appointed valley, the diverted stream, following the contour of the hills, would flow southward into Travancore. At this point, again, a training wall of rough-hewn stones diverts the flow of water to the east, and about 1,000 feet about the plains the stream joins the Parattaiyār, a tributary of the Nambiyār. From the point at which the natural flow of the river is first diverted, its bed continues northwards and is filled by a number of tributary streams pouring down from the west. Thus re-formed, the river perseveres till it reaches another dam known as Kumāraswāmi Pillai's anicut.

The origin of this irrigation work is unknown. Briefly described, it consists of a masonry dam, 21 feet high, which is designed to bar the passage of the river completely. Just above it, on the right-hand side of the river, a deep channel, rather less than a mile in length, is cut through the wall of the valley; passing through this opening, the stream, known thereafter as the Nettēri-kāl, is carried down a natural valley to the village of Kalakkād in the plains. In the seventies of the last century both the anicut and channel were found to be in a state of complete dilapidation; and, largely owing to the efforts of the ryots interested in the scheme, the work of restoration was taken in hand. It was finally completed in 1892 at a cost of nearly Rs. 20,000.

Continuing northwards through dense jungle, the river-bed is again re-filled from a considerable catchment area. After about seven miles the river, once more re-formed, meets with another dam, the Karumāndi-amman anicut, formed partly of natural rock and partly of masonry. Here again the waters of the Manimuttār, which are preparing to tumble down the northern slopes of the hills into the Ambāsamudram taluk, are forced to take an easterly course down to the plains of Nāngunēri. The channel so formed, known as the Karumāndi-amman-kāl, gives off on its right bank in the plains another channel known as the Sīvalappēri-kāl, from which again the Nāngunēri channel branches. The surplus of the Karumāndi-amman-kāl loses itself in the Pachaiyār. The Sīvalappēri-kāl, in its turn, joins the Nettēri-kāl in the village of Sīvalappēri.

The course of the Kīla Manimuttār continues northwards and joins the Kusankuliyār in the Singampatti hills (see p. 11)

[1] The inscription, which is to be found under the *Rāya gōpuram*, relates that this irrigation work was built in Andu 235 (= A.D. 1060) and was renewed in Andu 848 (= A.D. 1673).

CHAP. IV. IRRIGATION.

The Karumanaiyār.

With the exception of the comparatively small amount of water that flows northwards to the Pachaiyār (and thence to the Tāmbraparni), the drainage of all the country supplied by these channels branching from the Kīla Manimuttār as well as a part of the drainage of the Nambiyār system is absorbed in what is generally known as the Karumanaiyār basin. It is mostly through the large tanks of Nānguneri and Vijayanārāyanam that this drainage is received, and a wide tract of country, converging eastwards towards Sāttānkulam (Tiruchendūr taluk) from Mūlaikaruppatti on the north and Vijayanārāyanam on the south and containing innumerable rain-fed tanks, forms the upper reaches of this basin. As Sāttānkulam is approached, the valley closes in, and from that point the Karumanaiyār first assumes definite shape as a river. Before reaching this place the watercourse carrying the Vijayanārāyanam surplus is obstructed at two points by rough masonry dams for the benefit of a few tanks lying within its reach; between Sāttānkulam and its mouth at Manappād the river is barred by seven dams, mostly temporary constructions of earth.

This fitful river, which is dry throughout the greater part of the year, is subject to one or two torrential floods during the north-east monsoon; as a rule the floods last but a day or two, and the tanks within its basin, being mostly small and weak, are unable to take full advantage of these supplies. The entire scheme of irrigation is a crude one and possesses none of the characteristics of an ordinary river-system. In the recent resettlement all tanks within the basin, whether supplied by channels from the river or not, were rated as fourth-class sources and thus placed on the level of ordinary rain-fed irrigation.

Area irrigated.

The area irrigated by tanks which are nominally supplied by channels from the Karumanaiyār is :—

Taluk.	Single crop.	Double crop.	Total.
	ACS.	ACS.	ACS.
Nānguneri	62	106	168
Tiruchendūr	837	221	1,058
Total ...	899	327	1,226

A project relating to the Puttantaruvai.

Between the valley of the Karumanaiyār on the east and the lower reaches of the Nambiyār on the west lies an extensive tract of country, a great part of which consists of rolling sand-dunes—the *tēris* already referred to. In the western part of this area are a number of tanks of small capacity, dependent for their supply on a precarious rainfall; further east, the

CHAP. IV. IRRIGATION.

rain falling on the sand-hills added to the drainage of the country to the west forms the land-locked lakes—*taruvais,* as they are called—around which, as the water subsides, cultivation is raised in the way described on page 17.

An attractive scheme was suggested in 1869 by Dr. Caldwell, then at Idaiyangudi, for turning to account the immense volume of water which annually goes to flood the largest of these lakes, the so-called Puttantaruvai. The area which it was intended to benefit is roughly triangular in shape, having the Karumanaiyār and Nambiyār rivers as its sides and the coast-line as its base, the big Vijayanārāyanam tank forming the apex. Bisecting the triangle is a stream of surface drainage which supplies a number of small tanks in the neighbourhood of Idaiyangudi. To supplement this supply, the water remaining in the Nambiyār below the Kōvankulam anicut—the last on that river—was to be led round to the *taruvai*, supplying on its way any of the numerous small tanks of the neighbourhood which it might be found possible to reach. The western or upper half of this *taruvai* was to be bunded up to form a tank the other half being drained and irrigated from the tank. The fatal objection to the scheme was found to be the great depth of the bed of the lake, which is about mean sea-level; to dispose of the flood waters of the newly-formed tank, it would have been necessary to cut, at an almost prohibitive cost, a channel which would lead off in a south-westerly direction to the Nambiyār. An attempt made thirteen years previously to drain the neighbouring Vairavan *taruvai* (in Sāstāvinallūr) in the interests of the cultivators into the Karumanaiyār had proved a failure; and any further efforts which might be made to carry off the surplus water of the Puttantaruvai in this direction, even if otherwise practicable, would simply have meant flooding the land in the eastern half of the *taruvai* which it was intended to bring under irrigation.

Another project. A more modern proposal affecting the Vairavan *taruvai* has recently been under consideration. The idea is to intercept the channel from the Karumanaiyār which helps to supply this lake, and thus not only to prevent the frequent floods to which the *taruvai* is subject but to utilize the surplus water in a small scheme of irrigation. The project, however, is beset with difficulties.

Rain-fed irrigation. There are just under 35,000 acres of land under the irrigation of 1,142 rain-fed tanks maintained by Government. The Nānguneri and Tiruchendūr taluks each account for more than one-fifth of the total area so watered, but the Tiruchendū figures include two other classes of irigation, the sand-hill springs and the *taruvais* (referred to on page 17), both of which afford, as a rule, a better supply than any rain-fed tank. Two-thirds of the total number of tanks in the district irrigate extents of less than 50 acres each, and only fifty of them have ayakats exceeding 100 acres.

Wells.

The irrigation under private wells has been referred to above (p. 157).

ECONOMIC CONDITION OF THE AGRICULTURISTS.

It remains to add a few remarks in regard to the economic condition of the fifty-seven in every hundred of the population who make a living out of the cultivation of the soil. The position of affairs varies greatly in the different parts of the district.

Tenures.

The most valuable landed asset of Tinnevelly is the river-irrigated double-crop land under the first seven anicuts of the Tāmbraparni, and of this area it may safely be said that at least two-thirds is leased by its ryotwari owners to tenants By far the commonest form of lease is the *kattukuttagai*, under which a fixed rental is paid either in money or, far more generally, in kind; the *vāram* lease, by which the ryot and his tenant share the crop in a fixed proportion, is relatively rare in this tract and is confined to those few lands whose irrigation is precarious. Under the *vāram* system the tenant's share in the lands referred to is usually one-third of the gross produce. Under both kinds of tenure the tenant supplies the seed and bears all the expenses of cultivation—ploughing, manuring, watering and weeding—and is allowed to keep the straw.

Next in value to the Tāmbraparni wet lands of the Ambāsamudram and Tinnevelly taluks come the river-fed wet lands of Srīvaikuntam, Tiruchendūr and Tenkāsi. In these areas rather more of the land is in the hands of classes who are themselves cultivators; and leases more often take the form of *vāram*. Irrigation is less certain, and consequently the rental or the "share" received by the landowner is smaller. The peculiar kind of tenure known as *pēru*, which is so common in the precarious wet lands east of Srīvaikuntam, is in effect a compromise between direct management and the *vāram* system. The landowner provides the farm stock and seed, and the "tenant" receives a small proportion, usually one-seventh, of the outturn.

In the case of the minor river-systems, the *kattukuttagai* tenure is confined to the very best lands; elsewhere, as also in the case of all rain-fed irrigation, *vāram* is the standard form of lease.

It is only in respect of a certain typical portion of the upper Tāmbraparni valley that exact figures have been gathered to

CHAP. IV. ECONOMIC CONDITION OF THE AGRICULTURISTS.

Position of the tenant.

illustrate the proportion of land that is leased, the rates generally at which leases are granted, the proportion of the profit that goes to the landowner and the actual net income earned by the tenant. Except in regard to the proportion which leased land bears to the whole, there is no reason to believe that the conditions which prevail in the Tāmbraparni villages do not equally represent the state of affairs in all the irrigated country of the district. In the rain-fed areas and in the tracts watered by the smaller rivers of Tenkāsi, Sankaranainārkōil and Nāngunēri, a greater proportion of the wet lands than elsewhere is in the hands of cultivating owners; the economic aspect of these lands will be considered hereafter.

Under the seven upper anicuts of the Tāmbraparni, fixed rentals in kind for the two crops together range from thirteen *kōttais* of paddy an acre downwards (i.e., at the present rate of exchange value, about Rs. 130), and money rents are on the same scale. They often amount to, and even exceed, eight times the assessment payable, and many represent as much as three-quarters of the net profit derived from the land. The average size of a tenant's holding is about two acres, and, after defraying all expenses, he may look for a net profit at the rate of about Rs. 30 an acre.

Before, however, concluding that these figures indicate rack-rent, it is necessary to remember that a tenant occupies no permanent position in regard to his holding; his lease practically never runs for more than a year, and he is not dependent on it for his livelihood. Though called a tenant, he is in fact, both in the scale of social economy and in the eyes of his landlord, little better than a labourer paid directly out of the fruits of his exertions. In fact half the number of tenants are also in other capacities hired labourers; of the remainder some follow the hereditary profession of their caste, as oilmongers, palmyra-climbers and artisans, or even own a little land of their own. A tenant seldom "relapses" to the position of a simple labourer, and it must be inferred that, poor as his returns appear to be, the cultivation of lands on lease must possess some positive fascination for him. As a tenant he has little to pay for, and the labour is supplied by himself, the members of his family and, in exchange for similar service, by his fellow-tenants. If, as is too often the case, he wants to borrow money, he has his prospective share of the crop as security and is in a stronger position than the mere labourer.

The "non-cultivating owner."

At the census of 1911 six in every hundred of the agriculturists returned themselves as "non-cultivating owners." It

CHAP. IV
ECONOMIC CONDITION OF THE AGRICULTURISTS.

would certainly be wrong, however, to infer that all the leased land of the district is in the hands of this minute fraction of the population and that consequently two-thirds of the best wet lands is owned by a still smaller class. On the other hand, as statistics amply prove, really large ryotwari properties are extremely rare, and the average holding amounts to less than six acres. The truth must therefore be that many "non-cultivating owners" have either wrongly returned themselves as "cultivating owners" or in all sincerity have adopted this classification on the ground that they reserve a portion of their holdings for cultivation at their own expense. Consequently, if we are to form an estimate of the number of persons among whom all the leased lands are distributed, it is necessary to deduct in favour of "non-cultivating owners" a portion of the class (amounting to one-half the total number of agriculturists) who have described themselves as "cultivating owners." Even after this deduction—admittedly conjectural—has been made, it may be safely inferred that the leased lands are the property of a relatively small community. In this small class Brahmans, who abound especially in the wet lands of the Tāmbraparni valley, are undoubtedly the most numerous; in many cases their property, descending often from the days of Nāyakkan, or even Pāndya, benefactors, is ancestral, and the owners of the present day have reaped to the full the benefits of the enormous rise in the value of land and its produce which began some sixty years ago and has steadily continued until within recent years. Yet frugal though he is in many ways, the Tinnevelly Brahman is generally a poor economist; he spends inordinate sums on marriages, and there are signs everywhere that the Brahman owner of but a few acres is giving place to the thriftier Vellālan, his next competitor in wealth, and to the hard-working and poorer castes of Shānāns, Idaiyans, Pallans and Maravans. The modern Brahman who still owns his fifteen or twenty acres is in an impregnable position. He has no anxieties; the rain comes in its seasons—"fundit humo facilem victum justissima tellus"—leases follow the *māmūl* scale and, with all his extravagance, a surplus is assured. Wet lands, in which the irrigation-works and the uninstructed Pallan do all the work that is required, are no longer a profitable investment for one who does not cultivate; the Brahman becomes a banker or a cloth merchant and, on a system of credit which provides a safe return of 20 per cent and with a little risk 36, soon joins the ranks of the comfortably rich.

CHAP. IV. ECONOMIC CONDITION OF THE AGRI-CULTURISTS.

The "cultivating owner."

The holdings of the real "cultivating owners"—those who cultivate with their own hands and those who direct their own cultivation—are to be found here and there in the Tāmbraparni valley, especially towards the tail-end of the Srīvaikuntam anicut system, in a few villages irrigated by the Chittār (Andipatti and Tippanampatti are good examples), more commonly under smaller river-systems and in the rain-fed areas of all the taluks; in all parts of the unirrigated red soil tracts—the Sankaranainārkōil taluk in particular—and, last of all and most important, throughout the length and breadth of the black-cotton country. All these are the places where it is not enough that the landowner shall wait for the season and then give orders to a "tenant." The supply for the wet lands is precarious, and, if it does not come or comes out of season, resource and patience are needed; a gingelly crop must be sown in the nick of time in place of the paddy that has failed, or the last drop of water left in the tank must be husbanded and led to the field at the critical moment; the land is by the register entitled only to a dry crop, but the united labour of a family will lower it till water is bound to reach it, and fearless of "penal rates" the peasant owner will turn a dismal waste into a smiling garden. In many places the tank fills only during *pisānam* and to the non-cultivating owner the value of such land is but one crop in the year. The cultivating owner can make double, or even three times, that income; wells are sunk, and, by the steady labour of himself, his family and joint owners, precious crops—chillies, onions, brinjals and cholam, exceeding in value even the paddy of *pisānam*—fill up the interval between the paddy seasons. In the dry lands a well, with cultivation almost continuous throughout the year, denotes the field owned by its cultivator; such lands are plentiful in all the red soil tracts, and the figures given above (p. 157) will show how rapidly they are extending. The amount of land still available for cultivation is in all taluks negligible, and the growing tendency towards intensive methods is the most satisfactory feature of the economic outlook. Foremost among those who till their own lands (the black soils excepted) are the Shānāns; if there is water below ground, he will find it, and, if it is within reach on the surface, he will tap it. Pallans, Idaiyans and, in many parts, Maravans are close competitors. These farming classes are the back-bone of the agricultural population; they turn the soil to full account, acquire a surplus and are always in search of more land.

CHAP IV

Economic Condition of the Agriculturists.

The black soil country—the country *par excellence* of peasant-proprietors—is practically the close preserve of the three Telugu-speaking castes, the Reddis, Kammavans and Kambalattāns. Their methods of cultivation have been described elsewhere. Well-farmed cotton land will yield on an average 450 to 500 lbs. of raw cotton to the acre, and in the present state of the market any ryot may expect to realise Rs. 50 for his crop. His surplus will be invested in land or cattle; his grain-store will serve the needs of his family and dependants, and it is seldom that he has much cash in hand. A few who hoard their savings dabble in cotton-dealing and often burn their fingers in the process; others play the part of the village sowcar, always, however, with the object of ultimately buying more land.

The agricultural labourer.

The transition from tenant to labourer is, as has been seen, very slight; and even of the relatively small number—fifteen in every hundred agriculturists [1]—who returned themselves at the last census as field-labourers, it is doubtful whether some should not have assumed the more distinguished style of "cultivating tenants." In pre-British times the field labourer was, frankly, a slave, and it is still one of the proudest boasts of the modern Shānān of the Tiruchendūr taluk that he used to traffic in Pallans and Paraiyans; the labourer was included in official returns among the assets of his master, a male being valued at any price up to Rs. 30 and a female at Rs. 10 and under. They were well treated and, provided they returned at the time of cultivation, were allowed during the offseason to take up other jobs. Fifty years ago the condition of the field-labourer was (by Mr. Puckle) reported to be remarkably good. They were better fed, housed and clothed than similar classes elsewhere, and a male labourer was given in grain the equivalent of four annas, or even, in harvest times, six annas a day. In the greater part of the district there is still no difficulty in procuring labour at the old rates, and the exodus from the land, of which so much is heard, scarcely affects the best irrigated areas. Even if as many as fifteen in every hundred agriculturists are landless, there is still left the large class of labourer-tenants whom the attractions of life on the land bind down to the soil in a state of fair contentment. So far as wet lands are concerned, it is in eastern Srīvaikuntam and Tiruchendūr and in the valleys of many of the smaller rivers, where the Palla labourer largely gives place to the Shānān, that labour is more fully mobile and

[1] The corresponding figure for all other Tamil districts together is 23.

CHAP. IV. ECONOMIC CONDITION OF THE AGRICULTURISTS.

the cultivator, be he also a tenant or not, is in a better position to dictate his terms. It is from these regions and still more from the unproductive country of Nānguneri, Tiruchendūr and Srīvaikuntam that members of the labouring classes migrate in thousands every year to the tea and rubber estates of Ceylon. To these distractions may be added employment in the cotton and sugar factories of the district. The Tinnevelly labourer is generally reputed to be better off than his fellows in most of the Tamil districts, and the theory is probably right.

Indebtedness of agriculturists.

The general indebtedness of the agricultural classes is a thorny subject. Enquiries showed that in one typical tract about one-half of the tenant population were debtors, and it is probable that the same would apply to ryots. Borrowing, however, is largely a habit, and in most cases the sums borrowed are more than covered by substantial assets. The Brahman, constantly beset with huge outlays on the purchase of sons-in-law, is perhaps the worst offender; all classes are far too prone to the expensive amusement of the law-courts. The professional money-lender sometimes advances his loan on the condition that it shall be repaid at harvest time in paddy rated at a money value far below the current market price; whatever be his method, the interest he demands varies from 12 to 50 per cent. The money-lending pattadar seldom demands more than 18 per cent and, when he can be found, is naturally preferred. More harmless methods of borrowing money are provided by the familiar *ēlanithis* and *pūchits*, which form so common a feature of village life in all parts of the district.

CHAPTER V.

FORESTS.

Early methods—The "license and voucher" system—Beginnings of conservation—The "Special Department"—Mr. Puckle's measures—Private forests—Reservation in the plains, 1871-1884—A Forest Committee, 1878—The Madras Forest Act; "reserved forest"—Demarcation—The new methods—Working-plans—The Ghat forests—The Nāngunēri forests—The forests of Ambāsamudram and Tenkāsi—The Kadaiyanallūr and Vāsudēvanallūr forests—Their general characteristics—Reserves in the plains—The Kuthiraimoli *tēri* reserve—The Gangaikondān reserve—The Vaippār reserve—Grazing—Unreserved lands—Fuel and timber; supply and demand—Minor produce—Large timber—Forest revenue—Forest administration.

Early methods.

FOR many years after the assumption of the district the forests attracted but little serious attention from the Government. Timber when felled was subject to a tax, which, in the absence of all supervision, was easily evaded. It appears that from the earliest times ryots were allowed to cut without permission wood for agricultural implements only and bundles of firewood not exceeding a head-load at a time. "Hill rents," which conveyed the right to collect the minor produce and to fell trees other than "valuable" ones for stakes, rafters, firewood and so on, formed a regular, though insignificant, item of the annual land revenue. In the leases, however, no definition of what constituted a "valuable" tree was attempted, and it is not surprising to find that the renters not only made a practice of felling valuable trees but even claimed the sole right to do so.

The "license and voucher" system.

In 1842 Sir H. Montgomery, the Collector, notified a list of "valuable" trees and prohibited their removal except on the receipt of permission from the Tahsildars and on payment of their value at fixed rates. In the interests of the hill-tribes, who, it was thought, were being oppressed by the lessees, the hill rents were in 1854 discontinued under the orders of the Government; at the same time the privileges which had belonged to the renters of felling small trees for firewood and general domestic purposes was extended to all classes. The rules regarding valuable or "classed" trees—afterwards known as the "license and voucher" system—remained undisturbed and continued to be in force until the methods of more modern times took its place. Relying as it did for its

CHAP. V. FORESTS.

success on the village headman, the system proved ineffectual to arrest the denudation of the ghats. Coffee-planting had already helped to increase the destruction; and by the middle of the last century considerable areas on the hills overlooking the Nāngunēri and Tenkāsi taluks had been granted or appropriated for this purpose. The danger thus involved to the rainfall and to the irrigation dependent on mountain streams was forcibly urged in 1865 by Mr. MacGregor, then Sub-Collector at Sērmādēvi, and it was owing largely to his efforts that a block of 500 acres in the Pāpanāsam forests escaped, though narrowly, from the demand of an European coffee prospector.

Beginnings of conservation.

Meanwhile the Madras Government had taken the subject of forest conservation seriously in hand; and in 1864 Captain (afterwards Colonel) Beddome was sent down to the district. Various parts of the ghats, amounting in all to about half the forest of the district, were, it was found, claimed as private property by no less than ten zamindars; a valuable tract of jungle to the west of the Ambāsamudram taluk was claimed as *kāval māniyam* by the *kāvalgārs* of Alvārkurichi. This extravagant claim had been questioned by the Government so long before as 1837; the forests were miles away from the village of Alvārkurichi; the watching service was a pretence, and the fees levied from the purchasers of forest produce were nothing but blackmail; moreover the endowments of the *kāval* from other sources were ample. The claim was rejected, and Government took possession of the forest. The Kalakkād forests were claimed by the Tirukkurungudi mutt; and, though Government overruled these pretences and assumed control of the forests, the mutt persevered in its claim for many years.[1]

These and such of the Pāpanāsam forests as remained unclaimed by zamindars, together with the resumed forest of Alvārkurichi, extending northward to Kuttālam, were brought under the recently devised conservancy rules and, on the Collector's suggestion, were placed in charge of a duffadar and two or three peons under the direct supervision of the Sub-Collector stationed at Sērmādēvi. North of Kuttālam the two forests of Vāsudēvanallūr and Watrap (the latter is now in the Rāmnād district), over which no private rights were asserted, were placed under an overseer of the newly-formed "Special Department."

[1] The main claim of the mutt was rejected at the Forest Settlement. The final decision in regard to some subsidiary claims, which was in favour of Government, was given on appeal by the High Court so recently as 1909.

CHAP. V. FORESTS.

The "Special Department."

The arrangements, however, proved unsatisfactory; the revenue officers had no time to attend to forest work, and the overseer had to supervise all the forests of Madura as well. Mr. Puckle, who had come to the district as Collector in May 1866, declared that the only remedy was to hand over the complete charge of all the ghat forests to the "Special Department." The proposal was accepted, and Captain Fullerton was appointed to the combined charge of the Madura and Tinnevelly forests. All authorities were agreed as to the pressing necessity of the systematic conservation of the forests, and in 1857 Mr. Puckle forcibly described the situation:—

Mr. Puckle's measures.

"The prosperity of the river-irrigated section of Tinnevelly extending through five taluks, from the Western Ghats to the sea, is dependent on a continuous flow of water in the rivers that rise on the Western Ghats. Now this continuous flow has notably decreased of late years, and the decrease commenced with the destruction of much of the forest that formerly clothed the ghats and protected the heads of the streams; the rich shola land in the ravines down which the streams descend, attracted coffee planters, who destroyed the magnificent timber and thus let in the wind, which has extended the mischief done by the axe. Thousands of trees lie prostrate, and the coffee gardens, as might be expected, are mostly wind-blown and useless. Where the ground was once moist continuously, it is now parched and dry, and the courses of the numerous little rivulets that once fed the larger streams are now rocky nullahs without a drop of water in them.

"The mischief, however, is done so far and cannot now be repaired, but what we can do is, to conserve the remaining forest most carefully, and see if we cannot increase the volume of water in the streams. Almost all the streams descend the ghats in the Tenkāsi and Ambāsamudram taluks between Kuttālam and Kallidaikurichi. The area to conserve is thus very limited, and in the Tenkāsi taluk I have visited every village and have made most careful arrangements. The people themselves are unanimous in their wish for conservancy, as even at the foot of the hills they now begin to suffer, and lower down the streams there is always an outcry for water."

Mr. Puckle's zeal for conservancy outran even that of the Forest department. He proscribed the issue of all licenses to cut timber; he forbade cultivation (except coffee) and charcoal-burning in the forests and restricted cattle-grazing and the cutting of firewood to certain limits defined separately for

CHAP. V. FORESTS.

each village. Captain Beddome felt that forest revenue was endangered and preferred a system of regulated felling. Mr. Puckle went away from the district, and the rules were relaxed. Finding on his return what had happened, he overrode the local forest officers and re-issued orders, in 1872, on the lines he had previously followed. The irrigation of the district, he again urged, and in particular the Srīvaikuntam anicut scheme, then in hand, was being jeopardized; and the Government, when appealed to, warmly supported him. The task of conservation was, however, an uphill one; and Captain Beddome, who again visited the district five years later, agreed that the best efforts of everyone had failed to secure anything that might properly be called conservation.

Private forests.

The problem of the so-called private forests still remained unsolved. The claims most prejudicial to the new policy of Government were those of the Singampatti and Chokkampatti zamindars. The Singampatti forests commanded the upper waters of the Tāmbraparni and the sources of a number of affluents of that important river. In the *ayakat* accounts, on which at first he had relied, the zamindar was allowed 59 square miles of jungle; his claims, when tested by "occupation" and "possession", extended to four times that area. There were several alternatives: to take the forests on lease; to resort to the civil courts; to acquire the property under the Act; or to override the zamindar's very doubtful claim and to assume the property. Unfortunately, the zamindar was at the time a minor under the Court of Wards, and the position of Government was an embarrassing one. After much correspondence it was decided that, during the ward's minority, the forest should be worked according to the conservancy rules, its ultimate treatment being left for future decision. In 1879 the zamindar's claim came up for decision under the Survey and Boundaries Act, the zamindar, who was then a minor, being represented by the Collector as the agent of the Court of Wards. A great part of the forest claimed was decreed to the zamindar. In 1881 he attained his majority and, dissatisfied with this partial success, appealed against the decision to the District Court. By that court the appellant was declared to have no right of ownership over any part of the forest which he had originally claimed; some exclusive rights of easement in regard to pasture, the collection of produce and the felling of timber were admitted not only over the tract which the survey officer had allowed the zamindar but also over a tract which that officer had refused him. On a further appeal in 1885 to the High Court, the zamindar was entirely successful in establishing all the claims he had originally set up, a decision which was ultimately confirmed, on appeal, by the Privy Council.

A "private forest" situated in the Pāpanāsam range of hills and claimed by the Chokkampatti zamindar was an estate called Kattalaimalai, which drains into the upper reaches of the Tāmbraparni. To secure this tract various expedients were tried, and it was not till 1876 that the project was finally abandoned. The other "private forests," viz., those belonging to the zamindars of Chokkampatti and Sivagiri, all of which lay to the north of Kuttālam, were considered of less importance, and no attempts were made to contest the zamindars' claims or to secure control over them.

Reservation in the plains, 1871–1884.

With the progress of conservation the demand for fuel and small timber not only continued but threatened to increase; and, to relieve the toll taken on the ghat forests, a scheme of development and reservation of tree growth in the plains was taken up in 1871. The immediate end in view was to supply fuel to the "Great South Indian Railway", the extension of which to the Tinnevelly district was then in contemplation. There was but little indigenous jungle in the district, and a start was made with five blocks of open land near Palamcotta. The scheme of plantation failed and was given up. Attention was then concentrated mainly on tank-beds, where the natural growth of the various species of acacia (especially *Acacia arabica)* was fostered and extended. The revenue and forest authorities disagreed over the management of these reserves, particularly in regard to the restriction which the Forest department wished to enforce as to the rights of villagers to fell timber and to graze their cattle. The reserves continued for some years under the charge of the Forest department but never paid for the expense of their maintenance and supervision. In 1881–82 the whole area, estimated (though unsurveyed) at about 18,000 acres, was transferred to the Collector as head of the "Jungle Conservancy," a department instituted in 1861–62 for the establishment and maintenance of topes and avenues in the plain country. This system of management did not last long; and by 1884, the reserves were again transferred to the Forest officers.

In the ghat forests the old system of allowing ryots to help themselves to small timber and firewood and to graze their cattle in all "conserved" areas free of charge continued; but the permission of the Tahsildar was now, in theory at least, required. In the Tenkāsi taluk Mr. Puckle, when conducting the settlement, had marked off by a clearly cut ride the lower

CHAP. V. FORESTS.

slopes, which he intended should serve as "village forests." The scheme received the warm approval of Government but was not extended to other taluks. Illicit felling, however, still continued, and, in the absence of any law on the subject, the prosecutions which were attempted proved of little use. The important work of demarcation, recently begun, had made little progress; and in 1878, a Committee, consisting of Captain Walker, the Collector, and the District Forest Officer, was appointed to consider this subject and the forest policy of the district generally.

A Forest Committee, 1878.

The commissioners accepted the principle first adopted by Mr. Puckle of dividing by a clear boundary the forests to be reserved from those which were to be assigned for grazing purposes and fuel; the whole ghat forest of the district was to be divided into five blocks, and arrangements were to be made to secure the conservation of private forests at the hands of their owners. Government accepted the proposals, but nothing further was done until 1882, when the Madras Forest Bill, which had for some years been under discussion, was passed into law.

The Madras Forest Act; "reserved forest."

In the next year 286 square miles of the upper ghats between Kalakkād and Vāsudēvanallūr were declared "reserved forest." From 1892 onwards the lower slopes, which had till then been merely "protected" under the designation of "reserved lands," were brought completely under reservation and added to the main ghat forests. Most of the subsequent additions to the reserved forest area have been contributed by the plains. The area now under reservation is divided into 27 blocks and is distributed among the various taluks as shown in the following table:—

Taluk.	Area. (Sq. miles.)	Percentage of forest to total area of the taluk.
1. Ambāsamudram ...	139·7	28·0
2. Kōilpatti [1]	4·7	0·46
3. Nānguneri	87·3	12·6
4. Sankaranainārkōil ...	42·6	6·2
5 Srīvaikuntam [1] ...	9·2	2·5
6. Tenkāsi	39·9	9·9
7. Tinnevelly [1]	7·6	2·3
8. Tiruchendūr [1] ...	24·7	7·6
Total ...	355·7	8·2

[1] Forests in the plains only. In the remaining taluks, forests are confined almost exclusively to the ghats.

Demarcation.

The demarcation of the boundary between the reserved forest and Travancore was taken up in 1878 and, with the exception of a few details which remained for some years in dispute with Travancore, was completed in 1883. Subject to two deviations, one to include the Shencotta enclave and the hills above it with Travancore, and the other, where to the south of Mahēndragiri, according to arrangements made in 1851 and again in 1871, the dividing line turns down the eastern face of the hills, the watershed was taken as the boundary. The frontier between the Singampatti forests and Travancore still remains unsettled.

The new methods.

From 1882 onwards the work of conservation of the forests has been one of steady progress. The old system by which permits to fell timber were issued by the Tahsildar was soon stopped, and in 1887 the important principle was adopted of restricting the cutting of timber to located areas. The weakness of the method, however, was that the areas selected were scattered and difficult to control, whilst the best growth was always being felled. From 1891 the system of allotting coupes by rotation was introduced, and "working-plans," conforming to the modern principles of forestry, were taken in hand. Four years later a small working-plan for 3,046 acres—an area thenceforward known as the "Pādarmalai working-circle"—was sent up; and since then the greater part of the workable area of the forests has been similarly dealt with. At the present time there are 28 working-circles, 19 for the ghats, 3 for the detached hills of the Ambāsamudram taluk, and 6 for the "forests" of the plains. The "unreserved lands" (see below) have also been classed in nine "series," and are worked under a somewhat similar system.

Working-plans.

The object of the working-plan is by a system of allotting areas or "coupes" in a regular order to meet, as far as is consistent with the conservation of the forest, the demand of the people for fuel, in the form of firewood and charcoal, and for small timber. Pasture is also provided for. A block varying in size from a few hundred to six thousand acres is formed into a "working-circle", which is again sub-divided into "coupes." The method of treatment is that known as "coppice with standards," the standard trees being carefully marked and recorded before any felling is allowed. They are retained at the rate of about twenty-five to an acre, with a view to giving shade and seed and also timber of larger dimensions than can be obtained from the coppice during a single rotation. The period of rotation usually adopted is

CHAP. V. FORESTS.

twenty-five years, but varies according to the quality of the forest and its ability to coppice.

The Ghat forests.

The reserved area of the ghat forests falls geographically into four blocks, which may be separately considered.

The Nānguneri forests.

First are the southernmost forests which command the Nānguneri taluk and, with its outliers, Manpothai and Kolundumāmalai, a part of the Ambāsamudram taluk. They form a strip, about fifteen miles long, rising from above Panagudi to the Mahēndragiri watershed and widening gradually towards the north to include the dense sholas which hold the sources of the Nambiyār, the Kīla Manimuttār and the Pachaiyār. The outer slopes are often very precipitous and rise in places to about 3,000 feet; between them and the higher hills which rise to the watershed are the evergreen forests, interspersed with bare grass slopes.

The forests of Ambāsamudram and Tenkāsi.

Separated from this block by the forests of the Singampatti zamindari is the great mass of hills which overlooks the Ambāsamudram and Tenkāsi taluks. For many miles of its course the Tāmbraparni marks the boundary between the Government and the zamindari forests; and it is in the great square southern block of the Ambāsamudram ghats that this river and all its upper affluents take their rise (see page 8). This is the most extensive forest tract of the district, the watershed lying at a distance of some 12 miles behind the base of the hills. Behind the steep rocky faces of the lower hills extend the undulating plateaus in which are comprised most of the workable areas of the forests; above them, less sharply than elsewhere, towers the great irregular range whose summit marks the boundary of Travancore. The chief peaks of this fine mass have been referred to in Chapter I. Unlike most of the other ghat forests of the district, the higher slopes of this range enjoy the full force of the south-west monsoon, frequent showers during January and February, and occasional bursts of rain during April and May. Consequently they are exceedingly damp during the greater part of the year and seldom dry at any season. Northwards from Sivasailam within the Ambāsamudram taluk and extending on past Kuttālam, the forests decrease in width, dwindling ultimately to little more than the side of a hill, which thrusts a narrow wedge down to the plains just near Shencotta. These hills contain the sources of the Jambunadhi, the Gatanānadhi, the Rāmanadhi and the Chittār, all of which join the Tāmbraparni in the level country. Here, as elsewhere, their inaccessibility has largely saved the evergreen forests from destruction, and the protection which these afford to the head-waters of innumerable streams constitutes their chief value. The best growth of the range is to be found in the hills above Kuttālam, which are visited by heavy storms of rain during the south-west monsoon.

The Kadaiyanallūr and Vāsudēvanallūr forests.

North of Shencotta (omitting the two small and unimportant reserves of Vadagarai Mēlapidāgai and Kīlapidāgai) are the Kadaiyanallūr forests, which face the Tenkāsi taluk from the north-west; and north of these again, but separated by the hills comprised in various Chokkampatti mittas, are the Vāsudēvanallūr forests, which command the Sankaranainārkōil taluk. The northern boundary of this tract is the river Pālaiyār, the greater part of whose catchment area lies within these hills. Descending to the plains, it irrigates a small extent of Government land and also extensive areas in the Sivagiri estate, making it for its size the most valuable zamindari of the district. Both these blocks consist of steep and somewhat poorly wooded hills, which rise abruptly to the watershed. The streams which rise in their slopes are referred to on page 13.

Their general[1] characteristics.

The general characteristics of all these forests are light deciduous growth about the lower slopes, from an elevation of 1,000 feet upwards, higher up dense masses of *Beesha Travancorica* interspersed with bare grass hills, and above this again the evergreen forests rising from an elevation of about 3,000 feet or even less. The peaks which mark the watershed are mostly bare and rugged.

The deciduous forests contain few species which possess any value except as fuel and small timber. Among the trees most commonly met with in this region are: *Albizzia amara* (Turinji), *Chloroxylon swietenia* (Satin wood), *Grevia rotundifolia* and *Grevia asiatica*, *Nephelium longana*, *Careya arborea* with a few *Azadirachta indica*, *Albizzia lebbek* and *Albizzia procera*. Teak, which is also common, seldom grows to more than "pole" size and forms, especially above Kalakkād and in Aladiyūr, patches of forest in which hardly any other species occur. Ascending, still in the dry forests, we find *Buchanania latifolia*, *Albizzia odoratissima*, *Terminalia chebula*, *Terminalia paniculata*, *Anogeissus latifolia*, *Pterocarpus marsupium* and, near the streams, *Eugenia jambolana*, *Mesua ferrea*, *Pongamia glabra*, *Diospyros*, two or three species. These gradually pass into evergreen forests, containing *Pterospermum* (two species are common), *Hopea parviflora*, *Balanocarpus utilis*, *Gluta travancorica*, various species of *Eugenia*, *Pœciloneuron pauciflorum*, *Elceodendron serratum*, *Elceodendron glaucum*, *Elceodendron*

[1] For this section I am indebted to Mr. H. A. Latham, of the Imperial Forest Service.

CHAP. V. FORESTS.

oblongum, *Calophyllum tomentosum*, *Ormosia travancorica*, *Dichopsis elliptica* and *Dichopsis Bourdilloni*, *Beilschmiedia*, and numerous trees belonging to the natural order *Lauraceæ*, including *Cinnamomum zeylanicum*. Mention must also be made of *Bentinchia coddapana*, a palm peculiar to the Tinnevelly-Travancore hills, and *Podocarpus latifolia*, the only indigenous conifer in southern India. The shrubs are very numerous, the commonest on the lower slopes being *Cassia auriculata*, *Dalbergia multiflora*, *Gmelina asiatica*, *Randia dumetorum*, *Canthium parviflorum*, *Dodonœa viscosa*, *Euphorbia antiquorum* and prickly-pear; whilst higher up we get *Murreya exotica*, *Mundulea suberosa*, *Phœnix farinifera*, *Isonandra stocksii*, and many others.

In the forests of the plains, where the rainfall is slight and the soil scanty, the most noticeable feature of the flora is its poverty. In these "forests" we find *Dalbergia multiflora* (the Vallanād reserve contains little else) with *Acacia planifrons*, *Acacia latronum*, *Acacia lencophlœa*, a few margosa (*Azedirachta indica*), *Dalbergia paniculata* and such shrubs as *Dodonœa viscosa*, *Calotropis gigantea* and prickly-pear.

Reserves in the plains.

Names of the forest reserves in the plains.

1. Kolunthumāmalai.
2. Mānpothai.
3. Kāvalkutti.
4. Kōttaimalai.
5. Tālaiyūthu.
6. Gangaikondān.
7. Wolf Hill.
8. Mēlapāttam.
9. Sivalappēri.
10. Vallanād.
11. Kaliyāvūr.
12. Mīlavittān
13. Pannampārai.
14. Kōttamadakki.
15. Kuthiraimoli *tēri*.
16. Virisampatti.
17. Vaippār.

With a hot and exceedingly dry climate, forestry in the plains * is in this district a task of special difficulty.[1] It is generally believed that in former times—perhaps no more than a hundred and fifty years ago—most of the bare low hills scattered over the plain country and indeed a great deal of the extensive areas of high ground till then uncultivated were covered with jungle. The reclamation of these areas to their old condition is necessarily slow; and some of the reserves, such as Mēlapāttam (Tinnevelly taluk) and Kolunthumāmalai (Ambāsamudram taluk), are still mainly valuable as quarries. Others yield, besides small timber and fuel, leaves suitable for manure, grass for thatching purposes, babul pods and gums. In the Vaippār and Mīlavittān areas a considerable revenue is derived from the salt-wort known as umari (*Suœda nudiflora*), which yields a valuable mordant used in the process of dyeing; the wood of the *Acacia latronum* and *A. planifrons*, which many of the reserves produce in abundance, is in great demand as firewood and especially for use in boiling jaggery. The regulation of

[1] The question of abandoning some of these reserves is now (1914) under consideration.

grazing, particularly in regard to the omnivorous goat, is everywhere a difficulty; while the Mīlavittān, Vallanād and Vaippār areas are frequently infested by herds of half-wild and apparently unowned cattle.[1]

The Kuthiraimoli *tēri* reserve.

Reference has already been made (in Chapter I) to the peculiar Kuthiraimoli *tēri* reserve. The object of the Forest department is by means of plantation to fix this great mass (some 21 square miles) of drifting sand-dunes and so to save the cultivated lands on the east from the encroachment of sand with which they are threatened every year by the furious winds of the south-west monsoon. Attempts to secure this object date, as already stated, from 1848, when by the offer of favourable terms Mr. E. B. Thomas encouraged ryots to plant trees, palmyras in particular, on the sand-hills. Since 1884 the Forest department have tried various expedients. In the early years an attempt was made to combine sylviculture with agriculture; seeds of various kinds, *Acacia planifrons*, *Dalbergia multiflora* and *Dodonea viscosa*, were sown, with ragi and other dry grains, but the results were negligible. A system of penning goats fed on pods of *Acacia planifrons* was tried and was only slightly more successful. For many years past the Forest department have concentrated their main efforts on the planting of palmyras. Though their growth is exceedingly slow, they are sufficiently bushy in places to arrest the movement of the sand, and some hundreds of acres of sand along the western side of the *tēri* may be considered fairly fixed. In some low situations on the eastern side casuarina has done well, and near Kānam a thriving plantation of cashew is serving a good purpose; on the same side the birds (probably bulbuls) have in a most striking way assisted in the propagation of the margosa. It is difficult, however, to say whether the results have, on the whole, been commensurate with the labour expended. There is, indeed, a feeling in some quarters that a reversion to the system of private plantation would possibly prove more effective.

The Gangaikondān reserve.

An interesting reserve is that of Gangaikondān, in which from year to year portions have been ploughed up and sown with seeds of *Acacia planifrons*, *A. arabica*, *A. eburnea*, *Albizzia amara* and *A. lebbek*. The whole area of about two square miles is slowly converting itself into a most promising jungle.

The Vaippār reserve.

The Vaippār reserve (four square miles) is unlike any of its class. It lies near the sea and contains an old salt factory. The tidal area contains a poor growth of *Avicennia officinalis*, and attempts have been made to introduce the common

[1] See also p. 35 above.

CHAP. V. FORESTS.

mangrove. The lowground which once contained the salt-pans produces umari *(Suœda nudiflora)* in abundance; on the higher ground are found the usual acacias and bushes.

Grazing.

The regulation of grazing in the forests has always been in this, as in other districts, a troublesome problem. It appears that even in the earliest years of the century forest pasturage was nowhere enjoyed as a matter of right. Express permission was required; sometimes it was given free, and sometimes on payment of insignificant fees. The damage done by cattle owners, who took the opportunity while "grazing" of cutting saplings and burning the jungle, was one of the earliest difficulties with which Captain Beddome had to contend. In the course of the revenue settlement (that is, between 1866 and 1872) Mr. Puckle, as already observed, defined for the Tenkāsi taluk (in which area he personally carried out the settlement) the limits of the ghats beyond which grazing should not extend; the same procedure was suggested for the remaining taluks but was not carried out. There grazing-grounds had not been definitely allotted, forest-grazing was in some places allowed on payment of fees, but the system varied in different parts of the district.

Mr. Puckle's plan worked smoothly till 1877, when Mr. A. J. Stuart, the Collector, with the object of alleviating the distress caused by the famine, applied for permission to throw open "the whole of the range of the Western Ghats from the confines of Madura to Cape Comorin for this one year only to the people for grazing their cattle." Government's reply was: "The Collector speaks as if general orders excluding all cattle from grazing in the Western Ghats had been passed. His Grace, however, is not aware of any such restrictions on the use of the forests having been authorized. If the local officers have imposed any such restrictions, they will consider such orders cancelled and not merely suspended during the present season of drought. His Grace the Governor however is prepared to sanction such restrictions in special cases, e.g., authorized reserves." In spite of this important reservation, the ghat forests were thrown open for pasture and remained open for the next four years.

On receipt of the report of the Forest Committee (referred to above) the Government directed the extension to all the ghat forests of the system which Mr. Puckle had introduced in the Tenkāsi taluk. Free grazing was now authorized on all the lower slopes, subject to such conditions as regards fire and other forms of damage as the Collector might impose. Grazing on any terms was prohibited in the "upper" forests after their reservation in 1883–84. In 1887 the lower slopes were declared "reserved lands," but free grazing continued. The system presented obvious difficulties; and it came to be agreed that it was the duty of the forest officers gradually to obtain as full control over grazing in the reserved lands as in the reserved forests. By 1888 considerable progress had been made in this direction, and, subject in both cases to the payment of fees, grazing came to be permitted both in the reserved lands and forests. In 1892 the distinction between reserved lands and reserved forests, which had already become difficult to define, was abolished, and with it disappeared the last possibility of varying the treatment of grazing claims in the different areas under reservation.

The system introduced between 1892 and 1894 has been followed to the present time. Briefly stated, the arrangement is that for grazing purposes the forests are divided roughly into compartments, which are alternately opened and closed to cattle and sheep. Goats are not admitted. Fees are charged on a scale lower than the maximum, and the revenue derived under this head was, in 1913–14, Rs. 5,754.

Unreserved lands. Besides the reserved forests there are a number of areas in the plains, chiefly tank-beds, over which, under the provisions of the rules framed under section 26 of the Madras Forest Act, the forest officers exercise a form of limited control. These are the plantations which, as we have seen, were taken in hand in 1871, with the primary object of supplying fuel for the expected railway. They are generally known as "unreserved lands." Their chief growth consists of acacias of different kinds, the wood of which is in great demand for purposes of fuel and agricultural implements. The trees are felled in accordance with a working-plan; but a villager who wants wood for his agricultural implements may, on obtaining a permit from the Forest department and payment at seigniorage rates, cut sufficient wood for his purposes. No restrictions in regard to grazing are enforced in the case of "unreserved lands."

Fuel and timber; supply and demand. In the supply of fuel for the ordinary domestic purposes of the ryot the forests of the district play a relatively unimportant part. Cotton stalks, castor stalks, cowdung beaten up with chaff into the form of "bratties," palmyra leaves and stalks, and refuse of all sorts form, as a rule, the material with which the ryot makes his fires. From the villages situated near the hills women and, less often, men go and spend their time in the coupes, collecting on payment of three pies head-loads of fuel, which they take to the plains for sale. Were the coupes as a rule more accessible, the demand for fire-wood

CHAP. V. FORESTS. would probably be brisker; and it is the policy of the department to distribute its coupes as widely as possible and so to bring firewood close to the ryots' doors. At the present time, many contractors find it pays them to convert their large firewood into charcoal before removal from the forest.

The demand for small timber, on the other hand, is considerable; and the "unreserved lands" afford the ryot special facilities in this line. Further demands for this class of wood are met by the supplies of the open market. Attempts have been made from time to time to open depots for the sale of forest firewood and small timber in one or two centres, such as Tūticorin, Tinnevelly and Sankaranainārkōil. The wood was felled, carted and sold by the department. It was found impossible, however, to obtain a price which would cover the cost incurred, and since 1908 departmental depots have been abandoned. The district in fact is peculiarly situated, the trade in timber of all kinds being practically free. The supplies received from Travancore are enormous, and there is also the competition of the zamindari forests and, to some extent, of patta lands. No one, and least of all Government, possesses the monopoly of supply, and market rates are, therefore, as low as they can possibly be. Almost all large timber comes from Travancore or Burma.

Minor produce. The minor produce of the ghat forests, the right to collect which is annually leased to contractors, consists of honey, wax, cardamoms, grasses of many kinds, leaves used as manure, wild dates, roots and fibres. In the forests of the plains, the leases convey the right to collect umari *(Suæda nudiflora)*, grasses, āvāram bark, palmyra produce, and sometimes to quarry stone.

Large timber. During the last two years no sales of large timber apart from such as the coupes may yield have taken place; even in previous years the annual income derived under this head amounted only to a few hundred rupees.

Forest revenue. The total revenue derived from the forests of the district in 1913–14 was as shown below:—

Source of revenue.	Amount.
	RS.
1. Timber	1,750
2. Firewood and charcoal	65,189
3. Bamboos	539
4. Minor produce	24,616
5. Grazing revenue	5,754
Total ...	97,848

CHAP. V. FORESTS.

Forest administration.

The District Forest Officer, who is also in charge of the Government forests of the Rāmnād district, has his headquarters at Palamcotta. For administrative purposes the forests of the district are divided into four ranges, each being under the immediate supervision of a range officer. The Kuttālam range embraces all forests in the Sankaranainārkōil and Tenkāsi taluks; the Ambāsamudram range, the forests south of these and north of the Tāmbraparni; the Nānguneri range, the forests of the Nānguneri taluk and that part of the Ambāsamudram which lies to the east of the Singampatti zamindari; to the Tinnevelly range belong the forests of the plains, scattered over the four taluks of Tinnevelly, Srīvaikuntam, Tiruchendūr and Kōilpatti. Five deputy rangers, seven foresters and over a hundred and thirty guards and watchers complete the outdoor establishment.

CHAPTER VI.

OCCUPATIONS AND TRADE.

OCCUPATIONS. ARTS AND INDUSTRIES—Production and treatment of cotton—Hand-spinning—Spinning mills; at Pāpanāsam—The "Tinnevelly Mills" near Pāpanāsam—The "Coral Mill"—The Kōilpatti Mill—Cotton-ginning; by hand—By machinery—Pressing—Cotton-weaving; castes employed—State of the industry—Products—Silk-weaving—Looms—Lace thread—Dyeing—Mat-making; from palmyra leaves—Grass mats—Pattamadai mats—The palmyra—Its uses—Palmyra-tapping—Jaggery and palm-candies—Production and demand—The tapper—Sugar refineries—Oils—Strings and ropes—Baskets, etc.—Bangles—Bell-metal—Brass-work—Iron-smelting—Jewellery—Tanning—Printing-presses—Industrial schools—Fishing—Pearl-fishery—Its importance in ancient times—The Paravans and the "Moormen"—The Portuguese, 1532-1658—The Dutch, 1658-1796—Father Martin's account—Decline of the fisheries—The Nawāb and the English—Fisheries since 1801—The Tinnevelly pearl—The chank-fishery—Uses of the chank—Chank-cutting in the district in early times—The chank trade. TRADE—Exports—Imports—Internal trade; markets—Cattle-markets. WEIGHTS AND MEASURES—Foodstuffs—Metals—A "standard" table—Grain—Liquids—Measurement of area—Lineal measures—Time—Money.

CHAP. VI.
OCCUPATIONS.

THE percentage of the population which makes its living out of agriculture and pastoral occupations is only 58, a figure considerably below the corresponding percentage for the Presidency (68). As explained below, however, an allowance should here be made for the ninety thousand persons, representing 5 per cent of the population, who in the census of 1911 were returned as deriving a complete or partial livelihood from the palmyra. Amongst landowners six in every hundred (double the corresponding figures for all the Tamil districts taken together) have returned themselves as owning land without cultivating it. Agricultural methods have been discussed in chapter IV.

ARTS AND INDUSTRIES.

The arts and industries of the district and the callings connected with them have now to be considered. The ordinary artisans, the carpenter, the goldsmith, the blacksmith and the potter exist in most village communities, and their work, which is much the same as elsewhere, calls for no special notice.

The industries connected with the treatment of cotton are the most important and may first be dealt with.

CHAP. VI. ARTS AND INDUSTRIES.

Production and treatment of cotton.

In the year 1913–1914, an average season, there were 294,000 acres of land in the district under cotton cultivation; and, to judge by previous years in which exact figures were recorded on the point, it may be estimated that at least seven-eighths of this area was planted with one or the other of the indigenous varieties. Three large spinning-mills, thirteen ginning-factories, and six steam-presses are employed in the treatment of the product; in addition to these, there are numerous hand-gins *(manai)*, worked either by cotton-growers on their own account or owned and controlled by small capitalists; hand-looms for the production of carpets, blankets and cloths of all kinds exist in hundreds throughout the district. In all its various stages after harvest cotton provides employment and a means of subsistence for one out of every twenty-five of the population of the district.

Hand-spinning.

Hand-spinning as a serious industry has long been extinct, the few spindles which had survived the competition of imported machine-made yarn having fallen into almost complete disuse with the establishment in the district of the spinning factories, first at Pāpanāsam and later at Tuticorin and Kōilpatti. A few spindles may still be seen in cottages, and occasionally an old Shānān woman may be found whiling away her time at the art. Fishermen say they prefer hand-spun cotton, when they can get it, for their nets.

Spinning-mills; at Pāpanāsam.

The "Tinnevelly Mills" at Pāpanāsam (in the village of Vikramasingapuram, Ambāsamudram taluk), which are driven by water-power, represent a very great advance on an idea first put forward by Lord Napier, Governor of Madras, who, in 1869, visited the district and suggested a scheme for the utilization of the Tāmbraparni as a motive power to work a cotton mill. He selected a site between the Pāpanāsam falls and the temple, apparently at the point where the Kōdaimēlalagiyan dam crosses the river. It was considered that in all seasons the water would suffice both for irrigation and for the mill; and in any case the irrigation reservoir[1], then under consideration, would meet any possible deficiency of water during the dry season. Accordingly in the same year M. Duval, a French engineer stationed at Pondicherry, was engaged by Government and sent down to Tinnevelly to examine the project scientifically. He finally selected a spot on the island of high ground which is enclosed by three of the streams in which the Tāmbraparni flows above and just below the Kōdaimēlalagiyan dam. The southernmost arm,

[1] See pp. 178 foll.

CHAP. VI. ARTS AND INDUSTRIES.

by means of a dam, was to supply the factory, whilst the northern arm was to serve as a waste weir, a channel being cut through the island to effect direct drainage from the one to the other. The site possessed the advantage of being below the irrigation channels, and the horse-power available was estimated between a maximum of 2,900 in November and a minimum, in April, May and August, of 217. M. Duval calculated that a capital of forty lakhs invested in a cotton-mill would give a return of 35 per cent and reported enthusiastically in favour of the scheme.

This very sanguine report was referred by Government to the Madras Chamber of Commerce, who replied by pouring extremely cold water on it. "The public at large," they observed with some sarcasm, "are at present afflicted with a possibly morbid, but insuperable, distrust of calculations showing so abnormal a rate of profit." They added that, if instead of 35, Government would guarantee a dividend of five per cent, the capital for one, or fifty, such mills would be at once forthcoming. It appears that the project was allowed to drop.

The "Tinnevelly Mills" near Pāpanāsam.

In 1883 Mr. Frank Harvey, at that time engaged in the cotton trade of the district, conceived a far more scientific scheme. His proposal was to build a mill at the foot of the hills and, by diverting the river above the Pāpanāsam fall, to utilize to the full the immense power developed by the water in its descent from the crest of the hills to the plains. The permission of Government was obtained for the free use of the water (a charge was first imposed in 1899), and in 1885 the "Tinnevelly Mills Company, Ltd.," was formed. A mill was built (in Vikramasingapuram) at some distance from the right bank of the river; the water was carried off above the fall by a channel a mile and a half long and thence by a cylindrical iron pipe to the factory. Work started in 1885 with 10,000 spindles; three years later six thousand more were added. A second and much larger mill was opened in 1908, the total number of spindles now at work in the two factories exceeding forty thousand. To supply the second mill a channel running parallel to the original one was added; and, in view of a reservation made by Government that the amount taken by the mill should not in a day of 24 hours exceed a fixed proportion of the water passing down the river, the company subsequently established at the top of the hill a reservoir in which to store during seasons of low water the supplies diverted during the night. The supply thus obtained works two sets of turbines, which develop between them a horse-power of 1,100, and after use returns to the river below the Kōdaimēlalagiyan dam.

The mills consume in a year over 3,000 tons of cleaned cotton, mostly the produce of the Tinnevelly and Rāmnād districts, and turn out 2,800 tons of yarn, in counts varying from 12 to 44. The yarn is sold chiefly within the Madras Presidency, a fair amount being exported to Shanghai. The present registered capital of the company is Rs. 12 lakhs; the shares with a nominal value of Rs. 250 now stand at a very high premium, and the dividend paid in 1913 was 20 per cent.

The "Coral Mill."

The "Coral Mill" of Tuticorin was started in 1888 and, like the Pāpanāsam factory, is under the management of Messrs. A. and F. Harvey. It has nearly doubled in size since its formation, being now slightly larger than the other factory. It is worked by an engine of 1,100 horse-power; it employs daily 1,800 hands and turns out in a year 2,500 tons of yarn. The factory is the property of a limited company with a capital of Rs. 15 lakhs.

The Kōilpatti Mill.

The cotton factory at Kōilpatti near the railway station contains nearly 15,000 spindles and employs, when working, about 800 hands. It was started by some Muhammadans as a limited company with a capital of five lakhs. The concern did not pay, and the company went bankrupt and was wound up in 1908. The property came to court sale and was bought by two Nāttukōttai Chettis for nearly seven lakhs of rupees. After having lain idle for a year and a half the mill re-opened as a purely private concern, which went under the style of the "Kāmākshi Mills." So things continued till July 1911, when a new company, calling itself the "Srī Chidambara Vināyakar Mills, Ltd.", was floated with a nominal capital of seven lakhs. The original owners hold two-thirds of the shares, the remaining capital having not yet been called for. From the point of view of the cotton trade it is probable that no better site for a spinning-mill could be found in the district. A small amount of ginning is also done in the factory.

Cotton-ginning; by hand.

The hand-gin consists of two wooden rollers fixed horizontally one above the other across a frame. By means of a handle attached to the side the cylinders are made to revolve in opposite directions; the raw cotton, or *kappās*, is placed between the rollers, which allow the lint to pass while the seed is detained. In every important village of the cotton-country there were formerly large hand-gin factories *(pirais)* owned and managed by dealers, each of whom employed fifty to a hundred coolies. Ryots also ginned their own cotton; and a hand-gin until recent years formed a regular

CHAP. VI. ARTS AND INDUSTRIES.

wedding-present to the bridegroom among the Kammavans and other cultivators of the black soil country. A good number of *pirais* still survive in the Kōilpatti taluk, but hand-ginning at home is now rare.

By machinery.

The steam-ginning factory was first introduced in the district in 1894. There are now thirteen gins worked by machinery, and most of the raw cotton now finds its way to one or other of these. The largest factory is that owned by Messrs. Ralli Bros., at Tuticorin. It possesses 40 double-roller gins, each of which can turn out 750 lbs. of cleaned cotton in a day of twelve hours. Other large factories of the kind are those of Messrs. Dymes & Co., Ltd., one at Kàdambūr, the other at Tuticorin; at Nālāttinputtūr (a village on the railway in the Kōilpatti taluk) Messrs. Volkart Bros. have a factory; in Tuticorin, besides those already mentioned, are steam-gins belonging to Messrs. A. and F. Harvey, the New Berar Company, and a factory leased to Messrs. Ralli Bros., by its Indian owners. The remaining factories, mostly small, are distributed over the cotton country.

Pressing.

The pressing of cleaned cotton with a view to reducing its bulk is a necessary preliminary to its storage or its export by sea. According to Dr. Caldwell[1], who obtained the particulars at first hand, the first press or "screw" (as the machine was then called) erected in Tuticorin was set up in 1832 by a Mr. Groves, an English merchant of the place. Before this, the Commercial department of the East India Company had their own screw at Kokkarakulam (p. 484), and Mr. G. A. Hughes (p. 487) owned one at Tachanallūr. An improved specimen of the old machine may still be seen in the "Bravi Senna Press" at Tuticorin. The press at Tuticorin owned by the Tinnevelly Cotton Press, Ltd., and managed by Messrs. Dymes & Co. was originally such a screw. The oldest steam press in the place (that now managed by Messrs. Gaddum & Co.) was originally set up in 1840 by Messrs. Arbuthnot & Co., from whom it passed to its present owners, the New Berar Company, Ltd. Altogether there are six steam presses in Tuticorin, all owned by European firms, the largest and most efficient being that belonging to Messrs. Ralli Bros. The density obtained by the steam press as compared with the old screw is as 5 to 3, the outturn by the more modern method being, of course, incomparably greater.

Cotton-weaving; castes employed.

The weaving of cotton cloths is the hereditary employment of the Kaikkilaiyans, Pattāsālaiyans and Pattunūlkārans and

[1] *History of Tinnevelly*, pp. 83, 84.

forms the chief occupation of a large number of Muhammadans and Iluvans and a few Kōliya Paraiyans. Wide streets lined with double rows of trees to give shade to the workers at the long line of outstretched warp are the familiar signs of a settlement of weavers; and in many of the taluks it is seldom necessary to go far to find one. The most prosperous centre of the industry is the Ambāsamudram taluk; and here, in Ambāsamudram itself, in Kallidaikurichi, Vīravanallūr and many neighbouring villages, Kaikkilaiyans (with their caste-title Mudali) are found in large numbers. In the Tenkāsi taluk, the headquarter town and Kadaiyanallūr are their chief centres; large numbers are found in the town of Tinnevelly, and in various places in the Sankaranainārkōil taluk. Pattāsālaiyans (whose caste-title is Adavi) are found chiefly in the Ambāsamudram taluk, Vīravanallūr and Pattamadai being their important centres. Pattunūlkārans (who assume the title Ayyar and pose as Brahmans) are numerous in Vīravanallūr and Palamcotta. Muhammadan weavers are found all over the district Pottalpudūr (Ambāsamudram taluk), Mēlappālaiyam (Tinnevelly), Eruvādi (Nangunēri), Kadaiyanallūr (Tenkāsi), Kāyalpatnam (Tiruchendūr) and Seydinganallūr (Srīvaikuntam) being their more important stations. Iluvans are commonest perhaps in the Ambāsamudram and Srīvaikuntam taluks; a large settlement exists also in Puliyangudi (Sankaranainārkōil taluk). Kōliya Paraiyans are most numerous in the Ambāsamudram taluk but are found elsewhere, as, for instance, at Sawyerpuram (Srīvaikuntam taluk).

State of the industry.

In the time of the Dutch, who possessed the monopoly of the sea-borne trade in cloths, weaving must have been an industry of first-rate importance. The Dutch had weavers bound by contract to work for them in various centres, and the broadcloth of the district found a ready sale in the markets of Europe. From the time of its formation till its abolition in 1831 cotton piece-goods accounted for a great part of the "investment" of the Commercial department of the East India Company; weavers who accepted the Resident's terms and agreed to supply cloths for his trade were exempted from the loom tax; with the disappearance of the department the tax (repealed finally in 1860) was reimposed, the importation of machine-made cloths soon started, and the weavers' struggle had begun. At present it is only in a few centres, where the existence of a class of capitalists has rendered possible a combination of workers and a fairly large and continuous output of woven fabrics, that weaving can be called a profitable industry. In all the important weaving centres of the

CHAP. VI. ARTS AND INDUSTRIES.

Ambāsamudram taluk the rich Brahmans of Kallidaikurichi (in which town alone there are over a thousand looms) have their *taragans* or brokers. They advance money to the local weavers and buy the finished products from them, at a price which makes allowance for the sum advanced *plus* interest and leaves a margin both for the broker's commission and the seller's profit. In Kallidaikurichi and Sērmādēvi these Brahmans have set up cottage factories on a small scale, employing Iluvans and, in one case, Marava boys to work the looms. In Ambāsamudram itself the richer Kaikkilaiyans have recently made an attempt to break the Brahman monopoly by the employment of their own castemen as brokers; handicapped however by the lack of capital, they are unable to offer the weavers as good terms as the Brahmans can afford, and their efforts are not likely to succeed.

In Eruvādi (Nāngunēri taluk), Tenkāsi and Kadaiyanallūr (Tenkāsi taluk) Muhammadan weavers are similarly under the control of Muhammadan capitalists of Mēlappālaiyam, and considerable profits accrue to the employers from an extensive export trade to Ceylon and Singapore. Where capital is absent, weaving, as a rule, does no more than supply local demands, any surplus products being hawked about in the neighbouring markets.

Products.

The cotton cloths woven vary greatly in quality. That produced in the largest numbers, by all classes of weavers, is the rough cloth, known as *muri*, which is used either as a sort of towel or upper cloth or as both. Large quantities of these cloths are sent to Travancore from all parts of the district, and the bulk of the Kallidaikurichi trade consists in the manufacture and export of this article. Their selling price ranges between Rs. 6-8-0 and Rs. 8 per *kachai* of 48 yards. The cotton cloths worn by women are made by every class of weaver in all parts of the district. They vary much in quality and are, as a rule, sold locally at prices ranging from Rs. 2 to Rs. 15. The cheapest are the white ones, produced mostly by Iluvans.

A superior kind of cloth for the use of men is made from cotton of the higher counts by the Pattāsālaiyans of Sērmādēvi, Vīravanallūr and Kallidaikurichi. The Pattunūlkārans also produce a similar article in a few centres. Like the *muris*, these garments, known as *mundus*, are sent, but on a very much smaller scale, to the west coast, the trade being entirely in the hands of Brahmans. The cloths are usually ornamented with borders of silk and lace and may cost anything from Rs. 3 to Rs. 25 apiece.

The plaid or check, known usually as the "Singapore cloth," is the exclusive manufacture of Muhammadan weavers, and is produced in large quantities in Mēlappālaiyam, Eruvādi, Kadaiyanallūr and Tenkāsi; the cloths are bought up by merchants of Pēttai and are either sold in the district or exported by way of Tuticorin to Ceylon and the Straits Settlements.

For all the ordinary cloths the yarn used is that produced by the mills of the district; only for the finer kinds of *mundu* and *sēlai* (women's cloth) foreign thread is obtained in the Madura market.

Silk-weaving. Cloths of pure silk are not woven in the district. The Pattāsālaiyans and Pattunūlkārans make to order cloths for women out of a mixture of silk and cotton.

Looms. The looms used for weaving of all kinds are mostly of the old indigenous pattern and need no description. Fly-shuttles, favoured chiefly by Iluvans, are to be found here and there in the important centres of the Ambāsamudram taluk, Kallidaikurichi and Sērmādēvi being instances. The Pattāsālaiyans, Pattunūlkārans and Kaikkilaiyans seldom use them and declare that for weaving the better kinds of cloths the fly-shuttle is unsuitable, being apt to damage the warp. One or two machine looms, in which the whole business is done by treadles, are to be found in the Ambāsamudram taluk.

Lace thread. Lace thread is made by a few Muhammadans at Vīravanallūr. Gold and silver wires are beaten out in flat strips on an anvil and then twisted round cotton threads. For the manufacture of gold lace the thread should first be dyed red. The silver wires, after they have been hammered out, are usually subjected to a process, which for a time at least gives them the appearance of gold. A perforated pot is placed bottom upwards over a mixture of smoking straw and saffron, and the wires are laid across the top. The colouring so obtained, though not lasting, is generally considered to enhance the value of mere silver wire. A *tiri* of 180 yards of gold lace fetches about a rupee, silver lace being valued at half the price. The lace is used for borders and for the *chutti*, the longitudinal V-shaped mark which most purchasers, and above all the Malayālis, look for in the corner of their cloths.

Dyeing. Dyeing as an industry is almost extinct in the district. Its gradual disappearance is within the memory of the present generation, who attribute it to the increased importation of dyed yarns from Madura. A few Pattāsālaiyans in the Ambāsamudram taluk, some Sāyakkārans in Sīniyāpuram

CHAP. VI. ARTS AND INDUSTRIES.

Tenkāsi and Vallanād (Srīvaikuntam taluk) and in one or two other places, and some Muhammadans in Mēlappālaiyam and Kayattār still do a little dyeing, mostly in blue and red.

If yarn is to be dyed red, a mixture is made of gingelly-oil and sheep dung, to which is added a solution of the ashes of umari[1] *(Suœda nudiflora)* and water. In this mordant (known as *kāram*) the yarn is soaked and dried alternately for seven days. It is then placed in running water, and after some hours the thread becomes perfectly white and ready to receive the dye. An aniline pigment (known locally as *sennir*) mixed with dried *kāsān* leaves *(Memecylon edule)* is applied to the yarn, which is then boiled in water for some hours. The yarn is taken out and placed again in running water and, if a specially fast dye is required, may again be boiled as before and soaked in water several times. A final immersion in a solution of *vēmbādam* bark *(Ventilago madraspatna)* completes the process and renders the dye fast.

Blue dyes are obtained from the indigo plant.

Mat-making; from palmyra leaves.

Mats of varying degrees of coarseness are made from the leaves of the palmyra, in almost all parts of the district where that tree is plentiful. In those regions where the palmyra is the chief product of the soil the manufacture of these articles forms a regular employment for the womenfolk of the tappers' families during the off-season. From Kulasēkharapatnam large numbers are bought up at the rate of one rupee a hundred, shipped to Tuticorin and the west coast and thence often to Bombay, where they are used in the bazaars to sit on or are sold to steamship companies for the use of pilgrims going to Mecca. Mats of still coarser texture (which means that the leaf is maturer) are manufactūred in large quantities, mostly by the poorer Muhammadan women, the chief centre of production being the Srīvaikuntam and Tiruchendūr taluks. They are sent as a rule to Pēttai and Tuticorin for local distribution or export, and are used chiefly in packing goods for transport.

Grass mats.

Mats of *kōrai* grass are made, mostly by Muhammadans, in several villages throughout the district, the chief being Pattamadai, Alvārkurichi (Ambāsamudram taluk), Kayattār, Aiyanārūttu (Kōilpatti taluk) and Kalakkād. For the ordinary

[1] This salt-wort is a product of the sandy country near the coast of the Kōilpatti and Srīvaikuntam taluks. The plants are cut and bundles of them are heaped over a pit and set on fire. As the stack burns, a black molten stream flows down into the pit; thence it is drawn off by a drain into another hole, where it coagulates into a substance of extreme hardness. This is the mordant which is usually known as *sārakatti* and is used largely by the Madura dyers.

mats, the *kōrai* is obtained from the beds of tanks and channels in the district, the right to gather it being sold in auction by Government. It is dyed to a variety of colours and woven by hand on to a warp, which is usually made of aloe fibre. The finished articles are sent in large quantities to Pēttai, whence they are distributed within the district and beyond it, large numbers being sent to Negapatam and Tuticorin for export to Burma and the Straits Settlements.

Pattamadai mats.

A mat of very superior composition and considerable reputation is produced at Pattamadai. Its manufacture, which is now the monopoly of four or five Muhammadan families, appears to be of purely indigenous origin and to have evolved itself from long experience in the production of the coarser varieties. The excellence of these mats has been acknowledged by the award of medals to their makers at several public exhibitions, amongst them the Delhi exhibition of 1902. So fine is the texture of the best of them that, though crumpled in the hand like a pocket-handkerchief, they will remain undamaged. In spite of their artistic merits, however, it is difficult to see that the mats are of much practical value; they form a delightful spread to sleep on, especially in the hot weather, but for all the uses to which mats are generally put they are by their very fineness and delicacy less suitable than the ordinary coarser articles. Their production is expensive, and for a mat about 6 feet by 3 feet a price varying according to the texture of the article from ten to thirty-five rupees is asked. There is unfortunately no real demand for them and consequently no market; the few sales that are made are usually the result of hawking on the part of the makers themselves.

Their manufacture, though similar in most respects to that of the cheaper and coarser kinds, that is, mats costing from Rs. 1½ to Rs. 5, is a great deal more elaborate. The *kōrai*, which is found in swampy grounds in Travancore at the foot of the hills, is cut when fully grown; after being dried in the sun for two hours each culm is split lengthwise into two strips, which are again left to dry for a day. The strips are then bundled up and taken home and stored in a dry shaded place. Six weeks later the bundles are taken out and untied and left in the open for fifteen days and nights. This stage should be timed to occur somewhere between December and February so that the grass may have the benefit of the sun and dew alternately. After this the grass, which will have lost all trace of greenness, is taken in again and stored. A fortnight later it is immersed for a few days in running water in a shady

CHAP. VI. ARTS AND INDUSTRIES.

place, care being taken to see that the weight which keeps the stalks in their place is constantly changed from one end to the other. The single grasses are then taken and split lengthwise into as many strands, varying from three to seven, as they will bear. This is the most difficult and delicate part of the whole process, the elimination of the slightest roughness with the knife requiring the most precise care. The strands are sorted into bundles and are now ready to form the woof of the mat. Cotton yarn forms the warp, and a split bamboo needle takes the place of the ordinary shuttle. The fineness of the mat is estimated according to the number of longitudinal threads *(kan)* used for a span's width of the warp, the figure varying from 16 to 120. The figure 42 is generally considered to mark the dividing line between "ordinary" and "superior"; a mat of 42-*kan* standard costs about Rs. 5.

The mats are usually picked out with patterns, the coloured threads being inserted as the work of weaving progresses. The dyeing process is applied to the strands when ready for the loom. The red dye is obtained from a mixture of *sappan* and *ḳāsān*, with which the grass is mixed and boiled. The black dye is sometimes obtained by first colouring the material red and then immersing it in a solution of iron refuse and gall-nut powder; the use of chemical powders, which are simple and efficient, is, however, usually preferred.

The palmyra.

There is no single product of the district which provides an occupation for so large a number of its inhabitants as the palmyra; there are nearly nine millions of them, and roughly it may be said that one in every twenty of the population depends for his livelihood, either entirely or to a great degree, upon this tree. Loose red soil (and, if there are subsoil springs, so much the better) is the country best suited to the palmyra; hence it grows in abundance over the greater part of the Nāngunēri taluk, flourishing chiefly in the sandy tracts of the south of that taluk and of Tiruchendūr. The sandy country lying behind the whole length of the eastern coast yields palmyras by the thousands; and throughout the red-soil country the tree is to be seen scattered over the fields and villages and clustering often in thick masses in the foreshores of tanks or in patches of high ground rising above the level of surrounding paddy fields.

Its uses.

The palmyra *(Borassus flabellifer)* is an erect palm, diœcious, of an average height of 40 to 50 feet, with a terminal crown of fan-shaped leaves, which it produces at the rate of twelve a year. Instances have been known in which a single tree has combined the characteristics of the male and female, but the phenomenon is extremely rare. Every scrap of the tree can be turned to account. An ancient Sanskrit poem enumerates 801 uses to which the tree can be put, and a Tamil proverb grandiloquently declares that the palmyra lives a thousand years and continues to live, when cut, another thousand. The timber, though it splits easily, will bear a severe cross-strain and is used largely to serve as rafters; it is hollowed out to form water-pipes, sluices and aqueducts. Its leaves when young are worked up into fine baskets, an industry commonly pursued by women in the villages in the south of the Nānguneri and Tiruchendūr taluks. The leaves are cut into strips and dried in the sun and are then often dyed to a variety of colours. Fancy articles, such as models of processional cars and animals, are also made. When the leaves are more mature, they are cut and plaited to form mats and baskets or are twisted to serve as water-buckets. Fully-matured leaves are used for thatching purposes and go a long way towards making a complete shelter for the poorer classes. The stem of the leaf is a most valuable item. From the part of it nearest the tree (the *pattal*) a useful fibre is extracted; the black species, which is the best and fetches as much as Rs. 20 a cwt., is obtained from the convex side of the stalk, the most serviceable tree for the purpose being a fully-grown one of, say, 20 years or more. The fibre when beaten out is twisted into yarn and ropes; and from Tisaiyanvilai (Nānguneri taluk), the most important centre of this industry, large quantities of fibre are produced under the supervision of a European company and exported by them to Europe for use in the manufacture of ropes and brushes. The so-called *mattai,* a higher part of the stalk, yields two kinds of fibre or string; that obtained from the concave side is smooth and broad and is used largely in the manufacture of chairs, mats and native bedsteads; the other fibre, forming the outer edge or binding of the stalk, possesses great strength and serves rougher purposes. When not used in any of these ways, the stalk serves in the formation of palings, pandals or the cross-beams of small houses; at the worst the whole or part of it makes excellent fuel. The web which envelopes and conceals the base of the stem is used for this last purpose alone.

The fruit *(nongu)* of the female tree contains when young a jelly-like fluid and in this state is often cut into strips and eaten with great relish, especially by the fishermen on the coast. The juice of the fruit is believed to be a cure for defective or sore eyes and is often applied to the eyes during small-pox. The ripe fruit is planted for the sake of the edible shoots it puts forth after three months' growth. It is just buried in a pit under a thin layer of earth and occasionally watered. The shoots *(panai kilangu)*, which are either baked or pounded to a powder before they are eaten, form a common article of diet in all parts of the district in which palmyras grow. The fruit, if left in the ground a year or so, produces what is known as a *pili*; when after another year or so the leaves begin to stand clear of the ground, the young tree is called a *vadali*, a name which it retains for the next 12 or 15 years.

Palmyra-tapping.

But it is as a producer of juice that the palmyra is most important; and in this connection it is necessary that the difference between the male and female tree should be understood. The female tree when left to produce fruit is known as a *kāy* or "fruit-tree"; if tapped for juice, it becomes a *paruvam*. A male tree which is tapped is known either as an *alagu* or *kattupālai* according to the method of its treatment. A male tree which is not tapped and yields only leaves is called an *ōlaivettu*, i.e., "a tree whose leaves are cut." After six months' growth in concealment the flower-stalk or spathe, from which the juice *(pathanīr)* is obtained, begins in October or November to put forth an appearance; and, provided good rains have fallen in the preceding March and April, which for the palmyra is the most critical period of the year, more important even than the monsoon months of November and December, the spathe will be fully developed by February. The seasons vary in the different parts of the district; and for convenience those ruling in Nānguněri, Tiruchendūr and Srīvaikuntam are here referred to. It should be remembered, however, that the seasons of Tenkāsi and Sankaranainārkōil are roughly a month in advance of the southern taluks.

A tapper who believes in lucky days will climb one or two of his trees during the feast of Pongal, in the second week of January, to examine the growth of the spathe and even perhaps to tap one here and there. But the serious business of tapping does not begin till March. With regard to his male trees the tapper has then to decide which he will treat as *kattupālai* and which as *alagu*. The experience of previous seasons coupled with a consideration of present needs decides the case. The trees which are to be treated as *kattupālais* are the first to be tapped. Three is the average number of spathes put forth; and, as soon as any one of them is about a foot long, it is squeezed with a pair of wooden pliers and snipped at the end and wrapped round with a strip of palmyra leaf. The snipping is continued for a day or two; an earthen pot is attached to the end of the spathe, and in a week from the beginning of the operation the sap begins to flow. The daily yield of a normal male tree varies between half a Madras measure and one measure, according to the number of spathes yielding juice at one time. Left to itself, the juice quickly ferments; and, if fermented juice or toddy *(kallu)* is not required, the pot is lined with lime. Toddy pots are removed both morning and evening, the danger being that, if they are left longer, the fumes and froth of the fermented liquor will damage the spathe. The sweet juice is removed only in the early morning; but during the period of actual tapping, which in the case of an individual tree may last three weeks or a month, the spathes have to be cut twice a day.

The *alagu* can, at least in the tapping season, be readily distinguished from the *kattupālai*. To render the spathes of the *kattupālai* accessible to the climber, all the lower leaves together with the web encircling their stems are cut away, the tree being made to resemble nothing more nearly than a gigantic shaving-brush. With the *alagu*, on the other hand, the spathes are allowed to grow till they develop clusters of fruits like elongated fingers; these fall clear of the lower leaves, which in consequence the tapper need not remove. It is these fingers (sometimes as many as thirty or forty) that are tapped and the season of yield in the case of the *alagu* is consequently later, usually by two months, than that of the *kattupālai*.

About the same time the female tree is ready to be tapped. The spathe, which is thicker than that of the male and, if left to grow, produces round juicy fruits *(nongu)*, is pressed, cut and tapped as soon as it is about eighteen inches long; and the tree will continue to yield juice for 20 or even, in some cases, 40 days. The *paruvam* produces any number of spathes up to twenty or thirty.

The quantity and duration of yield are in the case of all kinds of palmyra most uncertain. The *paruvam*, whose tapping season lasts for three or four months, and the *alagu*, whose season is only slightly less, give more juice than the *kattupālai*, which seldom yields for more than two months.[1] *Alagu* juice is often said to be superior to that of *kattupālai*; and it is generally agreed that the juice of the *paruvam* is superior to both.

Jaggery and palm-candies.

Only a small proportion of the juice produced in the district is required for consumption either as a sweet drink or as

[1] Roughly it may be said that the annual yield of a tree may vary between 20 gallons (for a *kattupālai*) and 40 (for a *paruvam*).

CHAP. VI. ARTS AND INDUSTRIES.

fermented liquor, and the rest is boiled to produce either the coarse sugar known as jaggery or, more rarely, palm-candies of different kinds. To make jaggery the sweet juice is boiled to a semi-solid state and then poured out either into cocoanut shells or into pits dug for the purpose. In half-an-hour the juice hardens and, when cooled, it is removed from its case. The lumps are then tied up either in sacks or matting, the latter method being employed only when the jaggery has been thoroughly well dried and the juices are consequently not liable to run. The "mat jaggery" is sold for home consumption, being used largely to sweeten tea and coffee and in the manufacture of sweetmeats of all kinds. The "sack jaggery" is bought up extensively for use in sugar refineries and distilleries, in and beyond the district. A certain amount is sent to Sivakāsi for use in the curing of tobacco. A superior kind of jaggery produced in a few villages of the Tiruchendūr taluk, notably in Kāyalpatnam and, under the supervision of the Jesuit missionaries, in Adaikalāpuram, is that known as *sillukarupatti* or *puttu*. The juice is allowed to stand until it becomes slightly acid and is then filtered through a cloth and boiled. When it has become sufficiently thick, it is poured generally into small squares or cones cut in wooden planks and is left to cool and solidify. Spices are often added to flavour it, and the product is highly prized as a sweetmeat. A certain amount of it is eaten at marriages and festivals, the greater part being exported to Colombo. A still more refined article made from palmyra juice is the sugar-candy produced in a few villages of the Tiruchendūr taluk.

Production and demand.

The amount of jaggery annually produced in the district is enormous; but it is impossible to estimate it with any degree of accuracy. Exports by rail beyond the district from Tinnevelly Bridge, which is the chief collecting centre of the district, amount in a year to over 11,000 tons, nearly half of which is accounted for by the purchases made by the local agent of the East India Distilleries Company for consignment to the firm's factory at Nellikuppam. Of the remainder a great part is distributed to all parts of the Presidency and beyond it for domestic consumption. Account has also to be taken of the enormous and rapidly increasing amount that is bought up and retailed for household purposes within the district and of the purchases made by the three local sugar factories, in Tinnevelly, Kulasēkharapatnam and Alvārtirunagari. The growing demand for jaggery as an article of domestic consumption has not, it seems, been accompanied by a larger output, and the stronger competition thus created has within the last fifteen years sent up the price of the article from Rs. 15 per candy (of 500 lbs.) to Rs. 20. It is even alleged that the outturn of the district is on the decline; and, difficult as it is to estimate the truth of such a statement, there are undoubted signs in some quarters of the district that palmyra-tapping as a profession is falling into disfavour.

The tapper.

Tapping is the monopoly of the Shānān caste, and no other caste, however much it might profit them, is willing or able to take up the vocation. The tea and rubber estates of Ceylon, Malay and Travancore, the breeding of sheep and fowls for the Colombo market, shop-keeping and garden cultivation at home, offer superior attractions; and the spread of education, chiefly through the agency of Christian missions, has opened up a new field of activity for a most adaptable and enterprising community. Enormous tracks of trees in the taluks of Tenkāsi, and Ambāsamudram, in the "palmyra forest" of Nāngunēri and Tiruchendūr and, in fact, all over the district are never tapped; and were it not for the influx of Shānāns from Nānjanād in Travancore, which occurs annually in April after the tapping season of that country is over, many more thousands of good trees in the taluks of Nāngunēri, Tiruchendūr and even parts of Srīvaikuntam would be perpetually unproductive. These foreigners arrive just at the season when the *paruvam* and *alagu* are ready to be tapped. They build their little leaf-huts in the topes, tap the trees according to the terms made with the owners and having finished with one tope move on to another. The tapping of the *paruvam* and *alagu*, the two most difficult kinds of palmyra to tackle, is fortunately their speciality; and even the Tinnevelly Shānān admits the superiority of his Travancore cousin in this respect.

The tapper's existence is certainly a severe one. As a rule he will have during the season anything from 25 to 40 trees to climb twice a day; rain and wind may be too much or too little or may come at the wrong season, and misfortunes repeated in two or three consecutive years may mean the death of his trees. Though he may not be the owner (and as a rule he is not), the terms on which he generally contracts with the owner render him equally susceptible with his master to the vicissitudes of the season. A popular form of lease is that known as *vāram*, the "sharing system," by which tapper and owner each get one day's yield in alternation. Absentee owners prefer a system of fixed rental paid as a rule in money, rarely in jaggery. Under all these systems the tapper has to contend with the local dealer, himself probably the dependant of an agent who buys on commission for a firm, and many are the stories told of the wiles and dodges to which the tapper has to submit. If only the factory recently established by the East India Distilleries Company at Kulasēkharapatnam can, as its object is, to some extent eliminate the middleman, the prospects of the tapper over at least one large palmyra tract should be considerably improved. Even as matters stand, there is reason to believe that in recent years the tapper generally has improved his position; he is seldom content with the traditional share under the *vāram* system and usually claims and secures additional money payments.

Sugar refineries.

Four factories are engaged in the district in refining jaggery into sugar. The oldest of these, known as the "Lakshmi Sugar Mill," Alvārtirunagari (it lies actually within the limits of the village of Tirukkalūr), was founded in 1890 by a native of Attūr. Being unable to work it successfully, he sold it to a vakil of Srīvaikuntam, who again sold it to a Tinnevelly vakil, and from the latter it came to the Nāttukōttai Chetti who at present manages the concern. The factory is a small one, employing during the working season about 40 hands. The sugar is sent to Tinnevelly, Pēttai and Tuticorin, the molasses being bought up mostly by the tobacco merchants of Sivakāsi (Rāmnād).

The Pēttai Sugar Mill Company, Ltd., whose factory is situated in Tinnevelly, was founded in 1895 by a family of Muhammadans. A dividend was declared in one year only; and in 1910, being unable to repay their loans or to raise fresh capital, the directors closed the mill. Since then the Chetti through whose financial help the factory was for many years kept going has been put into possession of the concern and has lately (1913) started work.

The Sārangapāni Sugar Mill Company, Ltd., opened a factory in Tinnevelly in 1898 and owing to financial trouble closed it in 1902; since then the buildings have lain vacant.

Reference is made on page 501 to the sugar refinery recently established in Kulasēkharapatnam by the East India Distilleries Company. The produce of the factory, which is of two kinds, soft white sugar and white crystal sugar, is shipped to Tuticorin and thence to all parts of Southern India. The crystal sugar is largely used in the manufacture of sugar-candy.

Oils.

The chief oil produced in the district is that obtained from the gingelly plant. It is expressed by Vāniyans in the ordinary country mill (*chekku*), the gingelly being, as a rule, obtained locally. Pēttai is a great collecting centre for this article and supplies not only the numerous Vāniyans settled

CHAP. VI.
ARTS AND INDUSTRIES.

in the place but distributes large quantities over the various taluks. The oil is used for the purposes of bathing and cooking. The waste is given to cattle or sometimes is taken fresh from the press, mixed with jaggery and eaten.

The use of kerosine oil for lamps is almost general in the towns and is fairly common in rural parts.

Castor oil, used for lighting purposes and also, compounded very often with herbs, as a medicine, is obtained by boiling the seeds of the plant after they have been pounded and then skimming off the oil as it rises to the surface.

The oil of the iluppai (*Bassia longifolia*) also is used for lamps, the crushed husks serving the purpose of soap for the removal of oil from the body after a bath.

The oil extracted from the seeds of the pinnai (*Vateria indica*) is used for lighting purposes only, the seeds being occasionally (as in the Tiruchendūr taluk) imported from Colombo.

Almost all the cocoanut oil used in the district comes either from Malabar or Colombo. Margosa oil is regarded as a valuable medicine and is often given to infants in convulsions.

Strings and ropes.

String of some sort or other is perhaps the easiest thing to obtain at a moment's notice in any part of the district. Agriculturists generally make the string required for everyday uses—tying up their cattle, strapping up bundles and binding broken implements—out of aloe, sunn-hemp, *pulichai nār* or palmyra fibre according to the locality. All stronger ropes are imported.

Baskets, etc.

Throughout the palmyra country baskets are made out of palmyra leaves. Some are made (chiefly by Katasans) out of the mid-ribs of palmyra leaves; others consist of leaves only or a combination of leaves with fibre obtained from the stem. In many villages in south Nānguneri and in the Srīvaikuntam and Tiruchendūr taluks Shānān and Muhammadan women make nice fancy baskets, suitable for betel and tobacco boxes, out of young palmyra leaves, which they dye in a variety of colours. The ornamental specimens of basket work to be found in the same parts, such as representations of animals and cars, are the work of the magician caste of Kaniyāns. Fish-traps are the speciality of the Katasans.

Bangles.

Wax bangles (*kankanam*) worn by women of practically every caste are made by the Kavarai Nāyakkans[1] of Māramangalam (Srīvaikuntam taluk), who also import glass bangles from Bombay and retail them.

[1] They adopt the title "Chetti."

CHAP. VI. ARTS AND INDUSTRIES.

Bell-metal.

Bell-metal vessels are made in a number of villages in various parts of the district, the chief centres of the industry being Vāgaikulam and Mannārkōil (Ambāsamudram taluk), Seydinganallūr and Eral (Srīvaikuntam taluk), Tinnevelly and Narasinganallūr (Tinnevelly taluk) and Sankaranainārkōil. The industry is the monopoly of the Kannāsāri section of the Kammālan caste, and generally speaking, may claim to be a fairly prosperous one. The products of Vāgaikulam, which include lamps, temple-bells, and the usual vessels of domestic use, are the best known, and the demand for them is brisk. An earthenware core is first coated with clay and then with wax. The wax is carefully shaped to the required design, and over it are laid further coatings of clay. As soon as the covering has hardened, the whole thing is placed on the fire, and, as the wax melts and runs away through an aperture provided in the clay case for the purpose, the molten alloy is poured into the hollow space and assumes the shape desired. In twelve hours the metal hardens; the clay is broken, and after a little polishing the vessel is ready.

Brass-work.

Brass vessels are made out of plates of metal, which are heated and beaten out on the anvil; sections are then welded together and reduced to their final shape by a process of gentle hammering. The plates are imported. Workers in brass are Kannāsāris and are usually found alongside the bell-metal workers. Hindu idols are produced at Vāgaikulam; elsewhere the productions are chiefly domestic vessels.

Iron-smelting.

The extinct industry of iron-smelting has been referred to on page 27.

Jewellery.

The jewellery and ornaments worn in such abundance by Hindu women, and especially by members of the Vellālan, Paravan and Shānān castes, are produced by the Tattāsāri in all parts of the district. The so-called Kavarai Chettis of Māramangalam have acquired a distinct reputation for their traffic in gold ornaments set with stones. The jewels are obtained from Upper Burma, where these traders have established agencies of their fellow-castemen.

Tanning.

Some half-dozen tanneries exist in the district. The bark of the *āvāram* plant (*Cassia auriculata*), which plays an important part, can be obtained in large quantities in almost any part of the district, and the process of tanning is much the same as elsewhere. Leather of a good quality, which is exported to Europe, is produced in a tannery near Pudukkōttai; other factories meet the needs of local consumption only. The slippers (*seruppu*) made by Tinnevelly "chucklers" are appreciated both in the district and beyond it for their strength and neatness; shoemakers were imported by the Dutch from Tuticorin to their settlements on the west coast in the eighteenth century.

Printing-presses.

There are no less than twenty-five printing-presses in the district, fifteen of which are distributed over the three municipal towns. They are mostly engaged in the printing of leaflets, notices, official and semi-official records, and, more rarely, philosophical writings.

Industrial schools.

The industrial schools of the district are referred to in Chapter X.

Fishing.

Fishing is the occupation of hundreds of Paravans in the sea-coast villages, and the value of the total catch made during a year at Tuticorin, the best market for fish on the coast, has been estimated at nearly half a lakh of rupees. The hauls made at some other villages, Manappād, and Alantalai, for instance, are probably not far behind this figure; from these and other villages large quantities of salted fish are sent into the interior and even shipped to Ceylon. The vālai (*Chirocentrus dorab*) is the commonest fish of all; others are sardines, jew-fishes, the Indian rock-cod (*kalavai*), the seer, the sea bream (called *vellamin*) and the red mullet. The boats chiefly used are dug-out canoes improved by "spreading" and by the addition of a weather-board to each gunwale; "catamarans" (*madī*) are found only towards the south in places where surf has to be negotiated.

Pearl-fishery.

An industry of great commercial and historical interest is the pearl-fishery, to which reference has already been made in Chapter I.

Its importance in ancient times.

Of the antiquity of the fisheries of the Gulf of Manaar there is abundant evidence. Speaking of the ports of the Indian coast, the unknown author of the *Periplus Erythraei Maris* (about A.D. 80) says:—

"Upon leaving Ela-bakara, we come to the Ruddy[1] Mountain (Pyrrhos) towards the south; the country which succeeds is under the Government of Pandian; it is called Paralia (Purali) and lies almost directly north and south; it reaches to Kolkhoi[2] in the vicinity of the pearl-fishery. But the first port after leaving the Ruddy Mountain is Balita and next to that is Komar[3] which has a port and a harbour . . . From Komar the district extends to Kolkhoi, and the pearl-fishery, which is conducted by slaves or criminals condemned to the service, and the whole southern point of the continent

[1] Apparently the red cliffs south of Quilon.

[2] The modern Korkai (see also p. 429). The other names mentioned in this tract have not been identified with certainty.

[3] Cape Comorin.

CHAP. VI. ARTS AND INDUSTRIES.

is part of the Pandian's dominion. The first place that succeeds after leaving Kolkhoi is the Bay of Argalus connected with a district inland (of the same name). Here and there only the pearls obtained in the fishery at the island of Epidorus are perforated and prepared for the market and from the same island are procured the fine muslins sprinkled with pearls."[1]

Ptolemy (A.D. second century) also alludes to the pearl-fishery and in connection with it mentions the towns of Sosikourai [2] and Kolkhoi. The old Tamil work *Kaluvettu* refers to the pearl-fisheries in the following passage : "Vidanarayanen Cheddi and the Paravu men who fished pearls by paying tribute to Alliyarasani, daughter of Pandya King of Madura, who went on a voyage, experienced bad weather in the sea, and were driven to the shores of Lanka, where they founded Karainerkai (Karativo) and Kutiraimalai. Vidanarayanen Cheddi had the treasures of his ship stored there by the Parawas, and established pearl fisheries at Kadalihilapam (Chilavaturai) and Kallachihilapam (Chilaw) and introduced the trees which change iron into gold." The *Madurai-Kanchi* speaks of Korkai as the chief town of the Parathavar and the seat of the pearl-fishery and describes the Paravans as the most powerful people of the country. It was no doubt largely owing to its importance as a centre of the pearl trade that Korkai rose in greatness and became (as we have seen elsewhere) the head-quarters of the Pāndya rulers. In the later days of that dynasty the great prosperity of the fishery may be gathered from the fact that in A.D. 1330, according to Friar Jordanus, no less than 8,000 boats were employed in the fisheries of Tinnevelly and Ceylon.

The Paravans and the "Moormen."

Tradition thus points unmistakably to the Paravans as having from time immemorial conducted the fisheries; and in return for tribute paid from the produce of the fisheries they obtained, it appears, from successive rulers the protection of their industry and immunity from further taxation. With the weakening of the paramount power of Vijayanagar and the rise to power of Muhammadan immigrants from Arabia, the privileged position of the Paravans was seriously threatened.

"The Moors [3] who had spread themselves over India, and principally along the coasts of Madura, were strengthened by

[1] For a full account of these pearl-fisheries see *Report on the Indian Pearl-Fisheries* by J. Hornell, F.L.S. (Government Press, Madras, 1905) from which the present account is abstracted ; see also *Ind. Ant.*, April 1879, p. 111.

[2] Believed by Mr. Hornell to be identical with "Tuticorin."

[3] Extract from a Report, dated 19th December 1669, by two Dutch Official in Tinnevelly to the Governor of Ceylon.

the natives professing Mahomedanism and by the Arabs, Saracens, and the privateers of the Sammoryn,[1] and they began also to take to pearl-diving as an occupation, but being led away by ill-feeling and hope of gain, they often attempted to outreach the Parruas, some of whom even they gained to their party and to their religion, by which they obtained so much importance, that the Rajas joined themselves to the Moors, anticipating great advantages from the trade which they carried on and from their power at sea; and thus the Parruas were oppressed although they frequently rose against their adversaries, but they always got the worst of it, until at last in a pearl fishery at Tutucoryn, having purposely raised a dispute, they fell upon the Moors, and killed some thousands of them, burnt their vessels and remained masters of the country, though much in fear that the Moors, joined by the parties of Calicut, would rise against them in revenge."

The Portuguese, 1532–1658.

It was shortly after this, in 1532, that the Portuguese, who had already formed a settlement in Cochin in 1502, appeared on the scene to champion the cause of the Paravans against the "Moormen" of the coast; the Paravans (pages 88–89) became Christians and subjects of the king of Portugal. The Muhammadans were chastised, and by the time that Xavier arrived on the coast (1542) the control of the pearl-fishery was completely in the hands of the Portuguese. Within a few years the new-comers had established themselves at Manappād, Punnaikāyal, Tuticorin and Vēmbār, their chief settlement being Punnaikāyal, where a hospital and a seminary were founded in 1551.[2] Punnaikāyal subsequently declined in importance, and its place was taken by Tuticorin. The new settlers with their Parava converts constituted themselves from the first into an independent community and, to judge from the scanty records which survive, managed to derive considerable profits from the pearl-fishery. They acknowledged no master save the king of Portugal; and it was, presumably, in order to collect the tribute due to the central government that the emissaries of Vijayanagar and of his Nāyakkan lieutenants—the "Badages" (or Vadugans) to whom Xavier so often refers—were constantly descending on the coast.

With their policy of defiance towards Vijayanagar and Madura the Portuguese combined an intolerant hatred of the "Moormen." These Muhammadans, bringing with them from the coast of Persia the valuable experience of their native pearl-fisheries, were a force to be reckoned with. They obtained

[1] The Rāja of Calicut.

[2] Caldwell's *History of Tinnevelly*, p. 67.

the support of the Nāyakkan ruler and were soon strong enough to establish themselves independently of the Portuguese in their own town of Kāyalpatnam.[1] The Nāyakkan demanded and obtained "free stones"[2] for himself and conferred similar privileges on the Mussalman headman of the re-formed settlement; he further directed that one of the headman's residences should be "near Marie Amman's Chapel at Tuticorin." The Portuguese in the end were forced to make contributions to the Nāyakkan in return for the protection afforded by that sovereign to the merchants in their journeys to and from the fisheries.

The relations between the Nāyakkan and the Portuguese assumed a stormy character; and to the attempted interference of the Madura ruler the Portuguese replied with heroic measures. On one occasion at least they removed all their native Christian subjects from the Madura and Tinnevelly coast to Manaar and to the islands skirting the coast as far north as Pāmban and then blockaded the Nāyakkan's sea-board; "with their boats they pillaged the sea-coast, which they disquieted so effectually that the renters and overseers [of the Nāyakkan] on account of the great loss they suffered in their revenues were obliged to request the Nāyakkan to call the Portuguese back again."

The Dutch, 1658–1796.

But the Portuguese success was short-lived. In 1658 Tuticorin (apparently their only remaining settlement) together with the pearl-fisheries came under the power of the Dutch. The Portuguese system of control, subject to the concession of "free stones" to the Nāyakkan of Madura and the Sētupati of Rāmnād, was continued; "free stones" were also allowed to the Parava *pattangattis*, or headmen, and to the headman of the Mussalmans.

Father Martin's account.

To this period belongs the vivid description by Father Martin, a Jesuit, of a fishery held in 1700 off the Tuticorin coast. Space permits of the quotation of only a brief extract. "Enormous crowds of people," he writes, "assembled on the coast on the day appointed for the commencement of the fishery; traders came there with wares of all kinds; the roadstead was crowded with shipping, drums were beaten, and muskets fired; and everywhere the greatest excitement prevailed until the Dutch Commissioners arrived from Colombo with great pomp, and ordered the proceedings to be opened with a salute of cannon. Immediately afterwards the fishing

[1] See p. 499.

[2] I.e., the privilege of employing divers. A diver lets himself down by a stone, as explained further on.

vessels all weighed anchor and stood out to sea, preceded by two large Dutch sloops, which in due time drew off to the right and left and marked the limits of the fishery, and when each vessel reached its place, half of its complement of divers plunged into the sea, each with a heavy stone tied to his feet to make him sink rapidly, and furnished with a sack into which he put his oysters, and having a rope tied round his body, the end of which was passed round a pulley and held by some of the boatmen. Thus equipped, the diver plunged in, and on reaching the bottom, filled his sack with oysters until his breath failed when he pulled a string with which he was provided, and the signal being perceived by the boatmen above, he was forthwith hauled up by the rope, together with his sack of oysters. No artificial appliances of any kind were used to enable the men to stay under water for long periods; they were accustomed to the work almost from infancy, and consequently did it easily and well. Some were more skilful than others, and it was usual to pay them in proportion to their powers, a practice which led to much emulation and occasionally to fatal results."

If in the place of the Dutch Commissioner with his pomp we substitute a Superintendent of Police and a company of reserve constables, we have an account which very fairly describes a pearl-fishery of the present day.

Decline of the fisheries.

This fishery was a disastrous one, and seems to have been no exception to the general rule of the Dutch period. Manucci (1653—1708) mentions that "already the seas of Tuticorin and Mavar [Manaar] no longer yield the quantity of pearls that they anciently did"; and the Dutch authorities began to wonder whether the fishery were not "more glitter than gold, as many things are which belong to the Company which shine uncommonly but have no real substance." They decided to give up the expensive system of direct management and to rent the fishery, all "free stones" being abolished. In 1747 a long period of sterility closed, and the fishery of that year fetched £5,000.

The Nawāb and the English.

In 1736 the Nāyakkan of Madura had given way to the Nawāb, and the Dutch found themselves faced with the most insistent demands from that monarch for tribute from the proceeds of the fishery. For some years the banks continued unexploited, until (in 1786) the Nawāb, under pressure from the English Government, secured the recognition of his right to half the proceeds of the fisheries. After much further correspondence the control of the banks, both on the coast of India and Ceylon, passed in 1796 to the British. The "Lords of

CHAP. VI. ARTS AND INDUSTRIES.

the Pearl Fishery" were in 1801 the masters of the whole of the Carnatic; and with this change disappeared the concessions of "free stones", which were no longer required to secure from local potentates protection to the pearl merchants. The only survival of the principle is seen in the custom, last ratified by Government in 1891, by which the Jāthitalaivaimore, or headman of the Paravans, is allowed on the occasion of every fishery a small number of boats fixed in proportion to the number of boats employed by Government.

Fisheries since 1801.

Between 1801 and the present time thirteen fisheries have been held. The most productive of the series occurred in 1807, when the Tulāyiram pār yielded a net revenue to Government of nearly three lakhs of rupees. The last fishery (held in 1908) was the least successful of the period. All the business connected with the pearl-fisheries is under the direction of a Superintendent, stationed at Tuticorin.

The Tinnevelly pearl.

The Tinnevelly pearl, like that obtained in the Ceylon waters, though generally of small size, is in regard to colour and lustre unrivalled, save perhaps by the pearl of the Persian Gulf. The buyers of oysters at the fisheries come mostly from the Dēvakōttai country in the Rāmnād district; from their hands the pearls pass in large numbers to Bombay and are either sold there or shipped to London and Paris. The oyster is so small that its yield of mother-of-pearl is almost negligible; excellent lime is extracted from the shells, and it is for this purpose that they are usually purchased.

The chank-fishery.

Another most important commercial product of the Gulf of Manaar is the sacred chank or conch *(Turbinella pyrum)*[1]. Like the pearl-fishery, this fishery is a Government monopoly and is conducted from Tuticorin under the supervision of a Superintendent of Marine Fisheries. The shells are found near the pearl-banks in about 7 to 10 fathoms of water, either buried in the sand on the sea-bottom or in sandy crevices between blocks of coral rock. The fishery goes on from October to May and is worked by divers, who weight themselves with stones and descend to the bottom with a net round their waist. Unlike the pearl-oysters, which are found in clusters, the shells of the chank are scattered about, so that divers have to move about from place to place to find them. At the close of the day's fishery the chanks are brought on shore and tested with a wooden gauge having a hole two and three-eighths inches in diameter. Those shells which pass through this hole are discarded and returned to the sea on the

[1] Much of what follows is taken from *Pearl and Chank Fisheries and Marine Fauna* by Edgar Thurston. Madras Government Museum Bulletin, 1894.

chance that the animal may revive and continue to grow; the larger ones are stacked in a storehouse, where the animal substance is got rid of by the process of putrefaction in which flies and other insects play their part. The shells are sold by auction to the highest bidder.

Uses of the chank.

Not only is the chank valued as an ornament for the foreheads of bullocks and as a musical instrument in Hindu ceremonies, but it is also cut into bracelets and other instruments, an industry which at the present day is located almost entirely in Bengal.[1] From the place of fishery the chanks are sent to Calcutta and are distributed thence to Dacca and a number of places in Bengal. A few go occasionally to Chittagong, where bracelet-cutting is carried on by a few Muhammadan workmen for supply to the neighbouring hill-tribes. The business of importing and distributing the chanks is chiefly in the hands of Dacca families, a few Muhammadans from the Tamil coast having been admitted to partnership in the wholesale trade in view of their special local knowledge. The demand for the chank bracelet comes from the women of Thibet, Bengal and Assam. The most richly carved and highly polished bangles are used by the women of Bengal; the Thibetans and other hill-tribes prefer strength and quantity to fine finish and are satisfied with the plainest bracelets. Writing in the sixteenth century, Garcia da Orta says: "And this chanko is a ware for the Bengal trade and formerly produced more profit than now. . . . and there was formerly a custom in Bengal that no virgin in honour and esteem could be corrupted unless it were by placing bracelets of chanko on her arms; but since the Patans came in this usage has more or less ceased, and so the chanko is rated lower now."

In the south of India the use of the chank bangle, at one time apparently common,[2] is practically unknown at the present day; and, with the exception of a few rough specimens which are produced by the Muhammadans at Kīlakarai in the Rāmnād district, the industry of chank-cutting does not exist in this Presidency.

Chank-cutting in the district in early times.

Mr. J. Hornell has collected some interesting evidence to show that, during the early centuries of the Christian era, an important chank-cutting industry existed in the ancient Pāndya kingdom. His researches, based on ancient Tamil

[1] For assistance with what follows I am indebted to Mr. J. Hornell, F.L.S., Superintendent of Marine Fisheries, Tuticorin.

[2] Chank bangles have frequently been met with in prehistoric sites—See p. 409.

CHAP. VI. ARTS AND INDUSTRIES.

writings, received important confirmation from some discoveries he made on the site of the ancient cities of Korkai and Kāyal. Fragments of chanks, bearing distinct evidence of having been sawn by an instrument similar to that which is in use at the present day in Bengal, were unearthed in both these places. The circumstances in which this important industry disappeared from the south of India and transferred itself to a centre 1,500 miles away may never be satisfactorily explained; but it seems reasonable to suppose, with Mr. Hornell, that it was during the Muhammadan invasions of the fourteenth century and the disorganization of Hindu institutions which accompanied them that the stoppage of the industry occurred.

The chank trade.

The annual export of shells from Tuticorin amounts to about 250,000—roughly one-eighth of the total Bengal consumption—the other chief sources of supply being Ceylon and Rāmēsvaram. The relative importance, however, of the Tuticorin production is not to be judged from its numerical ratio. These shells are the very best of their kind on account of the purity of their colour and the readiness with which they can be polished; and, while the price obtained by the Ceylon shells ranges between Rs. 30 and Rs. 100 a thousand, the Tuticorin chanks, as also those from Rāmēsvaram, fetch on an average about Rs. 160 a thousand. During a period of twenty years ending with 1912 the Government made an average annual net profit from the fishery of Rs. 11,777; and, in spite of the increasing difficulty of obtaining divers and securing their services throughout the season, the latest returns show no decline of revenue.

TRADE.

The trade of the district may be considered under three heads: imports, exports, and internal commerce.

The details and value of articles imported and exported at Tuticorin and at the minor ports of Kulasēkharapatnam and Kāyalpatnam may be seen in table XXIV of the appendix and some account of the trade of Tuticorin will be found in the notice relating to that place (page 440). The figures of this trade are of course enormously swollen by the through consignments made to and from all parts of southern India, and it is impossible to separate the proportion which represents the trade of the district. Nor are district statistics available of the amount and value of imports and exports conveyed by road and railway.

Exports.

With the exception of cotton, which goes to Europe and Japan, and jaggery, which is sent in large quantities to the South Arcot district and other parts of the Presidency, most of the surplus produce of the district is sent to Ceylon,

Singapore and Travancore. To Ceylon are exported cattle, gingelly-oil, onions, chillies, palmyra mats and fibre, candy, check-cloths and occasionally rice; to Singapore, *kōrai* mats, chillies, hides, and cloths; to Travancore, cloths (especially *muris*), palmyra fibre, and paddy (from Kalakkād and Tirukkurungudi). *Kōrai* mats are sent to Negapatam for export to Madras.

Imports.

Imports by sea consigned to the district are, besides paddy from Rangoon and dry grains from Bombay, mostly manufactured articles, such as piece-goods, hardware, and kerosine oil and matches. By land, consigned mostly in the first instance to Pēttai, come "dry" grains and pulses from the Northern Circars and Bombay; from Malabar and Travancore come cocoanuts, pepper, ginger, ropes and timber.

Internal trade; markets.

The weekly markets held in more than sixty villages and towns throughout the district play a most important part in circulating products within the district, collecting goods for export and distributing imports. The most important centres outside the municipal towns are: in the Tiruchendūr taluk, Udangudi and Sāttānkulam; in Nānguneri, Tisaiyanvilai and Valliyūr; in Ambāsamudram, Mēḷa Ambāsamudram; in Tenkāsi, Pāvūr Chattram; in Sankaranainārkōil, the head-quarter town and Tiruvēngadam; in Kōilpatti, Kayattār, Kalugumalai and Ettaiyāpuram; and in Tinnevelly, Mēlakallūr. The important centre of Pēttai, frequently referred to in this chapter, is included within the limits of the Tinnevelly municipality.

Cattle-markets.

Important cattle fairs are held twice a year at Kalugumalai (Kōilpatti taluk) and annually at Sīvalappēri (Tinnevelly taluk), Muthulāpuram and Pasurantanai (Kōilpatti taluk), at Alvārtirunagari and Tiruchendūr, and at Sankaranainārkōil. At Singikulam (Nānguneri taluk), Mēlakallūr (Tinnevelly taluk) and Madathupatti (Sankaranainārkōil taluk) a large trade in cattle is conducted at the ordinary weekly markets.

WEIGHTS AND MEASURES

The intricacies of the weights and measures current in the district are such as to baffle the most resolute understanding.

Foodstuffs.

With foodstuffs weight is usually expressed in terms of *palams* and *tulāms*. A *palam* is the weight of Rs. 5½, but *tulāms* are of two kinds, one (known as *vadapadi*) containing 144 *palams*, the other containing 100 *palams* and called *sirupadi*. For the weighment of eatables of local production, e.g., chillies, jaggery, tamarind fruits and onions, the *sirupadi* is preferred, imported foods being, as a rule, measured by the *vadapadi tulām*. But even to this general rule there are exceptions. Vegetables, for instance, are often weighed by the *idai*, the

CHAP. VI. WEIGHTS AND MEASURES.

equivalent of 25 *palams*. The term *rāttal* (which equals seven *palams* or one English pound) is used with reference to potatoes. Grain and salt are invariably sold by measure.

In the place of the usual scales the old fashioned *vellikōl*, or weighing-rod, is used largely in rural parts for the weighment of vegetables, fish and jaggery.

Metals.

Workers in brass calculate in terms of a *padi* which is equivalent to 34 *palams*; bell-metal workers speak of a *seer* containing 4¼ *palams*. Gold and medicine are weighed by the *kalanji*. which is equivalent to 20 *manjadis*, one and a half *kalanjis* being the equivalent in weight of a sovereign.

A "standard" table.

The table of weights in use in all railway stations and already in use to some extent amongst shop-keepers is as follows :—

3 tolas [1]	...	...	...	=	1 palam.
8 palams	...	...	...	=	1 seer.
5 seers	...	...	...	=	1 viss.
8 viss	...	...	...	=	1 maund.
20 maunds	...	...	...	=	1 candy.[2]

If weights are ever to be standardized by enactment, it would appear that this table offers the best chances of success.

Grain.

The indigenous and prevalent system of grain measurement is as follows :—

8 ālāks	...	...	...	=	1 seer padi.
8 seer padi	...	...	...	=	1 (kundu) marakkāl or kuruni.
21 (kundu) marakkāls			...	=	1 kōttai (168 seer padis).

The *kōttai* contains 112 Madras measures, and the Madras measure is therefore equal to 1½ *seer padis*.

Liquids.

Liquids, such as milk and oils, are measured either in terms of the *seer padi* or the Madras measure.

Measurement of area.

The terms used in the table of grain measures are applied also to areas of wet lands. A *kōttai* of land (commonly called a *kōttai viraippādu*) is the equivalent of 1 acre and 62 cents, and a *marakkāl* (or *kuruni*) is almost exactly equal to 8 cents. The connection between the measurement of grain and the measurement of space is found in the theory that the amount of seed required to sow a *kōttai* of land is a *kōttai* of seed and that a *marakkāl* of land requires a *marakkāl* of seed.

The measurements of dry arable land are now generally referred to in terms of acres and cents; in the northern parts

[1] A tola is the weight of a rupee. [2] A candy weighs 500 lbs.

of the district the old district term *sangili* (3·64 acres) is often heard and, more rarely, the *kurukkam*, which is the rough equivalent of an acre.[1]

In regard to building sites, the unit of square measurement generally employed is a *kuli*, which is the square of a "carpenter's cubit" *(tachumulam)* of 33 inches.

Lineal measures.

For lineal measurement the yard, foot and inch are often used, but more commonly the native terms. These are—

2 spans	...	...	...	=	1 mulam.
2 mulams	...	...	...	=	1 gajam.

Fortunately, a *gajam* is equivalent to an English yard. *Kūppidudūram*, "the distance a shout can be heard," is a common expression, the vagueness of which commends it especially to witnesses in the law-courts. Longer distances are expressed as often in terms of miles and furlongs (the latter unit being used far more commonly than in English) as of *nāligai-vali*, roughly a mile, or the distance walked in an Indian hour, or *nāligai*, of 24 minutes.

Time.

Length of time is generally calculated in English hours and minutes, and points of time are generally indicated by reference to the clock. Popular expressions to denote periods and points of time are numerous: "the time it takes to crack a nut"; "the twinkling of an eye"; "when the sun is a palmyra tree high", a phrase which is very variously interpreted; "when the crows go home"; and so on.

Money.

A local peculiarity in regard to the calculation of money is the general use of the word *duttu* (four pies) and fractions and multiples of it, when small sums of one or two annas or less are spoken of. A pie is referred to by some as a *dampadi*, and half a pie is sometimes conceived of and called a *kāsu*. In many parts of the district the term *panam* (3 annas 4 pies) is commonly used, and in the markets of the south the price of grain is habitually quoted with reference to this unit. In the cotton country cotton is commonly used in small transactions as a substitute for money.

[1] In the centre and south of the district the word *kurukkam* is seldom heard. In the Tenkāsi taluk it is sometimes used to denote the equivalent of about half an acre.

CHAPTER VII.

MEANS OF COMMUNICATION.

ROADS—Their maintenance—Avenues—Road materials—Former condition of the roads—Serious work begins—Bridges—Captain Horsley—Culverts, etc.—Ferries—Travellers' bungalows—Chattrams. RAILWAYS—The South Indian Railway—District Board railways—The Tinnevelly-Tiruchendūr scheme—The Virudupatti-Tenkāsi project—Motor services.

CHAP. VII. ROADS.

THE latest returns show that the district possesses 814 miles of metalled road. From Tinnevelly and Palamcotta, which lie together in the very centre of the district, main routes radiate in all directions. Following the direction of the hands of a clock, these are the roads :—

(1) to Ambāsamudram and Tenkāsi, with a branch to Pāpanāsam.
(2) to Ravanasamudram (joining No. 1).
(3) to Tenkāsi *via* Alankulam and from Tenkāsi to Quilon (Travancore) and Sivagiri.
(4) to Sankaranainārkōil (Srīvilliputtūr and Madura).
(5) to Kōilpatti (and Madura).
(6) to Sīvalappēri, Ottappidāram and Vilāttikulam.
(7) to Tuticorin (branching from No. 8).
(8) to Tiruchendūr.
(9) to Nānguneri, Panagudi (and Nagercoil, Travancore).

Besides these there are the important trunk roads connecting Tuticorin with the black cotton country and a few other roads connecting the main roads with one another.

The best roaded part of the district is the western part of the Tenkāsi taluk, and after that comes the Ambāsamudram taluk; worst are the *tēri* regions of the south, where cart traffic is never possible and the wide strip of sand and swamp which forms the eastern and seaward boundary of the Tiruchendūr, Srīvaikuntam and Kōilpatti taluks. For the *tēri* country the most hopeful solution is offered by the possibility of developing a system of light railway lines such as the East India Distilleries Company has already laid in this tract for the purpose of conveying palmyra juice and jaggery from the surrounding villages to its sugar refinery at Kulasēkharapatnam. The Company has already obtained permission to convey passengers over that section of the system which connects Kulasēkharapatnam with Tisaiyanvilai (Nānguneri taluk); and in the interest of trade and public convenience it is to be hoped that a further extension of this railway may yet be made. Hundreds of rough tracks traverse all the dry country and serve the purposes of cart-drivers almost all the year through; in the *tēri* regions and the sandy country towards the coast pack-bullocks are used for transport purposes, lighter loads being carried by coolies on their heads or in baskets suspended from the ends of a pliant stick slung across the shoulders. The familiar pace, neither a walk nor a run, at which these carriers of burdens proceed is sustained for hours at a stretch.

Their maintenance.

The problem of road maintenance in this district is an undoubtedly difficult one. A dry season of nine continuous months, during which, in many parts of the district, it is almost impossible to obtain water, fierce dry winds raging at intervals during the same period, heavily-laden springless carts with wheels five feet in diameter and narrow tires habitually driven in the same grooves, shy labour and limited funds—all these circumstances combine to tax the resources of the most energetic and competent engineers.

Avenues.

Many of the roads are shaded by avenues, the usual trees being banyan, *maruthai*, tamarind and portia *(pūvarasu)*; the best shaded roads are to be found in the Tenkāsi and Ambāsamudram taluks. The comparative paucity of fruit-growing trees may be judged from the fact that, in 1913-14, the total income derived by local boards and unions from avenues was only Rs. 8,963.

Road materials.

In the western half of the district the numerous out-crops of granite provide excellent materials for the construction of the roads; towards the centre and south-east quartz and gneiss are used according to the locality; in the black-cotton land hard limestone is met with and is often used in combination with the gneiss which is obtained at intervals throughout this tract. The overground quarries of Brahmadēsam (near Ambāsamudram) yield a dark green basalt, well-known for its extreme hardness, and in the Nānguneri taluk a fine white granite and a blue basalt are obtained.

Former condition of the roads.

Roads, in the ordinary sense of that term, are of comparatively recent origin. When the Company came into possession of Tinnevelly, there were no roads fit for wheeled traffic, and,

CHAP. VII. ROADS.

apart from the existence of many miles of avenues of trees—the *sālais*, several of which exist to the present day—there was nothing to show that any capital had ever been sunk in road-making. The roadways beneath the trees had never been properly formed or drained, no bridges or culverts had been built; they had become the drain of all the country through which they passed and so much more rugged than the land on either side that they served merely as a rough guide to travellers, who took a course as nearly parallel to them as the ground permitted. "Mangammāl *sālai*" is the name by which these fine old avenues are usually known, and all are indiscriminately ascribed to the bounty of that famous Nāyakkan queen. In the *tēri* country they are at the present time most numerous and complete; and many survivals may be seen throughout the district. There is a *sālai*, for instance, which, with occasional breaks, connects Tinnevelly with Srīvilliputtūr (Rāmnād district); *sālais* run alongside the modern road from Sērmādēvi to Kalakkād and beside that from Alvārkurichi to Sivasailam ; the old route from Tinnevelly through Vaippār to Rāmēsvaram was such a *sālai*, and traces of it may be seen at frequent intervals near the line of the present road.

The old routes were thus, as a rule, useless ; and the problem was not one of maintenance but of construction. For some years the roads were left to look after themselves, and till 1824 the only money spent on them was a few hundred rupees found necessary to keep in repair the road from Palamcotta to Kāyalpatnam, by which the cotton and piece-goods of the Commercial department were sent to that port. Even the important military road through Kōilpatti to Palamcotta was almost impassable where it went through black-cotton soil, and peons and labourers had to be sent out to help in extricating the regimental carts ; during four months of the year the transport of guns was out of the question, and the post was frequently received in Palamcotta two days late.

Between 1826 and 1830 a start was made with an average yearly outlay of Rs. 2,300, and a few years later Government consulted the Collector on a proposal to levy a tax on carts or to set up tolls. The roads, the Collector replied, were execrably bad, and "a toll would be an additional infliction on those whose duty or pursuits entail upon them the necessity of passing through the district." In 1836 Captain (afterwards Colonel Sir Arthur) Cotton suggested that the problem of communications might be solved by a system of cheap rail-roads to be worked by cattle, a scheme which had already been tried for the purpose of bringing materials for the roads into the town of Madras. By this method Palamcotta was to be linked up with Madura, and plans for a system of 5,000 miles had been worked out for the Presidency. The Madras rail-road, however, was not a success, and the idea of extending the scheme was abandoned in 1839.

Serious work begins.

In 1846 a "Superintendent of Roads" was appointed to relieve the Board of Revenue of the supervision of the trunk roads of the Presidency, and an allotment of Rs. 4 lakhs a year was set apart for expenditure on them. But Tinnevelly got none of this. In the same year general permission was given to utilize on roads the accumulated surplus of the *tiruppani* or temple funds, and in this district a lump sum of a lakh of rupees was allotted from this source and set apart for the construction of a road to connect Tuticorin with the cotton country. In 1850 an estimate exceeding Rs. 1 lakh (subsequently augmented) was sanctioned for a road from Srīvilliputtūr to Sāttūr (both now in the Rāmnād district) and from Kōilpatti *via* Ettaiyāpuram to Tuticorin. Allotments on what would now be considered a meagre scale continued to be made by Government for the other roads, and in 1853 the Collector was authorized to spend for this purpose the few hundred rupees fetched each year by the sale in auction of the right to collect reeds and grasses in tanks and swamps. In 1856 work was started on a new road from Palamcotta to Tuticorin, Rs. 67,000 being allotted for the purpose.

The new works progressed slowly and took six or eight years to complete. Including the money spent on them, the average annual expenditure on roads for the years 1854 to 1864 was under Rs. 40,000. "It is evident," wrote Mr. Silver, the Collector, in 1865, "that almost everything has yet to be done in the matter of the roads to give the district a fair chance." "Cart hire," he added, "is 25 per cent higher here than in any other district." Want of money was the real obstacle; and it was not till the formation of a permanent fund, derived from the cess which the Local Funds Act of 1871 authorized, that any real progress was made. The average amount spent on the roads during the past ten years is Rs. 2,18,854.

Bridges

The bridges of the district, which are few in number, were almost all constructed about the middle of the last century. Amongst these may be mentioned that over the Tāmbraparni connecting Tinnevelly with Palamcotta, built in 1843 at the expense of Sulōchana Mudaliyār, a Naib Sarishtadar of the Collector's office; that over the same river at Ambāsamudram,

CHAP. VII. ROADS. provided by local subscriptions at a cost of Rs. 17,275 in 1841; the bridge over the Chittār on the Tinnevelly-Sankaranainārkōil road, built by public subscription in 1852; and the bridge over the Nambiyār near Dalapatisamudram, completed in 1861. The bridges at Tinnevelly and Ambāsamudram were seriously damaged by the floods of 1869 and were subsequently repaired (1873). The bridge over the Chittār at Gangaikondān was constructed in 1844 at the expense of the zamindar of Ettaiyāpuram; that over the Hariharānadhi (near Tenkāsi) was built in 1853 by public subscription. The bridge over the Tāmbraparni at Vikramasingapuram (Ambāsamudram taluk), which was built in 1891 by the Tinnevelly Mills Company, Ltd., to serve their own purposes, is open to the public. The bridge across the same river at Srīvaikuntam, which is carried across the anicut, was built by the District Board in 1890 from funds which had been subscribed for the purpose in 1867.

Captain Horsley. From 1841-55 Captain Horsley, R.E. (afterwards Chief Engineer), was District Engineer of Tinnevelly, and his name deserves to be held in grateful remembrance by all connected with the district. During that period of fifteen years he constructed five[1] important bridges and started another (that over the Nambiyār); he almost completed the system of roads connecting Tuticorin with the cotton country; he rebuilt (though these facts are irrelevant to this chapter) the Kannadiyan anicut and submitted the earliest proposals ever made for an anicut at Srīvaikuntām.

Culverts, etc. Innumerable under-vent bridges or culverts which allow the surface drainage of the surrounding country to pass under the roads exist in all parts of the district, and their number is constantly being added to.

Ferries. There are in the district ten public ferries, controlled by the District Board, almost all of which cross the Tāmbraparni. Some are provided with contrivances for transporting carts, and it is only during seasons of excessive floods that the ferries cannot be used.

Travellers' bungalows. A reference to table II in the appendix to this volume will show how scanty is the provision made by local boards in the way of travellers' bungalows. In the three taluks of Tenkāsi, Tinnevelly and Srīvaikuntam these boards maintain no bungalows at all; in each of the three taluks of Nānguneri, Sankaranainārkōil, Ambāsamudram and Tiruchendūr there is one such bungalow; in the Kōilpatti taluk there are four.

[1] He also built a great part of the bridge over the Vaippār at Sāttūr, which then belonged to this district.

Fortunately, the rest-houses and inspection sheds of the Public Works and Forest departments make up the deficiency to a small extent; and by the courtesy of the Church Missionary Society a number of bungalows belonging to that body in various parts of the district are available for the use of European travellers. At Kōilpatti the zamindar of Ettaiyāpuram owns a bungalow, which he allows travellers to occupy. The bungalow maintained at the same place by the Agricultural department may be used by certain classes of Government officials.

Chattrams.

Upwards of seventy chattrams, most of which are supported by endowments made either by their founders or by the old native Governments, afford accommodation in varying degrees of comfort to Indian travellers. Of these, twenty-four are controlled by the taluk boards, the rest being under private management.

RAILWAYS.

The South Indian Railway.

The South Indian Railway (metre gauge) enters the district from the north and terminates at Tuticorin (49 miles); this section and that which branches from it at Maniyāchi to Tinnevelly Bridge (18 miles) were opened for traffic on the 1st January 1876. This latter section was extended in 1902 to Kallidaikurichi and in the next year as far as Shencotta (Travancore territory), thus tapping the richest part of the district. The extension to Quilon was completed in 1904.

District Board railways.

In 1903, at the instance of the District Board, which desired to construct a railway of its own, the Madras Government sanctioned the reconnaissance survey of a line which it was proposed to lay from Sērmādēvi (on the South Indian Railway) to Panagudi near the boundary of the Nānguneri taluk and Travancore. While the Railway Company were starting on the work, the Travancore Durbar announced that it would object to any extension into the territory of that State, and the scheme was in consequence abandoned.

The Tinnevelly-Tiruchendūr scheme.

Later in the year the District Board substituted a proposal to construct a railway line connecting Tinnevelly Bridge station with Tiruchendūr; they resolved to impose a railway cess and to allow the funds so raised to accumulate. The line was surveyed; estimates were drawn up and revised more than once, with the result that the minimum cost was found to be Rs. 20½ lakhs. Lengthy correspondence ensued between Government and the South Indian Railway Company regarding the settlement of terms, and by the time their discussion showed signs of closing it was discovered, in 1912, that the work estimated for in 1905 would now cost over Rs. 23 lakhs. It was then decided to reduce the cost by lowering the grade

CHAP. VII. RAILWAYS.

of the line, and the estimate was once more revised. A new survey was made, and it is expected that work will start immediately. The cess has been levied since 1st July 1903, and the accumulated funds amounted in March 1915 to over Rs. 8½ lakhs. The last revised estimate amounts to a little over Rs. 17 lakhs. It is proposed to issue debentures bearing interest at 4½ per cent to the extent of Rs. 6 lakhs.

The line, which will be 38 miles long, is to pass through Palamcotta (the station being situated on the extreme eastern side of the town), Seydinganallūr, Pudukkudi, Alvārtirunagari, Nazareth, Kurumbūr and Kāyalpatnam, terminating in Tiruchendūr on the outskirts of the town. The prospects of the line are distinctly good. For twenty miles or so it will pass through or near rich paddy country; it will skirt the great jaggery-producing region of the district and serve a most important centre of the salt industry, Kāyalpatnam. The pilgrim traffic to Srīvaikuntam, Alvārtirunagari and, especially, Tiruchendūr is considerable.

The Virudupatti-Tenkāsi project.

A railway offering perhaps still better prospects of success is a metre-gauge line of 76 miles which it has recently been proposed to construct, from Imperial funds, between Virudupatti (Rāmnād district) and Tenkāsi. The length of the line in this district would be 37 miles, and its route (as at present designed) would be through Sivakāsi and Srīvilliputtūr (Rāmnād district), and (in this district) Karivalamvandanallūr, Sankaranainārkōil and Kadaiyanallūr.

Motor services.

Privately owned services of motor-omnibuses ply between Palamcotta and Nagercoil (Travancore), between Palamcotta and Tiruchendūr, and between Sankaranainārkōil and Ettaiyāpuram.

CHAPTER VIII.

RAINFALL AND SEASONS.

FAMINES AND SCARCITIES—In pre-British days—In 1811 and 1847—The great famine of 1877—January, 1877—March, 1877—June, 1877—September, 1877—Effects of the famine. RAINFALL. FLOODS—In 1810—In 1827—In 1847—In 1867—In 1869—In 1874—In 1877—In 1895—In 1914.

CHAP. VIII. FAMINES AND SCARCITIES.

In pre-British days.

TO judge from the letters of the Jesuit priests, famines, more or less severe, were of constant occurrence during the seventeenth and eighteenth centuries. The writings of the former century relate more particularly to the Madura district, and it is not possible to say whether the distress recorded for the years 1646–47 and 1687 extended to Tinnevelly; in the eighteenth century famine is spoken of as having swept away large numbers in this district on seven occasions between 1709 and 1735. Writing of the famine of 1770, Fr. Bertram says that "millions of people" perished.

In 1811 and 1847.

Within British times the district has experienced little of famine or scarcity. In 1811 the ravages of the epidemic fever (p. 258) were succeeded by widespread agricultural distress, to which the unseasonable weather also contributed. In 1847 we read that the north-east monsoon failed; and, with the exception of the Tāmbraparni valley and the villages on the upper Chittār, the district experienced severe drought, vast areas both of wet and dry land being left uncultivated. Remissions to the extent of three-quarters of the assessment in the case of wet lands and half the assessment in dry lands were granted, the cultivation of tank beds was allowed, and the frontier-duties on grain were suspended. No mortality is recorded.

The great famine of 1877.

The most serious difficulties which within British times the district has had to face occurred during 1877, when almost every district of the Presidency was in the grip of famine. In the neighbouring district of Madura, as in most other districts, grave distress began with the failure of the south-west monsoon in 1876. In Tinnevelly, as has been seen, the rainfall of that period of the year is normally slight, and the river-fed rice lands dependent for their supply on the rain received along the ghats yielded crops only slightly below

CHAP. VIII. FAMINES AND SCARCITIES.

the average. The local rainfall, however, had been sadly insufficient, the amount received between April and September in the three taluks of Sankaranainārkōil, Ottapidāram (roughly the present Kōilpatti) and Nāngunēri taken together being only 3¾ inches, that is 2¾ inches below the usual low average. Sankaranainārkōil had fared worst, receiving less than three inches.

The north-east monsoon started well enough in this taluk and in Nāngunēri, and the area there brought under cultivation during October and November actually exceeded the average of the four preceding years. In the Kōilpatti taluk the area of cultivation had fallen only a little short; but by December the monsoon came to an abrupt end, Ottapidāram (Kōilpatti) having by the end of November received less than 5 inches, Nāngunēri 8·80 inches, Sankaranainārkōil 10·37 inches. More than half the dry cultivation of the district begins in November, and the prospects of saving the dry crops of these three taluks began to appear very slight. The rain-fed tanks and even the smaller rivers of Nāngunēri and Sankaranainārkōil taluks were beginning to dry up, and by January it was estimated that remissions of revenue to the extent of about Rs. 7½ lakhs on wet and dry lands would be necessary. The price of paddy had advanced by over 50 per cent; that of cumbu, the staple food of the people over a great part of the Kōilpatti taluk, had more than doubled. Small ryots and labourers began to emigrate to Ceylon in larger numbers than usual, but, owing to the prevalence of cholera and fever in the island, most of them soon returned to their homes. A sum of Rs. 23,000 had already been sanctioned, so far back as May, for the opening of relief-works, should they be found necessary; but for the time being minor works, ordinarily carried out from local funds, were found sufficient to meet the situation.

January, 1877.

By January regular relief-works were opened in Nāngunēri, Ottapidāram and Sankaranainārkōil, these taking the form chiefly of the collection of road materials and the sinking of wells. The district was divided up into four charges, the Collector, Mr. A. J. Stuart, looking after Sankaranainārkōil, the Sub-Collector, Nāngunēri and Ambāsamudram, and the Head-Assistant, Ottapidāram. The two taluks of Sāttūr and Srīvilliputtūr (now belonging to the Rāmnād district), in which also pressure was severe, were entrusted to a Deputy Collector. A system was organized of watching villages closely and drafting to the relief-works people in danger of starvation. Two annas was the daily rate of pay offered; but, in spite of this comparatively high scale of wages, the Nāngunēri works failed to attract any labourers in January, while the average number employed daily during that month in the other two taluks, Ottapidāram and Sankaranainārkōil, amounted only to 1,727. At the end of January the rate of wages was, in accordance with instructions received from the Government of India, reduced to 1½ annas; the numbers fell still lower, and it was evident that pressure was not yet very severe. Gratuitous relief was from January forwards extended to those incapable of work either in their villages or in chattrams at the headquarters of the three distressed taluks; but, as may be seen from the figures below, which indicate the general course of the famine until its close, the number of persons seeking this relief was small:—

Month.	Daily average number of persons on			
	Gratuitous relief.		Relief works.	
1877.	No.	Cost. RS.	No.	Cost. RS.
January	215	234	17,127	2,903
February	99	305	1,223	2,924
March	311	635	1,405	5,079
April	1,216	724	1,388	4,179
May	692	1,237	487	1,417
June	879	2,122	23	87
July	1,990	4,337	...	...
August	8,596	18,467	...	...
September	22,331	59,503	1,806	1,315
October	9,669	28,368	4,139	4,722
November	2,449	7,040	2,494	1,403
December	1,102	3,585	1,002	715
1878.				
January	447	944	125	79
February	83	364	...	...
March	34	36	...	...

March, 1877.

On the 16th March two inches of rain fell. The cotton of Ottapidāram was greatly benefited, and some of the tanks in this and the other two affected taluks were half filled. All the other dry crops, however, had perished, and the ryots began to sow gingelly, a crop requiring little rain. Pasture was improved; but cattle disease had already broken out, and large numbers, especially in Ottapidāram, had died. Cholera appeared, and in the last fortnight of May as many as 492 persons died of the disease.

With June the south-west monsoon set in; the Tāmbraparni received even better floods than usual, and the tanks and

CHAP. VIII. FAMINES AND SCARCITIES.

June, 1877.

channels at the foot of the hills, in the Sankaranainārkōil, Tenkāsi and Nānguneri taluks, received a normal supply. The crops sown on the dry lands and under rain-fed tanks in March did fairly well in Sankaranainārkōil; in Nānguneri little survived except the cultivation under wells. Ottapidāram was bare once more; and, when it became known in September that a bumper crop had been reaped in the river-valley, crowds began to flock in that direction from all the dry taluks.

September, 1877.

In September Mr. Puckle, then a Member of the Board of Revenue, visited the district, and a vigorous programme of relief-works, designed partly to check the inroad on the river valley, was started in each of the three distressed taluks. In Ottapidāram new distributary channels at the tail-end of the north-main were dug, and improvements were made to the Tuticorin water-supply; in Nānguneri numerous tanks and channels were repaired, and in Sankaranainārkōil the road from Tinnevelly to Rājapālaiyam was laid out. Relief camps had been opened in March in three centres in the Ottapidāram taluk, at Ottapidāram, Vilāttikulam and Ettaiyāpuram (the last-named was managed by the zamindar); and in the end of May a camp was started in Nānguneri. At first they attracted very few, the Nānguneri camp being almost empty even throughout the worst months.

September marked the climax of distress; and in that month the number of persons daily in receipt of gratuitous relief, whether in camps, or in the villages, rose to over 22,000, nearly three times the daily average of the preceding month. In October relief-works began to attract larger numbers, and, for some reason or other, possibly owing to a severer test of indigence, the numbers on gratuitous relief greatly declined. On the last day of the month the north-east monsoon broke; rain fell in torrents, and famine was succeeded by floods.

The famine had carried away 54,000 of the population, and cholera another 14,400. The cost to the State was Rs. 8,43,000: in remissions of land revenue, Rs. 7,15,000, and in gratuitous relief, Rs. 1,28,000.

Effects of the famine.

The figures for the census of 1881 proved clearly the disastrous effects of the famine; the three taluks directly affected, Ottapidāram, Nānguneri and Sankaranainārkōil, showed a marked decline of population,[1] and, in spite of an exceptional increase in some of the other taluks, the figures for the whole district (that is, the old Tinnevelly district)

[1] So also did the Tinnevelly taluk.

showed only a very slight advance (0·3 per cent) on those recorded in 1871. The census of 1891 indicated a rapid recovery, the rebound in the case of Ottapidāram (26 per cent) and Sankaranainārkōil (18 per cent) being especially remarkable. The famine left little impression on the economic condition of the district. The holdings of wet lands were nowhere affected; and it was only in the Ottapidāram taluk that the dry lands suffered a set-back. The occupied area contracted but began to recover almost immediately.[1]

RAINFALL.

The appended table gives statistics of the average rainfall for the district as a whole and for each of the recording stations for as long a period as registers have been kept. For purposes of comparison, figures are given for each of the four periods into which, from a meteorological point of view, the year divides itself.

Number.	Stations.	Years recorded.	January to March.	April and May.	June to September.	October to December.	Total.
1	Tenkāsi	1870—1914	5·48	5·10	9·45	20·29	40·32
2	Kadaiyam	1906—1914	4·31	2·47	5·46	25·22	37·46
3	Sivagiri	1905—1914	4·75	3·86	4·54	23·35	36·50
4	Ambāsamudram ...	1870—1914	5·87	3·62	3·14	22·42	35·05
5	Kadayanallūr	1905—1914	3·87	2·44	4·70	21·38	32·39
6	Kōilpatti	1902—1914	1·29	5·29	5·24	17·42	29·24
7	Nānguneri	1870—1914	4·15	3·14	3·10	18·67	29·06
8	Palamcotta	1870—1914	3·42	3·93	2·27	18·12	27·84
9	Kayattār...	1904—1914	1·69	3·98	3·61	18·27	27·55
10	Rādhāpuram	1878—1914	3·00	2·78	4·10	16·82	26·70
11	Kulasēkharapatnam ...	1880—1914	3·16	1·84	0·85	20·43	26·28
12	Sankaranainārkōil ...	1870—1914	3·09	4·27	2·50	15·77	25·63
13	Kūttankuli	1893—1914	2·77	2·37	3·82	16·49	25·45
14	Srīvaikuntam	1870—1914	2·83	2·87	2·05	17·44	25·19
15	Kāyalpatnam	1893—1907	2·92	2·63	0·62	18·54	24·71
16	Ottapidāram	1870—1914	2·06	2·90	3·24	16·45	24·65
17	Sāttānkulam	1902—1914	1·48	1·77	1·66	19·50	24·41
18	Vilāttikulam	1880—1914	1·97	2·66	4·08	15·43	24·44
19	Arasadi	1894—1914	2·70	2·38	1·22	16·75	23·05
20	Tuticorin	1870—1914	2·56	2·49	1·11	15·95	22·11
21	Kīranūr	1897—1914	2·55	1·82	0·57	17·02	21·96
	Mean average for the district.	1870—1914	3·41	3·27	3·10	17·79	27·57

What is wanted during the north-east monsoon is rain to fill the tanks and saturate the dry fields; and in a normal year

[1] The taluks of Sāttūr and Srīvilliputtūr were more severely affected, and holdings recovered comparatively slowly.

CHAP. VIII. RAINFALL.

three-quarters of the rainfall is received in these three months and is sufficient to bring a crop to maturity. From January to March the ryot welcomes showers to keep his dry crops alive and to freshen the shooting paddy crop; but still more valuable than these and, as the Tamil proverb says, "worth their weight in gold" are the *kōdai* rains of April and May, which bring forth grass for the cattle, enable the farmer to plough his lands, both wet and dry, after harvest and, in the more favoured parts of the river-valley where freshes can be expected early in June, to sow his seed broadcast for the coming *kār* crop. In an average year [1] rain falls on only 41 days, and seasonable distribution is, therefore, of more importance than quantity.

The stations are given in descending order of their rainfall; and, as might be expected, the first five stations are those lying nearest to the hills. Between June and September, the period of the south-west monsoon, the district as a whole receives just over three inches of rain, a smaller fall than that experienced during that season by any other district. The high figure for Tenkāsi during this period is due to the fact that, owing to its situation near the Ariyankāvu pass, it receives frequent showers blown through this gap by the south-west winds.

The highest district average recorded for a year was 47·80 inches in 1914; in that year Kadaiyam received 74·73 inches (the highest fall ever recorded for any station in the district), Tenkāsi 65·29 inches, Ambāsamudram 63·97 inches; Kulasē-kharapatnam, Kadayanallūr, Tiruchendūr and Sivagiri all registered over 50 inches. Other years of heavy rainfall were, in descending order: 1877 (46·86), 1902 (44·91), 1891 (41·11) and 1896 (38·96). Against these may be set the 15·35 inches of 1892, the 16·14 of 1876, and the 17·16 of 1890. The lament of the present generation for the "good old days" when rain fell in abundance is probably not peculiar to this district; and the following table, which compares the figures for each of the past three decades, goes some way to show how unfounded this familiar conception of a golden age really is—

Years.		Average rainfall for district.
1871–1880	... ...	26·41
1881–1890	... ...	27·16
1891–1900	... ...	23·83
1901–1910	... ...	26·24

Still, judged by its rainfall, the district as a whole is one of the driest in the Presidency [2] and, save for the valleys of

[1] Average for 1870–1912.

[2] Four districts only have a lighter rainfall, viz., Coimbatore, Kurnool, Anantapur and Bellary.

the Tāmbraparni and Chittār and the narrow belts of country lying along the Sankaranainārkōil and Nāngunēri ghats, is at the mercy of the seasons. In the drier tracts of Nānguneri and Srīvaikuntam the palmyra, though affected by bad seasons, will survive a drought or two; its "cultivation" involves no outlay, and it is seldom that the owner of these trees has any loss of capital to face. Here, as elsewhere in the red soil country, the experience of bad seasons has given of late years a stimulus to well-sinking; and it is in those parts, south Nānguneri, Sankaranainārkōil and south Tiruchendūr, where the rainfall is scantiest, that well-cultivation is now most general.

FLOODS. Floods, confined mostly to the valley of the Tāmbraparni, have been fairly frequent, the most serious having occurred in the years 1810, 1827, 1847, 1867, 1869, 1874, 1877 (two floods), 1880, 1895 and 1914. With the exception of the flood of 1847, all these visitations occurred during the period of the north-east monsoon.

In 1810. In 1810 rain began to fall on the 6th December, continuing with unprecedented violence for 30 hours. On the night of the 7th the river-valley was inundated; many lives were lost, and more than a thousand houses swept away, 500 being destroyed in Alvārtirunagari alone. Most of the main channels, many large tanks, including the large tank of Srīvaikuntam, were breached, and for miles the river-valley was an unbroken sea of water.

In 1827. The disaster of 1827 exceeded any that had occurred within people's memory. For three days Tinnevelly and its neighbourhood were under water, the inhabitants being with difficulty rescued from their house-tops in boats. Cattle were swept away in hundreds, and hardly a single article of property in the town was saved. In the Srīvaikuntam and Tiruchendūr taluks the work of devastation was even more complete. "The whole face of the country," wrote the Collector, "was so changed that, though formerly quite familiar to me, it was with difficulty that I could recognize some of what used to be the most prominent objects. Tanks and watercourses were almost obliterated. Whole villages were under water for several days and as the water retired, the roofs were seen reposing in lines upon the banks of slime which had once composed the walls of the houses." The Assistant Engineer, who was at the time in Srīvai kuntam, was marooned for three days in the *gōpuram* of the local temple.

In 1847 The flood of 1847, which occurred during April, was on a comparatively small scale: the country on the lower reaches

CHAP. VIII. FLOODS. of the river suffered most, Attūr being under water for some days.

In 1867. In 1867, after a downpour of 24 hours, the river rose to a height of 24 feet at Ambāsamudram and 16 feet at Palamcotta. For miles the river, fields and channels presented a continuous sheet of water; the bridge over the Gatanānadhi at Ambūr, then under construction, was washed away.

In 1869. The cyclone of November 1869 exceeded all its predecessors in violence. At Tuticorin the sea rose to the level of the road, damaging it considerably, and the new lighthouse in progress on Hare Island was completely destroyed. At Palamcotta the river reached the unprecedented height of 26 feet; the bridge was wrecked, the four middle arches being swept away. The large Krishnappēri tank to the north-west of the Tinnevelly town breached, and the streets were flowing with four feet of water; four of the eleven arches of the bridge at Ambāsamudram were carried away, and not a trace was left of the bridge over the Nambiyār at Tirukkurungudi which had been completed only five months before. Innumerable channels and tanks not only in the river-valley but throughout the district were breached; water stood five feet deep in the Srīvaikuntam streets, and the newly completed road from Palamcotta to Tuticorin was seriously damaged. Fortunately no lives were lost. The loss of land revenue alone was estimated at Rs. 6 lakhs.

In 1874. In 1874 the north-east monsoon, which had held off for weeks, broke on the 24th November with great suddenness and violence. On the night of the 26th the river rose at Palamcotta by 8 feet reaching a total depth of 23 feet—only three feet less than the flood of 1869. The Tinnevelly channel and the Krishnappēri tank breached, and the town of Tinnevelly was again flooded. It was decided to cut the bund of the Nainārkulam, which threatened to burst over the town; but before this could be done it breached itself; the water poured in a deluge over the paddy fields down to the railway embankment, which it topped, escaping finally to the overflowing river below the bridge. Tinnevelly was completely cut off for a time from Palamcotta. Over 200 houses, mostly of the more unsubstantial dwellings of the poor, were destroyed in the town; but there was no loss of life. At Srīvaikuntam the river, augmented by heavy floods in the Chittār, rose to 17 feet, a foot higher than the flood of 1869; seven tanks under the north main channel breached, but, in spite of the worst fears, the great Kadambā tank held an example, which all the tanks on the south side followed. The Kōrampallam tank gave way and submerged the surrounding country, Tuticorin fortunately escaping. Though the local rainfall was heavy, most of the water came from the hills, and the country outside the Tāmbraparni valley suffered comparatively little damage. Even in the river-fed area the crops were only slightly injured, and no loss of life occurred anywhere.

In 1877. Three years later, following almost immediately on the famine of 1877, the north-east monsoon, which had made a vigorous start five weeks previously, burst with tremendous and sudden violence on the 5th December. By ten o'clock in the morning of the 6th the river rose to 10 feet at Palamcotta; at two o'clock the next morning the flood was over 27 feet, the highest figure that had ever been recorded. Hundreds of persons in Tinnevelly were rendered homeless in the night; and the Collector was confined helpless to his bungalow with the flood very nearly up to the basement floor. Over a hundred tanks in the Nānguněri taluk breached, the headquarter town being saved by the action of the Tahsildar, who pluckily made a cut in the eastern side of the big tank. In the Rādhāpuram division alone eighty tanks had breached in the heavy rains of the previous month, and many which were still depending on ring-bunds again collapsed.

Scarcely had the floods subsided, when on the night of the 17th the Tāmbraparni brought down another deluge exceeding that of the previous week and all recorded floods. At the Tinnevelly bridge the river rose 15 inches higher than on the night of the 7th and established a "record" which has never been equalled; the Collector's office, which on the former occasion escaped by a few inches, was swamped, and the great Marudūr anicut was breached. At Sērmādēvi for a whole day the Sub-Collector looked out on nothing but a sea of water dotted here and there with tree-tops. The repairs which had been put in hand in various parts of the district after the previous inundation were completely undone; and the additional damage done to irrigation works alone was estimated at Rs. 1¾ lakhs.

In 1895. The next serious flood occurred in 1895 on the 30th and 31st December. Beginning at midnight on the 29th, the river reached in twelve hours a depth of 27 feet at the Tinnevelly bridge, thus equalling the record of the first flood of 1877. Thirteen persons who were sleeping in the big *mantapam* in the river-bed just above the bridge were cut off and swept down the stream, all being drowned except one boy who managed to cling to a tree lower down and save himself. A great part of the town was flooded, mud houses were swept

CHAP. VIII. FLOODS.

away, the Collector's and Judge's compounds were washed out, roads, tanks and channels, throughout the river-valley and especially in the Srīvaikuntam taluk, were damaged. At the Srīvaikuntam anicut the water rose on the night of the 30th to 20 feet; and for a distance of seven miles below this anicut the inner flood bank on the left side of the river was washed away, the mud houses between the two banks were destroyed and ten lives lost. The outer flood-bank on the same side of the river, which forms also the right bank of the north main channel, breached in four places, and the right flood-bank in five. In Srīvaikuntam the floor of the tahsildar's office was under 4 feet of water; the hospital was flooded out, and some of the Apothecary's boxes were afterwards recovered at Eral, 9 miles down the river. In the Nāngunēri taluk, where 13 inches of rain fell in three days, the rivers came down in torrents, and nearly two hundred tanks were breached. The crops suffered less injury than might have been expected, and, coming as they did after a long drought when a general failure of crops under the rain-fed tanks was expected, the torrential rains proved themselves a blessing in disguise to the district as a whole.

In 1914.

The last flood of the series occurred in December 1914. Unusually heavy rainfall in October was succeeded by four weeks of exceptionally short supply. On the 28th November abnormal rains set in; Tiruchendūr received over 7 inches on the 1st December and another heavy fall on the 4th; Kulasēkharapatnam recorded in the first five days of December three tremendous downpours, including 9·58 inches on the 4th; at Srīvaikuntam, 11·68 inches fell in 18 hours on the 4th and 5th. Nāngunēri registered 5·80 inches on the 1st and 7·08 inches on the 4th; in every part of the district rain of apparently cyclonic origin was recorded.

The Tāmbraparni was in high flood from the 30th November till the 8th December, reaching its maximum on the 4th, when 26 feet of water—2¼ feet less than the figure recorded in the second flood of 1877—passed under the Tinnevelly bridge. The railway bridge at Sērmādēvi was wrecked. Minor irrigation tanks in all parts of the district were breached. By an odd but fortunate chance, the highest flood in the Chittār came down later. This river was in flood from the 7th to the 9th and reached its maximum of 17 feet at Gangaikondān on the 9th. On the 4th the Tāmbraparni had already risen to 20½ feet at the Srīvaikuntam anicut—exceeding the "record" of 1895 by 6 inches—, the right flood-bank gave way in the night at Alvārtirunagari, and at the same time the left flood-bank breached in two places in the village of Appankōil. A cut had to be made in the Kadambā tank to save it; and the consequent rush of water added to the inundation from the river damaged a number of channels, overspread fields with spoil, washed away many mud houses and wrecked long stretches of embanked road between Alvārtirunagari and Tiruchendūr. For several days communications between this part of the district and Palamcotta were cut off. On the north side of the river numerous tanks and channels below Srīvaikuntam were breached, and serious damage was done to the roads and paddy fields. Floods in the Nambiyār and Karumanaiyār coincided with those of the Tāmbraparni. Over a hundred tanks in the Nānguneri taluk were breached, and the Kumāraswāmi Pillai's anicut was seriously damaged. Sāttānkulam, the point at which the Karumanaiyār definitely takes shape as a river, was flooded; torrents of water poured into the large Sadaiyanēri tank in Megnānapuram and reduced its bank to ruin. The deluge swept over the wet lands into the low-lying valleys comprised in the villages of Megnānapuram, Mānād and Paramankurichi, and formed among the sand-hills an enormous land-locked lake of some four or five square miles. All the *taruvais* of the *tēri* country were flooded to the brim, and in the case of some the waterspread increased to twice its normal size. Many hundreds of houses were washed away in parts of the Srīvaikuntam and Tiruchendūr taluks, but fortunately the people everywhere had warning, and throughout the whole district only two lives were lost in the flood.

The damage done to major irrigation tanks alone was estimated at over two lakhs of rupees; local fund properties suffered damage to the extent of well over a lakh. Cultivation was, on the whole, not seriously affected. The dry crops on the red soils perhaps suffered most; where necessary, ryots had time, both in the wet lands and in the cotton country, to re-sow their crops.

CHAPTER IX.

PUBLIC HEALTH.

GENERAL HEALTH—Fever—The epidemic of 1811—Cholera—Small-pox. MEDICAL INSTITUTIONS—Hospitals controlled by district and taluk boards—Municipal hospitals : Palamcotta—Tinnevelly—Tuticorin.

CHAP. IX. GENERAL HEALTH.

TINNEVELLY is not known for any particular disease, and the district as a whole is healthy enough. The ailment known as "sore-eyes" (conjunctivitis) is perhaps commoner here than elsewhere, and prevails, as is natural, chiefly during the period of fierce winds and dust storms which lasts from June to September.

Fever.

Malarial fever accounts, in ordinary years, for about one in six of the total number of deaths in the district ; but, as the diagnosis of these cases, except in the towns, rests solely with the village headman, who is responsible for the returns and, if in doubt, finds "fever" the easiest explanation, full reliance cannot be placed on the figures. In the low-lying country towards the coast, at Kulasēkharapatnam, Kāyalpatnam and to a smaller extent in Tuticorin and in and around Tiruchendūr, malaria is undoubtedly common. The severe outbreaks of this disease which have in recent years occurred, chiefly amongst the cultivators of the betel-vine, at Eruvādi (Nānguneri taluk) are referred to in Chapter XV. The epidemic first appeared in a virulent form in February 1912 ; a temporary dispensary was opened in the place, and as many as 3,500 cases were treated. In seven months the disease accounted for over two hundred deaths. A similar outbreak occurred in the following year, and every effort was again made by the medical authorities to combat it. The valuable betel-gardens of the place afford an exceptionally favourable breeding-ground for the mosquito ; and, though there has been no serious recurrence of the disease since 1913, it is feared that its reappearance is only too probable. For one or two months preceding the arrival of the monsoon in June the country at the foot of the hills is sometimes found malarial by Europeans ; otherwise they rarely contract the disease.

The epidemic of 1811.

In the early years of the last century a very serious epidemic fever, which visited also the districts of Madura and Coimbatore at the same time, caused heavy mortality in almost all parts of the district. In 1810 heavy rain fell in

CHAP. IX. GENERAL HEALTH.

August and September, a most exceptional occurrence; and to the early rains of the north-east monsoon torrential floods, causing damage to life and property, succeeded in December. Heavy rain fell again in February, March and April 1811, and the whole of the low ground around Tiruchendūr was flooded; the waters of the largest lakes in the *tēri* country united; along the foot of the hills the country was similarly drenched and, to make matters worse, the usual winds of March and April failed altogether. The fever broke out first in Tenkāsi and immediately afterwards appeared in what is now the Tiruchendūr taluk. It quickly spread along the foot of the hills into the Nānguneri taluk and then attacked the centre of the district. From a village near the hills a peon who had been sent to get the revenue collections returned to say that he could find neither mirāsidārs nor karnam nor shroff nor any responsible person alive and that there were only three people who had not the fever. In Selvamarudūr out of a hundred houses inhabited by Lebbai weavers (described in the report as "the best fed people in the district") fifty were empty. In Brahmadēsam, in March, there were not sufficient persons alive to bury the dead; and in Kadaiyam the mortality was estimated at a thousand. The disease, as a rule, either terminated with death or took a turn for the better on the third day; it was calculated that nearly half the number of attacks ended fatally. Between February and June the epidemic carried off an eighth part of the population of the Tenkāsi taluk; in Ambāsamudram and Nānguneri and the south-east of the district the rate of mortality reached half this figure; elsewhere it was less severe. A committee of medical men, which was appointed to investigate and to report on the subject, attributed the epidemic to the exceptional conditions of the weather and, in particular, to the "miasmatic exhalations" arising during the early part of the year from the stagnant water with which a great part of the country was flooded. The disease broke out again in epidemic form in 1813, visiting the Tenkāsi taluk and the neighbourhood of Kalakkād with great severity.[1]

Cholera.

Cholera recurs every year and is, as a rule, most severe in the three towns of Tinnevelly, Palamcotta and Tuticorin. The most calamitous outbreak of recent times was in 1906, in which year the disease accounted for a fifth of the total

[1] The heavy inundations of December 1914 were followed, in the *tēri* country to the south of the Tiruchendūr taluk, by an outbreak a few months later of malarial fever in a mildly epidemic form. There is therefore every reason to believe that the epidemic of 1811 was in fact malarial fever.

CHAP. IX. GENERAL HEALTH.

number of deaths recorded for the district. Serious visitations occurred also in 1895, 1897, 1900 and 1908.

Small-pox.

Mortality from small-pox is, as a rule, slight but is liable to very great fluctuations. As with cholera, it is usually heaviest in the three large towns. Vaccination is compulsory in the municipalities and in nineteen union towns.

MEDICAL INSTITUTIONS.

Twenty-six hospitals and dispensaries (a list of which will be found in table XXVIII of the appendix to this volume) are maintained by public bodies. Of the six institutions controlled by the municipalities, three (one in each of the three towns) are hospitals and admit in-patients, whilst of the twenty institutions managed by local bodies six have accommodation of this kind. The remaining three municipal and fourteen local fund institutions are dispensaries. In addition to these, two dispensaries[1] and a hospital maintained by missionary bodies and a dispensary at Pudukkōttai owned by the mittadar of the place receive annual contributions (aggregating Rs. 1,400) from the taluk boards.

Hospitals controlled by district and taluk boards.

The Raja Sir Rāmaswāmi Mudaliyār's hospital for women and children, situated in Vannārpet on the edge of a great stretch of paddy fields, was constructed in the year 1901 at a cost of about Rs. 25,000. It owes its name to its chief benefactor, who contributed towards its foundation a sum of Rs. 10,000, the balance being provided by the two municipalities, the District Board and private subscriptions. An institution of the kind known as the Lady Dufferin Dispensary had previously existed for some years in unsuitable premises and surroundings near the Tinnevelly Bridge railway-station. The present hospital is managed by the District Board and maintained from the joint contributions of that body and the municipalities of Tinnevelly and Palamcotta. It has recently undergone considerable improvement both in regard to its buildings and its staff; an extension of the site is now under consideration.

The remaining five hospitals maintained from local funds are managed by the taluk boards. They date their foundation from the years 1879 to 1882, during which period local subscriptions were raised and small endowments established for their support. Most of these investments were subsequently sold out, and all the hospitals are now wholly or mainly maintained from the general revenues of the taluk boards.[2]

[1] Dispensaries at Idaiyangudi (Sērmādēvi taluk board) and Sawyerpuram (Tuticorin taluk board) and a hospital at Nazareth (Tuticorin taluk board).

[2] The Ambāsamudram and Ottapidāram hospitals still possess endowments of Rs. 4,200 and Rs. 1,000 respectively.

The local boards contribute a sum of about Rs. 4,500 annually towards the maintenance of the municipal hospitals and pay an annual subscription of Rs. 100 to the Pasteur Institute, Coonoor.

Municipal hospitals: Palamcotta.

The history of the Palamcotta hospital goes back to the middle of the last century. In 1849 the exertions of Mr. C. J. Bird, the Collector, brought into existence in Palamcotta a society the objects of which were to afford "relief to the poor in their sickness and old age." This "Friend-in-need Society," as it was called, was managed by a committee of twelve and was supported by voluntary subscriptions, most of the European officers, civil and military, paying monthly subscriptions. An institution which received the name of the "Palamcotta Lungarkhana" was established by the society on the site of the present hospital; separate buildings were erected for the different classes of patients, and a detached "*kanji* house," on the other side of the Tiruchendūr road, was maintained for the support of the friendless and aged. Medicines were supplied by Government, and the institution, which by 1864 possessed a funded capital of Rs. 7,000, served the purposes both of a hospital and a relief-house. At the same time there existed in the town of Tinnevelly a Government civil dispensary, in charge of which was the Zilla surgeon. In 1863 Government issued a general ruling to the effect that the in-patient departments of civil dispensaries should be self-supporting and that otherwise the dispensaries should be closed altogether. The Tinnevelly dispensary could not satisfy the requirement and was in danger of extinction. The Collector wrote to the Board of Revenue pointing out the existence of the self-supporting "lungarkhana," and recommending that the Tinnevelly dispensary should be amalgamated with it. The proposal was accepted. In May 1864 the transfer was effected, and the "lungarkhana," which had hitherto been under the medical charge of the regimental surgeon, was handed over to the Zilla surgeon. The committee of management continued as before, and a first-class (in place of a second-class) supply of medicines was sanctioned by Government for the enlarged institution. After some further correspondence the out-patient department of the Tinnevelly dispensary was allowed to continue its existence. To provide an endowment to meet the increased needs of the "lungarkhana," the Collector, Mr. J. Silver, issued a circular notice inviting subscriptions; money poured in, and in less than five months an amount of Rs. 83,000 had been collected. A sum of Rs. 81,500 was invested in the name of the Collector and the Zilla surgeon in

CHAP. IX. MEDICAL INSTITUTIONS.

Government promissory notes, and the interest derived from this sum, added to occasional donations and monthly subscriptions, sufficed to maintain the institution and to provide some improvements. In 1868 its compound wall, composed of stones from the dismantled fort, was built; an asylum for lunatics was added, and the existing buildings were enlarged. Monthly grants were paid to the Tinnevelly dispensary, and substantial contributions were made towards the foundation of dispensaries at Srīvilliputtūr (then in the Tinnevelly district) and at Idaiyangudi. The feeding of the poor was replaced by a system of pensions, and in 1868 the old "*kanji* house" was sold. There are still a few aged pensioners in receipt of small monthly allowances. In 1871, under the provisions of the Towns Improvements Act, the Palamcotta dispensary (as it was now called) was formally transferred to the newly-formed body of municipal commissioners, who thus became the trustees of the fund. One-third of the interest from this source was allotted to the Tinnevelly municipality in aid of their dispensary, which similarly passed to the control of the commissioners for that town and gradually developed to its present condition as a hospital.

Tinnevelly.

The site of the Tinnevelly hospital near the old taluk office building had frequently been condemned, and in 1901, when the council first moved in the matter, it was found that the old premises were incapable of extension. A proposal, which in 1902 received the approval of Government, was made that a combined hospital should be provided for the two towns and that it should be located in Palamcotta. The Tinnevelly council demurred and said the hospital ought to be in their town, and for years several sites were discussed. In 1909 it was finally decided to demolish the existing Palamcotta hospital and to place the new buildings there. Additional land to the north of the present hospital compound is to be acquired, and the whole scheme is estimated to cost Rs. 1,39,000. Government have made a grant of Rs. 1 lakh, and the District Board and the two municipalities are subscribing the remainder.

Tuticorin.

The Tuticorin "Pereira hospital" derives its name from a resident of the town who, in 1874, provided the site on which it stands. A dispensary, opened by the municipality in 1870, had previously been located in the old travellers' bungalow which stood on the site now occupied by the Sub-Collector's office. The hospital since its foundation has on many occasions been enlarged and improved, the latest addition being a maternity ward constructed by the municipality in 1913.

CHAPTER X.

EDUCATION.

CENSUS STATISTICS—Figures by religions and taluks—Literacy in English. EDUCATIONAL INSTITUTIONS—The C.M.S. College—The Hindu College—The Sarah Tucker College—School for the blind—Secondary schools for boys—High schools—At Palamcotta—At Tuticorin—At Megnānapuram—At Ettaiyāpuram and elsewhere—Sanskrit schools—Incomplete secondary schools—Secondary schools for girls—Elementary schools—Training schools—School for the deaf and dumb—Industrial schools.

CHAP. X. CENSUS STATISTICS.

JUDGED by the census returns of 1911, Tinnevelly stands fourth among the districts of the Presidency in regard to the literacy of its population as a whole; if males alone are considered, the district rises to third. In every 10,000 of its males 2,290 were returned as able to read and write, the corresponding figure for the year 1901 being 1,952. Women too have advanced in education, the number of "literates" among them having risen in the same ten years from 127 to 260 in every 10,000. Excluding the districts of Madras and Anjengo and the Nilgiris, Tinnevelly comes second in regard to women's education, Malabar ranking above it.

Figures by religions and taluks.

The Christians are by far the most advanced in literacy. Next come the Mussalmans and a little way after them the Hindus. The ratio of "literates" amongst the Christians is double what it is amongst the Hindus, a fact which is largely due to the advanced state of women's education amongst the former. The progress of education amongst the Christians is further illustrated by the fact that the proportion of "literates" among them of school-going age is three times that found in the case of Mussalmans and Hindus.

In point of general literacy Tiruchendūr, containing some important missionary centres, comes first amongst the taluks; next come the taluks of Tinnevelly, Srīvaikuntam and Ambāsamudram, the others following a good way behind.

Literacy in English.

If the exceptional districts of Madras and the Nilgiris are excluded, the Tinnevelly district comes fourth in regard to "literacy in English," and is rapidly closing up the gap which in 1901 separated it from Tanjore and Chingleput. Christians

CHAP. X. CENSUS STATISTICS.

(excluding Europeans and Eurasians, of whom there are 397 in the district) are in this respect by far the most advanced, as the following figures will show :—

	Number per mille of literates in English.	
	Males.	Females.
Christians	41	15
Mussalmans	7	...
Hindus	12	0·2

Tinnevelly, as is natural, heads the taluks in English education, Srīvaikuntam, Ambāsamudram and Tiruchendūr coming next. The rest are far behind.

EDUCATIONAL INSTITUTIONS. The C.M.S. College.

The Church Missionary Society's College, Tinnevelly, represents a later development of the old Palamcotta High School which is referred to below. About 1870 this school was amalgamated with the English section of a training school maintained by the Society; in 1878 college classes were added, and the institution (from which the training school was shortly afterwards detached) was affiliated to the Madras University as a second-grade college. In 1880 the college department was transferred to Tinnevelly, and school classes were opened to supplement it, the old high school being left in Palamcotta, where it has since remained. The college itself was at first a failure; and the conversion of a Brahman pupil to Christianity during the early days of its existence did not help to increase its popularity. After three years of disappointment the Principal urged the committee of the Society to abolish it and to retain only the high school, in which department fair success had been attained. The proposal was however rejected; and by 1885 the numbers had increased to such an extent that a new building was found necessary. Two Hindu schools then joined with the college, and in 1897 an extension of the premises was found necessary. By 1900 the handsome building which the college now occupies, midway between the Tinnevelly Bridge railway-station and the town, was erected, Government contributing over Rs. 14,000. At the present time the pupils of the college (school classes included) number more than six hundred.

The Hindu College.

The Hindu College, Tinnevelly, owes its existence to an uncomfortable state of feeling brought about by the successful proselytising efforts of the old Palamcotta High School managed by the Church Missionary Society. A meeting of the principal Hindu inhabitants was called; and their deliberations resulted, in 1859, in the establishment on a very small scale of

CHAP. X. EDUCATIONAL INSTITUTIONS.

an "Anglo-Vernacular school" in the town of Tinnevelly. In 1861 it was moved to a site midway between Tinnevelly and Palamcotta, in Vīrarāghavapuram, which, till the advent of the railway in 1876, was a comparatively unimportant suburb. At a meeting convened by Mr. Silver, the Collector (1859–65), a fund was raised to endow the school, and a fixed constitution (revised in 1878) was established for its management. In 1868, when Lord Napier visited Tinnevelly, the people pressed unsuccessfully for the establishment in Tinnevelly of a Government Zilla school; and in the course of another ten years the efforts of this purely indigenous institution had proved so far successful that it was raised to the status of a second-grade college and affiliated to the Madras University. The college, which maintains in addition to its higher classes the full complement of elementary and secondary forms, numbers about six hundred pupils on its rolls; it is managed by a committee of Hindu gentlemen and possesses a small funded capital. The construction of a hostel is now under consideration.

The Sarah Tucker College.

The Sarah Tucker College in Palamcotta, maintained by the Church Missionary Society, is one of the most important institutions of its kind in the Presidency. Affiliated to the Madras University as a second-grade college, it is intended only for Christian girls; a training school and a high school form part of the institution, in immediate dependence on which are two village boarding-schools, one at Nallūr (Tenkāsi taluk), the other at Suvisēshapuram (Nānguneri taluk). A large number of village schools have been opened throughout the district by the authorities of this college, which supplies trained teachers to staff them. The institution, which derives its name from a sister of the Rev. John Tucker, for many years Secretary to the Church Missionary Society in Madras, was started in 1862 as a primary training school; it soon developed to the middle school standard and before 1890 had risen to the first grade. In 1890 Miss A. J. Askwith (whose name in more recent years is chiefly associated with work among the blind) assumed the management of the institution and in the same year opened the high school classes. In 1896 a college class was opened, and the institution became recognized as a second-grade college. Several English ladies are employed on the teaching staff; the Indian teachers are provided with houses in the premises, and all the pupils, numbering nearly four hundred, are boarders.

Schools for the blind.

In 1890 work among the blind was begun, the pupils being accommodated in the college compound. During 1909 and

CHAP. X. EDUCATIONAL INSTITUTIONS.

1910 new and ample buildings, in which the blind pupils are taught and housed, were erected apart from the Sarah Tucker College. After passing the primary examination, girls are employed chiefly as teachers under the supervision of the college Principal; boys are taught to become teachers, to weave mats or to make themselves generally useful as gardeners, punka-pullers, and so on.

Secondary schools for boys.

The secondary schools for boys fall (with a few unimportant exceptions) into two main groups. First, there are what may be called the Brahman schools, situated mostly along the river-valley and managed, as a rule, by committees of Brahmans or of Brahmans and Vellālans together; and the bulk of the pupils are Brahman boys. The other group is that composed of mission schools. These are found either at the important centres of the district, e.g., at Palamcotta and Tuticorin, or in remote villages. Of the latter class, examples are found at Nazareth, Megnānapuram, Dhōnāvūr, Pannaivilai, Surandai and Sawyerpuram. Outside these groups stand the Ettaiyāpuram high school and the "incomplete secondary" school at Sankaranainārkōil.

High schools.

There are nine high schools for boys, two at Palamcotta, two at Tuticorin and one at each of the following places: Megnānapuram, Pattamadai, Ambāsamudram, Gōpālasamudram and Ettaiyāpuram.

At Palamcotta.

Of these nine the oldest institution is that maintained by the Church Missionary Society at Palamcotta. It started life in 1844 as an evangelistic agency under a well-remembered blind Eurasian teacher named Cruikshanks. Till 1870 he was at the head of the institution; and it was under his instruction that many families of the higher castes in Palamcotta turned Christians. In 1878, as we have seen, college classes were added and in 1880 were removed to Tinnevelly town, the high school remaining in Palamcotta.

The St. Xavier's High School, maintained at Palamcotta by the Jesuit mission, was founded in 1880 as a primary school and attained its present status in 1883; it is the largest of its kind in the district, having very nearly five hundred pupils, the great majority of whom are boarders.

At Tuticorin.

At Tuticorin, the St. Xavier's School, started in 1883, is maintained by the Jesuit mission; the Caldwell High School is managed by the S.P.G. In a sense, the origin of the latter school may be ascribed to the late Dr. G. U. Pope, who in 1842 founded at the little village of Sawyerpuram an important seminary comprising both college and school classes. In 1883 the college department was transferred to

CHAP. X. EDUCATIONAL INSTITUTIONS.

Tuticorin, and Dr. Caldwell left Idaiyangudi to take charge of it. In 1894 the college classes were closed, the institution continuing as a high school. Two hostels, one for Christians and the other for Hindus, are now under construction.

At Megnānapuram.

The Megnānapuram high school, provided with a boarding establishment, traces its foundation to the year 1847; in 1856 the boarding-school at Sāttānkulam was joined to it, and the present building was erected. Nearly all the pupils are Christians, and most are boarders.

At Ettaiyāpuram and elsewhere.

The Ettaiyāpuram high school is maintained by the zamindar; the remaining three schools are managed either by local committees or by their owners.

Sanskrit schools.

In the class "secondary schools" are comprised five Sanskrit schools maintained by the taluk boards—at Tenkāsi, Alvārtirunagari, Srīvaikuntam, Tirukkurungudi and Kallidaikurichi. All are supported from endowments which the local boards administer.

Incomplete secondary schools.

There are sixteen "incomplete secondary" schools, eight of which are maintained by the two Anglican missionary societies. The local boards do not maintain any secondary schools.

Secondary schools for girls.

One high school (apart from the Sarah Tucker institution) is maintained for girls (St. John's school, Nazareth), and there are four incomplete secondary schools. All five are the property of missionary societies.

Elementary schools.

According to the latest returns there are more than 1,700 elementary schools, including 119 for girls only. Local boards and municipalities are responsible for 163 of the total number. Of the "aided" schools the majority are maintained by missionary societies; too many are managed by persons who have failed in other walks of life and have an unfortunate tendency to regard school-managing as an easy way of securing a livelihood. Some three hundred and seventy of the elementary schools receive no assistance either from Government or local boards.

Training schools

Training schools (including "sessional schools") for male teachers number five, one of which, in Tinnevelly, is maintained by Government; the C.M.S. have one at Palamcotta, and the S.P.G. have one at Nazareth. The District Board manages two "sessional schools," one being stationary at Palamcotta, the other being itinerant. At Nazareth the S.P.G. maintain a training school for mistresses; the training school which forms part of the Sarah Tucker College has already been referred to.

CHAP. X. EDUCATIONAL INSTITUTIONS.

School for the deaf and dumb.

An institution of particular interest is the orphanage for the deaf and dumb at Palamcotta, which is maintained by private subscriptions supplemented by Government grants. Started in 1899 by Miss Swainson, who still manages it, the school is composed of over a hundred pupils drawn from all parts of India and from all classes of the population. Every child is taught a trade or some means of self-support; the boys learn tailoring, carpentry, weaving or book-keeping; the girls, sewing and cooking.

Industrial schools.

The first public industrial school in the district was opened in 1887 by the Tinnevelly municipality. It was located at the Pennington market and was intended to afford instruction in carpentry, blacksmith's work and rattan work. It attracted very small attendance and was closed four years later.

In 1889 the District Board, with the consent of the taluk boards and municipalities (except Palamcotta), had proposed to open in Vīrarāghavapuram a "Central Industrial Institution" combining with it the "Normal School" which, since 1885, the District Board had been managing in Palamcotta. The normal school was accordingly removed in 1890 to Vīrarāghavapuram; and after some discussion it was decided, in 1893, to give the industrial school a trial, locating it in a rented building and placing it under the supervision of the headmaster of the normal school. The industrial institution did not come into existence till 1895; it and the normal school were then united and styled the "Board Technical Institute." From the beginning, however, the progress of the institute was not satisfactory; and in 1899 the normal school was detached and taken over by Government. In 1905 the District Board appointed a sub-committee to examine the condition of the industrial school; and, in his inspection report of the next year, the Inspector of Technical Schools condemned the institution. During the year 1908–09 the charges exceeded the receipts by Rs. 7,160; even its poor attendance had declined; the accounts were badly kept, and the management was beyond the powers of the District Board executive. In 1908 the President of the District Board urged on Government the desirability of transferring the institute to the charge of the Director of Industries, a step which was sanctioned by Government in 1910. There was already an older Technical Institute in the important commercial centre of Madura; the Director reported to Government that the Tinnevelly school was unnecessary, and in April 1911 it was closed.

Besides the schools for the blind and for the deaf and dumb, there are now three industrial schools in the district,

EDUCATIONAL INSTITUTIONS.

situated at Nazareth, Idaiyangudi and Kūdankulam and managed by the S.P.G. At these places girls are taught lace-making, an industry started at Idaiyangudi by Mrs. Caldwell in 1844; at Nazareth boys are instructed in carpentry, printing and blacksmith's work. The lace made at the schools has a wide reputation; but it is unfortunate that, in the absence of expert supervision, the study of the quickly-changing fashions is impracticable, and the patterns which were introduced a generation or more ago are still being turned out. Much waste of labour is involved; for it is by no means the case that lace which costs most to produce will fetch the highest price in the market. Few of the pupils trained in the schools practise in later life the trade they have learned, and the industry seems scarcely susceptible of much expansion.

CHAPTER XI.

LAND REVENUE ADMINISTRATION.

REVENUE HISTORY—THE PĀLAIYAMS—The Permanent Settlement—The Tinnevelly zamindaris—Their subsequent history—The mittas—The forfeited palaiyams—Impartible estates. THE SIRKAR LANDS—Pre-British revenue system; the Muhammadan period—The "Renter"—Beginnings of English interference—Cession to the Company—Mr. Lushington's settlement. THE WET LANDS—The *amāni* system—Mr. Hodgson's deputation—Triennial village leases, faslis 1218–1220—The decennial lease—Attempts at a ryotwari system—The *olungu* settlement—Adoption of new principles; survey and classification—The revenue system unsatisfactory—End of the *olungu* system. THE DRY LANDS—Pre-British system—Mr. Lushington's settlement, and subsequent changes—Distribution of pattas and subsequent confusion of accounts—Attempted remedies—Lands under private wells. MISCELLANEOUS CHARGES—*Dēsakāval* fees—*Nilavari*—Taxes on trees—"Extra sources of revenue"—Official language. THE MOTTAFAISAL—The A and B registers—Effects of the new system—Disappearance of *mirāsi*. SURVEY AND SETTLEMENT—Mr. Puckle appointed Collector and Settlement Officer—His first scheme-report; the *nirārambam*—The principles of the Settlement—The second scheme-report; the "palmyra forest"—Settlement of the Tinnevelly and Tenkāsi taluks—Departure of Mr. Puckle—Settlement of the Tenkarai taluk—Settlement of the Ambāsamudram taluk—Settlement of the Nānguneri taluk—The other taluks—Financial results of the Settlement—Economic conditions of the period—Other measures carried out during the Settlement—"Puckle's Settlement." THE RESETTLEMENT—Economic progress of thirty years—Principles of the resettlement—The wet lands—Classification of irrigation sources and readjustment of rates—The new rates—Other changes—The dry lands. PALMYRAS—Early history—Mr. Puckle's reforms—*Sāsvatham* trees—"Other item" trees—After settlement—At resettlement—"Palmyra mediation"—Other taxed trees—Conclusion of the resettlement—Its financial results. MISCELLANEOUS—The special revenue staff—Fishery-pattas. INAMS—Kinds of Inam—The Settlement of 1863—Temple revenues—Their administration—Withdrawal of Government from management—Creation of district committees, 1864—Commutation of dastik allowances—Religious institutions and their funds at present. VILLAGE ESTABLISHMENTS—Old system—Mr. Pelly's scheme—Mr. Puckle's revision. ADMINISTRATIVE CHARGES—In early times—Subsequent changes—Present divisional charges. APPENDIX—List of Collectors.

CHAP. XI. REVENUE HISTORY.

THE leading feature of the land-revenue system revealed by our earliest historical view (in the eighteenth century) of the district as a whole is that a large part of the country is divided up amongst poligars,[1] to whom is entrusted the duty of collecting what they can from the inhabitants of

[1] See p. 71.

their allotted portions or pālaiyams, whilst at the headquarters of the district a "renter," appointed by the central government or "Sirkar," is responsible for exacting on behalf of that government tribute, or peshkash, from the poligars and for remitting also a stipulated amount of rent from the territories under his direct management. As these two classes of land, the pālaiyams and the "sirkar lands," were each from the outset on a distinct footing and developed on different lines, it is necessary to deal with the two classes separately.

THE PĀLAIYAMS.

Besides the resources they drew from their pālaiyams, the semi-independent poligars had, during the early years of the eighteenth century, usurped immense revenues from the sirkar villages which were nominally under the direct management of the renter; they had appropriated the office of *stalam kāval* and consequently its fees; they had invented and corrupted a new system of police known as *dēsakāval,* for which they extorted payment; they levied land-duties, taxes on ploughs, looms, shops, labourers and, above all, they were armed with a rabble of desperate marauders to enforce obedience. Against these armed mobs the renter was powerless; and it was only by the intervention of military force that any contribution to the central exchequer could be exacted from the poligars. It was the refractory behaviour of these freebooters that first brought the Nawāb and his allies, the English, into contact with Tinnevelly, and the whole of that half-century which followed is occupied with expedition after expedition designed to suppress the rebellions of one confederacy after another and to extort the payments due by defaulting poligars.

Finally, as has been seen (Chapter II), the poligars were, by the treaty made with the Nawāb in 1792, placed under the authority of the East India Company. The agreement, afterwards officially described as "disgraceful to the character of the Company's Government and destructive of the peace and prosperity of the country" produced, by the dual control it created, a situation as full of difficulties as that which had preceded it. On the 12th July of that year Mr. Benjamin Torin (who under the "Assumption" of 1790 had already been appointed "Collector of Tinnevelly and the dependent poligars") received a new commission under the style of "Collector of Zamindar and Poligar Peshkash in the Tinnevelly, Madura, Trichinopoly, Rāmanādhapuram and Sivaganga districts." Mr. Landon succeeded him in the same year and proceeded to make enquiries and to report on the claims to all sorts of extravagant fees which the poligars were asserting.

CHAP. XI.
THE PĀLAIYAMS.

Mr. Powney followed in 1794, and Mr. Jackson in 1797. The Nawāb had his own Renter, Muhammad Eitbar Khan, at Tinnevelly, and the nominal authority of that sovereign, as preserved to him by the treaty of 1792, left an open door for his interference in the management of the poligars. The Nawāb complained that the poligars did not respect his renter, whilst the Collector of Peshkash found that the Nawāb was taking upon himself to issue instructions direct to the poligars without reference to the Company's Government.

The usual rebellions marked the period, and spasmodic attempts were made to disarm the poligars; but it was not till 1799 that any drastic measures were carried out. After the fall of Pānjālankurichi in that year and the execution of the poligar a proclamation was issued requiring that the poligars should be disarmed and relieved of all police and military duties and that their forts should be destroyed. The estates of the six poligars who had united in the last outbreak, viz., Pānjālankurichi, Kulattūr, Kādalgudi, Elāyirampannai, Kōlārpatti and Nāgalāpuram, were sequestered. The Pānjālankurichi pālaiyam, containing 104 villages, was divided into two parts, one being presented to the Ettaiyāpuram poligar and the other to Maniyāchi, in recognition of the good services rendered by these two chieftains during the rebellion; the two small estates of Kulattūr and Kādalgudi, comprising altogether 29 villages, were for a similar reason conferred on the poligar of Mēlmāndai. The remaining three pālaiyams were confiscated.

Mr. Lushington (who had succeeded Mr. Jackson on the 12th January 1799) proceeded to make a settlement with the remaining twenty-five poligars. No reliable records could be found on which to base the assessments, and, in the absence of any guarantee that the estimates finally obtained were reasonable, it was decided that the settlement of 1799-1800 should be regarded as temporary. All the lands which had been improperly annexed to the poligars' villages were resumed, and the total peshkash newly imposed on all the pālaiyams together exceeded by as much as 117 per cent the maximum which they had ever previously paid. The increase, however, was largely due to the credit taken for the sums at which, by the surrender of the *dēsakāval*, the poligars' military services were commuted. Sooner than accept the new terms eleven of the poligars * surrendered their

Naduvakurichi.	Sandaiyūr.
Maniyāchi.	Urkād.
Surandai	Singampatti.
Sennalgudi.	Mannārkōttai.
Mēlmāndai.	Avudaiyāpuram.
Attankarai.	

villages to the Collector until the exact amount of their incomes should be ascertained.

The next serious insurrection, the last of the series, occurred in 1801 and was crushed in the same year. The orders issued in 1799 for the disarmament of the poligars and the demolition of their forts, which had been but partially carried out, were now reiterated and successfully enforced.

The Permanent Settlement.

In September 1802 Mr. Lushington (who on the cession of the Carnatic province to the East India Company had taken charge at Tinnevelly in 1801 as "Collector of Tinnevelly and the Maravars") submitted to a special commission appointed for the settlement of "the southern pālaiyams" a comprehensive scheme. A careful valuation was made of each pālaiyam, based on the estimate made by himself in 1800 and by previous Collectors of Poligar Peshkash, the result being a slight decrease in the total demand now settled as compared with that fixed in 1800. The eleven estates which had been assumed were handed back to their owners; subject to a readjustment in the distribution of the Pānjālankurichi villages as between Ettaiyāpuram and Maniyāchi, the arrangements made in regard to the three sequestered pālaiyams of Pānjālankurichi, Kulattūr and Kādalgudi were recommended for final ratification; and the sale at public auction, subject to the annual payment of peshkash, was proposed for the three confiscated estates of Elāyirampannai, Kōlārpatti and Nāgalāpuram. "The nature of the permanent settlement," Mr. Lushington reported, "and of the system of law and security by which it is to be enjoyed by themselves and handed down to their posterity has been repeatedly explained to the poligars; and they now await with anxious solicitude the confirmation of a blessing which is to soften them to the remembrance of former sacrifices." The proposals were accepted in their entirety by Government in 1803; and in the same year twenty-five poligars received the *sanad-i-milkiyat-i-istimrar*, or deed of permanent settlement, and thenceforward became zamindars. The three confiscated pālaiyams were divided up into nine mittas and sold.

The *dēsakāval* fees had already been appropriated to Government after the rebellion of 1799[1]; and now the extensive salt, sayar and abkāri revenues, which most of the poligars had formerly drawn from their estates, were also resumed. The remaining income was taken as the gross annual value of the pālaiyams, and on this amount the

[1] This was modified by the arrangements of 1800. See page 333.

CHAP. XI. THE PALAIYAMS.

The Tinnevelly zamindaris; their subsequent history.

peshkash, in proportions varying from 30 per cent (in the case of the small and unproductive Alagāpuri) to 65 per cent (Urkād, with its valuable wet lands), was calculated for each estate.[1]

The following table gives the names of these twenty-five zamindaris and the district in which the territory of each is now situated:—

Tinnevelly.	*Rāmnād.*
1. Ettaiyāpuram.	1. Mannārkōttai.
2. Mēlmāndai.	2. Sennalgudi.
3. Attankarai.	3. Kollapatti.
4. Kadambūr.	4. Sēttūr.
5. Maniyāchi.	5. Pāvali.
6. Sivagiri.	6. Kollankondān.
7. Talaivankōttai.	*Madura.*
8. Avudaiyāpuram.	1. Pēraiyūr.
9. Naduvakurichi.	2. Elumalai.
10. Alagāpuri.	3. Sandaiyūr.
11. Uttumalai.	4. Sāptūr.
12. Surandai.	
13. Chokkampatti.	
14. Urkād.	
15. Singampatti.	

The six estates now in Rāmnād passed to that district on its creation in 1910. Three out of the four Madura zamindaris, Pēraiyūr, Elumalai and Sāptūr, which, though surrounded by Madura territory, had for administrative purposes been attached to the Tinnevelly district, were transferred in 1859 to the Madura Collectorate; Sandaiyūr, which adjoined the Tinnevelly country, was handed over at the same time. Of the fifteen estates included in the present Tinnevelly district only ten[2]—Ettaiyāpuram, Attankarai, Kadambūr, Sivagiri, Talaivankōttai, Alagāpuri, Uttumalai, Urkād, Singampatti and Maniyāchi (a part)—have descended by inheritance to the lineal heirs of the original sanad-holders; a large part of the old Maniyāchi zamindari was alienated in 1870 (p. 386). It is only these ten estates, therefore, that may now be properly designated zamindaris.

The mittas.

The following table shows how the remaining five estates and the alienated portion of Maniyāchi have either been broken up into subdivisions, or mittas, or otherwise

[1] For the figures of peshkash payable by zamindaris (and the "proprietar estates"), see table No. XIV of Vol. II.

[2] Some account of each of these zamindaris will be found in Chapter XV.

disposed of. With the exception of a small part of the old Avudaiyāpuram estate (the Nelkattanseval and Panaiyūr portions in the list below) which, though not inherited, is now in the possession of a descendant of the first zamindar, the famous Pūli Tēvan, all these mittas have passed out of the families of the original holders :—

Original zamindari.	Mittas into which subdivided.	Taluk.
Mēlmāndai	Mēlmāndai (two-thirds)	Kōilpatti.
	Mēlmāndai (one-third)	
	Vēlāyudapuram	
Maniyāchi (alienated portion).	Kārkurichi	Srīvaikuntam.
	Pērūrani (two-thirds)	
	Pērūrani (one-third)	
Avudaiyāpuram (formerly called Nelkattanseval.)	Avudaiyāpuram (*alias* Nelkattanseval.	Sankaranayinār kōil.
	Gūdalūr	
	Panaiyūr	
	Sivagnānapuram, East	
	Do. West	
	Vayali	
Naduvakurichi	Naduvakurichi Minor division ...	Do.
	Do. Major do. ...	
	Poigai Kuttālappēri Akilāndapuram.	
	Nochikulam	
Chokkampatti	Tirumalaināyakkan Pudukkudi	Do.
	Tiruvettanallūr	
	Vīriruppu	
	Kulasēkharamangalam	
	Vellālankulam	
	Ichanda	
	Chokkampatti	Do.
	Vairavankulam	
	Nayinār Agaram	
	Kambanēri Pudukkudi	
	Umēni Alagiyān	
	Kunnakkudi	
	Vallam	
	Sillaraipuravu	
	Sivan Ādanūr	
	Minnadisēri	
	Kulayanēri	
	Anaikulam...	
Surandai [1]	......	Do.

[1] Bought in by Uttumalai and annexed to that estate in 1874.

CHAP. XI.
THE PALAIYAMS.
The forfeited pālaiyams.

The territories of the three pālaiyams which were forfeited and presented to other zamindars lie within the present Tinnevelly district. The present mittas of Kārkurichi and Pērūrani represent that portion of the Pānjālankurichi estate which was conferred on the Maniyāchi zamindar; the remainder of the old Pānjālankurichi pālaiyam, that which was known as the Puthiyamputtūr division, still forms part of the Ettaiyāpuram zamindari. The Kulattūr and Kādalkudi estates, which were conferred on the Mēlmāndai zamindar, were alienated by its owner early in the nineteenth century; Kādalkudi now comprises nine mittas,[1] Kulattūr three.[2] Of the three estates which were confiscated and sold, each in three lots, Nāgalāpuram alone lies wholly within this district (Kōilpatti taluk); it consists now of two mittas, one of which was in 1886 bought by the Ettaiyāpuram zamindar. [3]A part of one subdivision (called Sevvalpatti) of the old Elāyirampannai estate is situated in the Sankaranainārkōil taluk; the remainder of that estate is now in the Rāmnād district. The Kōlārpatti estate lies wholly in Rāmnād.

Impartible estates.

The ten zamindaris and the Avudaiyāpuram section of the old Avudaiyāpuram estate have been declared impartible under Act II of 1904 (Madras).

THE SIRKAR LANDS.
Pre-British revenue system.

As to the way in which the old native governments managed their revenues, and the rates at which they assessed the lands under their direct superintendence, we have, unfortunately, no information. Favourable grants to Brahmaṇs—which survived for many years under British rule in the form of *pāttam, poruppu, chaturbāgam*, and so on—were a feature of the Hindu system, and it is generally believed that the Muhammadan rulers were on the whole more exacting than their Hindu predecessors.

The Muhammadan period.

An interesting record[4] has preserved for us some important details of the revenue administration of the district during the period that it was, nominally at least, under the control of the Nawāb of Arcot. Dry land contributed a very small proportion of the revenue and was comparatively little accounted of. The usual procedure was to hand over such lands to the ryots of the village for a lump sum called

[1] Kādalkudi, Mallīsvarapuram, Rāmaswāmipuram, Kumārachakkanapuram, Vadamalaipuram, Subramanyapuram, Sundarapachaiyāpuram, Muthaiyapuram, Ariyanāyakkapuram.

[2] Kulattūr north, Kulattūr south and Kulattūr east.

[3] The other is the small estate of Pudūr.

[4] A report dated 24th September 1807 by Mr. Hodgson, printed with the *Fifth Report of the Select Committee*, p. 678.

kattukuthagai, leaving it to them to apportion the amount amongst themselves according to the extent of each man's cultivation. In regard to the wet lands, which were the object of chief interest to the government, the practice in almost every year, from 1739 to 1800, had been to divide the produce between the sirkar and the cultivators. The apparent exception to this rule was the period 1760 to 1763, when, under the management of Muhammad Yūsuf Khān, the assessment was collected in money according to current prices. As, however, this method consisted simply in handing over to the cultivators to sell the grain as it was cut, it could scarcely be called a rent.

The leading principle throughout the period was to raise revenue by any means that greed and ingenuity could devise. In 1739 the villainous device was invented of using a smaller measuring-rod than in previous years; in 1745 the demand, which had been in the case of the best fields at the rate of seven *kōttais* for a seed-*kōttai*[1] of land, was raised to eight; in 1746, a new tax, the *yāvana*, was invented and added to the demand on wet lands. In 1758 a smaller rod was used, but the *yāvana* was increased and a new impost, "the channel cess," created. In 1764 the *yāvana* was doubled, and the *nuzzer* invented. For six years, 1770–75, the sirkar share was fixed at 60 per cent of the produce, and the *yāvana* was temporarily abolished. During part of this time the sirkar grain was thrust on the ryots at a rate of commutation which exceeded the current selling price, and, by way of consolation to the people, a slightly longer measuring-rod was used. Under Mr. Irwin's management, in 1783 and 1784, the district was divided up into groups of villages, or "mittas," which were leased to renters. Mr. Torin followed the same plan in 1790 and 1791. From 1793 to 1799 the country was under *amāni*; and in 1800 the Nawāb rented the district for three years to seven renters, whose lease was cut short by the unforeseen change of government which occurred in 1801. During the sixty-one preceding years the land revenue collected from the district had varied between sixteen and thirty lakhs of rupees.

The poligar is a favourite object of abuse with all historians and it is interesting, therefore, to read the estimate, formed by a contemporary writer,[2] of his rival in extortion, the renter.

[1] A seed-kōttai of land is 1·62 acres; and a kōttai of seed (112 Madras measures) is considered to be the amount of seed required for sowing the area called a "seed-kōttai."

[2] Col. William Fullarton, M.P. *A View of the English Interests in India*, republished at Madras, 1867.

CHAP. XI.
THE SIRKAR LANDS.

The "Renter."

"The established practice throughout this part of the peninsula has for ages been, to allow the farmer one-half of the produce of his crop for the maintenance of his family, and the re-cultivation of the land; while the other is appropriated to the Circar. In the richest soils, under the cowle of Hyder, producing three annual crops it is hardly known that less than forty per cent of the crop produced has been allotted to the husbandman. Yet renters on the coast have not scrupled to imprison reputable farmers, and to inflict on them extreme severities of punishment, for refusing to accept of sixteen in the hundred, as the proportion out of which they were to maintain a family, to furnish stock and implements of husbandry, cattle, seed and all expenses incident to the cultivation of their lands. But should the unfortunate ryot be forced to submit to such conditions, he has still a long list of cruel impositions to endure. He must labour week after week at the repair of water-courses, tanks, and embankments of rivers. His cattle, sheep, and every other portion of his property is at the disposal of the renter, and his life might pay the forfeit of refusal. Should he presume to reap his harvest when ripe, without a mandate from the renter, whose peons, conicopolies and retainers attend on the occasion, nothing short of bodily torture and a confiscation of the little that is left him, could expiate the offence. Would he sell any part of his scanty portion, he cannot be permitted while the Circar has any to dispose of; would he convey anything to a distant market, he is stopped at every village by the Collectors of Sunkum or Gabella who exact a duty for every article exported, imported or disposed of. So unsupportable is the evil, that between Negapatam and Palghautcherry, not more than three hundred miles, there are about thirty places of collection, or, in other words, a tax is levied every ten miles upon the produce of the country; thus manufacture and commerce are exposed to disasters hardly less severe than those which have occasioned the decline of cultivation.

"But these form only a small portion of the powers with which the renter is invested. He may sink or raise the exchange of specie at his own discretion; he may prevent the sale of grain, or sell it at the most exorbitant rates; thus, at any time he may, and frequently does, occasion general famine. Besides maintaining a useless rabble, whom he employs under the appellation of peons, at the public expense, he may require any military force he finds necessary for the business of oppression, and few inferior officers would have weight enough to justify their refusal of such aid. Should anyone, however, dispute those powers, should the military officers refuse to prostitute military service to the distress of wretched individuals, or should the Civil Superintendent remonstrate against such abuse, nothing could be more pleasing to the renter; he derives, from thence, innumerable arguments for non-performance of engagements, and for a long list of defalcations. But there are still some other not less extraordinary constituents in the complex endowments of a renter. He unites, in his own person, all the branches of judicial or civil authority, and if he happens to be a Brahman, he may also be termed the representative of ecclesiastical jurisdiction. I will not enlarge on the consequences of thus huddling into the person of one wretched mercenary all those powers that ought to constitute the dignity and lustre of supreme executive authority."

Muhammad Yūsuf Khān was apparently an exception. "While he ruled those provinces," says Colonel Fullarton, "his whole administration denoted vigour and effect. His justice was unquestioned, his word unalterable; his measures were happily combined and firmly executed, the guilty had no refuge from punishment. His maxim was 'that the labourer and the manufacturer should be the favourite children of the Circar,' because they afford strength and comfort to the public parent; but that the Polygar and the Colliery, though equally entitled to truth and justice, have no pretension to indulgence, because they are the worthless prodigals who waste their own means and ravage those of others."

Beginnings of English interference.

The earliest interference of the civil officers of the East India Company in the revenue administration of the district occurred in 1781, when, by treaty with the Nawāb, the revenues of the Carnatic were assigned to the Company and "Receivers of Assigned Revenue" were appointed and sent to the district. The Nawāb's renters still continued during 1781–82; and, though nominally subordinate to the "Receivers," these "ministers of public exaction" paid scant heed to the orders of their superiors. In 1783 the Company's "Receiver" or "Superintendent," Mr. Irwin, supplanted the renter and assumed full control for two years of the revenues of the district. In 1790 and 1791, under the "Assumption," Mr. Benjamin Torin as "Collector of Tinnevelly and the dependent Poligars" occupied a similar position. The tyranny of the renter, however, outlived all these changes. In 1800, the year before Tinnevelly passed to the Company, Major Macaulay, who was commanding Palamcotta, was surprised to receive reports of a scarcity of grain. On enquiry it was

CHAP. XI. THE SIRKAR LANDS.

found that the villages round Palamcotta had been mortgaged by the Nawāb to an European adventurer and that he and six companions were holding up the grain of the whole district. The country was swarming with dubashes and "conocopolies," gangs of "badge-peons" and guards of sepoys; and numbers of defaulters had been thrown into prison by these tyrants. Macaulay gave four of the principal offenders the option of going to jail or to Madras; and they chose the latter. Government, to whom Macaulay reported his action, entirely approved his efforts "to frustrate the machinations of interested and unprincipled individuals who fatten on the spoils of an artificial famine, in the extorted wealth of the people and in the wreck of public prosperity."

Cession to the Company. Mr. Lushington's settlement.

When Mr. Lushington took charge of the district in August 1801, the *kār* crop was on the ground; and, though anxious to form a village settlement, he decided, with a view to collecting all possible information with regard to outturn and prices, to keep the crop under *amāni*. He revived in fact the method that had been followed from 1793 to 1799. The *pisānam* crop was dealt with in the same way. In regard to the dry lands, money collections were made in accordance with the numberless rates and measurements which had long existed. Their treatment was from the outset different from that of the wet lands; and they will be dealt with later on.

THE WET LANDS.

The Collector toured through the district and started a rough survey of the wet lands (completed apparently in 1805); he made advances to ryots for their *pisānam* cultivation, a pernicious, but apparently necessary, practice, which persisted till 1856. Judged by the fact that it showed an increase of revenue over the previous faslis of 22 per cent, the settlement of 1211 was an eminently successful one. In faslis 1213 and 1214 the same system was continued, with the very slight modification that for the *pisānam* crop about half the assessment was received in money; in other words, the ryots sold their paddy to Government at its estimated value in money and then paid their kists from the price received.

The *amāni* system.

It is difficult now to conceive the vexatiousness of an *amāni* management. What happened apparently was this. As soon as the crop began to ripen, the country was flooded with a host of *sibbendy* peons, who proceeded to measure the extent of actual cultivation and to form an estimate of the expected produce. In the case of the *pisānam* crop this process began in February or March, and the "settlement" was in consequence not completed till May or June. By this time the *kār* cultivation was beginning, and the *sibbendy* staff had now to set to work to stimulate the ryots to cultivate their fields and then to measure up the cultivation as it progressed. The *amāni* staff scarcely left the village at all throughout the year. The sirkar share in *pisānam* was three-fifths, and the practice soon established itself of requiring payment in money for this crop. The contribution was in the first instance received in grain; and this was kept under guard until the ryots had disposed of their share. This they had to do with all possible speed in order to be able to pay their kists by the end of June. The grain market was glutted, and the ryots had to content themselves with a price lower than that at which the sirkar share had, on an estimation made earlier in the year, been commuted. The glut soon subsided, and Government, whose granaries had been stocked with the produce of the preceding *kār* crop, was able to sell at a profit. For all that the ryots apparently clung to the system, and received with coldness a suggestion made in 1803 that money rents should be introduced. They had no capital, and the least variation in the season might spell ruin for them; if Government withdrew from the monopoly of grain, the ryots realized that the money-value of grain would fall; as it was, home-grown paddy was very cheap and was actually being undersold by imports from Bengal.

Mr. Hodgson's deputation.

The rival merits of the ryotwari system and a system of rents was now under discussion in high quarters, and in 1807 Mr. Hodgson, a Member of the Board of Revenue, was sent on deputation to the district to examine the local revenue system. He sent up an exhaustive report (reference has already been made to it), which concluded with a strong recommendation in favour of a system of village-leases. The contracts with the ryots should, he considered, be made for a period of three or five years; and if the ryots declined them, "mittadars" might be brought in to rent villages either singly or in groups.

Triennial village leases, faslis 1218—1220.

Government accepted the recommendation and directed the introduction from 1808–1809 of a system of village-rents for three years (faslis 1218—1220). The difficulty was to find a figure on which to base this rent; revenue had fluctuated from year to year, and, as about one-fourth of the revenue was usually paid after the close of the fasli, the receipts of one year were mixed up with those of another. The rates of lease were finally fixed in April 1809, and, as it was obvious that the ryots could expect to get but little for their grain in the few remaining months of the fasli, the rents were put at a low figure. In the first year the revenue fell by more than a lakh below the average of the six preceding faslis.

CHAP. XI. THE WET LANDS.

The decennial lease.

The system, however, was evidently considered satisfactory enough; for in 1811 Government ordered the introduction of a decennial village-rent, intending thus to pave the way for the establishment of permanent leases. The Court of Directors, on learning of these arrangements, strongly disapproved and directed that the system of village-leases should be withheld. They expressed their great surprise that the Board of Revenue, who had issued circular instructions on the subject to Collectors, should have sanctioned such an arrangement and should have assumed such "extraordinary and unwarrantable discretion." The decennial lease had been actually introduced in fasli 1222 (1812–13); and the Madras Government pointed out in reply that it was impracticable, at any rate in the case of the wet lands, to adopt a ryotwari system. They were prepared to follow such a system in regard to dry lands.

Ninety per cent of the wet villages accepted the lease in the first year, and in the next year the *amāni* system had almost disappeared for a time. An extension of cultivation was followed in 1817 by an almost unprecedented slump in the price of grain, and heavy balances of kist beyond the fasli became the rule. But the most distressing feature of the system to modern minds was the absolute subjection to a few rich plunderers, which was the lot of the mass of the peasant population. "The village," wrote the Collector, "was entirely in the hands of the karnam and mirāsidārs. If their exactions were tolerably moderate, the ryot was told that the demand against them was no more than the amount of rent of the lands he held. If this did not satisfy him, he was told that so much was for village charges; and if this again appeared inadequate to the amount, he was informed that the charges had been unusually swelled by bribes to the taluk and Huzur servants to procure some general remission or avert some intended addition to the beriz of the village or to purchase some other advantage to the community."

Attempts at a ryotwari system.

In 1815 the most positive orders, directing the discontinuance of rents and the introduction of a ryotwari system, reached the Madras Government, and in 1817 a definite attempt was made to introduce a ryotwari settlement in one wet village—Peruṇkulam (Srīvaikuntam taluk). A survey and classification of the lands were made, but the ryots absolutely declined to accept the arrangement. They demanded, first, that the assessment should be fixed at a figure 25 per cent below the average rates imposed by the decennial lease, and, secondly (it is interesting to notice), that the *kāvalgārs* should be required to make good the value of all stolen properties. The people of Vallanād began to realize that the decennial lease had ruined them and attempted to form a kind of ryotwari settlement among themselves. They found the remedy, however, worse than the disease and, in common with an increasingly large number of other villages, resolved to recur to the old *amāni* system. The mirāsidārs of Sērmadēvi fled the country to Travancore; and even after the days of the decennial lease were over could only be coaxed into returning by a promise from the Collector that he would rebuild their houses. The Board, adhering to its old position, made a last protest against the introduction of a system which, in their opinion, threatened to break up the community of interest on which the village system depended. "To dissolve this unity of interest and common stock of labour by requiring each to take, instead of the share which he possessed and owned, a defined part of the whole land of the village, would not be very different from dissolving a Joint Stock Company in England, and requiring each proprietor to trade upon his own portion of it in order that it might be separately taxed."

The *olungu* settlement.

The decennial lease ran its full course to fasli 1231 and was succeeded by a system which, for convenience, was known as the *olungu* settlement. The instructions were briefly to this effect. First of all, the quantity of the *mēlvāram* or government share for the year in each village was to be fixed and then commuted into money, either at the "standard price" or at a figure which, according to variations in the current selling price of the year, should be a certain percentage above or below the standard price, thus: If the selling-price of the year should not have risen 10 per cent or fallen 5 per cent, in comparison with the standard price, then the commutation rate should be fixed at the standard price. If it should have risen 11 per cent, the calculation should be made at 1 per cent above the standard. If it should have fallen 6 per cent, the commutation rate should be calculated at a price 1 per cent below the standard. The settlement was to be made with "each individual mirāsidār" unless any of them did not raise cultivation; and in that case it was to be made with "the cultivating ryot." If both mirāsidārs and ryots declined the terms, a stranger might be brought in to contract.

The Collector pointed out several objections and difficulties involved in the system; and the Board vouchsafed the unanswerable reply that he did not understand it. The method by which the "standard price" and the rate of *mēlvāram* were to be arrived at had not been explained; and when the

CHAP. XI. THE WET LANDS.

Collector reported that for fasli 1235 he had adopted, with reference to actual calculation, the assumed produce of seven *amāni* years (faslis 1211 to 1217) as the basis on which to estimate the *mēlvāram* and for the "standard price" had adopted the average selling price (Rs. 2-11-4 per *kōttai*) of a number of years during which the decennial lease was in force, the Board said that the settlement had been made "more in conformity with the instructions." An apparent, but by no means real, reform consisted in the fact that, while *muchilikās* or agreements were now, as a rule, obtained from the mirāsidārs or leading landowners, pattas were from 1826 onwards issued to individual ryots, "limiting the demand against them." The head ryots still remained responsible to Government for the kist and merely entered into agreements with the small ryots for the payment of their dues.

For this and other reasons the new settlement was little more than a village rent in disguise. A "standard" *mēlvāram* had been fixed on a calculation of the average outturn of the village, but, in those villages at least where irrigation was precarious, the standard was bound to work unfairly in adverse seasons. Allowing, however, that it was possible to arrive at a fair standard of outturn, the sum found to be due by the wet lands with reference to the *olungu* price was assessed in lump on the whole wet ayakat of the village, all fields being assumed to be equally productive. The fields had not been classified, and the old survey, which was already out of date, could not be adopted as a basis on which to work out a field classification. What happened in practice was that the head ryots and the cultivators worked out among themselves some sort of distribution of dues according to the quality of the fields which each man cultivated.

Reviewing the Tinnevelly land-revenue system in 1827, Government observed: "No good system of revenue management appears to have been established in Tinnevelly. The system, such as it was, is calculated to keep the Collector in ignorance of the state of the district and seems to have had in a great measure that effect. There are no detailed accounts or even abstracts in his Cutchery that can be depended upon. The karnams execute many of the duties which properly belong to the Collector and the Tahsildars. They distribute the assessment; they assess ryots as they please by entering their lands under a class of higher or lower rate of assessment. Orders regarding money settlement have been entirely misunderstood. The orders to fix money rent upon the average produce and price of a number of years have been interpreted to mean that, after ascertaining the average of any village, the whole of the lands of the village, whether good or bad, are to be assessed at the same rate instead of being assessed according to the relative produce."

Adoption of new principles; survey and classification.

The Board issued orders for the classification of the wet lands, and Mr. Drury, who became Collector in 1828, adopted a system which his predecessor, Mr. Kindersley, had initiated in the previous year. The wet lands were divided into *kannārs*, or blocks; accounts were prepared which showed the fields in consecutive order, the extent of each, and the standard of its productivity in terms of *kōttais*. By 1835 one hundred and forty-six villages in the taluks of Tinnevelly, Tenkāsi, Ambāsamudram and Sankaranainārkōil, had been treated in this manner; in the remaining villages the apportionment of the assessment still remained with the mirāsidārs. The *amāni* system had, by 1839 at least, disappeared altogether. Between 1842 and 1844 an experimental survey and settlement, more or less according to the modern system, were carried out by Mr. E. B. Thomas, the Collector, in four villages; a commutation rate of Rs. 2¼ for a *kōttai*[1] was adopted; the settlement was apparently popular, and its adoption actually resulted in a slight increase of revenue. It was felt, however, that the rates adopted were too low; and in the light of subsequent events it is satisfactory that the scheme was not extended. The opportunity was taken of anticipating some of the reforms which were adopted in the subsequent settlement of the district.

The revenue system unsatisfactory.

In spite of all the patchwork that had been attempted, the revenue system remained most unsatisfactory. There were no less than 300 wet rates in force for *kār* and *pisānam* together; the average of the wet assessment was higher than in any other district in the Presidency, and, under the best irrigation sources, wet lands paid twice as much as the average wet rate prevailing in Coimbatore, the district next most highly assessed. As late as 1855 it was calculated that one-third of the cultivable wet land was permanently waste, some because the rates made cultivation unremunerative, and some because it ought never to have been classed as wet at all. In the river valley a second crop on double-crop lands often paid as much as 80 per cent of the first-crop charge; and in the case of lands registered as single crop the assessment due on a second crop varied according to the caprice of local custom. As a result of the arrangement by which the ryots themselves

[1] The selling price of a *kōttai* of paddy during the recent settlement was between Rs. 10 and Rs. 12.

CHAP. XI. THE WET LANDS.

apportioned the assessment, gross irregularities disfigured the accounts; the poor man's land was at a disadvantage with that of the rich, and scarcely a trace of the ryotwari system was to be found. The *olungu* system, based on a principle apparently sound, in that it accommodated itself to current prices, was not proof against the effect of sudden rises of the market, and, during the period of high prices which set in with 1853, actually raised the assessment to an almost impossible figure. There were no less than 146 different *olungu* rates in force in the various parts of the district; and, as the market price of grain was not fixed until the end of April towards the close of the fasli, the ryot never knew what the demand against him would be until he was called upon to pay it.

End of the *olungu* system.

During the first fifty years of the century, that is, through the periods of *amāni* management, triennial lease, decennial lease and finally the *olungu* settlement, the land revenue derived from ryotwari lands, though subject to fluctuation, had averaged about Rs. 17 lakhs. From 1843 onwards the price of grain had showed a marked upward tendency, but the increase was not sufficient to deprive the ryots of the benefit of the *olungu* principle. In 1853 prices went up with a bound and in that year were nearly double what they had been ten years before. By 1857 they had advanced by another 40 per cent, and they again increased by nearly 25 per cent in the following year. The demand now stood at the alarming and unprecedented figure of Rs. 28 lakhs.[1] The *olungu* system was clearly doomed and in the next year (1859–60) was abandoned in favour of a new settlement, called the *mottafaisal*. Before dealing further with this subject, however, it is necessary to refer to certain other features of the old revenue system.

THE DRY LANDS. Pre-British system.

As has been seen, the pre-British custom in regard to the dry lands had been to levy a lump sum known as *kattukuthagai* on each village and to make a few leading inhabitants responsible for its payment. According to Wilkes, the sum demanded was, as a rule, the equivalent of one-third of the gross produce of the soil.

Mr. Lushington's settlement, and subsequent changes.

Mr. Lushington found that in the accounts the dry lands were roughly divided into four classes, known, in descending order of fertility, as *karisal*, *veppal*, *pottal* and *sevval*, and were assessed at different rates accordingly. He adopted both the recorded classification and rates and made the ryots apportion

[1] That is, only slightly less than the demand for the whole district (including the Rāmnād taluks of Sāttūr and Srīvilliputtūr) as it stood after the recent resettlement.

CHAP. XI. THE DRY LANDS.

the assessment among themselves according to the quality of the land each man cultivated. In the next year the rates were increased to five in number and were somewhat reduced; a survey was put in hand, and the ryots of one village were told off to classify the lands of the next. Most of the ryots, as might have been expected, did the work in their own homes and classed the best lands in the lowest tarams. In 1804 the Collector had to start the work once again and at the same time added a fifth class. The rates were once more raised and, on the completion of the survey, were finally fixed in 1808 at figures which thereafter remained unaltered. They varied between Rs. 2-5-0 and As. 10 an acre.[1] To these rates were added a number of miscellaneous charges, professional taxes and village dues of all kinds, so that the original rates became unrecognizable.

Distribution of pattas and subsequent confusion of accounts.

In 1806, in spite of the opposition of the "nāttāmaikārans," the leading men of the villages, pattas were distributed to the ryots in nine out of the nineteen taluks of the district. What further progress was made in the issue of pattas is not clear; but the theory prevailed, at any rate, that from about that year the settlement of the dry lands of the whole district was in accordance with ryotwari principles. It appears, however, that, during the period of the triennial and decennial leases, a lump sum, as in the case of the wet lands, was levied from the head inhabitants, the ryots being left to distribute the payments amongst themselves with reference to the entries contained in the village accounts or in the pattas previously issued. At any rate, no jamabandi was conducted during these years; and, to judge from the confessions of Mr. Munro, after he had been for three years Collector of the district, it may be inferred that no trace of any ryotwari system remained after the lease-period was over. "Your Board believed," he wrote in 1826, "and I was given by Jivan Row [the Sheristadar] to believe that the punjai lands of this district had been measured, classed and assessed and pattas given for each field. There remain some imperfect traces of this arrangement, but the whole system of accounts kept with it is irreparably mutilated. Very few ryots can produce a patta. The village accounts are either lost or falsified and if, by chance, there is a village safe and entire, the corresponding documents in the taluk and the Huzur Cutchery are either altered or missing. It is probable that this general mutilation of the accounts was gradually effected during the decennial lease. The headmen of the villages, mirasidars, nattamaigars, karnams, and their friends have got possession of the best lands, whilst an

[1] The unit of measurement was the "chain" of 3·64 acres.

CHAP. XI. THE DRY LANDS.

average collection[1] has been made according to the extent of the lands tilled by each cultivator without any regard to its quality, much to the injury of the poorer ryots."

Attempted remedies.

The karnams were ordered to re-write the accounts or to revise those that survived. They drew up lists of fields by numbers; but the notation meant nothing, and even the karnam himself could not identify on the ground the fields entered in his account. One year he numbered them off from north to south and in the next year from east to west; boundaries of fields were never mentioned, and, though occasionally the name of the occupying ryot was entered, the account as a rule merely showed the *total* extent under cultivation in each "class." The classes, moreover, had come to have very little meaning; for, after the various miscellaneous charges (see below) had been added, there were (according to a calculation made in 1855) as many as 497 different acreage rates.[2]

Lands under private wells.

In the case of lands irrigated by private wells the old practice had been to levy assessment according to the nature of the crop grown. In 1841 it was felt that this amounted to taxing improvements, and orders were consequently passed that lands irrigated by privately-owned wells should pay only *punjai* rates. In application the order was taken to mean that wells sunk after the year (fasli 1251) in which the new rule came into force should have the benefit of the concession; lands under "old" wells continued to pay at the old varying rates.[3]

MISCELLANEOUS CHARGES.

In addition to the ordinary assessment levied on wet and dry lands, a number of charges, classed for convenience as "ready money collections," were included under the general head of land revenue. The *yāvana* (abolished in 1807), an additional cess on wet lands, accounted annually, whilst it was in force, for considerably more than a lakh of rupees. The *nanjai-mēl-punjai* was, in theory, the assessment levied on lands classed as "wet" but fit to produce only "dry" crops, such as ragi, onions and senna; it was in practice often confused with the charges levied, under the names *bagayat* or *vanpayar*, on certain crops grown on wet lands, such as betel, sugar-cane, tobacco, turmeric and plantains. A crop classed in one village as *vanpayar* was registered in another as *nanjai-mēl-punjai*. Under the *amāni* system it had been impossible with most of these crops to divide the produce; consequently money-rents, differing

[1] A recognized system, which came to be known as *ivu taram*.

[2] In some parts of the district a charge was levied for a second crop on dry lands. The charge was abolished in 1857.

[3] The anomaly was not removed until 1883, that is, until after the settlement. The lands irrigated by "old" wells were at the settlement classified as "permanently improved" and assessed at special rates, higher than the ordinary dry rates. In 1883 ordinary dry rates were imposed.

CHAP. XI. MISCELLANEOUS CHARGES.

from village to village, had been usually demanded, and these survived under subsequent systems, subject to the salutary rule that, if the *nanjai* rate were higher, that should be paid. The tax on betel gardens was a specially vexatious one. In addition to the assessment the cultivator had to pay a transit duty (see p. 325) before he might pluck a single leaf; and it was calculated that the average taxation, including assessment and duty, to which this species of produce was subject, amounted to Rs. 40 an acre. In 1842 the rule was introduced that all *nanjai-mēl-punjai* lands, if irrigated, should pay ordinary wet assessment; and in 1855 eight specified kinds of cultivation, which fell properly under the class of *vanpayar* or *bagayat,* were declared liable to two full "wet" rates.

The charges known as *pāttam* and *poruppu* were in the nature of favourable "quit-rents" imposed on lands granted, or believed to have been granted, subject to certain conditions in regard to reclamation.

Dēsakāval fees.

A vexatious charge which from the earliest times had been levied in certain villages as an additional cess on the wet and dry lands was the *dēsakāval* tax. It represented the fees formerly levied by the poligars on the lands of the sirkar villages on the pretext of "watching fees." [1] Some villages paid it and some were exempt, and the rates at which it was calculated appear to have been numberless. Proposals to abolish the tax were sent up from time to time, but it was decided finally that the matter should lie over for the coming settlement. The cess was abolished then.

Nilavari.

A curious additional impost on the land was the tax known as *nilavari* which was levied on dry and wet lands alike; and, from the accounts preserved of the method by which it was assessed, it seems unlikely that even the large sums, varying between one and two lakhs of rupees, which were annually credited to this head, represented the whole of the collections made under the pretext of this tax. *Nilavari* included, we are told, fees paid to the village servants; charges incurred by the villagers in buying limes when the headman went out to receive persons in authority; presents given to the huzur accountants at the time of jamabandi; travelling allowances for village headmen; fees paid by the *mahājanams* to the taluk office gumastas in order that they might be given their proper titles in the accounts; fees to shroffs; fees to "sastris, poets, musicians, jugglers, and tumblers" for the performances they gave when high officials came to the village; and a host of other payments. The tax was abolished in 1857.

[1] See p. 334. This tax is to be distinguished from the "moturfa" *dēsakāval* fees referred to on page 326.

CHAP. XI. MISCELLANEOUS CHARGES.

Taxes on trees.

The taxes on trees, which survive, in a modified form, to the present day, underwent an important reform about this time. They are dealt with below (pp. 306 foll.).

"Extra sources of revenue."

Unconnected with the land, but lumped occasionally under the general head of "land revenue," were the taxes which in the early records are referred to as *swarnadāyam* and came to be known generally as *moturfa*. These taxes, as well as those comprisсd under the heading "extra sources of revenue," are dealt with in Chapter XII.

Official language.

A reform of some importance, which was carried eut in 1854, was the discontinuance of Mahratti as the official language of correspondence between the offices of the Collector and the Tahsildars. During the earliest years of the Company's rule two sets of accounts, one in Mahratti and the other n Tamil, were kept in the revenue offices, and in 1814 the Tamil accounts were discontinued. Persian, which had been the medium of correspondence, was in 1804 replaced by Mahratti; Tamil was substituted in 1813 but in 1827 gave way to Mahratti. The village accounts had always been kept in Tamil, which was also the language used in addressing zamindars and in police correspondence. The revenue offices were thus until 1854 the close preserve of a very small class.

THE MOTTAFAISAL.

By 1859, therefore, the revenue system had been purged of many of its worst vices, and the new system of *mottafaisal*, which, as has been seen (p. 286), was introduced in that year, started under favourable conditions. By the new system (which had already been tried in Tanjore) the *olungu* standard price was adopted as the unalterable commutation rate. Although the price of grain actually fell in 1859–60 by over 30 per cent, the result of the adoption of the fixed standard price was a saving in that year to the ryots of Rs. 5 lakhs as compared with what they would have had to pay under the old system.

The A and B registers.

With a view to the determination of the amount due by each ryot both on wet and dry lands, two important accounts, described as the A and B registers—the precursors of the modern settlement register—were put in hand. The B register was the important one. It exhibited the total extent of land in the occupation of each ryot, not only that which he had cultivated in the last preceding fasli, but also that which, though fallow, had been at any known period in his occupation. The register was completed in 1864; and from that year onwards each ryot was responsible for the assessment on the extent of land entered in his name and received a patta showing the demand against him. The individual fields had in most villages not been surveyed, and, even where this had been roughly attempted, there was no notation by which thev could be specified; consequently the entry made against each ryot's name was the total assessment due on his entire holding. In the case of wet lands this sum was calculated at the commutation rate, either with reference to the standard *mēlvāram* rate of the village, or, if the village had been classified, according to the "block rate"; in the case of the dry lands the taram rates were adopted. When the system first came in, the Collector was given a large discretion to grant remissions in the case of uncultivated fields; but, as soon as the registers were completed, the ryot was given the option of paying assessment or relinquishing what he could not cultivate. In spite of the concession, the ryots chose to retain in their pattas as much as 250,000 acres of uncultivated land.

Effects of the new system.

The effects of the new method of assessment and registration were seen in an increase, between 1860 and 1865, of 18 per cent in the figures of cultivation, for wet and dry lands together, accompanied by a corresponding rise in revenue. In 1865, a year in which the price of grain reached an unprecedented figure, it was calculated that, had the old *olungu* system still been in force, the revenue demand would have been greater by Rs. 32 lakhs, a sum which, it may be presumed, could never have been collected.

Disappearance of *mirāsi*.

One most important economic result of the new system was the blow it dealt to the old obstructive claims of *mirāsi* right. When in 1826 orders were passed requiring the issue of pattas, the question arose who should receive them: should they go to the mirāsidārs or to the cultivating ryots? It was reported that in the entire district there were only thirty-six villages in which *mirāsi* was unknown and that, since the early years of the century, the claim had become by degrees more widespread. Three classes of villages were distinguished at the time: the *panguvāli* villages, in which the mirāsidārs, the virtual owners of all the land, enjoyed their own shares in rotation; the *pattavritti,* those in which the mirāsidārs enjoyed their fixed portions; the few *parumpattu* villages, in which there was no intermediary (besides the headman, or "nāttāmaikāran," appointed by Government to receive the revenue) between the Sirkar and the cultivator. In practice those responsible for the revenue, both in the dry villages and in the wet, whether under leases or under the *olungu* system, were in almost all cases the mirāsidārs; and it may readily be understood that in the presence of such excellent opportunities the *mirāsi* claim was not slow to assert itself. There is no question that the village lease system gave a strong impetus to this process. The *mirāsi* claim extended itself not only to the lands which the mirāsidār was able himself to cultivate or get cultivated but also to the waste land of the

CHAP. XI. The Motta-faisal.

village. If a cultivator, or *purakudi,* chose to bring waste under the plough, he paid a fee known as *swāmibhōgam* (believed to have been the equivalent of about 5 per cent of the gross produce) to the mirāsidār. By degrees, as the issue of pattas became more general, these extravagant claims received a set-back; and, by 1850 or perhaps earlier, the practice was established that, if a mirāsidār left land uncultivated for as much as five years, any person might apply for it and obtain registry. Just about the time that the system inaugurated by the B register was coming into force, a suit on the subject of *swāmibhōgam* had gone against the mirāsidārs of a village. The *pangālis* still objected before the Collector to the issue of pattas in favour of the *purakudis* and, failing to secure their object, appealed to the Board of Revenue. The Board, following the decision which the court had already given, declined to interfere. A few instances in which exception was taken to the issue of patta, on the ground that the objectors received *swāmibhōgam* from the occupants, arose even during the recent resettlement; most of these claims were either rejected on their merits or compromised on terms which gave the occupants their pattas. It may fairly be said that for the past half century *mirāsi* and *swāmibhōgam* have been unknown to the revenue system.[1]

[1] A curious survival of this tenure exists, however, in what are known as "Company *pannai* lands," that is, the "home-lands of the (East India) Company." In 1799 an arrangement (finally ratified in 1803) was made by which the confiscated pālaiyam of Pānjālankurichi was conferred on the poligars of Ettaiyāpuram and Maniyāchi (p. 272), the former receiving four *māgānams* or divisions and the latter two. A few lands, for the reason apparently that they were scattered and consequently fell into none of the six divisions, were not included in these gifts. Having been confiscated, they remained the property of the East India Company both as Government and zamindar, and on this account received the appellation of "Company *pannai.*" At first the lands were given on lease for varying periods to the highest bidder. Subsequently, before the settlement, ryotwari pattas were issued; but, to mark the occupancy right of Government, a charge of *swāmibhōgam* in addition to the assessment was levied from the pattadars. Mr. Puckle offered the ryots the chance of redeeming their *swāmibhōgam* by the payment of a capitalized sum; but they refused. The matter came again to notice on one or two occasions; and finally, in 1878, a few ryots of the Srīvaikuntam taluk, owning altogether 28 acres, accepted an offer of redemption similar to that made by Mr. Puckle. Other ryots declined the proposal; and "Company *pannai*" lands still exist to the extent of 1,408·75 acres in the three taluks of Kōilpatti, Srīvaikuntam and Tiruchendūr. They are distributed thus:—

Taluk.	Area.	Swāmibhōgam due.		
	ACS.	RS.	A.	P.
Kōilpatti taluk	1,386·76	139	15	3
Srīvaikuntam taluk ...	96·98	688	7	8
Tiruchendūr taluk ...	25·01	81	3	4

CHAP. XI. SURVEY AND SETTLEMENT.

In 1861 Government decided that the district should be surveyed with a view to its settlement on the latest ryotwari principles. Demarcation began in 1862, and in 1866 Mr. R. K. Puckle was appointed to the district as Collector and Settlement Officer.

Mr. Puckle appointed Collector and Settlement Officer.

For the purposes of his settlement, Mr. Puckle dealt with tracts of country, not with taluks, and divided the district into its four natural divisions: (1) the *nirārambam*, a stretch of country comprising the country (at that time 345 villages) irrigated by the Tāmbraparni and its affluents and running in narrow strips through the five taluks of Tinnevelly, Tenkāsi, Ambāsamudram, Tenkarai and Nānguneri; (2) the *kādārambam*, a region not so irrigated, extending from the north to the south of the district and containing 409 villages; (3) the sandy tract of country generally referred to in the settlement records as the "palmyra forest," in which palmyras largely take the place of cultivation. This region, extending from the mouth of the Nambiyār eastwards for about forty miles with an average breadth of ten miles from north to south, comprised 68 villages lying in the south-west of Nānguneri and the south of Tenkarai (now Tiruchendūr); (4) the plain of black-cotton soil (the modern Kōilpatti and north Srīvaikuntam) and Sāttūr [1], comprising 188 villages.

His first scheme report; the *nirārambam*.

Mr. Puckle's first scheme, embodied in an exhaustive report which he sent up in 1868, dealt with the first-named of these four tracts but was not disposed of by Government until 1872. For the calculation of his money rates for wet lands Mr. Puckle had adopted as a commutation rate the average of the selling prices of paddy during the previous 98 years; the Government took exception to this and sent the scheme back for revision on this point. In all other essentials the proposals were accepted and warmly approved. Less than a month later Mr. Puckle sent in his revised scheme, suggesting two alternative commutation rates, one based according to the instructions of Government on the prices of twenty years (1846–1865) immediately preceding the beginning of settlement operations, the other deduced from the prices of the years 1844–1863. Mr. Puckle preferred the second alternative, as the prices of 1864 and 1865 had been exceptional and their inclusion raised the rates to a dangerously high figure. The Board and Government agreed with Mr. Puckle, and his proposals were finally accepted without further modification.

The principles of the Settlement.

The principles of the settlement need only be briefly stated. The five prevailing soils (black loam, sand and clay and red loam and clay) were divided, not, as had been the

[1] Now in the Rāmnād district.

CHAP. XI. SURVEY AND SETTLEMENT.

practice elsewhere, into three, but into five classes or "sorts"—best, good, ordinary, inferior and worst. Mr. Puckle decided that the "best black loam" was undoubtedly superior to any other soil; "good black loam" was classed as equally productive with "best red loam"; and the "best" black and red sandy soils were considered equivalent to the "good" red loams. Soils of similar yield having thus been bracketed together, seven "tarams" or classes were obtained for wet soils and seven for dry, with the addition of two separate tarams at the top of the table of dry rates for *olappēri*, or "permanently improved" lands.[1] Each village was divided into blocks of 10 to 50 acres, a taram being allotted to each block according to its soil situation and, in the case of wet lands, facilities for irrigation.

The tract having thus been laid out in groups, the villages in blocks and the soils in classes, the next step was to ascertain the yield of each variety of soil. Experiments in this direction had already been made in 1865 in regard to wet lands in all the taluks of the district under the supervision of the Collector, Mr. Banbury. Mr. Puckle made further experiments, compared his results with those previously obtained and those now obtained by the ryots themselves and finally fixed the average outturn per acre, on the best wet land, at the comparatively lenient figure of 1,200 Madras measures. The estimated yield of land in the lower tarams was graded proportionately. No experiments, however, were made in the case of dry lands. The bulk of these lands were poor and seldom cultivated; it was difficult to determine what the "staple" crops were, and it was not thought worth while, in any case, to repeat the experiments which had already been made in the case of similar soils in Salem and Trichinopoly. As a matter of fact, the bulk of the dry lands of the tract were assessed in the two lowest tarams.

The yield of each quality of soil having been ascertained, the money assessment had to be determined for each class. The average of the market prices of paddy for twenty years, 1844 to 1863, was struck. This being the merchants' price, a deduction of 15 per cent was made to cover the cost of cartage, sellers' profits and so on, and in the end a commutation rate of Rs. 3-9-0 a *kōttai*, or Rs. 108 a garce, was obtained. The application of this rate to the yield set against each taram gave the gross produce of the soil; a deduction was then allowed for expenses of cultivation, at the rate of Rs. 15-4-0 an acre for land in the first taram and at one rupee

[1] See foot-note on p. 288.

less for each succeeding taram. The remainder was divided by two; and from the half so obtained a deduction of 5 per cent was made for "unprofitable areas," such as channels, banks and paths. The resultant net figure was taken to represent the amount due as assessment.

The rates so obtained were applied only to villages in the "first group" (see below) and were modified to suit the circumstances of villages in the lower "groups," in such a way as to give a table of ten rates. The assessment thus arrived at was for a single crop only, that is, the *pisānam* crop. The old system, in the case of lands which regularly grew two crops a year, had been to charge a full *kār* assessment for the second crop; those on which a *kār* crop was occasionally raised paid half the *kār* assessment. This distinction was now abolished, and the second-crop charge was fixed, according to circumstances, at two-thirds, one-half, one-third, and one-quarter of the first-crop charge, a uniform rate being applied to each block. The total charge thus made was treated as a consolidated rate of composition; and it was further laid down that lands which were not compounded for in this way would, in the event of their raising a second crop, be charged *faslijāsti* at the rate of three-quarters the charge due on the first crop. Lands irrigated by baling from a Government source were charged half the full wet rates.

With reference to soil, situation, irrigation, and abundance or scarcity of labour, the villages of the *nirārambam* were divided into four "groups." Sixty-four exceptionally good villages, irrigated from the Tāmbraparni by the Kannadiyan and Pālaiyan channels, were placed in the first group; over a hundred villages irrigated by other Tāmbraparni channels and by the main channels from the Chittār, Pachaiyār and other affluents of the Tāmbraparni fell into the second group; a third group was made up of 131 villages situated at the tail-end of these channels or irrigated by "jungle streams;" 19 villages possessing especially poor irrigation composed the fourth group. Four villages which, though possessing no wet lands, were comprised in the scheme were not placed in any group.[1] The dry lands of all villages were unaffected by the grouping of the villages in which they were situated.

[1] As this system of grouping was ultimately applied to the whole district, it may here be stated that the first group extended along the river-valley from Ambāsamudram nearly to Palamcotta; the fourth group included the village of the *tēri* and the black-cotton country; the bulk of the district thus fell into the second and third groups. About 80 villages, possessing no wet lands, were not grouped at all,

CHAP. XI
SURVEY AND SETTLEMENT.

The following table shows the acreage rates adopted both in wet and dry lands—10 single crop rates, 10 double crop rates and 9 dry rates. In the case of the compounded wet lands it will be noticed that the rate of composition was made dependent on the taram[1]:—

Taram.	Wet Lands. First group. Single crop.	Wet Lands. First group. Compounded double crop.	Wet Lands. Second group. Single crop.	Wet Lands. Second group. Compounded double crop.	Wet Lands. Third group. Single crop.	Wet Lands. Third group. Compounded double crop.	Wet Lands. Fourth group. Single crop.	Wet Lands. Fourth group. Compounded double crop.	Dry Lands. (No grouping.)	
	RS. A.	RS. A.	RS. A.	RS. A.	RS. A.	RS. A.	RS. A.	RS. A.	RS. A.	
1	12 0	20 0	10 8	17 8	9 0	13 8	7 8	10 0	5 0	"Permanently improved" series.
2	10 8	17 8	9 0	13 8	7 8	10 0	6 0	7 8	3 8	
3	9 0	13 8	7 8	10 0	6 0	7 8	4 8	5 10	2 8	
4	7 8	10 0	6 0	7 8	4 8	5 10	3 8	4 6	1 8	
5	6 0	7 8	4 8	5 10	3 8	4 6	3 0	3 12	1 0	
6	4 8	5 10	3 8	4 6	3 0	3 12	2 8	3 2	0 12	
7	3 8	4 6	3 0	3 12	2 8	3 2	2 0	2 8	0 8	
8	...	...	...	..	...	...	...	...	0 6	
9	...	...	...	...	...	. .	...	...	0 4	

The second scheme-report; the "palmyra forest."

The next tract of country dealt with was the division numbered (3) above, the "palmyra forest." The report was submitted in 1872, before orders had been passed on Mr. Puckle's first scheme for the *nirārambam*, and was approved by Government in 1874. The treatment of the palmyras (a subject dealt with on pp. 306 foll.) of the tract, estimated at nearly a million, was the leading problem of this country. For the wet lands, amounting in all to less than 3,000 acres, the same scale of rates was adopted as had been sanctioned for the river-valley. The first three groups were not used at all in the case of villages containing wet lands; for the loose red sand of the *tēri* country a sixth "sort," described in settlement parlance as "worse than worst red sand," was added, and rated at As. 3 an acre. Otherwise the dry lands were treated on the same lines as had been followed in the *nirārambam*.

[1] The lands in the first two "primary tarams," i.e., lands bearing the two highest of the ten single crop rates, were compounded at two-thirds, those in the third "primary taram" at one-half, those in the fourth at one-third, and those in the fifth and all below it at one-fourth.

Settlement of the Tinnevelly and Tenkāsi taluks.

The first introduction report was sent up in 1874. It related to the two taluks of Tinnevelly and Tenkāsi, and their settlement was the work of Mr. Puckle himself. In addition to the villages covered by the scheme-report relating to the *nirārambam*, 35 villages not irrigated by the Tāmbraparni were included in the settlement. Of the river-irrigated lands more than one-third was assessed at rates ranging from Rs. 10 to Rs. 20; nearly 80 per cent of the total wet area was compounded for as double-crop, and the average wet rate, Rs. 8-13-1, was still considerably higher than that of any other district in the Presidency. The rate on the dry lands averaged only As. 8.

Departure of Mr. Puckle.

In 1874 Mr. Puckle was appointed to act as Director of Settlement but retained the general supervision of the settlement work of the district, the immediate charge of the work being left with Mr. A. T. Arundel, who, as additional Sub-Collector, had been conducting the settlement of the Ambāsamudram taluk, and with T. Venkatāchāri, a "Special Assistant," who had been engaged in Tenkarai. On Mr. Puckle's promotion to the Board of Revenue in the same year, the charge of the settlement work devolved on the Collector, an arrangement which was terminated in October of the next year by an order issued to Mr. C. Rundall, the new Director, to assume charge of the work in Tinnevelly. In 1876 Mr. Puckle reverted to the post of Director of Settlement and continued to supervise the Tinnevelly settlement until its close in 1878.

Settlement of the Tenkarai taluk.

The settlement of the Tenkarai taluk was conducted under Mr. Puckle's directions by his Special Assistant, T. Venkatāchāri. Besides those parts of the taluk which were comprised in the *nirārambam* and the "palmyra forest," there were 56 villages which fell into the tract described as *kādārambam;* these were settled on the lines already sanctioned for the river-valley villages. The new rates were introduced in fasli 1284 (1874-75); and, owing mainly to the benefits derived from the newly constructed Srīvaikuntam anicut, the revision showed a net increase of Rs. 30,800. The only departure made from the general principles sanctioned by Government was that, in compounding wet lands in the first taram in second-group villages, the rate adopted in the case of villages under the Srīvaikuntam anicut was one-half instead of two-thirds of the first-crop charge; that is, the rate imposed on such lands was Rs. 15-12-0 instead of Rs. 17-8-0. Over 90 per cent of the river-irrigated land was compounded for, and on the total wet area of the taluk the average rate was as much as Rs. 10-9-8,

CHAP. XI. SURVEY AND SETTLEMENT.

that is, higher than in the two taluks previously settled. Of the dry lands more than 80 per cent was assessed at rates varying from As. 8 downwards.

Settlement of the Ambāsamudram taluk.

Ambāsamudram, which was settled by Mr. A. T. Arundel, was the next taluk reported on. Five-sixths of the river-irrigated area, which comprises the finest paddy land of the district, was assessed at consolidated rates for two crops, and of this compounded area as much as two-thirds fell into the two highest tarams.[1] In Sērmādevi alone, though almost all the land of the village was now assessed at Rs. 20, the new settlement involved a decrease of Rs. 2,000. The settlement included 33 villages which had not been covered by the *nirārambam* proposals.

Settlement of the Nānguneri taluk.

Of the Nānguneri taluk 81 villages in the river-irrigated area and 14 villages of the "palmyra forest" had been dealt with in Mr. Puckle's reports. The remaining villages, 118 in number, including those irrigated by the Nambiyār and Hanumānadhi, were dealt with on the principles sanctioned for the river-valley; and in 1877 the report on the settlement of the whole taluk was sent up by the Special Assistant, T. Venkatāchāri. As anticipated, the result was a considerable drop in the revenue demand, the average wet rate per acre falling from Rs. 9–3–6 to Rs. 6–11–11. More than half the area of dry lands was now assessed at rates varying between 3 and 6 annas, the average rate on the total dry area of the taluk being just under 5 annas. Though the poorest taluk of the district, its average incidence of assessment per head of the population had been second only to Ambāsamudram.

The other taluks.

By 1877 the classification of two of the remaining four taluks[2] had been completed, and Mr. Puckle undertook to visit the district, complete the classification of the remaining two taluks and close the settlement of the district within the following fasli. He urged that a detailed scheme report with an estimate of financial results was unnecessary. Government approved. A "completion report" for the Ottapidāram taluk was submitted in 1877, and for the three other taluks in the following year.

Financial results of the Settlement.

Though the survey of ryotwari lands (which was completed in 1872) showed a total increase for the whole district of 7 per cent over the area previously recorded, the settlement resulted

[1] The average rate on all the wet lands of the taluk was Rs. 12–8–10 an acre.

[2] Ottapidāram, Sankaranainārkōil, Sāttūr and Srīvilliputtūr. Of these, the two last named were in 1910 transferred to the Rāmnād district.

(as the following table will show) in a reduction of the previous demand by 2 per cent :—

Taluks (1)	Fasli in which settlement was introduced. (2)	Assessment: Before settlement. (3)	Assessment: As fixed at settlement. (4)	Difference. (5)	Percentage. (6)	Increase of palmyra assessment. (7)	Net result. (8)
		RS.	RS.	RS.	RS.	RS.	RS.
1. Tenkāsi ...	1283	1,79,478	1,72,050	— 7,428	— 4	1,500	— 5,928
2. Tinnevelly ...	1283	8,32,928	3,22,778	—10,150	— 3	2,500	— 7,650
3. Ambāsamudram.	1284 1285	3,71,108	3,74,271	+ 3,163	+ 1	6,087	+ 9,250
4. Tenkarai ...	1284	4,76,685	4,98,625	+ 21,940	+ 5	8,860	+30,800
5. Nānguněri	1286	3,49,065	2,73,838	—75,227	—22	9,435	—65,792
6. Ottapidāram ..	1287	1,31,874	1,39,167	+ 7,293	+ 6	1,242	+ 8,535
7. Sankaranainārkōil.	1287	1,65,268	1,65,868	+ 600	...	787	+ 1,387
8. Sāttūr ...	1287	1,90,622	1,95,063	+ 4,441	+ 2	140	+ 4,581
9. Srīvilliputtūr.	1287	3,28,338	3,31,738	+ 3,400	+ 1	307	+ 3,707
Total ...	...	25,25,366	24,73,398	— 51,968	— 2	30,858	—21,110

It was the fortunate result of many circumstances that a greater sacrifice of revenue was averted. The *mottafaisal* system of 1860, the security of tenure imported by the principles of the B register, the suppression of *mirāsi* claims, the abolition of vexatious taxes and the general rise of prices had helped to introduce a new era of economic progress. Mr. Puckle wrote in 1867 : " It is little more than twenty years ago that ordinary land was hardly worth holding. The tax was high, the market prices were low, the crop was often sold before it was reaped, and small land-holders frequently left their lands and fled the country to avoid debts which they knew they could not meet. Only the best irrigated and garden lands had a marketable price and they were not worth generally more than Rs. 100 an acre.

Economic conditions of the period.

" Now, the worst irrigated lands are worth as much as the best were twenty years ago and the best are now worth upwards of Rs. 1,000 an acre.[1] In fact, land is so valuable that there

[1] They now change hands at Rs. 4,000 and over.

CHAP. XI. SURVEY AND SETTLEMENT.

is literally no waste in some taluks, all being held on patta. The increased value of land has led to improved cultivation. Communications have been improved, and prices in neighbouring districts have consequently been equalized. The gradual abatement of taxation and restrictive enactments, the abolition of fluctuating charges on the land, the stricter supervision of native subordinates have all tended to a certain degree to increase the value of rent."

Other measures carried out during the settlement.

Advantage was taken of the settlement to abolish certain old-fashioned remissions known generally as *chaturbāgam* (amounting in all to over half a lakh of rupees annually) granted without consideration to certain privileged classes, mostly Brahmans. A village cess of one anna in the rupee of assessment was levied; and this, added to the fixed deductions which had customarily been made from the revenues under the heads *dupati māniam, stalam kāval* and karnams' salaries, was formed into a fund which paid for the new village establishments. Lands held in common enjoyment were in numerous villages divided amongst the shareholders; 38,000 transfers of patta were effected; many new fishery-pattas were issued, and, where such a patta stood in the names of numerous shareholders, some absentees, some dead and forgotten, each of whom was still shown to possess a petty fraction, a new deed was issued in the name of the village temple or the Sāsta on the tank bund, the remaining sharers being left to apportion the proceeds among themselves. Grazing-grounds aggregating 10,000 acres were provided in numerous villages, and in the Tenkāsi taluk a strip of the lower ghats was set apart for a similar purpose. A number of small rain-fed tanks (particularly in the Tinnevelly and Nānguněri taluks), the maintenance of which by Government was disproportionately expensive, were handed over with their ayacuts on special acreage rates to the pattadars.

"Puckle's Settlement."

This settlement—"Puckle's settlement" as it is rightly called—forms the most memorable epoch in the modern history of Tinnevelly; and even to-day the phrase "Puckle Dhurai"—"familiar in his mouth as household words"—conveys at once to a Tinnevelly ryot visions of spacious days and of the district's greatest benefactor. Combining in himself the offices of Collector and Settlement Officer, Mr. Puckle adopted from the outset the policy of enlisting the co-operation of the people in executing at their own cost works of public utility which they had long desired but for want of a lead had been unable to accomplish. Once awakened, the clamour for the repair of tank bunds and sluices, the construction of "Mount roads"

CHAP. XI. SURVEY AND SETTLEMENT.

and the planting of trees became so insistent that even Mr. Puckle thought it wiser to obtain the sanction of Government to the course he had adopted. "This is an opportunity," the Board wrote to Government on the subject, "which will never occur again. Under such circumstances any judicious Collector might work wonders with a very small expenditure, but Mr. Puckle's antecedents, and especially the evidence that he had deservedly won the trust of the people, afforded by the project [1] to which they have subscribed large sums, show that he is pre-eminently fitted for such work." The permission was granted, "subject to no restrictions except this: that Mr. Puckle shall promise to see personally that the subscriptions are voluntary and the money properly spent."

In the Tenkarai taluk Rs. 40,000 was subscribed by ryots, especially those of Tentiruppērai, for the head-sluice and channel at the right flank of the Srīvaikuntam anicut; a sum of Rs. 60,000 realized by the sale of waste lands, newly brought within reach of irrigation, paid for sixteen miles of roadway, five tanks and over fifty miles of channels. In the Tinnevelly taluk a road eight miles long was laid out from the Tinnevelly bridge to Tiruttu along the south bank of the river; from the bridge past the Collector's office to Mēlanattam another road was made; from Udaiyārpatti (near Tachanallūr) a road was taken along the north bank of the river as far as the Chittār; in some villages broad roads were formed across the paddy fields to replace the swampy tracks that had served before; irrigation tanks and sluices were repaired. In the Ambāsamudram taluk (this was Mr. A. T. Arundel's charge) Rupees 20,000 was spent on an anicut in the Rāmanadhi river; numerous masonry sluices were built to replace the old hollow palmyra trunks; over thirty miles of road were laid out across the paddy fields; village-sites and *teppakulams* were improved. The Tinnevelly and Ambāsamudram bridges, which had been seriously damaged in the flood of 1869, were rebuilt by public subscriptions amounting to upwards of a lakh of rupees. By means of the Jungle Conservancy Fund trees were put down along the road-sides. More than a hundred topes, many of which are pointed out to this day, were planted; and, before he left the district, Mr. Puckle was contemplating the establishment of a "model farm." [2]

THE RE-SETTLEMENT.

The period for which this settlement was to be in force was declared to be thirty years; and in fasli 1313 (1903–1904) the

[1] The Srīvaikuntam anicut.

[2] Mr. Puckle was made a C.I.E. in 1878. He is now the senior member of that Order.

CHAP. XI. THE RE-SETTLEMENT.

two taluks of Tinnevelly and Tenkāsi became due for a resettlement. A resurvey of the district was found necessary and was put in hand in 1904. Mr. D. T. Chadwick was appointed to the district as Settlement Officer, and in 1905 he sent up his proposals [1] for the treatment of the three taluks of Tinnevelly, Tenkāsi and Ambāsamudram.

Economic progress of thirty years.

The result of enquiries made in all parts of the district was to show that the economic history of the district during the preceding thirty years had been one of marked progress. The settlement had been followed by a striking increase of cultivation (as the figures in the marginal table indicate); and of this increase a most satisfactory feature was the expansion which had occurred in the cultivation of the more valuable crops. In all parts of the district wells had greatly multiplied, the most conspicuous taluks in this respect being Tenkāsi, Nānguneri and Sankaranainārkōil. Paddy and cholam had largely displaced sāmai and varagu; in Ottapidāram the proportion of the total cultivated area under cotton had, at the expense of cumbu, risen to nearly one-third, in Sankaranainārkōil the area under this crop had doubled, and in the Sāttūr taluk the expansion of cotton cultivation was even more remarkable. The proportion of waste land to the total classified area was considerably lower than in any other district, and investigations showed that it was to the cultivating classes rather than to the the money-lender or the absentee owner that the newly-occupied land had as a rule passed. The expansion of holdings had increased the revenue by Rs. 40,000. During the thirty years the prices of paddy and of most agricultural produce had risen 43 per cent; land had advanced enormously in value, and in Tenkāsi its price had doubled. As judged by the incidence of taxation on the occupied area, Tinnevelly had been before Mr. Puckle's settlement the most highly assessed district in the Presidency; in 1904 it stood tenth in the list, with an average incidence per acre of Rs. 2-11-0. Communications of all kinds had been improved; in 1876 the main line to Tuticorin and Tinnevelly Bridge was opened, and by 1903 the extension to Tenkāsi was completed.

Taluk.	Percentage in fasli 1312 of increase of cultivation since settlement.
Tinnevelly ... ... } Tenkāsi ... ... } Ambāsamudram ... }	19
Srīvaikuntam	14
Nānguneri	21
Ottapidāram	38
Sankaranainārkōil ...	29
Sāttūr	55
Srīvilliputtūr	50

[1] Printed with G.O. No. 304, Revenue, dated 31st January 1908.

CHAP. XI. THE RE-SETTLEMENT.

Principles of the resettlement. The wet lands.

As the whole district was ultimately resettled on the same principles, these may here be briefly recapitulated.[1] It will be convenient to deal with the subject under three main heads:—(1) wet lands, (2) dry lands, and (3) trees, mainly palmyras.

(1) *Wet lands.*—It was clear that a rise of prices during the preceding thirty years by 43 per cent justified an enhancement of the assessment. In districts recently settled Government had foregone a part of the increment to which they were reasonably entitled, and on this occasion they decided to limit the general enhancement of the rates to 12½ per cent.

Classification of irrigation sources and readjustment of rates.

The difficulties of applying this general increase to the wet rates and of removing at the same time the anomalies which existed in the old system are fully discussed in Mr. Chadwick's report printed with G.O. No. 304, Revenue, dated 31st January 1908. Mr. Puckle's method of "grouping" villages which contained wet lands possessed some obvious drawbacks. As the grouping of a village was determined mainly by the general character of its irrigation, it followed that, where good irrigation sources existed in a third-group village and poor sources existed in a first-group village, the soil classification had to be "manipulated" a good deal in order that appropriate money-rates might result in each case. Again, if during the currency of a settlement lands under rain-fed tanks were brought under river-channel irrigation, no change could be made in the money-rate unless the soil classification were "modified." The more modern method which overcomes these and other difficulties is to classify sources of irrigation according to their individual capacity; and at the resettlement Government directed the introduction of this system. Under it the ratio of the charge for a second crop to that levied on the first crop is regulated, as is only logical, by the ability of the irrigation source to provide water sufficient to mature a second crop. The system of "grouping" villages entirely precluded the application at the previous settlement of these sound principles, with the result (as has been seen) that Mr. Puckle had to make his composition charge dependent on the "primary taram," that is, in fact, on the first-crop charge. Thus, by compounding his two single-crop rates of Rs. 12 and Rs. 10-8-0 at two-thirds he obtained double-crop rates of Rs. 20 and Rs. 17-8-0. Under these two tarams there were, as a matter of fact, no single-crop lands, and the important point in regard to these

[1] In 1909 a scheme report was sent up for Srīvaikuntam and Nānguneri; a report dealing with Ottapidāram, Sankaranainārkōil, Sāttūr and Srīvilliputtūr was sent up in 1910.

CHAP. XI. THE RE-SETTLEMENT.

lands, therefore, was to find a reasonable double-crop rate. When irrigation sources are classified, the ratio of the second-crop charge to the first cannot, under the rules, exceed a half; consequently in applying a double-crop rate which would bear the percentage increase desired, it was necessary to enhance the single-crop rate—albeit a purely hypothetical one—by considerably more than 12 ½ per cent. Again, the bulk of irrigation of the district fell into the second and third "groups", and within this area there were a large number of irrigation sources which on classification would fall into the first "class"; for these villages there were only eight single-crop rates and eight very irregular double-crop rates available. So irregular in fact were the double-crop rates that it was found impossible, in the case of lands under "first-class" sources situated in "second-group" villages, to raise the assessment mechanically by one taram and thus to bring it to the level of the charge which would be leviable on similar land in a "first-group" village. For these and similar reasons it became necessary, with the classification of irrigation sources, to construct a new table of wet rates.

The new rates.

Mr. Puckle's rates, though few, inelastic and, in some respects, irregular, had proved on the whole extremely fair. His "first group" undoubtedly comprised what is still the finest and most valuable stretch of paddy land in the district; and, generally speaking, the market value of the wet land throughout the district was found to vary in proportion to the settlement rate it bore.[1] While the application of the new principle of the classification of sources and the removal of some of the old anomalies made it necessary that the rates should be recast and amplified, care was taken to preserve, by the adjustment where necessary of the soil classification, the original tarams and consequently the old proportion between assessment and land values. Irrigation sources were divided into four classes; channels and tanks supplied by rivers and a few exceptionally good rain-fed tanks fell into the first three classes; the fourth class comprised rain-fed tanks only and included half the total number of sources in the district.[2]

[1] Many of the wet villages of Tenkāsi formed an exception. Assessments were found to be very low in proportion to the value of the lands, and a scheme for the reclassification of some villages was sent up. The proposal, however, was negatived by Government.

[2] The detailed principles of this classification will be found in the resettlement notifications relating to the various taluks. For particulars of sources and irrigated areas, see appendix B to the introduction report of the Sankaranainārkōil and Kōilpatti taluks, printed with B.P. No. 113, R.S., dated 23rd April 1913.

Cf. also table on p. 168 above.

CHAP. XI. THE RESETTLEMENT.

The following table of rates was finally adopted [1] :—

—	First class.				Second class.				Third class.				Fourth class.			
	Single.		Double.		Single.		Double.		Single.		Double.		Single.		Double.	
	RS.	A.	RS.	A.	RS.	A.	RS.	A.	RS.	A.	RS.	A.	RS.	A.	RS.	A.
IV-1	15	0	22	8	13	2	17	8	11	8	14	6	8	8	10	4
IV-2, VII-1	13	2	19	12	11	8	15	4	8	8	10	10	6	12	8	2
III-1, IV-3, V-1, VII-2, VIII-1	10	2	15	4	8	8	11	6	6	12	8	8	5	0	6	0
III-2, IV-4, V-2, VII-3, VIII-2	7	8	11	4	6	12	9	0	5	0	6	4	4	0	4	12
III-3, IV-5, V-3, VII-4, VIII-3	5	10	8	8	5	0	6	10	4	0	5	0	3	6	4	0
III-4, V-4, VII-5, VIII-4	4	4	6	6	4	0	3	4	2	6	4	4	2	12	3	4
I, I-5, V-5, VIII-5 ...	3	6	5	0	3	6	4	8	3	12	3	8	2	4	2	10

Other changes.

Other changes introduced were: the charge for a second crop raised on single-crop land was reduced from the old district rate of three-quarters of the first-crop charge to one-half; in the case of wet lands irrigated by baling water the usual deduction of one rupee an acre (Rs. 1–8–0 in the case of double-crop lands) was substituted for the old remission [2] which amounted to half the assessment; and such lands were, where necessary, reclassified; the general rule by which half a full rate is charged for water taken from a Government source of irrigation to raise a second wet crop on dry land replaced the old peculiar district rule which required the payment in such a case of a full rate.

The dry lands.

(2) *Dry lands.*—Here again the old settlement had been peculiar. Mr. Puckle made no such calculations of outturn and prices in regard to dry lands as had been made in the case of wet lands, and it became impossible, therefore, at the resettlement to work out percentage variations of price in the usual manner. The average prices of grains had, however, greatly increased, and it was decided by Government that, as in the case of the wet lands, an enhancement of the old rates, calculated to yield a percentage increase of 12½ per cent, should be

[1] For a special concession to some single-crop wet lands falling in the third "primary taram" in the Nānguneri and Srīvilliputtūr taluks, see G.Os. No. 2753, Rev., dated 19th August 1910, and No. 785, Rev., dated 18th March 1911.

[2] A rule introduced in 1852. Till then "baling-wet" lands had paid full rates.

CHAP. XI. THE RE-SETTLEMENT.

made. The rates in the three lowest tarams were not disturbed. The following table[1] was sanctioned :—

Settlement.							Resettlement.	
RS.	A.						RS.	A.
5	0	...	...	...	...	...	5	10
3	8	...	...	...	...	...	3	15
2	8	...	...	...	...	...	2	13
1	8	...	...	...	...	...	1	11
1	0	...	...	...	...	...	1	2
0	12	...	...	...	...	...	0	13
0	8	...	...	...	...	...	0	9
0	6	...	...	...	...	...	0	6
0	4	...	...	...	...	...	0	4
0	3	...	...	...	...	...	0	3

PALMYRAS.

(3) *Palmyras.*—A résumé of the literature dealing with taxes levied on trees, and in particular the palmyra, in this district would of itself fill a fair-sized volume. The subject has been admirably summed up in Mr. Chadwick's report on the subject, printed with G.O. No. 304, dated 31st January 1908; and the account which follows is only a brief abstract of that paper.

Early history.

From the days of the Nawāb, and probably from a much earlier period, all palmyras had been assessed separately from the land, and the Government had full right to the timber of the trees.[2] Under the Nawāb these trees were leased out over large tracts for a lump sum to the "head inhabitants," who were left to collect the amounts from the "inferior ryots." Mr. Lushington had the palmyras counted, classed and assessed at so much a hundred, and there seems little reason to doubt that many of the curious rates which at the time of the recent resettlement were still found existing in various villages actually dated from those early times. The "palmyra tax" formed from the beginning of the Company's rule an important item of the revenue (they were classed as "ready money collections") contributing over a lakh of rupees annually. Besides the palmyra, 38 kinds of trees enjoyed the dignity of taxation and brought in a further revenue of about Rs. 27,000.

[1] The first two resettlement rates were not used. The corresponding settlement rates, which were in reality special rates, had been applied to the *olappāri* lands, and were abolished in 1883 (See p. 294 and foot-note on p. 288).

[2] Palmyras (and other "taxable" trees), which at the present day are exempt from assessment on the ground that they stand within the limits of house "compounds," may perhaps have been even then an exception. It has been thought, however, that this exemption developed itself, if it did not originate, during the ill-administered period of the decennial lease.

CHAP. XI. PALMYRAS.

Mr. Puckle's reforms.

From 1843 onwards the subject of the Tinnevelly tree tax was continually before Government, but no change was made in the old system. Mr. Puckle was the first to take the matter seriously in hand. He divided palmyras, for revenue purposes, into two classes: (i) *sāsvatham* and (ii) "other item" trees.

Sāsvatham trees.

Palmyras belonging to the owner of a survey field in which there were not also trees belonging to other persons were declared to be *sāsvatham*, and in respect of these the land-owner was given complete ownership on payment of a tax in addition to the land assessment. This tax, which was based on the figures recorded in the existing accounts, was consolidated in the land patta with the land assessment and was unalterable during the currency of the settlement; the pattadar might cut and sell his trees or plant new ones without incurring any further charge. In this way Government parted with its right to the timber of nearly six million trees, including seedlings.

"Other item" trees.

"Other item" trees included all trees for which separate pattas were issued, viz., (1) trees which stood on patta land and would have been *sāsvatham* but for the fact that one or more persons other than the land pattadar also possessed trees on the same survey-field; (2) trees standing on patta land and enjoyed not by the land pattadar but by some one else; (3) trees standing on poramboke land and enjoyed by a ryot who had a tree patta for them; and (4) trees which were similarly held on patta and stood on unoccupied assessed land. All these four kinds of "other item" trees were at the settlement divided in the accounts into five "botanical" classes: *paruvam*, a female tree which has been tapped; *kāy*, a female tree which has not been tapped but bears fruit; *kattu*, a male tree which has been tapped; *ōlaivettu*, a tree of either sex which has hitherto served no purpose but to provide leaves; *vadali*, a young tree not more than six feet high. In all these "other item" trees Government continued to have the full right to the timber, and anyone who cut a tree without permission was liable to a penalty. Before settlement the taxes imposed on palmyras had varied according to the sex, age and usefulness of the trees; the rates were innumerable and varied from village to village. Mr. Puckle fixed a uniform scale for "other item" trees of each of his first four "botanical" classes: for a *paruvam* one anna; *kāy* and *kattu*, six pies; *ōlaivettu*, three pies; for *vadalis* no pattas were issued and consequently no charge was made. The number of trees for which "other item" pattas were issued at the settlement was about six millions. In regard to these

CHAP. XI. PALMYRAS.

trees, the old system, by which they were re-classified and recounted periodically, was continued, and Government, as before, claimed the right to the timber.

After settlement.

Difficulties of all kinds, however, continued to beset the system. The periodical inspection of trees, a necessary feature of the scheme, was generally a farce; it was often impracticable, when "other item" trees in mixed holdings were "missing," to determine who was the pattadar responsible; and, if a penalty was to be imposed, there were numerous contradictory "rulings" as to what the right penalty was;[1] "other item" trees sometimes passed to the enjoyment of the land pattadar, and it was uncertain in such cases whether their new owner should not pay their value before he was to be allowed to enjoy them. Fortunately the tendency for the ownership of trees and land to become merged progressed so far during thirty years that at the resettlement the number of trees held on separate patta was about one-third of the number so held in Mr. Puckle's time.

At resettlement.

Many important changes were made at the resettlement. The old classification of trees according to age and sex was given up. All palmyras, whether on patta-lands, porambokes or assessed wastes, were counted and divided into two classes: (1) "smooth" trees; that is, those which had been prepared for tapping, the evidence of this fact being that the bark had been smoothed; and (2) "rough" trees; those which had not been so treated. *Vadalis* were ignored. The district was divided up into "groups" according to the general quality and value of the palmyras which each contained, and a uniform scale of rates (as shown in the table below) was imposed on all palmyras, on whatever kind of land they stood:—

Taluks.	Rate for	
	Smooth trees.	Rough trees.
(1)	(2)	(3)
	PIES.	PIES.
First group—33 villages in the "palmyra forest" of Tiruchendūr.	8	3
Second group—36 villages in Nānguněri, 56 villages in Srīvaikuntam, and 37 villages in Tiruchendūr.	6	3
Third group—Tenkāsi, Ambāsamudram, Tinnevelly, Kōilpatti, Sankaranainārkōil, 47 villages of Nānguněri, 16 villages of Srīvaikuntam.	4	2

[1] The theory gradually grew up that in certain circumstances the tree pattadar was entitled to a share with Government of the value of the timber. Zamindars and other "proprietors" still retain an exclusive right to the timber of all palmyras (whether on patta land or not) within their estates.

PALMYRAS.

In respect of all palmyras standing on patta lands Government waived their right to the timber. To meet the problem of "mixed holdings," that is, holdings in which there were trees held on patta by a person other than the land pattadar, it was decided that separate tree pattas for "other item" trees on occupied land should no longer be issued and that such trees, as well as any *sāsvatham* trees which might exist in a survey field, should be entered in the patta of the landowner only. The assessment fixed on all trees found at the resettlement to exist on patta lands was consolidated with the land assessment and declared unalterable during the currency of the settlement. Thus all "other item" palmyras standing on occupied land become *sāsvatham* trees, and the policy started by Mr. Puckle was driven to its logical conclusion.

In the case of trees standing on assessed waste land, pattas exhibiting a consolidated assessment both for the land and trees were, as a rule, issued to the tree pattadars; if the trees were confined to a portion of the assessed waste field, a subdivision was made, and, where tree holdings were intermixed, joint pattas were given. With regard to palmyras on poramboke lands, and on assessed waste lands which for some reason or other were not given on patta, Government retained their right to the timber; and for these trees alone the issue of tree pattas was continued. They are still re-counted every third year.

"Palmyra mediation."

In order to induce the ryots to effect by mutual arrangement a transfer of rights and to terminate the system of "mixed holdings," special officers were at the resettlement appointed to act as mediators under the supervision and guidance of the Settlement Officer. In regard to no less than two-and-a-quarter millions of trees, which stood on patta lands and had been held on "other item" patta, agreements between the pattadars of land and trees were by the exertions of these officers effected and recorded. As a rule the land pattadar bought the palmyras from the tree pattadars; in other cases the tree pattadar bought the land; in a few instances joint pattas were issued in the names of the pattadar of the land and the former pattadar of the trees; in some cases, with the land pattadar's consent, the portion of land containing the "other item" trees was subdivided off and assigned to the tree pattadar; sometimes the tree pattadar, after paying for the Government share of the timber, was allowed to cut and remove his trees; in fact, compromises of every kind were effected, with the object of securing a consummation, for which the ryots as a body were no less eager than the revenue officers. The result attained was perhaps the most remarkable achievement of the resettlement, and was largely due to the personal exertions and influence of Mr. Chadwick.

Other taxed trees.

From 1851 the only trees besides the palmyra which were taxed were the cocoanut, iluppai, tamarind and mango. Mr. Puckle remitted the charge for fruit-trees growing on patta land, except for such as were owned by others than the land pattadars. For these and for fruit-trees on poramboke lands and assessed wastes he fixed a scale of charges and issued "other item" pattas. At the resettlement pattas issued for fruit-trees standing on patta land were cancelled; for trees of these four kinds standing on poramboke and assessed waste land the old system of "other item" pattas was continued.

Conclusion of the resettlement.

In 1910, while the resettlement was still in progress, the two taluks of Sāttūr and Srīvilliputtūr were transferred to the newly-formed district of Rāmnād, and from that year their revenue history ceases to belong to Tinnevelly. At the same time the Ottapidāram taluk, after surrendering some villages on the south and undergoing a readjustment of its frontier on the north, became the modern taluk of Kōilpatti. The Srīvaikuntam taluk, enlarged on the north by the addition of a strip of country from Ottapidāram, was divided into the two existing taluks of Srīvaikuntam and Tiruchendūr. With the introduction of the new rates into the two taluks of Kōilpatti and Sankaranainārkōil in fasli 1321 (1911-12) the resettlement of the modern district was completed.

Its financial results.

The financial results of the resettlement (which is in force for thirty years) are summarized in the following table:—

Taluks.	Fasli in which the resettlement was introduced.	Percentage increase, due to application of new rates, on occupied lands and palmyras.				
		Wet lands.	Dry lands.	Palmyras.	Dry lands and Palmyras together.	Total.
(1)	(2)	(3)	(4)	(5)	(6)	(7)
Tenkāsi ...	1318	14·81	7·63	27·16	11·61	13·90
Ambāsamudram	1318	11·08	1·10	10·82	5·41	10·35
Tinnevelly ...	1318	12·24	3·35	12·6	5·65	11·28
Srīvaikuntam ...	1319	12·04	3·70	4·52	4·01	10·00
Tiruchendūr ...	1319	11·92	4·55	7·52	6·49	9·96
Nānguněri ...	1320	11·46	1·22	19·26	6·69	9·86
Sankaranainārkōil.	1321	12·99	9·05	62·55	9·73	11·10
Kōilpatti ...	1321	12·41	9·90	23·71	10·10	10·29
District Total ...	...	12·04	5·53	12·44	7·63	10·66

The total land revenue demand for the whole district (as revised in 1910) rose from Rs. 22,65,000 to Rs. 25,56,000.[1]

The special revenue staff. Through the agency of a special staff, which was first organised in 1906, the revenue registry underwent a thorough revision; the new registers, together with sketches also prepared by this staff, were put into the hands of the surveyors for their guidance, and every effort was made to ensure that, before the new accounts were furnished to the district revenue officers, the registry agreed as far as possible with enjoyment and that both agreed with the survey records. Important communal lands such as cart-tracks and main irrigation channels, many of which had been measured in with patta lands at the previous survey, were at the resurvey subtracted and registered as poramboke.

Fishery-pattas. The old fishery-pattas were continued, the settlement charge being enhanced by 12½ per cent.

INAMS. The preparation of a register in 1814 under the orders of Mr. Cotton represents the earliest methodical attempt to deal with the inams of the district. The Inam Settlement of 1863 and the following years proceeded on the basis of this account and of statements prepared at the successive jamabandis of later years. An account of the various kinds of inams then found in existence will be seen in the report of the Inam Commissioner, dated 27th February 1863, read in G.O. No. 1405, dated 28th July 1863.

Kinds of inam. The land inams are of the same kind as elsewhere and need no description.

The so-called *dittam* was a deduction of a fixed extent, and the *ivu* of a percentage, from the annual cultivation of the village, the proportionate revenue demand on which was paid over, in cash, to the inam-holder. Most of these inams were enjoyed by village servants.[2] The *pāttam* lands were wet lands which paid a low assessment in grain; the *poruppu* were lands, both wet and dry, which paid a low assessment in money in proportion to the extent of the actual cultivation of the village. Similar remissions were the *chaturbāgam*,[3] a deduction from the assessment allowed to the *panguvālis* or mirāsidārs, and the *mahājana shrōtriyam*, a similar, though smaller, allowance.

[1] The approximate cost of the resurvey and resettlement of all the taluks of the old Tinnevelly district was Rs. 18 lakhs. On the same area the increase of revenue amounted to Rs. 2,89,644, a percentage increase of 10·61. The resettlement closed in fasli 1322.

[2] See also p. 315.

[3] Most of these payments were resumed and credited to the village service cess fund—see p. 316.

CHAP. XI. INAMS.

According to tradition, these concessions were originally conferred by the Madura Nāyakkan rulers on the numerous Brahman settlers whom they introduced from the north. The *ardhamāniyam* paid half the full assessment; *kattukuthagai* lands were grants made subject to a fixed favourable assessment. The "whole inam" villages were 171 in number.

The Settlement of 1863.

All these inams were settled on the same principles as elsewhere. Inams paid by deduction from the village beriz, with the exception of those rare cases in which they were commuted into land inams, were not dealt with.

The extent and value of the land inams[1] settled by the Commissioner are shown in the following table :—

Object of inam.	Extent.	Assessment.	Quit-rent imposed.
	ACS.	RS.	RS.
1. Hindu religious institutions ...	133,428	2,60,763	39,398
2. Mosques, etc.	4,991	18,528	2,359
3. Churches	22	244	2
4. Charitable institutions	31,747	53,853	10,959
5. Personal	74,494	1,52,983	51,844
Total ...	244,682	4,86,371	1,04,562

Temple revenues.[2]

An important item of land revenue, which from the earliest times was collected and managed by Government officers, was that connected with the temples of the district. The fund[3] was derived from two main sources :—(i) the *dēvastānam*, consisting of *dastik* and of *māniyam* revenues; and (ii) the *tiruppani*. Under the old Hindu Government lands had been set apart for the support of a number of Hindu temples; and, fifty years before the assumption of the district by the English, the Nawāb took possession of these lands and substituted for the income derived from them an allowance in money. In Mr. Lushington's time (fasli 1211) this fund amounted to Rs. 1,79,691; the practice continued of deducting this amount annually from the land revenue collections and apportioning it amongst the temples. This was the *dastik* allowance.

[1] See note on p. 311.

[2] For assistance with this section I am indebted to M.R.Ry. Rai Sahib V. T. Krishnama Achari Avargal.

[3] This whole fund is often (incorrectly, it seems) referred to in the revenue records as the *dēvastānam* fund. The *dēvastānam* revenue, as will be seen, contributed the greater portion of the general temple fund.

CHAP. XI. INAMS.

The *māniyam* revenues, derived from lands the assessment due on which had been alienated in favour of temples, were also collected by the district officers and disbursed by them to the various institutions. An annual income of about Rs. 26,000 was derived from this source.

The *tiruppani,* which yielded a yearly income of about Rs. 21,000, was derived mainly from a payment known as *pōrpichai,* "alms from the heap," a deduction made from the gross produce of wet lands before the division was effected between the ryot and Government. A similar payment levied in the case of dry lands only and known as *khētwari* also contributed to the fund. The proceeds of *dēvastānam* and *tiruppani* were spent on the maintenance of 350 temples scattered throughout the district.

Besides these resources the temples held a large number of lands under the designation of *sarvamāniyam* and *kattukuthagai,* either free of assessment or on favourable tenures; many of the institutions also possessed ordinary ryotwari lands.

Their administration.

From the earliest times the control of the district authorities extended to all details connected with the temples, the collection of their revenues, the management of their lands, the regulation of their daily expenses and periodical festivals, the maintenance of their fabric—in fact, to every item of receipt and expenditure. At first the *tiruppani* was collected by Tahsildars and disbursed by them at pleasure; but from 1806 this fund, like all other branches of temple revenue, was paid into the treasury and entered in the district accounts. Of the temples thus managed by Government, the majority received support from the *dēvastānam* fund, a few had lands only, a few only *tiruppani;* others had combinations of two or more of these sources of revenue.

Withdrawal of Government from management.

About 1840 Government resolved to withdraw from the management of the temples, a decision which, it appears, was received with general dissatisfaction. According to the Collector's report, the people asserted that "the relinquishment of Government control would be speedily followed by the destruction of the institutions themselves." In 1841 the 350 temples then under Government management were divided into two classes, "village temples" and "district temples." The former were handed over to village committees; of the latter, which numbered nine[1] altogether, seven were handed over to trustees and two, the Nānguneri and Tirukkurungudi temples, to Jeers.

[1] This figure includes the temple of Srīvilliputtūr, now in the Rāmnād district.

CHAP. XI.
INAMS.

The question then arose as to what should be done with the temple lands and with the surplus lying in the Government treasury to the credit of the *dēvastānam* and *tiruppani*. In 1843 a lakh of rupees was spent from the *dēvastānam* fund on the construction of roads in the black-cotton country; and in 1845, under the orders of the Government of India, the Madras Government disposed of the remaining surplus funds by transferring them to the general education fund of the Presidency. The management of the lands belonging to the temple was handed over to their committees or trustees in 1849. The payment of the *dastik* allowances continued, the annual amount being fixed, in 1846, at Rs. 1,81,368. With regard to the *pōrpichai* and *khētwari* payments, which constituted the bulk of the *tiruppani,* some difficulty was felt. The payments were, in theory at least, of a purely voluntary character, and by compelling ryots to continue them Government placed itself, it seemed, in a false position. It was ultimately decided (in 1860) that the collection of these fees on the part of Government should cease entirely and that any trustees who were willing to do so might receive good cultivable waste land in compensation; otherwise they might themselves collect the old contributions from the ryots.

Creation of district committees, 1864.

In 1864 two district committees, one for Saivite and the other for Vaishnavite temples, were created; and, with the exception of the Nānguneri and Tirukkurungudi temples, which still continued under the control of their Jeers, those temples which until 1841 had been under Government management were handed over to the newly-formed bodies. The arrangement continues to the present day.

Commutation of *dastik* allowances.

About 1865 a suggestion was made that the *dastik* allowances should be converted into assignments of land revenue. The matter was left for consideration at the settlement of the district; little progress was made, however, and the matter continued under correspondence for years. Title-deeds conveying inams with a total annual revenue of about Rs. 14,000 had, by 1895, been issued in the place of *dastik* allowances; of these inams some were again commuted into *dastik* allowances, with the result that at the present day a very small fraction (less than 7 per cent) of the original *dastik* allowance is now enjoyed in the form of land revenue assignments.

Religious institutions and their funds at present.

At the present time two hundred and ninety-eight temples under the control of the two committees receive annual allowances which, inclusive of the revenue foregone on inam lands, amount to about Rs. 2,75,000; temples not so controlled are subsidized to the extent of Rs. 20,000. Mosques receive Rs. 11,000, and churches Rs. 200.

VILLAGE ESTABLISHMENTS. Old system.

In early times the remuneration of the various officials and artificers, who went to make up the "village establishments," was derived from payments in grain and cash contributed by the ryots and the Government alike and from the profits on lands held on favourable terms by office-holders. The post of karnam, or village-accountant, was, as a rule, restricted to certain families, the members of which held the office in turn. In 1807, when the old *yāvana* was abolished, a new fund called the "karnams' *marah*" was constituted from deductions made from general revenues, and karnams were paid from the funds so raised in their respective villages. In 1836 the payments made under the *marah* were constituted (for a time only it appears) into a general district fund, and a new establishment of karnams on fixed scales of pay was created in some villages. There still remained many villages in which karnams continued to enjoy also fees paid by ryots (known by the general name of *sittuvari*) and the proceeds of lands held free of assessment. Other important officials of the village were the headmen, variously known as the mirāsidārs or nāttamaikārans. Munsifs were comparatively few; sometimes the munsif was a mirāsidār, sometimes not. They were appointed on the nomination of the people by the magistrate and depended for their remuneration entirely on fees and inams.

Mr. Pelly's scheme.

In 1860 Mr. Pelly, a Member of the Board of Revenue, was placed on special duty to revise the village establishments and to systematise their payment. He proposed an establishment for the district which would cost about Rs. 1½ lakhs a year; but, taking into account fees in grain and cash then paid by Government and also the proceeds of inam lands, he could only point to assets amounting to about half the estimated cost. The scheme was accordingly dropped and the matter left for consideration at the forthcoming settlement of the district.

Mr. Puckle's revision.

Mr. Puckle sent up proposals for the various taluks from 1874 onwards, and during 1878 and 1879 the new establishments were introduced into all the taluks of the district. Under Act IV of 1864 (Madras) a village service cess at the rate of one anna in a rupee of assessment was imposed at the time of settlement, that is, from 1874 onwards. The village service land inams,[1] which, as well as all customary cash

[1] That is, inams registered under the headings, *mirāsi*, *nāttāmai*, karnam, *kāvalgār*, *nirganti*, *tōtti*.

CHAP. XI. VILLAGE ESTABLISHMENTS.

payments, had been investigated and recorded by the Inam Commission of 1863, were (between 1875 and 1885) enfranchised; the cash payments [1] were resumed, and these sums, added to the proceeds of the enfranchised inams and the amount realised as cess, constituted the new village service fund. The system was subsequently modified by Act IV of 1893 (Madras); and by Act IV of 1907 (India) the village service cess was finally abolished. The establishments created in 1878 have continued, subject to occasional local modifications, to the present time. Neither the office of karnam nor that of village munsif was considered hereditary until 1853, in which year orders were received that they should be so regarded.

ADMINISTRATIVE CHARGES. In early times.

Mr. S. R. Lushington, when appointed Collector of Tinnevelly in 1801, still retained charge of the pālaiyams of Sivaganga and Rāmnād. His Head Assistant, Mr. Parish, was in 1803 appointed Collector of the newly formed "Zilla of Rāmnād," which included also the zamindari of Sivaganga, the districts of Dindigul and Madura and also the zamindaris of Tinnevelly. In 1808 the district of Rāmnād was abolished, and the twenty-five Tinnevelly zamindaris (of the original 31 pālaiyams, three had been confiscated and sold, and three had been conferred on other zamindars) were incorporated in the Tinnevelly district.

Subsequent changes.

When the English first came into possession of Tinnevelly, the district was divided into 19 taluks. These were afterwards reduced to eleven; and the redistributions of areas subsequently made are shown in the following table:—

Old taluks.	1838.	1860.	Since 1910.
Nadumandalam ...	Sāttūr	...	Transferred to Rāmnād district.
	Srīvilliputtūr ...	...	
Sankaranainārkōil ...	Sankaranainār-kōil.	Sankaranainār-kōil.	Sankaranainār-kōil.
Alvārtirunagari	Ottapidāram [2] ...	Ottapidāram ...	Kōilpatti (1911). [3]

[1] The total value of these allowances amounted (in 1872) to Rs. 63,637. They consisted mainly of *ivu* and *dittam* allowances: karnams' salaries (the old *marāh*): *chaturbāgam* and *dupati maniyam*, remissions granted to mirāsidars.

[2] The new Ottapidāram taluk consisted of a portion of the Alvārtirunagari taluk, the rest being incorporated with Srīvaikuntam.

[3] In the formation of these two taluks, 10 ayan villages of the old Ottapidāram taluk, including Tuticorin, and eight mitta villages, were transferred to Srīvaikuntam; and the common frontier of the Ottapidāram and Sāttūr areas also underwent change.

CHAP. XI.
ADMINISTRATIVE CHARGES.

Old taluks.	1838.	1860.	Since 1910.
Srīvaikuntam	Srīvaikuntam ...	Tenkarai (name changed to Srīvaikuntam in 1893).	Srīvaikuntam. Tiruchendūr. (1911.)
Panchamahāl	Panchamahāl ...		
Kalakkād ...	Nānguneri ... Valliyūr ...	Nānguneri ...	Nānguneri.
Nellaiyambalam ...	Nellaiyam-balam.	Tinnevelly ...	Tinnevelly.
Vidugrāmam [1]	Vidugrāmam ...		
Tenkāsi	Tenkāsi	Tenkāsi ...	Tenkāsi.
Sērmādēvi	Sērmādēvi ...	Ambāsamud-ram.	Ambāsamudram.
Brahmadēsam	Brahmadēsam ...		

Present divisional charges.

The existing divisional charges are as follows:—The Srīvaikuntam and Tiruchendūr taluks, constituting the Tuticorin division, are under the charge of a Sub-Collector stationed at Tuticorin; a Sub-Collector at Tinnevelly is in charge of the Tinnevelly and Tenkāsi taluks, which form the Tinnevelly division; the Sērmādēvi division, comprising Ambāsamudram and Nānguneri, form the division of the Sub-Collector, Sērmādēvi; the Kōilpatti division, made up of the taluks of Kōilpatti and Sankaranainārkōil, is under a Deputy Collector, whose headquarters is at Kōilpatti.

Appended is a list of Collectors who have held charge of the district since 1790, the year of the "Assumption."

[1] Headquarters, Murappanād-Pudugrāmam, now included in the Srīvaikuntam taluk.

CHAP. XI.
APPENDIX.

APPENDIX.

List of Collectors.

Date of taking charge.			Names.
1 Sep.	1790	...	Benjamin Torin, "Collector of Poligar Peshkash."
	1792	...	J. Landon do.
17 July	1794	...	J. Powney do.
10 March	1797	...	W. C. Jackson do.
12 Jan.	1799	...	S. R. Lushington do.
8 Aug.	1801	...	Do. Collector.
12 Jan.	1803	...	George Parish, Acting Collector.
5 Nov.	1803	...	J. Cochrane, Collector.
14 May	1806	...	J. Hepburn, Collector.
16 Jan.	1807	...	J. Hanbury, Acting Collector.
21 March	1807	...	J. Hepburn, Collector.
18 June	1810	...	J. Hanbury, Acting Collector.
25 Oct.	1810	...	J. Hepburn, Collector.
15 Aug.	1812	...	J. G. Turnbull, In charge.
18 Aug.	1812	...	J. Hanbury, Acting Collector.
26 Dec.	1812	...	No records.
26 Jan.	1814	...	J. Cotton, Collector.
8 Jan.	1816	...	E. H. Woodcock, Acting Collector.
29 Feb.	1816	...	J. Cotton, Collector.
1 Nov.	1819	...	R. H. Young, Acting Collector.
15 Jan.	1820	...	Do. Collector.
9 May	1820	...	J. Thomas, In charge.
29 May	1820	...	J. B. Hudleston, Collector.
6 May	1823	...	E. Bannerman, In charge.
2 July	1823	...	J. A. Munro, Collector.
23 May	1827	...	No records.
7 June	1827	...	H. W. Kindersley, Collector.
Dec.	1827	...	No records.
26 Feb.	1828	...	G. D. Drury, Collector.
9 Feb.	1832	...	A. Mellor, In charge.
......			R. Eden, Collector.
19 March	1832	...	T. V. Stonehouse, Acting Collector.
17 July	1832	...	J. Blackburn, Acting Collector.
26 Sep.	1832	...	Do. Collector.
18 Dec.	1832	...	No records.
30 Jan.	1833	...	R. Eden, Collector.
Jan.	1834	...	J. Bishop, In charge.
19 Feb.	1834	...	J. C. Wroughton, Acting Collector.
19 Jan.	1835	...	No records.
4 March	1837	...	J. Bishop, In charge.
14 June	1837	...	R. Eden, Collector.
22 Sep.	1837	...	J. Bishop, In charge.
26 Oct.	1837	...	E. P. Thompson, Acting Collector.
17 July	1839	...	R. Eden, Collector up to 8th Nov. 1839.
......			C. J. Bird, In charge up to 5th March 1840.
5 March	1840	...	E. P. Thompson, Collector.
16 Nov.	1840	...	W. C. Ogilvie, Acting Collector.
26 Aug.	1841	...	Sir H. C. Montgomery, Collector.

List of Collectors—cont.

Date of taking charge.				Names.
13	Sep.	1842	...	E. B. Thomas, Acting Collector.
1	April	1843	...	Do. Collector.
19	June	1843	...	C. Whittingham, Acting Collector.
26	July	1843	...	E. B. Thomas, Collector.
13	Feb.	1846	...	F. B. Elton, Acting Collector, In charge.
17	April	1846	...	R. D. Parker, Acting Collector.
25	March	1847	...	F. B. Elton, Acting Collector.
22	Jan.	1848	...	E. B. Thomas, Collector.
13	Dec.	1848	...	C. Whittingham, In charge.
22	Dec.	1848	...	F. B. Elton, Acting Collector.
17	July	1849	...	C. Whittingham, In charge.
10	Aug.	1849	...	C. J. Bird, Acting Collector.
7	March	1851	...	Do. Collector.
22	Oct.	1855	...	No records.
19	Nov.	1855	...	J. Silver, Acting Collector.
12	Feb.	1856	...	Do. Collector.
24	Feb.	1858	...	D. Mayne, Acting Collector.
23	Nov.	1858	...	No records.
20	Dec.	1858	...	V. H. Levinge, Acting Collector.
4	Nov.	1859	...	J. Silver, Collector.
31	Jan.	1865	...	G. Banbury, Acting Collector.
30	June	1865	...	A. Wedderburn, Collector.
17	May	1866	...	A. Macgregor, In charge.
31	May	1866	...	R. K. Puckle, Collector.
6	Oct.	1868	...	J. B. Pennington, Acting Collector.
21	Oct.	1868	...	C. T. Longley, Acting Collector.
1	Oct.	1870	...	A. J. Stuart, Acting Collector.
5	Oct.	1870	...	J. R. Arbuthnot, Acting Collector.
16	Nov.	1870	...	R. K. Puckle, Collector.
28	Feb.	1874	...	W. A. Happell, Acting Collector.
7	March	1874	...	W. H. Comyn, Acting Collector.
1	June	1874	...	R. K. Puckle, Collector.
23	Nov.	1874	...	W. H. Comyn, Acting Collector.
5	Oct.	1875	...	W. A. Happell, Acting Collector.
	......			J. B. Pennington, Collector.
18	Oct.	1875	...	A. J. Stuart, Acting Collector.
14	Jan.	1876	...	W. H. Glenny, Acting Collector.
21	Feb.	1876	...	A. J. Stuart, Acting Collector.
25	May	1877	...	J. B. Pennington, Collector.
18	March	1880	...	A. L. Lister, Acting Collector.
18	June	1880	...	J. B. Pennington, Collector.
29	June	1883	...	A. J. B. Atkinson, Acting Collector.
26	May	1884	...	J. Lee-Warner, Collector.
28	April	1885	...	H. M. Winterbotham, Collector.
14	May	1886	...	S. H. Wynne, Acting Collector.
15	Nov.	1886	...	J. Lee-Warner, Collector.
12	Nov.	1887	...	C. F. Maccartie, Acting Collector.
3	May	1888	...	F. A. Nicholson, Acting Collector.
7	Dec.	1888	...	J. Thompson, Acting Collector.
13	July	1889	...	F. A. Nicholson, Acting Collector.
12	Oct.	1889	...	J. H. A. Tremenhere, Acting Collector.
6	Nov.	1890	...	F. A. Nicholson, Collector.

CHAP. XI.
APPENDIX.

List of Collectors—cont.

Date of taking charge.				Names.
28	May	1891	...	G. S. Forbes, Collector.
25	June	1894	...	Bannatyne Macleod, Acting Collector.
21	Dec.	1894	...	A. W. B. Higgens, Collector.
13	Nov.	1897	...	R. B. Clegg, Acting Collector.
23	May	1898	...	A. W. B. Higgens, Collector.
23	Nov.	1898	...	E. Scott, Acting Collector.
9	June	1899	...	J. P. Bedford, Acting Collector.
7	Dec.	1900	...	L. E. Buckley, Acting Collector. (Made permanent on 9th Nov. 1903.)
12	Sep.	1904	...	R. F. Austin, Acting Collector.
30	Sep.	1904	...	L. E. Buckley, Collector.
28	Oct.	1905	...	D. D. Murdoch, Collector.
17	May	1907	...	F. A. Coleridge, Acting Collector.
2	Dec.	1907	...	L. M. Wynch, Collector.
3	Dec.	1908	...	S. W. G. I. MacIver, Acting Collector.
9	March	1909	...	L. Davidson, Collector.
8	March	1910	...	R. W. D'E. Ashe, Acting Collector.
12	April	1910	...	L. Davidson, Collector.
2	Aug.	1910	...	R. W. D'E. Ashe, Acting Collector.
23	June	1911	...	H. F. W. Gillman, Collector.
7	Nov.	1911	...	W. Francis, Collector.
10	Sep.	1912	...	J. C. Molony, Acting Collector.
20	Sep.	1913	...	G. H. B. Jackson, Acting Collector.
13	March	1914	...	C. G. Todhunter, Collector.
11	June	1915	...	F. R. Hemingway, Acting Collector.

CHAPTER XII.

SALT, ABKARI AND MISCELLANEOUS REVENUE.

SALT—Factories—Trade—Duty—Manufacture—Fish-curing yards—Salt earth. ABKARI AND OPIUM—Arrack—Toddy—Tapping—Foreign liquor—Opium—Establishment—Former sources of extra revenues. SEA CUSTOMS. CHANKS AND PEARLS. INCOME-TAX—The old "moturfa." STAMPS.

CHAP. XII. SALT.[1]

THE Madras Salt Act (IV of 1889), which now regulates the administration of the salt revenue, provides for manufacture and sale on two systems, namely "excise" and "monopoly."

The system of a monopoly, introduced by Madras Regulation I of 1805, was the earliest attempt made by the British Government to regulate the manufacture and sale of salt, which till that date had merely been subject to the payment of inland duties, the Government collecting the revenue on the salt passing out of the sirkar villages, the duties leviable in the pālaiyams being left to poligars. When the pālaiyams were settled, the Government resumed the salt revenue, a proportionate allowance being made in the peshkash fixed for each estate. Under the monopoly system the occupants of the salt-pans continued to manufacture salt but were required to deliver to Government the salt they made, receiving back the value of a share of the produce commuted into money rates which were determined from time to time for each factory. This share was known as the *kudivāram*, the portion appropriated by Government being the *mēlvāram*. The system, it will be seen, was based on the analogy of the land revenue system, by which Government and the occupants were regarded as entitled to their respective shares of the produce.

As early as 1854 the substitution of an excise system for the monopoly was suggested; and in 1865 the whole question of the salt administration in Tinnevelly was examined by Mr. Clarke, who was deputed to the district by Government for the purpose. In 1871 (Madras Act VI) the excise system was introduced by law, and between 1882 and 1886 the old monopoly method was definitely replaced in this district by the excise system, which, with some modifications, has continued in force to the present day.

Factories.

At one time there were as many as twelve salt factories in the district; in 1839 the number was reduced to eight, and, in

[1] For assistance with the Salt and Abkāri sections I am indebted to Mr. F. W. Gooch, Assistant Commissioner, Salt department.

CHAP. XII. SALT.

the interests of Government supervision and the improvement of the quality of the supply, the tendency of the past many years has been to the concentration of manufacture in a few large centres. The salt factories at present working in the district are situated at four places along the coast—Tuticorin, Kāyalpatnam, Kulasēkharapatnam and Kūttanguli. In and around Tuticorin are four factories—Kārapād, Sivandākulam, Sivandākulam extension and Levingepuram; a "sub-factory" is situated at Arasadi, three miles north of the town. The Kāyalpatnam "group" similarly comprises four factories, that at Kulasēkharapatnam, 14 miles to the south, being treated as a "subordinate" of Kāyalpatnam. The Kūttanguli factory is small and unimportant, existing solely in the interests of local consumption. Indeed so slight is the interest in the manufacture and so weak the demand for salt that, in the opinion of those best qualified to judge, the factory is hardly likely to survive much longer. Of the factories above enumerated that at Arumuganēri in the Kāyalpatnam "group" is held on a lease which is subject to conditions not usually applicable to excise licenses. The terms, though designed to secure the introduction of improved methods of manufacture and a high standard of chemical purity in the salt produced, have so far proved ineffective.

Trade.

Tuticorin, the terminus of the railway, is the main centre of the salt trade of the district. At Kāyalpatnam the salt is shipped and carried round to Tuticorin by sea. Thence it travels inland, finding favour, equally with the salt produced at Tuticorin, in the Rāmnād, Madura and Coimbatore markets.

Great assistance[1] is afforded to the trade at Tuticorin by the railway siding which connects the two largest platforms of the factory with the main South Indian line. In fact so valuable has this arrangement proved that the salt manufacturers of the Kāyalpatnam "group" are anxious to overcome by similar means the difficulties of land transport presented by the 18 miles of heavy sand and swamp which separate their factories from Tuticorin. Already several miles of trolley-lines have been laid in Kāyalpatnam connecting the factories with one another and running thence down to the sea.

Duty.

The rate of excise, which for many years had stood at Rs. 2-8-0 a maund, was reduced in 1903 to Rs. 2, in 1905 to Rs. 1-8-0 and again, in 1907, to Re. 1, a rate which remained in force until the general enhancement to Rs. 1-4-0 which

[1] The export from Tuticorin of salt of inferior grades to the Straits Settlements, formerly a trade of considerable volume, has of late years declined, being unable to compete with the low prices accepted for the salt conveyed from Aden to Singapore as ship's ballast.

took place with effect from March 1916. Though during the past ten years there has been a slight but steady rise in the total amount of salt sold at the Tinnevelly factories, the alleviation of the duty appears not to have contributed in the smallest degree to this result.

Manufacture.

The period of manufacture in this district is from February to September. As elsewhere, the salt is produced by the solar evaporation of sea-brine in shallow beds laid in stiff clay. The brine is led in from the sea by channels, which usually run around the entire factory; brine wells, yielding often a much stronger product, are occasionally used to supplement the supply of the channels. The brine collected in the pits is raised by a lift into condensing beds and, after attaining the required density, is thence run off by gravitation into troughs of tough well-rammed clay, where crystallization takes place. The crystals are scraped up from the ground and carried off to a platform, where the heaps are left to dry. The efforts continually being made by the Salt department to secure improvement in the methods of manufacture appeal but little to the local manufacturers. Salt is bought at the factory by weight and retailed in the bazaars by the measure; consequently, what the manufacturers are most anxious to produce is a light and large-grained salt which will yield the greatest possible number of measures to the maund.

Fish-curing yards.

There are five fish-curing yards: at Vēmbār, Sippikulam, Punnaikāyal, Ovari and Idintakarai—all fishing villages. At each of these enclosures salt is issued at cost price and free of duty to fishermen who care to bring their fish to the yards and cure them there. It cannot, however, be said that the two-fold object of Government, the encouragement of the fish-curing industry and the promotion of improved methods of curing, has been attained in this district. The duty is a negligible amount, and as much fish is cured outside the yards as in them; the methods followed outside the yards are those sanctioned by custom and show no tendency to change. Some of the yards pay their cost of maintenance.

Salt earth.

Saline soils are common in the district, and at many points along the sea-coast salt forms spontaneously. Prosecutions for the use of contraband salt were at one time very numerous but are now very rarely called for. Most of the salt-earth tracts are at present under cultivation.

ABKARI AND OPIUM.

The principal sources of abkāri and opium revenue are (1) country spirits or arrack; (2) toddy, the fermented juice of the various palms; (3) foreign liquors and (4) opium and ganja.

Arrack.

In very early times the distilling of arrack was the profession of the caste of Iluvans. The "arrack farm" was leased

CHAP. XII. ABKARI AND OPIUM.

by Government to a renter, to whom the distillers in their turn paid a fixed monthly sum for the right to manufacture and sell the spirit. So late as 1866 it was computed that arrack was distilled in 3,642 places in the district; and that was after continued efforts had been made to reduce the number of stills and bring them under some sort of control. The farm often went unsold, and in such cases the Tahsildars (and, in the zamindaris, the zamindars) were required to settle with the distillers individually. The system by which the manufacture of spirits was concentrated in large distilleries, arrack being issued from them on payment of an excise duty, was introduced in 1878–79. In 1884 the privilege of sale was separated from that of manufacture, and the sale of the right to vend in shops the arrack obtained from the licensed distilleries was introduced. The supply of arrack for this district is at present derived from a distillery at Tachanallūr owned by M.R.Ry. T. Guruswāmi Nādār.

Toddy.

The revenue from toddy, the fermented juice of the various kinds of palms, was in early times managed in much the same way as the arrack revenue. The "farm" conveyed to the lessee the right to receive fixed payments from those who climbed trees and drew juice intended for consumption in a fermented state; if no offers were received, licenses were issued by the Tahsildars to the individual tappers. The system of licensing shops was the first change; the present system of selling toddy-shops in auction was first adopted in the municipal towns in 1888 and was gradually extended to the whole district during the eight years following. The plan of issuing at the same time licenses to tap specified or "marked" trees was introduced in 1895. In this district toddy is obtained almost exclusively from palmyras, a few cocoanut trees also being "marked" in the Tenkāsi and Tiruchendūr taluks. Toddy-drawers are invariably Shānāns; the shop-keepers, though usually also Shānāns, are recruited from all classes. The liquor is transported from the trees to the shop either by the tappers themselves or by Pallan and Paraiyan employees of the shop-keepers. By a fortunate provision of nature the yield of the palmyra is greatest when the days are hottest; and it is during that season that the toddy shops are most popular.

Tapping.

Palmyras are tapped also on an enormous scale for sweet juice; and, to prevent the fermentation which otherwise will follow in a few hours, the pot into which the juice is drawn from the tree is coated with lime. The difficulty of preventing the drawing of fermented toddy under the guise of tapping for sweet juice led, in 1900, to an attempt on the part of the

Abkāri department to separate into blocks as far as possible the trees required for each purpose and to issue, in addition to the ordinary toddy-tapping licenses, licenses to tap for sweet juice also. The scheme met with much opposition and was soon abandoned as a failure. Besides illicit tapping the admixture of sweet juice with toddy is an offence with which the abkāri officers have constantly to contend; even though the juice be drawn off from the unlicensed tree in a lime-coated pot, numerous devices are known to the Shānāns by which, with little risk of detection, they can make a colourable imitation of toddy out of a blend of sweet and fermented juice.

Foreign liquor.

"Foreign liquor" covers all liquors imported into British India and all liquor, made by European methods in the Presidency, which has paid excise according to the scale of import duties; it includes also beers, methylated and rectified spirits.

Opium.

Opium is supplied to the District treasury from the Government Opium factory, Ghazipur, and taluk treasuries receive supplies from the District treasury for sale to shop-keepers. Ganja and bhang are supplied from the store-houses at Santavāsal (North Arcot) and Santaravūr (Guntūr). The consumption of drugs in the district is small.

Establishment.

An Assistant Commissioner of Salt and Abkāri, stationed at Palamcotta, is in charge of this district and a part of Rāmnād; under him within the district are four Inspectors, at Tinnevelly, Tuticorin, Kāyalpatnam and Nānguneri.

Former sources of extra revenues.

In addition to salt and abkāri, the "extra sources of revenue" of the early years of the last century comprised the inland transit duties which were described comprehensively as *sayar*. The duties were levied, at nine places in the district, on cloths, betel-leaves, tobacco, arecanut, jaggery, chanks and a host of other articles, the right of collection being farmed annually to renters. The tax was abolished in 1844. The so-called "chayroot farm" (abolished in 1844) conveyed the right to dig up and appropriate the little shrub known as sāyavēr *(Oldenlandia umbellata)*, which grows wild all over the sandy tracts of the east of the district and yields a red dye. "Other farms" comprised "hill-rents" (which ceased in 1854), the lease of the right to search for "jewels, booties and precious metals dropped in public places" (abolished in 1843) and, occasionally, "the cat's eye farm," that is, the right to collect cat's-eye stones, a species of chalcedonic quartz.

SEA CUSTOMS.

Customs duties are levied at the three ports of Tuticorin, Kulasēkharapatnam and Kāyalpatnam. While in regard to the total value of its trade Tuticorin ranks second among the ports of the Presidency, both Madras and Cochin yield heavier customs duties; a partial explanation is no doubt the

CHAP. XII. CHANKS AND PEARLS.

fact that cotton, which at Tuticorin is the chief article of export, is exempt from export duty.[1]

The revenues derived from the chank and pearl fisheries are referred to in chapter VI.

INCOME-TAX.

Figures regarding income-tax will be found in appendix XIX of the second volume. More people pay income-tax in Tinnevelly than in any other district of the Presidency (Madras excepted); eighty in every hundred of the assessees pay on an income of Rs. 2,000 or less, and in no other district is the incidence per head amongst the tax-payers so light. Excluding Madras, only two districts, Rāmnād and Tanjore, yield a greater amount of tax.

Tuticorin with its rich trading community, where the incidence of taxation per head of the population is as high as Rs. 1-2-0, accounts for nearly one-third of the total amount of tax drawn from the district. The general incidence for the district as a whole is As. 1-6.

The old "moturfa."

Historically the ancestor of the modern income-tax is, in this district, to be found in the old "moturfa," one of the items classed in the early records under the general head of *swarnadāyam*, or "cash payments."

The moturfa, which was one of the most unpleasant legacies of the native governments, was designed to tap the profits of trades and professions from which no contributions were made directly to the exchequer. It was divided under two main heads, *ayan* and *dēsakāval*, the former comprising the taxes levied by the Sirkar on the inhabitants of its own villages, the latter having its origin in the irregular levies which in pre-British times the poligars had exacted from the sirkar villages. By a proclamation of 1799 the Government suppressed the *dēsakāval* claims which the poligars had long enforced and thereafter continued to collect the fees as a tax on its own behalf.[2] Within their own estates the poligars had similarly collected moturfa from their own people; and, though by Regulation XXV of 1802 this levy had been forbidden, the amount derived by poligars from these fees was actually included in the assets on which their permanent peshkash was calculated, and the zamindars, in consequence, continued to collect the fees. In 1848 the practice was definitely prohibited, and, by way of compensation, the zamindars were allowed a reduction in their peshkash. From that year moturfa in zamindari villages was collected by Government on its own behalf.

It was calculated in 1842 that, out of 1,298 Government villages in the district, 168 paid moturfa under both heads, *ayan*

[1] There was formerly such a duty; it was repealed in 1847.

[2] See pp. 273, 334. *Dēsakāval* fees were also levied on lands. See p. 289

INCOME-TAX.

and *dēsakāval,* 743 paid *ayan* only, 17 *dēsakāval* only and 370 villages were exempt from moturfa of any kind. Almost every trade and profession, and members of every class of the people, except Brahmans, paid a tax of some sort under this general head. The main item was the tax on looms, which ordinarily contributed nearly a half; next came the taxes on houses and shops. Writing in 1818, Mr. John Cotton reported that the tax was levied under 110 distinct heads and yielded rather more than half a lakh annually. The number of heads was subsequently condensed to 68, but in spite of that the average annual receipts, for fourteen years ending with 1840, rose to well over a lakh of rupees. "It is difficult, if not impossible," wrote Sir Henry Montgomery, the Collector, in 1842, "to define the moturfa tax of the Tinnevelly district. It varies in almost every village, both in objects and rates of taxation and is regulated, if that term can be applied to anything so irregular, nominally by local custom, but in reality, mainly by the arbitrary decree of the village accountant, the acknowledged expounder and interpreter of what that custom is. A tax on the loom of the weaver, on the shop of the petty-dealer, on the artisan, and on the labourer gaining his livelihood by unskilled labour—it is a poll-tax, a house-tax, a cattle-stall tax, and a caste tax. The beggar is taxed because he is a beggar, the widow is taxed because she is destitute, while the chuckler receives his putta, and pays for the enviable privilege of sharing with the wild beasts of the jungle, the carcass of the cattle, which die within the limits of his village."

Included in moturfa were a poll-tax on palmyra-climbers and on Pallans, a tax on mat-makers, on the owners of pack-bullocks, on members of the "right and left hand" castes; one man in Tuticorin paid a tax on the pots he used in selling butter-milk; another paid for the exclusive right of receiving the heads of the sheep sacrificed to Kāliamman. The variations were infinite. In 1843 a partial reform was effected by the limitation of the demand to a tax on looms, shops and houses; but it was not until the passing of the first Income-tax Act[1], in 1860, that the moturfa taxes were abolished.

STAMPS.

Stamps, both judicial and non-judicial, are sold in the same manner as elsewhere. In respect of the revenue realised under this head Tinnevelly comes eighth among the districts of the Presidency.

[1] Act XXXIX (India) of 1860; repealed in 1868. At the same time arrangements were made for the payment from general revenues of certain assignments, amounting to about Rs. 5,000 annually, which had been made from moturfa fees in favour of temples and chattrams.

CHAPTER XIII.

ADMINISTRATION OF JUSTICE.

FORMER COURTS. CIVIL JUSTICE—Litigation—Registration. CRIMINAL JUSTICE. POLICE—The *kudikāval*—The *dēsakāval*—The treaty of 1792—Arrangements of 1800—*Dēsakāval* abolished—Subsequent history of *kudikāval*—Beginnings of a police force—The *kāval* system fails—Suggested reform—Reconstitution of police ; its effect on the *kāval* system—The *kāval* system of to-day—Criminal castes—The Maravans—The Nānguněri Maravans—Special measures for the repression of Marava crime—Methods of crime—Cattle-lifting—The Kuravans—The Pallans, and others—The Idaiyans—The Oddans—Crime—Sedition and riots, 1908—Murder of Mr. Ashe—The existing police force—Additional police forces. JAILS. APPENDIX—List of Judges.

CHAP. XIII. FORMER COURTS.

IN pre-British times there were no courts of justice except such as were occasionally held by the local poligars. Torture, mutilation and execution by the most savage methods were amongst the means employed by these mock tribunals. One man who had had his hand cut off by a poligar for suspected theft came in to Mr. Lushington ten years later and asked permission to file a civil suit against his mutilator for damages. The suspicion of being implicated in the plots of an enemy entailed the most horrible consequences. "A circle of peons armed with spears formed the ring into which the poor creatures were brought, and they were speared to death, precisely in the same manner as they do with a wild hog when out a-hunting."

On the establishment in 1802 of Courts of Circuit, Tinnevelly came under the jurisdiction of the Rāmnād court, which was shortly afterwards transferred to Madura. The Collector of the district, assisted by a "Register," exercised the powers of a magistrate and criminal court of first instance until 1806. In that year a Zilla Court was established in Tinnevelly, and the powers of the magistrate were transferred to the Judge. In 1816 the Collector once again became magistrate. The Tinnevelly Zilla Court was abolished in 1822, its functions being transferred to a similar court at Madura. In 1827 an Auxiliary Court was established in Tinnevelly, presided over by a civilian judge, who was assisted by a sadr amin, and continued, in subordination to the Madura court, until the rehabilitation, in 1843, of the Tinnevelly district court under the title of "Civil and Sessions Court." By the Civil Courts

Act of 1873 this court received its present title of "District and Sessions Court." Appended to the chapter is a list of Judges who have presided over the Tinnevelly court since 1806. CHAP. XIII. FORMER COURTS.

CIVIL JUSTICE.

The authority of the District Court extends, as elsewhere, over the whole district.

In subordination to this court are two Sub-Judges, one at Tinnevelly and the other at Tuticorin.

There are six courts presided over by district munsifs, two at Tinnevelly and one at each of the following places: Ambāsamudram, Srīvaikuntam, Tuticorin and Kōilpatti. Besides these a temporary additional district munsif's court, with no original jurisdiction, was established in Palamcotta in 1913, and still continues.

The limits of jurisdiction of the sub-courts and of the courts of the district munsifs are as follows:—

Court.	Place.	Jurisdiction.
Sub-court ...	Kokkarakulam (in Palamcotta).	Tenkāsi, Tinnevelly, Ambāsamudram and Nāngunēri taluks.
Do. ...	Tuticorin	Srīvaikuntam, Tiruchendūr, Kōilpatti and Sankaranainārkōil taluks.
District Munsif's Court.	Kokkarakulam (in Palamcotta).	Tinnevelly taluk.
Do.	Kokkarakulam (Additional District Munsif's Court).	Nāngunēri taluk, Sērmādēvi firka of Ambāsamudram taluk and Karungulam firka of Srīvaikuntam taluk.
Do.	Ambāsamudram	The remaining portion of Ambāsamudram and the whole of Tenkāsi taluk.
Do.	Srīvaikuntam	The kasba firka of Srīvaikuntam and the whole of Tiruchendūr taluk.
Do.	Tuticorin	The remainder of Srīvaikuntam and the Ottapidāram and Vilāttikulam firkas of Kōilpatti taluk.
Do.	Kōilpatti	The remaining portion of Kōilpatti and the whole of Sankaranainārkōil taluk.

There are nineteen bench courts constituted under Act I of 1889.

With the exception of Tanjore, more suits have been filed in this district before the village munsifs than in any other district of the Presidency.

Next to Tanjore, Tinnevelly is the most litigious of the districts, contributing in a year as much as 6 per cent of the total number of suits and appeals filed within the Presidency. Litigation.

CHAP. XIII. CIVIL JUSTICE.

Registration.

The Registration of Assurances is under the superintendence of a District Registrar stationed at Palamcotta. There are thirty-four sub-registrars, of whom one is stationed at each of the taluk head-quarters, the remainder being distributed over all parts of the district.

CRIMINAL JUSTICE.

The criminal tribunals consist, in ascending scale, of the courts of village magistrates, sub-magistrates, the divisional magistrates and district magistrate, and the sessions court. In addition to these, special magistrates have been appointed, at Kadaiyanallūr and Surandai (Tenkāsi taluk), Vīravanallūr, Sērmādēvi and Kadaiyam (Ambāsamudram taluk), Perunkulam (Srīvaikuntam taluk), Alvārtirunagari (Tiruchendūr taluk), Kōilpatti and Kayattār (Kōilpatti taluk), Puliyankudi (Sankaranainārkōil taluk), and other places, for the trial of offences under special and local laws; and in Tuticorin, Ambāsamudram and Sivagiri benches of magistrates exist to deal with minor offences. For Tinnevelly and Palamcotta together a bench court has recently (1915) been constituted, which exercises either first or second class powers according to the status of the presiding magistrate of the day.

As will be seen from table XXXI of the appendix, village magistrates rarely exercise their powers. The class of sub-magistrates, on whom falls the bulk of the second and third class cases of the district, dates its creation from 1861. Eight such appointments were then made to relieve the tahsildars, who, assisted by peshkars and head gumastas, had till that time performed the functions of subordinate police magistrates. The tahsildar dropped the title, which he had hitherto borne, of " head of the police " and, when acting in his magisterial capacity, came to be known as the "taluk magistrate." Though invested as a rule with second class magisterial powers, tahsildars now seldom exercise them. There are at present thirteen sub-magistrates, one at the head-quarters of each of the eight taluks, and one at each of the following places:—Palamcotta, Rādhāpuram, Tuticorin, Sāttānkulam and Vilāttikulam. These last-named five sub-magistrates are also deputy tahsildars. The four Divisional Magistrates and the District Magistrate possess first-class powers, and appeals from the subordinate magistrates lie to them. The decisions of the first-class magistrates are appealable to the Sessions Court, which exercises over the whole district the same powers as elsewhere.

POLICE. The *kudikāval*.

The basis of the ancient police system of Tinnevelly was the *kudikāval*, or *stalakāval*, the "village watch." Dating perhaps from the time of the formation of the village community itself, it represents the simple and effective device of a self-contained group of inhabitants for protecting their lives and property from the aggression of hostile or jealous neighbours. Theft is the commonest and most dangerous form of crime in a primitive community; and, should a theft occur in the village, it was the duty of the *kudikāvalgār*, the people's watchman, to trace and recover the stolen property or, if he failed in this, to recompense the owner from his own resources. The office of *kāvalgār*, when we first find it, is generally hereditary, and the watchman is paid by contributions made at the time of harvest by all the villagers. Though primarily a servant of the villagers and responsible to them, his value is recognized by the Sirkar, a central authority, and in recognition of this fact he is often allowed to enjoy lands on favourable tenure.

The *dēsakaval*.

With the institution of the poligar system—popularly ascribed to Viswanātha Nāyakkan (A.D. 1559-1563)—the innocent and peaceful institution of *stalakāval* suffered a blow from which it never subsequently recovered. Whatever may have been the intentions of their founder (if indeed the poligar system may be attributed to the deliberate action of a central authority), there is no doubt that the poligars soon usurped most of the authority of the government to which they were nominally subject and terrorised the country to a degree which in these days it is scarcely possible to realise. The strongest engine of their power was an institution invented by them which came to be known as *dēsakāval*. The earliest enquiries as to its origin (made in 1797 by Mr. Lushington) went to show that the system originated in the early years of the eighteenth century, when anarchy had reached its highest pitch, and that, during the convulsions which followed, it had developed and extended its power. It is quite possible, however, that the institution was a good deal older than this and that, from having been in its origin harmless and possibly necessary, it had by the eighteenth century degenerated to a system of plunder and extortion, in which it was impossible to recognize its original purpose. The *dēsakāval* was maintained by the levy of fees from the inhabitants of villages, whether belonging to the poligars or the Sirkar, theoretically for the performance by the poligars or their nominees of those duties of watching which it was beyond the power of the village-watchers to execute. The high roads, the jungles, tracts of uninhabited country, the district borders—in all these places gangs of marauders might be found; and to deal with law-breakers of this kind the poligars instituted their

CHAP. XIII. POLICE.

special constabulary. Like so many institutions of its kind, the *dēsakāval* soon lost its good features and developed its worst. The collections were made by armed peons, and, when the demands were not quietly submitted to, "torture and the whip are applied, the whole village put into confinement, every occupation interdicted, the cattle pounded, the inhabitants taken captive to, and not unfrequently, murdered in the *Pollams* and in short every outrage and violence and cruelty committed until their purposes are obtained." The contributions consisted of fees, fixed in lump on a village, "the people suffering considerably if the village is declining in its tillage, or population, because it then becomes divided upon fewer persons than when the village was in a thriving condition." Fees were levied also on ploughs, looms, shops and labourers; the poligar had allotments of land in the sirkar villages, on which he received the government share or assessment, a claim which he had no difficulty in enforcing against his rival in extortion, the Sirkar's renter. The poligar's methods were ingenious. Discontented sirkar ryots were easy enough to find; and if they chose to fly from the renter to the poligar, as the latter encouraged them to do, the poligar would pose as the champion of the sirkar village in question and demand from the renter the recognition of his *madisum*, or self-imposed duty of protecting the village from any "breach of faith" on the part of the sirkar servants. If this were denied the poligar, the discontented villagers would be settled in the *pālaiyam*, or the village bodily annexed, and the renter would lose a year's revenue. The *madisum* was recognized, the renter's demands were modified, and the *dēsakāval* of the poligar was fortified. In the hands of men who exercised, within their pālaiyams at least, the powers of life and death, the *dēsakāval* was a weapon of incalculable savagery.

But the power of the poligars did not stop with *dēsakāval*. Not only had they seized and appropriated large extents of the sirkar lands, but, in more than three-quarters of the total number of villages remaining to the sirkar, the poligars had usurped the power of appointing and controlling even the *stalakāvalgārs* and receiving from them "russoms", or fees. The exercise of this power led to other exactions, "hunting batta," contributions to marriage parties, and numberless fees of all sorts and sizes.

The treaty of 1792.

The treaty of 1792 placed the poligars under the Company's authority; but, when it was realized that the poligars dominated the sirkar villages only in a slightly less degree than their own, differences naturally arose between the parties to the agreement as to interpretation of its terms. The difficulties of the situation were explained by Mr. Landon and by Mr. Powney who succeeded him. Was the *dēsakāval* right with its fees to be admitted? If so, who was to collect the fees from the sirkar villages, the Nawāb through his renter or the Company through its "Collector of Peshkash"? The Nawāb might collect the fees and pay the amount to the Company; but the poligars, the suppression of whose excesses was the main object of the Company's control, would still exercise their tyranny over the sirkar lands. A sum of nearly three lakhs of rupees—which was the estimated value of the poligars' usurpations in the sirkar lands—represented an extensive and dangerous authority. It was suggested that, as had already been done in Madura, Government should resume the *kāval* lands and itself pay the actual *kāvalgārs* from the produce of the lands. This might have been practicable had the produce of lands been the only source from which the poligars derived their payments; it might also have been possible to levy an additional revenue from the poligars and relieve them entirely of the duty of maintaining their establishments, had not the treaty of 1792 fixed the peshkash amounts. The fact was that, so long as the dual control of the Company and the Nawāb continued, it was impossible to effect any satisfactory police arrangements.

Arrangements of 1800.

Finally, in 1800, after the suppression of the great poligar rebellion of the previous year, an agreement was effected with the Nawāb, by which the poligars were prohibited from collecting from the sirkar villages either *dēsakāval* or *stalakāval* fees; the Company undertook to perform the duties for which these fees had been paid, and the Nawāb was to collect the fees and reimburse the Company for the loss they sustained by the surrender of them.

In regard to the *dēsakāval*, the situation, though still difficult, was improving; the position of the *stalakāvalgārs* was, if anything, worse. "The power of the cavel carrahs," [i.e., *dēsakāvalgārs*] wrote Mr. Lushington, "has been so completely humbled, that the tullam cavel carrahs have no longer any dread of them; and from their interference I have no apprehension of any serious obstruction to the well-ordering of the watching services; but there are other circumstances, which, if suffered to take their course, would place the provinces in a greater state of confusion and insecurity of property and life than it was in the plenitude of the poligar power. I refer to the injuries which the cavel carrahs no longer protected by or connected with the poligars receive from the circar servants

CHAP. XIII. POLICE.

by the withholding of their "russoms" and being made responsible for thefts which have never happened. Under the pressure of such injuries it is obvious that men who have arms in their hands, who are well acquainted with all the lurking-places in the country, whose line of duty favours nightly excursions and to whom the hereditary office of protector as well as their long connection with the Poligar has naturally given a spirit of enterprise and independence will plunder and rob rather than starve. To disarm them would not be effectual; for a large bamboo with a piece of iron stuck on the top of it is all-sufficient for the purposes of robbery and plunder." The problem was not solved until 1801, when the undivided sovereignty of the whole district came into the hands of the East India Company.

Dēsakāval abolished.

The *dēsakāval* was immediately abolished by proclamation; the fees levied on this account, to the value of Rs. 1,92,500, were resumed; and the poligars, now finally disarmed, were prohibited from receiving "watching fees" on this account and from performing any duties connected with the police of the country. At the same time Mr. Lushington accomplished his design of "restoring the tullum caval to the intention of its institution and the enjoyment of the fees and privileges justly due to that service to the executors of that duty." A few years later Mr. Hodgson, who had been sent on a commission of enquiry to the district, was able to report: "the security of persons which has followed from the assumption of the cawelly from the poligars, from the punishment of the rebellious and the transfer of the country to the authority of the Company can only be estimated by those who were witnesses of the previous scenes of insecurity, robbery, plunder and murder."

Subsequent history of *kudikāval*.

Suitable, however, as the *stalakāval* system may have been to an age when the necessity of self-protection made the isolated village strong and when the interference of a feeble central government was confined to the periodical exactions of its renters, it possessed in itself all the elements which, having been excited by the inroads of plundering poligars, were to defy for years to come the best efforts of a strong and persevering Government to regulate.

Beginnings of a police force.

By Madras Regulation XXXV of 1802 a police force was created, and a number of peons, roughly at the rate of one peon to ten villages, were appointed under a few *tānādārs*. The Collector was the Magistrate and Superintendent of Police, whilst tahsildars received in the first instance all criminal complaints. The *kāvalgār* still performed both revenue and police duties. It was his task to guard the growing

CHAP. XIII. POLICE.

crops from thefts and, after harvest, to protect the share of Government and of the ryots. He received payment from Government, sometimes in money, more often in the shape of rent-free land. At the same time he was the servant of the people themselves, receiving fees from them, guarding their property from theft and making restitution should a theft occur. In 1806 the powers of magistrate were transferred to the Judge; criminal complaints were forwarded to him, and the police establishment with its newly appointed "darogas," who replaced the tahsildars for a time, were placed under the Judge's direction. Confusion naturally ensued in regard to the position of *kāvalgārs*, the Collector claiming their services for revenue duties and the Judge for judicial duties. The situation improved in 1816, when the Collector once more became the magistrate and the immediate control of the subordinate police was retransferred to the tahsildars, as "heads of the police," the darogas being abolished.

The *kāval* system fails.

But a serious change had occurred in the status of the *kudikāvalgār*. Practically all the posts of *kāvalgār* were held by Maravans; and, belonging as they did to the caste which by inherited tradition professed the art of theft, they were of all people most likely to be skilful in tracing and recovering stolen property. The Madras Regulation XI of 1816 entirely upset the contractual basis on which the system depended for its success; the *kāvalgārs* were no longer to be held responsible for the value of property stolen within the limits of their charges, and the special qualifications of the Marava watchmen were thus set free to benefit themselves and to rob the very persons whose protectors they were designed to be. In spite of the Regulations, it was found necessary to enforce the liability of the *kāvalgār*, and, on one occasion at least (in 1816), a proclamation to this effect was issued by the magistrate. With a view to checking crime, some magistrates required all *kāvalgārs* and Maravans to pass muster daily before the village headman and to obtain passports to leave their villages. Failure to do this meant punishment with stripes or imprisonment. These methods continued, apparently, till about 1825, when they were discontinued "as inconsistent with the Regulations." Attempts were then made at taking security from Maravans; but, as other Maravans gave it and as all Maravans throughout the district seemed to be related to one another and as the terms of the bonds were seldom enforced, the practice proved useless.

Suggested reform.

As early as 1830 Mr. F. Hall, Joint Magistrate in charge of the district, anticipating a reform that was to be carried out

CHAP. XIII. POLICE.

forty years later, suggested the resumption of *kāval* fees and the establishment of a competent village police to be paid in fixed monthly sums from the proceeds. The heads of villages, who from the earliest times had never in Tinnevelly had any connection with the police, were under this scheme to be appointed "superintendents." The Board of Revenue was called upon by Government to compute the value of the *kāval* fees, and it suggested in reply that the pay of the *kāvalgārs* (admittedly most irregular) should be improved. The Government of India did not approve. It was found, on a computation made in 1855, that there were in the district about 9,000 *kāvalgārs*, whose total emoluments, consisting of grain, land and money, amounted to over a lakh of rupees. Of this sum, however, the greater part was contributed by the people themselves. Mr. Bird pointed out that it was no good attempting to reform the village watch, unless the establishment of village headmen and karnams were also put on a systematic basis; even if carried out, the reform would leave the zamindari villages untouched. "The kāval system of Tinnevelly," he concluded, "without being anything like perfect is suited to the genius of its inhabitants. It is the ancient Hindu plan and exists in a district where Hindu institutions have been little broken in upon by foreign conquerors."

Reconstitution of police; its effect on the *kāval* system.

Shortly after this the district police, which, as we have seen, had its humble beginnings in 1802, was entirely reconstituted. In 1861 Superintendents were appointed to relieve the District Magistrates of the police duties they had hitherto performed; and in 1862 the first Tinnevelly Superintendent of Police took charge. A feature of the new scheme was the organization of bodies of "village servants," with a view to their acting as a "village police" in co-operation with the district force. This step involved the entire reconstitution of the village establishments, but it was not till the time of Mr. Puckle's settlement that the reform was taken in hand. The cess which, under the provisions of Act IV of 1864, was to pay for these establishments was first imposed (in the Tenkāsi taluk) in 1873, and the appointment of the new "vettis" and "talaiyaris" (as the village policemen were called) proceeded from this year. The *kāvalgārs* were no longer required by Government; their inams were enfranchised, and their fees resumed. But the *kāvalgār* still remained, and the two services, known as *kudikāval* and *sirkār kāval*, the latter paid at a fixed rate of three or four rupees a month, existed side by side. The village police were poor creatures, "playing the hypocrite by day by being living protests against kāval, while they shared its profits in the night." They were, like the *kāvalgārs*, mostly Maravans, sometimes simply the old *kāvalgār* in a new disguise —"new vetti's but old kāvalgār writ large," it might often have been said; but the new men had the positive disadvantage of being in no sense the nominees of the villagers. To put down the old system, the Act declared that the payment of fees as "being due by custom" to *kāvalgārs* was illegal; but the fact was they were due by contract, sometimes written, and it seemed difficult to declare that such contracts were illegal.

CHAP. XIII. POLICE.

The results of the new system were alarming; in one year alone, 1878, the amount of property lost in robberies in the Ambāsamudram taluk amounted to over Rs. 15,000. If they were not always successful in detection, the old *kāvalgārs* were at least fairly good at prevention; the new village police could neither prevent nor detect. The impracticability of entirely suppressing the *kāval* system was at length recognized, and the policy laid down by Government in 1881 of ensuring that "active terrorism and exaction are punished" has, with increasing success, been followed to the present time.

The *kāval* system of to-day.[1]

Even as it stands to-day, however, the *kāval* system is responsible for most of the serious crime that occurs in the district. The introduction of railways and the consequent incursions of alien thieves have tended perhaps to make matters worse; and even the conscientious *kāvalgār* is no longer able to prevent or make good the losses incurred by thefts or to detect the offenders. The *kāvalgārs* therefore resort to crime to replace lost property, or make out in favour of the persons looted promissory notes, which are never redeemed; the villagers at last, disgusted with the worthlessness of the services rendered, dismiss their watchmen. Deprived of a living, the *kāvalgārs* at once prey on the community they hitherto pretended to protect, until the villagers are forced in self-defence to re-establish them in their posts.

An incident which illustrates the dangers which villagers run when they try to oust their *kāvalgārs* occurred in 1908 in Kāyalpatnam (Tiruchendūr taluk). The inhabitants of the village, all Muhammadans, decided in 1908 to get rid of their Marava watchmen owing to their inefficiency, and imported some Kambalatta Nāyakkans to supplant them. The Maravans objected, and assaulted the Nāyakkans; the Muhammadans interfered, and a riot ensued. Knives and guns came into play, and the police who interfered were forcibly disarmed. In 1899 an effort was made in Srīvaikuntam to put an end to the

[1] For most of what follows on the subject of *kāval* and criminal castes I am indebted to Mr. F. A. Hamilton, a former Superintendent of Police, Tinnevelly.

Marava *kāval*. The villagers themselves disagreed on the subject and, taking advantage of the tacit support of one of the parties, the Maravans called in their friends of the neighbourhood and descended on the village by night with torches, looted several houses and tortured some of the inmates. The *kāval* has been discontinued, but the Maravans are still resentful.

Generally speaking, however, the *kāvalgārs* have been continually extending their hold on the villages until, realising that safety lies in submission, the peace-loving ryot allows the Maravans to hold undisputed sway. The institution has at least the sanction of antiquity and has established itself firmly on a basis which is considered legal. The Maravan has set up his own courts for the trial of offences against the system, has introduced trial by ordeal for the discovery of persons suspected of crimes within his *kāval* limits, and exercises over all the castes a tyranny which is beyond belief.

It is in the Nānguneri taluk that the *kāval* organization is most complete. By the establishment of sub-*kāvalgārs*, who hold their villages at an annual rent payable to the head-quarter village from which they came, the Arupangunāttu Maravans [1]—who boast that they are the first immigrants of their caste—have taken the whole taluk into their grasp. The rent is payable in cash and varies from Rs. 20 to Rs. 80. The sums thus accumulated are devoted to a certain festival in the Nānguneri temple, the celebration of which rests with this sect of Maravans. It is not the case, however, that all *kāvals* are mischievous; in many villages the "watch" is conducted peacefully and efficiently. Recognizing its good features, the police have done their best to foster it and to purge it of its evil tendencies. Among the most successful *kāvals* are the few which are held by the Shānāns. The Shānāns, or "Panikkans" (as they style themselves), of Chidambarapuram (Nānguneri taluk) are the holders of a *kāval* which extends over the neighbouring villages of Kalakkād, Pattai, Kōilpatti, Nāngulam, Singampatti and Vijayarājapuram. According to a copper-plate in the possession of the head Panikkan, bearing the date *Saka* 1422 (A.D. 1500–01), the right was originally granted to the Shānāns of the place by Tirumēni Mālandan, who may have been the representative of the Travancore ruler at a time when he was in possession of a portion of the Tinnevelly district.[2] Four of these villages, the

[1] A purely local name borne by the Kondaiyankōttai Maravans of this taluk. The tradition is that the immigrant party consisted originally of six brothers, each of whom took a group of villages under his charge (*āru*, six, *pangu*, share).

[2] That the grantor was a representative of Travancore is only a conjecture. Can Mālandan be a form of Mārtānda?

kāval of which the Shānāns had allowed the Maravans to annex, have lately been restored to their rightful protectors by the intervention of the police. At Kuttam, again, in the Nānguneri taluk, and at Kadaiyam (Ambāsamudram taluk), the *kāval* is in the hands of Shānāns, or "Panikkans." Muhammadan *kāval* exists in a few places; more numerous are the Kambalatta Nāyakkan *kāvals*, found chiefly in the Ettaiyāpuram zamindari.

Criminal castes—The Maravans.

Amongst the criminal classes of the district the Maravan holds easily the first place. Belonging as he does to one of the tribes which formed the "fierce colleries" of Orme's history, he inherits the marauding instincts of his freebooting forefathers. It is during the stirring times of the eighteenth century that we first come upon any historical account of the Maravans as a fighting race; and it is doubtless to the centuries of anarchy of which that period was merely the closing scene that we may look for the experiences which have produced the modern Marava criminal, skilful in design, daring in execution and undaunted in defeat.

The Nānguneri Maravans.

According to one of the traditions of the castewhich) evidently forshortens past history) it was Kattaboma Nāyakkan of Pānjālankurichi who first gave the Maravans, in particular the Maravans of Nānguneri, their chances of distinction. That chieftain sent out a force against them and was at first successful; the Maravans, however, rallied and finally decimated the Nāyakkan force at Shenbagarāmanallūr (Nānguneri taluk). Thinking their friendship would be valuable, Kattaboma Nāyakkan offered terms and took the Maravans into alliance against the British. The tradition serves in a way to explain the fact that, at a time when all the Marava poligars, including even the reckless Pūli Tēvan of Nelkattanseval, were holding aloof from the last great poligar rebellion, we find Kattaboma Nāyakkan supported to the end by the Maravans from the south of the district. After the capture of the Pānjālankurichi poligars and the proscription of his chief agents, the "Dalavāy Pillai," and Sevattaiya Nāyakkan, every attempt to capture the outlaws was frustrated by the Maravans of Nānguneri. They were roaming the country in hordes, infesting the public roads, robbing travellers and looting the villages. Fifteen of the head *kāvalgārs* were transported, and seventy Marava bandits were placed in confinement at Kamudi. Before leaving the district Mr. Lushington released a large number and gave them settlements of land in the Rāmnād country and set them up with farm stock. Immediately sixty of them sold their cattle and returned to the Tinnevelly district, where they resumed their old habits. Sepoys and "sibbendy"

CHAP. XIII
POLICE.

peons were sent to round them up, but the Maravans escaped, either to Travancore or to the hills, which, wrote Mr. Parish, "they are in the habit of climbing with uncommon dexterity." After an exciting struggle the party was at last captured in the Kalakkād hills, and its members were transported. Then, as now, the Maravan, when captured and convicted, took his fate manfully. In 1804 two notorious marauders with an appalling record against them were brought up for execution. "The spectators assembled to witness the unhappy event were numerous, it being the day after the Tinnevelly feast. They seemed fully impressed with the justness of the sentence and many of them were even perceived to shed tears. The culprits behaved with becoming composure, adjusting the ropes that were to take away their lives about their own necks."

As early as 1798 Mr. Lushington had, owing to the "notorious profligacy and savageness of their character," deprived the Nānguněri Maravans of the *kāval* rights which they had usurped over the village of Nānguněri and its dependants and restored the privilege to its original possessors, the Shānāns. By 1816 the Maravans returned, ousted the Shānāns with great savagery and regained their stronghold. In 1880 it was computed that in the single village of Marukālkurichi (adjoining Nānguněri) there were as many as eighty Maravans maintaining themselves by plunder and theft alone. Dacoity was their main business, and their methods were highly organised. A band of fifty would move out from Marukālkurichi and, under cover of night, make for a village outside the taluk where the house of a rich man or of an enemy had been marked down. The gang was told off into parties, each with its duties to perform; and, while some terrified the villagers by raising yells, others kept them at bay by hurling stones in all directions, leaving free the storming-party armed with a bandy-axle to break in the door of the doomed house, the scene being lighted up by the flames of a cart or any material that came to hand. Once inside the house, they laid hold of jewels, vessels and cash. Torches carried by the dacoits or old cloths set on fire served as hand-lanterns. Were a hidden horde the object of the raid, an inmate of the house—usually a woman left unprotected by the menfolk—was caught and tortured till she revealed its resting place. A lighted wick placed between two tethered fingers or a torch applied to her nakedness, after she had been suspended by her feet from a beam, were ready persuaders. Then, armed with their booty, the raiders made off in the darkness.

Occurrences of this kind—torch-light-dacoities as they are called—are now comparatively rare. The absence of one Maravan from his village, much less fifty, is difficult in the presence of a police force more vigilant and perhaps less pliable than may have been the case a generation ago. It is only by trickery that the Maravan escapes surveillance, and the tactics which necessitated the holding of a village at bay are no longer possible.

Special measures for the repression of Marava crime.

The institution in 1901 of an additional police force at Marukālkurichi was the first determined effort in the long campaign of active police warfare which has been conducted against these turbulent Maravans of Nānguneri. At the same time similar forces were stationed at two other strategic points in the Marava country, Pūlam and Munnīrpallam. The forces have since been reduced; and their "punitive" character ceased in 1906, when the charges of their maintenance were placed on Government. Gangs whose common bond is *kāval* are being taken in turn and broken up; security is exacted from the more restless spirits, and every inducement is offered to the inhabitants themselves to assist the police in ridding the villages of their oppressors. The process is a long and difficult one, but there is evidence in recent years of distinctly increasing success.

Methods of crime.

Abandoning dacoity, the Maravan resorts, in modern times, to burglary as a safer and easier occupation. A regular ritual often precedes an expedition. Offerings are made to Sudalaimādan and Karuppan the night before; a crow-bar is placed before the image or *pūdam*, and a promise is made that further offerings will be made in proportion to the fruits of the outing. Omens are looked for anxiously during the ceremony and afterwards; the chirp of a lizard on the left, the hoot of an owl, a cat running across the path from left to right—these things foretell disaster, and the expedition must be postponed. Members of the party assume strange names; one is called "hatchet", another "knife", another "club", and the expedition is humourously referred to as "a hunt." Some carry stones in their waists and, when a hole has been bored in the house they are attacking, they drop one in to see if anyone is awake. If all seems well, the thinnest man—"knife" probably—struggles in, while the others await his signal to enter.

Another common method of house-breaking with the Maravan was till recently to bore a hole in the wall just near the bolt and then by inserting his hand to slip the bolt back. On his entrance into this district the Kuravan brought with

CHAP. XIII. POLICE.

him his special method, which the Maravan, considering superior, has not been slow to copy. A hole is bored in the door of the house just large enough to admit a finger, which then draws back the bolt. The Maravan, however, who has not yet attained the skill of the Kuravan, generally uses a larger and clumsier auger than his preceptor in crime. At the same time the Maravan has assimilated his taste in loot to the taste of the Kuravan. Silk cloths, jewels and cash are now what Maravans, like Kuravans, mostly fancy; and it is no longer possible to distinguish at sight the burglary of the Maravan from that of the Kuravan. In other directions too the Maravan has shown himself a careful student of crime and the methods of its detection. It has long been an axiom of police work that, if a hole in the wall of a house is larger on the inside than the outside, it may be inferred that the hole was made from the inside and, obviously, by the complainant himself. The Maravan has noted that cases have been treated as false on this ground and will, if he has time to stop, enlarge his hole from the inside of the house.

A pretty art developed by one member of this ingenious caste was that of catching fowls by means of a hook and bait.

Cattle-lifting.

As a cattle-lifter, the Maravan is an adept but in this department of crime has competitors—in the Paraiyan and the Lebbai. The Maravan takes his stolen cattle (except sheep which are stolen for food) to distant markets, in Travancore or in other taluks, and sells them. The Paraiyan, on the other hand, slays his cattle and the Lebbai trades in their skins. The Paraiyan and Lebbai consequently work together, and their dark conspiracies can, as a rule, be distinguished from the work of the Maravan.

The Kuravans.

Next to the Maravans, among criminal classes, but far below them in importance, come the Kuravans. Adept criminals and close students of police methods, they move about the country in gangs, committing burglaries and any kind of theft that opportunity offers. On the assumption that a part of a gang will be mistaken for the whole, the old men and women are sent about without concealment to divert the attention of the police, while the young stalwarts, taking close cover, depute themselves to conduct the serious business of the tribe. They are always armed with knives, which they do not hesitate to use in order to evade capture.

The Pallans, and others.

As dacoits, robbers and burglars, Pallans, who often ally themselves for the purpose with the Kambalattāns, contribute largely to the crime of the district. The Kambalattāns and

Kammavans of the black country are a hot-blooded people, and it is amongst them that riots, leading often to bloodshed and murder, most frequently occur. Disputes over land are often the cause, and the discovery of an intrigue on the part of one of their women with a member of another caste usually ends in disaster.

The Idaiyans. The Idaiyans, with whose womenfolk Maravans, it is said, often live on intimate terms, frequently associate themselves with Maravans in dacoities. Before the days of the railway from Tinnevelly to Tenkāsi gangs so constituted, hailing from near Alankulam, terrorized the neighbourhood and rendered the road to Kuttālam unsafe for travellers.

The Oddans. Oddans with their familiar trains of donkeys and pigs have from time to time appeared. Petty theft is their chief occupation; they dislike being watched and, sooner than endure it, they pass quietly out of the district.

Crime. In regard to burglaries and robberies, Tinnevelly, on a consideration of the figures of ten average years (1902–11), has the blackest record of any district in the Presidency. During that period burglaries averaged nearly 400 in a year, robberies ninety. Coimbatore and Nellore alone surpass Tinnevelly in dacoities; in respect of murders this district, with an annual average of 35, comes fourth among the districts, Coimbatore, Salem and Cuddapah (in this order) heading the list. Dacoities are common in the Ambāsamudram and Tuticorin circles, robberies and burglaries in Ambāsamudram, Kōilpatti, Srīvaikuntam and Tinnevelly. Speaking generally, crime occurs in the richest part of the district, the apparent exception being the position of Kōilpatti in regard to burglaries and robberies. This taluk borders on the Rāmnād district and is consequently exposed to the incursions of Kuravans who live immediately across the boundary. Nāngunēri and Sankaranainārkōil contain no fewer, and possibly more, criminals than any other circles, and their comparatively creditable place in the list of taluks is due to the fact that their burglars and robbers generally prefer to exploit more distant and richer territory. More than half the number of robberies, which contribute to give Tinnevelly so unenviable a position in the Presidency, is made up of cases in which women are attacked and stripped of the ornaments which they so often wear in heavy clusters in their ears.

Sedition and riots, 1908. A form of crime which made its first ugly appearance in the district a few years ago was sedition. In the beginning of the year 1908 several so-called "swadeshi lecturers" stumped the district, preaching veiled sedition under the guise of genuine "swadeshi" propaganda. Two of the most prominent orators, Chidambaram Pillai and Subramania Siva, delivered in Tuticorin a series of lectures, by means of which they contrived to cause extensive strikes in the mills of the place and to embitter local feeling most seriously. Europeans and some Indians were boycotted and openly insulted, and towards the end of February the situation became dangerous. Meetings were then prohibited, and proceedings were taken, in the interests of securing the peace, against the principal agitators and some of their local supporters. The two ring-leaders were subsequently prosecuted on charges of sedition and abetment, and after a protracted trial both were convicted and sentenced to long terms of imprisonment.

While the preliminary proceedings were being taken against these two agitators and the prosecution on the charge of sedition had not yet been begun, riots broke out simultaneously on the 13th March, 1908, in Tuticorin and in Tinnevelly. They were the immediate result of the inflammatory speeches and had been deliberately planned by a single body of conspirators. The hand of this organization was clearly visible in the methods followed by the rioters in Tinnevelly. The closing of the bazaars, invariably a symptom of serious disquiet in an Indian town, was carried out not spontaneously but by the forcible persuasions of a crowd set on for the purpose; the population as a whole was not greatly excited. A mob composed mainly of riff-raff and a number of boys and young men first formed in Vīrarāghavapuram, the locality generally known as "Tinnevelly Bridge," compelled the bazaarmen there to shut up their shops and moved on towards the town of Tinnevelly, smashing street-lamps, assaulting two Europeans and invading the Church Missionary Society's College on their way. Having reached the town, the rioters forced the shopmen to put up their shutters, destroying or looting the contents of their stalls in the event of refusal; they then entered the district munsif's court and made him close it, plundered and burnt the police-station, set fire to the municipal office and a municipal storehouse, burnt part of the post office and entered the hospital and broke up some of the furniture. The District Magistrate and Superintendent of Police, who had arrived in all haste with a party of reserve police, were repeatedly hemmed in and assaulted whilst attempting to make their way to the centre of the town; the mob was called upon to disperse, but to no purpose, and it became necessary to fire. The rioting was quickly suppressed. Fifty-three persons were arrested and charged, and most of them were convicted and sentenced to imprisonment. An additional police force was imposed on the town for six months.

The riot which occurred at Tuticorin on the same day was on a less extensive scale. Mr. Ashe, the Joint Magistrate, and the police were assaulted by a large and disorderly mob which they were endeavouring to disperse. The order was given to fire, and a few persons were shot. Thirty-six rioters were arrested and charged, and of these thirty-two were convicted. An additional police force of 100 men was quartered on the town for six months.

On the day following these two riots a disturbance occurred in Tachanallūr, a suburb of Tinnevelly. It was only an after-taste of the other outbreaks and confined itself to the limits of this little union town. Lamps were shattered by the mob, the union office was broken into, and some public property was burnt. A party of reserve police was despatched immediately from Tinnevelly; but the riot had subsided before their arrival. The inhabitants were punished by the imposition for six months of a force of additional police.

The seeds of sedition sown in the district in this year were not allowed to die down. It was not forgotten that four Hindus had been killed in the riot at Tinnevelly and that the two chief agitators had been convicted; and the completely erroneous belief still persisted that the failure of the "Swadeshi Steam Navigation Company," which Chidambaram Pillai had so freely used as a text for his seditious speeches, was the work of the British Government.

Murder of Mr. Ashe.

On the 7th June, 1911, Mr. R. W. D'E. Ashe, Collector of Tinnevelly, was murdered in the district at the Maniyāchi railway station. His assassin, a Brahman of Shencotta in Travancore, used an automatic revolver, and immediately afterwards shot himself dead with the same weapon. The investigation of the crime revealed the existence of a seditious conspiracy, initiated by a Tanjore Brahman, named Nīlakantam Ayyar, a young man of 21, with experience in journalism. As editor of a vernacular paper, the *Sūryōdhaya,* published in Pondicherry, he used the opportunity of disseminating seditious articles over the southern districts. In March, 1910, however, the paper was proscribed by Government; and Nīlakantam Ayyar and his supporters found it necessary to adopt other methods of spreading their propaganda. He visited Travancore, Coimbatore, and this district, to which, it appears, he was already no stranger. Meetings organized by him were held at Tuticorin, Tenkāsi and Shencotta, and on these occasions Nīlakantam expounded his views. Briefly stated, they were to the effect that the miserable state of the country and the injustice of Government made it necessary that the British should be driven out and *swarāj* obtained; previous endeavours to effect this object by means of preaching, pamphleteering and assassinations having failed, a new and drastic plan must be tried. The murder of a particular European was not an item in the programme of those recruited for the Tinnevelly district, but formed part of the scheme of the Travancore conspirators, of whom Vānchi Ayyar, the actual murderer, was a member. Fourteen persons were committed for trial before a Special Tribunal of the High Court on charges of abetment of murder and conspiracy; nine were convicted and sentenced to imprisonment for terms varying from one to seven years.

The existing police force. In 1862, as has been seen, a Superintendent of Police was appointed. The district force, which at that time consisted of two police amins (on Rs. 21 each), a "cutwal" (for Palamcotta town), fifteen "roysans," two duffadars, 253 peons, a drummer and one bugler, was shortly afterwards re-organized on the plan which, with some changes, has continued to the present day. The force is controlled by a Superintendent at Palamcotta, who is helped by two Assistant Superintendents, one at Tuticorin and the other at Kuttālam (Tenkāsi taluk). A Deputy Superintendent is usually stationed at the headquarters, in the capacity of Personal Assistant to the Superintendent. Inspectors are stationed in charge of "circles" at Tinnevelly, Ambāsamudram, Sankaranainārkōil, Kōilpatti, Tuticorin, Srīvaikuntam and Nānguneri, the charge of local stations being, as a rule, entrusted to Sub-Inspectors. Though competition for the post of constable is keen, the physique of the average Tinnevelly policeman is poor, and his standard of education is lower than is desirable. To a total force of constables numbering (reserve police included) over 1,300, Vellālans furnish twice as many men as any other community, Muhammadans coming next.

In addition to the usual "district reserve" (stationed at Palamcotta), "special forces," dating from 1908, exist at Palamcotta and Tuticorin. They are recruited to a large extent from Māppillas, largely ex-sepoys, and Hindu Malayālis of the West Coast, and attain an exceptionally high standard of physique and general efficiency.

Additional police forces.

Particulars of the additional police forces quartered in the district from time to time are summarized in the following table :—

PLACE.	PERIOD.
1. Kalugumalai ...	[1] February 1896 to February 1899.
2. Surandai	[2] 1899–1904.
3. Kōilpatti	
4. Marukālkurichi ...	[3] 1901–1906.
5. Pūlam	
6. Munnīrpallam ...	
7. Tinnevelly	[4] 1908 for six months.
8. Tachanallūr	
9. Tuticorin	

JAILS.

During the early years of British administration there was no regular district jail, and prisoners were accommodated within the fort at Palamcotta. A jail was subsequently provided in the town of Tinnevelly and was under the supervision of the District Judge, whose court, in 1810, exchanged places with the Collector's office and moved from the riverside at Kokkarakulam to the old building which still exists just south of the Tinnevelly temple. The new Auxiliary Court of 1827 was located in Kokkarakulam; and it was apparently before that date that the jail on the eastern wall of the fort (now used as the office of the deputy tahsildar and sub-magistrate, Palamcotta) was built.

The present jail, situated in Palamcotta, was begun in 1876, and took six years to complete. It contains accommodation for 437 prisoners, and its inmates turn out in a year work to the value of over Rs. 20,000. The articles manufactured include carpets, ropes, tape and coarse cloths.

There is a sub-jail at the headquarter station of each sub-magistrate, except at Palamcotta and Tinnevelly. At these two places the district jail serves the purpose.

[1] See p. 126.
[2] See p. 127.
[3] See p. 341.
[4] See p. 345.

CHAP. XIII. APPENDIX.

APPENDIX.[1]

List of Judges.

Date.			Name.
The Zilla Court was established in September 1806.			
14 May	1806	...	G. Stratton.
13 Feb.	1810	...	R. H. Young.
15 Jan.	1820	...	J. B. Hudleston.
19 May	1820	..	W. G. Monck.
On the 14th July, 1822, the Zilla Court of Tinnevelly was abolished, and the district came under the Zilla Court of Madura.			
	1822	...	W. O. Shakespear (Madura).
	1826	...	S. Nicholls (Madura).
In 1827 an Auxiliary Court was established in Tinnevelly.			
	1827	...	W. R. Taylor, Assistant Judge.
	1829	...	J. Horsley, do.
	1831	...	J. Horsley, do.
	1833	...	J. C. Scott, do.
	1834	...	G. Sparkes, Assistant Judge (Acting).
	1835	...	T. Prendergast, Assistant Judge.
	1839	.	J. Walker, do.
	1841	...	W. Dowdeswell, do.
	1843	...	D. R. Limond, Assistant Judge (Acting).
The Zilla Court was re-established in Tinnevelly on 16th May, 1843.			
...	1843	...	W. Douglas.
17 Jan.	1849	...	F. B. Elton.
13 Nov.	1849	...	Hatley Frere (Acting).
13 June	1851	...	Thomas Clarke (Acting).
2 March	1852		G. T. Beauchamp (Acting).
1 July	1852	...	G. T. Beauchamp.
26 Aug.	1856	..	V. H. Levinge (Acting).
17 Oct.	1856	...	V. H. Levinge (Acting).
19 Dec.	1856	...	E. Story.
30 Oct.	1857	...	A. Hatheway Acting).
30 Nov.	1857	...	R. G. Clarke (Acting).
9 June	1859	...	A. W. Phillips (Acting).
17 April	1860	...	W. Elliot.
15 Feb.	1861	...	J. H. Goldie.
22 July	1861	...	J. D. Goldinghan (Acting).
20 Sep.	1861	...	J. H. Goldie.
26 Feb.	1863	...	J. H. Blair (Acting).
8 Sep.	1863	...	W. Hodgson (Acting).
29 Aug.	1865	...	F. S. Child (Acting).
5 Sep.	1865	...	F. S. Child.
17 Dec.	1867	...	R. B. Swinton (Acting).
15 Aug.	1869	...	E. F. Webster (Acting).
1 Jan.	1871	...	F. S. Child.
1 Aug.	1871	...	W. T. Blair.
27 July	1871	...	F. C. Carr (Acting).
12 March	1872	...	F. C. Carr.

[1] This list was kindly compiled by Mr. H. Dodwell, Curator, Madras Record Office.

List of Judges—cont.

Date.			Name.
26 June	1874	..	W. H. Comyn (Acting).
23 Nov.	1874	...	F. C. Carr.
21 Aug.	1876	...	J. F. Snaith (Acting).

17th October, 1876, to 13th May, 1878, no records

13 May	1878	...	J. F. Snaith (Acting).
21 June	1881	...	E. Turner (Acting).
21 July	1881	...	J. F. Snaith (Acting)
25 Nov.	1881	...	H. C. Hughesdon.
21 April	1887	..	W. F. Grahame (Acting).
20 Aug.	1888	...	W. F. Grahame.
2 Feb.	1890	...	A. Thompson (Acting).
21 March	1890	...	W. F. Grahame.
14 Feb.	1892	...	T. M. Horsfall (Acting).
18 Aug.	1892	...	J. Hewetson (Acting).
11 Oct.	1892	..	T. M. Horsfall (Acting).
8 Feb.	1893	...	F. H. Hamnett (Acting).
9 March	1894	...	M. D. Bell (Acting).
22 Dec.	1894	...	B. Macleod (Acting).
25 Nov.	1895	...	H. T. Ross (Permanent).
22 June	1896	...	T. M. Swaminadha Ayyar (Acting)
11 July	1896	...	R. D. Broadfoot.
25 July	1898	...	K. C. Manavedan Raja.
22 Oct.	1898	...	J. W. F. Dumergue (Acting).
11 Oct.	1899	...	J. Hewetson.
16 Feb.	1903	...	W. W. Phillips (Acting).
7 March	1906	...	A. L. Vibert (Acting).
17 April	1906	...	H. Moberly.
10 July	1906	...	R. F. Austin (Acting).
3 Sep.	1906	...	C. G. Spencer (Acting).
1 Sep.	1908	...	A. C. Dutt.
2 Dec.	1908		E. H. Wallace (Acting).
25 Dec.	1908	...	A. C. Dutt.
8 March	1909	...	C. G. Spencer.
5 July	1910	...	K. Srinivasa Rao (Acting).
13 Dec.	1910	...	F. D. P. Oldfield.
6 Oct.	1912	...	D. G. Waller (Acting).
16 Sep.	1914	...	F. J. Richards (Acting).
16 Oct.	1914	...	D. G. Waller.

CHAPTER XIV.

LOCAL SELF-GOVERNMENT.

CHAP. XIV. THE LOCAL BOARDS.

THE administration of public affairs by local bodies dates in this district, as elsewhere, from the passing of the Local Fund Act of 1871. The district was divided into two circles, Tinnevelly and Sērmādēvi, for each of which a board was constituted. The Tinnevelly circle comprised the six taluks of Tinnevelly, Tenkarai (the modern Srīvaikuntam and Tiruchendūr), Ottapidāram (now Kōilpatti), Sankaranainārkōil and the two taluks transferred in 1910 to the new Rāmnād district, Sāttūr and Srīvilliputtūr. In the Sērmādēvi circle were included the three remaining taluks of Ambāsamudram, Nānguneri and Tenkāsi. The Collector was president of both the boards, the divisional officers at the headquarters of the two boards being vice-presidents; the members, non-official as well as official, were nominated.

District and taluk boards.

In 1884, when the next Local Boards Act was passed, the two boards were amalgamated and, in the following year, were constituted into a District Board, taluk boards being created in 1886.

Except for the areas controlled by the municipalities, the District Board has jurisdiction over the whole revenue district. It is composed of the Collector, as *ex-officio* President, and twenty-eight members, elected and nominated. One-half of the members are elected by the taluk boards, a power which these bodies have exercised since 1887. The jurisdiction of the taluk boards is conterminous with the revenue divisions. The divisional officer is in all cases the *ex-officio* president,[1] half the number of members being, as a rule, elected, and the rest nominated. The power of electing a vice-president was granted to the taluk boards in 1908, and the system of electing a proportion of members by popular vote was introduced in 1909.

Unions.

Provision for the formation of union panchayats was made in 1886. At the present day, there are 31 such bodies, the largest number to be found in any single district of the Presidency. With the exception of the Sērmādēvi panchayat,

[1] A non-official has since been appointed President of the Sērmādēvi Taluk Board.

to which three members are elected, both members and presidents are appointed by nomination.

Income.

The main sources of income for the district and taluk boards are the land cess and tolls; in the unions the house-tax, which in all cases is levied at the maximum rates, furnishes most of the revenue. In unions the incidence of taxation comes to As. 3–3 per head of the population; taxation for local boards involves a payment of As. 4–4 per head, a figure slightly above the Presidency average.

Objects of expenditure.

The only new work of first-rate importance carried out by the local boards since their creation is the construction, at a cost of a little over a lakh of rupees, of the bridge at Srīvaikuntam above the anicut. A large part of the cost was met by public contributions, money which had previously been subscribed for the anicut itself being diverted to the purpose. The work was begun in 1885 and closed in 1890. The chief objects of local fund expenditure are, as usual, hospitals, schools and roads, some details regarding which will be found in preceding chapters. The district possesses an unenviable reputation for its roads; and it is probable that in the way of travellers' bungalows few districts provide accommodation either so sparse or so poor. The taluk boards maintain five annual cattle-markets and 36 weekly markets, no less than eleven of which are found in the single taluk of Nānguneri. Under their management also are various endowments, whose united annual income amounts to nearly half a lakh of rupees. From these funds they maintain twenty chattrams, five Sanskrit schools, a few "water pandals" and the Tirukkurungudi dispensary. Other dispensaries also receive contributions from this fund. The subject of the railway, which for some years the District Board has been contemplating, is dealt with in chapter VII. Details of receipts and expenditure of the local boards will be found in table XXVII of the statistical volume.

THE MUNICIPALITIES.

The three towns of Tinnevelly, Palamcotta and Tuticorin were constituted municipalities on the 1st November 1866. Each council, as then formed, consisted of the Collector, who was President, the Public Works Engineer of the division in which the municipality was situated, and a few members, varying in number from five to nine. The Collector nominated a vice-president, who was usually the divisional officer. In addition to the duties ordinarily associated with a modern municipality, these early corporations had the charge also of the local police. The Towns Improvement Act of 1871 modified the constitution of the councils to some extent;

CHAP. XIV. THE MUNICIPALITIES.

but it was not until the District Municipalities Act of 1884 introduced a system of election both for chairman and members that the councils were in a position to become in any sense popular bodies. These privileges were conferred on the councils in the following year; and since then they have exercised them without interruption. Details of the income and expenditure of the municipal bodies will be found in table XXIV of the separate volume.

The Tinnevelly municipality.

The Tinnevelly council consists of an elected chairman and twenty-two members, seventeen of whom are elected. The municipality comprised originally the town of Tinnevelly only. In 1901 the two suburbs of Pēttai, two miles away, and Mēlavīrarāghavapuram—generally referred to now as "Tinnevelly Bridge"—were incorporated. Tinnevelly town lies between these two suburbs; and the area which the municipality has to administer is considerable. The town is cut off from its suburbs by long stretches of paddy fields, and the problem of relieving its ever increasing congestion is one of great difficulty. To reclaim paddy fields, even could it be done successfully, is too expensive a task for a municipality; and it is now felt that an extension of this kind, which has recently been put in hand in the direction of Kandiyāpēri, should give way to a scheme for the regulation of a number of spontaneous extensions which are at present in progress and, if they are to be brought under control, have yet to be included within the municipal limits. Examples are to be found along the Kuttālam road, north of the railway at Pēttai, and in the river-side villages.

Sanitary conditions.

Tinnevelly has no drainage system. A few drains are found here and there, some discharging into paddy fields or other low ground, others into the irrigation tanks and channels which are the chief sources of drinking water for the town. Cholera recurs almost every year, chiefly during the months of November and December, after the setting-in of the north-east monsoon; during 1906-07 the epidemic lasted throughout the year and was responsible for four hundred and fifty deaths.

Water-supply.

To avert the danger arising from such a water-supply, various schemes have from time to time been proposed. One of the last of these schemes was to dig wells in the bed of the Vēppankulam, a tank lying two miles to the north of the town; a flow of subterranean water was expected, and this was to be raised to a reservoir, from which a supply was to be carried to the town in closed pipes. The investigation began in 1903 and continued for seven years. The experiments made were, however, unsuccessful; and by 1910 a new joint scheme for the three municipalities of Tuticorin, Palamcotta and Tinnevelly was brought forward by Mr. W. Hutton, Sanitary Engineer to Government.

Joint scheme for the municipalities.

The proposal was to lay down a gallery in the bed of the Tāmbraparni two miles below the Marudūr anicut. From this gallery, which was intended to tap only the subsoil flow, water was to be pumped to a place of storage on the neighbouring Vallanād ridge and carried thence to Tuticorin, a distance of 18 miles, through a steel or iron pipe. A main distributary pipe was to be laid from the pumping station at the river to Palamcotta, 10 miles away, conveying a supply for that town and for Tinnevelly. Reservoirs were to be provided at Tuticorin and Palamcotta for the purpose of regulating local distribution. The cost of the combined scheme was estimated at Rs. 35 lakhs. After a good deal of discussion, it was finally decided (in 1914) that the cost of thus providing the three towns with water was prohibitive; and only so much of the project as was designed to supply Tuticorin was sanctioned.

Institutions.

The council makes grants-in-aid to thirty-two schools, and maintains from its own resources two elementary schools, one for Panchamas and the other for girls. The last-named, known as "Puckle's Caste Girls' School," is an endowed institution, which the municipality took under its management in 1910.

The municipality manages two dispensaries, in Pēttai and Mēlavīrarāghavapuram, and a hospital in Tinnevelly town. The "Pennington market", opened in 1879 at a cost of Rs. 15,000 and named after the Collector of that time, is situated in the heart of the town. The meat market is in the north end of the town. The old municipal office building was fired by the mob in the course of the riot of the 13th March 1908 and severely damaged; all its records were destroyed. The new "Pentland Buildings" which now form the office were opened by His Excellency the Governor in 1914.

The Palamcotta municipality.

The municipality of Palamcotta covers, like Tinnevelly, an extensive area, and is composed of the town itself and a number of detached villages, between which large rural tracts intervene. The inclusion with Palamcotta of the outlying suburbs of Vannārpet, Kokkarakulam and Kīlavīrarāghavapuram, of Mēlappālaiyam some two miles to the south of the town, and of Kulavānikkapuram, a mile down the Nānguneri road, dates from the year 1902. The council is composed of an elected chairman and sixteen members, twelve of whom are elected.

CHAP. XIV.
THE MUNICIPALITIES.

Objects of expenditure.

As elsewhere, the chief objects of expenditure are roads, drains, education, hospitals and ordinary conservancy. The chief permanent improvement carried out has been the market built in 1869–70 at a cost of Rs. 5,540, to which numerous structural additions have subsequently been made. The market is assembled on Thursdays, when it is crowded with buyers and sellers of food-stuffs of all kinds, grains, vegetables, fish, mats and baskets made from the palmyra, cloths, and articles of all kinds. The Palamcotta hospital, now maintained by the municipality, is older than that body and is referred to on page 261. There is also a dispensary at Mēlappālaiyam. The council maintains three elementary schools, one of which is for girls, and also makes grants-in-aid to eighteen schools.

Water-supply.

The problem of a water-supply for the town has for many years exercised the minds of the authorities. In the suburbs near the river a fair supply is ready to hand, and in the region of the cantonment there are many public wells. The water is not, however, much appreciated by the people; it is considered hard and often turns brackish, and in the dry months many of the wells fail completely. The result is that the people of the town practically depend on the water of the Pālaiyan irrigation canal, which skirts the western side of the most populous quarter. The channel irrigates several thousands of acres of heavily-manured rice-fields; it receives the drainage of some thirty villages and, finally, of Mēlappālaiyam and Palamcotta; the banks and, so far as the water permits, the bed of the channel are polluted daily by hundreds; people bathe in the stream and wash animals and dirty clothes in it. As drinking-water, however, the channel-supply is preferred to anything else, and it is not surprising to find that, immediately the heavy freshes of November come down the river, cholera breaks out with almost mechanical regularity.

Improvements of a minor kind to existing wells and the sinking of new ones have been suggested, but the proposals were some years ago given up in favour of a scheme of some sort by which water should be brought from the Tāmbraparni. A scheme of this kind, estimated to cost Rs. 5 lakhs, was definitely formulated in 1909 and submitted to Government. It was in the next year that the joint scheme referred to above under Tinnevelly was brought forward; and, now that this scheme has been found impracticable, the problem of water-supply remains for the present unsolved.

The Tuticorin municipality.

The Tuticorin council is composed of an elected chairman and sixteen members, of whom the rate-payers elect ten.

CHAP. XIV. THE MUNICIPALITIES.

Objects of expenditure.

It maintains a hospital and three schools, one of which is for girls. Unfortunately for the municipality, all the markets of the place, of which there are three, are in private hands. Unlike the two other municipal towns, Tuticorin covers a very small area, the urban portion of the municipality covering less than a square mile and possessing less than twenty miles of metalled road. The extreme congestion of the place, which possesses a population of 40,185, can therefore be imagined; and no effective measures have hitherto been taken to relieve it.

Water-supply.

The problem of water-supply in Tuticorin is probably as old as the town itself. Even the theory that the town derives its name, *Turttu-kudi*, "the place where (the wells) dry up," from the scarcity of water which from the first beset it, possesses a respectable antiquity; it was certainly current in the days of the Dutch occupation. As long ago as the beginning of the last century women used to make a living by hawking water at a "duttu" (four pies) a pot [1]; and even to the present day, in spite of all that has been done to improve matters, the dry months of April and May are generally a time of great discomfort. The wells either dry up or become intolerably brackish, the supply in the reservoir runs perilously low, and those who can afford to do so import their drinking water from Colombo.

The first serious attempt to face the problem appears to have been made in 1846. Undertaken, it appears, like most enterprises of the time, on the advice of Captain Horsley, the experiment, which aimed at finding artesian springs, was conducted by some European merchants of the place in a private compound.[2] At a depth of twenty feet a whitish clay was met with, below this a foot of blue clay and sand and then four feet of the same substance with the addition of gravel and petrified shells. Coral rock was found at 25 feet and at 31 feet a change in the water, which hitherto had been salt, was observed. The boring continued to 42 feet; and here the experiment ceased, because, the record states, the owner of the compound (a Mr. Mather) suddenly left Tuticorin. It was the belief of the experimenters that fresh water existed at the depth reached, "sufficient to supply the port and shipping," the only necessary precaution being to construct a well to this depth in such a way as to keep out the salt water. The abandonment of the experiment, especially for the very inadequate reason adduced, seems at first sight to have been

[1] "Survey Account" of 1823.

[2] It has not been possible to identify the scene of this experiment.

CHAP. XIV. THE MUNICIPALITIES.

unfortunate. It appears, however, that the expectations then formed were unjustified; for a few years later, between 1849 and 1851, similar borings which were undertaken in the town proved a failure, owing to the percolation of salt water. For many years longer Tuticorin had to be content with its brackish and precarious wells and the supplies imported from beyond Mēlūr.

One of the features of the Srīvaikuntam anicut scheme (p. 173) was the supply to Tuticorin of drinking-water from the Kōrampallam tank, the last tank benefited by the new irrigation system; and in 1874 the town received its first supply from that source. An open channel, five miles long, led the water to an open masonry reservoir on the outskirts of the town; thence by means of small conduits and pipes the water was laid on to a number of wells in the town. The Kōrampallam tank had its duties also as an irrigation source, and during the dry weather the town got nothing. To remedy this difficulty, a cross-bund was constructed, and a part of the tank was set apart to serve as a reservoir; at the same time, in order to save the loss due to percolation, a closed masonry conduit was substituted for the open channel. These improvements were completed in 1905, and cost just over a lakh of rupees.

A proposal was subsequently made to filter the water when it reached Tuticorin and to distribute it by means of pipes and fountains. A scheme which was to cost nearly Rs. 2 lakhs was actually drawn up; but, before it was sanctioned, it was found that, owing to the sandy nature of the soil, the leakage in the reservoir at Kōrampallam was enormous and the storage consequently insufficient. The remedy suggested was to raise the bunds of the reservoir; but, in view of the interference caused to the irrigation, the expense of buying out vested rights and, finally, the comparatively impure nature of the supply, all attempts to improve the existing system were finally abandoned in favour of the scheme of a joint water-supply referred to above.[1] As stated there, the scheme, so far as it relates to Tuticorin, has been sanctioned; its estimated cost is Rs. 18¼ lakhs. Government have promised to contribute half the amount and to advance the remainder on loan to the municipality.

[1] pp. 352-53.

CHAPTER XV.

GAZETTEER.

AMBASAMUDRAM TALUK.

CHAP. XV.
AMBASAMUDRAM TALUK.

AMBASAMUDRAM is the most mountainous of all the taluks; one-half of its entire area is composed of ghat forests (Government and zamindari together), and of the Government land forests account for one-third. The Tāmbraparni and many of its most important affluents take their rise in these hills; and the sharp contrast, so common in this district, between the rich green irrigated paddy lands and the dull brown dry fields is nowhere so clearly to be seen as from any point of the hills enclosing this taluk. Of the total area usually cultivated one-fourth is under irrigation from the Tāmbraparni and its tributaries; besides this are 4,613 acres divided up into 256 minute patches, each watered by a tank dependent on rain for its supply. In and around Sērmādēvi and Ambāsamudram are to be found the most fertile wet lands of the district, the best of which (at the present exchange value of paddy) fetch for their owners an annual net rental of Rs. 150 an acre. Agricultural profits have provided the capital (mostly owned by Brahmans) which

CHAP. XV. AMBASAMUDRAM TALUK.

supports the prosperous banking and weaving concerns of the taluk; the concentration of wealth is indicated by the fact that nearly one-half of the entire population is contained in seven river-valley villages.

Apart from the woven cloths, in which quantity is studied rather than quality, the most notable industrial product consists of the mats made at Pattamadai. Large quantities of paddy are sent to the Nāngūnēri taluk and to the great exchange market of Pēttai. There are six weekly markets, two of which (at Sērmādēvi and Kallidaikurichi) are the property of the taluk board. The private market at Ambāsamudram is an important centre of cattle trade. Metalled roads are plentiful, and the South Indian Railway traverses the taluk from east to west. The best known temples are those at Pāpanāsam, Tiruppudaimarudūr, Brahmadēsam, Sērmādēvi (Baktapriyar); and, in another class, the Sorimuthayyan (Sāstā) temple in the forests of the Singampatti zamindari. The taluk contains seven out of the thirty-one unions of the district:—Kadaiyam, Ambāsamudram, Kallidaikurichi, Vīravanallūr, Sērmādēvi, Pattamadai and Mēlasevval. Burial urns have been found at Ṣērmādēvi, but no traces of any are at present visible on the surface.

Ambāsamudram: forming with Urkād a union (population 14,207), is the headquarters of the taluk and, besides the tahsildar's office, contains a local fund hospital, a travellers' bungalow, a high school, the offices of a sub-magistrate, sub-registrar and a police inspector, and a district munsif's court. The chief industries are weaving, in which large numbers of Kaikkilaiyans and a few Iluvans are engaged, and stone-cutting, the work of Kammālans. Exceptionally fine granite is obtained in the neighbourhood, and a large number of massive columns ready carved are exported to Rāmēsvaram at the expense of the Nāttukōttai Chettis. An important market is held in the place every Saturday.

The Erichā-udaiyār temple, situated near the river half a mile away from the town, contains two *vatteluttu* inscriptions of Māranjadaiyan, a Pāndya ruler of the ninth century. From these records, it appears that the old name of the place was "Ilangōkkudi" (*kō* = Brahmans, *ilam* = next to, *kudi* = habitation), "the habitation of the caste next to Brahmans," i.e., apparently, Vaisyas; and the tradition of the local Kaikkilaiyans that they settled in the place as guardians of this temple on the invitation of a Pāndya (named Pulimati Rāja) affords a possible explanation of this old name. In the same temple Vīra Pāndya of the tenth century, "who took the head of the Chōla king',—has left an inscription, also in *vatteluttu* characters. Other interesting inscriptions are one by Rājarāja (A.D. 985—1013), the great Chōla conqueror, and one by Sundara Chōla-Pāndya, the viceroy of Rājēndra Chōla (A.D. 1011—44).

By the side of the main road are two old stones on which are carved in relief the figures of armed warriors. The Kaikkilaiyans, or "Sengunda Mudaliyārs", as they describe themselves, assert that they represent the two survivors of the twelve heroes of their caste who went out to subjugate an invader.

Brahmadēsam (population 3,861): 2 miles to the north of Ambāsamudram, from which side alone it is accessible by road, was until 1861 the headquarter town of a taluk of the same name. The prosperity of its Brahman inhabitants, who are the chief landowners of the place, is reflected in the exceptional grandeur of many of the houses around the *teppakulam* and elsewhere. To the west of this tank stands an imposing temple dedicated to Kailāsanāthaswāmi enclosed in a high compound wall. Within the building almost every facet of stone is adorned with vigorous carving, marred in most cases, however, either by the dirt of ages or the brush of the whitewasher. Two *yālis*, half elephant, half lion, hold in their mouths each a stone ball, which, though movable, cannot be taken out[1]; a similar triumph ingenuity is the three-linked chain with bell attached suspended from the roof, roof slab, chain and bell being carved out of a single stone.

The Sōmavāra *mantapam* situated on the northern side of the outer circuit is especially worthy of notice; and the two monkey figūres to which the worshippers point with the greatest pride are by no means the finest specimens of the sculptor's art in this rich gallery. Livelier than all these are the figures, mounted men, birds, beasts and serpents, carved in relief, as if by afterthought, along the sloping roofs of the two shrines of Subramanya and Vignēswara which guard to right and left the main approach to the temple.

Kadaiyam: a union (population 13,798) comprising the villages of Terku, Mēla and Kīla Kadaiyam and Ravanasamudram and the inam village of Pottalpudūr, contains a police-station and the office of a sub-registrar. Terku Kadaiyam, the headquarters of the union, is prettily situated

[1] A similar *Yāli* is found in the Krishnāpuram temple, Tinnevelly taluk.

on the Jambunadhi, whose banks are heavily clothed with clusters of mango, *pinnai*, cocoanut and tamarind trees. The river, after winding round the south and west of the village, joins the Rāmanadhi about half a mile above Ravanasamudram, which, with Pottalpudūr, lies on the left bank of the Rāmanadhi.

The chief interest of this union centres in the well-known Pottalpudūr mosque, which in respect of sanctity claims to rank not below Nāgore (in the Tanjore district) and second only to Baghdad. The mosque, which is an old one (said to have been founded in 1674), is built on an ample scale, strongly suggesting in its design the plan of a Hindu temple. It has its annual festival (*Kanthūri*); but throughout the year it is a popular resort of not only Muhammadans but also Hindu and Christian pilgrims. In the way usual amongst Hindus vows are made by all classes to the Andavar and the daily contributions in money and in models of limbs once afflicted by disease are evidence of the frequency with which the prayers of the faithful are fulfilled. The greater number of the Andavar's devotees are Hindus, and many of the ceremonies performed in the mosque are of a purely Hindu character. With Hindus the taking of sacred ashes (*vibūthi*) is an important ritual; here holy ashes of another kind (obtained from tamarind bark, ghee and flowers and called *nērsa*) are distributed by the priest (*lebbai*) to all worshippers, both Muhammadans and Hindus, the latter being admitted a few feet within the mosque for the purpose on the last day of the yearly festival. Sheep and fowls are brought by all classes, just as if the Andavar were an Amman or a village deity; the Lebbai slays them in honour of the god, and the flesh is divided between the worshippers and priest. Hindus, who prefer to do so, bring fruit, obtain for it the Lebbai's blessing and then distribute it amongst the worshippers. Sandal paste is prepared on a large scale at the time of the *kanthūri*; the pot is sent to the Hindu village of Ravanasamudram, three-quarters of a mile away, and brought thence with pomp to Pottalpudūr. At the mosque it is offered to the Andavar and then distributed to eager crowds of Hindus and Muhammadans.

Kallidaikurichi (population 17,263, sub-registrar's office, a secondary school and a Sanskrit school): on the opposite side of the Tāmbraparni to Ambāsamudram, with which it is connected by a bridge, is for its size the richest town in the district. The original bridge erected in 1841 was partially destroyed by the floods of 1869 and was rebuilt by subscriptions in 1873. The wealth is almost entirely in the hands of Brahmans; and long streets of substantial Brahman houses with their banks and cloth shops are the distinctive feature of the place. Besides their profits from agriculture—the village possesses some of the most valuable wet lands in the district—the income derived by Brahmans from money-lending and from the cloth-trade is enormous. Practically all the cloths made by the numerous local weavers, Kaikkilaiyans, Muhammadans and Iluvans, like those made at Ambāsamudram, Sērmadēvi and Vīravanallūr, are intended for the Travancore market; the Brahmans advance money to the weavers, export the finished cloths to the west coast, where they maintain their agencies, and thus practically control the trade. Money-lending pure and simple is found even more profitable; and, when a man has amassed sufficient capital in the cloth-trade, he becomes a banker. One Brahman runs a small factory of ten fly-shuttle looms and one high power loom; otherwise the use of the fly-shuttle is practically unknown. Amongst the richest of the Brahmans of the place is a sect of Smārthās locally known as "Annāvis." They are believed to have been the earliest settlers of their caste and at one time (it appears from the old "Survey Account" of Thos. Turnbull) were not above doing cultivation. They still have a reputation for parsimony and in some circles are regarded as "inferior."

There are a number of temples and well-endowed chattrams in the place. Among the temples may be mentioned one dedicated to Vishnu, in which that god, in memory of an incarnation which he once assumed, is represented with the face of a pig. The Nāgēswaramudaiyār and Kīrkrishnan temples contain Pāndya inscriptions, some of which are ascribed to Jatāvarman Kulasēkhara I (A.D. 1190—1214) and others to Māravarman Sundara-Pāndya I (A.D. 1216—1235).[1]

The Kulasēkharamudaiyār temple contains an inscription of Vīrappa Nāyakkan, the Madura ruler.

Mēlasevval: a village of spacious streets, constitutes with Kīlasevval, Dēsamānikkam, Sokkalingapuram, Nainārkulam, Gōpālasamudram and Pirānjeri a union having a population of 10,071. It lies on the road from Palamcotta to Ambāsamudram ten miles from the latter place. Brahmans are numerous; and here, as in many other places, tradition declares that many of them are the descendants of colonists imported by the Nāyakkan rulers of Madura. The large Saivite temple dedicated to Aditya Varnēswarar, "the god of shining brightness," which, as is right and usual, stands in the

[1] *Govt Epig. Ann. Report* for 1908, pp. 71–72.

CHAP. XV. - AMBA-SAMUDRAM TALUK.

north-east corner of the village, and the smaller Vishnu temple in the south-west, contain a number of sculptured figures forming the supporting pillars of *mantapams.*

There is a high school (in Gōpālasamudram) maintained by a Brahman landowner. The chief industry of the place is the manufacture, by Saluppans, of sacking from sunnhemp fibre. The products are, as a rule, sent to Narasinganallūr (Tinnevelly taluk), whence they are distributed in and beyond the district by members of the same caste. Turmeric, a crop which is very little cultivated in the district, is raised here and in the neighbourhood. Before the seed is put in, the ground is well trenched as for betel-gardens; the plants are carefully manured as soon as they come up and remain in the ground for a year.

Pāpanāsam, or, more correctly, Pāpavināsam (Sanskr. *pāpa* = sin, *vināsam* = destruction): a hamlet of the village of Vikramasingapuram (population, 6,543), is deservedly famous for the magnificent cascade—the *kaliyānatirtam*—by which the Tāmbraparni, after a journey of some fifteen miles through the forests, finally descends to the plains. Thence pouring over great boulders in a succession of foaming rapids, the river divides into three arms; on the left-hand stream, less than a mile from the great fall, is the Saivite temple of Pāpavināsēswara, which, with its mantapams, choultries and matams, composes the hamlet. The *kaliyānatirtam* is formed by a drop of about 300 feet over an almost sheer wall of rock; part of the flood in its fall is caught inside a deep cleft of the rock and thence hurled sideways from its course to join the main torrent before the base is reached; in times of heavy flood the whole becomes one unbroken cataract. Guarded on both sides by rocky hills and forest, the fall and the reach of rapids at its base have the advantage of a setting of extreme beauty; and nature has appropriately arranged that the fall is fully visible to none but those who actually go to Pāpanāsam. It is enclosed in an angle of the hills, and the high rocks which line the river's right bank serve to screen the glory of the cascade from the plain country beyond.

To the Hindu the great attraction of the fall is its power (as illustrated by many stories) of washing away human sin. Among the best known of these tales is one which relates how at one time there lived near the place a Pāndya king. He was converted to Buddhism and oppressed his people so severely that many fled the country. Among the fugitives was a man who had a son and a daughter. Wandering to Chōladēsam, which was then the scene of war, brother and sister parted, as it seemed, for ever; after many years they chanced to reach Benares on the same day and halted in the same choultry. Not recognizing one another, they fell in love and married. Discovering later the sin they had committed, they sought advice of the learned men of the place. Bidding them clothe themselves in black and wander in search of expiation to all the bathing-places of the earth, the wise men added that, in the place where their black clothes turned white, salvation would be found. After many years they came to Pāpanāsam and there they bathed. Their clothes turned white; and God appeared and granted them the blessing of everlasting happiness.

The temple receives the offerings of thousands of pilgrims, who resort to the place from all parts of the Presidency. The great festival of the year is celebrated on the ten days ending with *Chittirai Vishu*, when the god—Pāpavināsēswara—is taken with pomp to Vikramasingapuram and back; and his efficacy may be judged from the number of *ex voto* limbs and cradles hung up in the temple. Though possessing no special architectural merits, the temple is spacious and well maintained; broad flights of steps lead down to the river, where several mantapams are provided for the use of bathers. The hundreds of large carp in the neighbouring reach of the river which are fed daily by the temple are extraordinarily tame; to feed them on recovery from an illness is a form of vow commonly taken by pilgrims. If taken from the river, they turn to blood and injure the eye-sight of him who takes them. The fact is proved by a story, told with great wealth of detail, of the fate once suffered by a European who, not knowing the properties of the fish, hooked one of them.

At the foot of the fall is—as might be expected—a shrine dedicated to Agastiswara—the *rishi* Agastya. When Siva was being married in Kailāsam, Agastya had to be sent on urgent business to the south; to compensate the *rishi* for missing so thrilling a ceremony, Siva promised that with his consort Pārvathi he would appear to Agastya in the full splendour of his marriage-robes. Here in Pāpanāsam, in commemoration of Siva's fulfilment of the promise, Agastya is brought every year from his shrine to witness the marriage of the god and goddess of the local temple.

A walk of four miles by a bridle path up through the forest takes one to the forest bungalow of Mundanthurai, beautifully placed on the right bank of the river Sērvaiyār just above its confluence with the Tāmbraparni. Eleven miles further on by the same forest road, at a height of

CHAP. XV. AMBASAMUDRAM TALUK.

2,550 feet, is the little forest station of Kannikatti, set in the heart of deep jungle. The journey to this place leads through a privately owned estate, called Kattalaimalai, which now belongs to the Jesuit Missionary Society. The land was originally granted in pre-British times as an endowment to the Pāpanāsam temple, the old Chokkampatti poligar being the trustee. The services required by the grant were not rendered; the land went through many vicissitudes of mortgage, and no money ever reached the temple. The endowment was finally resumed by Government, and, in 1911, a ryotwari patta was issued to its occupants, the Jesuit missionaries. The question of acquiring the property with a view to its reservation as Government forest was much discussed at the time when the general subject of a forest policy was first taken up some forty years ago; the idea, however, was long ago abandoned. At one time a great part of the property was planted up with coffee by European lessees, and the bushes, which remain but receive little attention, still yield a small amount of coffee reputed to possess a fine flavour. The estate produces also a few oranges, guavas and pomeloes, and, though it has been badly denuded in the past, the forest still contains a good deal of teak and *kongu*. Passing Kannikatti the forest track continues to the Travancore frontier, eight miles away, and descending the other side leads ultimately to Trivandrum.

Overlooking Kattalaimalai from the north is the great bare hill known as Kōttaimalai, "Fort Hill," on which substantial remains of what must at one time have been a considerable fort are still to be seen. Though nothing, unfortunately, is known regarding its past history, it may fairly be assumed that it served the Travancoreans as a place of refuge during the many incursions into the Tinnevelly country which they are known to have made from the fifteenth to the eighteenth centuries. Sērmādēvi, as we know from inscriptions, was at one time in the occupation of Chēras, and the site of this fort would have lain almost in the course of the shortest route to that district from south Travancore. Referring to the mutual incursions made into one another's territory by the "Maliaver," that is, the Travancore ruler, and by the poligar of Vadakarai (Chokkampatti) in 1759, Orme speaks of the invasions on both sides as having been led through "the pass of Shencotta which lies fifteen miles to the south of Vadagherri." The entrance to the Kattalaimalai pass is certainly fifteen miles south of Vadakarai, while Vadakarai itself stands at the mouth of the Shencotta gap. It seems likely, therefore, that the pass actually used on that and similar occasions was not Shencotta but Kattalaimalai.

Pattamadai: forms with Kēsavasamudram a union, having a population of 6,290. The obvious conjecture that the name originates from the number of sluices which irrigate the village (*pattu* = ten, *madai* = sluice) is discounted by the fact that there are in fact eleven. The alternative theory is therefore preferred. Before the Kannadiyan channel was cut there was, it is said, a tank in the village from which the water was led to the wet fields by a "pot-hole sluice" *(pattalmadai)*: hence the name of the place. The village is two miles from Sērmādēvi, and the approach to it from that place is marked by the prominent Maradiya Sāstā set on a pinnacle of rock. It contains a privately-owned high school, to which Hindus alone are admitted. Mats of very diverse qualities are manufactured from *kōrai* grasses by the Muhammadans of the place. Some account of the industry will be found on pages 219–20.

Sērmādēvi: a union with a population of 12,150, the headquarters of a Sub-Collector whose charge comprises the two taluks of Ambāsamudram and Nānguneri, contains the offices of a sub-registrar and of a sub-divisional officer of the Public Works Department, a police station, and a hospital maintained from local funds. The original form of the name, Cheranmahādēvi-Chaturvēdimangalam, found in Pāndya inscriptions of uncertain date in four of the local temples, leaves no room for doubt that the place was at one time under the occupation of the Chēra or Travancore sovereign. The villages comprised in the union are—besides Sērmādēvi—Kūniyūr and Vadakku Kāraikurichi to the west and Sērankōilpattu on the south. The headquarter village consists of several distinct blocks of houses, between which lie stretches of wet fields irrigated by the Kannadiyan channel. Sērankōilpattu alone of all the component units consists chiefly of dry lands; and immediately to the south of it towers up conspicuous for miles the great rugged hill, Kolundumāmalai, a hunting-ground for medicine-men in quest of herbs.

Brahmans, temples and good wet lands are the distinguishing features of Sērmādēvi. Palayagrāmam to the north near the ancient Rāmaswāmi temple, which contains inscriptions of the Chōla kings, Rājarāja and Rājēndra Chōla I (p. 48), is by repute the oldest settlement of the caste; southward from this extending to the Kannadiyan channel, are four streets in which live the descendants of Brahmans who, tradition asserts, were imported by Kumārakrishnappa Nāyakkan, the feudatory at Madura of the Vijayanagar

CHAP. XV. AMBASAMUDRAM TALUK.

king [1], and given an acre apiece of wet land to be held free of assessment.

Besides the innumerable temples dedicated to the minor gods and goddesses, one at least of which presides over each separate colony, sometimes over single streets, there are in the whole of the main village no less than twelve temples belonging to the Trimūrti, eight of which may be called ancient. Most interesting of all is the beautiful, but sadly neglected, Bhaktapriyar temple, situated on the bank of the Tāmbraparni about a quarter of a mile east of the main road. The stone carvings which adorn the outside wall of the building are of remarkable delicacy and recall the similar sculptures of Manappadaivīdu and Tenkāsi. Kulōttunga I (A.D. 1074—1118), the last great Chōla king, has left an inscription in the temple. Vīra-Pāndya (A.D. 1252--1267), who boasts that he "took Ilam (Ceylon), Kongu and Sōlamandalam, conquered the powerful chiefs and was pleased to perform the anointment of heroes and victors at Perumbarappuliyur (Chidambaram)," has left six inscriptions here.[2] Close by is a bathing-ghat, to which thousands resort once a year at the time of the January new moon, as it is believed that then the Ganges enters the Tāmbraparni at this point. The Alagiyappar temple, also on the river bank but to the west of the road, has a chattram attached to it, which possesses a wide reputation for the excellence of the pepper-water served to its Brahman "free-fooders." It contains inscriptions of Pāndya and Vijayanagar kings. Sōmanāthaswāmi, the presiding deity of the temple just to the east of that dedicated to Alagiyappar, is famous for his power of providing rain in times of distress. The ceremony—known as *varunajapam*—consists in placing a vessel of water with a hole in it over the head of the god and allowing the contents to trickle down for a period of eight days. If water fails, milk is substituted; and if both fail, the Brahmans stand in water and call in a loud voice on all the elements in turn. This ritual, even after the most desperate remedies, including the pepper bath of the Pillaiyār (referred to below), have been tried in vain, has never been known to prove ineffectual. The richest of all the temples, that dedicated to Ammanāthaswāmi, contains an inscription of the

[1] Incidentally it may be noted that an inscription (No. 187 of *Govt. Epig. Ann. Report* for 1895) in the Appan temple of this place distinctly describes Vīrappa Nāyakkan of Madura (A.D. 1573—1595) as the feudatory of the Vijayanagar king, Srīranga II.

[2] *Govt. Epig. Ann. Report* for 1911-12, pp. 44, 71 and 72. See also p. 54 above.

great Chōla king, Rājarāja, and two relating to the Chōla Pāndya viceroys of the eleventh century.

A deity possessing more than a local reputation is the Pillaiyār—"Pepper Pillaiyār" he is called—whose shrine is situated beside the peaceful little tank at the south end of the village. When water is lower than it should be in the Kannadiyan channel, his image is plastered with a paste of pepper and water, and his little temple is then filled with water. A stopper is removed from the floor, and the mixture flows out by a passage into the channel which flows just past the shrine. If the rite is properly performed, water will come down the channel in flood next day. The temple has an endowment from Government, and contributions towards the ceremony are eagerly volunteered by the villagers when a failure of water is threatened.

On the opposite side of the tank is the prettily-situated bungalow which, from 1860 onwards, was for fifty-four years occupied by successive Sub-Collectors. The building, which is little better than an odd jumble of most incommodious rooms, was evolved originally out of a few old *mantapams.* The work was begun by Mr. (afterwards Sir Vere) Henry Levinge (the first resident Sub-Collector), who obtained a grant of the site on patta and became the owner of the buildings. They were occupied by his successors, and, before his death (which occurred in 1885), Sir Vere Levinge made a present of the property to Government. The building, in spite of repeated patch-work, was never satisfactory; and a new residence, completed in 1914, has been constructed on the dry land to the south of the railway station.

Weaving is the occupation of the Pattāsālaiyans, Kaikkilaiyans, Iluvans and Kōliya Paraiyans of the place and forms the chief local industry. In addition to the ordinary fabrics, cloths of somewhat fine texture with silk borders, the *angavastirams* of the better-dressed Hindus, are produced by the Pattāsālaiyans and Kaikkilaiyans. It is interesting to note that, in a cottage factory owned by some Brahmans just near the railway station, one or two Marava boys are to be found working at the looms. The local market (in Sērankōilpattu), which belongs to the taluk board, assembles on Thursdays.

Singampatti (population 1,267): picturesquely situated on the right bank of the Manimuttār, two miles from the base of the hills, is the seat of a zamindar, whose estate is one of the ancient pālaiyams converted by the East India Company into a zamindari by a sanad of 1803. The estate comprises four villages and over 90 square miles of ghat forests. The wet

CHAP. XV. AMBASAMUDRAM TALUK.

lands, which extend to upwards of thirteen hundred acres, are irrigated by a channel—the Perunkāl—diverted from the Manimuttār by an anicut at the foot of the hills. A few miles before reaching the plains the river tumbles in a fine cascade; and, should the supply of water threaten to fail, it is to this fall that propitiatory ceremonies should be performed. A basket containing rice, flowers, a new cloth and beads is placed in the basin at the foot; above the fall a sheep's head is thrown into the stream. The offerings disappear at once from sight, and within a week abundant floods will descend. The forests possess much valuable timber, and, as they contain the sources of the Pāmbār and many smaller affluents of the Tāmbraparni river, their proper conservation is of immense importance. The present zamindar is said to be working his property on methodical lines, and forest revenue now forms one of his most important resources. The history of the litigation by which the forests were finally decreed to the estate in 1882 is referred to on page 198.

The zamindar's residence is comfortable, spacious and airy; close by in a pleasant retreat, the "Singāra Bāgh," well stocked with fruit-trees, is a bungalow which the zamindar maintains for the accommodation of his friends. On the estate is a small tile-factory.

When in 1792 the East India Company appointed their Collectors of Poligar Peshkash, it was found that the Nawāb's renter, Kuppu Ayyangār, was claiming the Singampatti pālaiyam as the property of his employer. The Company disallowed the claim, and in 1798 Mr. Jackson, after examining the resources of the estate, demanded a peshkash amounting to eight times that which had previously been levied. Sooner than accept the new terms, the zamindar surrendered his estate to the management of the Collector so that its actual resources might be ascertained. The property was in the Collector's hands when Mr. Lushington succeeded in 1799; the amount fixed by Mr. Jackson was found reasonable, and in 1803 the Special Commission, whose proposals were ratified by Government, adopted practically the same figure. After five years' management the estate was handed over to the zamindar, Nallakutti Tēvar. In 1830 the peshkash fell into arrears, and the Collector attached and held the zamindari till 1832. Two years later the zamindar, Periyaswāmi Tēvar, died, and, a dispute arising as to the succession, the estate came once more under the Collector's management, who transferred it in 1836 to a supposed widow of the late zamindar. The peshkash was not paid, and in 1842 the Collector once more attached the zamindari. In 1845 the estate was released, and Sankaravadivammāl, the previous holder, who had successfully established by a law-suit her claim as a widow of Periyaswāmi Tēvar, succeeded to the property. On her death in the same year disputes followed regarding the succession, and the management of the property passed to the Collector, who retained it for five years. In 1852 Sudalaimuttu Ammāl, the mother of the deceased Periyaswāmi Tēvar, was put in possession, and she retained it till 1856, when her daughter's son, Siva Subramanya Tēvar, succeeded. He died in 1860, and, his son being a minor, the Collector assumed the management. After six months the minor's mother was appointed to the charge of the estate; and when she died in 1867, the estate came under the Court of Wards. In 1881 the zamindar, who was described at the time as a gentleman of good character and capable of managing his estate, attained his majority, and the estate was handed over to him. During the Court's management debts to the extent of over half a lakh were cleared off, and the irrigation works of the estate were set in order; in 1881 a substantial balance was handed over to the zamindar. It was in the next year that the zamindar pressed and succeeded in his claim to the forests. On his death in 1893 his son, Thennāttupuli Nallakutti Sivasubramanya Tēvar, the present zamindar, succeeded.

Tiruppudaimarudūr (population 1,170): is situated on the right bank of the Tāmbraparni just opposite the point where that river is joined by the Gatanānadhi. The goddess Gōmati Amman, whose shrine is in the Nārambunāthaswāmi temple, has a great reputation as a healer of diseases, especially those peculiar to women. In this respect she is second only to the goddess of the same name at Sankaranainārkōil; indeed it is said that in some cases where the latter goddess has failed this Amman has been known to succeed. Women possessed of devils sit in the *manimantapam* for days together and, while worship is being performed, fling and roll themselves about, screaming for deliverance. Vows are made for the cure of all diseases and for safe delivery in childbirth; and, to mark their fulfilment, models of the parts of the body cured, cradles, and images of infants, are hung before the Amman's shrine. The *thaipūsam* festival held (in January) in honour of the god Nārambunāthaswāmi is celebrated with great enthusiasm and attracts worshippers from all parts of the district.

The temple contains a *vatteluttu* inscription of Sadaiyan Māran, an ancient Pāndya ruler who is believed to have existed

CHAP. XV. AMBASAMUDRAM TALUK.

not later than the tenth century. His name appears also at Sivalapperi. The famous Chōla Rājarāja has also left two (Tamil) inscriptions, in which he records a naval victory. Perhaps the allusion is to his conquest of Ceylon and "the twelve thousand ancient islands of the sea."

Urkād (population 3,132): the headquarters of one of the zamindaris permanently settled in 1803, is an insignificant village and forms with Ambāsamudram, a mile away, a union. The local Sāstā temple, perched on a conspicuous rock, attracts a large number of worshippers including Brahmans, a fact which gives colour to the local tradition that Brahmans once lived here but, owing to the disorder created by the Maravans, left the place.

The zamindar's family, who belong to the Periyatāli sect of the Kottāli Maravans, came originally, according to their own tradition, from the Rāmnād country. The estate is a small one, comprising somewhat less than two thousand acres in addition to an unimportant coffee estate in the hills above Mattalampārai. Its rent-roll is about Rs. 60,000.

The great grandfather of the present zamindar (a minor) married three wives and died in 1862, leaving sons by two of them. During his lifetime the question of succession had already come under dispute, and a declaratory suit was accordingly filed by one of the claimants. In 1863 the High Court on appeal dismissed the suit on the ground that it was not sustainable during the zamindar's lifetime. Before the decree was passed, however, the zamindar died, and the estate had, in view of the disputes, come under the management of the Collector on behalf of the Court of Wards. Meanwhile Sivananainjaperumāl, the eldest son of the third wife of the late zamindar, filed a suit for possession and, though unsuccessful in the lower court, succeeded in the High Court in 1866. The eldest son of the first wife, the ward of the Court, died in 1865. Thus Sivananainjaperumāl succeeded to the zamindari. But complicated disputes arose over the division of the "partible" estate, and for some time that part which did not belong to Sivananainjaperumāl remained under the Collector's management. In 1872 the zamindar died, leaving two minor sons, and in the same year the Court of Wards took over the property. The debts of the zamindari amounted in that year to half a lakh of rupees; by 1881, when the property was restored, the debts had been cleared, and a balance of Rs. 72,000 was handed over to the zamindar. He died in 1907 leaving an infant child, the present zamindar, who was placed under the care of the Court of Wards.

Vīravanallūr (population 15,966): a union, comprising also Harikēsavanallūr, Giriyammālpuram, Pudukkudi and a part of Attālanallūr, is one of the many rich country-towns of the river valley; it contains a sub-registrar's office and a secondary school. It is perhaps the most important weaving centre of the district, possessing more than 1,500 looms. Amongst the weavers Pattunūlkārans and Pattāsālaiyans (whose title is Adavi) preponderate; after them come the Kaikkilaiyans and last and by much the least the Iluvans. *Muris*, rough cloths with coloured borders, form the bulk of the products; they are manufactured by all classes of weavers and, through the agency of Brahmans, as elsewhere, are exported in large quantities to Travancore, Alleppey, Quilon and other places on the West Coast. A superior and more expensive garment with silk borders called the *angavastiram* is also manufactured, as at Sērmādēvi, by the Pattunūlkārans. The Pattāsālaiyans weave a large number of the ordinary coloured cloths that women wear and occasionally take special orders for superior ones. Dyeing in black and red, which once formed the occupation of the local Sāyakkārans, is now practically extinct, dyed yarn being imported from Madura and abroad. The manufacture on a small scale of mats and of bell-metal articles completes the list of local industries.

The Kannadiyan channel winds through the village and irrigates a large extent of land which annually yields two heavy crops.

KOILPATTI TALUK.

CHAP. XV. KOILPATTI TALUK.

THE KOILPATTI TALUK as an administrative area dates from 1911, its creation forming part of the general scheme of re-distribution of taluks consequent on the constitution of the new Rāmnād district. It is the largest of all the eight taluks.

The most chāracteristic and interesting part of this country is the great black-cotton plain which, including the zamindari of Ettaiyāpuram, occupies perhaps two-thirds of the taluk. Save for a few big trees denoting villages and for the unlovely, if useful, acacia, it is a treeless tract devoted to the serious business of producing good crops once a year and, in particular, the famous Tinnevelly cotton. The irrigated land is less than in any other taluk, amounting to only two per cent of the total area; wet land indeed is little accounted of in the land of *karisal* (black loam).

Except the Vaippār, which enters the taluk on the north and falls into the sea beside the village of the same name, there are no rivers; heavy rains produce short-lived torrents, which escape by the shortest route they can find to the sea. A few of these drainage channels have carved out well defined courses, notably the Uppōdai in the south-west of the taluk which joins the Chittār in the Tinnevelly taluk, and the Uppār odai which, starting to the west of Ottapidāram, carries the drainage of a large tract of country through the Kōrampallam tank to the sea just south of Tuticorin.

Two-thirds of the taluk consists of zamindari, the proportion of land held on that tenure being larger here than in any other taluk. The Ettaiyāpuram estate, which alone comprises half of the taluk, is the largest zamindari in Tinnevelly and contains some of the finest black-cotton soil of the southern districts.

Historically, the taluk is of interest as having been the theatre of the last and most serious of the poligar rebellions. The memories of that troublous time are still preserved in folk-songs, of which in almost every village a part at least is known and sung; the forts of poligars with which, as is clear from the old records, the face of the country was once studded were obliterated at the beginning of the last century and are, as a rule, no longer traceable; in Pānjālankurichi, that "Gibraltar of the insurgents," which was razed to the ground and sown with castor seed and salt, clear traces remain of former habitations.

Relics of the Jains are, or seem to be, commoner here than elsewhere; and the enthusiasm which marks the ceremony of *kaluvēttal*[1] finds keener expression in the Saivite temples of Kalugumalai and Vilāttikulam than elsewhere in the district.

The taluk is one of the most thinly populated, and between 1910 and 1911 the number of its inhabitants increased by only 3·6 per cent. The prevailing castes are the three Telugu-speaking communities, Kambalattāns and Kammavans (both of whom adopt the suffix Nāyakkan) and Reddis. The other usual castes are also found, but in smaller numbers than elsewhere. Curiously enough, the three castes named seem to have made a sort of territorial division of the country. West of a line drawn north and south through Ettaiyāpuram is the land of the Kammavans; eastward of this line, occupying the heart of the Ettaiyāpuram country, live the Kambalattāns, divided into two main sub-castes, Sillavans and Tokkulavans, according as they were of old the followers of Ettaiyāpuram or of Pānjālankurichi; eastwards again as far as the sea coast, where palmyras and Shānāns flourish, is the territory of the Ayōdhi Reddis. All are good cultivators, but the Reddis and Kammavans, in this order, excel the Kambalattāns; their habitations are as a rule small villages in which they live devoted to the labour of the soil. The country is essentially one of peasant proprietors. Farming in the black cotton country demands patience and close attention; and it is only a man whose tenure is secure, for preference one who owns the land he cultivates, that will turn the earth to full account. It is therefore no matter for surprise that Brahmans, whose experience of agriculture is, as a rule, limited to giving lands on lease, are very few in the Kōilpatti taluk. Wet lands are scarce, and few of these are valuable; and the narrow margin of profit will not attract a tenant or repay a landlord. Brahmans are confined to a small number of villages; and even here the general story is that, where fifty years ago there were thirty or forty families, there are now but five left. Such Brahmans as are found make their living, as a rule, as *purōhits*, whose function is to tell the lucky days from the unlucky and to assist at marriages; others are cooks or shop-keepers.

Temples dedicated to the Trimūrti are few, and none of them are noteworthy.

Besides the ginning and spinning of cotton there are few industries in the taluk. Grass mats are made at Kayattār and at one or two other places; the Kaikkilaiyans in Kalugumalai,

[1] See page 100.

Ettaiyāpuram and Vilāttikulam weave the ordinary cloths for local sale. Kōilpatti, Kayattār and Ettaiyāpuram are the only unions.

Sepulchral urns have been found at Kadambūr; and it is probably for want of exploration that they have not been discovered elsewhere.

Attankarai (population 2,601): situated on the left bank of Vaippār, is the headquarters of an ancient zamindari, which measures about sixteen square miles and consists almost entirely of dry lands. It bears a rent-roll of rather more than Rs. 8,000. The zamindar belongs to the Kambalattān caste and ascribes the foundation of his greatness to the bounty of the Vijayanagar sovereigns. The forefather of the present holder received his sanad in 1803.

Ettaiyāpuram (population 8,636): a union, nine miles from Kōilpatti, with which it is connected by a maintained road, is a small unattractive town situated in the midst of black-cotton country and calls for notice chiefly as being the seat of the zamindar of that name. It contains the office of a sub-registrar, a police station, a local fund hospital to which the zamindar makes a substantial annual contribution, and a chattram which is his property. The boys' high school and the school for girls are also maintained by the estate. The square tank faced with stone to the north of the town by the roadside, deriving its supply from a larger reservoir two miles away, provides the town with its drinking-water and was constructed in the thirties of the last century by the great-grandfather of the present zamindar. The two temples, the older one dedicated to Siva and the other to Vishnu, are, according to local tradition, the foundations of former poligars. A small weekly market is held on Saturdays; but the chief business of the place is the export of cotton to Tuticorin. There is a fairly large colony of Kaikkilaiyans who weave cloths of the coarser kinds for men and women, chiefly for local markets.

The zamindar's residence, which is at the eastern end of the town, consists of a series of heterogeneous buildings set in a rough square to which there are entrances on each side. On the left, as one enters by the western or main gate, is the spacious "kalyāna-mahāl" and on the right the durbar hall. Beyond this are the offices and private apartments of the zamindar. The buildings are fitted with modern furniture and lighted throughout by electricity.

The zamindari, which was granted under an Istimrar Sanad in 1803, comprised originally 185 villages, 79 of which belonged formerly to the Pānjālankurichi pālaiyam and were, on the sequestration of that estate, presented to Ettaiyāpuram (see p. 272); to these were added, by purchase on the part of the present zamindar's great-grandfather, 162 villages which at one time formed parts of other zamindaris. In more recent years another 75 villages, including forty-three which belonged to the Guntamanāyakkanūr zamindari of the Madura district, have been bought. The whole estate, which thus comprises 422 villages in and beyond this district, covers an area of 647 square miles. The peshkash payable by the zamindar is Rs. 1,32,018, his rent-roll being more than three times that sum. Less than 3 per cent of the cultivated area lying within the district is irrigated, the rest consisting of a small amount of "garden" and a vast area of "dry" land. The finest black soil in the district is to be found within the estate, and it is probable that this zamindari accounts for more than half the total output of the indigenous cotton of the district. The estate is traversed by a few roads and is skirted by the railway. The chief markets are those held at Nāgalāpuram and Kalugumalai (q.v.).

The traditional account[1], as preserved by the family, of the origin of their greatness is typical of the stories related by many of the Nāyakkan zamindars of the district. If not historical, it may at least be taken as indicating in a general way the migrations of the troubled period which followed the downfall of the Vijayanagar kingdom. When the Muhammadans overthrew the king of Vijayanagar, Kumāramuttu Ettappa Nāyakkan fled with his followers from Chandragiri (in the present North Arcot district) and took refuge with the Pāndya king at Madura. That sovereign appointed him to subdue Kallan outlaws and gave him a strip of country for his maintenance. In the course of time the settlers moved southwards and took possession of many villages in the Tinnevelly country, making their headquarters at a place which in honour of their leader they called Ettaiyāpuram. If the general outline of the story be accepted, we may assign the settlement at Ettaiyāpuram to the 16th century. In explanation of the curious name Ettappan it is related that, in response to a challenge, an ancestor of Kumāramuttu overcame by an exceptional feat of strength a muscular warrior named Sōman, the watchman of one of the gates of the Vijayanagar fort. The Nāyakkan floored his opponent and cut off his head. When Sōman's eight surviving brothers in their turn craved protection, the Nāyakkan in a passing fit of magnanimity spared their lives. Having thus become the protector

[1] *Ettaiyapuram Past and Present*, by W. E. Ganapathi Pillai, Madras, 1890.

CHAP. XV. KOILPATTI TALUK.

or "father" of these eight, the victorious hero received the title of "Ettappan," "father of eight."

If we may believe the Madura records, the poligar was not at all times a faithful vassal; for in the time of Tirumalai Nāyakkan the Sētupati of Rāmnād was deputed to suppress a rebellious confederacy of poligars in which Ettaiyāpuram had taken the lead. The rising was put down, and the leaders executed. A hundred years later we find the poligar spoken of as the dependant of Pānjālankurichi, who by this time had assumed the leadership of all the "eastern," that is, generally speaking, the Nāyakkan, poligars of the district. Hostages for good conduct and payment of tribute were demanded and received from both Ettaiyāpuram and Pānjālankurichi by Colonel Heron during his campaign of 1755; and it was this measure which accounted, apparently, for the fact that both these chieftains held aloof from the great confederacy organized by the Pūli Tēvan in the following year. Muhammad Yūsuf evidently reckoned on the potential value of Ettaiyāpuram as an ally; for, though pressed for money during his campaign a few months later, he considered it not politic to compel the poligar to redeem the hostages who were still in confinement at Trichinopoly. It was not, however, till about 1797, at a time when all the eastern poligars were banded together in defiance of the Company's authority, that the political importance of Ettaiyāpuram became manifest. His abstention from this dangerous confederacy was alone an immense source of strength to the English at a most critical moment, and it is difficult to calculate the lengths to which the poligar wars might have dragged had he thrown in his lot with the enemy. Ettaiyāpuram had definitely resolved to ally himself with the British. When after the assault of 1799 the Pānjālankurichi rebels escaped, the Ettaiyāpuram poligar, in response to Major Bannerman's request, sent out a party of troops, who, with their knowledge of the country, rendered valuable service in leading the pursuit of Kattaboma and his followers. They found him at Kōlārpatti; some skirmishing ensued before the cavalry arrived, and Kattaboma escaped. Subramanya Pillai, as dangerous a man as the poligar himself, was captured. Major Bannerman expressed his gratitude by presenting the poligar with two shawls and a horse, and in the following year Government conferred on him six divisions (comprising 79 villages) of the forfeited Pānjālankurichi pālaiyam.

In the last Pānjālankurichi rebellion (1801) the poligar sent a thousand men to assist Major Macaulay; and, whilst the

British attacked on the west of the fort, these "brave and faithful allies" (as Colonel Welsh calls them) made many unsuccessful and costly attempts at an escalade on the east. In the pursuit which followed the final assault the Ettaiyāpuram troops again played a spirited part.

In 1803 the estate received its permanent settlement as a zamindari. The most conspicuous of the line was, perhaps, the zamindar referred to by the Collector of the time as "the most considerable and at the same time well-disposed and liberal-minded native gentleman in the district"—who died in 1853. He built two important bridges, one over the Chittār at Gangaikondān and the other over the Uppār Odai, a mile south of Kayattār; he set apart for the use of travellers a bungalow of his (its foundations may still be seen) on the left bank of the river just below the Tinnevelly bridge. On his own estate his greatest monument is the fine *mantapam* beside the temple at Kalugumalai. In 1872, on the motion of Mr. Puckle, the estate was rescued by the intervention of the Court of Wards from mismanagement at the hands of an uncle of the minor heir. The revenue administration which was in a state of confusion was put on a sound basis; the sharing-system was abolished in favour of money rents, boundary disputes in regard to adjoining ryotwari lands were settled, the revenue establishment was improved, most of the estate was surveyed, and an experimental farm, which is still maintained, was established in 1876. During the period of management, which lasted six years, the balance to the credit of the estate rose from under a lakh of rupees to nearly three and a half lakhs.

The death of his father in 1891 left the present zamindar a minor, and the estate again came under the Court of Wards. The boy was educated by English tutors both at Ettaiyāpuram and at "Newington," Madras. A number of new buildings were erected, including the zamindar's bungalow at Kuttālam; many temples on the estate were restored, the survey begun during the previous wardship was completed, and a surplus of nearly three lakhs of rupees was handed over to the zamindar on his assuming charge in December 1900.

In 1911 the Government of India conferred on the zamindar as a personal distinction the title of Rāja. The direct management of the estate is in the hands of an officer, styled the Diwān, who at the present moment is a retired Deputy Collector. The zamindar's family belongs to the Sillavar section of the caste of Kambalattāns or Tottiyans,

CHAP. XV. KOILPATTI TALUK.

Ilavēlankāl (population 2,541): on the main railway line, deserves notice on account of the remarkable series of sculptured stones which stand in a field near the village. There are ten of these stones, each about 4 feet high, and on them are carved in relief scenes representing the successive phases of a conflict between two warriors. One party wears the peculiar high slanting top-knot, usually associated with the Kondaiyankōttai Maravan of past times, fights on foot, is armed with bow and arrows and carries a shield on the left arm. His antagonist appears to be the royal warrior; he wears a crown and fights on horseback. A shield, a sword and a lance form his armour. The result of the fight is clear. At the first onset the Maravan is dashed to the ground; recovering himself, he seizes his opponent's horse by the bridle and thus dodges the thrust which the horseman is preparing to deliver with his lance. A well-directed arrow pierces the horse, and another transfixes the warrior in the waist. The horseman falls to the ground, and the fight is ended.

Most of the stones bear Tamil inscriptions, some of which are now illegible; all are dated Saka 1469 (A.D. 1547). The translation of one inscription is: "In Saka 1469 Kīlaka year, 10th Panguni, when Vettumperumāl Rāja,[1] the Tinnevelly Perumāl, came to Ilavēlankāl and when Vengala Rāja led a force against him, a Kondaiyankōttai Maravan . . put (them) to death" [i.e., presumably, Vengala Rāja's men].

Kadambūr (population 5,119, railway station, sub-registrar's office): is a small village with a very busy bazaar. Messrs. Dymes & Co. have a cotton gin here, and another small one owned by a local Nāyudu is worked by Messrs. Ralli Brothers on a lease; a Paravan of Tuticorin owns a bone-crushing factory.

The place is the seat of a zamindar who belongs to the Kondaiyankōttai section of the Marava caste. His estate, which was permanently settled under an Istimrar Sanad, dated 22nd April 1803, is a small one, comprising thirteen villages with a total area (it has not been surveyed) of approximately twenty-eight square miles. All rents are, and apparently always have been, paid entirely in money. Land is divided, as was once the case in ryotwari areas, into three classes, "wet" (only about fifty acres), "dry" and "garden," the acreage rate of assessment in the last-named class running in some cases as high as Rs. 12 and over.

In 1858 the zamindarni, who was the last in the direct line of descent from the original sanad-holder, died without issue,

[1] See under Kayattār (pp. 381 foll.).

and, with the sanction of Government, a descendant of the first zamindar's sister succeeded. He was followed by his son in 1897, who died ten years later leaving two minor sons. The estate was then taken under the Court of Wards and continues in that state at present. During this period the debts due by the estate have been cleared, outstandings, where realizable, have been collected, and a handsome surplus has been invested on behalf of the minors. The boys are being educated at the Hindu College, Tinnevelly.

Kalugumalai, "the hill of the vulture" (population 6,381): a half-way station on the twenty-four miles of local fund road which connects Kōilpatti with Sankaranainārkōil, may be located for miles around by the massive dome of naked rock, some 300 feet high, which overlooks the village. On three sides it is almost a sheer precipice, and it is only with some difficulty that it can be ascended from the fourth. The place is deservedly famous for its rock-cut temple, *Vettuvān Kōvil*, as it is locally called. In the face of a great ridge of the rock a passage open to the sky forming three sides of a square has been hewn; enclosed in it, but separated from the solid rock by a space of three feet, was left the solid lump, which was subsequently hollowed out within and adorned with carvings. The building, which faces outwards from the hill, consists of the two compartments usual in small temples, the outer hall for the worshippers and a *garbagraha* or inner shrine for the god. The interior is perfectly plain. Surmounting the *garbagraha* is a dome which, like the walls, is rich in sculptures. The recess in which the building lies goes some forty feet into the rock, the depth from the base of the cutting to the top being about thiry feet. Most of the sculptured figures are in a sitting posture; some are carved with particular delicacy, whilst here and there are rows of figures of the ultra-cherubic type, with thick round limbs and sometimes humourous expressions. A type of sculpture which seems peculiar are a few "vignettes" carved in relief and set in semicircular embrasures. The work is unfinished; probably, as Fergusson suggests, because the person who commenced it did not live to complete it, and it was nobody's business to finish what was of no use and was intended only to glorify him who made it. The rock is of extreme hardness, and the masterpiece has consequently withstood time; it now serves as a Pillaiyār temple for the villagers. Fergusson's account of Kalugumalai is unfortunately most confused and seems to have been based on an inaccurate report. Apart from this account, the learned have

CHAP. XV. KOILPATTI TALUK.

not pronounced upon the origin of the temple; but, from the general posture of the sculptured figures, from the fact that one or two of them hold up the right hand with the two first fingers extended in the familiar attitude of benediction or instruction, and from the existence a little way up the rock of numerous figures of undoubted Jaina origin, it seems reasonable to assign to this extraordinary creation a Jaina origin.

The figures of devotees referred to—*tirtankarar*—are a little higher up and are carved in relief on two separate smooth faces of the rock; they are ranged generally in two rows and number well over a hundred altogether. Almost all are seated figures with the legs tucked up and crossing one another: the hands with palms upturned rest one over the other on the legs, and above the head of each is the triple crown or canopy. Each devotee has a separate niche about two feet high, and, with a few exceptions, all are of one size and design. One or two larger figures are surmounted by haloes of elaborate tracery and what appear to be guardian spirits; in attendance on some are women with chowries in their hands. Below the figures are inscriptions in the old *vatteluttu* character, each recording, it is said, the name of the village at whose expense the figure above it was carved.

The Pāndya king, Māranjadaiyan (whose records are found also at Mānūr, Gangaikondān, and Tirukkurungudi), has left an inscription on the same rock. As stated elsewhere, he is for the present identified with the Varaguna Varman who ascended the throne in A.D. 862. An inscription of the same ruler, in which he refers to an expedition into the Tondai-nādu, at that time the territory of the Chōlas, is to be found on a stone slab in the Kosakkudi street. The potters of the neighbourhood make offerings to it.

Just near the Jaina figures is a cave which forms an admirable shelter from sun and rain. It is large enough to form a comfortable habitation and is evidently appreciated by the Sūdra *sanyāsi* who has chosen to live there in peace and seclusion for many years past.

On the other side of the rock at its foot is the temple of Subramanyaswāmi, the property of the zamindar of Ettaiyāpuram. The peculiarity of the building is that, to form the innermost shrine and two porticoes immediately in front of it, the rock itself has been scooped out. Europeans may not see this part of the temple; but from accounts received the work amounts merely to a somewhat elaborate extension of a natural cave, the original rock having been left here and there to serve as pillars. Within its precincts is a fine tank revetted with cut stone, the work of a former zamindar; overlooking the tank is an ample *mantapam* to which the god is brought at times of festival.

The local cattle-market, which is famous, assembles in the well-kept enclosure to the south of the Sankaranainārkōil road. The fair is held twice annually at the time of temple festivals, one in *Thai* (January-February) and the other in *Panguni* (March-April). Ten thousand cattle, at least, it is said, are brought on each occasion, one-half of which consist of animals from Madura, Salem, Coimbatore and Mysore. Buyers come from all parts of the Tinnevelly black-cotton country and from the adjoining taluks of the Rāmnād district; and the local temple, to which the proceeds go, is said to make Rs. 4,000 out of each fair.

The place belongs to the Ettaiyāpuram zamindari, and the zamindar has a residence here. In addition it contains a police station and a sub-registrar's office. A stone lying in the compound of the sub-registrar's office bears an inscription of Jatāvarman Sundara Pāndya-dēva, who was appointed by his father Rājēndra Chōla (A.D. 1011–1044) to the post of viceroy in the Pāndya province (see page 49). There are two chattrams, one maintained by the Kāsukkāra Chettis of the place, the other by the Rājus of Rājapālaiyam. A weekly market is held on Tuesdays, the income of which goes to the Subramanya temple.

An account of the riot which occurred here in 1895 between the Shānāns and other castes will be found on page 126.

Kāyattār: a small union of 3,955 inhabitants, lies 18 miles from Palamcotta on the main road connecting that place with Madura and eight miles from the two nearest railway stations, Gangaikondān and Kadambūr. It contains a police station, the office of a sub-registrar (who is also a third-class magistrate with limited powers), a travellers' bungalow, a chattram and a large elementary school, all maintained from local funds. The chattram was endowed by a Huzur Sarishtadar named Nāna Rao; and a tablet outside it, surmounted by a lamp, commemorates its construction and acknowledges the assistance given towards its foundation by Mr. J. Silver, the Collector of the time (1855–65). The weekly market, which is held on Thursdays and serves a large tract of country, is one of great local importance and brings in a handsome revenue to the taluk board which owns it. It serves as a regular mart of exchange between the interior and the great distributing centre of Pēttai.

The Roman Catholics have a large church in the village. Their congregation, which dates from the 17th century (during which time we read of persecutions in the letters of the Jesuit Fathers), includes a large number of converts from the Vellāla caste.

The temple which stands in the village is of no particular architectural interest; evidence of long neglect is seen in the embankments of earth which have been thrown up on two sides to prevent the outer walls from collapsing. One wall has recently been renewed, the dilapidated shrines have been restored, and the wild growth which had been allowed to overrun the court-yards within has been removed. During the operations, which began in 1908, a number of brass and stone images were dug up and are now preserved in the temple.

The ancient temple of the locality appears to be that dedicated to Kōthandarāmēswarar, standing picturesque and isolated on elevated ground on the right bank of the Uppār Odai, a stream which flows to the west of the village. Unlike the temple in the village this foundation possesses its *stalapurāna*; and this, added to the fact that clear traces of habitations exist in its immediate neighbourhood, suggests that the original village of Kayattār was considerably to the north of the modern place. According to the story, Rāma, when in pursuit of the deer alluded to in connection with Alankulam (p. 453), stopped at Kayattār; being thirsty, he bade the Gaja-nadhi, "the Elephant river," now known as the Uppār Odai or salt stream, flow from the Elephant mountain. The hunter-god bathed in the stream but found it too brackish to drink; whereupon he shot his bow into the ground close by, and the Ganges welled up. This is the origin of the spring of good water which now exists within the temple. Gajanadhi became in Tamil Gajattār: hence "Kayattār." The temple contains two inscriptions, dated A.D. 1536 and 1538, of Māravarman Sundara Pāndya, one of the later race of Tinnevelly rulers.[1] Immediately in a line with the temple on the opposite side of the road are the streets along which, it seems, the temple car was dragged. Tradition has it (and the general configuration of the ground supports the view) that the habitations of men once existed here; but no remains are traceable. Immediately adjoining this site on the south are the clear remains of a fort about a quarter of a mile square. On the south and east the mud walls exist in a mutilated state; within the enclosure is a mound of earth, thirty feet high, a place of outlook; not far from this are the remains of a Perumāl

[1] See pp. 53, 57.

temple, of which the ruined shrine with its decrepit *gōpuram* and the foundations of the outer walls still exist; elsewhere are the broken masonry remains of what is believed to have been a Siva temple and close by the wreckage of yet another building. Marking the position of the four gates, outside the fort itself, are the temples or remnants of temples dedicated to minor gods; that on the south belonging to Sāstā and that on the north to Angala Iswari are preserved and held in great veneration.

When or by whom the fort was built, it is, as usual, impossible to ascertain. Local tradition ascribes it to a king called Vettumperumāl Rāja, who is believed to have had his headquarters at Kayattār. The inscription at Ilavēlankāl,[1] dated A.D. 1547, refers to "Vettumperumāl Rājā, the Tinnevelly Perumāl"; and there too the general belief is that the king in question ruled at Kayattār. It is therefore permissible to attribute the origin of this fort to one of the company of Pāndyas who, from the frequent occurrence of their inscriptions in this district, seem to have exercised local authority even after the establishment of a suzerain power at Madura.

Coming to more historical times, Kayattār is chiefly remembered as the place where Kattaboma Nāyakkan, the rebel poligar of Pānjālankurichi, was hanged in 1799 (16th October). The memory of that event is kept alive in a peculiar manner. The site of execution is on the left-hand side of the trunk road about three-quarters of a mile to the north of the village. Here stands a great pile of stones of all sizes, which represents the accumulated offerings by wayfarers of the past hundred years for the repose of the soul of the victim. To the present day those who go past the spot contribute a handful of small stones and go on their way comforted. The exact motive is hard to understand but can perhaps best be explained by reference to the general feeling which prompts men to erect *pūdams*, or shapeless emblems of worship, in commemoration of those who were terrible in their life-time or met with unnatural deaths. If repose is desired for the spirit of Kattaboma Nāyakkan, it is such repose as will ensure for the passer-by freedom from the torment of his visitations. Offerings of sheep, cooked rice, and fruits are also made for the cure of diseases or for the disappearance of blight from the fields. Shoes are hung up in the tree overhanging the heap (not the tree of execution, for it has disappeared) for the use of Kattaboma, who, like all active spirits, goes hunting by night; so hard in fact does he hunt that a new pair hung up

[1] See p. 378.

CHAP. XV. KOILPATTI TALUK.

at night is worn out by the next morning. On one side of the heap may be seen a specially selected stone, bigger than the rest, about which devotees tie chaplets.—*Stat magni nominis umbra.*

During the struggles with the poligars Kayattār was regularly used as a station for troops. According to tradition, the site of the cantonment was the open ground, still partially shaded by many trees of great age, immediately to the south of the travellers' bungalow. The cantonment was given up in 1798, the garrison being removed and concentrated in Palamcotta. For troops marching out from Palamcotta to Pānjālankurichi the place afforded a half-way halt; and it was here on the 27th March 1801 that the force of three thousand men, artillery, infantry and cavalry, under Major Colin Macaulay assembled on their way to reduce that stubborn fortress. The village continued to serve as a halting-place for troops on the march; and just near the travellers' bungalow is a tomb covering the remains of a young lieutenant of 28, who died at the place in 1830. In the old fort-site is another tomb, now surrounded by cultivation, which records the death of an ensign of His Majesty's 89th regiment, aged seventeen, whilst on his way to join his regiment at Quilon.

The chief industry of the place is mat-making, which forms the employment of Muhammadan women. The trade, which is managed by their male relations, is of considerable value, amounting, it is calculated, to over Rs. 10,000 a year. The products go to Negapatam, Rangoon and Madras. The same community do some business in dyeing yarn. Red is the usual colour, and the finished article is consumed chiefly by Tinnevelly Kaikkilaiyans in the manufacture of cheaper cloths for women.

Kōilpatti (population 5,016): which in 1911 gave its name to the taluk then newly formed, was at the same time made the headquarters of a new revenue division, composed of the two taluks of Kōilpatti and Sankaranainārkōil. Until the Rāmnād district was formed, in 1910, the place fell within the limits of the old Sāttūr taluk, the greater part of which went to Rāmnād. New buildings for the divisional officer, tahsildar, sub-magistrate, sub-registrar and district munsif have just (1915) been completed. Till recently Kōilpatti had been little more than a big village of no particular importance; in the last few years tiled houses have sprung up on all sides, and land has increased a hundred-fold in value. Its site is one admirably adapted to meet the needs of a growing settlement. The town itself lies partly in the level plain and partly on the outskirts of an extensive and well-drained gravelly ridge, the whole forming, together with the country for a few miles round, one of the few large tracts of red soil that occur towards the north of the taluk.

As is so common, the place (according to the *stalapurāna*) begins its history as a forest in which *rishis*, or saints, in large numbers were doing penance. Agastya on his way from Kailāsam in the north stayed in the place and set up a *sivalingam*, and it was on this spot that in later days a Pāndya king built the temple. The curious spring which wells from the rock into the prettily situated bathing tank beside the temple was the creation of Agastya, a fact which is commemorated by the image of the saint carved just beside it.

It is round the temple, situated on high ground to the south, that the original village is believed to have existed. As is usual in this taluk, there is here the sad tradition that Brahmans, whose houses (apart from newly imported officials and their followers) can now be counted on the fingers of one hand, were once abundant; just north of the temple a few Sūdras settled on the low ground; in 1876 the railway came, and a bazaar grew up; in 1891 the cotton mill was opened; the place has now become an important official centre and is on its way to greatness.

About a mile and a half to the south of the village, in the barren ridge which runs in continuation of the Kōilpatti high ground, is a somewhat remarkable and evil-smelling chasm with many ramifications of dark cavernous passages. The formation is probably natural in part but has clearly been worked at by man. The roof has been roughly hewn out to the shape of a flattish dome, and it seems probable that, like the rock shelters in Kalugumalai, it was at one time inhabited. The entrance to the cave, which is at the base of a striking solitary mass of perpendicular rock, is clearly visible from the railway. Near by are the ruins of the old punitive police lines which were demolished, with the removal of the force, in 1904. The local agricultural station is referred to on page 160 and the spinning mill on page 213.

Kulattūr (population 4,209): 14 miles east of Ottapidāram and about three miles from the sea, deserves a note on account of a Jaina image which is to be found there. It stands in an open place in a Sūdra street to which it has given its name *Samanar teru*, "Jain street." The stone is about three feet high, its two sides converging to an apex. The figure, carved in relief, is that of a man sitting with his legs tucked up and crossing one another inwards; his palms are turned upwards,

CHAP. XV. KOILPATTI TALUK.

and about his head is the usual conical canopy. Two small maid-servants bearing chowries are sculptured by his side. It is a singular fact that the Vellālans and Kammālans of the neighbourhood make vows to the image and present offerings of rice and cocoanuts, and even, when cows are calving, money.

The village, which is mainly populated by Shānāns, was the head-quarters of the old rebellious poligar whose estate was sequestered in 1799 (see p. 272). A portion of the pālaiyam, including this village, was conferred on the zamindar of Mēlmāndai, from whom it passed by court sale to Mr. G. A. Hughes (p. 487). It now belongs to some Vellālans of Tinnevelly.

Mandikulam (population 1,280): four miles south of Vilāttikulam off the main road, contains a Jaina image differing from the one referred to under Kulattūr only in the fact that the stone is rounded at the top and not pointed. Here, however, the image is not worshipped. In 1908 some brass images of Hindu deities were found by a potter whilst digging near his house. Three of them were acquired by Government for the Madras museum, the rest being handed over to the finder.

Maniyāchi (population 1,964): a dingy little village, situated near the railway junction of the same name, contains a police station and deserves mention only for the reason that it is the seat of a zamindar. His estate, about 12 square miles in area, comprises nine villages and consists almost entirely of dry lands. Rents on dry and garden lands are paid in money; on the wet lands (which are irrigated by rain-fed tanks and amount to only 100 acres) the zamindar and tenant divide the produce equally. Cotton, cumbu and chōlanāttu on the black soil, horse-gram and sāmai on the red, are the chief dry crops; wells are few. Exclusive of wet lands, the rent roll of the estate is about Rs. 6,600. On his death in 1866 the father of the present zamindar left the estate encumbered with a debt of more than one-and-a-half lakhs of rupees; suits were filed, and an application was made by the civil court to the Collector, Mr. Puckle, for the sale of the two divisions of Kārkurichi and Pērūrani which originally formed part of Pānjālankurichi and were in 1799 conferred on this zamindar (see page 272). Mr. Puckle, with less success than attended a similar effort of his at Sivagiri, did his utmost to stave off the evil day from the estate. He went on leave, and Mr. Longley took his place. Mr. Puckle's scheme was declared unworkable, and in 1870 the Kārkurichi and Pērūrani portions of the zamindari were sold.

The present zamindar's father married seven wives and left five sons, all minors. The only son of a senior wife was allowed to succeed, and the estate was taken under the management of the Court of Wards on his behalf. The litigation usual in such cases ensued, and two years later the civil court declared the deceased zamindar's eldest son, the child of a junior wife, to be the heir. He was still a minor, and the estate continued under the charge of the Court of Wards. On his death in 1873 the present zamindar, Subramanya Talaivar, the eldest surviving son, then aged eleven, succeeded. The management of the Court of Wards ceased in 1882. The zamindar belongs to the Kondaiyankōttai section of the Marava caste.

Ottapidāram (population 3,867) : formerly the headquarters of the old Ottapidāram taluk (abolished in 1911) has just (1915) been disinherited in favour of Kōilpatti. There is a local fund hospital in the place. Its large tank and many acres of paddy fields present, during part of the year, a refreshing contrast to the bare country of the neighbourhood. The village is a small one, consisting of two parallel streets of Brahman houses, a temple dedicated to Siva and one to Vishnu, and a few houses of Sūdras. The most dearly-prized possession of the place is the temple of Ulagamman, whose power to avert cholera from the village is notoriously great.

Just to the north of the village in the midst of the paddy fields, is an enclosure containing the tombs of four officers and a gunner who fell in the assault made on Pānjālankurichi on the 5th September 1799.

In the village of Rājānkōvil, four miles to the south-east, is a stone on which is carved in relief the figure of a warrior, in an attitude of readiness to fight, with a short sword in his right-hand and a shield in his left. His hair is bunched into a high top-knot; he has fierce moustaches and distended ear-lobes. Below the figure two cocks are represented fighting. A *sati* stone of the usual type is found on the same site.

Two miles to the north of Ottapidāram is the site of PANJALANKURICHI, the stronghold of the famous line of poligars each of whom is known to history under the name (it is in reality a family title) of Kattaboma Nāyakkan. The earliest poligar of historical times succeeded in 1709; and it was against him that the first of a long series of expeditions was directed in 1755. The leader was Colonel Heron, the first British Commandant to enter Tinnevelly; it was however a half-hearted affair, and the troops never reached the place. As the party approached, Kattaboma Nāyakkan sent out a part

CHAP. XV. KOILPATTI TALUK.

of his tribute, the enforcement of which was the object of the campaign; and the troops were withdrawn. During the time of Muhammad Yūsuf Khān, Pānjālankurichi seems to have given no trouble. On the recall of that powerful commander the poligars were immediately up in arms and refused to pay their dues, foremost among them being the Kattaboma Nāyakkan of the day who had succeeded in 1760.[1] In 1767 Major Flint marched with a strong force against the place. An assault was made but was unsuccessful. Having lost several men, including eight Europeans killed, Major Flint decided on a blockade, but during the night the defenders made good their escape to their Dutch allies at Tuticorin and Vaippār. The next attempt to reduce Pānjālankurichi was in 1783, the expedition being led by Colonel Fullarton. The assault was a failure, and the storming party had to retire with considerable loss. On this occasion again the poligar's men, who had also suffered heavily, evacuated the fort as soon as the storming party advanced. The stronghold contained a large quantity of guns and ammunition and forty thousand pagodas, a sum which was distributed among the troops. The most interesting find was the original of a treaty between Kattaboma Nāyakkan and the Dutch Government of Colombo. The next clear opening for Kattaboma Nāyakkan came with the Ramnad rebellion of 1797. A regular confederacy was formed by almost all the poligars (Ettaiyāpuram was an exception) throughout the east of the district. Kattaboma Nāyakkan's followers were plundering every part of the country; Srīvaikuntam and Alvārtirunagari were looted, and their principal inhabitants taken prisoners; the chief people of Kurumbūr (Srīvaikuntam) and Mānād (in the present Tiruchendūr taluk) were carried off—all apparently on the pretext that the *kāval* fees claimed by the poligar had not been paid. Mr. Jackson, who was appointed Collector of Poligar Peshkash in 1797, issued order after order to the poligar to appear before him at his headquarters, Ramnad. He appeared finally on the 10th September 1798, when the unfortunate incident referred to on page 80 occurred. The poligar was called on to explain and gave a lengthy, largely irrelevant and unconvincing account of the affair, affirming that he did not commit the murder and that it was done without his knowledge or consent. A small commission was appointed to enquire into the matter, with the result that the poligar was acquitted and Mr. Jackson removed. Mr. Lushington succeeded and immediately addressed a pompous communication

[1] Died in 1791.

on the subject of his acquittal to Kattaboma Nāyakkan, adding a homily on the duties of a poligar. From March till June the Collector issued orders at frequent intervals to the poligar either to appear before him or to return to his pollam. Realizing that he now had the upper hand, Kattaboma entirely ignored the Collector and amused himself by ransacking the country. Reports of his depredations were pouring in from all sides.

In September 1799 Major John Bannerman, who had been specially appointed to take command in Tinnevelly, reached Pānjālankurichi; the attack was at once made but failed; and in the night the poligar and his people once more fled from the fort. Kattaboma Nāyakkan, largely owing to the assistance rendered by the Tondamān (of Pudukōttai), was captured in October; he was taken to Kayattār and there hanged,[1] and Subramanya Pillai, his chief adviser, suffered the same fate at Nāgalāpuram.

To the last the poligar maintained an attitude of cool defiance. "The manner and behaviour of the Poligar," wrote Major Bannerman, "during the whole time of his being before those who were assembled yesterday at the examination which took place was undaunted and supercilious. He frequently eyed the Ettaiyāpuram Poligar who had been so active to secure his person and the Poligar of Sivagiri with an appearance of indignant scorn; and when he went out to be executed he walked with a firm and daring air, and cast looks of sullen contempt on the poligars to his right and left as he passed. On reaching the foot of the tree in which he was hanged he regretted that he left his fort in the defence of which it would have been better for him to have died."

The story of the capture of the fugitives, their subsequent escape from jail, their flight to Pānjālankurichi, the unsuccessful attempt made on March 31 by Major Colin Macaulay to storm the fort and its final capture and reduction, on May 23, 1801, by Colonel Agnew has been narrated in chapter II. The resistance offered by the defenders was remarkable, and to the methods they employed it would probably be difficult to find a parallel in history. "To us, who had suffered so severely in our unsuccessful assault," wrote Captain Welsh,[2] describing his impressions on entering the fort after its capture, "a sight of the interior of this abominable dog-kennel was most acceptable; the more so, as this was the first time it had ever been taken by storm, though

[1] See also p. 81.

[2] Col. Jas. Welsh's *Military Reminiscences* (London, 1830).

CHAP. XV. KOILPATTI TALUK.

frequently attempted. Nothing could equal the surprise and disgust which filled our minds at beholding the wretched holes under ground, in which a body of three thousand men, and for some time their families also, had so long contrived to exist. No language can paint the horrors of the picture. To shelter themselves from shot and shells, they had dug these holes in every part of the fort; and, though some might occasionally be out to the eastward, yet the place must always have been excessively crowded. The north-west bastion, our old breach, attracted our particular attention; and a description of it will therefore serve for every other in this fort. It was about fifteen feet high on the outside, and nearly square: the face we breached was thirty feet long, and a parapet of about three feet thick at the summit, gradually increased sloping down into the centre, which was barely sufficient to contain about forty men; the passage in the gorge being only wide enough to admit two at a time. The depth in the centre being originally on a level with the interior, was increased as the top mouldered down, so as to leave the defenders entirely sheltered from everything but the shells and shot, which we had latterly used, more by accident than design. These were, of course, thrown over from the outside, and nothing else could have secured us the victory, since every man in the last breach was killed and the passage blocked up, before our grenadiers obtained a footing above. Their long pikes, used in such a sheltered spot, must be most powerfully effective. No wonder then, that every man who got to the top was instantly pierced and thrown down again. He could never get at his enemy, and indeed could scarcely tell from whence the blow was inflicted. The system of defence adopted by these savages would have done credit to any engineer. Nothing could surpass it but their unwearied perseverance. Had the bastions been solid, or their defensive weapons only musquets and bayonets, we should not have had the mortification to be before it for two months; and had our cavalry been more efficient, we should not have had a continuance of this warfare for six months longer."

The moving spirit of the last rebellion was the remarkable deaf mute[1]—"Umai," as he was called in consequence—the younger of the two brothers of the poligar who was hanged at Kayattār in 1799. A tall slender delicate-looking lad, he commanded the adoration of his followers. His least sign was an oracle, and obedience to his command was instant. To represent the English he would take a few pieces of straw

[1] The account which follows is taken from Colonel Welsh's *Reminiscences*.

and place them in the palm of his hand; with a whizzing sound from his mouth he would draw the other hand across and sweep them off and—"so perish the English!" During the pursuit of the fugitives from the fort, Umai fell covered with wounds. On the entreaty of a comrade some women picked him up, covered his body with a cloth and set up a funeral lamentation of the usual kind. The Ettaiyāpuram pursuers on coming up asked what had happened; and, receiving the answer that a poor young fellow had just died of small-pox, hurried on.

As already stated, when the fort was demolished in 1801, the site was ploughed over. The work, however, was imperfectly done; for to the present day there remain clearly visible the foundations of buildings of all sizes. Amongst the remains is a circular floor of fine masonry on which, it seems impossible to doubt, stood a shrine of Sakka Dēvi (her temples are always circular), the household goddess of the poligar's caste. To the west, beyond the tank bund, at a distance of six hundred yards from the fort site, are the remains of the mound which was built, after the failure of the assault in March, and used as a breaching-battery in the final attack and, later in the year, as the place of execution of Kattaboma and his brother Umai. A quarter of a mile to the north is an enclosure, containing in three divisions the tombs of 9 officers, 8 non-commissioned officers and 27 private soldiers who were killed in the two last assaults of the 31st March and the 24th May. At a little distance to the south, and not far from a building which appears to have been a powder-magazine, are the tombs of native officers.

The name of Kattaboma is still famous in the district and is generally mentioned with respect. A long poem called "The Great Epic of the Kaliyuga," in 40 cantos aggregating 4,000 distiches, relates the origin of the Kattaboma family and their relations with the English from the days of Mr. Jackson to the final triumph—not defeat—of the last poligar. The "epic" is historical to the extent that real persons and a few true incidents are introduced; it is full of wild exaggerations, and the sequence of events is often most confused. The dialogue, however, is lively and often humorous, the scene-changing rapid and dramatic; and, when delivered by a reciter skilful enough to conceal the deficiencies and irregularities of the metre, the poem goes with a most attractive lilt. Copies of the work exist on cadjans and may even be found in manuscript; snatches of the song are known almost everywhere.

The present representative of the family, who lives at Sekkārakkudi, receives a small pension from Government and is entertained in most places by the members of his caste with the honours generally shown to a zamindar. In the Tokkalava subdivision of the Kambalatta caste he is regarded as the leading member, corresponding to the zamindar of Ettaiyāpuram in his relation to the rival subdivision of Sillavars. His adherents speak of him as "zamindar" and his residence as *aranmanai*, pay him for his visitations and take their disputes to him for decision.

Vilāttikulam (population 4,031) : a small village, 20 miles by a direct road from Kōilpatti, contains the offices of a deputy tahsildar (who is also a sub-magistrate) and of a sub-registrar, but otherwise possesses no importance. A few families of Kaikkilaiyans weave the cloths worn by women, coarse towels and a class of bedsheet known as *rettu*. They used to do their own dyeing but now import coloured yarn from Madura.

NANGUNERI TALUK.

CHAP. XV. NANGUNERI TALUK.

NANGUNERI, second in size among the eight taluks, occupies the south-western corner of the district and marks the southern limit of British India. As far south as Panagudi a magnificent barrier of hills divides it from Travancore on the west, the actual boundary following the watershed as far as Mahēndragiri; thence the boundary drops south-east to the plain country, continuing more or less due south till it meets the sea four miles east of Cape Comorin. The negotiations which led to the final settlement of this last section of the boundary were prolonged and intricate. For many years the frontier as laid down along the watershed by Messrs. Ward and Connor, who had surveyed the Travancore boundary between 1817 and 1820, was, apparently, accepted by both the parties affected. In 1856 the Travancore Durbar set up the contention that they had been enjoying a considerable extent of land east of the Arāmboli pass and demanded that the boundary should be re-aligned so as to include with Travancore this territory and also some lands west of Karunkulam between the pass and Cape Comorin. The demand was at first resisted, but the matter remained still under discussion. In 1868 Mr. Puckle met Sir T. Madhava Rao, the Diwan, and, following the *uti possidetis* principle, they came to a settlement, which, in 1871, Government finally ratified. Between Mahēndragiri and the Arāmboli pass the base of the hills was adopted as the frontier; south of this point the old line laid down by Ward and Connor was adhered to.

The sea-coast fronting the Gulf of Manaar consists mostly of rolling sand-dunes, the exception being a few excrescences of granitoid rocks, at Idintakarai and westwards. The taluk is on the whole a dry one, only a little more than one-eighth of the total ryotwari area being irrigated. Palmyras are generally abundant; and in some parts, particularly in the six large villages comprised in the "palmyra forest," these trees dominate the dry lands to the exclusion of cultivation. Where the soil is sandy or poor, a crop of sāmai, gingelly or horse-gram is raised once in two or three years; elsewhere dry crops are attempted whenever the rain is sufficient and seasonable. Along the western edge of the taluk, especially

CHAP. XV. NANGUNERI TALUK.

the region of Panagudi, Palavūr, Karunkulam, and further east towards Rādhāpuram and again north of Nāngunēri, well-cultivation is common'; in and around Selvamarudūr towards the south-east large quantities of first-class plantains are grown in this way. The rainfall of the taluk is below the district average, and the effect of a short or unseasonable supply is soon seen in an increased number of emigrants to the tea-estates of Travancore, to Ceylon and the Straits Settlements, and in a general advance in the price of local labour. Nāngunēri seems always for one reason or another to have been the "Cinderella" of the taluks. In 1874 Mr. Puckle wrote:—

"The good old revenue system now in force has assessed this impoverished tract, where rainfall is less than anywhere else in the Presidency, at higher rates than prevail in even the most fertile parts of the Cauvery or Tāmbraparni; and were it not for the assistance afforded by the palmyra forest on the east of the taluk, the coffee estates on the hills to the west, and the charities of Travancore to the south, the poorer tracts of this taluk would have been depopulated years ago."

Even to-day, after every possible consideration has been paid in the recent re-settlement to its conditions, the average incidence per acre of the assessment paid by its rain-fed wet lands is higher than in any other taluk; its river-fed lands, though more lightly assessed than those of the Tāmbraparni valley, bear a much heavier average rate than those of the Tenkāsi taluk. It was one of the first taluks to feel the effects of the famine of 1877 and suffered more than any other from the torrential rains which followed in the north-east monsoon of 1878.

It continues to be the most sparsely populated taluk of the district, and, in the ten years ending with 1911, its inhabitants increased by only 3·60 per cent.

The weekly market held at Tisaiyanvilai is probably the largest in the district. Paddy from the river-valley, dry grains of all kinds, garden produce, baskets and other articles manufactured from the palmyra and cocoanuts from the west coast are sold in enormous quantities.

Means of communication leave much to be desired. In the extreme south of the taluk nothing better than a cart-track is to be found; a road to connect Nāngunēri with Srīvaikuntam and one from the east of the taluk, say from Vijayanārāyanam to Sāttānkulam, would be greatly appreciated by traders. Nāngunēri, the largest place in the taluk, is a union; so also are Kalakkād, Eruvādi and Tirukkurungudi. The temples at Nānguneri and Tirukkurungudi, both Vaishnavite, are noteworthy.

Eruvādi:[1] a union with a population of 2,033, situated five miles from Nānguneri on the road to Tirukkurungudi, is famous for its betel-gardens, the cultivation of which belongs, as usual, to the caste of Ilaivāniyans. In normal seasons, it is calculated, as much as three or four tons of betel-leaves is exported from the place in a month. The village has recently suffered from a severe outbreak of malarial fever, in which the Ilaivāniyans have been the worst sufferers.

On the other side of the Nambiyār, included in the union, lies the Muhammadan settlement of PULIYANJUVANAM. It is a large weaving centre containing about 1,000 looms, almost all the workers being the employees of Muhammadan capitalists of Mēlappālaiyam, who supply the yarn and merely pay the weaver for his work. The cloths woven are of the "tartan" style, large quantities of which are exported to Ceylon and Singapore.

Idaiyangudi (a hamlet of the revenue village of Tisaiyanvilai): situated in the south-east corner of the taluk, is accessible by road only from the north. On the south the village is shut in by great rolling dunes of brilliant red sand dotted with palmyras; on other sides the sandy soil is relieved, where water has been found, by patches of cultivation; otherwise palmyras and thorn-trees are the only products of the soil. The village is a Christian settlement and memorable chiefly as having been for 43 years the scene of the labours of Dr. Robert Caldwell, missionary, scholar and bishop.

Born on the 7th August 1814 of Scottish parents, Robert Caldwell[2] received his University education at Glasgow. There he attached himself to the sect of Congregationalists and, after taking his degree, joined the London Missionary Society. In 1838 his Society sent him out to Madras, where for over two years after his arrival he devoted his time mainly to the study of Tamil. Caldwell soon felt an inclination to join the Church of England and decided to take orders and enlist himself in the service of the Society for the Propagation of Gospel. Tinnevelly was the field in which he elected to work, and in July 1841 he set out on foot from Madras to find the country of his choice. On the way he visited Pondicherry, Kumbakōnam and Tranquebar; at Tanjore he met the veteran missionary Kohloff; thence travelling by Trichinopoly and

[1] For assistance with many of the topographical notices relating to this taluk I am indebted to Mr. D. N. Strathie, I.C.S.

[2] *Reminiscences of Bishop Caldwell*, edited by Rev. J. L. Wyatt, Madras, 1894.

CHAP. XV. NANGUNERI TALUK.

Mettupālaiyam, still on foot, he made his way up to Ootacamund, where he received ordination at the hands of Bishop Spencer. He bought a horse to take him the rest of the way, but soon discarded his mount and continued to journey on foot by way of Coimbatore and Madura. Finding shoes an encumbrance, he walked bare-footed through the black-cotton plains of Madura and Tinnevelly. Idaiyangudi was reached in November.

Christianity here dated from the time of Jaenicke and Satyanāthan, but had received so little attention from missionaries of later years that in 1841 there were practically no Christians there at all. A confused collection of mean houses, tortuous lanes, a small church and a one-roomed bungalow constituted the village. Caldwell set himself at once to buy up the whole site together with a few adjoining fields. Regular streets were laid out running east to west and north to south, the young missionary himself climbing to the top of a convenient tree to see that his plans were carried out correctly. Trees were planted, wells dug, scrub jungle was cleared, and a site was marked out in the sandy waste for the mission buildings and the church of the future. "You have spoiled my city," murmured a testy old Nādān, one of the community from whom Caldwell had bought the land; and it was some time before the improvements were appreciated.

Within three years twenty-one congregations had been formed, nine schools had been established, and 2,000 persons were under Christian instruction. In 1844 Caldwell married; and in the same year, through Mrs. Caldwell's efforts, a school for girls was started, and the lace industry for which Idaiyangudi is now famous was introduced. These revolutionary practices provoked sarcastic comment. "What are these girls learning to read for?" asked the "educated" father of ignorant daughters. In 1847 the foundation stone of the present handsome church was laid, and, until its dedication in 1880, Caldwell took the keenest interest in its building, shaping in clay the tracery of the windows and the mouldings of the roofs so that masons and carpenters might work from his models. After seventeen years in India, Caldwell—pastor, doctor and magistrate among his people—was obliged by ill-health to return for a time to England, where he took three years to recover. Till then he had made it his custom during the hot months to move with all his pupils to a little place called Ilunjunai on the sea-coast, just near Idaiyangudi; temporary school buildings were run up, and the remains of "Dr. Caldwell's bungalow" (so marked in the old survey maps) still recall the days when

Kōdaikānal had not been "invented." With only two more short breaks for leave to England Caldwell spent the rest of his life in India.

As missionary work extended, it was felt that the district should have a bishop of its own; if this proposition were admitted, each of the two societies, the S.P.G. and the C.M.S., it was thought, must have its bishop; and at the same time a bishop in Tinnevelly must be subordinate to the Bishop of Madras. It was decided finally that a bishop from each Society should be appointed; and in 1877 Dr. Caldwell for the S.P.G. and the Rev. E. Sargent for the C.M.S. were made Assistant Bishops to the Bishop of Madras.

In 1884 Bishop Caldwell, on the advice of the Metropolitan, moved to Tuticorin with a view to making that place the centre of the work of the S.P.G. in Tinnevelly; the transfer of the College department of the Sawyerpuram institution and its rehabilitation in Tuticorin as the "Caldwell College" formed part of the scheme. There Bishop Caldwell continued actively engaged in missionary and educational work until, in January 1891, he was compelled by advancing age to resign. He retired to Kōdaikānal, where, after a very short illness, he died on the 28th August. His remains were conveyed to Idaiyangudi and buried beneath the altar of his own church.

From the time of his first arrival in India Caldwell devoted himself with rare enthusiasm to the study of Indian philology, ethnology and history. He taught himself German in order to read works of German scholarship; he ransacked Greek and Roman writers and geographers from Herodotus down to Byzantine times and during his absence from India spent much of his time in the British Museum. In 1856 he produced his first book, "A Comparative Grammar of the Dravidian and South Indian Family of Languages." The work, which soon ran into a second edition, covers a wider field than its title implies. In recognition of its merits, the University of Glasgow conferred on its author the degree of LL.D., an honour which Durham followed up in 1873 with the degree of D.D. Dr. Caldwell's next book, produced in 1881, was his "History of Tinnevelly." It was published by the Madras Government at their expense and is now, unfortunately, out of print. Its value can best be appreciated by those who have attempted to study in the same sphere; and the obligations under which Dr. Caldwell has laid the present writer cannot be sufficiently acknowledged. In 1881 appeared Dr. Caldwell's last book, "Records of the Early History of the Tinnevelly Mission of the S.P.C.K. and the S.P.G." In addition to these books,

Dr. Caldwell found time for numerous pamphlets, the best known of which are those relating to demon-worship in Tinnevelly.

At the present day Idaiyangudi appears much the same, it may be supposed, as Dr. Caldwell left it—a village of straight and well-kept streets, church, bungalow, and schools for boys and girls standing at one end in ample compounds. It is the headquarters of a mission "district" and still the residence of a European missionary.

Kalakkād (population 4,766): a union, 8½ miles from the taluk headquarters, with which it is connected by a metalled road, is situated at the foot of the ghats on the road leading from Sērmādevi to Travancore. Lying in the midst of well-watered paddy fields and shaded by thick clusters of cocoanut trees, the little town possesses every natural advantage of situation and scenery. There is a P.W.D. rest-house in the place and one-and-a half miles away, up the valley, is a forest bungalow. There are three chattrams: one maintained by local funds, one by the temple, the other being a private institution.

The Saivite temple dedicated to Sathyavāgīswarar is popularly believed to have been founded by Vīra-mārtānda Rāja, one of the kings of Travancore; it contains an inscription of the early years of the sixteenth century which records grants from a ruler (obviously a Chēra) named Mārtāndan and another inscription which mentions the same name.[1] His statue, which stands within the temple, is worshipped daily. The foundation of the Vishnu temple, dedicated to Varadarāja-perumāl, as also of the Vīramārtānda Pillaiyār temple, is ascribed to the same king. Each of the two main temples celebrates two festivals annually, a singular fact being that, on the fourth day of the Saivite festival celebrated in *Vaikāsi* (May-June), the ceremonies are conducted by a Muhammadan of the place who is the trustee for some of the temple lands.

The little Roman Catholic church to the south-east of the village was built about 1808 by a subadar of the old 18th regiment named Kastūri, whose faithful services (in connection with the Vellore mutiny, it is said) were rewarded by a grant of 30 *kōttais* (about 48 acres) of land in the village, free of assessment. The "subadar mānibam," as it is called, though reduced in extent, continues to the present day.

A lower secondary school, known as the Edward Coronation School, which was established by public subscription, is managed by a local committee. There is also a privately-owned

[1] *Govt. Epig. Ann. Report* for 1904–05; inscriptions Nos. 131, 132.

Sanskrit school, in which Brahman boys are educated and fed free of cost. The C.M.S. maintain a school for girls.

A little cloth weaving is done by Iluvans and Muhammadans; the latter also weave grass mats, which are sent to Mēlappālaiyam and Pēttai. The heaps of slag near the village point to an iron-smelting industry which existed before the days of cheap imported iron (see p. 27).

Traces of an old fort, the origin of which is ascribed to a Travancore king, may be seen to the south of the village. The remains of an inner and an outer wall and a moat are still clearly visible. The tradition as to its origin is probable enough; for we know that, at intervals during the fifteenth and sixteenth centuries and subsequently during the eighteenth century, large portions of the Tinnevelly district were occupied by the Travancoreans. In 1756 Muhammad Yūsuf expelled them from this fort, only to find on his return two years later that the treacherous Māhfuz Khān, who had taken the Travancoreans into alliance, had handed back to them this stronghold and the adjoining districts. Muhammad Yūsuf marched on the place and drove the foreigners back to their own country. By 1765 the Travancore troops were once more in possession of the "Kalakkād district," which embraced Tirukkurungudi and Panagudi, and had compelled the small garrisons that had been left in these places to retire to Palamcotta. Two successive detachments of troops were sent out under British officers, who succeeded ultimately in forcing the invaders to retire within the Arāmboli lines. A settlement was effected in the next year, by which, through the intervention of the East India Company, the Rāja of Travancore agreed with the Nawāb to relinquish his claims to the "Kalakkād district." After the assumption of Tinnevelly by the Company the place was used as a station for the troops engaged in watching the movements of the freebooting Nānguněri Maravans. From the records of that time it is seen that the fort was of a considerable size, 900 by 600 yards square, with walls six feet high and fifteen feet thick. It was repaired in 1802, but seems to have been abandoned soon after.

A journey of eight miles up the hill by a well-kept bridle-path leads to the Sengaltēri forest bungalow, standing at an elevation of 2,880 feet and commanding magnificent views. Close by is an old coffee estate, one of the many small plantations that were opened up on these hills from 1850 onwards. No attempt is made at cultivation, but the Brahman who owns it occasionally sends up coolies to pick any coffee-berries or pomeloes that may happen to be growing. Some of the old buildings and machinery still remain and, strangest of all, several English rose-bushes. Seven miles again from Sengaltēri is the Kumāraswāmi Pillai's anicut (see p. 186), beside which is a rest-house maintained by the Public Works Department.

Nānguneri (population 4,817): a union 19 miles from Palamcotta on the road to Travancore, has been the headquarters of the taluk since 1819, when, owing to the epidemic fever then raging along the foot of the hills, Kalakkād was dethroned from this position. The present form of the name of the place is comparatively modern, the name appearing in the early English records variously as Nangancheri (the name generally used to the present day by the natives of the taluk) and Nangalancheri. The place contains all the offices usually found in a taluk headquarter station. The taluk board maintains a travellers' bungalow, a choultry and an elementary school.

As the headquarters of the Vānumāmalai mutt (known in the northern districts as the Tōdādri mutt), whose Jeer is the religious head of the Tenkalai Vaishnavites, Nānguneri enjoys a wide rēputation. The Jeer also exercises supreme control over the local temple, which, owing to the prestige of the mutt, attracts financial support from all parts of the Presidency. In 1841, when the management of the temples was abandoned by Government, the funds of this temple were handed over, not to trustees as was done in most cases, but to the Jeer. The office appears always to have carried with it the control of the temple. A brass plate inscription, dated *Kollam Andu* 622 (A.D. 1447), in the possession of the mutt records that in that year a Vaishnavite ascetic came to Nānguneri and, on the request of the Nambūdiri Brahmans who were then controlling the temple, took over the management. He appears at the same time to have assumed the position of Jeer and is regarded as the first of his line. Whether he actually founded the mutt is not clear; the record referred to makes no allusion to this point. Every Jeer names his own successor, his powers of selection being absolutely unfettered and not open to question. Throwing his mantle on the shoulders of his nominee and handing him the rod which is the emblem of office, he declares that the appointment is made. At death his body is carried out in a palanquin to the place where all Jeers are buried; the deceased is buried in a covering of salt, and cocoanuts are broken on his head; his successor then proceeds to the mutt in the same palanquin. The good deeds of many of the Jeers have been recorded. The first toured through India and won many disciples; the fourth built the *gōpuram;* the nineteenth spent vast sums on the temple and built the *sivili mantapam* and acquired many of the temple jewels; the twenty-first obtained for the temple the coffee estate above Tirukkurungudi, which the mutt still owns; the twenty-fourth built the golden car. The present Jeer is the twenty-fifth of the line. The resources of the temple and the mutt (separate accounts for each are kept) are enormous. Besides the annual *dastik* allowance of Rs. 8,694 which the temple receives from Government, both temple and mutt own extensive properties in land, inam and *ayan;* two hundred subordinate mutts scattered over India contribute their surplus revenues, and the subscriptions of pious pilgrims must reach a high figure. All this wealth is at the absolute disposal of the Jeer.

Situated close beside the bund of the large irrigation tank, the temple is almost shut in on its other sides by blocks of houses. The *mantapam* by which one enters contains some good specimens of life-sized sculptures, carved, together with the pillars they adorn, out of single blocks of stone. The *sivili mantapam* is in reality a series of four long corridors which form a circuit round the inner temple; flanked on either side with the familiar rows of *yālis* supporting the stone roof, it produces a fine effect of symmetry and grandeur. The temple possesses a large collection of jewels, a number of vehicles *(vāhanam)* on which the gods are carried in procession, and a car decorated with gold. The mutt is within the temple precints. It maintains a Sanskrit school, which provides free education and board for Brahman pupils. Two festivals are celebrated in the year, one in *Panguni* (March-April) and the other in *Chittirai* (April-May).

The chief export of the place is paddy, mostly of the poorer kinds. The mutt, which owns much of the wet land, consumes, by means of its pilgrims and Brahman adherents, enormous quantities and exchanges a good deal of the locally-grown grain for the superior produce of the Tāmbraparni valley. The surplus goes mostly to the Tisaiyanvilai market and to Travancore. A market is held every Monday.

About five miles to the south-west off the main road is the village of RAJAKKALMANGALAM, where excellent stone for use in pavements and pillars is quarried in large slabs. Lying about on the ground are numerous blocks of stone with figures carved on them. The largest is about 9 feet high by 4 feet broad and represents, the villagers say, a king named Hiranya Rāja, who once ruled here. The site looks as if it would yield much to excavators.

CHAP. XV. NANGUNERI TALUK.

Panagudi: population 4,565 (the name is popularly believed to be a corruption of *Panam-kudi*, "the money-place" or "treasury") is situated on the banks of the Hānumānadhi, 14 miles south-west of Nānguneri, on the road to Travancore. It contains a local fund hospital, a choultry managed by the Sērmādēvi taluk board and two private choultries, one for Muhammadans, the other for Hindus. The principal temple is one dedicated to Siva under the name Rāmalingaswāmi; curiously enough, it contains a small Vaishnavite temple inside it. A history of its foundation, which is ascribed to a king of Tenkāsi in the fourteenth century A.D., is preserved on cadjan leaves by a Vellālan of the place. The taluk board maintains a school for Muhammadans, a community represented by about a hundred families; in addition there are three schools maintained by missionary bodies and one other private school. The chief exports of the place are jaggery, palmyra fibre, paddy, cotton and firewood. A weekly market is held on Wednesdays.

Rādhāpuram (population 2,373): 19 miles from Nāngunēri, situated in a dry open plain seven miles from the sea, contains a police-station and the offices of a deputy tahsildar (who is also a sub-magistrate) and of a sub-registrar. Two choultries, built by public subscription on the occasion of the coronation of King Edward VII, are already in a state of sad disrepair, waiting apparently for the helping hand of an already overburdened taluk board. The old name of the place, as evidenced both by local tradition and by brass plate inscriptions preserved in the Siva temple, was *Rāja-rāja-puram*. It is impossible to know what king is here commemorated or even to decide whether he was a Pāndyan or a Chēran. The connection of Travancore with the place is seen in a brass plate inscription preserved in the temple which records a gift in the year *Kollam Andu* 715 (A.D. 1540) of lands by a Chēra prince, and there is every reason to believe that the place lies within the area occupied at frequent intervals from the fifteenth century onwards by the rulers of Travancore. One other inscription contained in the temple is interesting as throwing light on a detail of pre-British revenue administration. It is dated *Kollam Andu* 956 (A.D. 1781) and records the assignment to the temple by Dānappa Mudaliyār[1], the Nawāb's renter, of the tax levied on a newly opened shop.

At the western end of the village is a half-ruined Vishnu temple in which, oddly enough, pūja is performed by a

[1] Presumably an alternative name of Dalavāy Tirumalaiyappa Mudaliyar, who rented the district from the Nawāb from 1780 to 1782.

Smārtha Brāhman. Traces of an abandoned village, believed to have been the original settlement, are to be found in an open field about a quarter of a mile to the north-east of the Siva temple. The remains consist of paved stones, broken pieces of pottery, and grinding-mills.

Shenbagarāmanallūr (population 669): a small village, five miles east of Nānguneri, contains two large temples, one dedicated to Siva, the other to Vishnu, and a large stone-built tank. The sculptures of the Vaishnavite temple are similar, though inferior, to those found at Krishnāpuram. The Saivite temple contains an inscription dated *Kollam Andu* 765 (A.D. 1590). The high ground called *Māliatattu,* half a mile away from the village on the northern side, is traditionally supposed to have contained a fortified residence of a local ruler; substantial foundations of buildings are to be found a few feet below the surface.

Tirukkurungudi (population 2,183, union, sub-registrar's office, local fund dispensary, police-station, travellers' bungalow): is situated on the Nambiyār, two miles from the foot of the great Mahēndragiri range. The perfect cone of rock immediately to the south marks the position of the place for miles around.

Founded by the famous Udaiyavar, the author of Vaishnavism and the common priest of Vadakalais and Tenkalais, the local Vaishnavite temple attracts pilgrims from all parts of the south of India. The place possesses also peculiar sanctity as having been the last resting place of Tirumanja Alvār, known also as Kalla Alvār, a Maravan by caste, one of the twelve saints, or apostles, of Vaishnavism. After enlarging the Srīrangam temple by means of the loot acquired in the course of an adventurous career of free-booting, he prayed to the god Srīranganāthar to grant him heaven. The god bade him to go to "Tekkevīdu," "the abode in the south," meaning Tirukkurungudi. Thither the saintly warrior came, built a *prākāram* of the temple, and, dying in peace, obtained *mōksham*—salvation. As in Nānguṇēri, the temple has since 1841 been managed by a Jeer who has a Tenkalai mutt here; the adherents of this mutt, however, are comparatively few. The present Jeer is the ninth of his line, and the modern history of the temple he controls is largely composed of disputes in the law-courts between the Vadakalai and Tenkalai sects, the chief result of which has been the gradual impoverishment of the foundation.

The god Vishnu is represented in the place in five *avatārs,* or "incarnations." In the small tower beside the chattram he

CHAP. XV. NANGUNERI TALUK.

appears as Vāmanāvatāram—as a dwarf—the form in which he appeared before the unsuspecting Mahābali Rāja and asked for three feet of earth's space. In the temple itself three *avatārs* are depicted: first that of *Tiruviswarūpam*, the giant-form in which Vishnu, to the great discomfiture of Mahābali Rāja, measured out his allotted three-foot plot; the second attitude is that of the god sitting, and the third that of the god recumbent. The fifth *avatār*, the god standing, is found up the hills six miles away in what is called the Malai Nambi Kōvil, a favourite resort for the performance of vows.

A curious feature of the temple, one which is generally quoted as illustrating the breadth of view of its distinguished founder, is the existence within the Vaishnavite temple of one dedicated to Siva. Paramasivan, it is said, whilst wandering over the earth under the ban of a curse, came one day to Tirukkurungudi. There the god Nambi, an incarnation of Vishnu, treated him with kindness and promised his visitor that he should receive equal respect with himself. So the new god was established and received the name "Pakkanindrār," "he who stands by the side."

A *vatteluttu* inscription was removed from the temple to the Madras Museum in 1905. It is dated in the fourth year of the reign of King Māranjadaiyan, who is believed to be identical with Varaguna Varman, also called Māranjadaiyan,[1] the aggressive Pāndya ruler of the ninth century. Another record points to the connection (at a much later date) of the ruler of Travancore with the temple. This is an inscription dated *Kollam Andu* 644 (A.D. 1469), in Grantha characters, which is to be found on a large bell and records its presentation by Aditya Varma, prince of Travancore. We have seen (from Chapter II) that, during the fifteenth and sixteenth centuries, large portions of the Nānguneri taluk were constantly in the occupation of the Chēra ruler; and from the eighteenth century, at least, we have the evidence of Orme that Tirukkurungudi, amongst other places, was as frequently in the hands of Travancore as in those of the Nawāb. Its long association with Travancore is further borne out by the fact that to the present time the expenses of one day's celebrations during the *Panguni* festival are borne by the Durbar of that State.

The temple celebrates three festivals a year. During that held in the month of *Kārtikai* (November-December) a story connected with the temple is enacted in the form of a drama. A Paraiyan disciple of Udaiyār—his caste indicates again the master's broadminded teaching—was on his

[1] *Govt. Epig. Ann. Report* for 1904-05. See also pp. 45, 47, 358.

way to the temple to pray. He had reached the foot of Mahēndragiri, when he met a demon standing ready to devour him. Arguments ware proceeding, when Vishnu intervened, a compromise was effected, and the pilgrim was allowed to go to the temple on the condition that he should come back and be eaten then. He kept his promise; but meanwhile the monster's appetite had, through Vishnu's interference, so much abated that, instead of a feast of blood, he asked for the virtue of the pilgrim's offering. The devotee consented to give one-sixteenth part of it; and the demon, as soon as the holy water touched him, was restored to his normal human shape.

The inscription which refers to the building and restoration of the Venkayya Nāyakkan's anicut has already been mentioned (p. 185).

The so-called Tiruppālkadal Annadāna Nambirāyar chattram is the richest and best maintained institution of its kind in the district. The stone pillars in front of the building record its foundation and endowment in *Kollam Andu* 844 (A.D. 1669) by Shenbagamāran Kālatiyappa Pillai. Owing to mismanagement the Government assumed control in 1819; and, on the transfer of trust properties to the newly-created local bodies, the chattram passed under their management. It is now under the administration of the taluk board, and its finances are in a flourishing condition. From an income of about Rs. 20,000 food is supplied to travellers; allowances are given to the lame and blind; a yearly contribution is paid to the temple, and free board and tuition is given to fifteen Brahman students of Sanskrit; a primary school and a dispensary are maintained, and contributions are made to other charities.

Besides the Sanskrit and primary schools maintained by the chattram, there are in the place a Government school for Brahman girls, a girls' school belonging to the C.M.S. and a Panchama school, at Levingepuram on the south side of the river, maintained by another missionary body. The hamlet referred to derives its name from Mr. (afterwards Sir Vere) Levinge, who founded on the spot a *kanji pirai*, or "poor-house," for the refreshment of travellers of the poorer classes. This need is now supplied by the chattram itself, and the old building has recently been converted into a travellers' bungalow.

In NAMBITALAIVANPATTAIYAM, a hamlet on the other side of the river, is a half ruined Saivite temple, forming by its position on the top of a rock a conspicuous object as

CHAP. XV. NANGUNERI TALUK.

one approaches from Nānguneri. It is attached to the Tirukkurungudi mutt, and the Jeer receives a separate *dastik* allowance for its maintenance a Pūja, however, is no longer performed there, the idols having been removed to Tirukkurungudi.

In 1782, the year after the "Assignment," the leading Maravan of the place turned it into a fortress and, in imitation of the poligars of the north, started to plunder the neighbourhood. A force was despatched from Palamcotta, and the fort was captured and destroyed.

Up on the hills, eight miles from here, is a spot known as Nādugāni where there is a small rest-house. The building is situated in a clearing one mile from the Travancore frontier. The surrounding forest is threaded with elephant tracks, which alone make the dense masses of *ittikali (Beesha travancorica)* passable.

Vadakkankulam: the centre of a *pangu*, or parish, of the Jesuit mission, possesses the interest of being the place at which the Jesuits made their first converts amongst the Shānāns. Their Christianity dates from the closing years of the seventeenth century (see page 90); the conversion of Vellālans appears to have begun about a century later. For the last hundred years the history of the place has consisted largely of disputes between these rival sects of Christians. Both parties claimed the best seats in the church, and any arrangement which was suggested met with uncompromising opposition from one party or the other. The remedy finally adopted was the present handsome church, which was completed in 1872. The building consists in effect of two converging naves which meet in a common chancel; one side of the church is intended for the Shānāns, the other for the Vellālans. The solution of the trouble was by no means accomplished. Further disputes arose; petitions, counter-petitions and law-suits followed; and it is not known whether the decision given in 1913 by the District Court has restored peace to the community.

Valliyūr (population 7,661): was in 1839 made the head-quarters of a taluk of the same name, the old Nānguneri taluk being in that year divided into two. In 1860, when the divisions of the district were again re-constituted, the Valliyūr taluk was abolished, the present taluk of Nānguneri again coming into existence. The police-station and post office now occupy the old tahsildar's office. The local chattram managed by the taluk board was founded in 1844 by a tahsildar and is maintained partly from its own endowments and partly from the properties of an abandoned *matam*. The place is known for its Subrahmanya temple, which possesses unusual sanctity. Its shrine consists of a cavity in a rocky hill, in front of which stand the usual *mantapams*. Beside the temple are two beautiful *teppakulams* shaded by trees, which afford good shelter for a camp. During the festival held in *Chittirai* the temple is visited by thousands of pilgrims bearing *kāvadis*.

Around the Kāli temple about a mile from here the remains of a fort are clearly traceable, and legend connects with it the name of the Pāndya king, Kulasēkharaperumāl. Just to the south is a tank called Annāchikulam in which, it is said, the ladies of the royal house used to bathe. Remains of tiles and pillars have been dug up between the Amman and Siva temples. It seems certain that the place was once the residence of a king or local chieftain.

There is a tradition in the village that there used to be a Jaina temple here. The stones, it is said, were taken to re-line the tank, and the image removed "by a European."

Vijayāpati (population 5,333): on the sea-coast, seven miles from Rādhāpuram, possesses a ruined temple, whose exceptional sanctity attracts pilgrims twice a year. The furnace of holy fire before which a sage of old performed his *yāgam* is now a basin of water: to bathe first in this and then in the sea is a ritual which all worshippers perform. The old Kāli temple in the *tēri* to the east contains an inscription, which has not been deciphered and appears to be quite illegible.

SANKARANAINARKOIL TALUK.

CHAP. XV.
SANKARA-NAINARKOIL TALUK.

SANKARANAINARKOIL[1] occupies the north-west corner of the district and is the most rural of all the taluks. Its isolated position with its advantages of woods and mountain fastnesses rendered it, during the seventeenth and eighteenth centuries, the stronghold of the last of the Marava poligars who struggled to maintain against all opposition the ancient independence of their race. The whole area of the taluk was occupied by these chieftains. Pūli Tēvan of Nelkattan-seval, the most conspicuous amongst them, held the heart of the country, and around him were the poligars of Chokkam-patti, Uttumalai, Talaivankōttai, Sivagiri and Sēttūr, all Maravans and all prominent figures in the history of the eighteenth century. Even at the present time more than one-third of the taluk consists of zamindari land, and Maravans form the bulk of the population in this area.

The taluk is divided between the basins of the Vaippār and of two affluents of the Chittār, the Karuppānadhi and the Uppōdai. The streams which rise in the ghats and drain towards the Vaippār provide fair irrigation for a number of villages lying along the base of the hills; the rest of the taluk is but scantily supplied from rain-fed tanks. These adverse conditions have stimulated the energy of the ryots, and few taluks can show in recent years so rapid an expansion of well-cultivation.

There are no towns in the taluk; and even the five unions, Puliyankudi, Vāsudēvanallūr, Sivagiri, Kuruvikulam and Sankaranainārkōil, are little more than agglomerations of small villages. Important markets are held at Sankara-nainārkōil, Tiruvēngadam and Madattupatti; the annual cattle-fair at Sankaranainārkōil attracts dealers from all parts of the district.

The chief temples are the four members of the *Panchastala*, referred to under Sankaranainārkōil. The fifth temple of the series is at Dēvadānam, Srīvilliputtūr taluk, Rāmnād district.

[1] Mr. L. Cammiade, when Deputy Collector, Tinnevelly, some years ago, wrote for the Gazetteer an article on this subject which I have freely used. All the archæological information is derived from him.

The archæology of the taluk deserves attention. Burial urns have been found at Sivagiri, Panaiyūr, Vāsudēvanallūr, Karuvanallūr, Kārisāttān, Ariyūr. Ancient beds of ornamental stone and old coins are to be picked up on the sites of several old and forgotten townships, many of which adjoin the pre-historic cemeteries. Mr. L. Cammiade, who explored a number of these village-sites, writes :—"Quite a collection of strange beads may be had from this (Kārisāttān) and other old village-sites. The materials used, to name only a few, are crystal, garnet, opal, agate of various kinds, including banded agate, carnelian, jasper, green quartz, dark green steatite and lapis lazuli. Ancient glass and shell beads are also numerous. Glass bracelets of unusually fine workmanship are to be found. Some of the glass used has a resinous appearance and an opaque enamel has been fused into it. Others have a transparent blue enamel over the yellow glass which thus produces a green effect. The bangles found are absolutely dissimilar from anything now in use. Chank bangles are very numerous. Precious stones were not unknown, to judge from a much damaged ruby found in one of these old sites. Porcelain and glass are very rare; only minute fragments are to be found. Most of the bits produced are Chinese ware. Numerous lumps of a dark blood-coloured stone with a glassy lustre are usually to be picked up on the village-sites. The natives call them *kōli iral-kal*, "fowl's liver stone," from their appearance. Some of them have been neatly flaked. These may have served for striking fire. Bits of bronze and pewter ornaments have been produced. But it is difficult to get admissions from the finders that any metal ornaments exist. They have an ineradicable fear lest they will get into trouble if they admit finding gold or silver, or any metal. Ornaments, seals, etc., of baked clay also occur. Coins are found in the more recent sites, but seem to be totally absent from the more ancient ones.

"The extraordinary abundance of these remains in the midst of broken pottery and ashes suggests that the places where they were found were suddenly ravaged by an enemy and the populations massacred in their homes. At Kārisāttān bits of human bones are to be found mixed with the rest of the débris.

"The places where the old sites have been noticed by me are Palankōttai, Sāyamalai,[1] Kuruvikulam, Nāluvāsal-kottai,

[1] On this site there are, amongst other remains, the ruins of a Vishnu temple, a Pillaiyār temple, a *teppakulam* and a *mantapam*. A Siva temple and an Amman temple are still in use.

Sankaranainārkōil, Perunkōttur, Perumbattūr, Kuvalaikkanni, Marattōni, Karivalamvandanallūr, Kārisāttān, Panaiyūr, Ariyūr (foot of the hill), Gūdalūr, Vāsudēvanallūr, several places, east of Gūdārapēri, beyond Sivagiri, also south of Sivagiri town, Tenmalai, Dēvipatnam, Vīrasikhāmani and Kulasēkharamangalam. In fact the taluk (like the rest of the district) is full of town places. Below the town refuse at Kārisāttān at a depth of six or eight feet, large funeral-urns have occasionally been met with indicating possibly an antiquity considerably greater than that of the nameless city that grew over them."

Alagāpuri (population 1,954): seven miles to the north-east of Sankaranainārkōil, is the headquarter village of the smallest of the ancient zamindaris. The estate, about 3 square miles in extent, comprises four patches of land which are grouped into two villages. Its rent-roll is about Rs. 4,500. The zamindar, like the Sivagiri family, belongs to the caste of Vanniyans.

In VADIKOTTAI is a small rock-cut temple, about 9 feet square and 6 feet high, hollowed out of the base of a hill. Two life-sized figures carved in the rock guard the entrance; unlike the similar temples at Vīrasikhāmani and Tirumalāpuram, the shrine contains neither *lingam* nor sculptures.

Karivalamvandanallūr (population 4,681). In explanation of this extravagant name it is said that once upon a time an elephant (Sanskr. *kari*) inspired by a deep sense of piety came from a neighbouring forest and performed the circuit of the temple in adoration of the *lingam*. Hence *Kari-valam-vantha-nallūr*, "the holy place round which the elephant perambulated." The inhabitants are proud of this polysyllabic name and pronounce it with due deliberation in the presence of strangers. Otherwise the place is generally referred to as Karuvanallūr.

Situated seven miles to the north of Sankaranainārkōil on the road to Srīvilliputtūr, which just north of the village crosses the river Nikshēbanadhi by a bridge, the place contains a local fund elementary school and a commodious private chattram. A *pirai*, or factory, in which about fifty cotton hand-gins *(manai)* are employed, has recently been started. The antiquity of the settlement is indicated by a custom still followed by many Sūdras of the district of bringing the ashes of their dead from distant places and burying them here on the banks of the Nikshēbanadhi. The temple is a large one and contains numerous inscriptions relating to the later Tinnevelly Pāndyas of the sixteenth and even of the seventeenth centuries. Specimens of stone carving intended to represent the details of wooden roofs, of the kind found at Tenkāsi, Sērmādēvi, Manappadaivīdu and other places, are to be seen on the outer surface of the walls of the inner shrine. The *lingam* is a rough block of white stone resembling chalcedony and, owing to its colour, has obtained the name "Pālvarnaswāmi," "the milk-coloured god.'

Though the village is old, it is apparently only an offshoot of a town which once existed at the foot of the Kārisāttān hill, three miles away to the east. The site, which is marked by broken pieces of pottery and one or two old wells, has for some years past been searched by Oddans and Pallans, who have discovered a large number of beads of a deep orange colour known as *pāpurapāsi.*

Nelkattanseval (or Avudaiyāpuram) (population 4,166): about seven miles to the north-west of Sankaranainārkōil, is chiefly memorable as having been in the eighteenth century the stronghold of the redoubtable Pūli Tēvan, who figured for many years as the leader of the Marava confederacy against the troops of the Nawāb and the Company. To the courage of the Marava warrior he added the wiliness of the Mahratta. He had a shrewd insight into the political situation of the time and was a veritable thorn in the side of the Nawāb's agents. Nelkattanseval (or "Nellitangaville" as spelt by Orme) was several times attacked, but Pūli Tēvan always succeeded in coming to terms before it was too late. Like Vāsudēvanallūr, the place appears to have had a considerable fixed population at a remote epoch. Old sites of habitations are to be found in many places in its neighbourhood; the most important are at Ariyūr, Periyūr, Panaiyūr, and Perumbattūr. At Ariyūr there is a long inscription on a rock, which does not appear to have been transcribed. Near by is the site of an old village, and old urn burials are to be found near the bed of a neighbouring stream.

The estate, which was granted on a deed of permanent settlement in 1803 to the poligar of that time, has since then passed through many vicissitudes of subdivision and sale, and no part of the ancient zamindari has descended by inheritance to the heirs of the sanad-holder. The headquarter village is in the possession of a lineal descendant of the first zamindar, but it had passed temporarily to strangers before it came to him. The name officially adopted in the deed of permanent settlement was Avudaiyāpuram, perhaps because the associations of the old name Nelkattanseval were too

CHAP. XV. SANKARANAINARKOIL TALUK.

unpleasant. The name Pānjālankurichi was expunged from all official records for a similar reason.

Puliyangudi: ten miles west of Sankaranainārkōil, forms with Mēla Puliyangudi, Chintāmani and Tirumalaināyakkanpudukudi a union, having a total population of 15,463. It contains a police-station, a sub-registrar's office and two local fund elementary schools. The local market, which is owned by the taluk board, is held on Mondays. About four hundred families are engaged in weaving; most of the weavers are Kaikkilaiyans, Iluvans coming next in number and, after them, Muhammadans. The wet lands of these villages, irrigated chiefly by the Vālamalaiyār, are amongst the most fertile in the taluk. An important product of the dry lands near the hills is the *kolinji (Tephrosia purpurea)* which is sent in large quantities to the villages in the valley of the Tāmbraparni for use as manure in the wet lands. Large quantities of paddy are sent to the neighbouring markets; rice to Travancore, cholam, gingelly and ragi to Pēttai.

In the Chokkampatti hills, three miles away to the south-west, is a remarkable cavern about 35 yards wide by 10 yards deep. Within it stand a temple dedicated to Karpaka Nāchi Amman and the shrines of minor deities. The cave occurs in a steep crevice enclosed by rocky hills, and, with the roof of the cavern for its bed, a stream descends from the forests. A channel leads the water to a *mantapam* which stands in a lower level in front of the cavern. When in flood, the torrent pours on to its roof or, at times, is shot clear over it.

Sankaranainārkōil: connected by a main road with Tinnevelly, from which it is 34 miles distant, is the headquarters of the taluk and the centre of a union with a population of 15,182. It contains the offices of a tahsildar, a second-class magistrate, a police inspector and a sub-registrar. There is also an "incomplete secondary" school under the management of a local committee. There are three chattrams in the place, one maintained by the taluk board, the other two being private institutions; the taluk board owns also a hospital and a travellers' bungalow. Weaving, which occupies a number of Kaikkilaiyans and a few Iluvans, is the chief industry of the place; two steam-gins which have recently been set up give employment to large numbers during the cotton season. A weekly market, owned by the taluk board, assembles on Thursdays. An annual cattle-fair is held at the end of July immediately after the *Adi tapasu* festival, half a mile away from the town, in a spacious enclosure neatly fenced and well shaded. The fair is among the largest in the district and brings into the taluk board which owns it an annual income of about Rs. 1,000.

The temple, conspicuous by its *gōpuram* for many miles around, boasts of great antiquity. According to the *stala-purana* in the possession of the trustees, king Ugra Pāndya, "Lord of Korkai, the vanquisher of the tiger-flag of the Chōlas and the bow-flag of the Chēras," used to go daily to Madura to worship. One day, on reaching the village of Perunkōttūr (two miles from Sankaranainārkōil), the elephant on which the king was riding plunged into a pit and refused to move. Whilst the king was marvelling at the portent, the god Ayyanār appeared and told him he need not go every day to Madura. At that moment a Paraiyan came and told the king he had found a cobra beside an ant-hill and on the king's request took him to the spot. There a *lingam* was found and a shrine was built. Such was the origin of the Sankaranainār-kōil temple. Here it was, the story goes on to say, that god Siva showed to his consort, Gōmati Amman, and to the two serpents, Sanka and Padma, who were quarrelling as to the relative importance of Siva and Vishnu, the unity of the two gods. The story, which up to this point had referred only to Siva, thus suddenly introduces in allegorical form a theological discussion of the type which originated with the great Rāmānujāchāriyār in the twelfth century. It is scarcely possible to doubt that this element of the story is a later interpolation, designed to associate the god Vishnu with the foundation of the temple and to lend support to the subsequent innovation by which the deity of the temple came to be called "Sankara Nārāyana" (i.e., Siva and Vishnu) instead of Sankara Nainār, "the Lord Siva." The plan of the building makes it evident that originally Vishnu had not a shrine in it. The temple consists of two main parts, the larger occupied by the *lingam*, the emblem of Siva, and the smaller by the goddess Gōmati Amman. Between the two a third small shrine has been inserted for Nārāyana. But the building did not lend itself to this addition; for, while the *lingam* and the Amman may, as is usual, be viewed from the main entrance through a continuous vista of doorways, so that the humblest worshipper may do homage from the street, it was found impossible to give the god Nārāyana similar accommodation. He has therefore been walled in and has no gateway. Instances of temples which, according to tradition at least, have been converted from the worship of Siva to that of Vishnu are not uncommon; the great temple of

CHAP. XV. SANKARA-NAINARKOIL TALUK.

Tirupati (North Arcot) and the Perumāl temple of Srīvilliputtūr (Rāmnād) may be quoted. In Sankaranainārkōil the attempt, which we may perhaps ascribe to the era of those ardent Vaishnavites, the kings of Vijayanagar, was met, it would appear, by the ingenious answer that already the temple contained both gods. Though the trustees of the present-day make much of the co-existence in their temple of the two gods and are particular in having the pattas for the temple lands made out distinctly in the name of Sankara Nārāyana, the newer god plays quite a minor rôle in the important rituals of the temple.

It is in fact mainly from Gōmati Amman, the consōrt of Sankara (Siva), that the temple derives its reputation. The ten days' festival in July, known as *Adi tapasu*, commemorating the penance done by Gōmati when she strove to see Siva and Vishnu as one God, is held chiefly in honour of the goddess and is the greatest local religious event of the year. The sick from all parts of the district and even beyond it flock to the temple in the hope of obtaining a cure from the goddess. Women suffering from hysteria prostrate themselves before her shrine, rolling and tossing their heads and continuing in her presence for days and nights together. In cases of bodily pain a dab of rice flour on a leaf is placed on the part affected; a hollow is scooped out in the paste and in it ghee is poured. The ghee is set alight, and, when it has burnt itself out, the cure is complete. Models of limbs, in wood or metal, are offered, some in the hope of a cure, some in gratitude for a cure already effected as the result of a vow made previously to the goddess. Products of the soil are given as a safeguard against pest and drought. Those who wish to keep their houses free from scorpions and snakes place images of these reptiles before the shrine; and such as cannot themselves go to the temple often send small money contributions through their friends to be placed in the *undil* box of the temple. Women hoping for safe delivery offer models of children and cradles. Victims of skin diseases throw salt and sugar in the square tank within the temple, hoping that their ailments may disappear as rapidly as their offerings are dissolved.

The temple is the chief of the *Panchastala*, "the five places," (four are within the taluk) each of which represents one of the five elements. The element here typified is earth; the other four temples, Dārukāpuram, Tenmalai, Karivalamvandanallūr and Dēvadānam (just across the border in the Rāmnād district) represent, in the order given, water, air, fire and ether.

In the main *gōpuram* of the temple is a clock (now out of repair) which is designed to ring the Indian hours (of 24 minutes), or *nāligais*.

Centrally situated as it was in the country of the Marava poligars, the place was used by the Company as a point from which to watch the movements of those restless marauders. A cantonment was established here in 1767 on the high ground to the north of the present travellers' bungalow. It was here that the main garrison of the district was encamped on the night of the 2nd February 1801, when the Pānjālankurichi prisoners broke out from the jail at Palamcotta and started the last of the poligar rebellions (p. 82).

Sivagiri: the headquarters of a zamindari (now in the hands of a receiver appointed by the Civil Court), is a union with a population of 12,257. It contains the office of a sub-registrar (who is also a special sub-magistrate with limited powers): a hospital and a local fund elementary school, to both of which institutions the zamindarni makes an annual contribution. The veterinary hospital and the agricultural farm (referred to below) which the estate maintains are also here. The little town, situated almost in a recess at the foot of the hills, lies in a fertile and well-watered strip of country. The zamindarni's residence consists of a collection of old buildings enclosed by a high and newly-built brick wall.

The zamindari, with a rent-roll (including its *dēvastānam* receipts) of about Rs. 2¾ lakhs, comes next in value, though not in size, to Ettaiyāpuram amongst the permanently-settled estates of the district. It covers an area of 129 square miles, exclusive of hill forests, which add another thirty. Of the cultivated area in the plain country a little less than one-third is irrigated, the remainder falling into the two classes, "garden" and "dry." The revenue system of the estate is extremely complicated, the rent on irrigated lands (of which there are four classes) being paid in some cases in kind, in other cases in cash, and again in other cases in both grain and cash together. Some progress in the substitution of money rents for payment in kind (a process begun in 1871 by Mr. Puckle) was recently made by the Court of Wards and is being continued. Certain kinds of "garden" crops, such as tobacco, betel, chillies, turmeric and so on, have "special" rates of assessment, the rates for the various crops differing even from village to village. The estate stands in the relation of trustee to a chattram at Viswanāthappēri, two miles away, and two temples, one at Sivagiri and the other at Tenmalai, five miles distant. The local temple is picturesquely situated

CHAP. XV.
SANKARA-NAINARKOIL TALUK.

on a rock overlooking the big irrigation tank; that at Tenmalai lies at the foot of a cluster of rocks beside the tank and is one of the *Panchastala* of the taluk, typifying "air." The institutions are maintained from a fund—the *dēvastānam,* or endowment fund—which is kept separate from the ordinary revenues of the estates.

The zamindarni, who belongs to the Vanniyan caste —to be distinguished from the sect of Maravans who call themselves Vannikutti Maravans—traces the foundation of her family's greatness to the favour of a "Pāndya king of Madura," who deputed a member of the family to command a tract of country around a place named Sundankulam. From Sundankulam, his first headquarters, the poligar (as he was styled) transferred himself in time to Tenmalai, twenty miles westward, and thence later on to Sivagiri. The family records, from which this account is derived, place the last migration in comparatively modern times, A.D. 1733–34. Tradition fixes the site of the old Tenmalai home as the open plain to the south of the hill so named; but no remains are now traceable. No explanation of the transfer of capital is given; but it is reasonable to suppose that, in those days of lawlessness, the necessity of possessing a stronghold less open to attack and more easily defensible than the exposed plain of Tenmalai dictated the move. The natural strength of Sivagiri was tested on at least three occasions within historical times. In 1767 the place was attacked by Colonel Campbell and the fort levelled; in 1783 Colonel Fullarton after a desperate encounter defeated the poligars' united forces of 8,000 men and received their submission; and again in 1792 the place was attacked and captured by Colonel Maxwell. On all these occasions the defenders fell back on the fortified ravine, or *kōmbai,* in the forests immediately to the west, from which it was only by outflanking manœuvres that they could possibly be dislodged. Colonel Fullarton has described his assault on the place—"as desperate as any contest in that species of Indian warfare"—in some detail[1]:—

"The attack commenced by the Europeans and four battalions of sepoys moving against the embankment which covers the wood. The Polygars, in full force, opposed us, but our troops remained with their firelocks shouldered, under a heavy fire, until they approached the embankment, there they gave a general discharge and rushed upon the enemy. By the vigour of this advance we got possession of the

[1] *A View of the English interests in India,* by W. Fullarton, M.P., 1785. Printed in Madras, 1867.

summit, the Polygars took post on the verge of the adjoining wood, and disputed every step with great loss on both sides.

"After reconnoitering, we found that the Comby could not be approached in front. We proceeded therefore, to cut a road through the impenetrable thickets for three miles, to the base of the hill that bounds the Comby on the west. The Pioneers, under Ensign Cunningham, laboured with indefatigable industry; Captain Gardiner of the 102nd, supported them with the Europeans, and Captain Blacker, with the 3rd and 24th Carnatic Battalions advanced their field pieces as fast as the road was cleared. These were strengthened by troops in their rear, forming a communication with those in front. For this purpose two other battalions were posted within the wood, and as soon as we gained the embankment, the camp moved near it and concentrated our force.

"We continued to cut our way under an unabating fire from 8,000 Polygars, who constantly pressed upon our advanced party, rushed upon the line of attack, piked the bullocks that were dragging the guns and killed many of our people. But those attempts were repulsed by perseverance, and before sunset we had opened a passage entirely to the mountain. It is extremely high, rocky, and in many places almost perpendicular. Having resolved to attack from this unexpected quarter, the troops undertook the service, and attained the summit. The Polygar parties posted to guard that eminence being routed, after much firing on all hands, we descended on the other side, and flanked the Comby.

"The enemy seeing us masters of the mountain, retreated under cover of the night by paths inaccessible to regular troops, and we took possession of this wonderful recess."

During the last quarter of the eighteenth century, before the rise of the Pānjālankurichi poligar to undisputed leadership among the poligars, Sivagiri was, next to the Pūli Tēvan, the most dangerous power in the district. At the time of Colonel Fullarton's expedition (1783) we find that he was at the head of a formidable confederacy which included practically all the poligars of the west and also Kattaboma Nāyakkan; in alliance with the Dutch at Tuticorin he had collected ammunition on a gigantic scale and had prepared his fort to resist, as he hoped, the most stubborn blockade. The actual holder of the pālaiyam at the time was a female, the management resting with Sendali Kalai Pāndyan, her husband. After 1792 the poligar, now an old man, seems to have ceased to give trouble; he appears henceforth as the helpless victim of a most troublesome son who, instigated by two notorious brigands of the

CHAP. XV. SANKARA-NAINARKOIL TALUK.

time, Māppillai Vanniyan and Sankaralingam Pillai, led a conspiracy to depose his father, and continued for a year or so to receive active assistance in his freebooting expeditions from Kattaboma Nāyakkan. In 1799 the son held aloof from the confederacy led by Panjālankurichi and in the following year, on the death of his father, was allowed to succeed to the pālaiyam. In 1803 he received the Istimrar Sanad. On his death in 1819 he was succeeded by his only daughter, Vīrammāl Nāchiyar, "in whom (wrote the Collector) a rare instance of education among the native women of India was found, being able to read and write." The management of the estate was left to her husband, who neglected it in favour of sport; and it was during the time of this zamindarni that the estate lapsed into a condition of indebtedness from which it took years to recover. Mismanagement and extravagance, added to the disastrous violence of a storm of 1827 which damaged most of the already neglected irrigation works, produced arrears of peshkash so heavy that, in 1827, the estate was attached by the Collector and remained under his management for eight years. By that time the arrears had risen to Rs. 2¼ lakhs. In 1841 the Collector reported that an improvement had set in; a great part of the arrear was paid, and the balance was written off. The zamindarni had died in 1835, and her husband continued as nominal manager till his death in 1844, when he was succeeded by his son. The new zamindar, "a weak and not very respectable character," was soon in a state of incurable indebtedness, and in a few years the estate was again under attachment. In 1870 the creditors of the estate obtained a decree for the sale of the property. Its division had been ordered, the peshkash due by the dismembered parts had been apportioned, and the formalities were complete, when the zamindar went with his son to Mr. Puckle and begged him to take possession of the estate and save it. After consulting the civil court, which assented, Mr. Puckle took the zamindari under his management and set to work to put its finances straight. Several villages lying isolated from the estate were sold outright; the substitution of money-rents for payment in kind was introduced; and the occupancy right in much of the home-farm, or *pannai*, lands was sold to the tenants. At the same time Mr. Puckle was engaged in a similar task at Ettaiyāpuram and, finding his hands too full, applied to the Board of Revenue for a paid manager. While commending Mr. Puckle's "zeal and good feeling," the Board pointed out that he should not have taken over the management of the estate without the sanction of Government. Mr. Puckle replied with an explanation, on the receipt of which the Board sanctioned the appointment asked for. In 1872 the civil court attached the estate; and the deputy tahsildar, whose nomination as manager the Board had approved, became receiver under the court. On the death of the zamindar, in 1873, his son succeeded; the debts were repudiated, and the receivership was terminated. His management, which lasted for twenty-three years, was marked by skill and energy. He was succeeded in 1896 by his son, Rāmalinga Varaguna Rāma Pāndya Chinnatambiyār, a boy of seven. The estate was taken under the Court of Wards, which continued to administer it until April 1910. The financial results of this management are interesting:—

	In 1896.	In 1910.
	RS.	RS.
Demand	1,76,791	2,77,506
Balance in hand	19,381	8,90,379

One-and-a-half lakhs were spent on irrigation works and general improvements; the estate (including the forests) was surveyed; in 1910 a veterinary hospital, which quickly became popular, was opened in the estate, and from 1901 onwards a demonstration farm of 250 acres, which had its humble beginnings in the time of the ward's father, developed, under the charge of its superintendent, M.R.Ry. A. Rama Rao, into one of the most successful and noteworthy institutions of its kind in the Presidency. The working of the zamin forests was set on a sound footing, the manager, on behalf of the zamindar, being vested with controlling powers under section 26 of the Madras Forest Act. The minor was educated at "Newington," Madras, and succeeded to the estate, on attaining his majority, on April 25th, 1910. He died in January 1914, having spent all the savings which the Court of Wards had accumulated for him and having incurred, in addition, personal debts to the extent of about Rs. 3 lakhs. The estate itself is said to be unencumbered. His mother succeeded; but, on the application of a rival claimant, a receiver, in the person of the zamindarni herself, has just (1915) been appointed by the civil court.

Talaivankōttai (population 3,085): is the headquarters of an ancient zamindari, about 10 square miles in extent, which comprises two villages and yields an annual rental of about Rs. 20,000. The proprietor owns also the inam village of Dārukāpuram. The last zamindar, who died in 1910, left an adopted minor son, and in the following year the estate was taken under the management of the Court of Wards. A reversioner appeared shortly afterwards, who challenged the

CHAP. XV. SANKARANAINARKOIL TALUK.

adoption and went to law on the point. The Court of Wards, therefore, divested itself of the management, and a receiver, appointed by the civil court, is now in charge. The family belongs to the Kondaiyankōttai section of the Marava caste.

Vāsuḍēvanallūr (called Vasanellore and Washinellore in the early records): is a thriving little town favourably situated at a short distance from the foot of the ghats and surrounded by rich and well-watered lands. It is a union with a population of 9,882, is the headquarters of a forest deputy range officer and contains a small bungalow available for travellers. The Siva temple is a large one and contains inscriptions; it is dedicated to Ardhanārīswarar, whose symbol is not a *lingam* but an image, half Siva and half Pārvati. The favourable situation of the place impressed the first British officers who visited these parts. Colonel Campbell, writing in 1767, declared the country around "to be as fine a grain country as he had met with." Originally the place belonged to the poligar of Nelkattanseval, and Muhammad Yūsuf was signally repulsed in 1760 in an attempt to capture the fort. Subsequently it came into the hands of the Nawāb, but no records are traceable to show how this happened. The Nawāb's occupation, however, was of very short duration; for in 1766 the place was again in the hands of the poligar. The next year Colonel Campbell laid siege to the place with a special force. For a whole week the besieged were pounded with shot and shell, cooped up in an enclosure 650 yards long by 300 broad. Throughout the bombardment the garrison conducted the defence with such gallantry that they earned the unfeigned admiration of Colonel Campbell and astonished him by their contempt of death and by the cool and prompt manner in which under a hot fire they went on quietly repairing with palmyras and straw breach after breach. At the end of the week one early morning the garrison resolved to abandon the fort. During a heavy fall of rain they rushed out at three points and quickly gained the neighbouring jungle, sustaining only a slight loss from a single volley from the besiegers.

Notwithstanding its small size, the fort was ranked by Colonel Campbell as the strongest he had seen during his campaign in the Tinnevelly district. Its strength was due in large measure to its position. On the west and south a dense jungle approached to within 1,300 yards of the fort, and beyond that rose the ghats. These woods were held by large bands of Maravans, who were able to watch unseen the operations of the beseigers and, at a decisive moment, rush out and strike effectively. The second defence consisted of a strong fence of vicious babul thorns, which, when firmly interwoven, can form an obstacle more formidable than barbed wire. Close under the south and east walls of the fort flowed the Pī-ār, which served as a further protection. The walls were not remarkable either for their size or thickness. They were built of sun-dried bricks, with a base of 15 feet, sloping upwards on both sides to a width of five feet, and were of such remarkable strength that, during Colonel Campbell's siege, upwards of five hundred shot were poured into it at one place without effect. The fort has now been levelled for over a century, and crops have ever since grown over it; but, notwithstanding all the soaking and exposure which this implies, the courses of the sun-dried bricks are still distinctly visible.

Iron-smelting was carried on to a considerable extent in the neighbourhood until the industry was destroyed by the importation of foreign iron.

A few of the local Muhammadans go in for a little pony-breeding. Some dolomite is quarried in the neighbouring hills; it is prepared into sticks and used in painting caste marks. Sepulchral urns have been found in the neighbourhood.

Vírasikhāmani (population 2,433): about eight miles south-west of Sankaranainārkōil, possesses considerable archæological interest. The tradition survives of a temple—the Mattan Kōvil—which once existed on the dry land to the east of the village. Finely cut stones, some of which bear Tamil inscriptions and Hindu carvings, are to be seen about the place, serving diverse useful purposes. A large number have been used to line wells with; others now form doorsteps or compose the surplus weir of the local tank.

On the edge of this tank is a large smooth rock, the eastern face of which has been excavated to form a little temple. The temple consists of two compartments: in the inner chamber is a *lingam*; in the outer are five large carved figures, two of which guard the entrance. Of the figures inside two are badly damaged; the rest are well preserved and are remarkable for the individuality of their expression, pose and type.

Higher up on the opposite side, sheltered by the overhanging rock, is a long ledge which has been hollowed out into a number of shallow rectangular beds similar to those found at Marugāltalai (p. 486). In another recess on the same ledge an eight-petalled lotus set in a square has been carved; in the centre of the lotus are the impressions of two feet cut in relief. At some height above this appears an inscription which records that a man named Avaiyan pukkān got the foot-prints of

CHAP. XV. SANKARA-NAINARKOIL TALUK.

Sachitānanda engraved. The epigraph has, on palæographic grounds, been assigned to the fourteenth century.[1] Even if the lotus and the inscriptions are synchronous, it does not of course follow that the beds are not older than both. The natives of the place call the five figures in the temple the *Pancha Pāndava*, and the beds (as at Marugāltalai) the *Pancha Pāndava padukkai*.

Similar stone caverns and beds are found also in the Madura district, and, with the exception of a few which contain Pāli inscriptions and are on that account ascribed to Buddhists (Marugāltalai is an example), all are thought to be the work of Jains. The rock-cut temple of Kalugumalai, believed to be of Jaina origin, contains no *lingam*, and it is difficult, on a Jaina hypothesis, to account for the presence of this Hindu symbol here.

At TIRUMALAPURAM also, a village about three miles away to the west, a cave temple has been carved out in the northern face of a steep rock. It is similar to that at Vīrasikāmani, but is in a better state of preservation and appears to be of later date. The six figures which adorn the walls, though well carved, are of a far more conventional type. The roof still bears signs of having been plastered, and traces may be seen of a neat mosaic executed in colour.

Another cave of the same type has been commenced on the opposite face of the rock, but, like the Vettuvānkōil of Kalugumalai, was left unfinished.

[1] *Govt. Epig. Ann. Report* for 1907–08, para. 98.

SRIVAIKUNTAM TALUK.

CHAP. XV. SRI-VAIKUNTAM TALUK.

THE SRIVAIKUNTAM TALUK as at present constituted dates from 1911. In that year the southern half of the area which had borne this name was made into a separate taluk, Tiruchendūr; the remainder, with the addition from the old Ottapidāram taluk of eight mitta and ten ayan villages, including Tuticorin, formed the new taluk of Srīvaikuntam. It comprises the usual variety of soil, cultivation and scenery. Nearly one-sixth of the total cultivable area is under irrigation, most of which is supplied by the Tāmbraparni. Practically the whole of the river-fed area pays a compounded assessment for two crops, the average incidence on an acre amounting, in the case of double-crop lands, to Rs. 6-11-0—a figure exceeded only in one other taluk, Ambāsamudram. The rainfed tanks, numbering 133 and commanding an average area of less than 40 acres each, are found in the north and in the south-west of the taluk. The general flatness of the country is relieved by the hills of Vallanād (1,052 feet) and Manakkarai, which together form a striking landmark, the low red ridge at Karunkulam conspicuous by the temple which crowns its rocky top, and adjoining this the rising ground of Adichanallūr. In the villages recently added from the old Ottapidāram taluk the soil is mostly black; southwards and towards the west it is red; inland from the sea for four or five miles sand predominates. In this low-lying sea-coast region roads do not exist; and for several months of the year the soil is so much saturated by the drainage of the wet lands under the irrigation of the Srīvaikuntam north main channel system that cart traffic is impossible.

Tēris—on a far smaller scale than in the Tiruchendūr taluk—with their familiar crops of palmyras and acacias, occur in and around Nattātti, Sāwyerpuram, and Pudukkōttai; and north of Tuticorin dunes of white sand cover a considerable area. Palmyras abound in all the dry lands and are most plentiful in the eastern parts.

Of the population more than four-fifths are Hindus; six-sevenths of the remainder are Christians, Muhammadans contributing the balance. The taluk is one of the most densely peopled areas of the district; and the percentage

CHAP. XV. SRIVAIKUNTAM TALUK.

increase of its population in the decade 1901-1911 was two and a half times as great as the increase recorded for the district as a whole. Tuticorin, a municipality, is the largest and most important town; Srīvaikuntam and Eral are unions. The best known temple is that at Srīvaikuntam dedicated to Vishnu. The Vēmbadi Sudalāimādaswami of Arumugamangalam has a great reputation; disputes in the law-courts and elsewhere are often settled by an oath taken before his shrine.

Adichanallūr, Korkai and Kāyal are sites of archæological and historic interest. In these and at least fifteen other places [1] sepulchral urns have been found.

Adichanallūr, or, more properly, Vēlūr Adichanallūr: 11 miles from Palamcotta on the road to Tiruchendūr, possesses considerable interest as an archæological field of exceptional richness. For many years the high ground to the west of the village had been known as a place where ancient burial-urns were to be found; but it was not apparently till the appearance on the spot, in 1876, of Dr. Jagor, a German antiquarian, that special attention was directed to the site. Some excavations were then carried out, and a number of articles—"upwards of fifty kinds of baked earthenware, utensils of all sizes and shapes, a considerable number of iron weapons and implements . . . and a great quantity of bones and skulls"—were taken away to Berlin. The discovery of these remains was assisted by the fact that the site was regularly used as a quarry. The matter was reported to Government, and orders were issued that the sites should be left undisturbed. Quarrying, however, continued as before. In 1900 the matter was taken seriously in hand; an area of over a hundred acres was definitely placed under reservation, and excavations were commenced by Mr. A. Rea of the Archæological Department. The more important finds were removed to the Madras Museum, where they are now exhibited. Mr. Rea's descriptions of the objects discovered are to be found in the annual reports of the Government Archæologist, for 1899-1900, 1900-1901, and (with illustrations) 1901-1902 and 1903-1904. A comprehensive account by the same writer, illustrated by photographs, is contained in the annual report of the Archæological Survey of India for 1902-1903. The following are extracts:—

"The objects (over 6,000 in number) yielded by these burial-sites, are finely made pottery of various kinds in great

[1] Agaram, Vadakku Vallanād, Vallanād, Murappanād, Vasavappapuram, Karunkulam, Vittilāpuram, Kongarāyakurichi, Srīvaikuntam, Tiruppuliyangudi, Pudukkudi, Vēlūr, Kālvāy, Appankōil, Māramangalam.

number; many iron implements and weapons; vessels and personal ornaments in bronze; a few gold ornaments; a few stone beads; boxes; and some household stone implements used for grinding curry or sandalwood. Traces of cloth and wood preserved by rust or oxidation in contact with metals are found. In a number of urns there were quantities of mica in pieces about an inch in size. Husks of rice and millet were found in quite a large number of pots inside the urns. All the implements and weapons are in iron; there are none in bronze.

"The vessels are mostly in earthenware, with a much smaller proportion in bronze. Lamps are of iron; no other vessels are of this metal.

"The comparative variety of bronze objects and their use for personal ornament, show that this metal must then have been scarce, highly valued and used only by the higher class of people. The only gold ornaments found in the tombs are diadems.

"Thus the people who made these objects appear to have been skilful in moulding pottery, in casting or brasing metals, in weaving, and in working stone and wood. That they were acquainted with agriculture is shown by the iron spades for digging, and the presence of husks of rice and millet. Some of the iron implements are for sacrificial purposes, others are for the chase or war. They have all been fitted with wooden handles. Their religion was probably devil worship, as evidenced by the various iron sacrificial implements discovered which are similar to those used in this form of worship.

"The attempts at art in casting animals in bronze and at ornamenting that metal, indicate a primitive workmanship. The ornamentation consists only of embossed dots, and incised lines for the most part in triangular or simple geometric designs.

"The domestic animals represented in bronze are the buffalo, goat or sheep, and the cock, while the wild animals are the tiger, antelope, and elephant.

"*Urns.*—The funeral urns are large, one-legged, elongated, globular pots of thick red earthenware, averaging less than a yard in diameter by a slightly greater height. They are similar to those found at Pallavaram and elsewhere. Around the mouth is a rim, in most specimens plain, but in some impressed with the thumb nail or incised with triangular and dotted ornaments. All have had flat conical covers, and on the preservation of these depends, to a large extent, the condition of the contents.

CHAP. XV.
SRI-VAIKUNTAM TALUK.

"In only a few instances do the urns contain the complete bones of a skeleton, and then the urn is always of large size, being nearly 3 feet in diameter. Generally the modern system of interring a selection of the bones only seems to have been the method followed. Such urns may contain a skull or parts of it only, or some other bones of the skeleton, and these occur either by themselves or in company with other articles in pottery or metal. The latter are occasionally very numerous, both outside and inside the urn.

"In those urns which contained complete skeletons, and which were thus preserved by the lid remaining intact, the position of the bones made it obvious that the body had been set inside in a squatting or sitting position. On its decay, the leg and arm bones fell over and rested against one side of the urn, while the skull, ribs and vertebræ dropped down to the bottom. . . .

"Many urns contained no traces of bones whatever. This may have been due to decay, or to the fact that none were buried. None of the bones were calcined. . . .

"Some complete skulls may offer a clue to the identity of the race to whom they belong. A few of the skulls have holes in the brow, which would indicate a violent death. Mr. Thurston of the Madras Museum has measured some of the skulls, and finds they belong to a dolichocephalic people. In a few urns were traces of ashes, but these did not appear to be the results of cremation. They were apparently due to the combustion of wood used during some ceremony of burial.

"*Objects in metal.*—The bronzes (consisting of ornamental vase-stands, bell-mouthed jars, sieves, decorated bowl-lids and bangles) exhibit a very high degree of skill in workmanship, and manipulation of the metal; this is also the case with iron implements. All this confirms historical accounts as to the early skill of the Indians in the working of metal. When bronzes are found, they are usually inside the urns, but not invariably; some instances occur of only one being placed inside, and half a dozen or so on the outside.

"Implements (hatchets and spades), arms (swords and daggers), or lamps of iron, are generally found in conjunction with bronzes and are, as a rule, placed outside; but they are found inside also. There are several swords from the inside, which have been bent by fallen débris before they had corroded, and have retained that shape.

"All swords, spears, arrows, and other weapons from around the urns, were always found point downwards, as if they had been thrust into the surrounding earth by the attendant mourners.

"Many of the iron weapons, through corrosion, are thickly encrusted with particles of gravel, but the metal is fairly firm and strong. Others again, either wholly or in part are simply a mass of fibrous black rust which it is impossible to remove or even touch without breakage. The metal of these could be crushed to powder between the fingers. Many of the swords and implements show traces of wood, permeated with rust at the handles and even along the blade. . . .

"*Gold diadems.*—When these ornaments were first discovered, it was thought probable that they were badges for affixing to the upper part of the arm, and formerly used by persons of rank. It now, however, seems certain that they are diadems. Diadems of the same shape were found at Mycenæ and are described as long, thin, oval, gold plates, bound round the head by a small gold wire, the holes for which are at each extremity. This description applies equally to the present examples, except as to the gold wire, of which none was seen. The tying material was probably thread of which I found traces in some bronze necklaces. Nowadays no custom is known in the neighbourhood of tying diadems on the dead. . . .

"In Adittanallūr, the custom could not have been a general one, for out of many urns excavated only a few gold ornaments were found. It must have been limited to persons of rank or importance. The urns in which they occurred, were invariably placed at a considerable depth, usually from 10 feet to 15 feet and protected by deposits of large stones or boulders extending from the surface right down to the urn. In other cases smaller urns were placed at some height over them either as a protection or representing a more recent burial. The urns containing them were always large and usually had considerable deposits, both inside and out, of pottery, bronze vessels and iron implements. When all these indications occurred, a gold ornament was almost sure to be found. In only two adjacent parts of the ground, so far as it has been examined, were these discovered. In most of the present examples, the diadems were lying at the bottom of the urn crushed and crumpled—apparently intentionally at the time of deposit. Their condition may possess some significance as others were produced unfolded. A few were in bronze, both folded and unfolded.

CHAP. XV. SRI-VAIKUNTAM TALUK.

"Some of these diadems are simple ovals, and others have thin strips of the gold extending beyond each extremity. A few are plain, but most of them have repoussé linear designs of dots. . . .

"*Pottery.*—[1] The great bulk of the deposits consists of pottery. Most of it is in almost perfect condition, due to the nature of the soil, but in some sites, where a clay soil exists, it is almost all in a fragmentary condition.

"It seems to have been placed indiscriminately both inside and outside the urns, a fact to which I have already referred in a previous paper on the subject. For the most part the pottery is well made, the clay being of a thin texture, in some cases red, in others black, or with the two colours combined. Only a few instances of applied colour occur and little or no ornament is used; such as there is, consisting of short dotted lines, is disposed diagonally around the rim. . . .

"The various types include pots, large and small, bowls; jars, long and small; cups, ringstands, both short and long, besides the urns above alluded to. Many present very little variation from such as are in use at the present day."

Less than a mile to the north of this place of burial in Kongarāyakurichi on the other side of the river Mr. Rea discovered traces of an ancient town site.[2] Numerous fragments of polished black and red pottery were found, identical with that found in the Adichanallūr tombs; most of the pottery, however, was of quite a different kind. Mr. Rea's theory is that this site once adjoined the cemetery and that subsequently the river changed its course and separated the one from the other. As stated in chapter II, the occurrence of town sites and burial grounds side by side can scarcely be a mere accident. Many instances of the kind are referred to in the notice relating to the Sankaranainārkōil taluk, and, were the matter thoroughly investigated, it is probable that some conclusion might be formed regarding this departed race of men. Of the buried dead we can at present only say, with Sir Thomas Browne: "Had they made as good provision for their names as they have done for their relics, they had not so grossly erred in the art of perpetuation. But to subsist in bones, and be but pyramidally extant, is a fallacy in duration."

Eral, "the rising ground" (population 4,920): is the name given to a locality now forming a union and comprising

[1] What follows is from the annual report of the Archæological Survey of India for 1903–1904, pp. 158–59.

[2] In spite of my best efforts I have been unable to locate this site.

portions of two revenue villages, Siruttondanallūr and Valavallān. The settlement is said to date from 1827, the year of a most destructive flood (p. 253), when the inhabitants of the low ground beside the river found refuge in this higher ground. To the present day there are a number of habitations further west, including the two large temples known as "Rettai Tirupati," which stand in what is now a part of the river-bed. With wet lands on three sides and the river on the fourth, the village stands on the metalled road from Srīvaikuntam to Arumugamangalam, 11 miles from the former place.

A curious institution of modern times is associated with the tomb of a former chairman of the union, named Arunāchala Nādān, who died a few years ago. His uncle possessed unusual skill in the cure of all diseases and snake-bite in particular. The gift descended to Arunāchala Nādān; but, though the nephew's skill was less, his reputation exceeded that of his uncle. One night, it is said, a Paraiya woman who was extremely ill was warned in a dream to walk round Arunāchala Nādān's tomb. Obedience brought its reward, and the news of her miraculous recovery soon spread. The tomb, situated on the edge of the river-bed, is now converted into a regular shrine, in which the "Chairman's" photograph is displayed in a gilt frame; Tuesdays and Fridays, still more the days of new moon and full moon, find the river sand thronged with people of all castes (Brahmans, perhaps, excepted) seeking from the spirit of the deceased cure of their diseases or good fortune for the future. Special facilities are offered to women possessed of evil spirits; in front of the shrine a carpet of rich mud is spread, in which the grateful victims grovel, gyrating their bodies from the hips, flinging their arms about them and swaying their heads with hair flowing loose, until a cure is effected.

The place is inhabited by Hindus, Christians and Muhammadans. The Roman Catholics (Paravans) are at work on a fine church.

The bell-metal industry of the place possesses some reputation.

Korkai: now an obscure village (population 2,573) on the north bank of the Tāmbraparni four miles from its mouth, has in modern times been identified with a town which, from references made to it by Greek writers and by the authors of various Tamil *purānas*, is known to have been at one time a seaport and a place of first-rate importance in South India. The correlation of the various facts which has led to this identification is of particular interest.

CHAP. XV.
SRI-VAIKUNTAM TALUK.

Korkai (the euphonized form of Kolkai[1]) is constantly referred to in the Madura songs.

மூசறு வண்டொமாலும் பசுந்தொங்கற்
பாசறுகொண்ட பகீரதிக்கு—வாசத்
தொடையெடுப்பான் சோழன்றுகிலெடுப்பான் சேரன்
குடையெடுப்பான் கொற்கையாகோன்.

To the sea, which has flowers inhabited by the humming bees,
He who brings scented flowers is the Sōran,
He who brings garments is the Sēran,
He who brings the umbrella is the king of Korkai.

Again in a poem written for the benefit of Chōla readers:

வீரர்க்குநிகராக மீனவனோவம்மா	னே
வெற்றிப்புலிக்கொடிக்கு மீனமோவம்மா	னே
ஊரிர்புகாதனக்கு கொற்கையோவம்மா	னே
ஒக்குமோசோழனுக்கு பாண்டின்காணம்மா	னே.

Does the fish banner equal the brave ?
Is the fish banner equal to that of the tiger ?
Korkai is not equal to Uraiyūr, town of praise.
The Pāndyan is not to be compared to the Chōlan.

The Madura *Aingurunūru* also refers to Korkai as a large seaport and the centre of the pearl-fishery.

Among Greek writers, the unknown author of the *Periplus Maris Erythraei* (probably about A.D. 80) and Ptolemy the Geographer (A.D. 130) both refer to Kolkhoi.[2] According to these authorities the place was the centre of the pearl-fishery and was the first port touched at by the Greeks after rounding Cape Comorin ; and, if only from the fact that they called the Gulf of Manaar "the Kolkhic Gulf," we may conclude that Kolkhoi was in their eyes a place of note.

Dr. Wilson, Boden Professor of Sanskrit at Oxford, had, in the thirties of the last century, identified the Korkai of the Tamil writers with the Kolkhoi of the Greeks and concluded that the place to which both sets of writers referred was Kīlakkarai, a seaport in the present Rāmnād district. The conjecture was even hazarded, in 1837, by the Rev. William Taylor, who disagreed on philological grounds with Dr. Wilson's conclusion, that the Korkai of the *purānas* might have some connection with the Gurkhas of Nepaul. In support of the

[1] This is the Tamil practice. Thus, the word கல் with the plural suffix கள் added becomes கற்கள். Dr. Caldwell (*History of Tinnevelly*, page 18) mentions that he found the form Kolkai in a Tamil inscription in the Tiruchendūr temple.

[2] For the quotation from the *Periplus* see p. 229 above.

idea he adduced a resemblance said to exist between the Tamil alphabet and that of Thibet and, also, the fact that Agastya, the father of the Tamil language, was according to tradition himself a Thibetan. In the following year an anonymous contributor to the "Madras Literary Journal" brought to notice the existence of the Tinnevelly Korkai, adding that the inhabitants of the place declared it to have been at one time the residence of Pāndya kings. The situation of the place, the writer observed, near the mouth of the Tāmbraparni, the relative nearness of Manappadaivīdu (q.v.), believed like Korkai to have been the seat of Pāndyan rulers, and the custom [1] that the earth used in the chief festival of the Nellaiyappar temple at Tinnevelly was brought from Korkai, contributed to the theory that Korkai was once a place of importance. This was a great step forward; but no attempt had yet been made to identify the Tinnevelly Korkai with the place mentioned both by the Greek and Tamil writers. This was Dr. Caldwell's contribution to the story of Korkai's rehabilitation. His inference was immensely strengthened by other facts to which he was the first to call attention. Kāyal (known generally as Palaya-kāyal), at present a village a mile from the mouth of the Tāmbraparni, was found on incontestable evidence to have been at one time (in the thirteenth century at any rate) a famous city and a centre of commerce. The same fate had overtaken both these cities. The continuous accumulation of silt at the mouth of the river gradually brought Korkai and Kāyal further inland and destroyed their value as ports. The Portuguese at first established themselves at Punnaikāyal, the successor of Kāyal, or "Old Kāyal" *(Palaya-kāyal)*, as it came to be called, but soon abandoned it in favour of Tuticorin, doubtless owing to causes similar to those which had rendered Korkai and Kāyal useless. Proof that the coast in these parts has extended itself at the expense of the sea is afforded not only by recent observation of the process but also by the abundance of sea shells, including deep-sea shells, such as the chank and pearl-oyster, found in the alluvial soil of all the villages included in the Tāmbraparni delta. For the ordinary shells there is no need to dig deep; any quantity may be picked up the surface of the ground. Dr. Caldwell found in Korkai three sepulchral urns containing small earthenware vessels, artistically shaped and endowed with an exceptional polish. One large urn 11 feet in circumference contained a complete set of human bones including a perfect skull. The most

[1] Now obsolete.

CHAP. XV.
SRI-VAIKUNTAM TALUK.

interesting discovery of quite recent times was made by Mr. James Hornell, F.L.S., who unearthed on the outskirts of the village a collection of chank workshop waste—17 pieces in all—the significance of which is of the highest importance.[1] Coins of Singhalese and Pāndya origin have been found in large numbers; and the name of an adjoining hamlet—Akkasālai, "the Mint"—is itself suggestive of vanished greatness. Two Jaina figures, it may be added, in the usual pose of contemplation, are to be seen in the place, one by the roadside and the other near the village.

The historical position may, therefore, thus be summarized. A place named Kolkhoi in the Gulf of Manaar was known to the Greeks; it was a well-known city and the centre of the pearl trade. By its geographical situation, the evidence of archæology, the important analogy of Kāyal (q.v.) and by local tradition, the present village of Korkai is shown to have been a port and a notable city. A place named Korkai is referred to in Tamil poems of uncertain date but undoubted antiquity, in a way which clearly implies that it was, if not the capital, at least a leading city, of the Pāndya kingdom. When all these facts are placed together, the conclusion seems irresistible that Korkai was the emporium referred to by the Greeks and one of the greatest cities of the early Pāndyas.

Palaya-kāyal or **Old Kāyal** (population 1,426): has already been referred to in the notice of Korkai. The word *kāyal* means a "lagoon" or "backwater", and the name seems specially appropriate to any place situated on the flats lying about the delta of the Tāmbraparni river. The little village, separated from the sea by two miles of swamp and sand, some of which is now under irrigation, is situated on the old track that leads south to north from Tiruchendūr to Tuticorin; from the west it can only be approached by an abandoned sandy road. In front of the Pillaiyār temple is a square *mantapam*, one of the series said to have been built by one of the Pānjālankurichi family [2] at regular intervals between Tiruchendūr and Ottapidāram. In all of them drummers were stationed, whose duty it was, beginning from Tiruchendūr, to communicate along the route for the spiritual benefit of that freebooter—somewhat after the style of the signals which conveyed across the Ægean the news of the fall of Troy—the performance of *pūja* in the temple of Subramanyaswāmi. Similar *mantapams* exist at Mukkāni and Arumuganēri.

[1] See also p. 236. [2] See pp. 387 foll.

The place, like Korkai, is now known to have had a glorious past; and, as with Korkai, it is to the late Bishop Caldwell that we are indebted for this discovery. Marco Polo, who visited this part of India in A.D. 1292, refers to "a great and noble city" which he calls Cail. Colonel Yule, the editor of this author, had, after some research but without visiting the locality, reached the conclusion that the place referred to was the existing town of Kāyalpatnam (q.v.). But the local traditions of the place are against such a theory; there is in fact no evidence of any sort to support it. Punnaikāyal, a curious little seaside village separated from Kāyalpatnam by an arm of the Tāmbraparni, appears first to have acquired importance under the Portuguese; and their period forms the furthest limit of time to which local tradition harks back. Like Korkai, Palayakāyal, its successor, has, owing to the accretion of land about the mouth of the Tāmbraparni, receded from the sea; other settlements have formed about the sluggish backwaters and, naturally enough, Kāyal, once "the city of the backwater," came to be known as "Old Kāyal."

Marco Polo's account of the place is so interesting that a lengthy quotation needs no apology.[1]

"Cail is a great and noble city and belongs to Ashar, the eldest of the five brother kings. It is at that city that all the ships touch that come from Hormos[2] and from Kis and from Aden and from all Arabia laden with horses and with other things for sale and this brings a great concourse of people from the country round about and so there is great business done in this city of Cail.

"The king possesses vast treasures and wears upon his person great store of rich jewels, he maintains great state, and administers his kingdom with great equity and extends great favour to merchants and foreigners so that they are very glad to visit his city.

"This king has some 300 wives for in those parts the man who has most wives is most thought of. As I told you before there are in this great province of Ma'abar five crowned kings[3] who are all own brothers born of one father and one mother and the king is one of them. Their mother is still living and when they disagree and go forth to war against

[1] *Ser Marco Polo*, translated and edited by Colonel Yule, C.B., II, 305.

[2] Curiously enough a fate exactly similar to that which overtook Korkai and Kāyal befell old Hormos (Hormuz) on the Persian Gulf. See Colonel Yule's *Ser Marco Polo*, Vol. I, p. 104 (notes).

[3] For the "Five Pāndyas" see pp. 41 (footnote), 55, 61.

one another their mother throws herself between them to prevent their fighting and should they persist in desiring to fight she will take a knife and threaten that if they will do so she will cut off the paps that suckled them and rip open the womb that bore them and so perish before their eyes. In this way hath she full many a time brought them to desist but when she dies it will most assuredly happen that they will fall out and destroy one another.

"All the people of the city as well as of the rest of India have a custom of perpetually keeping in the mouth a certain leaf called Tembul to gratify a certain habit and desire. They are continually chewing it and spitting out the saliva that it excites; the lords and gentlefolks and the king have these leaves prepared with camphor and other aromatic spices and also mix with quicklime and the practice was said to be very good for the health. If anyone desires to offer a gross insult to another when he meets him he spits this leaf or its juice in his face; the other immediately runs before the king relates the insult and demands leave to fight the offender; the king supplies the arms which are sword and target and all the people flock to see and there they fight till one of them is killed. They must not use the point of the sword for this the king forbids."

Speaking of the province of Ma'abar (i.e., Coromandel), Marco Polo says:—

"Here are no horses bred; and thus a great part of the wealth of the country is wasted in purchasing horses. You must know that the merchants of the Kis and Hormos, Dofar, and Soer and Aden collect a great number of horses, and these they bring to the territories of this king and of his four brothers. For a horse will fetch among them 500 *saggi* of gold worth more than 100 marks of silver and vast numbers are sold there every year. Indeed this king wants to buy more than 2,000 horses every year, and so do his four brothers who are kings likewise. The reason why they want so many horses every year is that by the end of the year there shall not be one hundred of them remaining, for they all die off. And this arises from mismanagement, for these people do not know in the least how to treat a horse; and besides they have no farriers. The horse-merchants not only never bring any farriers with them but also prevent any farrier from going thither, lest that should in any degree baulk the sale of horses, which brings them in every year such vast gains. They bring these horses by sea aboard ship."

Marco Polo's description of the pearl-fishery off the coast of Ma'abar is too long to quote.

Colonel Yule cites in a footnote a number of authorities, including Rashidudin, a Muhammadan contemporary of Marco Polo, who refer to a place in Ma'abar, variously spelt as *Kawal, Cahila* (Nicolo Conti) *Caell* and *Gael*; its situation opposite to Ceylon, its importance as a port and its pearl-fishery, are all mentioned by the writers referred to.

The site of the old town was evidently the high ground, locally known as Sūrankādu, to the north-east of the present village. Fragments of fine China porcelain and ancient pottery are to be picked up in any quantity; Dr. Caldwell speaks of having found in one day débris sufficient to fill a cart. Extensive foundations of buildings and bathing-tanks, it is said, have been discovered beneath the sand.

In the irrigation tank are two Jaina images of the familiar type; on one of them the local washermen beat the dirt out of their clothes.

Pudukkōttai (otherwise Kumāragiri): population 2,886: eight miles from Tuticorin, on the road to Palamcotta, is the headquarters of the Kārkurichi mitta, which dates its creation from 1870.[1] The Roman Catholic mission and the S.P.G. both own elementary schools in the place. In 1905 the mittadar opened a dispensary, which is still maintained by the estate and continues to do useful work. The local chattram was founded in 1880 by the grandfather of the present joint proprietors, Mr. Arunāchala Ayyar, who bought the estate from its original purchaser. Both the dispensary and the chattram have been substantially endowed with landed property. The mitta, about 25 square miles in extent, comprises eleven villages, which, for revenue purposes, are arranged in seven "groups." A large proportion of the irrigated lands (their total extent is rather less than two thousand acres) derives its supply from the lower reaches of the Srīvaikuntam north-main system; seven-eighths of the estate is unirrigated. Most of the land is held by tenants on permanent right of occupancy.

The Kārkurichi Maravans[2] point with pride to the rising ground (known as *Kōttai-tēri*), to the east of the road leading south from Pudukkōttai, as the site of a fort which once belonged to the leaders of their caste. In company with all proud things it disappeared, it is said, before the ravages of the Pānjālankurichi poligar.

[1] See p. 386.   [2] See pp. 132–34.

CHAP. XV. SRI-VAIKUNTAM TALUK.

In the neighbouring village of Kūttudankādu a Jaina image of the usual type is to be seen lying on the ground, apparently uncared for. Evidently, however, some importance is attached to it; for, when the mittadar a few years ago took it away and set it up on pedestal beside the road, the crops failed, and the ryots insisted on having the image back.

Sāwyerpuram (population 5,008): a settlement mainly of Shānān Christians, accessible only by sandy tracks, derives its name from a Portuguese merchant who, during the early years of the last century, was engaged in trade in Palamcotta and acted occasionally as an agent of the S.P.C.K. At a time when the position of new converts to Christianity was not always pleasant, Mr. Samuel Sawyer acquired for the mission the land on which his eponymous village stands. He died in 1816 and is buried in the Palamcotta churchyard. The smaller church, near the present school, was built in 1843 by Dr. G. U. Pope, then the resident missionary of the S.P.G. At the same time he founded in the place a theological seminary, which in 1880 was raised to the status of a second-grade college. Three years later the college department was transferred to Tuticorin, where it took shape as the Caldwell College, Dr. Caldwell moving from Idaiyangudi to take charge of it. The local institution became a lower secondary school and has since continued in that condition. The hospital, founded in 1857, is maintained from mission funds and contributions given by the taluk board. The large and handsome brick church opposite the school was completed in 1887, the foundation stone having been laid thirty-three years before. The place forms a "district headquarters" of the S.P.G. mission and is the residence of a European missionary.

Srīvaikuntam, "Heaven of Vishnu": forming with Pudukkudi, a union (population 11,005), is the headquarters of the taluk. The public buildings are the offices of the tahsildar, a sub-magistrate and a sub-registrar, the court of a district munsif, a telegraph office, a police station and a local fund hospital. A secondary school is owned and managed by a local committee; the taluk board maintains a chattram from the proceeds of a landed endowment. The town is situated on the left bank of the Tāmbraparni and is approached from the main road connecting Palamcotta and Tiruchendūr by a bridge (built in 1890) over the Srīvaikuntam anicut.

The chief temple of the place is that dedicated to Vishnu under the name Srīvaikuntapathiswāmi, a large and spacious building surmounted by a lofty *gōpuram*. The Tiruvēngadamudaiyār *mantapam*, situated on the right hand as the outer circuit is entered, is particularly rich in sculptures. The pillars bear carvings on every facet, forming themselves each one block with sculptures of *yālis*, elephants and terrific warriors; around the inner circuit of the *mantapam* runs a frieze presenting Vishnu in various postures, associated everywhere with a five-headed snake. In the roof may be seen specimens of the familiar type of stone-carving which is designed to represent wooden beams and rafters. A finely-carved double doorway, which is opened only on the *Vaikunta Ekādasi* day, leads into the *Ekādasi mantapam*, situated in the same circuit. The inner circuit of the temple—which a European may not enter—is said to contain good sculptures. Vīra-Pāndya-dēva,[1] one of the later line of Pāndya rulers of the Tinnevelly country, has left an inscription in the *mahā mantapam*, bearing the date A.D. 1438. The smaller temple dedicated to Kailāsanāthaswāmi and situated in the north-east corner of the town also contains inscriptions of the same Pāndya king.

The Vaishnavite temple served the company at one time as a fort and was one of the few strongholds which, during the critical months of 1801, held out against the attacks of Kattaboma Nāyakkan and his rebels. After the retreat of Major Macaulay's force from Pānjālankurichi to Palamcotta on the 9th February (p. 83) many of the smaller forts belonging to Government, together with considerable prizes of ammunition, fell into the hands of the enemy. "Strivygundam pagoda," wrote Colonel Welsh, "held out beyond example or expectation. To relieve this brave handful, Major Sheppard marched, at the head of the 1st Battalion of the 3rd Regiment, with two six-pounders. Arriving at Palamcottah, on the 13th of March, the heavy baggage was thrown in there, and on the morning of the 16th they came in sight of the pagoda of Strivygundam, on the opposite side of the river, and were immediately attacked by swarms of the enemy, through whom they forced their way to their comrades on the opposite shore. All the troops behaved well, particularly the grenadiers, who charged a large body of the enemy and put them to flight. The poligars, intent on capturing the place, had beset it on every side, and raised a large mound of earth to overlook the pagoda. They were all busy in making scaling ladders for an escalade, when our corps relieved them. The garrison was withdrawn, and on the march back to Palamcottah, the enemy annoyed them the whole way, though repeatedly charged by our soldiers. Our loss was not so heavy as might be expected, and the corps

[1] See pp. 53, 57.

remained resting at Palamcottah, till the stores necessary for a siege could be collected."

At the northern end of the town is an enclosure about 150 yards square, formed of mud ramparts 10 feet high, with a gate on each side, in which live one of the queerest races in the world. They call their enclosure a "fort" and themselves "Fort (*Kōttai*) Pillaimārs." They constitute a distinct sect amongst Vellālans and can marry only among their own people. The women never go outside the fort, and no male of any other caste (subject to the special exceptions noted below) may enter; within the fort itself no woman may be seen by any man except her closest relatives. A peculiar sect of Pattanam Brahmans are their household priests, and, when one of their number comes into the fort to perform a marriage, a curtain is placed between him and the bride. When a woman dies, her body is tied up in a sack (so that none may see it) and taken through the northern gate, which is opened only for this purpose, to the cremation-ground two hundred yards away. Menial duties are performed by a sect called Kōttaimārs who, it is said, followed their masters from their original home and, in spite of a serious quarrel which arose in 1840 (referred to below), are still regarded as their traditional servants. All domestic duties that a woman can perform are done by the women of this sect; when the services of a male are necessary, precautions to conceal the Pillaimār women are taken, and a Kōttaimār is called in. In spite of the obvious temptation of making their fort, to which no magistrate or policeman can be admitted, an asylum from the consequences of crime, the opportunity is never known to have been taken. English is known to none of them, and their contribution to the public service consists of one karnam and one village munsif. The community, as a whole, is very wealthy.

It is surprising that a society existing under these conditions should have survived to the present day. According to their own account they numbered originally 400 persons; at present they consist of 52 males and 42 females. "Of these 42 women 17 are widows and not being allowed to remarry are useless for the purpose of increase. Of 18 married women at least 6 are past child-bearing age. Seven unmarried women are aged 15 years and under. Of the 52 men, 18 are married, and 20 unmarried or widowed, between the ages of 20 and 50, obviously cannot find brides within the community. The hopes of the continued existence of these people rest then on 12 married women and 8 unmarried girls; but considering the fact that 16 married women had between them only 8 children in the last decade, these hopes cannot be considered particularly bright.[1]"

According to their own tradition, which in these latter days has been committed to print, the settlement is nearly a thousand years old. Residing in the Rāmnād country, this sect of Vellālans were the chamberlains of the Pāndya king and possessed the privilege of crowning the successive sovereigns. Some disagreement arose between them and their royal master, and the king determined to get rid of them. A rival ruler in the neighbourhood of Srīvaikuntam (perhaps at Korkai) came to their aid and established them in their present fort. In memory of their ancient custom the Kōttai Pillaimārs still retain the privilege of placing the crown on the head of the god Anavarathaswāmi in the Nellaiyappar temple at Tinnevelly on one of the days of the annual festival.

At one time the Kōttaimārs (already referred to) lived practically in the position of bondsmen in one corner of the fort. Contrary to custom (as their masters alleged) these dependants began to build stone houses and to tile them. The Pillaimārs went to law and obtained in 1839 an order restraining the Kōttaimārs from building any more such houses. The Pillaimārs next lodged a suit for damages and for an order that the four houses, which the Kōttaimārs had already built, should be broken down. The Kōttaimārs replied with the plea that their own ancestors had built the fort and that they were as good as—if not better than—the plaintiffs. The court found in favour of the plaintiffs, declaring in no uncertain terms the Kōttaimārs to be their slaves: "that there should be some distinction between masters and slaves is just and lawful and absolutely necessary and moreover it is usual in this country." At the same time the Kōttaimārs were ordered either to remain in the fort as subservient slaves or to break and take out of the fort the roofs and other materials of their houses. It appears that they preferred the latter course; for no Kōttaimār has within living memory resided within the enclosure. There are still more than fifty families of these Kōttaimārs living in the town, but only a few, who live quite near the western gate, continue to serve its residents as menial servants. The Kōttaimārs are Vellālans: they eat meat and by other members of this comprehensive caste are considered to rank comparatively low.

An allowance of Rs. 60 a year, originally granted by the native rulers, is still paid by Government for the upkeep of this

[1] From Mr. Molony's Census Report for 1911.

CHAP. XV. SRI-VAIKUNTAM TALUK.

odd fort. The payment continued unchallenged until 1843, when Mr. E. B. Thomas, the Collector, did his best to stop it. He withheld the money and reported the matter to the Board of Revenue. He painted the evils of the institution in very dark colours, describing the fort as liable to become "a second Alsatia, a safe harbour for any rogues or bad characters who can afford to pay for the refuge." He recommended that the walls should be dismantled and the annual payment stopped. The Government did not accept these alarmist views and ordered the continuance of the payment.

The village of PUDUKKUDI, "New Town," included in the union is situated on the other side of the river. It is said to derive its name from the fact that (like Eral) it was newly built to replace a village which was swept away in the floods of 1827. It contains a local fund choultry, and a rest-house maintained by the Public Works Department. The Kōttai Pillaimārs also own and maintain a chattram in the place.

Tuticorin (population 40,185): a municipal town and an important port, is the headquarters of a Sub-Collector, an Assistant Superintendent of Police, a Port Officer, a deputy tahsildar (who is also a sub-magistrate) and a sub-registrar; it contains also the office of the Superintendent of Pearl and Chank Fisheries, the courts of a Sub-Judge and a district munsif and the usual post and telegraph offices. It is geographically (though no longer officially) the terminus of the South Indian Railway, being 447 miles from Madras. Except on the south, the town is connected with the interior by good roads. The Tamil name of the place, Tūttukkudi, (of which the popular form is a corruption derived, apparently, from the Dutch) is, by some obscure process, popularly derived from *turttu*, "filling up," and *kudi*, "habitation," and is therefore said to mean "the place in which (the wells) dry up." The only obvious merit of this elaborate effort of philology is the appropriateness to the place of a word embodying the meaning thus extracted. The water troubles of the place have been referred to on pages 355-56 above.

The town contains a hospital, maintained from municipal and local funds, and an unusually large number of schools, among which may be mentioned the Caldwell High School maintained by the S.P.G., the St. Xavier's High School belonging to the French Jesuit Mission, a privately-managed "Anglo-Vernacular" school and the "Victoria Mary Elementary School" for girls. The municipality maintains three elementary schools, amongst which one is for girls, and another for Panchamas. In the Victoria Extension road is a convent school controlled by a sisterhood of French nuns. In addition, there are eighteen elementary schools belonging either to missionary bodies or private persons.

The two chief temples of the place, one dedicated to Siva and the other to Vishnu, possess no particular importance or interest. A memorial to the late Robert Ashe, I.C.S., a former Sub-Collector of the Tuticorin division and subsequently Collector of the district, who was murdered in 1911 at Maniyāchi, has recently been erected by public subscription at the eastern end of the Great Cotton road. It consists of an octagonal *mantapam* set in a garden, which is well cared for by the municipality.

The "English" Church,[1] erected by the Dutch East India Company in 1750 and bearing over its porch their monogram V.O.C., is a building of extreme plainness. For many years after the departure of the Dutch (in 1825) it remained unused and neglected. From about 1845 it began to be used by missionaries of the S.P.G., and in 1844 the Collector was appointed *ex-officio* trustee. The building was subsequently placed on the list of Government churches and is now served by missionaries of the S.P.G. The old Roman Catholic church situated towards the southern end of the beach and dedicated to "Our Lady of Snows" dates its foundation from the seventeenth century and, in spite of the strenuous efforts which, on their return in 1838, the Jesuits made to annex it, remains under the jurisdiction of the Bishop of Mylapore. The church of "The Sacred Heart" (near the railway-station), the property of the Jesuits, was completed in 1852.

Of Tuticorin before the arrival of the Portuguese we know only that it was a village inhabited by Paravans; and, as the Portuguese very soon abandoned their first headquarters, Punnaikāyal, in favour of Tuticorin, we may conjecture that the place had already proved its natural advantages for the navigation of small craft. The Portuguese first appeared off the coast in 1532, leading the crusade despatched from Cochin in defence of the Paravans against the Muhammadans of the sea board. The Paravans, as has been seen (page 89), were converted to Christianity, the power of the Portuguese was established on the "Fishery Coast," and, by 1543 at least, possibly earlier, Tuticorin was the seat of a Portuguese Governor. An interesting reference to Tuticorin contained in a letter of Francis Xavier [2] of the year 1544 relates to an attack made

[1] *The Church in Madras*, by Frank Penny, London, 1904, p. 581.

[2] The earliest extant letter of St. Francis Xavier written from the Tinnevelly Coast (28th October 1542) is dated from Tuticorin.

CHAP. XV. SRI-VAIKUNTAM. TALUK.

on the village by the "Badages" *(Vadugans)*, that is, the emissaries of the Vijayanagar rulers and their Nāyakkan subordinates of Madura. The Governor's ship was burnt, his house destroyed and pillaged, and he himself had to take refuge in the islands. The unfriendly relations of Madura with the Portuguese have already been described (pages 231–32). A curious relic (probably the only one) of the days of the Portuguese occupation is a tombstone bearing an inscription in Tamil characters and dated 2nd December 1618. The stone, which is at present lying in the compound of the Fort Press, commemorates "Susanna, daughter of Juan De Cruz, Syndic," and the inscription possesses the interest of being the oldest known mortuary legend in Tamil characters over a European or Eurasian.[1]

The Dutch, who made their first appearance in Ceylon in 1602, were during the first half of the seventeenth century constantly at war with the Portuguese. In 1658 they equipped a fleet, which entered Tuticorin harbour and captured the town, the possession of which they retained till 1784. The Dutch records of this period have unfortunately been lost, or, at any rate, have not yet been discovered; consequently the materials for constructing an account of their management of Tuticorin and of their other possessions in the Tinnevelly district, Vēmbār, Vaippār, Punnaikāyal, Palayakāyal, Kāyalpatnam, Manappād and Alvārtirunagari, are of the most meagre description. Their possessions in the Presidency comprised three groups, those of the Coromandel coast subject to Pulicat, those of the Malabar coast subject to Cochin and those of the "Madura coast" (as it was called) with headquarters at Tuticorin. They built a small fort in Tuticorin, about 100 yards square, and established a Resident there Like their predecessors, the Portuguese, they took possession of the pearl and chank fisheries and, after proving the futility of adopting towards the Paravans a policy of religious persecution, soon took them into the position of profitable friends and supporters; unlike the Portuguese, however, they exercised, it appears, no civil authority over them. To defend the fisheries a chain of armed ships was employed from Cape Comorin to Pāmban. "The Dutch," wrote Father Martin, in 1700, "draw considerable revenues from Tuticorin, though they are not absolute masters of it." By degrees they established an important export trade in the coarse cloths of the country and in the course of time began to claim the

[1] Mr. J. J. Cotton's *List of inscriptions on Tombs and Monuments.* Madras, 1905, p. 326. The stone has since been removed to the English Church.

monopoly of the entire cloth trade of the Madura and Tinnevelly coasts, searching all vessels and demanding passports for all cloth goods leaving the ports. In a number of villages in the interior the Dutch had their weavers who were under orders to work for them exclusively.

The political relations of the East India Company with the Dutch in Tinnevelly open in a most sensational way with the appearance at Tuticorin in 1760 (when Muhammad Yūsuf was waging war on the poligars) of a large Dutch force with field guns from Batavia. At the same time a Dutch force landed at Manappād. Muhammad Yūsuf demanded an explanation and himself led a large force against Alvārtirunagari, a Dutch trading-centre. The Dutch force immediately disappeared from the country. War having broken out in 1782 between the Dutch and the English in Europe, the commander at Palamcotta despatched a force to take Tuticorin. The mission was successful; seventeen guns were captured, and the Dutch garrison were taken prisoners. The Dutch and English came to terms in 1783, and, in consequence of a treaty then made, Tuticorin was restored to the Dutch in 1785. Ten years later, the Madras Government having in 1792 assumed the military control of the district, the surrender of the town was demanded. Colonel Donald Campbell and Mr. Powney, the Collector, received its submission; and a large quantity of stores, gunpowder and treasure was transferred to Palamcotta. At the same time all the other factories and stations in the district held by the Dutch were surrendered. Tuticorin remained an English possession till 1818. In 1801, during the last poligar wars, the Panjālankurichi rebel, with whom the Dutch had formed an alliance, managed to capture the town. The sepoys were disarmed, the English lieutenant in charge was compelled to take to the sea, and the Master Attendant, Mr. Baggot, was taken prisoner. At the close of the war Captain Welsh, the author of the *Military Reminiscences* frequently referred to in this book, was sent to restore order. The Dutch inhabitants, from their Resident, Mr. F. C. Vanspall, downwards, were put on the pension list of the Madras Government; they were not allowed to leave the town without obtaining passports from the Collector of Tinnevelly, and the position of most of them[1] was one of great distress amounting almost to destitution. The Dutch Resident appears to have been a helpless creature, quarrelling with his own people and the English of the place and constantly referring

[1] Mr. J. R. Cocq, father of Mr. C. H. R. Cocq, referred to elsewhere (p. 464) was a conspicuous exception.

CHAP. XV. SRI-VAIKUNTAM TALUK.

domestic, even matrimonial, squabbles to the Collector. The old fort had been left to decay; and that eccentric missionary, Ringeltaube, who visited it in 1806, records a lamentation over what was "formerly the abode of power and luxury, and now the refuge of a homeless traveller and thousands of bats suspended from the ceiling." . . . It was soon afterwards (in 1810 apparently) demolished by Colonel Dyce, commanding the district.

In 1818, in consequence of similar movements in Europe, it was decided to give back to the Dutch their former possessions. A Commission was appointed, and their settlements in Tinnevelly were handed over on 11th May 1818. The cession included Tuticorin and a number of dependent factories—Kāyalpatnam (occupied at that time by the Commercial Resident of Palamcotta), Alvārtirunagari, Punnaikāyal and Manappād; after much discussion, two of the seven islands off the coast were surrendered, namely Pāndi-Tīvu ("Hare Island"), on which the Dutch had erected an obelisk to serve as a landmark for ships, and Kranchi (Cronjee) Island, where they had settled a few artisans to repair their ships.[1] A right to appropriate one-third of the import duty levied on certain articles was claimed by the Dutch and admitted by the commission. But the settlement of claims was by no means ended. The various captures and recaptures of Tuticorin from 1543 onwards down to 1795 had occurred in an age when (with the exception of short periods) the Tinnevelly country was, nominally at least, under Hindu or Muhammadan rule; consequently the rights of the Dutch had not been defined with the same precision as had been the case with those factories which were surrounded by the territories of the East India Company. After infinite discussion and correspondence the Commission finally insisted that the Dutch were entitled to no part of the "native town" (by which at that time was meant the quarter now inhabited by Paravans and Kīlūr, the region north of the English church); they were to confine themselves to the territory formerly occupied by the old fort and its immediate surroundings, roughly a square whose eastern side would be formed by a line drawn from the southern limit of the church to the far end of the present post office. The Dutch claim to the salt factory was disallowed. The collection of a little root referred to in the old records as "chayroot"[2] *(Oldenlandia umbellata)*, from which a red dye

[1] Considerable masonry remains of what is traditionally believed to have been a Dutch jail are still to be seen on this island.

[2] Tamil—சாய வேர். The industry is now extinct (see p. 325).

was extracted, formed another bone of contention. The plant grows in abundance in the sandy soils of the neighbourhood, and the yearly auction of the right to collect it formed during the early years of the century an important item of district revenue; the Dutch claimed the right to lease the privilege in the neighbourhood of Tuticorin. This encroachment was after much difficulty stopped. In 1819 a serious disturbance occurred amongst the Paravans, which resulted in the temporary discontinuance of the chank fishery. The Dutch Government (of Ceylon) had, with a view to securing to themselves the control of this fishery, jobbed into the post of Jāthitalavaimore a person distasteful to the caste. The Paravans in alarm fled from Tuticorin, whilst the Dutch Resident captured the officials employed by the English Government in the fishery and refused to reply to the Collector's remonstrances. The Paravans, who hated and feared their Dutch masters, could not be persuaded to return, and the Collector was obliged to transfer the scene of operations to the place in which the Paravans had taken refuge. Quiet was finally restored, and the Dutch do not appear again to have interfered with the fishery. The Jāthitalavaimore, however, continued to be a thorn in the side of the Dutch; and in 1819 we find Mr. Vanspall, the Resident, writing to the Collector to complain that the barber at Punnaikāyal had "by the persuasion of the Jāthitalaivan and his party" refused to shave the Netherlands interpreter. The control of the import and land duties was another constant source of friction. The Dutch were allowed a remission of British import duties on articles intended for their own use. Ghee apparently was not on the list, and, in spite of his protests, the local English officers had compelled Mr. Vanspall to pay duty on this article. The Resident appealed to the Collector. "I cannot possibly conceive Mr. Hodgson," the Collector replied, "when he framed instructions for the collection of the duties, could ever have contemplated that an officer of such distinction as a Resident of His Majesty the King of the Netherlands, in the town of Tuticorin, should ever desire to import ghee for his own consumption free of duty." Disputes of all kinds were interminable, and questions which appeared at one moment to have been settled were soon re-opened. "It appears to me undoubted," wrote the Collector to the British Commissioner, summing up the situation, "that no general assurance of the Netherlands authorities, however sincere, can be looked on in any other light than as amiable expressions at the opening of a very intricate negotiation." So things continued until

1825, in which year, on the 1st of June, Tuticorin with its "dependencies" was transferred to the British. Except one or two families of mixed descent who preserve Dutch names, the church already referred to, a few commercial buildings, and their cemetery, with skull and cross-bones adorning the gateway, the Dutch have left no memorials of their occupation of the town.

Writing in 1700, Father Martin gives an impression of the place, which, with some obviously necessary changes, may be accepted as true to-day. "As you approach it from the sea," he says, "Tuticorin appears to be a handsome town. We observe . . . several spacious warehouses built by the water side which all look quite nice and pretty. But the instant you land, all this beauty vanishes and you find nothing but a town of hurdles." The hurdles survive here and there, but have almost entirely given place to walls of coral-stone; and the thatch that hurdles imply has been replaced by tiles. Still the streets and lanes behind the sea-front are narrow and irregular. The Great Cotton road, the main street of the town, is straight and wide above the average, but even so is inadequate to the traffic with which it is generally thronged. The sea-front, on the other hand, presents a fine array, three-quarters of a mile long, of substantial buildings, offices, churches, and private houses, which have succeeded, as they doubtless greatly surpass those which, to Father Martin's eyes, gave the town a meretricious beauty. The Beach road and the neighbourhood of the railway-station form the centre of the wholesale trade of the place, the Great Cotton road containing all the important shops. North of the railway station are the crowded habitations of all varieties of castes; and the *vādi* or "enclosure," which appears to be the most ancient Hindu settlement, is now one of the most insanitary quarters of the town. To the south live the Paravans, and further west, in the suburb called Mēlūr, is the superior residential quarter of the native town. The whole town does not cover a square mile. On the north Puckle's channel (named after the Collector who had it dug) and the sandy soil beyond it practically preclude expansion in this direction; south of the town the ground is swampy, and the western end, which seems the only outlet, is unattractive by its comparative remoteness from the centre of commerce. The congested state in which the local population of 40,185 persons live needs no demonstration.

The rise of Tuticorin to a position of importance in the world of commerce is a matter of comparatively recent history; it is probable that few ports in India have experienced so rapid a development. In the earliest years of the nineteenth century the sea-borne trade of the place amounted to a few hundreds of rupees in value, and, compared with Kāyalpatnam and Kulasēkharapatnam, the port was of no importance whatever. There were 16 ships engaged in the sea-traffic of the district, and the trade was chiefly in jaggery with Madras and cloth with Colombo. Kāyalpatnam gained importance from the fact that most of the cotton and cloths bought up by the Commercial Resident, amounting in value to three or four lakhs of rupees annually, were shipped to Madras from that port. So late as 1839 the "Madras Almanack" of the period remarked of Tuticorin: "this village being one of the nearest little sea-ports to Tinnevelly and Palamcotta there is some trade carried on by the native merchants and several vessels are employed in exporting bales of cotton, indigo,[1] etc., to the Presidency and also cloth of different kinds; but the chief importance of the place arises from the Pearl-Fishery." In 1835 a Bombay merchant sent an agent to Tuticorin to purchase cotton for the China market. He bought 3,000 bales, but could get no one to venture to take it from Tuticorin to China, as the harbour was uncharted. Ten years later we find seven cotton-screws (the first was set up in 1832 by a Mr. Groves of Liverpool)[2] at work in the place under the management of Europeans, prominent among whom was the well-remembered Dutchman, Mr. J. R. Cocq; in 1842 the harbour had been surveyed (it was again surveyed in 1879 and 1912) and a lighthouse[3] had been built to replace the old Dutch obelisk; and Tuticorin had suddenly leaped into the position of being the depot to the south for all the cotton ships for the China and English markets. By about 1851 the price of cleaned cotton, which had seldom exceeded Rs. 45 per candy or bale (of 500 lbs.), had risen to Rs. 60; between 1851 and 1861 the new roads connecting Tuticorin with the cotton country were laid out, and during these ten years the annual exports of cotton averaged 55,000 bales. During the American Civil War (1861–65) the price reached Rs. 100 a bale, and the trade with China almost completely disappeared in favour of London and Liverpool. The price soon fell again; but in 1889–90 the value of cotton exported amounted to Rs. 146 lakhs, and the price was steadily rising. In sixty years the trade of the port had multiplied itself by ten; and cotton in

[1] This cannot have been much; for Mr. Hughes, who alone made experiments with indigo, found it a failure (see p. 487).

[2] On the authority of Bishop Caldwell, *History of Tinnevelly*, p. 84.

[3] Replaced in 1874 by the present light. The old light was transferred to Muttam, in Travancore.

CHAP. XV. SRI-VAIKUNTAM TALUK.

1890 accounted for about three-quarters of the total exports. The railway line which was opened in 1876 has since brought to Tuticorin all the export trade of the southern districts of the Presidency.[1] During the five years ending with 1913-14 the average price of ginned cotton stood at the astonishingly high figure of Rs. 180. A reference to the separate appendix to this volume will give some idea of the trade of the place. At the present day the port ranks, within the Presidency, second in importance to Madras and, in the whole of British India, fifth. Its total volume of trade is nearly one-half of that of the Presidency town. Cotton, the chief article of export, is sent to Japan, England and Germany: yarn to China: senna to England and Germany: tea to Europe, Australia and America: coffee to Europe: cotton piece-goods to South Africa, the Straits Settlements and Ceylon: cattle, onions, chillies, rice and dry grains to Ceylon. The chief articles of import are machinery, cotton piece-goods, matches and kerosine oil.

The port has its own Chamber of Commerce, and a Port Conservancy Board has recently been formed for the regulation of local expenditure. There are ten European trading firms in the place: the Madura Company, agents for the British India Steam Navigation Company; Messrs. Volkart Bros., agents for the Asiatic Steam Navigation Company and exporters of cotton, fibre and senna; Messrs. A. and F. Harvey (managing directors of the Coral Mills, Ltd.), agents for three lines of steamers, and general traders; Messrs. Ralli Bros., who conduct an enormous export trade in cotton; the New Berar Company, exporters of cotton; Messrs. Shaw, Wallace & Co.; the Burma Oil Company; the Asiatic Petroleum Company; Messrs. Dymes & Co.; and Mr. Zellweger, general merchant. The Bank of Madras and the National Bank, Ltd., have agencies in the place. Indian traders and brokers—Paravans, Vellālans, Shānāns and Muhammadans—are innumerable. Besides its sea-borne trade, the town has extensive dealings with the taluks of Srīvaikuntam, Tiruchendūr and Kōilpatti, forming, like Pēttai further west, the important centre in the east and south for the distribution and collection of goods. The coolies recruited by the Ceylon Labour Commission are embarked and landed here and form the bulk of the 250,000 passengers who pass through the port in a year.[2] The Ceylon Government has a

[1] Since this was written the Dhanushkōdi route to Ceylon has begun to assert itself. It is also unnecessary to add that the conditions of trade described in this paragraph are those which existed before the out-break of the present war.

[2] The recently opened Dhanushkodi route has diverted much of this traffic.

substantial camp ten miles outside Tuticorin at Tattaparai where the intending emigrants are detained under medical observation before they are allowed to embark.

The harbour has already been described (see p. 20). As stated there, ships of 60 tons' burden and upwards anchor four to six miles away from the town, loading and discharging their cargoes by means of lighters. It was not till 1866 that the first pier—a primitive wooden jetty a hundred feet long and costing Rs. 1,200—was built. It was re-built and extended in 1873 and, though recently condemned, is still in use. In 1877 the Duke of Buckingham visited Tuticorin and was met by a deputation of merchants who pressed for the further improvement of their pier. In 1881 the jetty was considerably strengthened; six years later its width was doubled, and, in the following year, trolley rails were laid to connect it with the South Indian line. In 1894, the construction of a new pier supported on iron screw-piles was put in hand. At the same time considerable reclamation of the foreshore was found necessary to afford approaches to the new jetty, and the whole undertaking cost a little under two lakhs. The pier was opened on the 13th July 1895; and in 1899 the main line of the South Indian Railway was extended to the quay.

In spite of the natural disabilities of the harbour, the trade of Tuticorin continued to show marvellous progress, and Government and the interested merchants alike began to examine the possibilities of improving the port. Apart from the inconvenience that steamers had to anchor some five miles away in unsheltered water, the harbour itself, especially after the heavy rains of 1903 which brought down large quantities of black cotton-soil, was found to be silting up to an alarming extent.[1] One suggestion was to dredge a channel for ships from the anchorage to a point close in shore. A rocky bottom, however, was found, and the idea was quickly abandoned. An equally heroic proposal, which however seems not to have been seriously considered, was to carry the railway across to Hare Island and to provide wharfage near the lighthouse. At the same time the necessity of dredging the harbour had been much discussed, and, in 1904, a dredger was brought out from England at a cost of Rs. 3¼ lakhs. No sooner had the work been started than it was discovered that to accomplish the task proposed for it the dredger would take eight or ten years. To clear up the muddle into which the affairs of the port had drifted, a committee of merchants

[1] A comparison of the soundings recorded in the charts prepared in 1842, 1879 and 1912 illustrates this fact most strikingly.

CHAP. XV. SRI. VAIKUNTAM TALUK.

and officials was finally appointed in 1906, and it was then decided that the two evils for which a practical remedy must be sought were the inadequate length of wharfage and the insufficient depth of water for the navigation of boats.

To improve the wharfage, the construction of a new pier was finally recommended; and the proposal received the sanction of Government in 1910. Before this, it had been decided to employ the dredger in excavating a channel a hundred feet wide to a depth of nine feet; and in 1909 this work was put in hand. An interesting proposal, which received considerable attention at the time, was to run a stone bank straight out to sea opposite the railway station and, by means of a pump-dredger, to excavate the harbour to the south of it, to throw the material thus dredged on to the opposite side and ultimately to fill up in this manner the area to the north of the bank. The land thus reclaimed was to be joined up with the South Indian Railway line and, by the addition of a line of concrete pile-work, converted into a valuable wharf-frontage. The South Indian Railway, with the Pāmban-Ceylon railway scheme on their hands, declined to support the proposal, and no more was heard of it.

The new pier, 480 feet long, situated 100 yards to the north of the old pier, was completed in 1912. It is constructed of reinforced concrete piling and bracing, with no exposed steel, and a timber decking and fendering.

The main industries of the place are those connected with the treatment of raw cotton. Besides the large cotton-spinning factory known as the Coral Mill (p. 213) there are six cotton-presses and five ginning factories in the town. There is a "screw" of the old type, the "Bravi Press", used for pressing senna. There are three rice mills. The local pearl and chank industries are dealt with in chapters I and VI, and the salt-pans of the neighbourhood are referred to in chapter XII.

The work of cutting coral-stone from the bed of the sea occupies large numbers of Paravans; the stone is found about the coast of the islands of the neighbourhood and, after thorough exposure to sun and rain, makes a useful building-material. From the smaller débris lime is extracted, and the coast to the north of the town is littered with kilns employed for the purpose. The fisheries of the place are referred to in chapter VI.

TENKASI TALUK.

THE TENKASI TALUK, lying between Sankaranainārkōil on the north and Ambāsamudram on the south, occupies the westernmost extremity of the district. The country of which Kuttālam is the centre contains the most picturesque scenery to be found in the district. East of this, except for the strips of country watered by the Chittār and its affluents, the taluk consists of slightly undulating stretches of dry country, rising abruptly here and there to steep ridges and producing palmyras, in more or less abundance, almost everywhere. Half the total area of the taluk consists of ryotwari land, the north and north-east being occupied by the Chokkampatti mittas and the Uttumalai zamindari. Of the Government land one-fifth is composed of forests. Of the ryotwari irrigated land almost the whole is watered by the Chittār and its tributaries and of this river-fed area nine-tenths consists of double crop lands. The extent of rainfed wet land (ryotwari), about 650 acres, is less than in any other taluk.

In regard to density of population Tenkāsi comes fourth among the taluks and, during the decade 1901-11, showed a greater increase (11·8 per cent) than any taluk except Srīvaikuntam. The predominating castes are: in Uttumalai, Maravans; in the country south of the Chittār where palmyras are most plentiful, Shānāns; and in the fertile villages of the west, Vellālans, Muhammadans and Kavarai Nāyakkans. Weaving is the occupation of Muhammadans and Hindus, mostly Kaikkilaiyans, in Tenkāsi and Kadaiyanallūr; jaggery is manufactured by Shānāns in the palmyra tract to the south. Tenkāsi, Kadaiyanallūr and Surandai are unions.

In the western part of the taluk roads are plentiful above the average of the district and from Tenkāsi they radiate in all directions. In the north and east of the taluk, that is, in the Uttumalai and Chokkampatti country, practically no roads exist at all. The South Indian Railway enters the taluk on the south-west and, after leaving Tenkāsi, enters Travancore territory.

At Kuttālam, Ilanji, and Kadaiyanallūr (and possibly in other places which have not come to notice) sepulchral urns have been found.

CHAP. XV.
TENKASI TALUK.

Travancore possessions.

A considerable tract of level country in the west of the taluk, which geographically forms part of the Tinnevelly district, belongs to the Travancore State and is known as the SHENCOTTA TALUK. On the west it is bounded by the Ariyankāvu pass, which also lies wholly within the confines of that State. There are also in the west of the Tenkāsi taluk a few small isolated patches of land belonging to Travancore.

When in 1801 the English came into possession of Tinnevelly, the Shencotta taluk was found to be in the occupation of the Rāja of Travancore. Mr. Lushington held that the territory formed a part of the Tinnevelly district and consequently claimed that it should be ceded to the Company. An agreement binding himself to pay in respect of this tract a *nuzzernāmah* of 3,000 *cully chukrams* yearly had been executed by the Rāja in 1766 in favour of the Nawāb. Mr. Lushington's view was that this was rent due as from a dependent zamindar, and that, consequently, the Shencotta zamindari, like the pālaiyams of Tinnevelly, should pass under the control of the Company. Travancore insisted that the payment represented the tribute of a feudatory state and claimed that Shencotta formed part of the Travancore State. The question was complicated by the fact that the zamindar of Chokkampatti had for many years past exercised *kāval* rights over the Shencotta country and levied *dēsakāval* fees. By the treaty of 1792 the poligars came under the Company's control, and by the further agreement of 1800 (page 333) all *kāval* fees hitherto paid to zamindars were thenceforward assumed by the Company's Government. The argument that Shencotta should form part of the Tinnevelly district was soon dropped, and no "rent" was exacted from the Rāja; the claim to the *dēsakāval* fees, however, was insisted on. The fees were paid to the Collector of Tinnevelly until 1804, in which year the British officials engaged in collecting them were withdrawn. The fees, it appears, were no longer paid; but the question whether they were due or not, and, if so, whether they should be exacted, continued under correspondence between the Collector, the Board of Revenue and Government for many years. In 1825 it was finally decided that the claim should be waived.

Another dispute with Travancore, which arose at the time of the assumption of Tinnevelly by the Company, related to a number of scattered patches of country amounting in all to less than 1,000 acres—mostly enclaves in the Tenkāsi taluk—and to these Travancore asserted a claim. On the ground that they had been annexed "in an irregular way" to the Shencotta territory and really represented encroachments made in the past by Travancore on the Tinnevelly district, Mr. Lushington assumed control of these lands and included their revenues with those of the district. Travancore protested, and the question came before the Madras Government for final settlement together with the Shencotta *dēsakāval* dispute. Orders were passed, in 1825, to restore the lands to Travancore and to reimburse to that State the revenues collected.

A reduction of the tribute by Travancore was subsequently suggested in place of the surrender of these lands; and at one time it was hoped that some arrangement might be reached by which Travancore would be induced to relinquish its claim to all land on the Tinnevelly side of the ghats. The surrender to Travancore of the British possessions of Anjengo and Tangasseri and even of some territory in the south-west of the Nāngunēri taluk was suggested. The proposals, however, came to nothing; and in 1851 these bits of land, interspersed in a most inconvenient way in British territory, were definitely ceded to Travancore. One patch—a village named Malaiyankulam—lay in the Ambāsamudram taluk; and in exchange for this Travancore agreed to accept Puliyēri near the Shencotta taluk. The survey of these scattered portions of Travancore territory and of the Shencotta taluk was carried out in 1855.

Alankulam (population 3,090): 19 miles from Palamcotta on the Tenkāsi road, contains a police-station and chattram. Lying midway between Tinnevelly and Tenkāsi, it formed an important staging-place before the opening of the railway. A large chattram, which is an offshoot of Vengu Mudaliyār's Gnānamani Ammāl foundation at Vannārpet (Palamcotta), suffers neglect now that travellers are few; and the old travellers' bungalow has been left to decay. With the abandonment of this bungalow the only accommodation provided in the taluk by the local boards for European travellers has disappeared. The population consists almost entirely of Shānāns, who, forsaking the climbing of palmyras, have taken to cultivation. Excellent gardens of chillies, brinjals and, latterly, cambodia cotton are numerous. The temple dedicated to Rāma, Sīta and Lakshmana on the small hill called Okkanindrān Pottai, two miles to the north of the village, is believed to mark the spot where the gods assembled to greet Rāma after he had slain the deer which had long baffled his marksmanship. He first saw the deer *(mān)* in Māyamānkurichi (*māya*, "illusion") and lost it; he found it again at Mānūr, wounded it at Mudavakurichi (*mudava*, "lame"), and finally at Pattākurichi (*patta*, "perished") he slew it.

CHAP. XV. TENKASI TALUK.

Connected with Alankulam by a gravelled road is NALLUR, one-and-a-half miles to the north-east, a station of the Church Missionary Society. The girls' school of the place is under the management of the authorities of the Sarah Tucker School at Palamcotta. The local Shānāns own and manage a temple which is evidently of considerable age and is in all respects of exactly the same type as the ordinary Saivite temples managed by Brahmans. The temple contains all the usual subsidiary shrines and possesses two cars and vehicles *(vāhanams)* for the god's processions. Service is done by a Shānān priest, Brahmans being occasionally called in for special ceremonies.

Chokkampatti (population 6,553): once the headquarters of an important zamindari, is now a small village, inhabited wholly by Kondaiyankōttai Maravans, 14 miles from Tenkāsi on the road leading to Sivagiri. The ruins of the residence of successive zamindars and the remains of the mud walls which enclosed the old fort, a few acres in extent, are still to be seen.

In the early days of conflict between the poligars and the Nawāb's troops Chokkampatti (his pālaiyam is also referred to in the early records as Vadagarai or Vadhagerri)[1] was second only to the Pūli Tēvan of Nelkattanseval amongst the western poligars in power and in the stubbornness of his opposition. In 1758 he took a leading part in the great confederacy which united its forces with the firm determination of overthrowing Yūsuf Khān. Considering him to be the most dangerous of all the allies, the Nawāb's commander directed his first move against him in that year; the poligar's villages were burnt, and his fort was in danger, when suddenly Muhammad Yūsuf was recalled to Madras. The title of the poligar of the time, Chinnananja Tēvan, was disputed by Vellaiya Tēvan; and the final success of the latter in recovering the estate brought about a complete change in the relations between the Company and the pālaiyam. In 1779 Vellaiya Tēvan, obtaining the assistance of neighbouring poligars, attacked his rival's fort and compelled its surrender. Having got possession of the pālaiyam, he adopted the policy of actively supporting the Company and thus brought upon himself the active hostility of many of the poligars; in fact it was only on the intervention of Colonel Fullarton in 1783 that his fort was saved from extermination at their hands. On the surrender of

[1] The change of name and headquarters appears to have been made about 1767, when, after seven years' attachment, a reduced estate (excluding Vadagarai) was given back to the poligar. (See *Caldwell's History of Tinnevelly*, p. 138.)

the "Assignment" in 1785, Vellaiya Tēvan's position became hopeless. His enemies amongst the poligars easily persuaded Eitbar Khān, the Nawāb's commander, that Vellaiya Tēvan was a dangerous rebel; the troops of the Nawāb and the poligar combined and marched on Chokkampatti in 1787, and Vellaiya Tēvan had to fly. Chinnananja Tēvan was at once restored, and, on his death in 1790, the estate passed to his minor son. Meanwhile Vellaiya Tēvan continued his friendly relations with the Company and especially earned the thanks of Colonel Maxwell during his expedition and attempted settlement of 1792. His claims were brought by Mr. Powney in 1795 to the notice of Government, who decided that the restoration of Vellaiya Tēvan was "no less an act of justice than of policy"; he was accordingly reinstated in the following year. Chinnananja Tēvan was given a subsistence allowance, which continued to be paid till his death in 1825. Vellaiya Tēvan, who received his sanad as zamindar in 1803, died seven years later and was succeeded by his notorious son Valangapuli Tēvan. The new zamindar's payments of peshkash were from the outset invariably in arrear, and during the first fourteen years of his tenure his estate was taken eight times under attachment. In his own country he was an irresponsible tyrant and throughout the district was known and feared as a dangerous brigand. In March 1814 the Government treasury at Tenkāsi was plundered of Rs. 20,000; and, though the zamindar escaped conviction, it was the unanimous opinion of all disinterested persons at the time that Valangapuli Tēvan not only engineered the robbery but received the loot. His uncle who had taken a leading part in the crime showed a disposition to give information and promptly disappeared under the effects of poison. A confidential servant was convicted; and the money, though not recovered, was actually traced to the hands of the zamindar. In 1816 the Maravans of Nānguneri, who had been dispossessed of their *kāval* duties by Mr. Lushington in favour of the Shānāns, savagely murdered the head *kāvalgār* and regained their position. The leading offenders at once fled for refuge to Chokkampatti and, returning after a time with assurances of protection, successfully defied the efforts of the police to arrest them. In all parts of the district freebooting Maravans were wandering about, declaring themselves to be the zamindar's adherents; the police and subordinate magistrates were afraid to deal with them; the courts were filled with the zamindar's informers, who watched and reported all proceedings, and no witness dared give

CHAP. XV. TENKASI TALUK.

evidence. In 1818 Valangapuli Tēvan was charged with instigating a violent assault on the house of the Talaivankōttai zamindar and escaped with an order requiring him to give security. Land disputes brought him into conflict with his neighbours in Puliyankudi, and all Mr. Huddleston's attempts to secure a settlement were thwarted. In his own zamindari he had set up a court of criminal and civil jurisdiction before which persons were condemned to work in irons; and fines were imposed and property sold to realize the money. For this he was brought to trial in 1822, and the Criminal Judge of Madura (under whose jurisdiction Tinnevelly then was) recommended to Government that, under the provisions of Madras Regulation II of 1819 (State Prisoners), the zamindar should be deported. Government, however, were reluctant to take this step. "They impute," the order ran, "the irregularities of the Chokkampatti Poligar to his imperfect acquaintance with the regulations and express the hope that he will of his own accord make reparation of any injury which individuals may have suffered." The zamindar thus escaped; his depredations continued, and, by 1834, his arrears of peshkash amounted to Rs. 74,000. There was no prospect that he would be able to pay, and the sale of his estate was consequently ordered. At the same time, in view of the danger to life and property involved in leaving the dispossessed marauder at large, he was arrested and confined under Regulation II of 1822 (Criminal Procedure). The zamindari was put up to auction in 1834 and bought by Government for Rs. 8,000. Whilst under restraint, the zamindar executed a deed transferring the estate to his son; and the Collector strongly advised that Government should relinquish in his favour the property which they had bought and had now taken under their management. Government, however, declined to restore the estate and directed that it should be duly surveyed and assessed. Meanwhile the ex-zamindar's supporters were agitating for his release and in 1835 petitioned the Court of Circuit on the subject. The application was dismissed by the Judge on the ground that he could not interpose in the case of a State prisoner deported under Regulation II of 1819. "Why then," exclaimed the ex-zamindar, when the Judge subsequently visited the jail, "if I am a State prisoner, do not Government conform to their own laws by sending the warrant prescribed by Regulation II of 1819?" His "acquaintance with the regulations" was evidently not so "imperfect" as Government had supposed. Realizing his mistake, the Judge addressed Government with a recommendation that action under

Regulation II of 1819 should be taken. The proposal was accepted; a warrant was issued, and Valangapuli Tēvan was in 1835 sent to Gooty in the Bellary district and confined as a State prisoner. He memorialized the Madras Government and appealed to the Supreme Court without success; finally he submitted his case to the Government of India. That Government characterized the previous proceedings as irregular, and the prisoner was accordingly released on security in 1837. An allowance was made for his maintenance subject to the condition that he should not return to the Tinnevelly district.

The ex-zamindar's son had, since 1834, been doing all he could to secure possession of the estate. He sent repeated petitions to Government on the subject and finally laid his case before the Court of Directors. The matter was referred in 1851 to the Madras Government, who, accepting the views of the Board of Revenue, strongly opposed the idea of surrendering the estate and installing the petitioner. Peace and order had been restored; the land had been surveyed and settled on ryotwari principles, and private capital had been laid out on the assurance that the stable management of Government would continue. The Court however overruled the Madras Government and directed that the estate should be handed over to the ex-zamindar's son, Karunālaya Valangapuli Tēvan. On the 16th August 1859, the new zamindar was put in possession. By 1866 he was reduced to bankruptcy, and nine of the 18 villages comprised in the estate were sold in court auction. He had spent the whole of his income, which for this period amounted to Rs. 6 lakhs, and had incurred debts, mostly in dissipation, to the extent of another Rs. 7 lakhs. "Chokkampatti," wrote Mr. Puckle, "is a miserable collection of huts, filthy to a degree; and here the Zamindar has lived, surrounded by pigs and buffaloes while his estate was going to ruin and his ryots becoming more impoverished yearly." Three years later the remaining nine villages were sold in satisfaction of decrees, and the zamindari thus became extinct. An apportionment of the peshkash was made among the eighteen dismembered fragments of the old estate; they are known as "mittas" and are held by their various owners subject to the payment of a fixed peshkash. Twelve of them are situated in Tenkāsi and six in the Sankaranainārkōil taluk.[1]

The ex-zamindar spent his last days at Kuttālam, where he died in 1892.

[1] For the names of these mittas see p. 275.

CHAP. XV. TENKASI TALUK.

Three miles south-east of Chokkampatti is a large ruined Saivite temple known as the Shenbagarāmappērikōil. Its interior is richly carved; but the building has evidently been abandoned for many generations. A few hundred yards away is a small dilapidated Vaishnavite temple, whose situation by comparison with that of the other temple makes it evident that a village once existed on the site. Half a mile away are the remains of an old mud fort.

Kadaiyanallūr (population 17,077): situated ten miles north of Tenkāsi on the road to Srīvilliputtūr, is a union, and contains a police-station, a sub-registrar's office and a forest rest-house. A market is held on Thursdays, at which fish, vegetables and grains are sold. In population the place stands first in the taluk; more than one-half of the inhabitants are Muhammadans; and for their benefit the taluk board maintains an elementary school.

As in Tenkāsi, the main occupation of the Muhammadans is weaving; but here, in addition to the *muris* or coarse cloths provided for the Malayālam market, they make also the coloured cloths that the Singhalese, both men and women, wear. As weavers of these coloured cloths, the local Muhammadans are mostly the employees of their co-religionists of Mēlappālaiyam, who supply yarn and pay the weavers according to their outturn. The usual rate is about Rs. 8 for a *pā* of 77 yards, which represents (it is said) ten days' work for two men and two women. With the rise in the price of thread the manufacture of *muris* is apparently decreasing in favour of the production of coloured cloths on a system which requires no capital. Inspired by the "swadhesi" movement of recent years, the Chōliya Brahmans of the place started, in 1907, a limited company with a subscribed capital of Rs. 10,000 to form a weaving factory. Twelve looms were set up in a tiled building, and the manufacture of towels and carpets proceeded for two years. The project was then given up as a failure, and the factory with its looms has lain idle ever since.

Tradition asserts that the original village was situated two miles further west on the banks of the Karuppānadhi and was abandoned owing to the incursions of wild beasts. Traces of the old site are still distinctly visible, and forsaken idols may be seen lying about the ground. The name of the village is by tradition derived from the god Kadaiyālīswarar to whom one of the small Siva temples of the village is dedicated. The place, so runs the story, was once a jungle, in which shepherds used to pasture their flocks. A Brahman appeared one day and, asking the shepherds for some water to drink, was given a *kadaiyāl* (a bamboo cup) of milk. The Brahman drank the milk, put down the *kadaiyāl* and departed. Next day the shepherds went to pick up the cup, but it stuck to the ground. An axe was applied, and blood at once spurted out. The king, on being informed, came to the spot, found a *lingam* and built a temple to the god, whom he called Kadaiyālīswarar. This temple as well as the Vishnu temple facing the *agrahāram* contains inscriptions; but they have not yet been deciphered.

Four miles to the west of the village, at the foot of hills in Vairavankulam (mitta), is a small Sāstā temple called Periyaswāmikōil, the peculiarity of which is that the god is represented not, as is usual in such temples, by an idol in human shape but by a *lingam*. The temple was built and endowed by Chinnananja Tēvan, one of the Chokkampatti poligars of the eighteenth century.

Kuttālam (population 1,218): headquarters of an Assistant Superintendent of Police, is situated at an elevation of about 550 feet on the southern arm of a deep bay in the Western Ghats. Around the place is a network of branch roads connecting it by short routes with all the main roads of the neighbourhood. Possessing as it does fine waterfalls, delightful forest scenery, a temple of repute and, during certain months of the year, an exceptionally cool climate, Kuttālam has long been a favourite resort both of Europeans and Indians. Its annual rainfall is 58 inches, more than twice the average for the district. From June to September the hills which overlook the Kuttālam "bay" are overcast with storm-clouds beaten up through the Ariyankāvu pass by the winds of the south-west monsoon; and, at a time when the rest of the district gets practically no rain, heavy showers are constantly falling along the slopes of the hills and over a few square miles of the country at their foot. Whether rain falls or not, the wind blowing through the hanging clouds reduces the temperature by ten to fifteen degrees below the average of the district and substitutes a delightful climate for raging winds and sand storms.

During this season, as also from November to January, the period of the north-east monsoon, the waterfall—the "Vada-arivi"—one of the most striking natural beauties of the place, is in full flood. It is by this cascade of nearly 200 feet that the Chittār makes its final descent into the level country. Seen from the foot, the river comes first into sight rushing headlong from the forest above over a sheer precipice; nearly

CHAP. XV. TENKASI TALUK.

half-way down, a deep trough in the face of the rock, known as "the boiling sea" *(pongumākadal)*, breaks the fall, and it is beneath the mass of water issuing from this basin and in the pool (deepened to some extent by gunpowder) lying at the foot of the fall that all classes of people delight to bathe. "What conduces much", (so runs a medical report[1] of 1811) "to the restoration of the invalids at this singular abode, is the little waterfall, under which most of the Europeans daily bathe. This cataract is, by a division of a rock above, separated from the greater one; and is not more than thirteen or fourteen feet high. The falling of the water, after the first shock is over, gives an indescribable feeling of pleasure; by its constant beating, it quickens the circulation and produces a fine glow all over the body; and has, besides, the further good effects of dispelling languor, raising the spirits, exciting appetite, and promoting digestion in a superior degree to any other kind of bathing that we are acquainted with. It has, in consequence of these virtues, together with the delightful climate of the valley itself, been the happy means of rapidly restoring many to health and comfort who previous to their visit to Courtallam, appeared to be hastening to their graves." With Hindus the fall is equally efficacious as a means of washing away sins.

On the face of the rock are carved a number of *sivalingams*; and a few hundred feet from the bathing pool by the bank of the river is the temple of Kuttālanāthaswāmi, the "Lord of Kuttālam", who, on great feast days, is taken with musical pomp to the *tīrtavāri mantapam* just beside the pool. Thence the god is taken to the falls and bathed. Daily pūja is offered by the temple priests to the *sivalingams*, and on these and similar occasions the Chittār is considered to be the Ganges.

From its association with the waterfall the Kuttālam temple has attained a wide reputation as a place of pilgrimage. In the *stalapurāna* the place is referred to as "Trikūtāchalam," "mountain with three peaks," the god of the temple being "the lord of the mountain peaks," "Trikūtāchalapathi." That "Trikūtāchalam" should have become "Tirukūttālam" and thence "Kuttālam" seems probable enough; but the derivation of the name is uncertain.

The place is referred to in the Dēvāram (ascribed to the seventh century A.D.), and the temple, like so many others in the district, attributes its foundation to the *rishi* Agastya. At the time of Siva's marriage in Kailāsa guests and sight-seers

[1] Report of the Medical Committee appointed in 1811, see p. 259.

were assembled in thousands: the balance of the earth was disturbed, and the south began to rise up. At Siva's bidding Agastya, the shortest figure known to Hindu mythology, went to the south to right the balance. At Trikūtāchala he found a Vishnu temple and, bearing as he did the marks of a Saivite, was turned away from the door. Agastya went off to the Subramanya temple at Ilanji to ask the God's advice; and, accepting it, he returned next day with a *nāmam* and *dulasi* beads and easily obtained admission. By his touch he then converted the idol of Vishnu into a *sivalingam*.

The tradition that the temple was converted from Vaishnavism into Saivism is so generally accepted that it is presumably based on some historical fact. The temple contains inscriptions by Pāndya rulers of the fifteenth century, and to the south side of it stands an inscribed square column about six feet high, exactly similar to the pillar in front of the Tenkāsi temple.

About the foot of the fall and on the northern side of the river near the temple are a number of *mantapams* and kitchens for the convenience of pilgrims; the open spaces are paved with flagstones, and the northern bank of the river is revetted and walled, and a footbridge crosses the river. The two large *mantapams,* one containing the *kodimaram* and the other in front of the temple, are attributed to a Chokkampatti poligar of the eighteenth century, and in the former may be seen statues of the founder and (it is said) his brother, in full suit of armour. Belonging to this temple, a few hundred yards away on an open plateau, is a temple, known as *Chitra Sabhai* and dedicated to the God Natarāja (Siva as a dancer), the walls of which are decorated throughout with paintings. In front is a *teppakulam*, with an elaborately ornamented *gōpuram* in the middle, where, during January, a "floating festival" is celebrated. The large choultry situated on the left of the river near the temple, which provides food and shelter for Hindus of all castes and Muhammadans, was built about 1700 and endowed by the Chokkampatti poligar of that time. It is now under the management of the District Board, at whose expense a building containing a number of separate rooms for the accommodation of travellers has recently been added. The *mantapam* on the opposite side of the road known as the "Valangapuli Vilās," usually occupied by the Collector's office establishment when he halts at Kuttālam, was built by the notorious Periyaswāmi Valangapuli Tēvan, the father of the last zamindar.

CHAP. XV.
TENKASI TALUK.

Higher up the Chittār, within easy reach, are two more falls—"Shenbagādēvi arivi," about a mile from the foot of the hills: and about two miles further up again, "Tēnarivi," the "Honey-fall," a magnificent cascade descending a hundred feet through a vertical cleft which suggests the hollow contained by the three walls of a square chimney.

Though its waterfall and its temple must for centuries have attracted crowds of pious pilgrims, Kuttālam as a "residential resort" appears to have been the discovery of Europeans. From the earliest times of the Company's management we find Collectors holding their cutcherry at "Terucotallum," "Courtalam" or "Courtallam," the last being the form in which the name survives in general use to the present day.

No sooner had the place been discovered than the peculiar climate of its hills suggested the experiment of exotic cultivation. Between 1795 and 1800 nutmegs, cloves and spices of all kinds were imported from the Moluccas; and, largely through the untiring efforts of Mr. Casamajor, who was the Company's Commercial Resident from 1800 to 1806 and the name-giver of the little village of Kāsimēsipuram, a number of gardens on the slopes of the valleys draining into Kuttālam and its neighbourhood were planted up. A cinnamon garden was also established in Kokkarakulam, just next to the garden of the bungalow which is now occupied by the District Judge. It was ten or twelve years before the nutmegs in the Kuttālam gardens began to bear fruit; and in 1813 samples of the produce, nutmegs, cloves, cinnamon and coffee, were sent to Madras for the European market. The English merchants reported unfavourably; and, as the gardens did not promise to be a paying concern, Government transferred them from the Commercial Department, in whose charge they were, to the Revenue Department. Cinnamon had from the beginning been distinctly poor; and, in 1815, the cinnamon plantations, both at Tinnevelly and Kuttālam, were sold. The other gardens were retained for their experimental value. Further consignments were made a few years later to England; but the reception of the products was again disappointing. The nutmegs were pronounced to be unmarketable in Europe, their freight being far in excess of their sale value; the coffee too was poor and could not hope to compete with the produce of Java. The expenses of the gardens had invariably exceeded their receipts; but not eve an offer, made in 1835 by an European planter of Travancore, to take the gardens on lease for 12 years at Rs. 200 a year could induce Government to abandon their valued "experiment." In 1843 the Collector, Mr. E. B. Thomas, with his usual horticultural zeal, got to work on the gardens. He put down 1,000 nutmeg seeds, distributed seeds in Travancore and Salem; he pruned, manured and set the gardens thoroughly in order. Between 1840 and 1850, chiefly owing to his exertions, the number of trees enormously increased, and during the latter part of his time the gardens very nearly paid their way. The total area of the plantations was now between 40 and 50 acres; they were producing in addition to cloves, nutmegs and coffee, a few mangosteens, a little tea and some chocolate trees. Mr. Thomas made up some of this chocolate and gave it to his friends at Palamcotta, where, as he somewhat cryptically reports, "it was drunk without observation." Mr. Thomas left the district in 1848, and five years later Government decided to sell all the gardens. In spite of Mr. Thomas' comparative success, their maintenance had cost Government on an average about Rs. 3,000 a year; and it was becoming abundantly clear that the experiment was too expensive and could never prove fruitful. In 1853 all the gardens, with the exception of one above Panpuli (the most valuable of all, which, by way of settlement of a longstanding dispute, was handed over to Travancore) were sold for Rs. 9,841. Of the gardens sold (there were nineteen in all), ten retain their character as "spice plantations" to the present day; of the remaining nine, some have since been absorbed in the reserved forest, and some, being in the plain country, no longer preserve any distinctive character. Of the surviving ten plantations, one is the "Arivikkarai tōttam"—to give it its old name—situated at the head of the waterfall and owned by the zamindarni of Sivagiri. The remaining nine gardens (sold in one lot) form one group on the upper reaches of the Chittār about three miles above Kuttālam, and lie in a narrow valley enclosed between precipitous hills. Best known amongst them was the garden known as "Paradēsipudai" ("hermit's cell")—by a happy adaptation transformed to "Paradise estate"—and it is by this name that the modern estate comprising the nine gardens is known. The "cell" consists of a large cave, about thirty feet deep, formed between two rocks, a lower one being overhung by an immense umbrella-like spread of stone which completely excludes from the cave both sun and rain. At the entrance to this chasm is an inscription of fifteen letters which has not been yet explained. No tradition regarding the "hermit" survives; in early days, apparently, the cave often served as a "cooly line."

CHAP. XV. TENKASI TALUK.

This estate (of nine gardens) and the "Arivikkarai tōttam" were all bought by Mr. C. H. R. Cocq, a well-to-do Dutch merchant of Tuticorin, and with very short breaks continued in European hands through many vicissitudes of mortgage, redemption and court-sale until 1898, when they were sold to their present owners. Mr. Cocq added considerably to the estate, obtaining grants of land chiefly with a view to coffee-growing.

The other private estates on the Kuttālam hills are of more recent creation. The "Terkumalai estate," situated immediately above "Paradēsipudai" in the Chittār valley, and "Hope estate" in the valley of the Five-falls river represent the earliest clearances made in these hills for the definite purpose of coffee-planting. The sites were granted by Government in 1844 to Ramsingh of Tachanallūr, the natural son of Mr. G. A. Hughes (page 5); in 1869 both the estates came into the hands of Mr. Cocq, and thereafter the history of both of them, until 1898, is identical with that of "Paradēsipudai" and "Arivikkarai." In that year "Terkumalai" and "Paradēsipudai" came into the hands of one owner and now form one estate. Most of the other estates which were opened about this time have been since abandoned, the two small estates of "Kulirātti" above Mattalampārai and "Tirukutāchala parvatham" near "Paradēsipudai" alone remaining in private hands. Except to a small extent in the "Terkumalai estate," no coffee cultivation is at the present day attempted, and the only plantations which receive any attention at all are "Terkumalai," "Paradēsipudai" and "Arivikkarai tōttam." They still yield coffee, nutmegs, cloves, a few mangosteens and a little cinnamon.

From the earliest times Kuttālam was recognized as the "sanitarium" of the district and a place of regular resort for Europeans; the Collector, the Commanding Officer of Palamcotta and most of the civil and military officers owned bungalows here. The present Travancore Residency, now the property of the Government of that State, owes its origin to Mr. Lushington, the first Collector of Tinnevelly. In 1816 Mr. John Sullivan, Commercial Resident at Palamcotta, obtained the site on which he built the beautifully placed bungalow now owned by the family of the late M.R.Ry. Jagannātha Rao. The bungalow now belonging to the Mahārāja of Travancore descends from W. O. Shakespear[1] of the civil service, who was Assistant Collector in this district in the very early years of the last century. The property was bought

[1] Died in 1838 and was buried at Cannanore.

CHAP. XV.
TENKASI TALUK.

by Mr. Cocq, who gave it to his daughter, and from her it was bought by the Mahārāja. The "Kannādi" or "Glass" bungalow, now much modernised—so called, it is said, from the novelty of its possessing glass windows—was built by G. A. Hughes. On his death, in 1835, he bequeathed the house to his son, Rāmsingh, on the condition that he should always let it to the family of the Commanding Officer at Palamcotta.

So far as public officers are concerned, the habit of migrating to Kuttālam for long periods has been almost given up in recent years; and, with the exception of one or two bungalows belonging to missionaries, there are none now owned by Europeans. Besides the older bungalows of the place, which lie in ample gardens and are scattered over a wide area, a large number of houses of all shapes, sizes and colours—"Indian villas," they are generally called—have grown up in recent years along the edges of the road, concentrated as far as space permits in the neighbourhood of the waterfall and temple.

The natural scenery for which the place is justly famous is strongly reminiscent of the west coast. The road from Tenkāsi leads up a gentle incline through wide stretches of paddy fields, green for nine months of the year and fringed with dense topes of cocoanut, jack, mango and arecanut trees, which drink moisture from a network of channels. Nearer the hills the wet fields rise in tiers, deriving their supply from the numerous little tanks that intercept the hill streams before they join the Chittār.

To the botanist and the sportsman the jungle around Kuttālam is equally delightful. In 1835 Dr. Wight explored the neighbourhood and actually collected 1,200 species of flowering plants in an area of twenty square miles. He calculated that at least 2,000 species were to be found and that the ferns were almost equal in number [1]. Sambhur and, higher up the hills, ibex are fairly numerous; spotted deer are less common. Tigers make occasional descents, and pigs may be met with in the jungle at any time or place. Jungle-fowl and spur-fowl are plentiful.

Panpulipatnam. or **Panpuli** (population 3,679): seven miles north-west of Tenkāsi, deserves notice on account of its Subramanya temple, three miles north-west of the village. Built on the top of a bare steep rock, two or three hundred feet high, the temple with the detached shrines near it forms

[1] *Madras Literary Journal* for October 1835.

CHAP. XV. TENKASI TALUK.

a conspicuous object on the landscape for many miles around. The temple is approached from the south by some hundreds of steps cut in the solid rock, and by the side of the temple excavated in the rock is a large tank which traps all the rain that falls on the summit and is said always to contain water. The temple possesses no architectural merit and is much patched. The tamarind tree with an Amman at its foot is pointed out as the earliest symbol of religion on this rocky summit. The idol of Subramanyaswāmi was brought from the old fort—*kōttai tiradu*—near the river (see below); a small temple was built, and its enlargement to its present state is a work of comparatively modern times. The author of this work was an enterprising Marava woman who lèvied contributions of labour and money and recovered by law-suits the lands that were passing from the temple's hand. She died but thirty years ago; and already her tomb has become the scene of miracles, and pūja is regularly performed beside it. The temple is well-endowed and receives a substantial *dastik* allowance.

Half a mile to the south-east of the rock, by the southern bank of the Hanumānadhi, on the site called *kōttai tiradu*, or "Fort Raise," are clear traces of an old fort. The low broken mud walls indicating a square formation and remnants of bricks and chunam scattered about amongst the cholam cultivation remain to mark the site.

Panbuli ("Cumblipatnam" of the old records) was one of the places in which Mr. G. A. Hughes obtained a grant of land. Indigo and cotton were attempted here, but were soon given up in favour of paddy. He had a house south of the village, of which no traces survive.

Surandai: with the neighbouring village of Sundarapāndyapuram, is a union with a population of 13,149, and contains the office of a sub-registrar. It is connected with Alankulam, eight miles away, by a gravelled road; otherwise the place is accessible only by cart-tracks. Two markets are held weekly, at which considerable trade is done in dry grains, chillies, onions and garlic. The Muhammadans of the place make coarse mats, and the bell-metal work of the Kannāsāris has some local reputation. The village was the head-quarters of a small ancient zamindari, which was purchased in 1874 by the zamindar of Uttumalai[1] and ceased from that date to have a separate existence. The old family which received its sanad in 1803 is now extinct. In the union is included a Christian settlement controlled by the Church Missionary

[1] See p. 470.

Society. The colony has its church and school; the mission bungalow, which for many years has not had a European tenant, is usually available on application for occupation by travellers.

From January to March the large channel-fed tanks of Sundarapāndyapuram and Surandai are covered with duck and teal.

Tenkāsi (population 19,940): a union, situated on the railway, is the head-quarters of the taluk and contains, besides the office of the tahsildar, a stationary sub-magistrate's office, two sub-registrar's offices and a local fund hospital. There is a small rest-house maintained by the Public Works Department, about one and half miles from the town on the road to Kuttālam. Four schools are maintained by local funds, one a Sanskrit secondary school, and the others, elementary schools. The Church Missionary Society maintains an "incomplete secondary" school. About a quarter of the population are Muhammadans; they are engaged chiefly in weaving *muris*, or rough cloths, which are exported to Travancore. The Kaikkilaiyans, who form a large proportion amongst the Hindu population, weave the coloured cloths *(sēlai)* that Tamil women wear. There are a few families of Sāyakkārans in the town, whose hereditary occupation is to dye cloths; but, as the weavers prefer to receive the yarn ready dyed by foreign chemicals, the dyers now find no demand for their labour. A small market is held on Wednesdays. Paddy is the chief export of the place, most of it finding its way to the district exchange, Pēttai.

The reputation of Tenkāsi rests chiefly in its temple. The story of its building is related in an inscription on a four-sided pillar set up in front of the *gōpuram*. The god Visvanātha appeared to the king—Arikēsari Parākrama Pāndya—in a dream and bade him build for him a new temple at Tenkāsi ("South Benares"), as the permanent abode of the god in Vadakāsi ("North Benares") was going to ruin. Thereupon the king set to work, and in the next year, Saka 1369 (A.D. 1447), the central shrine, the *ardhamantapam*, and the *mahāmantapam* were finished, and the god was established in his shrine. Ten years later the building of the nine-storeyed *gōpuram* was begun; in the sixth year it was completed, and in the same year the king died (A.D. 1463). The temple contains numerous Pāndya inscriptions of the fifteenth and

[1] According to the *stalapurana*, Visvanāthaswāmi told the king, who was in the habit of visiting Benares to bathe in the Ganges and worship the god, that he would cause the Ganges to appear in the Chittār at *Ten-kāsi*, "South Benares."

CHAP. XV. TENKĀSI TALUK.

sixteenth centuries. A fire has reduced the upper storeys of the *gōpuram* to ruin, and the whole structure is dangerously cracked. Originally the tower had a striking clock, like the one still in existence, though out of order, at Sankaranainārkōil; but apparently this disappeared in the fire. It is curious that no record of the circumstances of this fire survives. The local account says no more than that it was "150 years ago" and that it broke out in the Nawāb's record room which was in the tower. The explanation of the origin of the fire is likely enough, for in British times a part of the temple served for many years as the taluk office; but the date of the occurrence is probably in the early years of the nineteenth century. From an entry, dated 12th February 1792, in the diary of the missionary Jaenicke, the *gōpuram* and its clock appear then to have been intact; according to the old "survey memoir" (1824–25) the tower at that time presented a "confused and deplorable appearance."

The temple contains some exceptional stone-carving. In the *mantapam* which forms the entrance to the temple are ten remarkable figures, eight of which are of colossal size and represent a series of warrior-gods wearing ferocious expressions and in some cases crushing demons under foot; each god has several arms and is clothed in the panoply of war. The remaining two figures, which face the temple, represent women in life-size posed with much grace and beauty. Each of the ten figures with the pillars to which they are attached form single blocks of stone. Twelve figures of a similar warrior type are to be found in the Perumāl *mantapam* just in front of a shrine originally dedicated to Vishnu but now used as a store-room. But the most striking architectural feature of the *mantapam*—and indeed of the temple—is the delicate stone-carving which gives the effect of elaborately finished woodwork. The Vishnu shrine stands next beside the shrine of Siva, and nothing is known about its abandonment beyond the tradition that the idol was transferred to the Vishnu temple which stands on the bank of the river. It is worth noticing that neither in the *stalapurāna* nor in the more historical inscriptions is any mention made of a Vishnu shrine. It was a little less than a century after the completion of the Visvanātha temple that king Achyutha of Vijayanagar led his victorious army, mainly directed against Travancore, to the south and "planted a pillar of victory in the Tāmbraparni." The Vishnu shrine was certainly a subsequent addition; and it seems not unreasonable to attribute its creation to the period when those well-known champions of Vaishnavism, the

Vijayanagar kings, were a real power in the south. During the ascendancy of Vijayanagar the Pāndyas were of small account and were probably little more than local chieftains.

In the street running past the front of the temple is a *mantapam*, the only interest of which is that it has for many years figured in a dispute which excites high feeling between the Muhammadans and Hindus of the place. The Muhammadans contended at one time that it was essential that the *taboot* procession of their annual *Kanthūri* festival should go through the *mantapam*; the Hindus objected, and a compromise is believed to have been effected recently on this point. Another disputed point of the route is the bathing ghat beside the "Elephant bridge" (on the Kuttālam road), at which, according to the Muhammadans, the procession should end. Feeling runs high on the point once a year; at other times Muhammadans and Hindus live together in peace.

Three-quarters of a mile away, on the road leading to Alankulam and Tinnevelly, is another Siva temple in a most dilapidated state. It contains inscriptions of the later "Tinnevelly Pāndyas" of the sixteenth century.

In and around Tenkāsi are a number of *sati* stones, six of which may be seen in the premises of the railway station. Though practically disregarded by the people, it is not thought right to take liberties with them. Two or three of these stones lay in the track needed for the permanent way of the new railway line, and to get them out of the way the railway workers buried them *in situ*. The first train that came down the newly-opened line stuck at the points outside the station, and it was not till the *sati* stones were unearthed and set up again beside the railway that attempts to get the train along proved of any avail.

Vīrakēralampudūr : (its name suggests a Chēra foundation), an obscure village (population 2,614) on the branch road connecting Surandai with the Tinnevelly-Tenkāsi road, calls for notice as having been from the early years of the eighteenth century the head-quarters of the Uttumalai zamindari. The place contains a police-station, a sub-registrar's office, a local fund dispensary and a chattram maintained by the estate. The estate, which is one of the zamindaris permanently settled in 1803, is the third in size in the district, measuring (though it has not been surveyed in detail) 126 square miles. It comprises 63 villages, twenty-two of which are irrigated in part by the rivers Chittār and Hanumānadhi; twenty-five villages possess rainfed tanks, and the remainder are composed entirely of dry lands. Along the eastern

CHAP. XV. TENKASI TALUK.

border of the estate runs the conspicuous Uttumalai ridge, and, except in the river valleys in the south and south-west, the country is bare and uninviting. The population (51,246), consisting chiefly of Maravans, is on the whole poor, ignorant and backward. In 1874, the small zamindari of Surandai which adjoins the Uttumalai territory came under the hammer, and three months after the sale the Uttumalai zamindar bought it from the court purchasers. The peshkash due by the two estates (including cesses) is as follows:—

	RS.
Uttumalai	40,484
Surandai	1,230

The estate is at present under the Court of Wards.

The family tradition traces the origin of the house to the Rāmnād country and the tenth century A.D. A more modern ancestor assisted the Pāndya king of Ukkirankōttai (near Mānūr) and in return obtained the Uttumalai estate.

The peshkash proposed by Mr. Lushington and recommended in 1803 by the Special Commission was accepted by Government; and it is interesting to note that the rental value of the estate was estimated then at Rs. 52,500. The present demand (fasli 1320) is Rs. 1,47, 215. At the time when the Collectorate of Rāmnād was abolished the estate was under the Collector's management, the zamindar having died in 1806. The succession was disputed by two sons of different wives. The elder, the son of the second wife, won his suit in 1812, but the arrears of peshkash were heavy, and the estate continued under management. The younger son then appealed and succeeded, but died in 1814. The balance remained unpaid; the estate continued under sequestration; and in 1816 the Collector proposed that the property should be subdivided and sold up. In 1817 the arrears amounted to nearly half a lakh of rupees, and the zamindari was on the verge of ruin. The estate was shortly afterwards restored to the zamindar only to be attached once more, in 1830. Again, in 1838, against the advice of the Collector, it was handed back to the zamindar, and an arrear of Rs. 1,70,000 written off. "The misery," wrote the Collector, "to which this event has subjected thousands cannot be concealed. . . . The landed proprietors are now led to believe that however bad their private character may be, however much they make their estates the asylum of robbers and thieves, and however little attention they give to the prosperity of their zamindaris or to the regular payment of their peshkash, the Government have not the will nor the power to deprive them of them. . . . This is the feeling and impression in the district consequent on the restoration to power of the most worthless and undeserving subject in the zilla of Tinnevelly." This zamindar—they are all called Maruthappa—died in 1850, leaving a minor son, on whose behalf his mother managed the estate until he came of age. The new zamindar appears to have been an improvement on his father. He died in 1891, leaving an adopted son, a minor, who died unmarried a few months later. The Court of Wards, which had taken charge of the estate during the life-time of the minor, now withdrew from management, and litigation at once ensued between the widows of the previous zamindar. The estate, already heavily encumbered, was put under the Collector as Receiver of the civil court; and by the time that the Privy Council, before whom the case was finally taken, had decided in favour of the junior widow, the adoptive mother of the deceased minor, the bill of charges had swelled the estate's liabilities to such a portentous figure—nearly six lakhs—that in 1901 it was notified for sale by the civil court. On the application of the zamindarni, however, the estate was once more assumed by the Court of Wards; and its creditors were disappointed. The Divisional Officer of Sērmadēvi was shortly afterwards made a Regulation Collector under Act II of 1902 to administer the property, and subsequently a special officer was appointed to the post. This arrangement continued until 1914, when the estate again came under the management of the District Collector. Considerable improvements have been made in the economic condition of the estate. In almost all the wet lands the old complicated system of payment of rent in kind has been replaced by money-rents; a number of irrigation works have been repaired, and the debts of the estate have been greatly reduced. The zamindarni has no direct heir.

TINNEVELLY TALUK.

CHAP. XV. TINNEVELLY TALUK.

THE TINNEVELLY TALUK occupies the very centre of the district, touching neither the ghats on the west nor the sea on the east, but lying enclosed by all the remaining seven taluks of the district except Tiruchendūr. Beyond the limits of the two municipalities of Tinnevelly and Palamcotta it contains no towns of any size or importance. The wealth of the taluk is concentrated chiefly on these two towns and on the strip of country, watered by the Tāmbraparni, which contains some of the most valuable wet lands of the district, perhaps of the Madras Presidency. Though three-fourths of the taluk is unirrigated, the wet lands yield nearly ten times as much revenue as the dry. Five tanks in the north and east of the taluk, the largest of which are those at Mānūr (ayakat 1,805 acres) and Gangaikondān (793 acres), are supplied by the Chittār, which joins the Tāmbraparni at Sīvalappēri in the extreme east of the taluk. The general flatness of the country is relieved by a number of striking quartzite ridges, the most conspicuous of which form an irregular circle round the two towns of Tinnevelly and Palamcotta.

Owing, no doubt, to the importance of its trade centres, Mussalmans are more numerous—the Tiruchendūr taluk comes next—than in any other taluk, accounting in fact for nearly one-fourth of the total Mussalman population of the district.

Tachanallūr is the only union.

Sepulchral urns have been found at Pālāmadai, Manappadaivīdu, Palamcotta, Krishnāpuram, Kīlanattam and Tiruttu. An illustrated account of the articles discovered at the two last-mentioned places will be found in the annual report of the Government Archæologist for 1903–04. The remains discovered at Tiruttu comprised pottery, iron instruments, bronze-wire bangles and cornelian beads.

Gangaikondān (population 3,495): twelve miles from Tinnevelly on the Madura road, is situated on the right bank of the river Chittār. The large tank is supplied from the last anicut on this river. The local Siva temple, dedicated to the god Kailāsapathi, contains inscriptions of both Pāndya

CHAP. XV. TINNEVELLY TALUK.

and Chōla kings. The Chōla rulers[1] represented are Rājarāja (A.D. 988—1013), Rājēndra Chōla (A.D. 1011—44) and Kulōttunga Chōla I (A.D. 1074—1118), all powerful rulers and well known to us. Jatāvarma-Sundara-Chōla-Pāndya-dēva, whom king Rājēndra appointed to the local charge of the Pāndya country, also has inscriptions here in the same temple. The name of the place occurs in one inscription in its full form—"Gangaikonda-Chōla-Chaturvēdi-mangalam"—and must owe its orgin either to Gangai-konda Chōla, who was appointed by his father Vīra-Rājēndra II (1062—70) to administer the Pāndya province, or to Rājēndra Chōla (A.D. 1011—44) who, by virtue of his conquests in the north, also bore the title Gangai-konda," he who conquered the Ganges" (p. 49). The Pāndya inscriptions give us the names of five kings. Of these, one is Māranjadaiyan—probably the king appearing as No. 11 in the list on page 45—who came to the throne in A.D. 862-63; his inscription is in *vatteluttu* characters. Other epigraphs refer to Māravarman Srīvallabha and Jatāvarman Srīvallabha, of whom we know nothing beyond the fact that they reigned in the twelfth century (p. 50). Māravarman Sundara Pāndya (III) also has an inscription bearing the date A.D. 1534 (p. 53).

Two miles south of the village, by the side of the road, is a mosque which, with a few other Muhammadan places of worship in the district, shares the peculiarity of attracting devotees from among Hindus. The fakir gives as *prasādham*, plantains to Brahmans and flour and sugar to Sūdras, and the gifts are eaten by the Hindus in the hope that their vows will be fulfilled. The explanation of the custom is that one night a Brahman woman was attacked by a footpad. She took refuge in this shrine and called to Allah for help, who replied by smiting the thief with blindness.

A peculiar caste, represented by two families, is found in the village. They call themselves Rājus or Kshatriyas and claim to be quite distinct from and superior to the other well-known caste which uses the same title. That they are distinct is clear; for, whilst these people speak Tamil, worship Siva and eat no meat, the other Rājus (as a rule) are flesh-eaters and Vaishnavites and speak Telugu. They are, they say, the sole relics of the Pāndya ruling house, and it is in keeping with this theory that they live in what they are pleased to call a fort, an enclosure formed by mud defences differing from the ordinary compound-walls only in being a little higher. Finding themselves threatened with extinction, this

[1] See pp. 47 foll.

CHAP. XV. TINNEVELLY TALUK.

proud race has in the last generation found itself obliged to go outside its pale in search of wives, its choice falling on women of the Vellāla caste.

The fine seven-arched bridge which crosses the Chittār was the gift of a previous zamindar of Ettaiyāpuram. It was built by Lieutenant Horsley and completed in 1844.

Buffaloes are sacrificed once a year in honour of the local goddess Ayirattamman. The same deity at Palamcotta is similarly honoured once in twelve years. These are the only examples of such a ritual in the district.

Krishnāpuram (population 406): situated on the Tiruchendūr road, six miles from Palamcotta, may be located by the striking temple which stands almost isolated in a dreary waste of red soil and palmyras. Closer inspection reveals a small village, for which "deserted" is the obvious epithet; and it is impossible to believe that it was for this scanty band of inhabitants that Krishnappa Nāyakkan of Madura founded this great temple. There is evidence, indeed, to show that the village was once a place of some importance. The existence of abandoned wells and foundations of houses in the neighbourhood suggests that the village was once populous, and it is significant that many persons gather here from outlying and even distant places to pay to the presiding deity of the temple the worship due to a household god. The foundation of the temple and the town is attributed in the Madura *purānas* to Krishnappa Nāyakkan (A.D. 1563–73), a tradition which is confirmed by the copper-plates preserved by the trustees of the temple.[1] "By Krishnabhūpathi" (the quotation is from the plate) "of sacred name . . . was built a temple at Krishnāpuram which was encircled by a wall of the shape of the *Pranava* and surmounted by a broad and lofty tower. It has a large *ranga mantapam* raised on a cluster of beautiful stone pillars and adorned with rows of rain-spouts. He built a car like the Mandara mountain and also broad roads around the temple for the propitiation of god Vishnu set therein." Neither the "broad and lofty tower" nor the car can now be accounted for; and it is generally believed that the wall (of which traces may still be seen) was demolished and the stones taken for the construction of the Palamcotta fort (see p. 478).

The temple is dedicated to Srī Venkatāchalapathi and contains some exceptionally good sculptures, the most noteworthy being the figures clustered round six of the pillars

[1] These plates are dealt with fully in *Epig. Ind.*, Vol. IX, p. 344.

which support the *ranga mantapam*. Two of these carvings, those on the second and fifth pillars as the temple is entered, are especially deserving of notice. One of them depicts a lively group, the meaning of which can hardly be mistaken. A gipsy woman is seen running off with a child on her shoulder and a young confederate is showing the child a toy to keep it quiet; the mother is at home consulting a palmist about her trouble. Meanwhile a horseman, hard in pursuit, appears to be on the point of capturing the child-stealer. In the other group a Kuravan (?) is kidnapping a princess. The prince with an attendant gives chase on horse-back and has caught and stabbed the thief. By some curious art of the sculptor a dull red streak, said to be indelible, has been let into the stone to represent the blood flowing from the gipsy's wounded breast. The dramatic setting of the groups, the clever attitudes and the accuracy of detail combine to produce a most effective triumph of art. The figures carved on the remaining four pillars, though well executed and worth examination, are of the more usual colossal type. In the *manimantapam*, the next enclosure, supported on seven pillars, are also to be seen a number of elaborate sculptures illustrating Hindu stories. An ingenious production in bas-relief above one of these figures is the representation of an elephant and a bull facing one another and so arranged that one head only appears. When looked at from the left side, the sculpture gives the impression of an elephant with trunk erect obscuring the head of a bull; from the right hand side the bull appears complete with head and horns and seems to be concealing the head of an elephant, whose body alone is visible.

Manappadaividu (population 719): deserves notice on account of its temple and its ancient traditions. That it was at one time an important centre of the Pāndya kingdom is clear from the fact that the tradition, whether oral or written, regarding the foundation of almost every village and temple of the taluk goes back in some way or other to the "Pāndyan of Manappadaivīdu." In common with Korkai, Kāyal and Adichanallūr, all situated on the Tāmbraparni and proved by evidence of one kind or another to have been important towns in the past, this place has long fallen into insignificance. It is scarcely possible to point to any visible evidence of its former greatness, unless it is to be found in a few bricks of exceptionally large size and good finish which were dug up, it is said, some years ago from the adjacent rice fields, and which now form a platform for Muniswāmi and his comrades near the river bank. Possibly too the large stones lying near the same spot, which show signs of having been worked, are the ruins of vanished buildings.

The most important feature of the present village is its Siva temple. The carving of the exterior of the *garbagraha*, or main shrine, is an admirable example of that peculiar style of architecture which is found also at Tenkāsi and Sērmadēvi (q.v.). Along the outer wall of the shrine runs an elaborate arrangement of columns, springing shafts and cornices, the whole combination being worked out of single blocks of stone. Similar work adorns the main walls of the temple. The work is extremely delicate and is well preserved.

A large number of sepulchral urns have been found in the neighbourhood, in Vellimalai and Kīlanattam, and, further away, in Tiruttu.

Mānūr (a police-station; population 1,142): nine miles from Tinnevelly on the road to Sankaranainārkōil, is another of the many small villages of the taluk traditionally supposed to have been at one time rich and prosperous. The foundations of a few old buildings may be traced in the paddy fields to the west of the village, but it is now impossible to account for the 1,008 Brahman houses which, according to local belief, once existed on the site. The legends of the place are in fact a study in this peculiarly sacred figure. In addition to the Brahman houses, there were 1,008 wells and—most astonishing of all—1,008 Siva temples. The beginning of the downfall came when Karūr Sidhar, a Saivite saint, asked a local Brahman one day for a meal of meat and liquor and obtained it. The other Brahmans resented the outrage, and the saint turned round and cursed the village.

In front of the Ambalavānaswāmi temple stands a granite pillar, about seven feet high, locally known as "Tiruvādipōthi." By a curious tradition it is supposed to contain the spirit of Muhammad, having been brought over from Mecca by a Pāndya king. It bears inscriptions in a mixed character, which have not been deciphered. Daily pūja is performed by the Othuvan of the temple, and the thick coating of ghee with which the stone is plastered is evidence of long-continued devotion. Vows for the cure of diseases and for rain in its season are made to the pillar, and, besides the ordinary offerings of milk and water, ganja and cheroots—the luxuries in which a Muhammadan would most delight—are placed for the spirit's consumption. The ritual is performed by Hindus only. Lying on the ground at the foot of this pillar are four stones, each with the figure of a warrior carved upon it in deep relief. Like the figures referred to under Ilavēlankāl (p. 378) and Rājānkōvil (p. 387), all have pendulous earlobes and wear their hair bunched into a knot above the ear.

Two inscriptions of Pāndya kings have been transcribed in the Ambalavānaswāmi temple, one (in *vatteluttu* characters) belonging to Māranjadaiyan, the other to Kōnērimaikondān. The former ruler, who is mentioned also in inscriptions at Gangaikondān, Kalugumalai, Ambāsamudram and Tirukkurungudi, is probably identical with the enterprising Varaguna Varman (A.D. 862–63) who is referred to in Chapter II, page 45. Kōnērimaikondān is perhaps the king who, with the additional names Kulasēkhara Dharmaperumāl (initial date A.D. 1550), is referred to in the Karivalamvandanallūr temple. In that case he would belong to the powerless race of Pāndyas who continued their nominal rule even after the establishment of the Nāyakkan dynasty.

Palamcotta (population 44,909): is the headquarters of the district and a municipality and (if the population of all its suburbs is included) is the largest town in the district. The municipality has been described in Chapter XIV, and some account of the various medical and educational institutions of the town will be found in Chapters IX and X. Comprising four revenue villages, it covers an area of 4½ square miles and falls, geographically, into three distinct parts: (1) Palamcotta proper, including Murugankurichi; (2) the suburbs of Kokkarakulam and Vannārpet beside the river; and (3) the village of Mēlappālaiyam, two miles south of the Tinnevelly bridge. The place contains all the offices usually found in the headquarter station of a district. The offices of the Collector, the Divisional Officer and the District Board, the courts of the District Judge, Sub-Judge and District Munsifs are located in Kokkarakulam, on the right bank of the river; the remaining public offices, the hospital (see p. 261) and a travellers' bungalow maintained by the municipality are situated in the main town of Palamcotta. The place is the headquarters for the Tinnevelly district of the Church Missionary Society and of the Jesuit mission; a Bishop, who is an Assistant to the Bishop of Madras and exercises jurisdiction over the Anglican missions in Madura, Rāmnād and Tinnevelly, is also stationed here. The District Judge resides in Kokkarakulam; and, with the exception of the Collector, whose bungalow is in Tinnevelly, the rest of the European population live in Palamcotta itself.

CHAP. XV.
TINNEVELLY TALUK.

At a time when almost the whole district was studded with the forts of numerous local chieftains, " Pālaiyamkōttai, " " the fort of the *pālaiyam* ", remained in the possession of the representative of the Nāyakkan ruler and of the Nawāb successively. The Palamcotta country thus constituted " the pālaiyam " *par excellence*—the territory which, unlike that controlled by the poligars, remained under the direct management of the central power; and Palamcotta itself was thus "the fort of the (Sirkar's) *pālaiyam*."[1] As to the origin of the fort nothing, unfortunately, is known. Tradition ascribes it variously to Hindu and Muhammadan builders. The Madura manuscripts tell us that it was built by Aryanātha Mudaliyār, the lieutenant of the famous Viswanātha Nāyakkan of Madura; a local tradition attributes it, reasonably enough, to Muhammad Yūsuf Khān, and adds that he obtained the stones by demolishing the great wall which once surrounded the temple at Krishnāpuram.[2] Bishop Caldwell appears to accept the theory that the fortress owes its origin to a man called Pālaiyan.

When incontestable history begins, in the eighteenth century, the fort was the strongest to the south of Madura. It was never tested by any serious attack, but merely served as an important place of refuge for the Nawāb's renter and later for the Company's troops. From 1765, at least, it was used as a garrison and a jail, and it was from its confines that the rebel captives made their memorable escape on February 2, 1801, and set on foot the last and most desperate of the poligar insurrections. Referring to the condition of the fort in 1756, Orme says: " the fort is spacious but the ramparts were in ruins, nevertheless capable of resisting an enemy which had no battering cannon." It formed a rectangle 900 yards by 840 yards and possessed neither ditch nor glacis. It consisted of a main inner rampart, 15 feet high and 15 feet thick, and a " fausse braie " or outer line, 9 feet high; both walls were surmounted by parapets. The ramparts were of earth, faced with massive cut stones. At irregular intervals there were square bastions, and at the angles of the fort the bastions were round. At the middle point of each rampart was a gate. The great square tower, on which the modern police-station now reposes in comfort and security, surmounted the western or "Tinnevelly" gate. Just beside the existing racquet court, which was built up against the southern

[1] In support of this theory is the use of the word " Paléam " in Jesuit writings of the seventeenth century, with reference, apparently, to Palamcotta.

[2] See p. 474

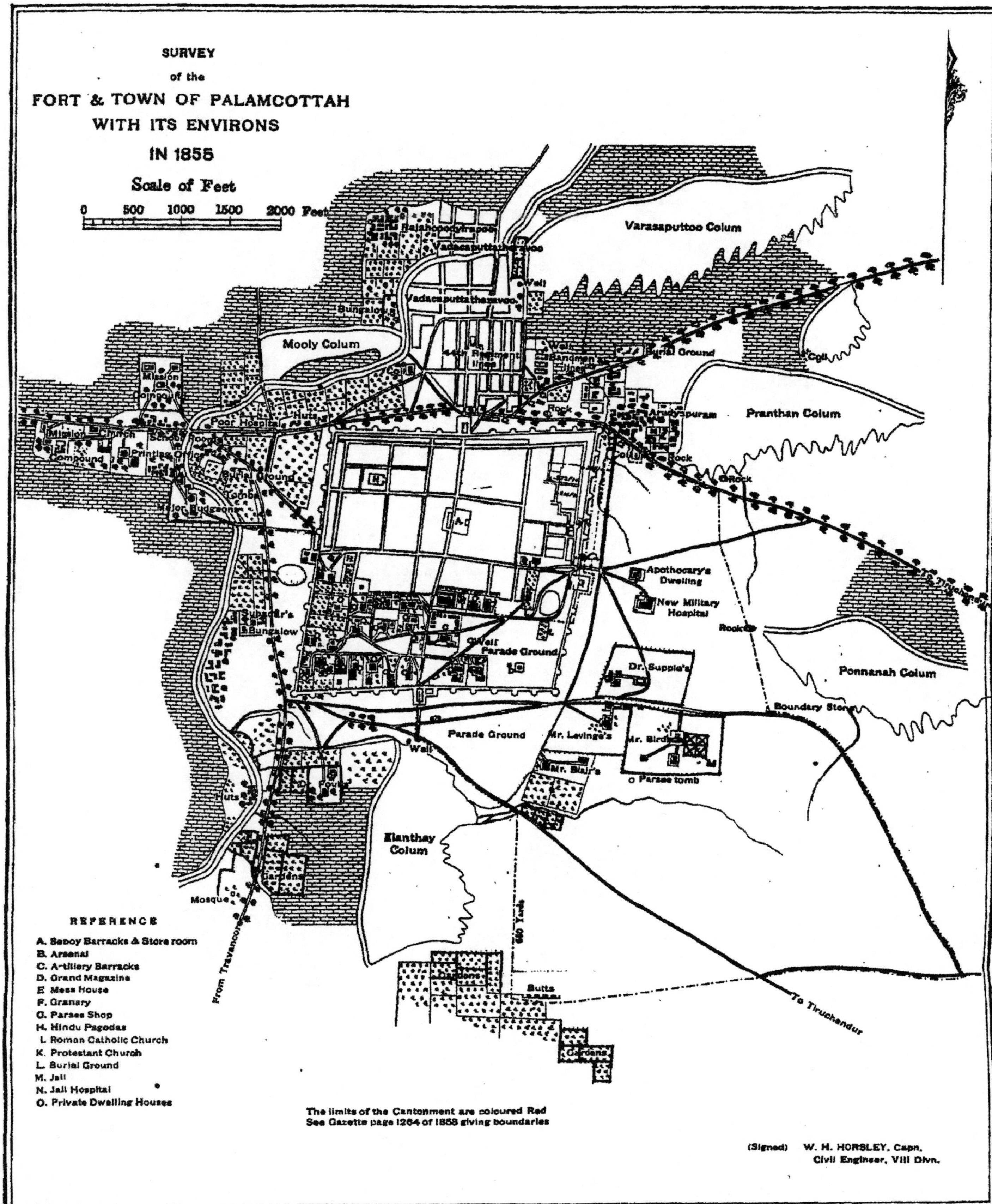

Reg. No. 2044
Copies. 510

Helio-Zinco., Survey Office, Madras.
1916

rampart, was the south or "Travancore" gate. The other entrances—the "Tiruchendūr" gate on the east (the site of which is now occupied by the sub-magistrate's court) and the northern or "Madura" gate (which stood on the site of the present market)—have disappeared. At the south-west angle of the fort a bastion has been preserved intact, and the foundations of the walls on the south and east are visible in many places.

The disappearance of the old fort was a gradual process. As early as 1840 a large quantity of stone had been taken from the outer wall for the purpose of building the foundations of the bridge at Tinnevelly. The eastern gate had been shut up, and on its site a civil jail (now the court of the sub-magistrate) had been built; the other gates were in existence, but there were innumerable breaches, especially on the west side, and pieces of wall were constantly collapsing. Mr. E. B. Thomas, the Collector, recommended in the interests of the public health that the outer wall at least should be completely removed, and, though the military authorities opposed the suggestion, its destruction was ordered in 1844 by Government. A few years later—in 1851—the demolition of the main wall on the east was put in hand, and permission was obtained to use the stones for public buildings. In 1860 the removal of the western wall followed; the southern wall was destroyed next and last of all the northern wall. By 1861 the fort had practically disappeared. The stones were sorted, good ones being retained for various public works and the best of all sent off to Srīvaikuntam for the new anicut. The rest were sold.

From the earliest years the place was garrisoned by native infantry, at least to the extent of one regiment, and by a detail of artillery. The artillery were removed in 1857; and with the removal of the sepoys in 1879 Palamcotta ceased to be a military station. The sepoys' lines were at all times outside the fort. First they were located on the north side just across the Tiruchendūr road; after 1855 new quarters were constructed to the north of the site now occupied by the offices of the Superintendent of Police and the Executive Engineer. The artillery barracks was the building, still popularly known as "Tillery," in which the post office is now located. The northern two-thirds of the fort was the crowded town it now is. In the remaining one-third in the south were the artillery (referred to), the mess-house and the bungalows of the military officers. The armoury, the building which now serves a similar purpose for the reserve police,

CHAP. XV. TINNEVELLY TALUK.

stood on the northern limit of this area. The parade-ground comprised the open land lying to the south of the present English church and also the site now enclosed by the hostel of the St. Xavier's high school. The Commanding Officer's residence was for some time on the site of the present high school itself; the other officers lived in the houses enclosing the open square to the west of the artillery barracks. "They are small but convenient bungalows:" (says an old account)[1] "one of them contains a public bath—which has been found to be not only a great luxury but conducive to health."

A curious survival of the bygone military days, to be seen near the line of the old north wall, is the mound of earth which is generally known as *dhamdhama mēdu*. The mound was within living memory a great deal bigger than what it is now and is generally reputed to have been a hundred feet high! *Mēdu* means "high ground", and *dhamdhama* suggests the noise of a tom-tom; and the story that the mound served as a place of look-out, from which warning was given to inmates of the fort of the approach of the enemy, seems probable enough.

"Military" and "civil" areas were thus intermingled, but no attempt was made for many years to define the limits of military and civil jurisdiction. Between 1850 and 1853 a cantonment was laid out, which included the southern or military part of the fort, the whole of the "maidan" of the present day and land extending northwards from it as far as the Tiruchendūr road. The "cantonment" has, of course, long ceased to have any real meaning.

It was shortly before this that one or two bungalows were built out in the region in which most European residents now live. As far as can be ascertained, the oldest of these houses is that which now serves the C.M.S. as an office. Captain Place of the 44th regiment, Native Infantry, built a house on the site and in 1849 transferred his ownership to Mr. C. J. Bird, the Collector. From him the bungalow passed in 1875 to Mr. F. C. Carr-Gomm, the District Judge of that time, who, in 1890, made a gift of it to the C.M.S. The residence is still known as "Carr House" in consequence. Until Mr. Bird's time the Collector had lived either in Kokkarakulam or Murugankurichi (apparently in the so-called Tennampillai Bungalow"), and even sometimes in one or other of the Vannārpet houses. Mr. Silver, the successor of Mr. Bird, began, as stated elsewhere (p. 490), the practice of occupying the bungalow in which Collectors now reside.

[1] Pharaoh's *Gazetteer*, 1855.

Another bungalow which claims to be almost coeval with "Carr House" is the one which the Assistant Commissioner of Salt now occupies. It started life as a thatched building and is still referred to by the older generation as "Pulipirai Bungalow" on that account.

In 1844 the building now occupied as an office by the Executive Engineer had been built to replace the old military hospital which existed in the congested region near the north wall of the fort; and eleven years later, as has been seen, the sepoys' lines were transferred to the open ground to the north of this new hospital. The officers' mess was transferred, about 1860, to the building which is now occupied on rent by the European club and formerly belonged to Mr. C. H. R. Cocq, of Tuticorin.

An odd relic of the past is the masonry foundation of what was once a Parsee tomb, on the edge of the "maidan" behind the compound of the C.M.S. office. There are records to show that in the very early years of the last century a Parsee liquor-merchant had a shop on the site (still known as "Paulanji's ground") which the Registrar's office now occupies. "Paulanji the Parsee" is still remembered, but there are now no Parsees in the place.

The first English church built in the place may still be seen, in a dilapidated condition, enclosed with the old burial-ground in a compound just near the more modern Christ Church. The little building was erected between 1780 and 1785 by public subscription, and owed its foundation chiefly to the efforts of a converted Hindu widow, who was given the name Clorinda. The famous missionary, Schwartz, dedicated the building in 1785, and the S.P.C.K. took charge of it. "Clorinda's church" (as it has always been called), served by missionaries and chaplains in turn, became the "official" place of worship of the station. The Court of Directors decided to terminate this system of joint management with the S.P.G. (which had succeeded the S.P.C.K.), and, in 1848, the construction of a Government church was ordered. A good deal of correspondence ensued between Government and the mission before the work was put in hand, and it was not till 1856 that the new church was completed and dedicated. A part of the eastern wall of the fort was removed to clear the site; and the adjoining churchyard, which, in addition to the burial-ground attached to the old church, had been in use from the earliest times, was subsequently enclosed by a wall built of fort stones. In 1857 the S.P.G. handed over Clorinda's church to Government.

CHAP. XV. TINNEVELLY TALUK.

Within the "civil" area once enclosed by the fort is the church of the Jesuit mission; it is dedicated to St. Francis Xavier and was completed in 1863. Near it is the residence of the Father Superior of the mission "district" of Palamcotta.

In the middle of the native town are two Hindu temples—one dedicated to Vishnu and one to Siva. The latter temple is dependent largely on endowments granted to it by the famous Tiruvakād Vengu Mudaliyār, who was for many years during the early part of the eighteenth century the dubash of the Commercial Resident of Tinnevelly (p. 484). In this capacity he amassed an enormous fortune, and prodigious stories are told about him. Like the Moghul emperors of Delhi, he is given the title *Pāsha*, and the memory of his deeds is preserved in a popular quatrain which links his name with three other well-remembered worthies of the period. He used to entertain the Europeans of the station in princely fashion, and his many bungalows were furnished with the most lavish decorations. He won a prize of a lakh of rupees, the story goes, in a lottery held in England, and under his instructions a sumptuous dinner was given in London to members of the Royal Family and Ministers of the Crown! The King of England was so pleased with Vengu Mudaliyār's munificent deeds that he presented him with a carriage adorned with the royal arms. In one night, it is said, he laid out the Vellai Kōvil road, leading from Palamcotta northwards to the river, so that his wife's body might be carried out in proper state to burial; he introduced from Madura the colony of Pattunūlkārans whose descendants still live in the place; and he is reputed to have been the originator of the local "barbers' band"! Many foundations and endowments which he made in the cause of religion and charity survive to the present day. The Brāndīswarar temple has been mentioned. The Brahman street beside the Rāmaswāmi temple owes its origin to his enterprise; he endowed lands for the support of *kattalais*, or services, in the Tiruchendūr temple; he founded and endowed the Gnānamani Ammāl chattram, in memory of a Brahman orphan girl whom he had adopted; the expenses of lighting Trinity Church are still met from the proceeds of land which he presented to the mission.

Westwards, on the other side of the bridge which crosses the Pālaiyan channel, is the little hamlet of MURUGANKURICHI, which may be described as the district headquarters of the C.M.S. Within it are contained a church, a high school, a training school, bungalows and other buildings, all belonging to the mission. The church—Trinity Church—was built by public subscription through the exertions of C. E. Rhenius in 1826; the tower was added in 1845. The tomb of this famous missionary (who died in 1838) lies in obscure surroundings near the right bank of the channel. The "Tennampillai Bungalow," prettily situated a little way up the channel on its left bank, was the property of Vengu Mudaliyār and is now in the possession of his descendants.

From this hamlet the high road, shaded by a fine avenue (believed to be the work of Mr. E. B. Thomas, Collector from 1842 to 1848), leads across the paddy flats to VANNĀRPET. The five bungalows, which, with their gardens, lie to the north of the road, were all at one time the property of Mr. G. A. Hughes (p. 487) and his descendants. Many of them were at various times occupied by civil officers, and the building next to that which now forms the Vannārpet club is still referred to in deeds as the "Police Bungalow." On the edge of the paddy fields, to the east of this group of buildings, the Women's Hospital[1] has replaced a bungalow which belonged to Vengu Mudaliyār. Further up this road, on the other side, a dilapidated arched gateway leads into a spacious enclosure, in the middle of which stand the ruined remains of a fine *mantapam*. This too was the property of Vengu Mudaliyār; and the festival of *taipūsam*, held here in honour of the god Brāndīswarar of Palamcotta, was celebrated in his days with a pomp and grandeur to which the present generation of worshippers are strangers.

The bungalow in which the District Judge now resides was built by Mr. Lushington on his transfer from Rāmnād in 1801. The site, for which he obtained a Company's grant, extended northwards across the present road to the so-called *Pillaipōttu-pilāpalam-edutta ōdai*. Just beside this property (apparently the site now occupied by the paddy fields between the present compound and the Mēlappālaiyam road) was a cinnamon garden, which had been planted by Mr. Torin about 1790 on behalf of the Company. Until the construction of the bridge in 1843 and the new alignment which that necessitated, the road leading up from the ford in the river passed through the avenue which is still to be seen to the south of the compound. From 1809 till 1826 the building was occupied by successive Commercial Residents[2]; about 1850 the property came into the possession of the C.M.S. and from that date was occupied at intervals by the District Judge. Government acquired it in 1907.

[1] See p. 260.

[2] It is still occasionally referred to as "Sullivan's bungalow" after Mr. J. S. Sullivan, who was Commercial Resident from 1814 to 1825.

CHAP. XV.
TINNEVELLY TALUK.

Next to Mr. Lushington's bungalow was a house called the "factory house," which had formerly belonged to the Commercial Resident and was turned by Mr. Lushington into a cutcherry. The site of this building is difficult to trace, but it appears to have stood on the ground now occupied by the court of the additional district munsif and the establishment of the district court. On Mr. Lushington's departure, the Collector's cutcherry was moved into the town of Tinnevelly to a building which until quite lately existed beside the more modern Pennington market; the "factory house" then became the court-house. In 1810 Collector and Judge again exchanged buildings. The Collector subsequently moved his office to Vannārpet and, in 1824 (the court having been abolished in 1822), again transferred it to the building in the town. The auxiliary court which was created in 1827 was for some years located in the Tinnevelly building. In 1831 the Company's investment in the trade of the district was withdrawn and the Commercial department abolished. Two warehouses and a cotton-screw, which had been erected between 1814 and 1819 on the ground to the south of the present Judge's bungalow, were handed over to the Collector for use as an office. One of the warehouses is now the Collector's record-room, and the other accommodates the court of the Sub-Judge and a branch of the Collector's office. The building occupied by the English and Accounts branch of the Collector's office is the old cotton-screw. Huddled together in a confused jumble with these buildings are others of later construction—the courts of the District Judge and district munsif, the office of the district board, the treasury, the district press and a number of subsidiary offices. Most of the buildings are ill-adapted to their purposes, and a scheme of reconstruction is now under consideration.

The main activities of the Commercial department in Tinnevelly were, from the beginning of the nineteenth century, devoted to the cotton trade; cleaned cotton was bought up from the ryots, pressed at Kokkarakulam and exported from Kāyalpatnam to Madras for shipment. Thence it went mainly to China. Weavers employed by the Company throughout the district furnished the Commercial Resident with cloths, which were exported in large quantities to China and the French islands. The earliest "investment" in Tinnevelly on behalf of the Company was made in 1793 or 1794, the pioneer in the field being a Mr. Martin of the Company's service. Till that time almost the whole of the cloth trade of the district had been in the hands of the Dutch of Tuticorin, who claimed, by virtue of an alleged concession from the Nawāb, an exclusive right to all cloths manufactured in the district. On one occasion, by way of asserting this claim, they actually seized Mr. Martin's boats off the Tuticorin coast on the ground that he was infringing their monopoly. To meet this opposition and also the encroachments of private traders, the Company secured from the Nawāb the concession that all weavers engaged by the Company should be exempted from the loom tax. The exemption (which involved a surrender of Rs. 25,000 a year) continued even after 1801; and it was from this time forward that systematic trade on a fairly large scale was undertaken. The annual investment during the thirty years varied between three and four lakhs of rupees.

MĒLAPPĀLAIYAM, a densely-populated settlement of Muhammadans, is situated at the point where the road from Tinnevelly to Nāngunēri crosses that leading from Palamcotta to Ambāsamudram. Most of the 14,500 Muhammadans returned at the last census under Palamcotta are crowded into this little suburb. Weaving, dyeing, tanning and foreign trade are the occupations of the inhabitants. The locally-made carpets are well known all over the district and are exported to Ceylon and to various parts of the Presidency. Check cloths, made here and also at Eruvādi, Tenkāsi and Kadayanallūr by the employees of Mēlappālaiyam capitalists, are shipped in large quantities to Ceylon. Yarn for the cheaper cloths is dyed in the place, foreign pigments alone being used; for the better cloth ready-dyed yarn is imported. Tanning is conducted on a small scale and appears to have fallen off of late. About one-fourth of the male population spend most of their time abroad as shopkeepers and general traders, in Rangoon, Mandalay, Kandy, Penang, Singapore, Bombay and many other places. No line of trade comes amiss to them, and many are adventurous to the point of recklessness. Their habit of investing in land the savings they bring home has greatly inflated the price of the wet lands of the neighbourhood.

Sīvalappēri (population 3,667): contains a police-station, a local fund primary school and a large private choultry. The choultry, which was built and endowed by one of the Dalavāy Mudaliyārs, renters under the Nawāb, is now under the management of the descendants of that family. Its annual income is said to amount to Rs. 20,000, and the institution is especially popular during the period of the cattle-fair in April. The village is situated on the left bank of the Tāmbraparni, at the point where it is joined by the Chittār, and lies on the old route from Tinnevelly and the south to Rāmēsvaram.

CHAP. XV.
TINNEVELLY TALUK.

The junction of these waters is generally referred to as *mukkadal*, "the place where three waters meet"; and, in justification of this name, local tradition asserts that the Kōthandarāmanadhi (popularly known as the Uppōdai), which now joins the Chittār at Gangaikondān, originally flowed direct to the Tāmbraparni at this place. The Tāmbraparni attains a great width at this point, and during most of the year a walk of a quarter of a mile through burning sand separates the villagers from their water supply. "Better," says the local proverb, alluding to the toilsome lot of water-carriers, "set your daughter to an oil-mill than give her in marriage to a man of Sīvalappēri."

The annual cattle-fair, which is held at the time of the festival celebrated by the Alagar temple, brings in to the taluk board the large revenue of Rs. 5,000, and is second only in importance to the annual market of the same kind held at Kalugumalai.

The Alagar temple contains Pāndya, Chōla and Chōla-Pāndya inscriptions. The Pāndya records (which are in the *vatteluttu* script) run in the name of Sadaiyan Māran, an ancient Pāndya king, whose date is still uncertain. His name is found also at Kallidaikurichi (q.v.). Eleven inscriptions (some in *vatteluttu* characters) relate to the great Chōla king, Rājarāja, who completely subdued the Pāndya country; two belong to his successors, Vīra-Rājēndra II and Kulōttunga I. Sundara-Chōla-Pāndya, who was appointed by Rājēndra I (A. D. 1011—44) to administer the Pāndya province, has two inscriptions.

A remarkable example of rock-carving,[1] believed to be of Buddhist origin, is to be found in MARUGALTALAI, a hamlet of the village. At the foot of an enormous mass of bare rock a series of what appear to be beds have been carved out in the solid stone. The beds—*Pancha Pāndava padukkai*, as they are called locally—lie almost horizontal and are overhung by a great brow of natural rock, some 200 feet in length, a part of which bulges over the beds and protects them. The face of the overhanging rock, which rises to a height of 40 or 50 feet, has been chiselled off to about half its height, the object apparently being to make the flow of rain-water fall clear of the *padukkai*. On a part of the chiselled surface appear inscriptions in Pāli characters, resembling those of the Asoka edicts. Local superstition has naturally peopled this curious spot with demons, and the rock is consequently bedaubed with smears of ashes and turmeric. The

[1] *Govt. Epig. Ann. Report* for 1906-07.

recess affords valuable shelter to sheep, and shepherds are especially forward in seeing to the propitiation of evil spirits. Nothing however will avail to save cattle; even when fenced in, they have been known to break away in terror and to bolt for miles.

Two miles from Sīvalappēri, in the little village of PADINALAMPERI, is a rock known as Andichipārai, "the beggar woman's rock," which has been hollowed out to serve, apparently, the purposes of a shrine. The cave is about five feet square and six feet high, and in the middle of the floor is a rude projection of rock which was evidently intended to develop into an image. To the left of the entrance are two roughly-carved images; but, as is the case with so many of the rock carvings of the district, the work here too was left uncompleted.

Tachanallūr (population 1,355): a union, is interesting as having been the chief centre of the many agricultural enterprises associated with the nāme of Mr. G. A. Hughes. In the early years of the last century Mr. C. W. Young, a "free merchant," had obtained a lease of extensive tracts of land in various parts of the district for the cultivation of coffee, indigo and cotton. Mr. G. A. Hughes, who was the son of a Madras civilian and had held the post of interpreter with the troops under Colonel Bannerman, entered into partnership with Mr. Young and, on the latter's death in 1809, became the owner of the properties. They comprised lands, amounting to upwards of 7,500 acres, distributed in Kuttālam, Panpuli, Ukkirankōttai, Valliyūr, Nāngunēri and Mānūr, and also about 18 acres of land in Tachanallūr; in 1821 Mr. Hughes obtained a further and more extensive grant in the same place in exchange for lands already assigned in Kuttālam. Till his death in 1835 Mr. Hughes was engaged in the cotton trade of the district, in which business he acted as the agent of Messrs. Binny & Co., Madras, and was the constant, often bitter, rival of the Company's agent, Vengu Mudaliyār[1]; his old cotton-screw and the remains of his indigo works are still to be seen at Tachanallūr. Coffee and indigo proved a failure; Bourbon cotton was for a time at least successful, but the senna which Mr. Hughes himself introduced from Arabia is cultivated with profit to the present day. Besides his bungalows and gardens at Vannārpet (see p. 483), Mr. Hughes owned houses at Tachanallūr, Kuttālam, Panpuli and Punnaikāyal; he bought the Kulattūr and Kādalkudi mittas and was a personage

[1] See p. 482.

CHAP. XV. TINNEVELLY TALUK.

of great influence in the district. His natural son, Ramsingh, succeeded him; and the question then arose whether the lease should be continued on the same favourable terms. The object of the original grant had been definitely to encourage exotic cultivation; but, as a matter of fact, the experiments had not justified themselves, and most of the lands granted had been planted up with the ordinary grains of the country. The lease was renewed for a limited period, and finally, in 1858, ordinary assessment was imposed and ryotwari pattas were issued. The memory of Ramsingh, who died in 1846, survives to the present day. Even before his father's death he had become the real manager of the family concerns; he was the terror of his tenants and wielded a dangerous authority throughout the district. Two years before his death he obtained grants of land in the Kuttālam hills for the plantation of coffee and opened up the "Terkumalai" and "Hope" estates. Ramsingh died much indebted, and the few surviving members of the clan, who live at Tachanallūr, retain but little of the family property in their hands.

Tinnevelly (Tirunelvēli—population 44,805): is the second largest town in the district. Its antiquity is evident from the fact that the place and its temple are referred to in the Dēvāram, a work usually ascribed to the seventh century A.D. The name Tinnevelly, as popularly understood, describes generally that part of the town which is massed around the temple of Nellaiyappar; and it would seem appropriate and satisfactory to allow the word *tiru-nel-vēli*, "the sacred paddy hedge," to refer to the continuous belt of paddy fields which surrounds this ancient settlement. But here, as elsewhere, mythologists have been at work and insist on the acceptance of a story which is now so popular that it must be repeated. In the days when the whole country was covered with forest Vēda Sarma, a devotee of Siva, used daily to collect and offer to the god such paddy as he could find among the clearings of the jungle. A famine arose, and no paddy could be got for the god, or (which was the same thing) for Vēda Sarma. After much searching he found a handful of grain and, taking it to Sindupūndurai, spread it in the sun on the river-bank and went down to bathe before performing the ritual of sacrifice. Whilst he was in the water, a terrible storm of wind and rain came on, and, fearing for his paddy, Vēda Sarma rushed back to the bank. There to his astonishment and relief he found that around the heap of grain a hedge had been formed, which parted the flow of water; over the paddy itself the sun still shone and no rain fell. "Lord, who madest the sacred hedge for the paddy!" he exclaimed, and added some expressions of natural gratitude. So *Tirunelvēli* obtained its name.

The town is a municipality, contains the residence of the Collector, is the headquarters of a taluk, and is served by three railway stations. The activities of the municipality have been referred to in Chapter XIV, its medical institutions in Chapter IX, its schools and colleges in Chapter X. The municipal town straggles over a stretch of country, roughly following one main road about five miles in length, and divides itself naturally into three distinct blocks. On the eastern extremity lies the area generally known as "Tinnevelly Bridge." Extending from the railway-station of that name on the west to the river on the east, this little suburb now forms perhaps the most important residential quarter of the municipality. Just across the river in Palamcotta lie almost all the district offices and law-courts; and "Tinnevelly Bridge," which owes its beginnings to two little villages, Vīrarāghavapuram and Sindupūndurai, naturally contains amongst its population a large proportion of Indian officials and vakils. The railway station (opened in 1876) and the growing congestion of the older part of Tinnevelly have been the most important factors in the rise of this suburb. In its turn "Tinnevelly Bridge," hedged in on three sides by paddy fields and on the fourth by the river, is becoming uncomfortably cramped. Even wet fields are now being converted into building-sites, a process which seems likely to continue.

The bridge across the Tāmbraparni, connecting the town with Palamcotta, was the gift of a citizen of Tinnevelly, Sulōchana Mudaliyār, who held the post of Naib Sheristadar in the Collector's office. The work was designed by Captain Faber and carried out by Lieut. Horsley, at the surprisingly moderate cost of just over half a lakh of rupees. The work was completed in November 1843, and the bridge was opened with befitting ceremony. A large elephant was the first passenger to cross; then followed a regiment of native infantry and a detachment of artillery; Sulōchana Mudaliyār came next, "supported (the record runs) by Mr. Douglas, the Judge, the Collector, Mr. Thomas, and Lieut. Horsley, the Engineer, and the whole society of the station." Government's contribution to the work consisted of the services of the engineers in charge, the labour of a hundred convicts, and stones from the dismantled fort for the formation of the piers. The bridge is supported on eleven elliptical arches, each of 60 feet

CHAP. XV. TINNEVELLY TALUK.

span, and resembles, in its design, the Waterloo bridge over the Thames. Its total length between the abutments is 760 feet or, between the extremities of the wings, 930 feet. The subject of bridging the river had been under discussion since 1836, and it is difficult now to realise the distress and inconvenience attending the days of the old ferry. "Both sides of the river," wrote the Collector in 1840, "are thronged with anxious crowds who have been waiting whole days to cross; and so great is the press that a guard of peons is obliged to be stationed on the spot to prevent accidents and the mob from becoming unruly." The obelisk just beside the Tinnevelly approach to the bridge, commemorating Sulōchana Mudaliyār's handsome gift, was erected in 1845 under the orders of Government. The bridge, it may be added, has provided those who look up the river as they cross with one of the most beautiful views to be found in the district.

The bungalow, which for many years has been occupied by the successive Collectors of the district, lies in ample and well wooded grounds on the left bank of the river, and is the property of the zamìndar of Ettaiyāpuram. The land was granted by Government on a 99 years' lease in 1806 to Mr. John Casamajor, the Commercial Resident of that time, and, after passing through various hands, came into the possession of a Muhammadan of the place named Hakim Ali Askar. The property descended to his widows and children, and from them and their alienees was bought up in two transactions, in 1840 and 1842, by the zamindar of Ettaiyāpuram. Mr. J. Silver, Collector from 1855 to 1859, was the first of his line to occupy the bungalow, an example which all his successors have followed.

Near the railway-station are two choultries maintained by the local board, one for Hindus and the other for Muhammadans, and yet another, which the Shānāns have recently built for themselves. The agency of Messrs. Parry & Co., also near the station, is mainly occupied in the collection and export of jaggery. The produce, which is obtained from all the taluks of the district except Kōilpatti and Sankaranainārkōil, is despatched to Nellikuppam (South Arcot), where it is used for the manufacture of sugar, sweetmeats and liquor. During the last ten or twelve years the demand for jaggery as an article of domestic consumption, for use in sweetmeats, tea and coffee, has noticeably increased, the result being that the control of the market and prices has more and more slipped from the hands of the wholesale buyer. The price of jaggery is now 20 per cent higher than it was ten years ago; and, though the balance left for export has in the same period reduced itself by half, Messrs. Parry & Co.'s Agent manages even at the present time to secure over 5,000 tons of jaggery in a year. Just beyond Messrs. Parry & Co.'s offices are the post office and a police-station, built (like the taluk office and the C.M.S. College further along) on land newly reclaimed from paddy cultivation.

From the neighbourhood of the railway-station a fine broad road, flanked on either side by rice fields and shaded by an avenue of *maruthu* trees, leads to the old town of Tinnevelly. Passing through a *mantapam* which, seen from a distance with the great *gōpuram* towering above it, appears to be the entrance of the great temple but is in reality a substantial arcade lined with bazaars, one arrives in front of the temple gates. Here the formation of the town, whose reconstruction is, by the Madura manuscripts, attributed to Aryanātha Mudaliyār, the lieutenant of Viswanātha Nāyakkan (A.D. 1559-63), can be made out. Around the temple run the four main streets; from these run other streets at right angles, east to west or north to south; beyond the main streets towards the west the design is lost in the congested habitations of the poorer classes, Idaiyans, Kaikkilaiyans and Muhammadans. Still further away lie the scattered dwellings of the Muhammadans of Kandiyāppēri, whose mosque, the "Kānumiah Pallivāsal" traces its comparatively rich endowments to the munificence of Queen Mangammāl.

The central feature of the town is, of course, the temple. Fergusson, in his "History of Indian and Eastern Architecture" (pp. 393 foll.), has dealt with it at some length. "Though neither among the largest," he says, "nor the most splendid temples of Southern India, that at Tinnevelly will serve to give a good general idea of the arrangement of these edifices; and has the advantage of having been built on one plan and at one time without subsequent alteration or change. . . . It has the singularity of being a double temple, the great square being divided into equal portions of which one is dedicated to the God Siva and the south half to his Consort Pārvathi. The general dimensions of the whole enclosure are 850 feet by 756 feet, the larger dimensions being divided into two equal portions of 378 feet each. There are three gateways to each half and one in the wall dividing the two. The principal gateway faces the east, the entrance to the temple, and the lateral ones are opposite each other. An outer portico precedes the great gateway leading internally to a very splendid porch, which, before reaching the gateway

CHAP. XV. TINNEVELLY TALUK.

of the inner enclosure branches off on the right to the intermediate gateway and on the left to the great hall of a Thousand Columns—63 feet in width by about 520 feet in depth.

"The inner enclosure is not concentric with the outer, and, as usual, has one gateway. The temple itself consists of a cubical cell, surmounted by a *vimāna* or spire, preceded by two mantapas, and surrounded by triple colonnades. In other parts of the temple are smaller temples, tanks of water, gardens, colonnades, etc., but neither so numerous nor so various as are generally found in Indian temples of this class. The inscriptions go back to the first half of the thirteenth century."[1]

The four sides of the god's temple immediately within the outer walls are flanked by raised corridors surmounted by rows of pillars. In the south-eastern corner of this circuit, or *prākāram*, is a small shrine containing a *sivalingam*, which is popularly known by the name of Anavaradhakhān. In explanation of this curious Muhammadan suffix it is said that a wife of one of the Nawābs fell sick one day and consulted the Brahmans of the place as to how she might be cured. The Brahmans prescribed some rites to be performed at the Nawāb's expense in the temple. The Nawāb consented; and his wife not only regained her health but soon after presented the ruler with a male child. The boy was given the name Anavaradha Khān, and the shrine was built in the corner of the temple, with an opening in the outer wall, so that the Muhammadan king and his son might without offence worship the god within. In the southern circuit are a number of life-size statues of the "Kartākkals", or Nāyakkan rulers, carved in one block with the pillars which support the roof of the *mantapam*. Following the *prākāram* round to the north-west corner, one comes to the shrine of the god Subrahmanya, where the god and his *vāhanam*, a peacock, are sculptured from one block of stone. The *mantapam* in the north-east corner, disfigured now by streaks of red and yellow paint, offers a good example of the stone carving which imitates the woodwork of beams and rafters. Guarding the entrance to the next enclosure and forming each a pillar, are four gigantic stone figures recalling the type met with at Tenkāsi. The gateway leads into the *manimantapam*, which none but a Hindu may enter; within this again is the dark narrow enclosure in which the god Vēnuvanēswarar is placed.

In the north-east corner of the first or outer circuit is a second *lingam*; and it is this god, Nellaiyappar, "Lord of

[1] As a matter of fact they go back to the tenth century—see below p. 494.

paddy," who gives his name to the temple and is regarded as its presiding deity. The traditional belief that this god formed the centre of an original and smaller temple is probable enough; for his enclosure, lying some feet below the general level of the temple, is now walled in by buildings, which ignore the position due to this god and must therefore be of later construction than the shrine itself. An inscription of Sundara-Pāndya refers to the deity of the temple under the two names "Vrīhi-Vritēswara," "Lord of the paddy hedge", and "Vēnuvanēswara," "Lord of the bamboo forest"; and a story which goes back to the days when Tinnevelly was a bamboo forest is related in the *stalapurāna* to explain the origin of the latter god.

Vishnu, in the person of Padmanābhaswāmi, has a shrine beside that of the "Lord of the bamboo forest."

From the precincts of the god the temple of the goddess is entered through the *Sangili mantapam*, supported on columns carved into figures of *yālis*. Beside the *mantapam*, on the left as one enters, is the Pothāmarai tank of stone, surrounded by a pillared cloister. On the other side of the *mantapam* is a well-kept "pleasure-garden", in which both god and goddess are placed during the six weeks of the *Vasantha* festival in the months of May and June. Returning to the entrance of the temple, one faces the *Unjal mantapam*, paved with polished marble, and from here is seen at the southernmost end of the temple the "thousand-pillared *mantapam*," with reference to which Fergusson observes: "The great thousand pillared portico in the temple is one of the least poetic of its class in India. It consists of a regiment of pillars 10 feet deep and extending to 100 in length without any break or any open space or arrangement. Such a forest of pillars does, no doubt, produce a certain effect; but half that number, if arranged as in some of the Chaulukyan or Jaina temples, would produce a far nobler impression. The aim of the Dravidians seems to have been to force admiration by the mere exhibition of inordinate patient toil."

Though the description is not quite accurate in its details—there is for instance in the middle of the mass of pillars a *mantapam* which breaks the uniformity of line to some extent, and the pillars do not stand ten by a hundred—it is impossible not to agree with Fergusson's general conclusion. The effect is further marred by the fact that, at the present time, a part of the "forest" has been walled off by a partition of mud to serve as a lumber room.

CHAP. XV. TINNEVELLY TALUK.

The temple is extremely wealthy; besides the *dastik* allowance of Rs. 18,000 received from Government it draws an enormous income from inams and other landed properties.

The great festival of the year occurs in June, when the car—the largest and most ornate in the district—is dragged round the streets and thousands assemble from all parts of the district.

The temple contains numerous inscriptions. The oldest are five *vatteluttu* records of Vīra Pāndya (about A.D. 950), who announces here, as at Ambāsamudram, that he "took the head of the Chōla king." Both Rājēndra Chōla I (A.D. 1011—44) and Kulōttunga I (A.D. 1074—1118) have left inscriptions, a fact which, incidentally, affords unquestionable evidence of the conquest of the Tinnevelly country by the Chōlas. Māravarman Sundara-Pāndya I (A.D. 1216—35), one of the founders of Pāndya greatness in the thirteenth century, speaks of himself in two of his numerous inscriptions as having "distributed the Chōla country" and, again, as having been "crowned at Mudikonda-Chōlapuram." The Pāndya, Māravarman Sundara-Pāndya II (A.D. 1238—51), has an inscription in which he refers to his Hoysala friend, Vīra-Sōmēsvaradēva. Jatāvarman Sundara Pāndya I speaks of victories over the Karnāta and Kākatīya kings. Other Pāndya rulers whose inscriptions occur here are Māravarman Kulasēkharadēva I (A.D. 1268—1308) and Māravarman Kulasēkharadēva II (A.D. 1314—21). Many of these records contain announcements of first-rate significance, and the selection of Tinnevelly for their publication clearly indicates the importance of the place in early times. Under the Madura Nāyakkans Tinnevelly appears to have been treated definitely as the headquarters of the southern part of their territories; Palamcotta, three miles away, was fortified and was regarded as sufficient protection for the capital. In the days of the Nawāb Tinnevelly was the residence of the renters; but, as we have seen, the possession of Palamcotta was essential to the maintenance of his authority.

The last division of the municipality is the important trading centre of PETTAI, two miles to the west of the main town. It has a railway-station, a police-station, a dispensary and two private chattrams. Muhammadans constitute one-half of the population. By its situation and character the place is entirely distinct from Tinnevelly proper. Almost all articles (except cotton and jaggery) exported from the west and centre of the district, most articles imported from outside the district, and products passing within the district between north and south or east and west, go through the hands of Pēttai merchants. Onions, chillies, bones, gingelly, grains of all kinds, pour in from all parts of the district for export either to another part of the district or beyond it; from Malabar and Travancore come ropes, pepper, ginger, areca-nut, cocoanut oil and mats, for distribution within the district; black gram and pulses from Bombay and the Northern Circars; paddy from Cocanada and Rangoon.

The monopoly of this trade, which once belonged to Muhammadans, has of recent years shown signs of giving way before the advance of the Vellālans and Ilaivāniyans. Large numbers of Muhammadans have migrated to Rangoon, Ceylon and Bombay and set up for themselves in centres with which they had already established trade connections.

The only important industry of the place is oil-pressing, the caste occupation of the Vāniyans. The gingelly is bought from the local merchants, and there are probably a hundred presses, of the usual primitive kind, employed in extracting the oil. An attempt made some twelve years ago to do the work by machinery quickly came to grief. Some Vellālans of Kadaiyam put together about Rs. 50,000 and set up a factory. The scheme did not pay, and the concern was sold to a Brahman, who fared no better than the originators and soon abandoned the enterprise.

TIRUCHENDUR TALUK.

CHAP. XV. TIRUCHENDUR TALUK.

THE TIRUCHENDUR TALUK, formerly a part of old Srīvaikuntam, dates its formation from 1911. It is a country of sharp contrasts, ranging between rich rice lands cropped twice a year and wildernesses of sand yielding little besides palmyras and acacias. More than three-quarters of the taluk is unirrigated; of the wet lands more than five-sixths derive their supply from the Tāmbraparni through the "mēlakāl", leading off at the Marudūr anicut, and through the Srīvaikuntam "south main" channel. East of the great Kadambā tank the channels, following the very slight fall of the country, branch southward away from the line of the river; and the immensity of the labour which has turned sand and palmyras into rice fields may be clearly judged by the large unproductive stretches which intervene between one paddy flat and the next. In the north-west of the taluk are a few rain-fed tanks, very few of which irrigate over 50 acres; the Karumanaiyār (see p. 187), a fitful stream of surface drainage, assists in the irrigation of about a thousand acres in the south-west of the taluk.

The "palmyra forest"[1]—as the great region of sand and palmyras to the south is called—has been referred to in chapter I; this taluk possesses more of this kind of country than any other, and travelling is consequently tedious and difficult. A traveller, however, who chooses his route with care will experience a curious joy at finding here and there the most refreshing patches of rich cultivation. These are the places where water lies near the surface and the villagers—almost certainly Shānāns—have drawn off water from the base of the sand-hills or have dug small wells in the valleys and transformed a pitiless waste into rich fields of paddy, chillies and betel-vine. Then again he may come upon that most beautiful of all the saving features of the *tēri* country—the *taruvai* or land-locked lake—which lies often in an amphitheatre of brilliant pink sand-hills crowned with palmyras.

[1] The "palmyra forest" appears first as a defined area in Mr. Puckle's settlement reports. Thirty-five out of the forty-one villages which now constitute that tract lie in this taluk. In "the forest" the density of palmyras exceeds 8,500 to the square mile.

During the north-east monsoon the water piles up and, as it evaporates during the dry weather, the sides of these basins, still saturated, are quickly planted up; water is baled, and abundant crops of all kinds—plantains, vegetables and paddy—soon form a fringe of luxuriant green around the lake. Roads do not exist; and pack-bullocks or men do almost all the work of transport. The sugar refinery at Kulasēkharapatnam has laid a light railway for the conveyance of its palmyra juice and jaggery; and the public have now the benefit of a part of this system (p. 241).

It was in these sandy regions that the earliest efforts of both Roman Catholic and Protestant missionaries were made; and, taking the taluk as a whole, Christians now number one-fifth of the total population and have increased here, since 1901, more rapidly than in any part of the district. Church towers are a conspicuous feature of the landscape, both inland and along the sea coast.

The rainfall (recorded for a long series of years only at Kulasēkharapatnam) is below the average for the district. Speaking generally, the villages in the lower reaches of the river-valley enjoy a cooler climate than those higher up; and the coast, which enjoys sea-breezes almost the whole year round, affords during the hot months of April and May a delightful resort.

The taluk contains six unions:—Tiruchendūr, Kulasēkharapatnam, Udangudi, Sāttānkulam, Alvārtirunagari and Kāyalpatnam.

Important markets are held weekly under the management of the taluk board at Udangudi, Sāttānkulam and Nazareth; the board owns markets also at Tattānmadam and Tenmāvadipannai. There are, in addition, eight private markets. The annual cattle-fair held at Tiruchendūr in *Māsi* (February-March) is one of the largest in the district; the fair conducted in *Vaikāsi* (May-June) at Alvārtirunagari is also well attended.

Ancient burial-urns have been found at Malavarāyanattam, Alvārtirunagari, Alagiyamanavālapuram, Tirukkalūr, Tentiruppēri, Poraiyūr, Angamangalam, Sugantalai, Nallūr, Kāyalpatnam and Vīrapāndiyanpatnam.

Alvārtirunagari, or Tenkarai: (often wrongly styled "Alwār Tinnevelly" in the old English records) forms, with the village of Alagiyamanavālapuram, a union (population 6,820). It contains a police-station, a sub-registrar's office, a privately owned "incomplete secondary" school and an elementary school maintained by the S.P.G. The local Gōvindappayyan chattram is supported from an endowment which the taluk board administers. At one time the place was the headquarters of a taluk of the same name, a position which it lost in 1838 (p. 316).

Situated on the south bank of the Tāmbraparni (whence its alternative name, *Tenkarai*, "south bank"), it is traversed by the main road from Palamcotta to Tiruchendūr. A long row of substantially built Brahman houses and *mantapams*, with flights of steps leading down to the river behind, flanks one side of the street; on the other side, concealed behind lines of houses, stands the important Vaishnavite temple dedicated to Adināthaswāmi. It is one of the largest temples in the district and receives a *dastik* allowance of Rs. 17,500 annually. On the roof of the lofty *mantapam* through which the temple is entered are a number of paintings, now rapidly disappearing, which depict scenes from the Rāmāyana. The *mantapam* to the left contains some remarkable examples of grouped pillars—it is scarcely possible to count them, but in one group there are said to be forty-eight—carved out of single blocks of stone. The temple owes its interest to its association with Nammālvār, one of the twelve *avatārs*, or incarnations, of Vishnu. The king and queen who ruled in Srīnagari, or (in Tamil) Tirunagari,[1]—the name the place bore before the days of the Alvār—were childless, and prayed to Vishnu for a son. The god replied that he would answer their prayer and that he himself would be born to them. "Like the coming of the rising sun, decked with *vakula* flowers," the infant Nammālvār was born and on the eleventh day was taken to be bathed in the river and thereafter to be presented in the temple of Adinātha. The child refused to return home with its parents and was left under the tamarind tree near by, which exists to this day but bears no fruit. There the young God in man remained for sixteen years, opening neither his mouth nor eyes nor ears, rapt in meditation on the Lord Vishnu. In the end, the God himself appeared before Nammālvār. So overjoyed was the disciple at the sight that his voice broke forth into verse; and this it was that came to be known as the *Prabandham*, or *Tiruvāymoli*, "the words of the sacred mouth," the standard exposition of Vaishnavite philosophy. The sage Madurakavigal, who was at the time lying prostrate at the feet of the Alvār, caught the verses from his master's lips and gave them to the world. According to general tradition the Prabandham, consisting of 4,000

[1] The account which follows is based on the local *stalapurāna*. For a theory as to the era and parentage of Nammālvār see *Govt. Epig. Ann. Report* for 1907–08, p. 69. The ancient name of Alvārtirunagari is there said to be Kurugūr.

verses, was the joint work of the twelve Alvārs, the contribution of Nammālvār, 1,000 verses, being the last instalment. The result of recent research is to place the era of this Alvār about the middle of the eighth century A.D.[1]

In popular esteem there is no question that Nammālvār eclipses the god Adināthaswāmi himself. Each has his separate car in the festival processions: and the feast in *Vaikāsi* (May-June), held in special honour of the Alvār, when the gods from nine temples [2] in the neighbourhood assemble to greet the Alvār and to join him in procession, is the grandest and most attractive event of the year.

The place was one of the trading stations occupied by the Dutch from the commencement of their establishment in the Tinnevelly district. With their other possessions in the district, they surrendered it in 1795 to the British. It seems clear that here, as elsewhere, the Dutch exercised no civil jurisdiction over the inhabitants; for in 1793 we find that a certain Captain Hamilton, who had been in the military service of the Nawāb, was appointed by that ruler to the command of the station. He continued to live in the place, apparently in great distress, even after the district passed to the English. Curiously enough his name (though not his memory) survives to the present day in a row of shops, known as "Ambaldan Chāvadi," in the eastern limits of the village.

The annual cattle-fair, which is timed to coincide with the *Vaikāsi* festival, is held in the sand of the river-bed.

Kāyalpatnam: a union (population 12,862), is a small port subordinate to Tuticorin; it is also the headquarters of an Inspector of Salt and Abkāri. The place is inhabited almost exclusively by Muhammadans, whose own account of themselves and the place is that they came from Arabia several hundreds of years—perhaps a thousand years—ago and, by the favour of a Pāndya king, obtained a tract of country four miles long and one and a half miles broad and there founded their settlement. They married Hindu women, chiefly of the Katasan caste. A copper-plate grant, which purports to have been issued by Tirumalai Nāyakkan of Madura to Mudaliyār Pillai Marakkāyar, the head of their community, throws some light on the subsequent history of the place. Kāyalpatnam, otherwise called "Sōnagarpatnam," had been almost deserted, and the Nāyakkan ruler bade the chief man of the place call together his scattered people and re-inhabit the site. To the Marakkāyar was assigned the

[1] *Govt. Epig. Ann. Report* for 1907–08.

[2] Known as the *Navatirupati*, or 'Nine Tirupatis.'

CHAP. XV. TIRU-CHENDUR TALUK.

duty of collecting and remitting to the central treasury the taxes levied on the chank fishery and the salt-pans, and in return he was given a present of rent-free land. But most important were the concessions made to the Marakkāyar in regard to the pearl fishery. The Muhammadans of the coast were already an important political factor in the rivalries which the aggression of the Portuguese had aroused; whilst the Portuguese with their allies and dependants, the Paravans, were threatening to assume the complete control of the fishery, the Nāyakkans won the Muhammadans to their side by the grant of important privileges.

To the present day, relying no doubt on their traditions, the upper circles amongst the local Muhammadans regard themselves, and indeed are generally regarded, as constituting a class apart from their fellow-religionists in the district. Their social customs and, often, their dress and appearance are distinctive. Venerable-looking figures with flowing beards and pointed features—many of the men look as if they had just newly immigrated from the land of the Prophet. Most of the families—perhaps three-quarters—in the place claim to be "pure-bred"; not, as is usual in the southern districts, on the ground that they "came from the north" in the train of some Moghul conqueror, but because their place of origin is Arabia. The "converts" live in separate streets according to their occupation—"snake charmers' street," "weavers' street," "fishermen's street"—and are not allowed to contract marriages with the "pure-bred" class. The study of Arabic or at least the Arabic script, an important mark of orthodoxy, enters into the curriculum of every boy's education. A fair number of the men claim to be able to speak and write the language, and most of them are familiar at least with Arabic characters.

The women (among the "pure-bred") observe the *gôsha* system; almost all the larger houses have their front doors opening not on to the street but into a side lane, so that when they must go out the women take no risk of being seen. Mosques, large and small, are very numerous, and the local estimate of forty appears to be not too high. The Mahabra Mosque, a particularly good specimen of modern work, is said to have been built after the design of an original in Baghdad. Taboots, mohurrum, carnivals and the wild *tamashas* in which less enlightened Muhammadans delight, are barred in Kāyalpatnam.

The trade of the place (see separate appendix) consists mainly of the export of salt, which is manufactured in the four factories lying in the immediate neighbourhood. In the trading days of the East India Company the cotton and piece goods bought up by the Commercial Resident were shipped from this port to Madras (see pp. 447, 484). The dilapidated remains of the old godowns of the Company may be seen down beside the beach. In the days of the Dutch, who occupied the place at intervals from 1658 to 1825, the dyers or cloth-painters of "Coilpatam" were well known.

Kulasēkharapatnam[1]: (police-station) forming with the adjacent village of Manappād a union (population 10,076), seven miles by a sandy track from Tiruchendūr, is situated on the southern apex of the bay enclosed between the headlands of Tiruchendūr and Manappād. The surrounding country is flat and composed entirely of sand, white within a distance of a mile or two from the sea and further inland red. Communications are therefore difficult, and at present almost all the trade of the place is by sea. As a port, the place was in the early years of the century of some importance; for native craft its harbour is superior to Tuticorin, being protected by a reef extending from beyond Manappād Point almost up to Tiruchendūr. For ships coming from the west coast it was the first port of call; goods going to the west coast were consigned to Kulasēkharapatnam and thence re-shipped to their port of destination. The old godowns near the present port point to the former importance of the place. With the development of foreign trade Tuticorin rose and Kulasēkharapatnam declined (see p. 447).

At the present day, the annual value of its trade amounts to about Rs. 17 lakhs. The chief exports are the various products of the palmyra, sugar, molasses, jaggery mats, baskets and fibre, which are sent to Tuticorin, and onions, a local crop of some importance, which go to Colombo. In the old days weaving and dyeing were fairly important industries, and, when the Dutch held Manappād, dyed and undyed broadcloth used to find its way from this place to Europe. The industries are now extinct.

In 1905 the East India Distilleries Company, Ltd., established a factory near the village for the manufacture of sugar not only from jaggery (the boiled juice of the palmyra) but also from the juice itself direct. Several miles of light rails have been laid traversing the surrounding palmyra country; juice is bought from the tappers, placed on trolleys and railed into a central station, from which it is pumped through a pipe to

[1] For assistance with this notice I am indebted to Mr. J. H. A. Weth, Agent of the E.I.D. Co., Ltd., Kulasēkharapatnam.

CHAP. XV. TIRU-CHENDUR TALUK.

the refinery. Palmyra juice must arrive at the factory fresh, and the produce of the villages lying off the line of rail has therefore to be converted into jaggery in the usual way before it can be transported.

The factory, the bungalows and casuarina plantations of the European Agent and his assistants, the numerous gardens which, stimulated by the example of their employer, the factory-hands have reared, have completely transfigured a site which, till a few years ago, was a wilderness of sand. An adequate supply of water was found at an easy depth, and land, hitherto regarded as worthless, has become valuable.

In the village are the ruins of what evidently was once a spacious palace of some kind, enclosed in a high compound wall. Tradition alleges that it was the residence of one of the old renters of the Panchamahāl taluk. A few hundred yards east of the village is a stone pillar bearing inscriptions on two faces, and on the third is carved in relief the figure of a man with his hands in the attitude of prayer. Above the figure a peacock and a *sūlāyudham* or dagger are embossed. A similar stone stands near the Pillaiyār temple in the east side of the village; it contains inscriptions but no carving.

Manappād, about a mile away on the other side of the river Karumanaiyār, is the other member of the union. It lies along the north side of the sandy promontory which runs out to form the southern arm of the harbour. Inhabited entirely by Paravans, it is one of the most striking villages of the district. The houses, largely copied, it is said, from models of English residences in Ceylon, are solidly built of stone: some are storied, all are tiled and well ventilated. Their owners spend most of their time trading in Ceylon, leaving behind them their families, to whom they return at intervals.

The lighthouse, whose white group-flashing light, visible for 18 miles, is marked by all ships passing between the West Coast and Ceylon, was set up in 1901 to replace an inferior light which had existed at the point since 1888.

The place figures constantly in the early history of the mission of the "Fishery Coast." It was one of the first villages visited by St. Francis Xavier, and a grotto is still pointed out on the seaward face of the cliff in which that Saint lived and prayed. For some years the College of the Coast was located here, having been transferred from Tuticorin about 1712. A church dedicated to the Assumption, one of the oldest of which there is any record, was converted by the Dutch into a ware-house; it was subsequently abandoned, and its ruins have now disappeared beneath the sand. The church of the Holy Cross, standing conspicuous at the head of the promontory, has the good fortune to possess a fragment of the True Cross, the exhibition of which at the annual festival attracts thousands of pilgrims. This church, as well as that dedicated to St. Jacob, belongs now to the Jesuit mission; the church of the Holy Ghost, recently enlarged, is under the jurisdiction of Mylapore.

Megnānapuram (population 2,215): an important Christian settlement, lying in the heart of the "palmyra forest" at the foot of the Kuthiraimoli *tēri*, possesses a special interest as having been from the time of its creation the special charge of a single family. The first of this line, the Rev. John Thomas, started work in the place in 1838. Before his death in 1870 he had extended Christianity to 125 hamlets of the neighbourhood; the Elliot Tuxford boarding school for girls (1842) and a boys' school (1846) were opened in the place; the beautiful church in Early English style, built of stone from Pannampārai, was completed in 1868; in the next year a dispensary was started. His son, the Rev. J. D. Thomas, who succeeded, was followed (till 1904) by a son-in-law. Miss Thomas, a daughter of the founder of the place, still superintends the girls' school and the embroidery work for which the place is well known.

Nazareth: a purely Christian settlement with a population of 4,280. It was in 1803 that the site of the village was purchased by the Rev. J. C. Kohloff of the S.P.C.K. for the settlement of the "Tanjore Christians." At first the place seems to have received the name of Mudalūr, "first town"; but very soon—by 1805 certainly—this had been changed to Nazareth, the name Mudalūr (occasionally in the form "Terku Mudalūr") remaining the exclusive possession of the four years older Christian settlement to the south, five miles from Sāttānkulam.

It is difficult to recognize in Nazareth of the present day, with its ample church, its spacious buildings and well-kept streets, the place where, in 1805, the missionary Ringeltaube found a mud church and a handful of Christians. The settlement now possesses two secondary schools, one of which is a high school for girls: two training schools for teachers of both sexes: two art industrial schools, one for boys and one for girls: and two orphanages. The orphanages were started during the famine of 1877; and, at the same time, in connection with them a large industrial school was founded. Instruction is now given in tailoring, carpentry, blacksmith's work, weaving, drawing and many other subjects; the girls are taught, amongst other things, lace-making.

CHAP. XV. TIRUCHENDUR TALUK.

Nazareth of the present day is the fruit of the labours of a long line of missionaries: David Rosen (1829—36), J. L. Irion (1836—38), A. E. Caemmerer (1838-39), Henry Pope (1859), T. Brotherton (1860—69), J. M. Strachan (1870—74), Canon Margoschis (1876—1908). The foundation stone of the church, which, with subsequent enlargements (the chancel was added in 1884), remains to the present day, was laid in 1829, and in the following year the church was opened. The bungalow occupied by the missionary in charge was built by J. L. Irion. The education of girls was begun by Mrs. Caemmerer, who opened a small school; in 1870 the hospital (rebuilt in 1892) was founded. Most remarkable, perhaps, of all this line was Canon Margoschis, who for 33 years, in spite of constitutional ill-health, managed and developed single-handed the diverse activities of this settlement.

In PRAKASAPURÁM, a neighbouring hamlet, is a small congregation owning a church, who style themselves "Hindu Christians" or "Jehovah Messianists." They observe the Jewish Sabbath and new-moons and make offerings to the Deity; their marriages and funerals are conducted on Hindu lines, but their priests take no part in the ceremonies. The sect dates from 1850, when their leader, a Shānān (who is still living), owing to some personal differences seceded from the S.P.G. and drew a large number of followers with him. At the present time his adherents number only a few hundreds and are scattered over three or four neighbouring villages.

A curious sect of Hindus, known as "five-letter people" (*ainthéluttukārar*), is found in the same hamlet. Their chief principles seem to be to eschew the use of images in their temples and the worship of the lower orders of Hindu gods. Hot cakes are placed as offerings at the feet of their priest, who for the time becomes the object of worship. Adherents of the sect are found in half-a-dozen villages of the taluks of Tiruchendūr and Srīvaikuntam and are mostly of the Shānān caste. Their priests are held in great veneration; and on their decease the mud of their tombs—*sivan kōvil* such a tomb is called—is regarded as efficacious in disease. This little hamlet is in fact a microcosm of religions. In addition to the two sects mentioned may be found Hindus of the ordinary type, Christians belonging to the C.M.S. and to the S.P.G. (the latter society has recently built a fine Gothic church here), and representatives of a sect known as "Seventh-day Adventists."

Sāttānkulam: union (population 7,440), contains a sub-registrar's office, a police-station, a local fund dispensary, two local fund schools and, since 1911, when the Tiruchendūr taluk was newly constituted, has been the headquarters of a deputy-tahsildar sub-magistrate. Local tradition asserts that the village originally belonged to five brothers of the Paraiya caste of whom Sāttān, the name-giver of the place, was one. The Vellālans, who served the family as accountants, rose against their masters and extirpated them. The names of four brothers are perpetuated in the rain-fed tanks of the village. Lying in the midst of sandy country, the village is accessible only from the north by a maintained road. The old sandy track—one of the "Mangammāl *sālais*"—from Tiruchendūr to Trivandrum passes through the village; but cart traffic, especially towards the east and south, is extremely difficult. Both the Jesuit mission and the C.M.S. have churches here, Christians forming a considerable section of the population. As in so many parts of the Tiruchendūr taluk, where local natural resources are poor, many have taken to trade in Ceylon, and most of the wealth of the place is derived from this source.

In the Vellāla quarter is a square stone pillar—known as a *kuttukal*—bearing an inscription, dated Andu 910 (A.D. 1735), which appears to record a gift of some sort to the Tiruvāduthurai mutt. The pillar is venerated, though not as a god; from it starts the annual procession to the Alagamman temple. The condition of the inscription speaks well for the qualities of the Pannampārai stone (obtained some four miles away), of which evidently the pillar is a specimen.

Tiruchendūr, "the beautiful city": a union, with a population [1], according to census, of 25,531 (tahsildar, sub-magistrate, sub-registrar, police-station and travellers' bungalow) was until 1860 the headquarters of the old Panchamahāl taluk and in 1911 was again restored to the equivalent of its old position as the capital of the newly-formed taluk of Tiruchendūr.

It was on his return from a hard-won conquest over Sūrapadman in his island fortress in mid-ocean that the god Subramanya landed at the spot and bade his followers, the Mukkāni Brahmans, build a place of habitation. On the sea front stands the famous temple dedicated to the divine founder of the place. The building is somewhat curiously arranged, the *Utsavar*, named Shanmugar, that is, the god whose idol is taken in procession, having a shrine with its full complement of *mantapams* separate from the shrine of the god Subramanya himself and facing an opposite direction. Within the last

[1] At the time when the census of 1911 was taken the *Māsi* festival was in progress here. At a rough conjecture, at least 10,000 of the recorded population may be taken to have been visitors.

CHAP. XV. TIRU-CHENDUR TALUK.

few years a handsome *mantapam*, carved in the traditional style, has been erected in front of the Shanmugar shrine. The original portion of the temple, containing the shrine of Subramanyaswāmi and his two Ammans, is cut out of the sand-stone rock; the cliff has been left as far as possible to form the circuit walls, pillars and reinforcements of stone being added to support the stone superstructure. At one point in the outer circuit, a shrine dedicated to Vishnu has been hollowed out of the rock itself. Wisely taking advantage of the cliff, the builders placed the great *gōpuram* apart from the temple and have thus provided a striking mark for miles around both by land and sea.

The temple is very richly endowed, and its income from offerings is also enormous. The great car festival (with which the local cattle-fair is made to coincide) occurs in February or March, when thousands assemble from all parts of the district and beyond it. Vows may be performed at any time, but they have their auspicious seasons. Parties of pilgrims bearing on their shoulders *kāvadis*—a *kāvadi* is a kind of yoke surmounted by a semi-circular hood and laden with offerings of sweet-meats, sandal or incense—may be seen constantly arriving; coins, images of limbs in silver, cradles of wood or metal, are offered to the god, and cattle who have recovered from sickness are surrendered to the temple's keeping. Cold rice when offered to the god has been known to appear steaming hot, and fishes dried and salted will revive and leap out into the sea. Even Muhammadans, it is said, occasionally make votive offerings to the god. Within a few feet of the temple is the sea; and bathing in its waters is beneficial to the worshipper and remunerative to the temple. Pillars have been set up at close intervals along the beach to mark the twenty *tīrtams* at which this course may be taken. Two hundred yards to the south of the temple near the sea is a remarkable spring of fresh water, to bathe in which is similarly meritorious.

A familiar local tradition runs to the effect that "about 300 years ago" a race of sea-faring men, called *Usilampadi*, descended on the place and took away the temple idol, thinking it was made of gold. Vadamalaiyappa Pillaiyan, the local renter of the Nāyakkan ruler, acting on the advice conveyed to him in a dream by the god, put out to sea and, following his instructions, recovered the image. In memory of this deed the Vadamalaiyappa *mantapam*, to which the god is taken in times of festival, was erected. *Usilampadi* is an unknown word, and is variously explained by those who tell the story as denoting the Muhammadans and the French. M. Rennel, the French author of a *Description, Historical and Geographical, of India*, published in Berlin, 1785, gives a picture of the temple, which, he says, he got from a soldier in the service of the Dutch Company; he relates an incident which offers a reasonable explanation of the Tiruchendūr tradition. "In a descent made by the Dutch on the coast in 1648," he says, "the Dutch halted in the temple and on leaving did their best to destroy it by fire and by a heavy bombardment. But they only partially succeeded and the tower defied all their efforts.[1]" Possibly the capture of the idol was one of their achievements.

The temple owns a rich collection of jewels; and a silver vessel presented to the temple in 1803 by Mr. S. R. Lushington, the first Collector of the district under the Company's rule, is still preserved amongst its properties. Mr. Lushington built a bungalow near here (the site is actually within the limits of the present village of Vīrapāndyanpatnam), which became the property of a long line of successive Collectors.

In the cliff of hardened sand-stone just beyond the temple, a cavern has been cut and fitted with pillars to serve as a temple. On the left-hand wall are some indistinct traces of figure-carving; the gaudily-coloured mud figures on the opposite wall were set up, it is said, to replace old sculptures.

The Mukkāni Brahmans, of whom there are probably not less than a thousand in Tiruchendūr, stand in a peculiar relationship to the Subramanya temple. When founding the place, the god Subramanya set up 2,000 families of this caste to attend to the services of the temple, a duty which they have ever since faithfully performed. Their functions consist mainly in making offerings and performing religious ceremonies—*kattalais* such services are called—on behalf of absentee worshippers. Distinguishable by their topknots of hair, which, very much like the Malayālis, they train to fall above their foreheads, they may be seen journeying in almost any part of the country, either to collect subscriptions for the temple festivals or fees from their tardy patrons. There is no doubt that the business is remunerative; they are generally well-to-do and lead a comfortable existence. A few have put their money into land, but none have yet found it necessary to invest in English education.

[1] As a matter of fact M. Rennel calls the place *Tutucurim*, but from the picture and an accompanying sketch-map it is clear that Tiruchendūr was meant. We know that about the period in question the Dutch were incessantly at war with the Portuguese on the coast.

CHAP. XV.
TIRU-
CHENDUR
TALUK.

The annual cattle fair, which brings in to the taluk board an annual revenue of about Rs. 1,700, is held in the extensive grounds reserved for the purpose to the north of the town.

Included in the union are the two coast-villages of VIRAPANDYANPATNAM and ALANTALAI, both inhabited almost exclusively by Parava Christians. The twin towers of the handsome church of the former village seem to vie with the Tiruchendūr *gōpuram* for pre-eminence on the landscape. St. Francis Xavier frequently visited both places and for a time resided at Alantalai.

Udangudi: a union (population 11,736), is accessible from Kulasēkharapatnam on the east by a poor road and on all other sides is surrounded by the heavy red sand of the "palmyra forest." Its weekly market, to which practically all wares are brought either by pack-bullocks or on the heads of coolies, is one of the most important in the district. Water is found here at an easy depth, and the garden cultivation of the place, mostly in the hands of Shānāns, is famous. The numerous rich Muhammadan residents derive most of their wealth from the trade which they conduct in Ceylon. The first of the "Tanjore" Christian converts outside Palamcotta hailed from Kālankudiyiruppu (included in the union), and the subsequent revival of mission work dates from the time of Christian S. Kohloff, a member of the S.P.G., who gave his name to the local settlement, Christianagaram. The church was completed in 1849.

INDEX

A

I

J

L

M

N

Q

R

S

U

V

DISTRICT GAZETTEERS OF INDIA {IN 245 BINDINGS}

ASSAM DISTRICT GAZETTEERS

11 VOLUMES

ISBN: 9788121285933 (PB Set)
Price: 6500/

BENGAL DISTRICT GAZETTEERS

52 VOLUMES

ISBN: 9789362089151 (PB Set)
Price: 35000/

GAZETTEER OF THE BOMBAY PRESIDENCY

27 VOLUMES
(IN 35 BINDINGS)

ISBN: 9788121285605 (PB Set)
Price: 90000/

CENTRAL PROVINCES DISTRICT GAZETTEERS

30 VOLUMES
(IN 33 BINDINGS)

ISBN: 9789362085399 (PB Set)
Price: 23000/

MADRAS DISTRICT GAZETTEERS

23 VOLUMES
(IN 25 BINDINGS)

ISBN: 9789362085627 (PB Set)
Price: 32000/

PUNJAB DISTRICT GAZETTEERS

36 VOLUMES
(IN 37 BINDINGS)

ISBN: 9789362084033 (PB Set)
Price: 46000/

RAJPUTANA DISTRICT GAZETTEERS

3 VOLUMES

ISBN: 9789362084781 (PB Set)
Price: 6000/

District
Gazetteers of India
{In 245 Bindings}
(Rs. 530000/- Hardcover)
(Rs. 370000/- Softcover)
Crown Size

UNITED PROVINCES OF AGRA AND OUDH DISTRICT GAZETTEERS

49 VOLUMES

ISBN: 9789362082183 (PB Set)
Price: 86404/